# *Multimedia:*
# COMPUTING, COMMUNICATIONS AND APPLICATIONS

# *Multimedia:*
# COMPUTING, COMMUNICATIONS AND APPLICATIONS

**RALF STEINMETZ**
**KLARA NAHRSTEDT**

PEARSON

ISBN 978-81-775-8441-7

First Impression, 2006
Twelfth Impression, 2012
**Thirteenth Impression, 2013**



Published by Dorling Kindersley (India) Pvt. Ltd., licensees of Pearson Education in South Asia.

Head Office: 7th Floor, Knowledge Boulevard, A-8(A), Sector-62, Noida – 201309, U.P, India.
Registered Office: 11 Community Centre, Panchsheel Park, New Delhi 110 017, India.

Printed in India by Chennai Micro Print (P) Ltd., Chennai.

*To my wife Martina and*
*my children Jan and Alexander*

— Ralf Steinmetz

*To my son Peter*

— Klara Nahrstedt

# Contents

# Foreword

Multimedia computing and communications are areas of intense current interest, software and hardware development, and future promise. Residential, institutional and business applications are emerging at a fast pace. Multimedia standards organizations are actively producing new standards for the field. Yet, the term "multimedia" and the subject areas it covers remain, to many people who hear, read and even use the term, clouded in mystery. Some recent books have attempted to define the essential elements of this fascinating area with various degrees of success.

This book is fully successful in its enterprise; it will certainly fill a void in the emerging field of multimedia. The book covers all the important topics involved in the new area, from the operating system and hardware aspects to the user interface, the applications and the programming abstractions. Such a wealth of information is not found in any of the few other books published thus far in the field.

The book is organized in 18 chapters, all of which are very informative and essential. The first five chapters define multimedia terminology and review the fundamentals of sound/audio, images and graphics, video and animation. An excellent treatise on image and video data compression follows, introducing and describing in detail such important standards as H.261, JPEG, MPEG-1 and MPEG-2. Chapters in optical storage media and computer technology give the reader up-to-date information about CD standards and pertinent hardware technology.

The chapter on operating system issues really makes this book unique. Resource and process management are covered in detail. All the important algorithms for real-time scheduling (rate monotonic, earliest-deadline-first and so on) are given.

File systems management is discussed in detail, and future aspects of multimedia operating systems are also covered.

Networking systems are the subject of another chapter. All the technologies relevant to multimedia networking are described. A chapter on protocols and quality of service issues follows, giving an overview of important multimedia protocols.

A brief description of multimedia databases is followed by a complete treatment of document architectures and standards such as ODA, SGML, hypertext and MHEG. Important design issues concerning multimedia interfaces are then presented. A very rich chapter on multimedia synchronization describes the heart of a multimedia system. This treatment is another major contribution of the authors that cannot be found in other books. A discussion of important programming abstractions follows, and the book concludes with an interesting chapter on multimedia applications and one on future directions.

We expect that this book will become a standard text in multimedia courses as well as a standard reference for all people working in the field. We congratulate the authors for their laborious but worthwhile and successful endeavor, and wish the readers a most pleasant journey into the field of multimedia!

Nicolas D. Georganas, University of Ottawa
Domenico Ferrari, University of California at Berkeley

February 1995

# Preface

There has been an explosive growth of multimedia computing, communication and applications during the last decade. Computers and networks process and transmit currently more than just text and images. Video, audio and other continuous media data, as well as additional discrete media such as graphics became part of integrated computer applications. In the future, all computers and networks will support multimedia computing and communication to provide appropriate services for multimedia applications.

This book aims to achieve a complete and balanced view on the multimedia field covering three main domains: *devices*, *systems* and *applications*. In the device domain, basic concepts for processing of video, audio, graphics and images are presented (Chapters 2 through 5). Because of the currently available technology and quality requirements, the original data rates of these media demand compression methods. The corresponding approaches are described in Chapter 6. Chapter 7 presents the optical storage media which have contributed significantly to the current development of computer-based multimedia systems. On the other hand, the high-speed networks, described in Chapter 10, with their higher bandwidth and transmission possibilities of all media kinds, have led to networked multimedia systems. In the system domain, Chapters 8 through 12 provide information on *computer technology* as an interface between the device and the system domain, *operating system*, *communication system* and *database system*. The application domain includes topics such as *programming abstractions* (Chapter 16), which represent the interface between the application and the system domain, *document handling* (Chapter 13), *tools and applications* (Chapter 17), and *user interfaces* through which the document handling, tools and applications are made accessible to humans. To all three domains, one area is common: the *synchronization* of multimedia. This topic is covered separately in Chapter 15.

This book has the character of a *reference book*, covering a wide scope. It has evolved from the first multimedia technology book, published in German in 1993 [Ste93b] (Figures fror this book were reused with permission of the Springer Verlag.) However, substantial areas have changed and enhancements have been made. The results, presented in this book, serve as groundwork for the development of individual components oua multimedia system. The book can be used by computer professionals who are interested in multimedia systems and applications. The book can also be used as a text for beginning or advanced graduate students in computer science, and related disciplines, although the absence of exercises for each chapter may put more load on the instructor. All discussions present the handling of multimedia in the corresponding domains and assume that the reader is familiar with the basic concepts of the systems: for example, scheduling in operating systems, layering in communication systems, etc. Since the amount of material in the book is too much for a one-semester course, it can be taught during two or more semesters. For example, the instructor could choose to emphasize the multimedia computing or communication aspect, including synchronization and application issues.

Many people have helped us with the preparation of this book. We would especially like to thank David Farber, Jonathan Smith, Ruzena Bajcsy, Craig Reynolds, Gerold Blakowski, Andreas Mauthe and Doris Meschzan. We would also like to thank Klara's colleagues from the Distributed System Laboratory for their comments and discussions during the writing process. Special thanks go to John Shaffer, Brendan Traw, Jean McManus and Anshul Kantawala. Acknowledgment is also due the National Science Foundation and the Defense Advanced Research Projects Agency (#NCR-8919038) for supporting Klara's research reported here.

Last but not least, we would like to thank our families for their support and patience.

# Chapter 1

# Introduction

*Multimedia* means, from the user's perspective, that computer information can be represented through audio and/or video, in addition to text, image, graphics and animation. For example, using audio and video, a variety of dynamic situations in different areas, such as sport or ornithology lexicon, can often be presented better than just using text and image alone.

The integration of these media into the computer provides additional possibilities for the use of computational power currently available (e.g., for interactive presentation of huge amounts of information). Furthermore, these data can be transmitted through computer and telecommunication networks, which implies applications in the areas of information distribution and cooperative work. Multimedia provides the possibility for a spectrum of new applications, many of which are in place today. On the other hand, one also has to keep in mind the problems of global communication, with its social and legal implications. However, these issues will not be discussed in this book.

One of the first and best-known institutes working on different aspects of multimedia is the MIT Media Lab in Boston [HS93]. Research is going on there on a variety of future applications, such as personal newspaper and holography [Bra87]. In the meantime, many research institutes, universities and computer and telecommunication companies work in the multimedia area.

## 1.1 Branch-overlapping Aspects of Multimedia

In addition to the strong interest in multimedia systems from the applications and technology viewpoints, one should not underestimate the ongoing migration process, and the evolution of the different industrial branches, as follows:

- *Telecommunication* began primarily with the telephone. Telephone networks changed gradually into digital networks, which are similar to computer networks. In the early days, intermediate switching systems had mechanical switching dials. Today, computers do the job. Now the telephone is becoming more and more of a computer, or is part of a computer (e.g., using an ISDN card).
- *Consumer electronics* contributed massively to the reduction of the price of video support in computers. Similarly, optical disc technology in computing is dependent on the success of the CD player. Consequently, the same companies very often produce CD drives for computer and stereo-systems, or both television and computer monitors.
- *Recording studios* and *TV producers* are pioneers in dealing with professional audio and video equipment. Today, professional systems are available for the digital cutting of TV movies. Some of these systems are standard computers extended through additional special cards. These information providers convey data through cable, satellite and plain old antennas, which will further allow them to serve as information providers via computer networks in the future.
- Many of the large *publishing houses* already offer their publications in electronic form. Further, there are many close relations between publishing houses and movie companies. These branches offer gradually more and more multimedia information.

This short overview shows that the different branches grow together because of coming multimedia technology and applications. However, to allow multimedia applications, many software and hardware components have to be adapted, extended or replaced.

From the technical perspective, besides handling the huge amount of data, the *timing requirements* among all components of the data computation is the major challenge. Traditional data computation tries to finish its task as soon as possible. Real-time systems must work internally within given time bounds, mostly as error-tolerant systems. The fault tolerance in multimedia is generally not the most important aspect.

Another challenge is the *integration requirement* of different types of media in a multimedia application. In such applications, the traditional media (e.g., text, image) as well as the continuous media (e.g., video, audio), must be processed. Moreover, if a timing requirement is set by a multimedia application, it should hold for both classes (traditional and continuous media) to achieve the timing specification of the application. These media are not independent of each other and therefore the integration requires concepts, which are more complex than just the integration of current concepts. In an integrated system, different components have to process both kinds of data, and moreover, different relations can occur in the form of *synchronization* among the media.

The notion of *multimedia* is often defined very differently in the literature in comparison to our (above) description. There is some need for clarification. The technology connections and binding different components, were considered only partially and in isolation from each other. Based on [Ste93b], we wrote this book to provide an integrated, consistent and total view.

## 1.2 Content

This book has the character of a *reference book*, covering numerous areas and allowing the reader to learn about a topic of interest without having previously studied extensively or having read areas previously covered in this book. Strong connections are provided among the different areas of this book through its *global structure*, which is shown in Figure 1.1. The results presented in this book serve as basis for the development of individual components of a multimedia system and suggest some general parameters one must keep in mind.

## 1.3 Global Structure

This book aims to achieve a complete and balanced view. Figure 1.1 shows the global view of this book with the main topics covered in it. Figure 1.1 was developed after many iterations of topic structuring. It shows schematically the main fields of multimedia systems. The basic idea of the figure is to express the interactions among the components through spatial proximity.

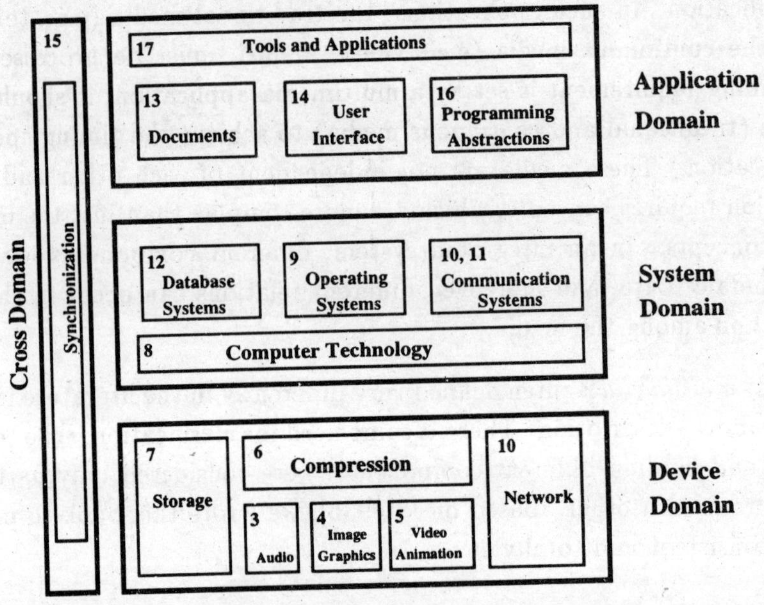


Figure 1.1: *The main topics covered in this book with chapter number information.*

The following areas can be distinguished:

- **Device Domain**

  Basic concepts for the processing of *digital audio* and *video* data are based on digital signal processing. Hence, these concepts are described and some possible practical implementations are presented. Different methods for the processing of *image*, *graphics* and *animation* are described. The audio techniques section includes music (MIDI) and speech processing. The understanding of video techniques is built mainly on TV development, including digital representation and HDTV. The originated data rates of these media demand, because of the current quality requirements and available technology, corresponding *compression* methods. The corresponding hardware and some software are briefly described.

The diminishing cost of *optical storage* space has contributed significantly to the current development of computer technology. Almost all developments are based on CD-DA (Compact Disc-Digital Audio), known from home electronics.

On the other hand, networks, with their higher bandwidth and their capacity for transmitting all media types, have led to *networked multimedia systems.* Not such a long time ago, local and distributed multimedia systems consisted of a set of external analog devices controlled by a computer. Today, development tends toward full digital working systems.

- **System Domain**

  The interface between the device domain and the system domain is specified by the *computer technology.* To utilize the device domain, several system services are needed. Basically, three services exist. These services are mostly implemented in software:

  - The *operating system* serves as an interface between computer hardware/system software and all other software components. It provides the user with a programming and computational environment, which should be easy to operate. In its function as an interface, the operating system provides different services that relate to the computer resources, such as: processor, main memory, secondary storage, input and output devices and network.
  - The *database system* allows a structured access to data and a management of large databases.
  - The *communication system* is responsible for data transmission according to the timing and reliability requirements of the networked multimedia application.

- **Application Domain**

  The services of the system domain are offered to the application domain through proper *programming abstractions.* Moreover, such abstractions can be, for example, part of a multimedia operating system, programming language or object-oriented class hierarchy.

Another topic embedded in the application domain is *document handling.* A document consists of a set of structured information, represented in different media, and generated or recorded at the time of presentation.

Many functions of *document handling* and other *applications* are accessible and presented to the user through a *user interface.*

- **Cross Domain**

  It turns out that some aspects, such as synchronization aspects, are difficult to locate in one or two components or domains. The reason is that *synchronization*, being the temporal relationship among various media, relates to many components across all domains.

## 1.4 Multimedia Literature

All individual topics mentioned in this work have been considered to some extent, and often in more detail, though in isolation, in the literature. Likewise, the groundwork for signal processing, audio, video, graphics, image and animation techniques and various networks have been published in relevant works. In this book, all the parts of an integrated multimedia system will be considered.

Some publications, such as [BD92, EH92, Gia92, Koe94], are composed of individual articles or chapters originated by different authors, with the goal of presenting the topics of user interfaces or applications from different points of view. In contrast to the present work, there was no attempt to provide a coherent integral presentation of the multimedia area.

Other publications serve as individual product descriptions, e.g., [BS92]. They present mostly the properties of individual products without giving a global view. In [Bur93] and [Ste92], besides the application and product descriptions, there is also some groundwork for audio techniques, video techniques, compression and optical storage media. But, in contrast to the present study, all scientific aspects, as well as an overall, integrated view, are neglected. This is the case also in [PF92, V. 93, Wod92].

Hypertext and hypermedia are documented in a large number of publications, most of which offer hypermedia document descriptions. A very good presentation is given in [Nie90a]. We consider hypermedia a part of multimedia.

Besides a number of national and international workshops in the multimedia area, new conferences such as ACM Multimedia Conference (first in August 1993, Anaheim, CA) and IEEE Multimedia Conference (first in May 1994, Boston, MA) evolved. Also, in addition to many product and commercial only oriented magazines, dedicated publications, such as the ACM Springer journal *"Multimedia Systems"* (end of 1993), *"Multimedia Tools and Applications"* (beginning of 1995) and the *"IEEE Multimedia Magazine"* (beginning of 1994) are being published.

# Chapter 2

# Multimedia: Media and Data Streams

The following chapter introduces terminology and gives a sense of the commonality of the elements of multimedia. The introduction of terminology begins with a clarification of the notion *multimedia*, followed by a description of media and the important properties of multimedia systems. Subsequently, characteristics of *data streams* in such systems and the introduction of the notion *Logical Data Unit* (LDU) follow.

One way of defining multimedia can be found in the meaning of the composed word.

- *Multi-* [lat.: much] many; much; multiple.
- *Medium* [lat.: middle] An intervening substance through which something is transmitted or carried on; A means of mass communication such as newspaper, magazine, or television (from American Heritage Electronic Dictionary, 1991).

This description is derived from the common forms of human interaction. It is not very exact and has to be adapted to computer processing. Therefore, we discuss in the next section the notion *medium* in more detail with respect to computer processing.

## 2.1 Medium

In general, one describes medium as a means for distribution and presentation of information. Examples of a medium are text, graphics, speech and music. In the same way, one can also add water and atmosphere to it (according to the above medium description from the American Heritage Dictionary).

Media can be classified with respect to different criteria [ISO93a]. We classify media according to perception, representation, presentation, storage, transmission, and information exchange.

### 2.1.1 The Perception Medium

Perception media help humans to sense their environment. The central question is: *How do humans perceive information in a computer environment?* The answer is that the perception of information occurs mostly through *seeing* or *hearing* the information, although tactile perception increases its presence in a computer environment.

There is a primary difference between *seeing* and *hearing* information when using a computer. For the perception of information through seeing, the visual media such as *text, image* and *video* are used. For the perception of information through hearing, auditory media such as *music, noise* and *speech* are relevant.

The difference among media can be further refined. For example, video can be further decomposed into different video scenes, which again are composed of individual images.

### 2.1.2 The Representation Medium

Representation media are characterized by internal computer representations of information. The central question is: *How is the computer information coded?* The answer is that various formats are used to represent media information in a computer. For example:

- A text character is coded in ASCII or EBCDIC code.
- Graphics are coded according to CEPT or CAPTAIN videotext standard. The graphics standard GKS can also serve as a basis for coding,
- An audio stream can be represented using a simple PCM (Pulse Coding Method) with a linear quantization of 16 bits per sample.
- An image can be coded as a facsimile (the group 3 according to the ISO Standard Specification) or in JPEG format.
- A combined audio/video sequence can be coded in different TV standard formats (e.g., PAL, SECAM, NTSC), and stored in the computer using an MPEG format.

### 2.1.3 The Presentation Medium

Presentation media refer to the tools and devices for the input and output of information. The central question is: *Through which medium is information delivered by the computer, or introduced into the computer?* The media, e.g., paper, screen and speaker are used to deliver the information by the computer (output media); keyboard, mouse, camera and microphone are the input media.

### 2.1.4 The Storage Medium

Storage media refer to a data carrier which enables storage of information. However, the storage of data is not limited only to the available components of a computer. Therefore, paper is also a storage medium. The central question is: *Where will the information be stored?* Microfilm, floppy disk, hard disk, and CD-ROM are examples of storage media.

### 2.1.5 The Transmission Medium

The transmission medium characterizes different information carriers, that enable continuous data transmission. Therefore, storage media are excluded from this kind of medium. The central question is: *Over what will the information be transmitted?* The answer is that information is transmitted over networks, which use wire and cable transmission, such as coaxial cable and fiber optics, as well as free air space transmission, which is used for for wireless traffic.

### 2.1.6 The Information Exchange Medium

The information exchange medium includes all information carriers for transmission, i.e., all storage and transmission media. The central question is: *Which information carrier will be used for information exchange between different places?* The answer is that information can flow through *intermediate* storage media, where the storage medium is transported outside of computer networks to the destination, through *direct* transmission using computer networks, or through *combined* usage of storage and transmission media (e.g., electronic mailing system).

### 2.1.7 Representation Values and Representation Spaces

The above classification of media can be used as a basis for characterizing the notion *medium* in the context of information processing. Here, the description of perception medium comes closest to our notion of a medium: the media appeal to the human senses. Each medium defines *representation values* and *representation spaces* [HD90, HS91], which involve the five senses.

Examples of visual representation spaces are paper or screen. During a computer-controlled slide show with simultaneous projection of the computer screen content, the whole movie screen counts as a representation space. Stereo and quadraphony determine the acoustic representation spaces. Representation spaces can also be considered part of the above described presentation media for information output.

Representation values determine the information representation of different media: while the *text* medium visually represents a sentence through a sequence of characters, this sentence will be represented by the *speech* medium in the form of a pressure wave. Some representation values are self-contained by their media. In other words, they can be properly interpreted by the recipient. Examples here are temperature, taste, and smell. Other media require a predefined symbol set, which the users must agree upon. Text, speech and gestures are examples of such media.

Representation values can be considered either as a continuum or a sequence of discrete values. Pressure wave fluctuations do not appear as discrete values; instead they determine the acoustic signals. Electromagnetic waves for human eye perception are not discrete values either; rather they are a continuum. Characters of a text and audio sample values in electronic form are sequences of discrete values.

### 2.1.8 Representation Dimensions

Each representation space consists of one or more *representation dimensions.* A computer screen has two spatial dimensions; holography and stereophony require an additional spatial dimension. Time can occur inside each representation space as an additional dimension, as it has central meaning to multimedia systems. Media are divided into two types with respect to time in their representation space:

1. Some media, such as text and graphics, are time-independent. Information in these media consist exclusively of a sequence of individual elements or of a continuum without a time component. Such media are known as *time-independent* (or *discrete*). Note, the notion 'discrete' is sometimes confusing, because a medium can also be discrete in value but continuous in time.). The text of a book is, for example, a discrete medium. Processing of discrete media should happen as fast as possible, but this processing is not time critical because the validity (and therefore correctness) of the data does not depend on any time condition.

2. The values of other media, such as sound and full-motion video, change over time. Information is expressed not only in its individual value, but also by the time of its occurrence. The semantics depend on the level of the relative change of the discrete values or of the continuum. Such media are *time-dependent.* Also, representation values caused by tactile or temperature sensors with threshold detectors are time-dependent, and therefore also belong to the time-dependent media.

Processing of these media is time-critical because the validity (and therefore correctness) of the data depends on a time condition. For example, a transmitted audio sample delivered too late is invalid if the following samples to the sample in question have already been played back.

Individual representation values occur in audio and video as a continuous sequence. We understand *video* as a sequence of plain images occurring periodically, as well as audio being a sequence of samples with periodic behavior. We call these media *continuous media.* Using this division, time-dependent representation values, which occur aperiodically, are not considered continuous media. Control commands for real-time systems are an example. In multimedia systems, we must also consider non-continuous sequences of representation values. Such sequences occur, for example, by transmission of information (e.g., mouse pointer position) in a cooperative application within a shared window.

Examples of continuous media are: *video* coming from natural source (e.g., video taken by a camera during a live video transmission) or from an artificial source (e.g., video disc); *audio*, which is mostly stored as a sequence of digitalized sound-wave samples; and *signals of different sensors*, such as those that sense air pressure, temperature, humidity, pressure or radioactivity.

These notions of time-dependent, discrete and continuous media do not have any connection to internal representation. They relate to the impression of the viewer or listener. For example, a movie as a representative of continuous media often consists of a sequence of discrete values, which change in representation space according to a time function. The inertia of the human eye only leads to the impression of continuity if a sequence of at least 16 individual images per second is provided.

## 2.2 Main Properties of a Multimedia System

### 2.2.1 Multimedia System Definition

If we derive a multimedia system from the meaning of the words in the American Heritage Dictionary, then a multimedia system is any system which supports more than a single kind of media. This characterization is insufficient because it only deals with a *quantitative* evaluation of the system. For example, each system processing text and graphics would be classified as a multimedia system according to this narrow definition. Such systems already existed before the multimedia notion was used in a computer environment. Hence, the notion *multimedia* implies a new quality in a computer environment.

We understand multimedia more in a *qualitative* rather than a quantitative way. Therefore, the kind rather than the number of supported media should determine if a system is a multimedia system. It should be pointed out that this definition is controversial. Even in the standardization bodies, e.g., ISO, a weaker interpretation is often used.

A multimedia system distinguishes itself from other systems through several properties. We elaborate on the most important properties such as combination of the media, media-independence, computer control and integration.

### 2.2.2 Combination of Media

Not every arbitrary combination of media justifies the usage of the term *multimedia.* A simple text processing program with incorporated images is often called a multimedia application because two media are processed through one program. But one should talk about multimedia only when both continuous and discrete media are utilized. A text processing program with incorporated images is therefore not a multimedia application.

### 2.2.3 Independence

An important aspect of different media is their level of *independence* from each other. In general, there is a request for independence of different media, but multimedia may require several levels of independence. On the one hand, a computer-controlled video recorder stores audio and video information, but there is an inherently tight connection between the two types of media. Both media are coupled together through the common storage medium of the tape. On the other hand, for the purpose of presentations, the combination of DAT recorder (Digital Audio Tape) signals and computer-available text satisfies the request for media-independence.

### 2.2.4 Computer-supported Integration

The media-independence prerequisite provides the possibility of combining media in arbitrary forms. Computers are the ideal tool for this purpose. The system should be capable of computer-controlled media processing. Moreover, the system should be programmable by a system programmer or even a user. Simple input or output of different media through one system (e.g., a video recorder) does not satisfy the requirement for a computer-controlled solution. Computer-controlled data of independent media can be integrated to accomplish certain functions. For such a purpose, timing, spatial and semantic synchronization relations will be included. A text processing program that supports text, table calculations and video clips does not satisfy the demand for integration if program supporting the connection between the data cannot be established. A high integration level is accomplished if changing the content of a table row causes corresponding video scene and text changes.

Such flexible processing of media is not obvious – even in many of the best available multimedia products. Therefore, this aspect must be emphasized in terms of an *integrated multimedia system.* Simply put, in such systems, everything can be presented with video and sound that is presented with text and graphics today [AGH90]. For example, in conventional systems, a text message can be sent to other users; but, a multimedia system with a high level of integration allows this function also for audio messages or even for a combination of audio and text.

### 2.2.5 Communication Systems

Communication-capable multimedia systems must be approached. A reason for this is that most of today's computers are interconnected; considering multimedia functions from only the local processing viewpoint would be a restriction, if not a step back. Another reason is that distributed environments enable particularly interesting multimedia applications. Here multimedia information cannot only be created, processed, presented and stored, but also distributed above the single computer's boundary.

## 2.3 Multimedia

Considering the first explanation of multimedia at the beginning of this chapter, it is apparent that the notion is insufficient. We derive the following definition for multimedia from the American Heritage Dictionary definitions and the above considerations with respect to the medium (Section 2.1) and to the main properties of a multimedia system (Section 2.2):

*A multimedia system is characterized by computer-controlled, integrated production, manipulation, presentation, storage and communication of independent information, which is encoded at least through a continuous (time-dependent) and a discrete (time-independent) medium.*

*Multimedia* is very often used as an attribute of many systems, components, products, ideas, etc., without satisfying the above presented characteristics. From this viewpoint our definition is deliberately restrictive.

Thus, two notions of multimedia can be distinguished:

- **"Multimedia", strictly speaking:**

  This notion was explained in Section 2.2 and will be used further. In this context, continuous media will always be included in a multimedia system. At the same time important timely marginal conditions (through the continuous media) for the processing of discrete media will be introduced. They have barely been considered in computer use until now.

- **"Multimedia", in the broader sense:**

  Often the notion *multimedia* is used to describe the processing of individual images and text, although no continuous medium is present. Many of the processing tasks in this environment will also be necessary in the multimedia system according to the restrictive definition. In any case, if more media are processed together, one can talk about multimedia according to this second notion.

## 2.4 Traditional Data Streams Characteristics

In Sections 2.1, 2.2, and 2.3 we clarified the multimedia notion from the local computer-based point of view. But the presented work also includes the consideration of multimedia communication systems. Therefore, we need to specify the multimedia notion from the communication point of view.

In distributed multimedia communication systems, data of discrete and continuous media are transmitted and information exchange takes place. Moreover, in each digital system, transmitted information is divided into *individual units* (in general, these are packets) and subsequently sent away from one system component (the source) to another (the destination). The source and destination can be located either on the same computer or on different machines. A sequence of individual packets transmitted in a time-dependent fashion is called a *data stream* (The term "data stream" will be used here as a synonym for "data flow".). Packets can carry information of either continuous or discrete media. An example of a continuous media data stream is the transmission of speech in a telephone system. The retrieval of a document from a database can be seen as setting up a discrete media data stream.

Transmission of information carrying different media leads to data streams with very different features. The attributes of *asynchronous*, *synchronous*, and *isochronous* data transmission come from the fields of computer communication and switching. They are also used, for example, in FDDI (Fiber Distributed Data Interface) networks for the description of different data transmission modes with respect to end-to-end delay of individual packets (see Figures 10.5 and 10.6).

### 2.4.1 Asynchronous Transmission Mode

The *asynchronous transmission mode* provides for communication with no timely restrictions. Packets reach the receiver as fast as possible.

Protocols of the worldwide Internet for electronic mail transmission are an example. In local area networks, Ethernet is a further example. All information of discrete media can be transmitted as an asynchronous data stream. Data of discrete media can also include time restrictions through the timely connection to continuous media synchronization. In this case an asynchronous transmission might not be appropriate. If an asynchronous mode is chosen for transmission of continuous media, additional techniques must be applied to provide the time restrictions.

### 2.4.2 Synchronous Transmission Mode

The *synchronous transmission mode* defines a maximum end-to-end delay for each packet of a data stream. This upper bound will never be violated. Moreover, a packet can reach the receiver at any arbitrary earlier time. Thus, an important claim of multimedia applications is satisfied: a maximal end-to-end delay can be guaranteed.

Additionally, an audio connection can be established over a local area network which supports synchronous transmission mode. The uncompressed transfer of video data in a retrieval mode is characterized by a high data rate and relatively high maximal end-to-end delay. Here the typical data rate is 140 Mbit/s and a maximal delay can be 1 second. In extreme cases packets arrive at the receiver 1 second too early and have to be stored intermediately. In our example, a receiver would need a temporary storage of about 17.5 Mbytes.

### 2.4.3 Isochronous Transmission Mode

The *isochronous transmission mode* defines, besides a maximum end-to-end delay for each packet of a data stream, a minimum end-to-end delay. This means that the delay jitter (in short, "jitter") of individual packets is bounded.

In this case, the necessary storage of video data at the receiver, mentioned in the above example, would be strongly reduced. These demands on intermediate storage must be considered in all components along the data route between source(s) and sink(s).

## 2.5 Data Stream Characteristics for Continuous Media

The following section describes data stream characteristics that relate to any audio and video data transfer in a multimedia systems (*multimedia data streams*). Moreover, we consider the effects of compression on data stream characteristics during data transfer. These data stream characteristics apply to distributed as well as local environments.

### 2.5.1 The Time Interval Between a Complete Transmission of Consecutive Packets

This first property relates to the time interval between a complete transmission of consecutive packets. Based on the availability of packets, we distinguish among the following possibilities:

- If the time interval between two consecutive packets is constant, a data stream is called *strongly periodic*. Therefore, in an ideal case, jitter has the value zero. Figure 2.1 shows such a data stream. An example is PCM-coded speech in

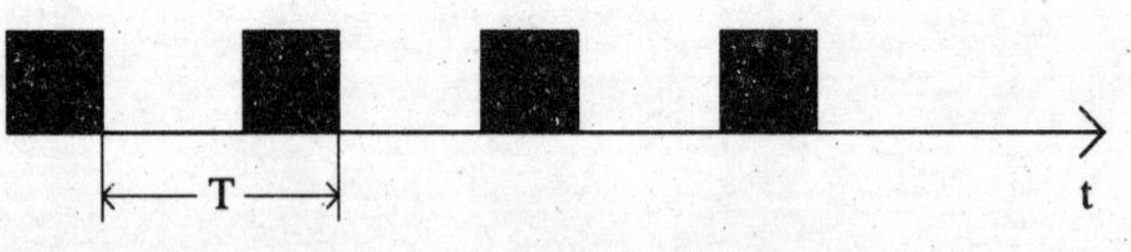


Figure 2.1: *Strongly periodic stream, (T-time limit between two consecutive packets), i.e., time intervals are of the same length between two consecutive packets.*

  traditional telephone switching systems.

- The duration of the time interval between two consecutive packets can be described through a periodical function with finite period, but the time interval between consecutive packets is not constant (otherwise it would be a strongly periodic data stream). The data stream is called *weakly periodic*. This case is shown in Figure 2.2.

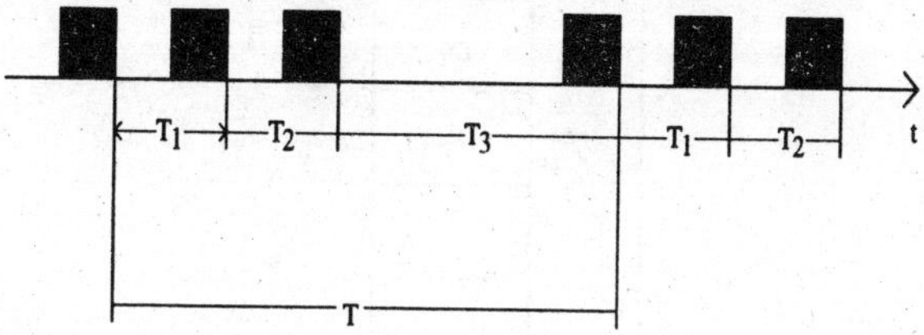


Figure 2.2: *Weakly periodic stream, i.e., time intervals between consecutive packets are of periodic nature.*

- All other possibilities of transmission with respect to time interval are known as *aperiodic data streams.* Figure 2.3 shows such a data stream.

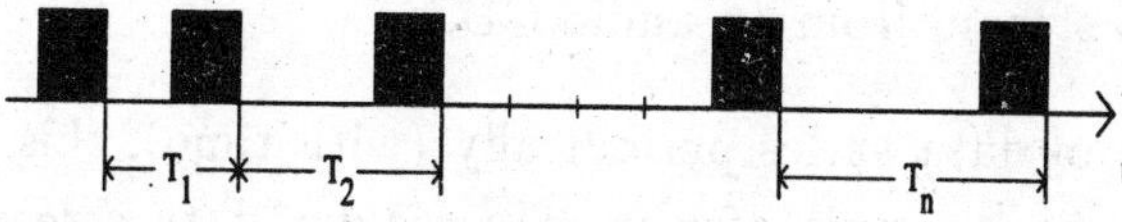


Figure 2.3: *Aperiodic stream, i.e., the sequence of time intervals is neither strongly nor weakly periodic.*

An example of an aperiodic data stream can be found in a cooperative application with shared windows. Very often, the status and actual coordinates of the user's mouse must be distributed among all participants of the multimedia conference. If this information is transmitted periodically, extremely high redundancy is present. Thus, given that an optimal system should transmit information only when necessary, after an initialization phase, data are exchanged only when a change in position or status occurs.

### 2.5.2 Variation of Consecutive Packet Amount

A second characteristic of data streams is the variation of the amount of consecutive packets.

- If the amount of data stays constant during the lifetime of a data stream, one calls the data stream *strongly regular.* Such a data stream is shown in Figure 2.4. This feature is typical for uncompressed digital data transmission.

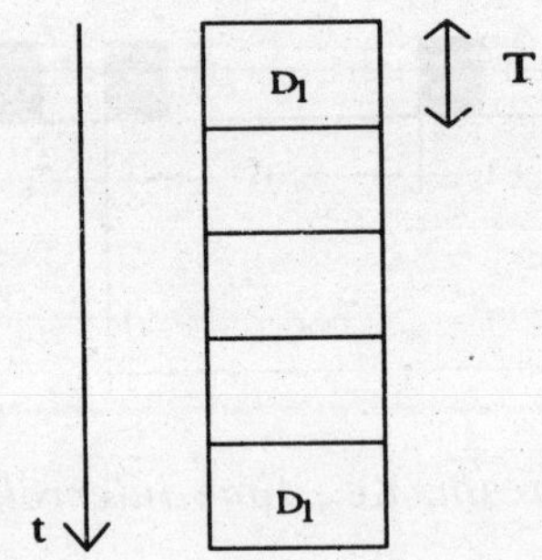


Figure 2.4: *Strongly regular stream, i.e., constant data size of all packets.*

Examples are the video stream taken from a camera in uncompressed form and the audio stream from an audio CD.

- If the amount of data varies periodically (with time), this is a *weakly regular* data stream. An example of a weakly regular data stream is a compressed video stream which uses a compression method as follows: individual images are coded and compressed as an individual, whole unit, which represents a relatively large packet inside the data stream (bounded packet length of network transmission is left out in this consideration.). Packets will be periodically transmitted, e.g., every two seconds. Inbetween the two second periods, additional packets will be sent which include the information about the difference of the two consecutive compressed images.

  An example of a compression method which works similarly to the above description is the MPEG compression method (see Section 6.7). MPEG differentiates among I, P and B images in a compressed video stream. I-images represent compressed individual images, while P- and B-images take into account image differences. With this approach the data rate is reduced essentially. There is no constant bit rate for individual I, P, B compressed packets, but the I:B:P relation of the created data amount for every image is known (often used value of the I:B:P relation is 10:1:2 for individual images.). Such a data stream can be characterized on average over a long time period as *weakly regular* (Figure 2.5).

- Data streams are *irregular* if the amount of data is neither constant nor changes according to a periodic function (see Figure 2.6). Transmission and processing

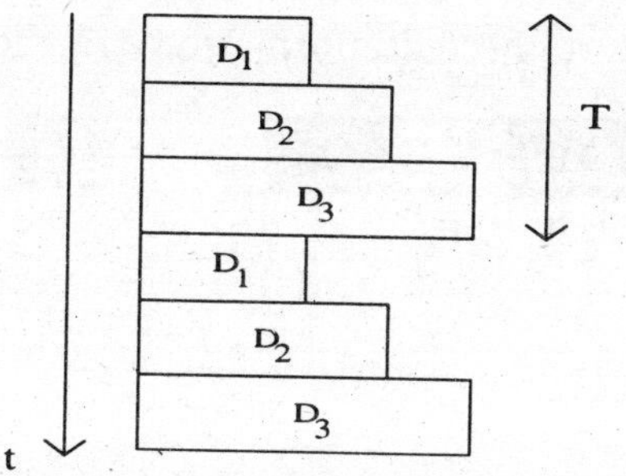


Figure 2.5: *Weakly regular stream, i.e., data size of the packets changes periodically.*

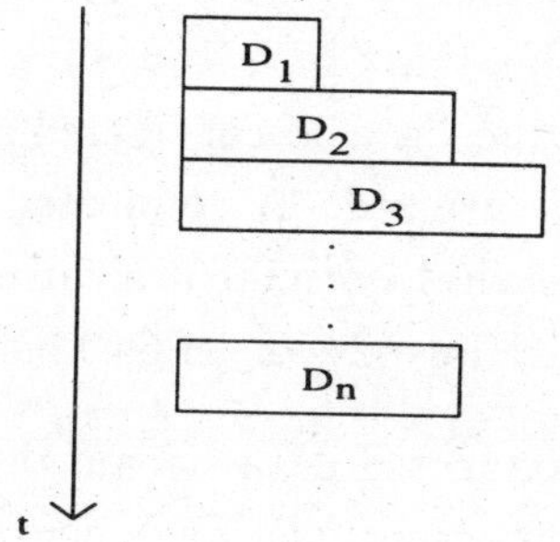


Figure 2.6: *Irregular data stream, i.e., data size of the packets is neither constant nor changing periodically.*

is more complicated in this case. In the case when a compression method is applied to the data stream, the data stream has a variable bit rate, and the size of an individual packet (derived from an individual image) is determined from the content of the previous changed image. The size of the created information unit is therefore dependent on the video sequence and the data stream is *irregular.*

### 2.5.3 Contiguous Packets

A third property characterizes *continuity*, or the connection between consecutive packets. Are consecutive packets transmitted directly one after another, or is there a gap between the packets? This can be seen as utilization of a certain system resource, such as a network.

- Figure 2.7 shows a *connected* information transfer. All packets are trans-

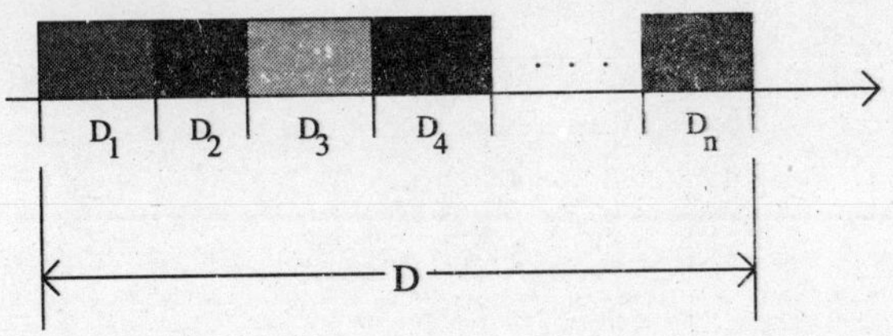


Figure 2.7: *Continuous stream, i.e., the packets are transmitted without intermediate gaps.*

  mitted successively without a gap. Necessary additional information (e.g., error control codes) of the data is considered. In this case, the considered system resource is 100% utilized. A connected data stream allows maximal data throughput and reaches optimal utilization of the system resource. A B-channel of ISDN with transmission of 64 kbit/s audio data is an example.

- The transmission of a connected data stream through a channel with a higher capacity leads to gaps between individual packets. A data stream with gaps between information units is called an *unconnected data stream.* An example is shown in Figure 2.8. However, it is not important if gaps exist among all

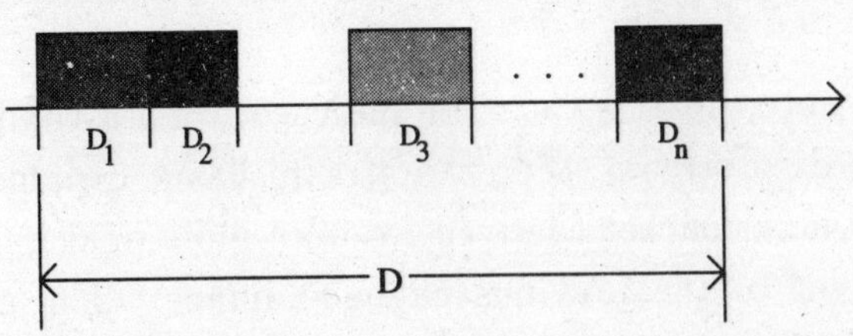


Figure 2.8: *Discrete stream, i.e., gaps exist among the packets.*

  packets or if the duration of the gaps varies. For example, the transmission of a data stream, coded with the JPEG method, with 1.2 Mbit/s throughput on average, will lead to gaps among individual packets on an FDDI network.

In the following example, the properties described above should be made clear: an NTSC video signal is captured from a video camera and digitized in a computer, yet no compression is done. The created data stream is strongly periodic, strongly regular and connected, as shown in Figure 2.4. There are no gaps among the packets. During the digitizing process, the DVI_RTV method for compression, using the ActionMedia II$^{TM}$card, is performed. The resulting data stream (considered over a longer period of time) is now weakly periodic, weakly regular, and, through transmission over a 16 Mbit/second Token Ring, unconnected.

## 2.6 Information Units

Continuous media consist of a time-dependent sequence of individual information units. Such an information unit is called a *Logical Data Unit* (LDU), which is close to a *Protocol Data Unit* (PDU). The meaning of the information and data amount of an LDU can be different:

1. Consider for example the symphony "*The bear*" by Joseph Haydn. It consists of four sentences: *vivace assai, allegretto, minuet* and *finale vivace*. Each sentence is an independent, self-contained part of this composition, consisting of a sequence of notes for different instruments. The notes are represented in a digital system as a sequence of samples (no compression is considered in our example.). With CD-DA quality, there are 44,100 samples per second, which are coded with 16 bits per sample. On a CD the samples are grouped into units of 1/75 second duration. One could take as the LDU the whole symphony, individual sentences, individual notes, grouped samples of 1/75 second duration or just individual samples. The particular application determines what is considered to be the LDU. For example, applications using output functions of the whole symphony will take the whole symphony as the LDU. Other applications use functions which consider the smallest meaningful units (in our case, notes). A digital system considers samples as the LDUs.

2. An example of an uncompressed video sequence consisting of individual video clips, which present a specific scene, is shown in Figure 2.9. Such a scene is comprised of a sequence of images. An image can be divided, for example, into 16x16 groups of pixels. Each pixel consists again of luminance and chrominance values. The image is therefore not the only possible LDU of a video sequence. A scene or a pixel can also be an LDU. In a video sequence, coded

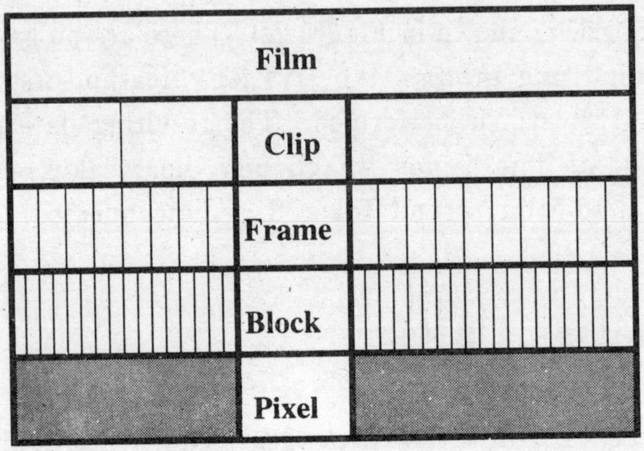


Figure 2.9: *Granularity of a motion picture sequence.*

with MPEG or DVI, existent redundancies can be used through applying an interframe compression method. The smallest self-contained meaningful units here are image sequences.

The notion of *granularity* characterizes the hierarchical division of audio or video data streams into their components. In our examples, the most general names and best-known information units are the symphony and the movie. Yet there exists also another classification of LDU with respect to duration. *Closed LDUs* have a pre-defined duration. An example of such an LDU stream is a data stream of audio samples in the computer. If the duration is not known in advance, we encounter an *open LDU*. An example of such an LDU stream is a data stream sent from a camera or microphone to the computer.

# Chapter 3

# Sound / Audio

Sound is a physical phenomenon produced by the vibration of matter, such as a violin string, or a block of wood. As the matter vibrates, pressure variations are created in the air surrounding it. This alteration of high and low pressure is propagated through the air in a wave-like motion. When a wave reaches the human ear, a sound is heard.

Sound methodology and audio techniques engage in processing these sound waves (acoustic signals). Important topics in this area are coding, storage on recorders or digital audio tapes, music and speech processing.

In this chapter a discussion of sound, music coding and speech processing is presented. Basic concepts and formats of sound, as well as representation of sound in the computer [Boo87, Tec89] are presented. Because multimedia applications use audio in the form of music and/or speech, music and its MIDI standard, as well as speech synthesis, speech recognition and speech transmission [Loy85, Fla72, FS92, O'S90, Fal85, Bri86, Ace93, Sch92], are described.

The topic of audio data storage on optical discs is presented in Chapter 7, for the reason that the principles and technology used are not restricted to audio. The compression of audio/video signals is also described separately in Chapter 6, because similar methods are used for compressing the data of different media. Further, the commonalities among the media are emphasized by being treated together.

## 3.1 Basic Sound Concepts

Sound is produced by the vibration of matter. During the vibration, pressure variations are created in the air surrounding it. The pattern of the oscillation is called a *waveform* (Figure 3.1 [Tec89]).

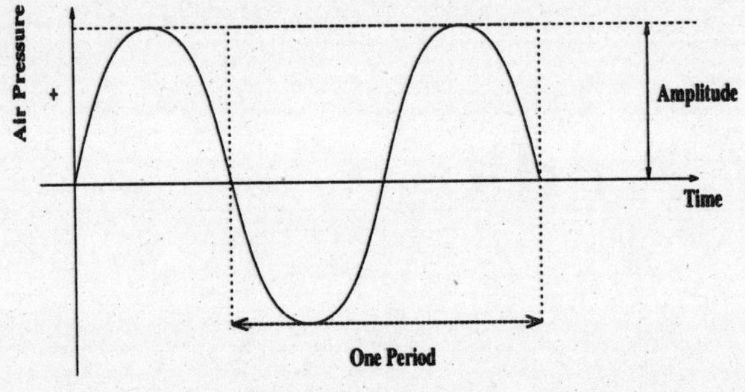


Figure 3.1: *Oscillation of an air pressure wave.*

The waveform repeats the same shape at regular intervals and this portion is called a *period.* Since sound waves occur naturally, they are never perfectly smooth or uniformly periodic. However, sounds that display a recognizable periodicity tend to be more musical than those that are nonperiodic. Examples of periodic sound sources are musical instruments, vowel sounds, the whistling wind and bird songs. Nonperiodic sound sources include unpitched percussion instruments, coughs and sneezes and rushing water.

### Frequency

The *frequency* of a sound is the reciprocal value of the period; it represents the number of periods in a second and is measured in *hertz* (Hz) or *cycles per second* (cps). A convenient abbreviation, kHz (kilohertz), is used to indicate thousands of oscillations per second: 1 kHz equals 1000 Hz [Boo87]. The frequency range is divided into:

| | |
|---|---|
| Infra-sound | from 0 to 20 Hz |
| Human hearing frequency range | from 20 Hz to 20 kHz |
| Ultrasound | from 20 kHz to 1 GHz |
| Hypersound | from 1 GHz to 10 THz |

Multimedia systems typically make use of sound only within the frequency range of human hearing. We will call sound within the human hearing range *audio* and the waves in this frequency range *acoustic signals* [Boo87]. For example, speech is an acoustic signal produced by humans; music signals have a frequency range between 20 Hz and 20 kHz. Besides speech and music, we denote any other audio signal as *noise.*

**Amplitude**

A sound also has an *amplitude*, a property subjectively heard as loudness. The amplitude of a sound is the measure of the displacement of the air pressure wave from its mean, or quiescent state

### 3.1.1 Computer Representation of Sound

The smooth, continuous curve of a sound waveform is not directly represented in a computer. A computer measures the amplitude of the waveform at regular time intervals to produce a series of numbers. Each of these measurements is a *sample.* Figure 3.2 illustrates one period of a digitally sampled waveform.

The mechanism that converts an audio signal into digital samples is the *Analog-to-Digital Converter (ADC).* The reverse conversion is performed by a *Digital-to-Analog Converter (DAC).* The AM79C30A Digital Subscriber Controller chip is an example of an ADC and is available on SPARCstations™. Desktop SPARC™systems include a built-in speaker for audio output. DAC is also available as a standard UNIX™device. For example, SPARCserver 6xx systems do not have an internal speaker, but support an external microphone and speaker.

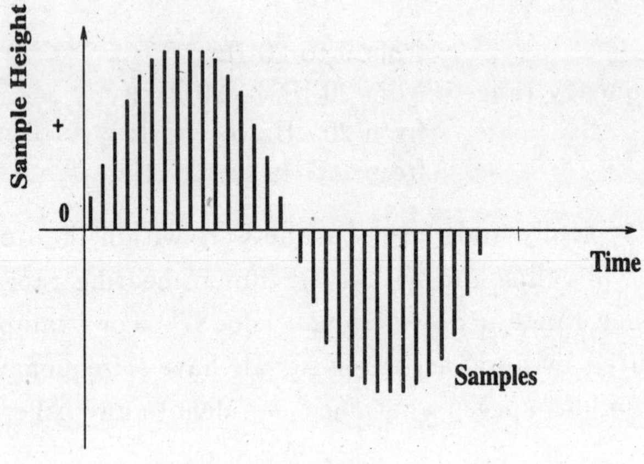


Figure 3.2: *Sampled waveform.*

### Sampling Rate

The rate at which a continuous waveform (Figure 3.1) is sampled is called the *sampling rate.* Like frequencies, sampling rates are measured in Hz. The CD standard sampling rate of 44100 Hz means that the waveform is sampled 44100 times per second. This seems to be above the frequency range the human ear can hear. However, the bandwidth (which in this case is 20000 Hz - 20 Hz = 19980 Hz) that digitally sampled audio signal can represent, is at most equal to half of the CD standard sampling rate (44100 Hz). This is an application of the Nyquist sampling theorem. ("For lossless digitization, the sampling rate should be at least twice the maximum frequency responses.") Hence, a sampling rate of 44100 Hz can only represent frequencies up to 22050 Hz, a boundary much closer to that of human hearing.

### Quantization

Just as a waveform is sampled at discrete times, the value of the sample is also discrete. The resolution or *quantization* of a sample value depends on the number of bits used in measuring the height of the waveform. An 8-bit quantization yields 256 possible values; 16-bit CD-quality quantization results in over 65536 values.

Figure 3.3 presents a 3-bit quantization. The sampled waveform with a 3-bit quan-

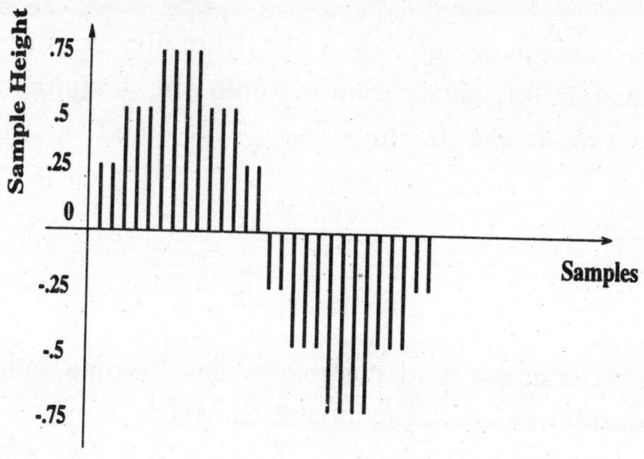


Figure 3.3: *Three-bit quantization.*

tization results in only eight possible values: .75, .5, .25, 0, -.25, -.5, -.75 and -1. The shape of the waveform becomes less discernible with a lowered quantization, i.e., the lower the quantization, the lower the quality of the sound (the result might be a buzzing sound).

#### Sound Hardware

Before sound can be processed, a computer needs input/output devices. Microphone jacks and built-in speakers are devices connected to an ADC and DAC, respectively for the input and output of audio.

### 3.1.2 Audio Formats

The AM79C30A Digital Subscriber Controller provides *voice-quality* audio. This converter uses an 8-bit $\mu$-law encoded quantization and a sampling rate of 8000 Hz. This representation is considered fast and accurate enough for *telephone-quality* speech input.

*CD-quality* audio is generated if the stereo DAC operates at 44100 samples per second with a 16-bit *linear PCM (Pulse Code Modulation)* encoded quantization [JB89].

The above examples of telephone-quality and CD-quality audio indicate that important format parameters for specification of audio are: *sampling rate* (e.g., 8012.8 samples/second) and *sample quantization* (e.g., 8-bit quantization).

## 3.2 Music

The relationship between music and computers has become more and more important, specially considering the development of MIDI (Music Instrument Digital Interface) and its important contributions in the music industry today. The MIDI interface between electronic musical instruments and computers is a small piece of equipment that plugs directly into the computer's serial port and allows the transmission of music signals. MIDI is considered to be the most compact interface that allows full-scale output.

### 3.2.1 MIDI Basic Concepts

MIDI is a standard that manufacturers of electronic musical instruments have agreed upon. It is a set of specifications they use in building their instruments so that the instruments of different manufacturers can, without difficulty, communicate musical information between one another [Loy85].

A MIDI interface has two different components:

- *Hardware* connects the equipment. It specifies the physical connection between musical instruments, stipulates that a *MIDI port* is built into an instrument, specifies a *MIDI cable* (which connects two instruments) and deals with electronic signals that are sent over the cable.

- A *data format* encodes the information traveling through the hardware. A MIDI data format does not include an encoding of individual samples as the audio format does (Section 3.1.2). Instead of individual samples, an instrument-connected data format is used. The encoding includes, besides the instrument specification, the notion of the beginning and end of a note, basic frequency and sound volume. MIDI data allow an encoding of about 10 octaves, which corresponds to 128 notes.

The MIDI data format is digital; the data are grouped into *MIDI messages.* Each MIDI message communicates one *musical event* between machines. These musical events are usually actions that a musician performs while playing a musical instrument. The action might be pressing keys, moving slider controls, setting switches and adjusting foot pedals.

When a musician presses a piano key, the MIDI interface creates a MIDI message where the beginning of the note with its stroke intensity is encoded. This message is transmitted to another machine. In the moment the key is released, a corresponding signal (MIDI message) is transmitted again. For ten minutes of music, this process creates about 200 Kbytes of MIDI data, which is essentially less than the equivalent volume of a CD-audio coded stream in the same time.

If a musical instrument satisfies both components of the MIDI standard, the instrument is a *MIDI device* (e.g., a synthesizer), capable of communicating with other MIDI devices through *channels.* The MIDI standard specifies 16 channels. A MIDI device (musical instrument) is mapped to a channel. Music data, transmitted through a channel, are reproduced at the receiver side with the synthesizer instrument. The MIDI standard identifies 128 instruments, including noise effects (e.g., telephone, air craft), with unique numbers. For example, 0 is for the Acoustic Grand Piano, 12 for the marimba, 40 for the violin, 73 for the flute, etc.

Some instruments allow only one note to be played at a time, such as the flute. Other instruments allow more than one note to be played simultaneously, such as the organ. The maximum number of simultaneously played notes per channel is a main property of each synthesizer. The range can be from 3 to 16 notes per channel.

To tune a MIDI device to one or more channels, the device must be set to one of the MIDI *reception modes.* There are four modes:

- Mode 1: Omni On/Poly;
- Mode 2: Omni On/Mono;

- Mode 3: Omni Off/Poly;
- Mode 4: Omni Off/Mono

The first half of the mode name specifies how the MIDI device monitors the incoming MIDI channels. If Omni is turned on, the MIDI device monitors all the MIDI channels and responds to all channel messages, no matter which channel they are transmitted on. If Omni is turned off, the MIDI device responds only to channel messages sent on the channel(s) the device is set to receive.

The second half of the mode name tells the MIDI device how to play notes coming in over the MIDI cable. If the option Poly is set, the device can play several notes at a time. If the mode is set to Mono, the device plays notes like a monophonic synthesizer – one note at a time.

### 3.2.2 MIDI Devices

Through the MIDI interface, a computer can control output of individual instruments. On the other hand, the computer can receive, store or process coded musical data through the same interface. The data are generated with a *keyboard* and reproduced through a sound generator. A *sequencer* can store data. Further, it may also modify the musical data. In a multimedia system, the sequencer is a computer application.

The heart of any MIDI system is the MIDI *synthesizer* device. A typical synthesizer looks like a simple piano keyboard with a panel full of buttons, but it is far more (more detailed information on synthesizers can be found in [Boo87].). Most synthesizers have the following common components:

- *Sound Generators*

  Sound generators do the actual work of synthesizing sound; the purpose of the rest of the synthesizer is to control the sound generators. The principal purpose of the generator is to produce an audio signal that becomes sound when fed into a loudspeaker. By varying the voltage oscillation of the audio signal, a sound generator changes the quality of the sound – its pitch, loudness and tone color – to create a wide variety of sounds and notes.

Internally, sound generation can be done in different ways. One way is to store the acoustic signals as MIDI data in advance. Afterwards, the stored MIDI data are transformed with a digital-analog adapter into acoustic signals. Individual notes are composed in a timely fashion. Another method is to create acoustic signals synthetically.

- *Microprocessor*

  The microprocessor communicates with the keyboard to know what notes the musician is playing, and with the control panel to know what commands the musician wants to send to the microprocessor. The microprocessor then specifies note and sound commands to the sound generators; in other words, the microprocessor sends and receives MIDI messages.

- *Keyboard*

  The keyboard affords the musician's direct control of the synthesizer. Pressing keys on the keyboard signals the microprocessor what notes to play and how long to play them. Some synthesizer keyboards can also signal to the microprocessor how loud to play the notes and whether to add *vibrato* or other effects to the notes. The sound intensity of a tone depends on the speed and acceleration of the key pressure. The keyboard should have at least five octaves with 61 keys.

- *Control Panel*

  The control panel controls those functions that are not directly concerned with notes and durations (controlled by the keyboard). Panel controls include: a slider that sets the overall volume of the synthesizer, a button that turns the synthesizer on and off, and a menu that calls up different patches for the sound generators to play.

- *Auxiliary Controllers*

  Auxiliary controllers are available to give more control over the notes played on the keyboard. Two very common variables on a synthesizer are *pitch bend* and *modulation*. Pitch bend controllers can bend pitch up and down, adding *portamento* (a smooth, uninterrupted glide in passing from one tone to another) to notes; modulation controllers can increase or decrease effects such as *vibrato*.

- *Memory*

  Synthesizer memory is used to store patches for the sound generators and settings on the control panel. Many synthesizers also have a slot for *external memory cartridges*. By using several memory cartridges, the musician can plug in a different cartridge each time s/he wants a set of new sounds for the synthesizer.

There are many other MIDI devices that augment the standard synthesizer in a MIDI system. Examples are drum machines which specialize in percussion sounds and rhythms, the master keyboard which increases the quality of the synthesizer keyboard, guitar controllers, guitar synthesizers, drum pad controllers and so on.

An important MIDI device is a *sequencer*, which can be a drum machine, computer or dedicated sequencer. A sequencer was used originally as a storage server for generated MIDI data. Today, a sequencer, being a computer, becomes additionally a music editor. Data can be modified in a proper way because of their digital data representation. There are several possibilities to represent musical data. The most common representation and manipulation of data are musical notes. The musical piece appears on the screen in the form of a sheet of music. The sequencer transforms the notes into MIDI messages (Sections 3.2.1, 3.2.3). Another representation is a direct input of MIDI messages. Here, the user specifies required musical events per channel with their time dependencies. This input depends on the keyboard type.

### 3.2.3 MIDI Messages

MIDI messages transmit information between MIDI devices and determine what kinds of musical events can be passed from device to device. The format of MIDI messages consists of the *status byte* (the first byte of any MIDI message), which describes the kind of message, and *data bytes* (the following bytes). MIDI messages are divided into two different types:

- *Channel Messages*

  Channel messages go only to specified devices. There are two types of channel messages:

  - *Channel voice messages* send actual performance data between MIDI devices, describing keyboard action, controller action and control panel changes. They describe music by defining pitch, amplitude, timbre, duration and other sound qualities. Each message has at least one and usually two data bytes that accompany the status byte to describe these sound qualities. Examples of channel voice messages are *Note On*, *Note Off*, *Channel Pressure*, *Control Change*, etc.
  - *Channel mode messages* determine the way that a receiving MIDI device responds to channel voice messages. They set the MIDI channel receiving modes for different MIDI devices, stop spurious notes from playing and affect local control of a device. Examples of such messages are *Local Control*, *All Notes Off*, *Omni Mode Off*, etc.

- *System Messages*

  System messages go to all devices in a MIDI system because no channel numbers are specified. There are three types of system messages:

  - *System real-time messages* are very short and simple, consisting of only one byte. They carry extra data with them. These messages synchronize the timing of MIDI devices in performance; therefore, it is important that they be sent at precisely the time they are required. To avoid delays, these messages are sent in the middle of other messages, if necessary. Examples of such messages are *System Reset*, *Timing Clock (MIDI clock)*, etc.
  - *System common messages* are commands that prepare sequencers and synthesizers to play a song. The various messages enable you to select a song, find a common starting place in the song and tune all the synthesizers if they need tuning. Examples are *Song Select*, *Tune Request*, etc.
  - *System exclusive messages* allow MIDI manufacturers to create customized MIDI messages to send between their MIDI devices. This coding starts

with a *system-exclusive-message*, where the manufacturer is specified, and ends with an *end-of-exclusive message*.

### 3.2.4 MIDI and SMPTE Timing Standards

MIDI reproduces traditional note length using *MIDI clocks*, which are represented through *timing clock* messages. Using a MIDI clock, a receiver can synchronize with the clock cycles of the sender. For example, a MIDI clock helps keep separate sequencers in the same MIDI system playing at the same tempo. When a master sequencer plays a song, it sends out a stream of 'Timing Clock' messages to convey the tempo to other sequencers. The faster the Timing Clock messages come in, the faster the receiving sequencer plays the song. To keep a standard timing reference, the MIDI specifications state that 24 MIDI clocks equal one quarter note.

As an alternative, the *SMPTE timing standard* (Society of Motion Picture and Television Engineers) can be used. The SMPTE timing standard was originally developed by NASA as a way to mark incoming data from different tracking stations so that receiving computers could tell exactly what time each piece of data was created [Boo87]. In the film and video version promoted by the SMPTE, the SMPTE timing standard acts as a very precise clock that stamps a time reading on each frame and fraction of a frame, counting from the beginning of a film or video. To make the time readings precise, the SMPTE format consists of *hours:minutes:seconds:frames:bits* (e.g., 30 frames per second), uses a 24-hour clock and counts from 0 to 23 before recycling to 0. The number of frames in a second differs depending on the type of visual medium. To divide time even more precisely, SMPTE breaks each frame into 80 bits (not digital bits). When SMPTE is counting bits in a frame, it is dividing time into segments as small as one twenty-five hundredth of a second.

Because many film composers now record their music on a MIDI recorder, it is desirable to synchronize the MIDI recorder with video equipment. A SMPTE *synchronizer* should be able to give a time location to the MIDI recorder so it can move to that location in the MIDI *score* (pre-recorded song) to start playback or recording. But MIDI recorders cannot use incoming SMPTE signals to control their recording and playback. The solution is a MIDI/SMPTE synchronizer that converts SMPTE into MIDI, and vice versa. The MIDI/SMPTE synchronizer lets the user specify different tempos and the exact points in SMPTE timing at which each tempo is to start, change, and stop. The synchronizer keeps these tempos and timing points in memory. As a SMPTE video deck plays and sends a stream of SMPTE times to the synchronizer, the synchronizer checks the incoming time and sends out MIDI clocks at a corresponding tempo.

### 3.2.5 MIDI Software

Once a computer is connected to a MIDI system, a variety of MIDI applications can run on it. Digital computers afford the composer or sound designer unprecedented levels of control over the evolution and combination of sonic events.

The software applications generally fall into four major categories:

- *Music recording and performance applications*

  This category of applications provides functions such as recording of MIDI messages as they enter the computer from other MIDI devices, and possibly editing and playing back the messages in performance.

- *Musical notations and printing applications*

  This category allows writing music using traditional musical notation. The user can then play back the music using a performance program or print the music on paper for live performance or publication.

- *Synthesizer patch editors and librarians*

  These programs allow information storage of different synthesizer patches in the computer's memory and disk drives, and editing of patches in the computer.

- *Music education applications*

  These software applications teach different aspects of music using the computer monitor, keyboard and other controllers of attached MIDI instruments.

The main issue in current MIDI-based computer music systems is *interactivity.* Music is a temporal art, and any computer program dealing with music must have sophisticated facilities for representing time and for scheduling processes to occur at a particular point in time. This capability of music applications became possible because of increased computational speeds (e.g., the computational speeds needed to execute compositional algorithms in real-time are available). Therefore, current computer music systems are able to modify their behavior in response to input from other performing musicians [Row93].

The processing chain of interactive computer music systems can be conceptualized in three stages:

- The *sensing stage*, when data are collected from controllers reading gesture information from human performers on stage.
- The *processing stage*, when the computer reads and interprets information coming from the sensors and prepares data for the response stage.
- The *response stage*, when the computer and some collection of sound-producing devices share in realizing a musical output.

Commercial manufacturers dominate in providing MIDI devices, such as MIDI controllers and synthesizers, for sensing and response stages. The processing stage has commercial entries as well, most notably MIDI sequencers. It is in processing, however, that individual conceptions of interactive music are most readily expressed, in any of a variety of programming languages with temporal and MIDI extensions.

Commercial interactive music systems appeared in the mid-1980s. Two groundbreaking efforts in this field were *M* and *Jam Factory* [Zic87]. Among the breakthroughs implemented by these programs was the graphic control panel, which allowed access to the values of global variables affecting musical output. Manipulating the graphic controls had an immediately audible effect. The sensing performed by *M* and *Jam Factory* centered around reading manipulations of the control panel and interpreting an incoming stream of MIDI events. Responses were sent out as MIDI.

In 1990, Opcode Systems released *Max*™, a graphical programming environment for interactive music systems. *Max* is an object-oriented programming language, in which programs are realized by manipulating graphic objects on a computer screen and making connection between them [DZ90].

An interactive computer music system, emphasizing composition and performance, is the MIT system *Cypher* [Row93]. The program has two main components: a listener and a player. The listener characterizes performances represented by streams of MIDI data, which could be coming from a human performer, another computer program or even *Cypher* itself. The player generates and plays musical material.

NeXT™ Computer has a music system based on MIDI that combines the synthesis power and generality of a mainframe computer with the performance flexibility of a keyboard synthesizer. The system, *Music Kit*, helps the composer or performer construct applications that create, organize, process and render music data [JB89].

## 3.3 Speech

Speech can be "perceived," "understood" and "generated" by humans and also by machines. A human adjusts himself/herself very efficiently to different speakers and their speech habits. Despite different dialects and pronunciation, the speech can be well understood by humans. The brain can recognize the very fine line between speech and noise. For this purpose, both ears are used, because filtering with only one ear is substantially more difficult for the listener. The human speech signal comprises a subjective lowest spectral component known as the *pitch*, which is not proportional to frequency. The human ear is most sensitive in the range from 600 Hz to 6000 Hz. Fletscher and Munson have shown that the human ear is substantially less sensitive to low and very high frequencies than to frequencies around 1 kHz. Speech signals have two properties which can be used in speech processing:

- Voiced speech signals show during certain time intervals almost periodic behavior. Therefore, we can consider these signals as *quasi-stationary signals* for around 30 milliseconds.

- The spectrum of audio signals shows characteristic maxima, which are mostly 3-5 frequency bands. These maxima, called *formants*, occur because of resonances of the vocal tract.

For description and modeling of human speech generation, see [All85, BN93].

A machine can also support speech generation and recognition. With computers, one can synthetically generate speech, where the generated signals do not sound quite natural but can be easily understood. An example of such an artificial sounding voice can be heard at the Atlanta (Georgia, USA) airport. On the other hand, a voice can sound natural but may be very difficult to understand. Speech recognition often uses matching rules or statistically based methods. Today, workstations and personal computers can recognize 25,000 possible words. Problems are caused when dialects, emotional pronunciation and environmental noises are part of the audio signal. There are, and will continue to be in the near future, considerable differences between the speech generation and recognition efficiencies/capabilities of the human brain and a high-performance computer [Ace93, Mam93].

In the following two sections we describe in more detail some crucial issues of computer-generated speech and recognition.

### 3.3.1 Speech Generation

Speech generation research has a long history. By the middle of the 19th century, Helmholtz had already built a mechanical vocal tract coupling together several mechanical resonators with which sound could be generated. In 1940, Dudley produced the first speech synthesizer through imitation of mechanical vibration using electrical oscillation [Fal85].

An important requirement for speech generation is *real-time signal generation.* With such a requirement met, a speech output system could transform text into speech automatically without any lengthy preprocessing. Some applications only need a limited vocabulary; an example is the spoken time announcement of a telephone answering service. However, most applications need a large vocabulary, if not an unlimited vocabulary.

Generated speech must be *understandable* and must sound *natural.* The requirement of understandable speech is a fundamental assumption, and the natural sound of speech increases user acceptance.

### Basic Notions

For further discussion we introduce some notions of importance:

- The lowest periodic spectral component of the speech signal is called the *fundamental frequency.* It is present in a voiced sound.
- A *phone* is the smallest speech unit, such as the *m* of *mat* and the *b* of *bat* in English, that distinguish one utterance or word from another in a given language.
- *Allophones* mark the variants of a phone. For example, the aspirated *p* of *pit* and the unaspirated *p* of *spit* are allophones of the English phoneme *p*.
- The *morph* marks the smallest speech unit which carries a meaning itself. Therefore, *consider* is a morph, but *reconsideration* is not.
- A *voiced sound* is generated through the vocal cords. *m*, *v* and *l* are examples of voiced sounds. The pronunciation of a voiced sound depends strongly on each speaker.
- During the generation of an *unvoiced sound*, the vocal cords are opened. *f* and *s* are unvoiced sounds. Unvoiced sounds are relatively independent from the speaker.

Exactly, there are:

- Vowels – a speech sound created by the relatively free passage of breath through the larynx and oral cavity, usually forming the most prominent and central sound of a syllable (e.g., *u* from hunt);
- Consonants – a speech sound produced by a partial or complete obstruction of the air stream by any of the various constrictions of the speech organs (e.g., voiced consonants, such as *m* from *mother*, fricative voiced consonants, such as *v* from *voice*, fricative voiceless consonants, such as *s* from *nurse*, plosive consonants, such as *d* from *daily* and affricate consonants, such as *dg* from *knowledge*, or *ch* from *chew*).

### Reproduced Speech Output

The easiest method of speech generation/output is to use prerecorded speech and play it back in a timely fashion [BN93]. The speech can be stored as PCM (Pulse Code Modulation) samples. Further data compression methods, without using language typical properties, can be applied to recorded speech (see Chapter 6).

### Time-dependent Sound Concatenation

Speech generation/output can also be performed by sound concatenation in a timely fashion [Ril89]. Individual speech units are composed like building blocks, where the composition can occur at different levels. In the simplest case, the individual phones are understood as speech units. Figure 3.4 shows the individual phones of the word *crumb*. It is possible with just a few phones to create an unlimited vocabulary.

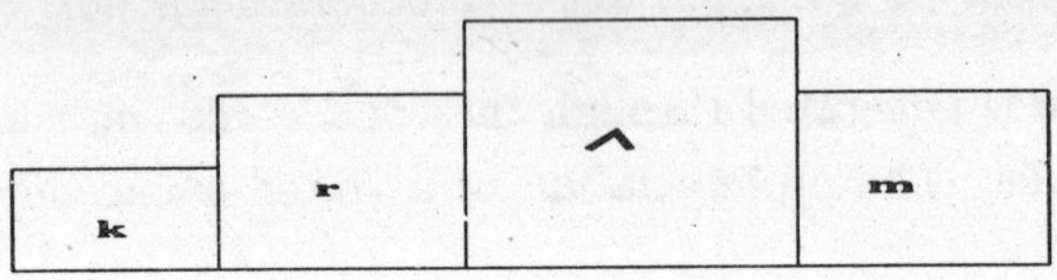


Figure 3.4: *Phone sound concatenation.*

However, transitions between individual phones prove to be extremely problematic. Therefore, the phones in their environment, i.e., the allophones, are considered in the second level. But the transition problem is not solved sufficiently on this level either. Two phones can constitute a diphone (from di-phone). Figure 3.5 shows the word *crumb*, which consists of an ordered set of diphones.

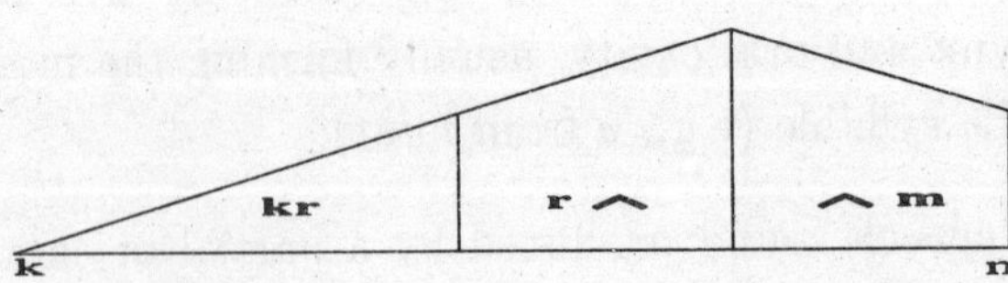


Figure 3.5: *Diphone sound concatenation.*

To make the transition problem easier, syllables can be created. The speech is generated through the set of syllables. Figure 3.6 shows the syllable sound of the word *crumb*. The best pronunciation of a word is achieved through storage of the

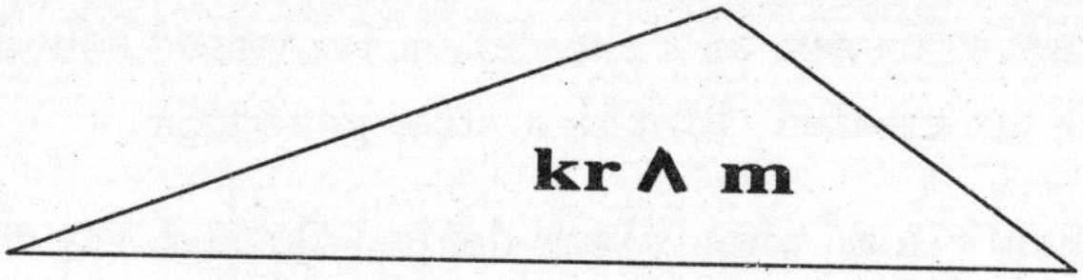


Figure 3.6: *Syllable sound.*

whole word. This leads toward synthesis of the speech sequence (Figure 3.7).

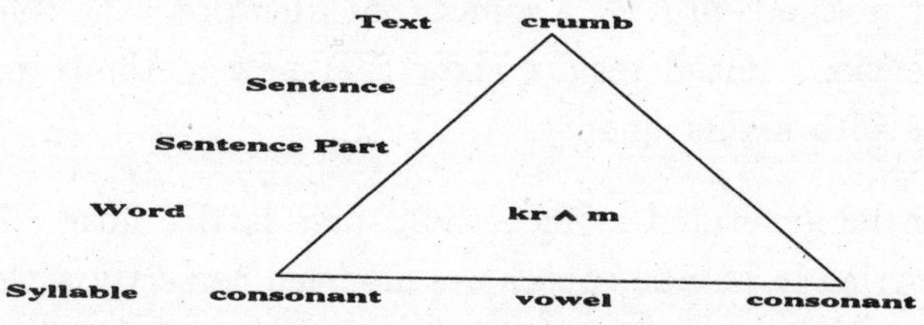


Figure 3.7: *Word sound concatenation.*

Transitions between individual sound units create an essential problem, called *coarticulation*, which is the mutual sound influence throughout several sounds. This influence between individual sound units arises because physical constraints, such as mass and speed of the articulator in the vocal tract, influence the articulation of consecutive phones.

Additionally, *prosody* should be considered during speech generation/output. Prosody means the stress and melody course. For example, pronunciation of a question differs strongly from a statement. Therefore, prosody depends on the semantics of the speech and this has to be taken into consideration during time-dependent sound concatenation [Wai88].

### Frequency-dependent Sound Concatenation

Speech generation/output can also be based on a frequency-dependent sound concatenation, e.g., through a formant-synthesis [Ril89]. Formants are frequency maxima in the spectrum of the speech signal. Formant synthesis simulates the vocal tract through a filter. The characteristic values are the filter's middle frequencies and their bandwidths. A pulse signal with a frequency, corresponding to the fundamental speech frequency, is chosen as a simulation for voiced sounds. On the other hand, unvoiced sounds are created through a noise generator.

Individual speech elements (e.g., phones) are defined through the characteristic values of the formants. Similar problems to the time-dependent sound concatenation exist here. The transitions, known as *coarticulation*, present the most critical problem. Additionally, the respective *prosody* has to be determined.

New sound-specific methods provide a sound concatenation with combined time and frequency dependencies. Initial results show that new methods generate fricative and plosive sounds with higher quality.

Human speech can be generated using a multi-pole lattice filter. The first four or five formants, occurring in human speech are modeled correctly with this filter type. Further, unvoiced sounds, created by vocal chords, are simulated through a noise and tone generator. The method used for the sound synthesis in order to simulate human speech is called the *Linear-Predictive Coding (LPC) method.* This method is very similar to the formant synthesis described above. A further possibility to simulate human speech consists of implementing a *tube model.* Here, a simplified mechanical tube model approximates the human tube as the speech generation system.

Using speech synthesis, an existent text can be transformed into an acoustic signal. Figure 3.8 shows the typical components of the system. In the first step, *transcrip-*

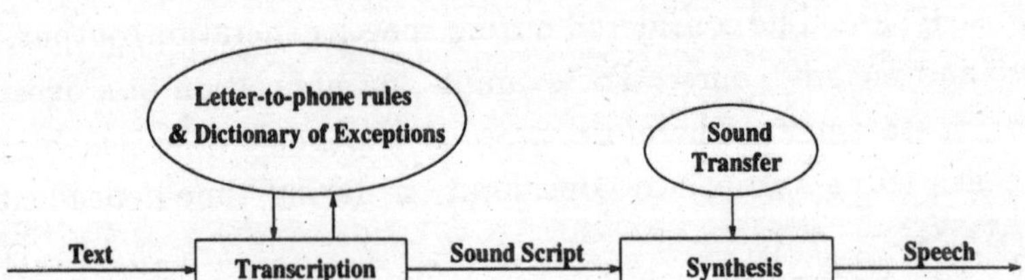


Figure 3.8: *Components of a speech synthesis system with time-dependent sound concatenation.*

*tion* is performed, in which text is translated into sound script. Most transcription methods work here with *letter-to-phone rules* and a *Dictionary of Exceptions* stored in a library. The generation of such a library is work-extensive, but using the interactive control of the user it can be improved continuously. The user recognizes the formula deficiency in the transcription and improves the pronunciation manual; therefore, his/her knowledge becomes part of the letter-to-phone rules and the Dictionary of Exceptions. The solution can be either individual or generally accessible rules and a Dictionary of Exceptions.

In the second step, the sound script is translated into a speech signal. Time or frequency-dependent concatenation can follow. While the first step is always a software solution, the second step is most often implemented with signal processors or even dedicated processors.

Besides the problems of coarticulation and prosody, ambiguous pronunciation must be considered. Pronunciation can be performed correctly only with additional knowledge of the content, i.e., it is semantic-dependent. An example is the word *lead.* It can be used as a noun to describe a metal, but when used as a verb (with a different pronunciation as the noun) it means "to guide people."

### 3.3.2 Speech Analysis

Speech analysis/input deals with the research areas shown in Figure 3.9 [Bri86]:

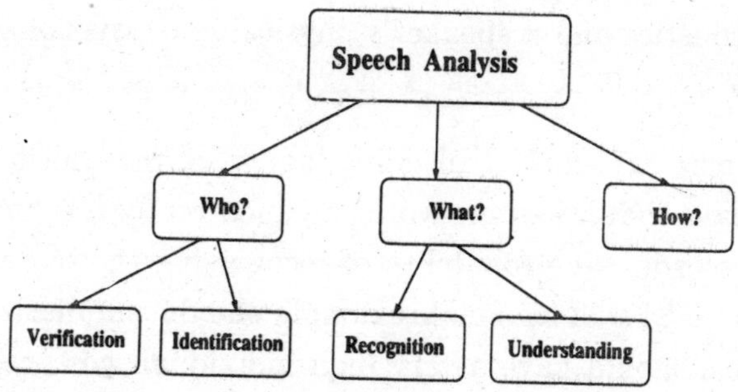


Figure 3.9: *Research areas of speech analysis.*

- Human speech has certain characteristics determined by a speaker. Hence, speech analysis can serve to analyze *who* is speaking, i.e., to *recognize a speaker* for his/her *identification* and *verification.* The computer identifies and verifies the speaker using an acoustic fingerprint. An acoustic fingerprint is a digitally stored speech probe (e.g., certain statement) of a person; for example, a company that uses speech analysis for identification and verification of employees. The speaker has to say a certain sentence into a microphone. The computer system gets the speaker's voice, identifies and verifies the spoken statement, i.e., determines if the speech probe matches the speaker's spoken statement.

- Another main task of speech analysis is to analyze *what* has been said, i.e., to recognize and understand the speech signal itself. Based on speech sequence, the corresponding text is generated. This can lead to a speech-controlled typewriter, a translation system or part of a workplace for the handicapped.

- Another area of speech analysis tries to research speech patterns with respect to *how* a certain statement was said. For example, a spoken sentence sounds differently if a person is angry or calm. An application of this research could be a lie detector

Speech analysis is of strong interest for multimedia systems. Together with speech synthesis, different media transformations can be implemented.

The primary goal of speech analysis is to correctly determine individual words with probability $\leq 1$. A word is recognized only with a certain probability. Here, environmental noise, room acoustics and a speaker's physical and psychological conditions play an important role.

For example, let's assume extremely bad individual word recognition with a probability of 0.95. This means that 5% of the words are incorrectly recognized. If we have a sentence with three words, the probability of recognizing the sentence correctly is $0.95 \times 0.95 \times 0.95 = 0.857$. This small example should emphasize the fact that speech analysis systems should have a very high individual word recognition probability. Figure 3.10 shows schematically a speech recognition system. The system is divided into system components according to a basic principle: "Data Reduction Through Property Extraction". First, speech analysis occurs where properties must be determined. Properties are extracted by comparison of individual speech element characteristics with a sequence of in advance given speech element characteristics. The characteristics are quantified where the concrete speech elements are present.

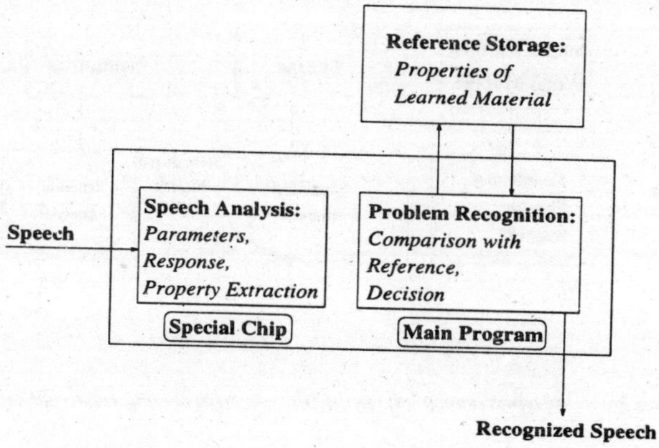


Figure 3.10: *Speech recognition system: task division into system components, using the basic principle "Data Reduction Through Property Extraction."*

Second, the speech elements are compared with existent references to determine the mapping to one of the existent speech elements. The identified speech can be stored, transmitted or processed as a parametrized sequence of speech elements.

Concrete implementations mostly use dedicated building blocks or signal processors for characteristics extraction. Usually, the comparison and decision are executed through the main system processor. The computer's secondary storage contains the letter-to-phone rules, a Dictionary of Exceptions and the reference characteristics. The concrete methods differ in the definition of the characteristics. The principle of "Data Reduction Through Property Extraction," shown in Figure 3.10, can be applied several times to different characteristics. The system which provides recognition and understanding of a speech signal (Figure 3.11) applies this principle several times as follows:

- In the first step, the principle is applied to a sound pattern and/or word model. An acoustical and phonetical analysis is performed.

- In the second step, certain speech units go through syntactical analysis; thereby, the errors of the previous step can be recognized. Very often during the first step, no unambiguous decisions can be made. In this case, syntactical analysis provides additional decision help and the result is a *recognized speech.*

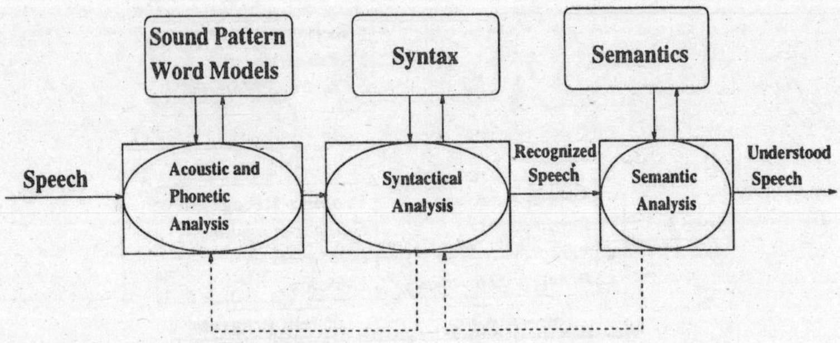


Figure 3.11: *Components of speech recognition and understanding.*

- The third step deals with the semantics of the previously recognized language. Here the decision errors of the previous step can be recognized and corrected with other analysis methods. Even today, this step is non-trivial to implement with current methods known in artificial intelligence and neural nets research. The result of this step is an *understood speech.*

These steps work mostly under the consideration of time and/or frequency-dependent sounds. The same criteria and speech units (formants, phones, etc.) are considered as in speech generation/output (discussed in Section 3.3.1).

There are still many problems into which speech recognition research is being conducted:

- A specific problem is presented by room acoustics with existent environmental noise. The frequency-dependent reflections of a sound wave from walls and objects can overlap with the primary sound wave.

- Further, word boundaries must be determined. Very often neighboring words flow into one another.

- For the comparison of a speech element to the existing pattern, time normalization is necessary. The same word can be spoken quickly or slowly. However, the time axis cannot be modified because the extension factors are not proportional to the global time interval. There are long and short voiceless sounds (e.g., *s*, *sh*). Individual sounds are extended differently and need a minimal time duration for their recognition.

Speech recognition systems are divided into *speaker-independent recognition systems* and *speaker-dependent recognition systems.* A speaker-independent system can recognize with the same reliability essentially fewer words than a speaker-dependent system because the latter is trained in advance. Training in advance means that there exists a training phase for the speech recognition system, which takes a half an hour. Speaker-dependent systems can recognize around 25,000 words; speaker-independent systems recognize a maximum of about 500 words, but with a worse recognition rate. These values should be understood as gross guidelines. In a concrete situation, the marginal conditions must be known. (e.g., Was the measurement taken in a sound deadening room?, Does the speaker have to adapt to the system to simplify the time normalization?, etc.)

### 3.3.3 Speech Transmission

The area of speech transmission deals with efficient coding of the speech signal to allow speech/sound transmission at low transmission rates over networks. The goal is to provide the receiver with the same speech/sound *quality* as was generated at the sender side. This section includes some principles that are connected to speech generation and recognition.

- *Signal Form Coding*

  This kind of coding considers no speech-specific properties and parameters. Here, the goal is to achieve the most efficient coding of the audio signal. The data rate of a PCM-coded stereo-audio signal with *CD-quality* requirements is:

  $rate = 2 * \frac{44100}{s} * \frac{16bit}{8bit/byte} = 176,400\ bytes/s = 1,411,200\ bits/s$

  Telephone quality, in comparison to CD-quality, needs only 64 Kbit/s. Using *Difference Pulse Code Modulation (DPCM)*, the data rate can be lowered to 56 Kbits/s without loss of quality. *Adaptive Pulse Code Modulation (ADPCM)* allows a further rate reduction to 32 Kbits/s.

- *Source Coding*

*Parameterized systems* work with source coding algorithms. Here, the specific speech characteristics are used for data rate reduction.

Channel vo-coder is an example of such a parameterized system (Figure 3.12). The channel vo-coder is an extension of a sub-channel coding. The signal is

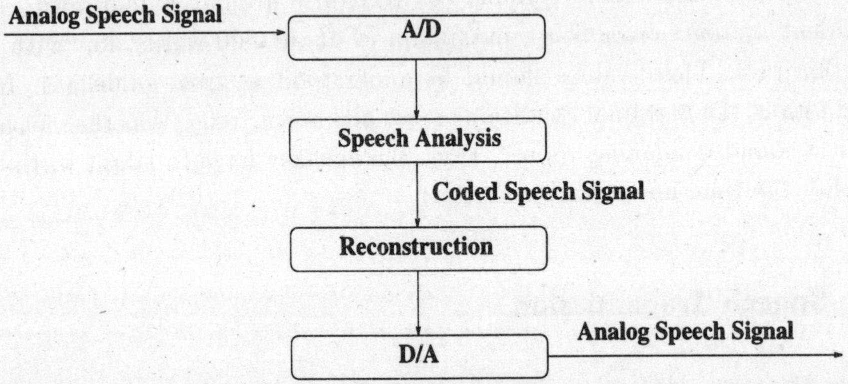


Figure 3.12: *Source coding in parametrized systems: components of a speech transmission system.*

divided into a set of frequency channels during speech analysis because only certain frequency maxima are relevant to speech. Additionally, the differences between voiced and unvoiced sounds are taken into account. Voiceless sounds are simulated by the noise generator. For generation of voiced sounds, the simulation comes from a sequence of pulses. The rate of the pulses is equivalent to the a priori measured basic speech frequency. The data rate of about 3 Kbits/s can be generated with a channel vo-coder; however the quality is not always satisfactory.

Major effort and work on further data rate reduction from 64 Kbits/s to 6 Kbits/s is being conducted, where the compressed signal quality should correspond, after a decompression, to the quality of an uncompressed 64 Kbits/s signal.

- *Recognition/Synthesis Methods*

  There have been attempts to reduce the transmission rate using pure *recognition/synthesis methods.* Speech analysis (recognition) follows on the sender side of a speech transmission system and speech synthesis (generation) follows on the receiver side (see Figure 3.13).

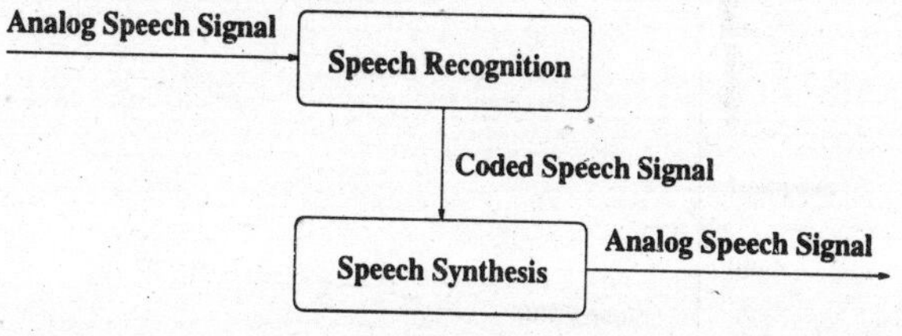


Figure 3.13: *Recognition/synthesis systems: components of a speech transmission system.*

Only the characteristics of the speech elements are transmitted. For example, the speech elements with their characteristics are the formants with their middle frequency bandwidths. The frequency bandwidths are used in the corresponding digital filter. This reduction brings the data rate down to 50 bits/s. The quality of the reproduced speech and its recognition rate are not acceptable by today's standards.

- *Achieved Quality*

  The essential question regarding speech and audio transmission with respect to multimedia systems is how to achieve the minimal data rate for a given quality. The published function from Flanagan [Fla72] (see Figure 3.14) shows the dependence of the achieved quality of compressed speech on the data rate. One can assume that for telephone quality, a data rate of 8 Kbits/s is sufficient.

  Figure 3.15 shows the dependence of audio quality on the number of bits per sample value. For example, excellent CD-quality can be achieved with a reduction from 16 bits per sample value to 2 bits per sample value. This means that only 1/8 of the actual data needs to be transmitted.

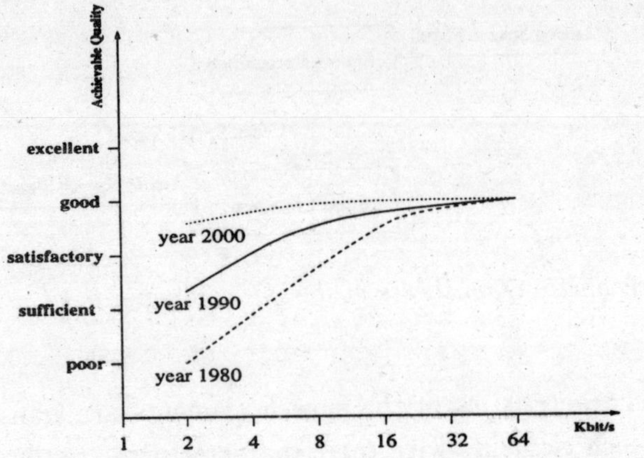


Figure 3.14: *Dependence of the achieved speech quality on the data rate.*

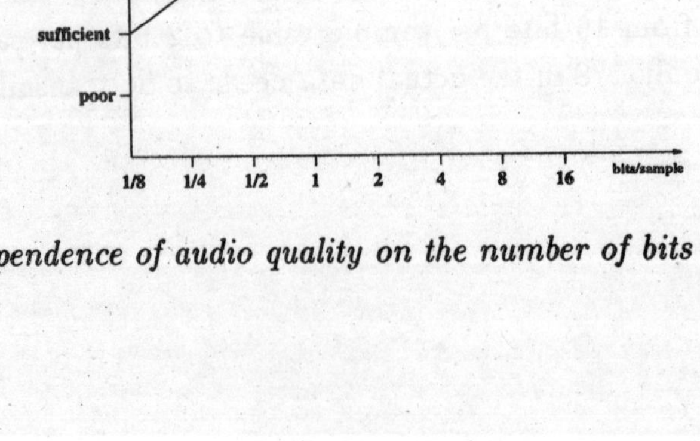


Figure 3.15: *Dependence of audio quality on the number of bits per sample value.*

# Chapter 4

# Images and Graphics

An *image* is a spatial representation of an object, a two-dimensional or three-dimensional scene or another image. It can be real or virtual. An image may be abstractly thought of as a continuous function defining usually a rectangular region of a plane. For example, for optic or photographic sensors, an image is typically proportional to the radiant energy received in the electromagnetic band to which the sensor or detector is sensitive. In this case, the image is called an *intensity image.* For range finder sensors, an image is a function of the line-of-sight distance from the sensor position to an object in the three-dimensional world; such an image is called a *range image.* For tactile sensors, an image is proportional to the sensor deformation caused by the surface of or around an object.

A recorded image may be in a photographic, analog video signal or digital format. In computer vision, an image is usually a recorded image such as a video image, digital image or a picture. In computer graphics, an image is always a digital image. In multimedia applications, all formats can be presented.

In this chapter, the digital image will be discussed; this is the computer representation most important for processing in multimedia systems. We present basic concepts of image representation. Further, computer processing of images is described with an overview of topics on image generation, recognition and transmission.

## 4.1 Basic Concepts

An image might be thought of as a function with resulting values of the light intensity at each point over a planar region. For digital computer operations, this function needs to be sampled at discrete intervals. The sampling quantizes the intensity values into discrete levels.

### 4.1.1 Digital Image Representation

A digital image is represented by a matrix of numeric values each representing a quantized intensity value. When *I* is a two-dimensional matrix, then *I(r,c)* is the intensity value at the position corresponding to row *r* and column *c* of the matrix.

The points at which an image is sampled are known as *picture elements*, commonly abbreviated as *pixels*. The pixel values of intensity images are called *gray scale levels* (we encode here the "color" of the image). The intensity at each pixel is represented by an integer and is determined from the continuous image by averaging over a small neighborhood around the pixel location. If there are just two intensity values, for example, black and white, they are represented by the numbers 0 and 1; such images are called *binary-valued* images. When 8-bit integers are used to store each pixel value, the gray levels range from 0 (black) to 255 (white). An example of such an image is shown in Figure 4.1.

It is common to use a square sampling grid with pixels equally spaced along the two sides of the grid. The distance between grid points obviously affects the accuracy with which the original image is represented, and it determines how much detail can be resolved. The *resolution* depends on the imaging system as well.

Digital pictures are often very large. For example, suppose we want to sample and quantize an ordinary (525-line) television picture (NTSC) with a VGA (Video Graphics Array) video controller, so that it can be redisplayed without noticeable degradation. We must use a matrix of 640 × 480 pixels, where each pixel is represented by an 8-bit integer. This pixel representation allows 256 discrete gray levels. Hence, this image specification gives an array of 307,200 8-bit numbers, and a total of 2,457,600 bits. In many cases, even finer sampling is necessary.

Figure 4.1: *An example of an image with 256 gray levels.*

### 4.1.2 Image Format

There are different kinds of image formats in the literature. We shall consider the image format that comes out of an image frame grabber, i.e., the *captured image format*, and the format when images are stored, i.e., the *stored image format.*

#### Captured Image Format

The image format is specified by two main parameters: *spatial resolution*, which is specified as *pixels* × *pixels* and *color encoding*, which is specified by bits per pixel. Both parameter values depend on hardware and software for input/output of images. As an example we will present image formats supported on SPARC and IRIS computers.

For image capturing on a SPARCstation, the *VideoPix*™card and its software [Sun90] can be used. The spatial resolution is 320 × 240 pixels. The color can be encoded with 1-bit (a binary image format), 8-bit (color or grayscale) or 24-bit (color-*RGB*). Another video frame grabber is the *Parallax XVideo*, which includes a 24-bit frame buffer and 640 × 480 pixels resolution. The new multimedia kit in the new SPARCstations includes the *SunVideo*™card (Sun Microsystems, Inc.), a color video camera and the CDware for CD-ROM discs. The SPARCstation 10 M offers 24-bit image manipulation. The new *SunVideo* card is a capture and compression card and its technology captures and compresses 30 frames/second in real time under the Solaris 2.3 operating system. Further, *SunVideo* offers capture and compression of video at resolution (320 × 240) pixels in several formats [Moo94]:

| | |
|---|---|
| CellB | 30 fps (frames per second) |
| JPEG | 30 fps |
| MPEG1 I frames | 30 fps |
| MPEG1 IP frames | 17 fps |
| Capture YUV | 30 fps |
| Capture RGB-8 | 30 fps |
| Capture RGB-24 | 12 fps |

IRIS™stations provide high-quality images through, for example, add-on *IndigoVideo* or *IndyVideo*™video digitizers and corresponding software [Roy94]. The IRIS video board *VINO*™is supported only on Indy™systems. It does not include image compression. *VINO* offers image resolution of 640 × 480 pixels at about four frames per second. Speed can be increased at the cost of resolution. The resulting formats are *RGB* and *YUV* formats (described in Section 5.1.1.).

### Stored Image Format

When we store an image, we are storing a two-dimensional array of values, in which each value represents the data associated with a pixel in the image. For a bitmap, this value is a binary digit. For a color image, the value may be a collection of:

- Three numbers representing the intensities of the red, green and blue components of the color at that pixel.
- Three numbers that are indices to tables of red, green and blue intensities.

- A single number that is an index to a table of color triples.
- An index to any number of other data structures that can represent a color, including $XYZ$ color system.
- Four or five spectral samples for each color.

In addition, each pixel may have other information associated with it; for example, three numbers indicating the normal to the surface drawn at that pixel. Thus, we consider an image as consisting of a collection of *Red, Green and Blue channels* (*RGB* channels), each of which gives some single piece of information about the pixels in the image.

If there is enough storage space, it is convenient to store an image in the form of *RGB* triples. Otherwise, it may be worth trying to compress the channels in some way. When we store an image in the conventional manner, as a collection of channels, information about each pixel, i.e., the value of each channel at each pixel, must be stored. Other information may be associated with the image as a whole, such as width and height, as well as the depth of the image, the name of the creator, etc. The need to store such properties has prompted the creation of flexible formats such as RIFF (Resource Interchange File Format) and BRIM (derived from RIFF) [Mei83], which are used in general attribute value database systems. RIFF includes formats for bitmaps, vector drawings, animation, audio and video. In BRIM, an image always has a width, height, creator and history field, which describes the creation of the image and modifications to it.

Some current image file formats for storing images include GIF (Graphical Interchange Format), X11 Bitmap, Sun Rasterfile, PostScript, IRIS, JPEG, TIFF (Tagged Image File Format) and others.

### 4.1.3 Graphics Format

Graphics image formats are specified through *graphics primitives* and their *attributes.* To the category of graphics primitives belong lines, rectangles, circles and ellipses, text strings specifying two-dimensional objects (2D) in a graphical image or, e.g., polyhedron, specifying three-dimensional objects (3D). A graphics package determines which primitives are supported. Attributes such as line style, line width, and color affect the outcome of the graphical image.

Graphics primitives and their attributes represent a higher level of an image representation, i.e., the graphical images are not represented by a pixel matrix. This higher level of representation needs to be converted at some point of the image processing into the lower level of the image representation; for example, when an image is to be displayed. The advantage of the higher level primitives is the reduction of data to be stored per one graphical image, and easier manipulation of the graphical image. The disadvantage is the additional conversion step from the graphical primitives and their attributes to its pixel representation. Some graphics packages like SRGP (Simple Raster Graphics Package) provide such a conversion, i.e., they take the graphics primitives and attributes and generate either a *bitmap* or *pixmap.* A bitmap is an array of pixel values that map one by one to pixels on the screen; the pixel information is stored in 1 bit, so we get a binary image. Pixmap is a more general term describing a multiple-bit-per-pixel image. Low-end color systems have eight bits per pixel, allowing 256 colors simultaneously. More expensive systems have 24 bits per pixel, allowing a choice of any of 16 million colors. Refresh buffers with 32 bits per pixel and a screen resolution of 1280 × 1024 pixels are available even on personal computers. Of the 32 bits per pixel, 24 bits are devoted to representing color and 8 bits to control purposes. Beyond that, buffers with 96 bits (or more) per pixel are available at 1280 × 1024 resolution on high-end systems [FDFH92]. SRGP does not convert the graphical image into primitives and attributes after generating a bitmap/pixmap. In this case, after the conversion phase, the graphics format is presented as a digital image format.

Packages such as PHIGS (Programmer's Hierarchical Interactive Graphics System) and GKS (Graphical Kernel System) [FDFH92] take graphical images specified through primitives and attributes, generate a graphical image in the form of pixmap and after image presentation, continue to work based on the object primitive/attribute representation. In this case, the graphical image format is presented after the generation phase as a *structure*, which is a logical grouping of primitives, attributes and other information.

## 4.2 Computer Image Processing

Computer graphics concern the pictorial *synthesis* of real or imaginary objects from their computer-based models. The related field of image processing treats the converse process: the *analysis* of scenes, or the *reconstruction* of models from pictures of 2D or 3D objects. In the following sections, we describe basic principles of image synthesis (generation) and image analysis (recognition). The literature on computer graphics and image processing presents further and detailed information [FDFH92, KR82, Nev82, HS92].

### 4.2.1 Image Synthesis

*Image synthesis* is an integral part of all computer user interfaces and is indispensable for visualizing 2D, 3D and higher-dimensional objects. Areas as diverse as education, science, engineering, medicine, advertising and entertainment all rely on graphics. Let us look at some representative samples:

- *User Interfaces*

  Applications running on personal computers and workstations have user interfaces that rely on desktop window systems to manage multiple simultaneous activities, and on point-and-click facilities to allow users to select menu items, icons and objects on the screen.

- *Office Automation and Electronic Publishing*

  The use of graphics for the creation and dissemination of information has increased enormously since the advent of desktop publishing on personal computers. Office automation and electronic publishing can produce both traditional printed documents and electronic documents that contain text, tables, graphs and other forms of drawn or scanned-in graphics. Hypermedia systems that allow browsing networks of interlinked multimedia documents are proliferating.

- *Simulation and Animation for Scientific Visualization and Entertainment*

Computer-produced animated movies and displays of time-varying behavior of real and simulated objects are becoming increasingly popular for scientific and engineering visualization. We can use them to study abstract mathematical entities and models of such phenomena as fluid flow, relativity and nuclear and chemical reactions. Cartoon characters will increasingly be modeled in computers as 3D shape descriptions whose movements are controlled by computers rather than by the figures drawn manually by cartoonists. Television commercials featuring flying logos and more exotic visual trickery have become common, as have elegant special effects in movies.

Interactive computer graphics are the most important means of producing images (pictures) since the invention of photography and television; it has the added advantage that we can make pictures not only of concrete, "real world" objects, but also of abstract, synthetic objects such as mathematical surfaces in 4D.

### Dynamics in Graphics

Graphics are not confined to static pictures. Pictures can be dynamically varied; for example, a user can control animation by adjusting the speed, portion of the total scene in view, amount of detail shown, etc. Hence, dynamics is an integral part of graphics (*dynamic graphics*). Much of interactive graphics technology contains hardware and software for user-controlled *motion dynamics* and *update dynamics*:

- Motion Dynamics

  With motion dynamics, objects can be moved and enabled with respect to a stationary observer. The objects can also remain stationary and the view around them can move. In many cases, both the objects and the camera are moving. A typical example is a flight simulator which contains a mechanical platform, which supports a mock cockpit and a display screen. The computer controls platform motion, gauges and the simulated world of both stationary and moving objects through which the pilot navigates.

- Update Dynamics

Update dynamics is the actual change of the shape, color, or other properties of the objects being viewed. For instance, a system can display the deformation of an in-flight airplane structure in response to the operator's manipulation of the many control mechanisms. The smoother the change, the more realistic and meaningful the result. Dynamic, interactive graphs offer a large number of user-controllable modes with which to encode and communicate information, e.g., the 2D or 3D shape of objects in a picture, their gray scale or color and the time variations of these properties.

### The Framework of Interactive Graphics Systems

Images can be generated by video digitizer cards that capture NTSC (PAL) analog signals and create a digital image. These kinds of digital images are used, for example, in image processing for image recognition and in communication for video conferencing. In this section we concentrate on image generation via graphics systems. We discuss in more detail image and video generation via video digitizers in Chapter 5.

Graphical images are generated using interactive graphics systems. An example of such a graphics system is SRGP, which borrows features from Apple's *QuickDraw* integer raster graphics package [RHA+85] and MIT's *X Window System*™[SGN88] for output; and from GKS and PHIGS for input. The high-level conceptual framework of almost any interactive graphics system consists of three software components: an *application model*, an *application program* and a *graphics system*, and a hardware component: *graphics hardware*.

The application model represents the data or objects to be pictured on the screen; it is stored in an application database. The model typically stores descriptions of primitives that define the shape of components of the object, object attributes and connectivity relationships that describe how the components fit together. The model is application-specific and is created independently of any particular display system. Therefore, the application program must convert a description of the portion of the model to whatever procedure calls or commands the graphics system uses to create an image. This conversion process has two phases. First, the application program traverses the application database that stores the model to extract the portions to be viewed, using some selection or query system. Second, the extracted geometry is put in a format that can be sent to the graphics system.

The application program handles user input. It produces views by sending to the third component, the graphics system, a series of graphics output commands that contain both a detailed geometric description of *what* is to be viewed and the attributes describing *how* the objects should appear.

The graphics system is responsible for actually producing the picture from the detailed descriptions and for passing the user's input to the application program for processing. The graphics system is thus an intermediary component between the application program and the display hardware. It effects an *output transformation* from objects in the application model to a view of the model. Symmetrically, it effects an *input transformation* from user actions to application program inputs that cause the application to make changes in the model and/or picture. The graphics system typically consists of a set of output subroutines corresponding to various primitives, attributes and other elements. These are collected in a *graphics subroutine library* or *package*. The application program specifies geometric primitives and attributes to these subroutines, and the subroutines then drive the specific display device and cause it to display the image.

At the hardware level, a computer receives input from interaction devices and outputs images to display devices.

To connect this high-level conceptual framework to our model shown in Figure 1.1, the application model and application program may represent applications, as well as the user interface part in Figure 1.1. The graphics system represents programming abstractions with support from the operating system to connect to the graphics hardware. The graphics hardware belongs to the device area in Figure 1.1; therefore, this is the main focus of the follwoing discussion.

### Graphics Hardware – Input

Current input technology provides us with the ubiquitous mouse, the data tablet and the transparent, touch-sensitive panel mounted on the screen. Even fancier input devices that supply, in addition to $(x, y)$ screen location, 3D and higher-dimensional input values (degrees of freedom), are becoming common, such as *track-balls, space-balls* or the *data glove.*

Track-balls can be made to sense rotation about the vertical axis in addition to that about the two horizontal axes. However, there is no direct relationship between hand movements with the device and the corresponding movement in 3D space.

A space-ball is a rigid sphere containing strain gauges. The user pushes or pulls the sphere in any direction, providing 3D translation and orientation. In this case, the directions of movement correspond to the user's attempts to move the rigid sphere, although the hand does not actually move.

The data glove records hand position and orientation as well as finger movements. It is a glove covered with small, lightweight sensors. Each sensor is a short length of fiber-optic cable, with a Light-Emitting Diode (LED) at one end and a phototransistor at the other. In addition, a Polhelmus *3SPACE* three-dimensional position and orientation sensor records hand movements. Wearing the data glove, a user can grasp objects, move and rotate them and then release them, thus providing very natural interaction in 3D [ZLB+87].

Audio communication also has exciting potential since it allows hand-free input and natural output of simple instructions, feedback, and so on.

### Graphics Hardware – Output

Current output technology uses *raster displays,* which store display primitives in a refresh buffer in terms of their component pixels. The architecture of a raster display is shown in Figure 4.2. In some raster displays, there is a hardware display controller that receives and interprets sequences of output commands. In simpler, more common systems (Figure 4.2), such as those in personal computers, the display controller exists only as a software component of the graphics library package, and the refresh buffer is no more than a piece of the CPU's memory that can be read by the image display subsystem (often called the *video controller*) that produces the actual image on the screen.

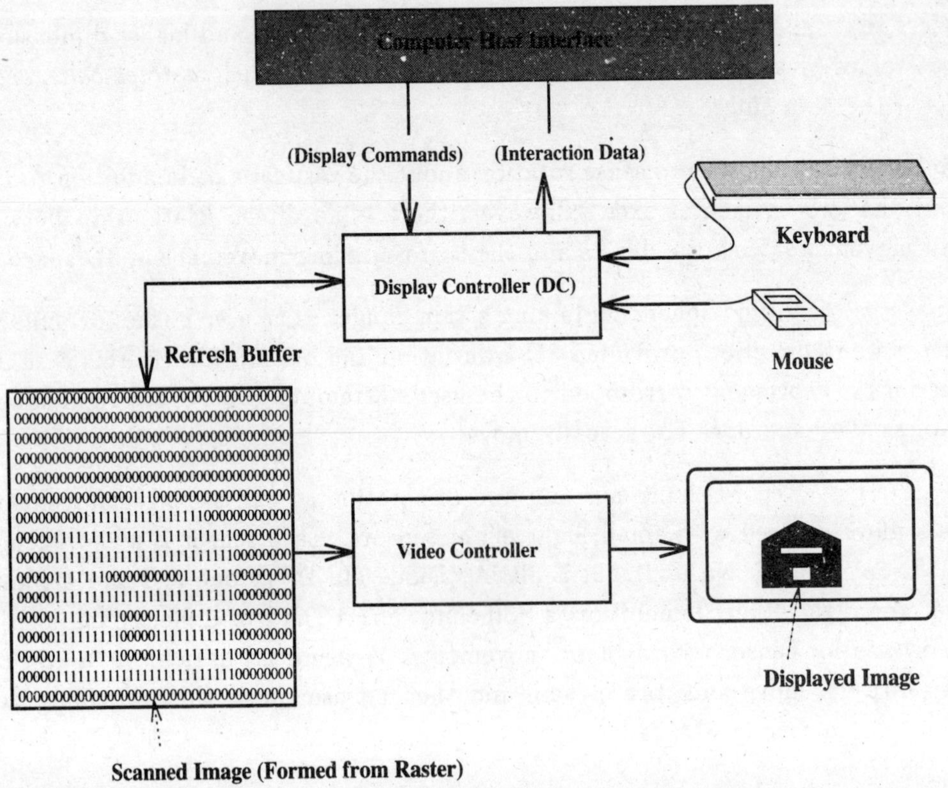


Figure 4.2: *Architecture of a raster display.*

The complete image on a raster display is formed from the *raster*, which is a set of horizontal *raster lines*, each a row of individual pixels; the raster is thus stored as a matrix of pixels representing the entire screen area. The entire image is scanned out sequentially by the video controller. The raster scan is shown in Figure 4.3. At each pixel, the beam's intensity is set to reflect the pixel's intensity; in color systems, three beams are controlled – one for each primary color (red, green, blue) – as specified by the three color components of each pixel's value (see Section 5.1).

Raster graphics systems have other characteristics. To avoid flickering of the image, a 60 Hz or higher refresh rate is used today; an entire image of 1024 lines of 1024 pixels each must be stored explicitly and a bitmap or pixmap is generated.

Raster graphics can display areas filled with solid colors or patterns, i.e., realistic

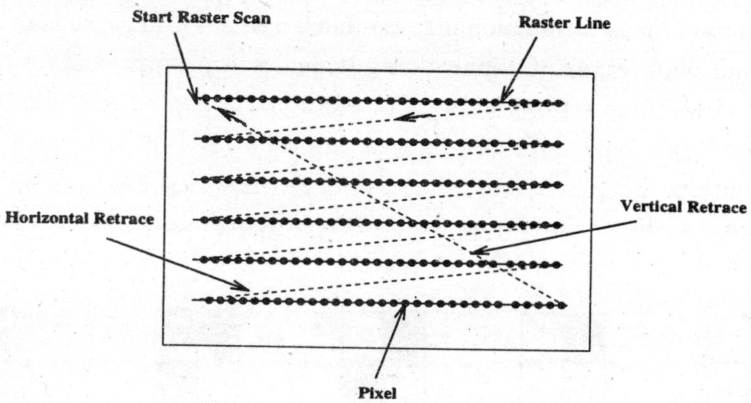


Figure 4.3: *Raster scan.*

images of 3D objects. Furthermore, the refresh process is independent of the image complexity (number of polygons, etc.) since the hardware is fast enough to read out each pixel in the buffer on each refresh cycle.

## Dithering

The growth of raster graphics has made color and grayscale an integral part of contemporary computer graphics. The color of an object depends not only on the object itself, but also on the light source illuminating it, on the color of the surrounding area and on the human visual system. What we see on a black-and-white television set or display monitor is *achromatic light.* Achromatic light is determined by the attribute *quality of light.* Quality of light is determined by the intensity and luminance parameters. For example, if we have hardcopy devices or displays which are only *bi-leveled*, which means they produce just two intensity levels, then we would like to expand the range of available intensity.

The solution lies in our eye's capability for *spatial integration.* If we view a very small area from a sufficiently large viewing distance, our eyes average fine detail within the small area and record only the overall intensity of the area. This phenomenon is exploited in the technique called *halftoning*, or *clustered-dot ordered dithering* (halftoning approximation). Each small resolution unit is imprinted with a circle of black ink whose area is proportional to the blackness $1 - I$ ($I$=intensity) of the area in the original photograph. Graphics output devices can approximate the variable-area circles of halftone reproduction. For example, a $2 \times 2$ pixel area of a bi-level display can be used to produce five different intensity levels at the cost of halving the spatial resolution along each axis. The patterns, shown in Figure 4.4, can be filled by $2 \times 2$ areas, with the number of 'on' pixels proportional to the desired intensity. The patterns can be represented by the *dither matrix.* This technique is used on

Figure 4.4: *Five intensity levels approximated with four* $2 \times 2$ *dither patterns.*

devices which are not able to display individual dots (e.g., laser printers). This means that these devices are poor at reproducing isolated 'on' pixels (the black dots in Figure 4.4). All pixels that are 'on' for a particular intensity must be adjacent to other 'on' pixels.

A CRT display is able to display individual dots; hence, the clustering requirement can be relaxed and a *dispersed-dot ordered dither* can be used. Monochrome dithering techniques can also be used to extend the number of available colors, at the expense of resolution. Consider a color display with three bits per pixel, one for red, green and blue. We can use a $2 \times 2$ pattern area to obtain 125 colors as follows: each pattern can display five intensities for each color, by using the halftone patterns in Figure 4.4, resulting in $5 \times 5 \times 5 = 125$ color combinations.

### 4.2.2 Image Analysis

Image analysis is concerned with techniques for extracting descriptions from images that are necessary for higher-level scene analysis methods. By itself, knowledge of the position and value of any particular pixel almost conveys no information related to the recognition of an object, the description of an object's shape, its position or orientation, the measurement of any distance on the object or whether the object is defective. Hence, image analysis techniques include computation of perceived brightness and color, partial or complete recovery of three-dimensional data in the scene, location of discontinuities corresponding to objects in the scene and characterization of the properties of uniform regions in the image.

Image analysis is important in many arenas: aerial surveillance photographs, slow-scan television images of the moon or of planets gathered from space probes, television images taken from an industrial robot's visual sensor, X-ray images and computerized axial tomography (CAT) scans. Subareas of image processing include *image enhancement, pattern detection and recognition* and *scene analysis and computer vision.*

Image enhancement deals with improving image quality by eliminating noise (extraneous or missing pixels) or by enhancing contrast.

Pattern detection and recognition deal with detecting and clarifying standard patterns and finding distortions from these patterns. A particularly important example is Optical Character R ecognition (OCR) technology, which allows for the economical bulk input of pages of typeset, typewritten or even hand-printed characters. The degree of accuracy of *handwriting recognition* depends on the input device. One possibility is that the user prints characters with a continuous-positioning device, usually a tablet stylus (a pen-based environment), and the computer recognizes them (online recognition). This is easier than recognizing scanned-in characters because the tablet records the sequence, direction and sometimes speed and pressure of strokes, and a pattern-recognition algorithm can match these factors to stored templates for each character. The recognizer may evaluate patterns without considering how the pattern has been created (a *static character recognition*) or it may focus on strokes, edges in strokes or drawing speed (a *dynamic recognizer*). A recognizer can be trained to identify different styles of block printing. The parameters of each character are calculated from samples drawn by the users. An architecture for an object-oriented character recognition engine (AQUIRE), which supports online-recognition with combined static and dynamic capabilities, is described in [KW93b]. A commercial character recognizer is described in [WB85, BW86].

Scene analysis and computer vision deal with recognizing and reconstructing 3D models of a scene from several 2D images. An example is an industrial robot sensing the relative sizes, shapes, positions and colors of objects.

### Image Recognition

To fully recognize an object in an image means knowing that there is an agreement between the sensory projection and the observed image. How the object appears in the image has to do with the *spatial configuration* of the pixel values. Agreement between the observed spatial configuration and the expected sensory projection requires the following capabilities:

- Infer explicitly or implicitly an object's position and orientation from the spatial configuration.
- Confirm that the inference is correct.

To infer an object's (e.g., a cup) position, orientation and category or class from the spatial configuration of gray levels requires the capability to infer which pixels are part of the object. Further, from among those pixels that are part of the object, it requires the capability to distinguish observed object features, such as special markings, lines, curves, surfaces or boundaries (e.g., edges of the cup). These features themselves are organized in a spatial relationship on the image and the object.

Analytic inference of object shape, position and orientation depends on matching the distinguishing image features (in 2D, a point, line segment or region) with corresponding object features (in 3D, a point, line segment, arc segment, or a curved or planar surface).

The kind of object, background, imaging sensor and viewpoint of the sensor all determine whether the recognition problem is easy or difficult. For example, suppose that the object is a white planar square on a uniform black background, as shown in the digital image (Table 4.1). A simple corner feature extractor could identify the distinguishing corner points, as shown in the symbolic image (Table 4.2). The match between the image corner features and the object corner features is direct. Just relate the corners of the image square to the corners of the object square in clockwise order, starting from any arbitrary correspondence. Then, use the corresponding points to establish the sensor orientation relative to the plane of the square. If we know the size of the square, we can completely and analytically determine the position and orientation of the square relative to the position and orientation of the camera. In

| 0 | 0 | 0 | 0 | 0 | 0 | 0 | 0 | 0 | 0 | 0 | 0 | 0 |
|---|---|---|---|---|---|---|---|---|---|---|---|---|
| 0 | 0 | 0 | 0 | 0 | 0 | 0 | 0 | 0 | 0 | 0 | 0 | 0 |
| 0 | 0 | 0 | 0 | 255 | 255 | 255 | 255 | 255 | 0 | 0 | 0 | 0 |
| 0 | 0 | 0 | 0 | 255 | 255 | 255 | 255 | 255 | 0 | 0 | 0 | 0 |
| 0 | 0 | 0 | 0 | 255 | 255 | 255 | 255 | 255 | 0 | 0 | 0 | 0 |
| 0 | 0 | 0 | 0 | 255 | 255 | 255 | 255 | 255 | 0 | 0 | 0 | 0 |
| 0 | 0 | 0 | 0 | 255 | 255 | 255 | 255 | 255 | 0 | 0 | 0 | 0 |
| 0 | 0 | 0 | 0 | 0 | 0 | 0 | 0 | 0 | 0 | 0 | 0 | 0 |
| 0 | 0 | 0 | 0 | 0 | 0 | 0 | 0 | 0 | 0 | 0 | 0 | 0 |

Table 4.1: *Numeric digital intensity image of a white square (gray tone 255) on a black (gray tone 0) background and symbolic image.*

| N | N | N | N | N | N | N | N | N | N | N | N | N |
|---|---|---|---|---|---|---|---|---|---|---|---|---|
| N | N | N | N | N | N | N | N | N | N | N | N | N |
| N | N | N | N | C | N | N | N | C | N | N | N | N |
| N | N | N | N | N | N | N | N | N | N | N | N | N |
| N | N | N | N | N | N | N | N | N | N | N | N | N |
| N | N | N | N | N | N | N | N | N | N | N | N | N |
| N | N | N | N | C | N | N | N | C | N | N | N | N |
| N | N | N | N | N | N | N | N | N | N | N | N | N |
| N | N | N | N | N | N | N | N | N | N | N | N | N |

Table 4.2: *Numeric digital intensity image of image's corners shown in Table 4.1 (N = noncorner; C = corner).*

this simple instance, the unit of pixel is transformed to the unit of match between image corners and object corners. The unit of match is then transformed to the unit of object position and orientation relative to the natural coordinate system of the sensor.

On the other hand, the transformation process may be difficult. There may be a variety of complex objects that need to be recognized. For example, some objects may include parts of other objects, shadows may occur or the object reflectances may be varied, and the background may be busy.

Which kind of unit transformation must be employed depends on the specific nature of the vision task, the complexity of the image and the kind of prior information available.

Computer recognition and inspection of objects is, in general, a complex procedure, requiring a variety of steps that successively transform the iconic data into recognition information. A recognition methodology must pay substantial attention to each of the following six steps: *image formatting*, *conditioning*, *labeling*, *grouping*, *extracting* and *matching* (Figure 4.5).

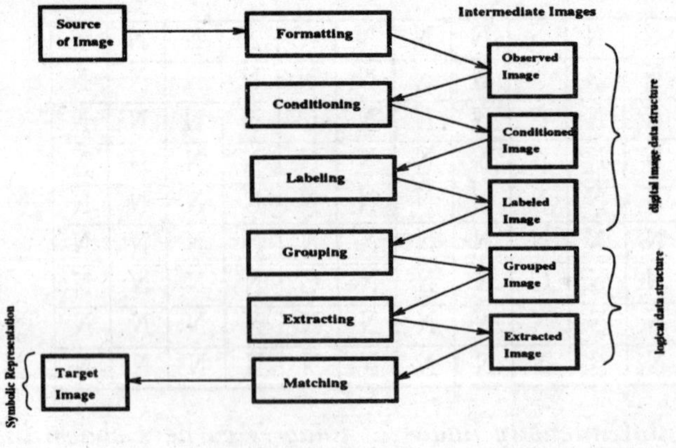


Figure 4.5: *Image recognition steps.*

### Image Recognition Steps

We will give a brief overview of the recognition steps, but a deeper analysis of these steps can be found in computer vision literature, such as [Nev82, HS92], etc.

Image formatting means capturing an image from a camera and bringing it into a digital form. It means that we will have a digital representation of an image in the form of pixels. (Pixels and image formats were described in Sections 4.1.1. and 4.1.2.) An example of an observed image is shown in Figure 4.6.

Figure 4.6: *Observed image (Courtesy of Jana Košecká, GRASP Laboratory, University of Pennsylvania, 1994).*

Conditioning, labeling, grouping, extracting and matching constitute a canonical decomposition of the image recognition problem, each step preparing and transforming the data to facilitate the next step. Depending on the application, we may have to apply this sequence of steps at more than one level of the recognition and description processes. As these steps work on any level in the unit transformation process, they prepare the data for the unit transformation, identify the next higher-level unit and interpret it. The five transformation steps, in more detail, are:

1. *Conditioning*

   Conditioning is based on a model that suggests the observed image is composed of an informative pattern modified by uninteresting variations that typically add to or multiply the informative pattern. Conditioning estimates the informative pattern on the basis of the observed image. Thus conditioning suppresses noise, which can be thought of as random unpatterned variations affecting all measurements. Conditioning can also perform background normalization by suppressing uninteresting systematic or patterned variations. Conditioning is typically applied uniformly and is context-independent.

2. *Labeling*

   Labeling is based on a model that suggests the informative pattern has structure as a spatial arrangement of events, each spatial event being a set of connected pixels. Labeling determines in what kinds of spatial events each pixel participates.

   An example of a labeling operation is *edge detection*. Edge detection is an important part of the recognition process. Edge detection techniques find local discontinuities in some image attribute, such as intensity or color (e.g., detection of cup edges). These discontinuities are of interest because they are likely to occur at the boundaries of objects. An edge is said to occur at a point in the image if some image attribute changes in value discontinuously at that point. Examples are intensity edges. An ideal edge, in one dimension, may be viewed as a step change in intensity; for example, a step between high-valued and low-valued pixels (Figure 4.7). If the step is detected, the neighboring

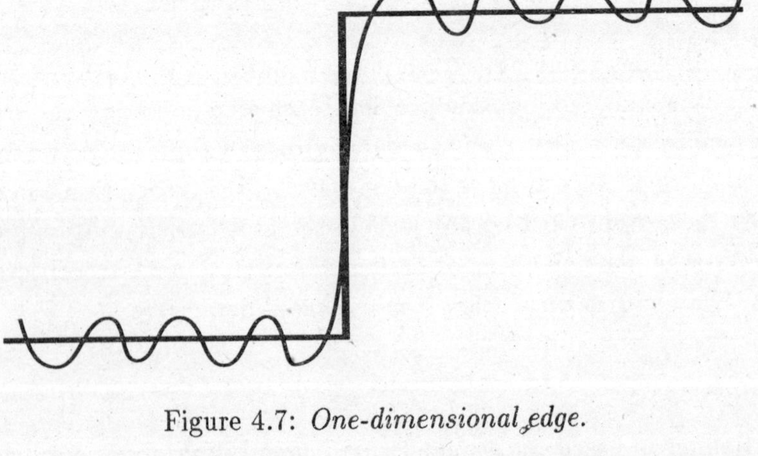

Figure 4.7: *One-dimensional edge.*

high-valued and low-valued pixels are labeled as part of an edge. An example of an image (Figure 4.6.) after edge detection is shown in Figure 4.8

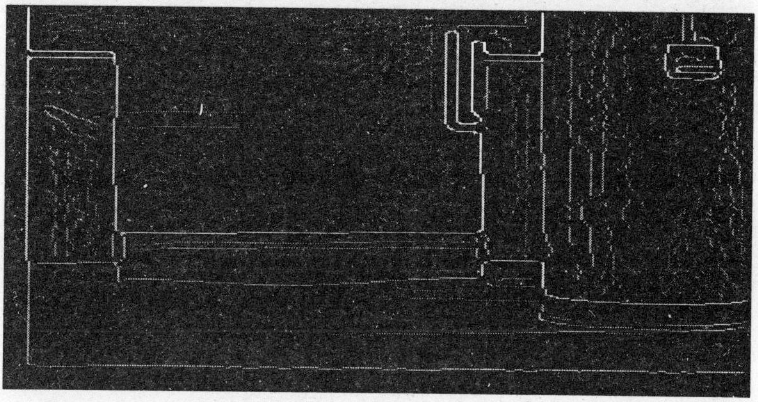

Figure 4.8: *Edge detection of the image from Figure 4.6 (Courtesy of Jana Košecká, GRASP Laboratory, University of Pennsylvania, 1994).*

Edge detection recognizes many edges, but not all of them are significant. Therefore, another labeling operation must occur after edge detection, namely *thresholding.* Thresholding specifies which edges should be accepted and which should not; the thresholding operation filters only the significant edges from the image and labels them. Other edges are removed. Thresholding the image from Figure 4.8 is presented in Figure 4.9.

Other kinds of labeling operations include corner finding and identification of pixels that participate in various shape primitives.

3. *Grouping*

The labeling operation *labels* the kinds of primitive spatial events in which the pixel participates. The grouping operation identifies the events by collecting together or identifying maximal connected sets of pixels participating in the same kind of event. When the reader recalls the intensity edge detection viewed as a step change in intensity (Figure 4.7), the edges are labeled as step edges, and the grouping operation constitutes the step edge linking.

A grouping operation, where edges are grouped into lines, is called *line-fitting.* A grouped image with respect to lines is shown in Figure 4.10. Again the

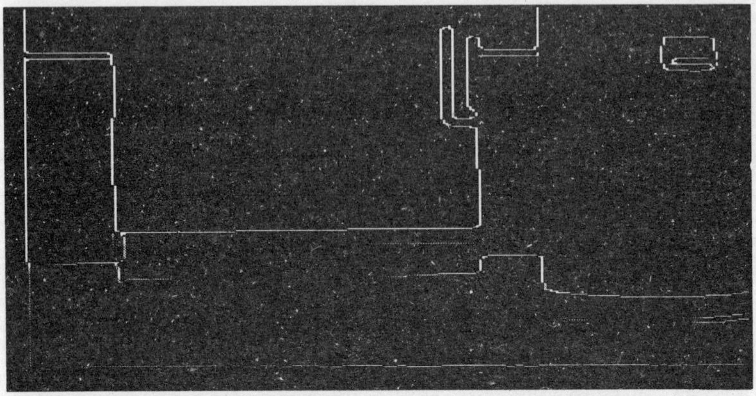

Figure 4.9: *Thresholding the image from Figure 4.8 (Courtesy of Jana Košecká, GRASP Laboratory, University of Pennsylvania, 1994).*

grouping operation *line-fitting* is performed on the image shown in Figure 4.8.

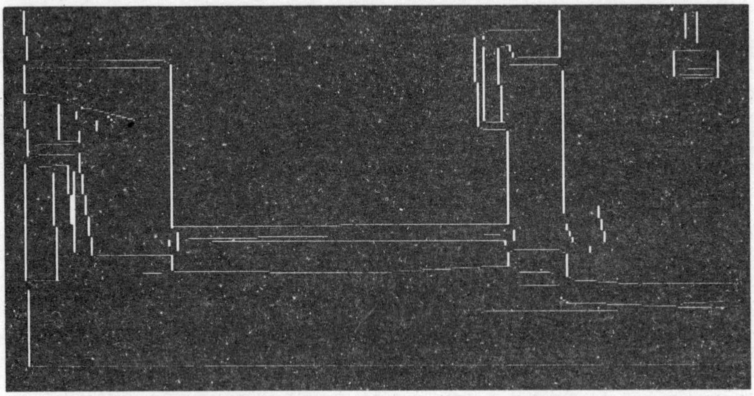

Figure 4.10: *Line-fitting of the image from Figure 4.8 (Courtesy of Jana Košecká, GRASP Laboratory, University of Pennsylvania).*

The grouping operation involves a change of logical data structure. The observed image, the conditioned image and the labeled image are all digital image data structures. Depending on the implementation, the grouping operation can produce either an image data structure in which each pixel is given an index associated with the spatial event to which it belongs or a data structure that is a collection of sets. Each set corresponds to a spatial event and contains the pairs of positions (row, column) that participate in the event. In either case, a change occurs in the logical data structure. The entities of interest prior to grouping are pixels; the entities of interest after grouping are sets of pixels.

4. *Extracting*

The grouping operation determines the new set of entities, but they are left naked in the sense that the only thing they posses is their identity. The extracting operation computes for each group of pixels a list of properties. Example properties might include its centroid, area, orientation, spatial moments, gray tone moments, spatial-gray tone moments, circumscribing circle, inscribing circle, and so on. Other properties might depend on whether the group is considered a region or an arc. If the group is a region, the number of holes might be a useful property. If the group is an arc, average curvature might be a useful property.

Extraction can also measure topological or spatial relationships between two or more groupings. For example, an extracting operation may make explicit that two groupings touch, or are spatially close, or that one grouping is above another.

5. *Matching*

After the completion of the extracting operation, the events occurring on the image have been identified and measured, but the events in and of themselves have no meaning. The meaning of the observed spatial events emerges when a perceptual organization has occurred such that a specific set of spatial events in the observed spatial organization clearly constitutes an imaged instance of some previously known object, such as a chair or the letter A. Once an object or set of object parts has been recognized, measurements (such as the distance between two parts, the angle between two lines or the area of an object part) can be made and related to the allowed tolerance, as may be the case in an inspection scenario. It is the matching operation that determines the interpretation of some related set of image events, associating these events with some given three-dimensional object or two-dimensional shape.

There are a wide variety of matching operations. The classic example is *template matching*, which compares the examined pattern with stored models (templates) of known patterns and chooses the best match.

### 4.2.3 Image Transmission

Image transmission takes into account transmission of digital images through computer networks. There are several requirements on the networks when images are transmitted: (1) The network must accommodate bursty data transport because image transmission is bursty (The burst is caused by the large *size* of the image.); (2) Image transmission requires reliable transport; (3) Time-dependence is not a dominant characteristic of the image in contrast to audio/video transmission.

Image size depends on the image representation format used for transmission. There are several possibilities:

- *Raw image data transmission*

  In this case, the image is generated through a video digitizer and transmitted in its digital format. The size can be computed in the following manner:

  $$size = spatial\_resolution \times pixel\_quantization$$

  For example, the transmission of an image with a resolution of 640 × 480 pixels and pixel quantization of 8 bits per pixel requires transmission of 307,200 bytes through the network.

- *Compressed image data transmission*

  In this case, the image is generated through a video digitizer and compressed before transmission. Methods such as JPEG or MPEG, described in Chapter 6, are used to downsize the image. The reduction of image size depends on the compression method and compression rate.

- *Symbolic image data transmission*

  In this case, the image is represented through symbolic data representation as image primitives (e.g., 2D or 3D geometric representation), attributes and other control information. This image representation method is used in computer graphics. Image size is equal to the structure size, which carries the transmitted symbolic information of the image.

## 4.3 Comments

We have described in this section some characteristics of images and graphical objects. The quality of these media depends on the quality of the hardware, such as frame grabbers, displays and other input/output devices. The development of input and output devices continues at a rapid pace. A few examples should give a flavor of this development:

- *New multimedia devices*

  New *scanners* of photographical objects already provide high-quality digital images and become part of multimedia systems. An introduction of a new multimedia device (e.g., scanner) implies new multimedia format because the new medium (e.g., photographical images) can be combined with other images and other media. An example of such a new multimedia format is the Photo Image Pac File Format introduced by Kodak. This format is a new disc format that combines high-resolution images with text, graphics and sound. Hence, it enables users to design interactive Photo-CD-based presentations [Ann94b].

- *Improvements of existing multimedia devices*

  New *3D digitizers* are coming to market which enable the user to copy 3D objects of all shapes and sizes into a computer [Ann94a].

# Chapter 5

# Video and Animation

Motion video and computer-based animation have become basic media for multimedia systems. In this chapter we present concepts and developments in these areas to develop understanding of the *motion video* and *animation* media. We describe current (analog) and upcoming (digital) video, and graphics animation with respect to the properties of human perception.

## 5.1 Basic Concepts

The human eye views pictures and motion pictures. The immanent properties of the eye determine, in connection with neuronal processing, some essential conditions related to video systems.

### 5.1.1 Video Signal Representation

In conventional black-and-white TV sets, the video signal is displayed using a CRT (Cathode Ray Tube). An electron beam carries corresponding pattern information, such as intensity in a viewed scene.

To understand later reasoning behind data rates of motion video and computer-based animation, we focus on the description of their respective signals rather than specific camera or monitor technologies. We analyze the video signal coming from a camera and the resulting pictures (using USA standards) [BF91].

Video signal representation includes three aspects: the *visual representation*, *transmission* and *digitalization*.

### Visual Representation

A central objective is to offer the viewer a sense of presence in the scene and of participation in the events portrayed. To meet this objective, the televised image should convey spatial and temporal content of the scene. Important measures are:

1. *Vertical Detail and Viewing Distance*

   The geometry of the field occupied by the television image is based on the ratio of the picture width $W$ to height $H$. It is called *aspect ratio*. The conventional aspect ratio is *4/3=1.33*. Figure 5.1 shows an example of aspect ratio.

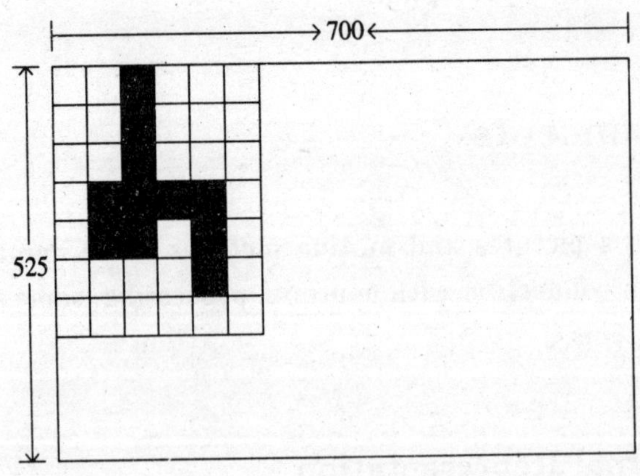


Figure 5.1: *Decomposition of a picture using an aspect ratio of 4:3 (NTSC standard).*

   The *viewing distance D* determines the angle $h$ subtended by the picture height. This angle is usually measured by the ratio of the viewing distance to the picture height ($D/H$).

The smallest detail that can be reproduced in the image is a *pixel.* Ideally, each detail of the scene would be reproduced by one pixel. Practically, however, some of the details in the scene inevitably fall between scanning lines, so that two lines are required for such picture elements. Thus, some vertical resolution is lost. Measurements of this effect show that only about 70% of the vertical detail is presented by the scanning lines. The ratio is known as the Kell factor; it applies irrespective of the manner of scanning, whether the lines follow each other sequentially (a progressive scan) or alternately (an interlaced scan).

2. *Horizontal Detail and Picture Width*

The picture width chosen for conventional television service is $4/3 \times picture\ height$. Using the aspect ratio, we can determine the horizontal field of view from the horizontal angle. Table 5.1 lists the resolutions and fields of view for different systems.

3. *Total Detail Content of the Image*

The vertical resolution is equal to the number of picture elements separately presented in the picture height, while the number of elements in the picture width is equal to the horizontal resolution times the aspect ratio. The product of the number of elements vertically and horizontally equals the total number of picture elements in the image.

4. *Perception of Depth*

In natural vision, perception of the third spatial dimension, depth, depends primarily on the angular separation of the images received by the two eyes of the viewer. In the flat image of television, a considerable degree of depth perception is inferred from the perspective appearance of the subject matter. Further, the choice of the focal length of lenses and changes in depth of focus in a camera influence the depth perception.

5. *Luminance and Chrominance*

Color vision is achieved through three signals, proportional to the relative intensities of Red, Green and Blue light (*RGB*) in each portion of the scene. The three signals are conveyed separately to the input terminals of the picture tube, so that the tube reproduces at each point the relative intensities of red, green and blue discerned by the camera. During the transmission of the signals from the camera to the receiver (display), a different division of signals in comparison to the RGB division is often used. The color encoding during transmission uses *luminance* and two *chrominance* signals. We will detail these signals later in this section.

6. *Temporal Aspects of Illumination*

   Another property of human vision is the boundary of *motion resolution.* In contrast to continuous pressure waves of an acoustic signal, a discrete sequence of individual pictures can be perceived as a continuous sequence. This property is used in television and motion pictures, i.e., motion is the presentation of a rapid succession of slightly different still pictures (frames). Between frames, the light is cut off briefly. To represent visual reality, two conditions must be met. First, the rate of repetition of the images must be high enough to guarantee smooth motion from frame to frame. Second, the rate must be high enough so that the persistence of vision extends over the interval between flashes.

7. *Continuity of Motion*

   It is known that we perceive a continuous motion to happen at any frame rate faster than 15 frames per second. Video motion seems smooth and is achieved at only 30 frames per second, when filmed by a camera and not synthetically generated. Movies, however, at 24 frames/s, often have a jerkiness about them, especially when large objects are moving fast and close to the viewer, as sometimes happens in a panning scene. The new *Showscan* technology [Dep89] involves making and showing movies at 60 frames per second and on 70-millimeter films. This scheme produces a bigger picture, which therefore occupies a larger portion of the visual field, and produces much smoother motion.

   There are several standards for motion video signals which determine the frame rate to achieve proper continuity of motion. The USA standard for motion video signals, NTSC (National Television Systems Committee) standard, specified the frame rate initially to 30 frames/s, but later changed it to 29.97 Hz to maintain the visual-aural carrier separation at precisely 4.5 MHz. NTSC scanning equipment presents images at the 24 Hz standard, but transposes them to the 29.97 Hz scanning rate. The European standard for motion video, PAL (Phase Alternating Line), adopted the repetition rate of 25 Hz, and the frame rate therefore is 25 frames/s.

8. *Flicker*

Through a slow motion, a periodic fluctuation of brightness perception, a *flicker effect*, arises. The marginal value to avoid flicker is at least 50 refresh cycles/s. To achieve continuous flicker-free motion, we need a relatively high refresh frequency. Movies, as well as television, apply some technical measures to work with lower motion frequencies.

For example, to run a movie with 16 pictures per second without any technical measures taken would be very disturbing. To reduce the flicker effect, the light wave is interrupted additionally two times during the picture projection, so that additionally to the original picture projection, the picture can be redrawn twice during the interruptions; thereby, a picture refresh rate of $3 \times 16\ Hz = 48\ Hz$ is achieved.

In the case of television, flicker effect can be alleviated through a *display refresh buffer*. The data are written in the refresh buffer at a higher frequency than the motion resolution requires (e.g., 25 Hz). The picture is displayed at a frequency so that the flicker effect is removed (e.g., 70 Hz). For example, the 70-Hz-motion frequency corresponds to the motion frequency of a good computer display. A full TV picture is divided into two half-pictures which consist of interleaved scanning lines. Each half-picture after another is transmitted, using the line-interleaving method. In the case of a full TV picture, where the transmission occurs at 30 Hz (actually 29.97 Hz), or 25 Hz in Europe, the half-pictures must be scanned at higher frequency of $2 \times 30\ Hz = 60\ Hz$, or $2 \times 25\ Hz = 50\ Hz$, to achieve the scanning rate of 30 Hz, respectively 25 Hz, for the full pictures. Figure 5.2 shows the situation described above

9. *Temporal Aspect of Video Bandwidth*

An important factor to determine which video bandwidth to use to transmit motion video is its temporal specification. Temporal specification depends on the rate of the visual system to scan pixels, as well as on the human eye's scanning capabilities. For example, in a regular TV device, the time consumed in scanning lines and frames is measured in microseconds. In an HDTV (High Definition TV) device, however, a pixel can be scanned in less than a tenth of a millionth of a second. From the human visual perspective, the eye requires that a video frame be scanned every 1/25 second. This time is equivalent to the time during which a human eye does not see the flicker effect.

The rates of scanning pixels are stated in video frequencies, but there is no one-on-one mapping. At best, during one cycle of video frequency, two horizontally adjacent pixels can be represented, so the scanning rate of, for example, 22.5 million pixels per second (HDTV scanning rate) requires video frequency up to 11.25 MHz.

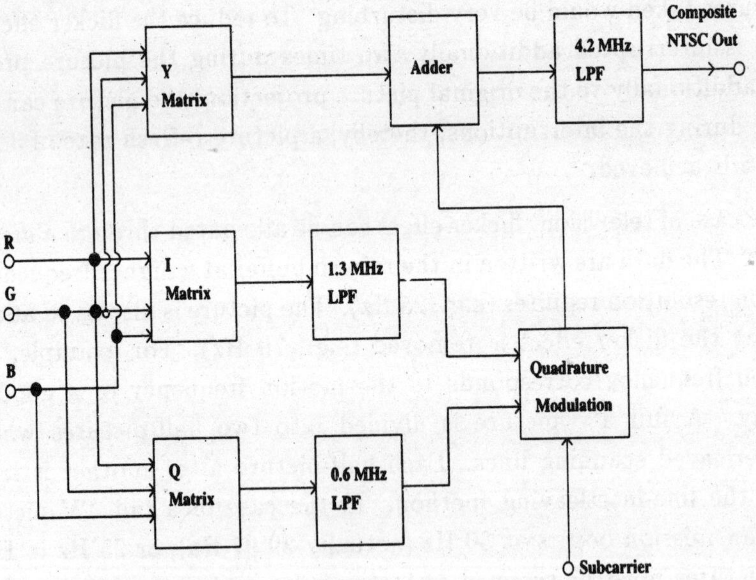


Figure 5.2: *Flicker-effect: Eye irritation by the motion frequency of 30 Hz and 60 Hz.*

### Transmission

Video signals are transmitted to receivers through a single television channel. The NTSC channel is shown in Figure 5.3.

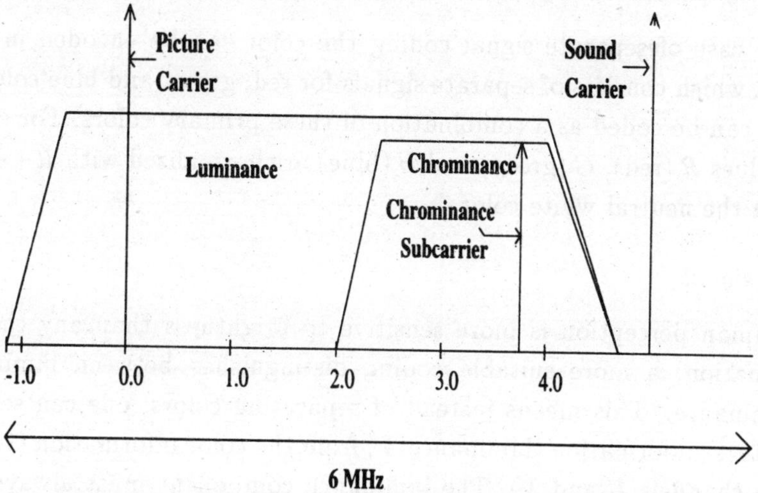


Figure 5.3: *Bandwidth of the NTSC system.*

To encode color, a video signal is a composite of three signals. For transmission purposes, a video signal consists of one luminance and two chrominance signals. In NTSC and PAL systems, the composite transmission of luminance and chrominance signals in a single channel is achieved by specifying the chrominance subcarrier to be an odd multiple of one-half of the line-scanning frequency. This causes the component frequencies of chrominance to be interleaved with those of luminance. The goal is to separate the two sets of components in the receiver and avoid interference between them prior to the recovery of the primary color signals for display. In practice, degradation in the image, known as *cross-color* and *cross-luminance*, occurs. These effects have pushed manufacturers of NTSC receivers to limit the luminance bandwidth to less than 3 MHz below the 3.58 MHz subcarrier frequency and far short of the 4.2 MHz maximum of the broadcast signal. This causes the horizontal resolution in such receivers to be confined to about 25 lines. The filtering employed to remove chrominance from luminance is a simple *notch filter* tuned to the subcarrier's frequency; currently it is the *comb filter*. The transmitter also uses the comb filter during the luminance-chrominance encoding process.

Several approaches of color encoding are summarized below:

- *RGB signal*

In the case of separate signal coding the color can be encoded in the *RGB signal*, which consists of separate signals for red, green, and blue colors. Other colors can be coded as a combination of these primary colors. For example, if the values $R$ (red), $G$ (green) and $B$ (blue) are normalized with $R+G+B=1$, we get the neutral white color.

- *YUV signal*

  As human perception is more sensitive to brightness than any chrominance information, a more suitable coding distinguishes between luminance and chrominance. This means instead of separating colors, one can separate the brightness information (luminance $Y$) from the color information (two chrominance channels $U$ and $V$). The luminance component must always be transmitted because of compatibility reasons. For black-and-white reception, the utilization of chrominance components depends on the color capability of the TV device.

  The component division for *YUV* signal is :

$$Y = 0.30\ R + 0.59\ G + 0.11\ B$$

$$U = (B\text{-}Y) \times 0.493$$

$$V = (R\text{-}Y) \times 0.877$$

  Any error in the resolution of the luminance ($Y$) is more important than in the chrominance $(U, V)$ values. Therefore, the luminance values can be coded using higher bandwidth than the chrominance values.

  Because of these different component bandwidths, the coding is often characterized by a ratio between the luminance component and the two chrominance components. For example, the YUV encoding can be specified as (4:2:2) signal. Further, the YUV encoding is sometimes specified as the Y, B-Y, R-Y signal because of the dependencies between U and B-Y and V and R-Y in the above equations.

  The CD-I (Compact Disc-Interactive) and DVI video on demand CD developments adopted the *YUV* signal decomposition.

- *YIQ signal*

  A coding similar to the YUV signal described above is the *YIQ* signal, which builds the basis for the NTSC format.

$$Y = 0.30R + 0.59G + 0.11B$$

$$I = 0.60R - 0.28G - 0.32B$$

$$Q = 0.21R - 0.52G + 0.31B$$

  A typical NTSC encoder is shown in Figure 5.4. It produces the $I$ and $Q$ signals, limits their passbands, uses them to modulate the subcarrier in a quadrature and adds the moduled subcarrier to the luminance $Y$, blanking and synchronizing signal waveform.

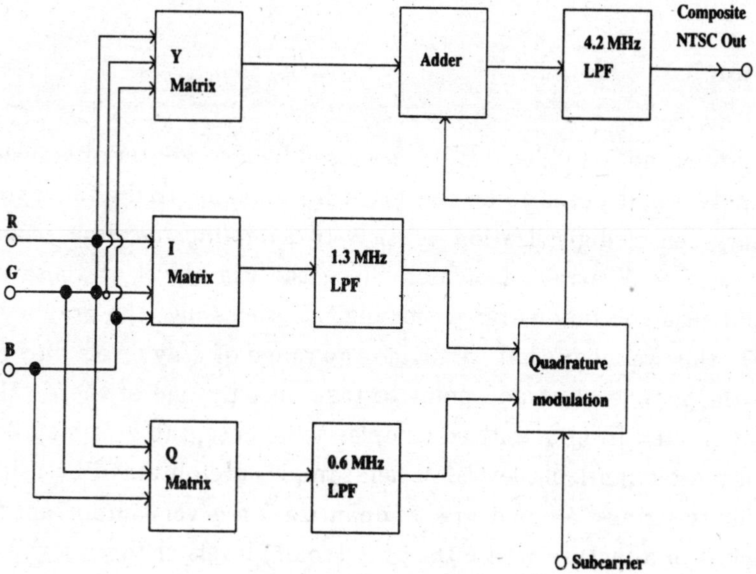


Figure 5.4: *YIQ encoding operations of an NTSC system.*

- *Composite signal*

  The alternative to component coding composes all information into one signal; consequently, the individual components (*RGB, YUV* or *YIQ*) must be combined into one signal. The basic information consists of luminance information and chrominance difference signals. During the composition into one signal, the chrominance signals can interfere with the luminance. Therefore, the television technique has to adopt appropriate modulation methods to eliminate the interference between luminance and chrominance signals.

The basic video bandwidth required to transmit luminance and chrominance signals is 4.2 MHz for the NTSC standard. In HDTV, the basic video bandwidth is at least twice of the conventional standard (e.g., NTSC). Moreover, in the separate component method of transmission, the bandwidths occupied by the three signals (*RGB* or *YUV*) are additive, so the total bandwidth prior to signal processing is of the order of 20-30 MHz.

### Digitalization

Before a picture or motion video can be processed by a computer or transmitted over a computer network, it needs to be converted from analog to digital representation. In an ordinary sense, digitalization consists of *sampling the gray (color) level* in the picture at $M \times N$ array of points. Since the gray level at these points may take any value in a continuous range, for digital processing, the gray level must be *quantized.* By this we mean that we divide the range of gray levels into $K$ intervals, and require the gray level at any point to take on only one of these values. For a picture reconstructed from quantized samples to be acceptable, it may be necessary to use 100 or more quantizing levels. When samples are obtained by using an array of points or finite strings, a fine degree of quantization is very important for samples taken in regions of a picture where the gray (color) levels change slowly [RK82].

The result of sampling and quantizing is a digital image (picture), at which point we have obtained a rectangular array of integer values representing pixels. Digital images were described in more detail in Section 4.1.

The next step in the creation of digital motion video is to digitize pictures in time and get a sequence of digital images per second that approximates analog motion video.

### 5.1.2 Computer Video Format

The computer video format depends on the input and output devices for the motion video medium.

Current video digitizers differ in digital image (*frame*) resolution, quantization and frame rate (frames/s). For example, as described in Section 4.1.2., IRIS's video board *VINO* takes NTSC video signal and after digitalization can achieve spatial resolution of 640 × 480 pixels, quantization of 8 bits/pixel (256 shades of gray) and a frame rate of 4 frames/second. The *SunVideo* digitizer from Sun Microsystems, on the other hand, captures NTSC video signal in the form of the RGB signal with frame resolution of 320 × 240 pixels, quantization of 8 bits/pixel, and a frame rate of 30 frames/second.

The output of the digitalized motion video depends on the display device. The most often used displays are raster displays, described in the previous chapter. A common raster display system architecture is shown in Figure 5.5.

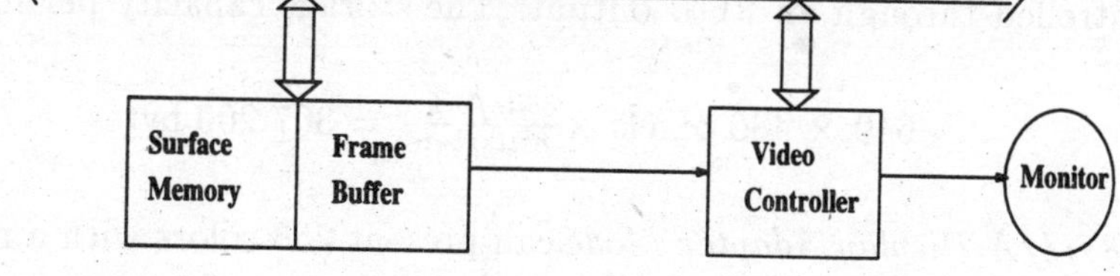


Figure 5.5: *A common raster display system architecture.*

The *video controller* displays the image stored in the frame buffer, accessing the memory through a separate access port as often as the raster scan rate dictates. The constant refresh of the display is its most important task. Because of the disturbing flicker effect, the video controller cycles through the frame buffer, one scan line at a time, typically 60 times/second. For presentation of different colors on the screen, the system works with a *Color Look Up Table (CLUT or lut)*. At a certain time, a limited number of colors ($n$) is prepared for the whole picture. The set of $n$ colors, used mostly, is chosen from a color space, consisting of $m$ colors, where generally $n << m$.

Some computer video controller standards are given here as examples. Each of these systems supports different resolution and color presentation.

- The *Color Graphics Adapter (CGA)* has a resolution of 320 × 200 pixels with simultaneous presentation of four colors. Therefore, the storage capacity per image is:

$$320 \times 200 \text{ pixels} \times \frac{2bits/pixel}{8bit/byte} = 16{,}000 \text{ bytes}$$

- The *Enhanced Graphics Adapter (EGA)* supports a resolution of 640 × 350 pixels with 16-color presentation. Therefore, the storage capacity per image is:

$$640 \times 350 \text{ pixels} \times \frac{4bits/pixel}{8bits/byte} = 112{,}000 \text{ bytes}$$

- The *Video Graphics Array (VGA)* works mostly with a resolution of 640 × 480 pixels. In this case, 256 colors can be displayed simultaneously. The monitor is controlled through an RGB output. The storage capacity per image is:

$$640 \times 480 \text{ pixels} \times \frac{8bits/pixel}{8bits/byte} = 307{,}200 \text{ bytes}$$

- The *8514/A Display Adapter Mode* can present 256 colors with a resolution of 1024 × 768 pixels. The storage capacity per image is:

$$1024 \times 768 \text{ pixels} \times \frac{8bits/pixel}{8bits/byte} = 786{,}432 \text{ bytes}$$

- The *Extended Graphics Array (XGA)* supports a resolution of 640 × 480 pixels and 65,000 different colors. With the resolution of 1024 × 768 pixels, 256 colors can be presented. In this case, we have the same storage capacity per image as the 8514/A adapter.

- The *Super VGA (SVGA)* offers resolutions up to 1024 × 768 pixels and color formats up to 24 bits per pixel. The storage capacity per image is:

$$1024 \times 768 \text{ pixels} \times \frac{24bits/pixel}{8bits/byte} = 2{,}359{,}296$$

Low-cost SVGA video adaptors are available with ***video accelerator chips*** that pretty much overcome the speed penalty in using a higher resolution and/or a greater number of colors [Lut94]. The role of video accelerator boards is to play back video that would originally appear in a 160 × 120 window at full screen. Hence, video accelerators improve the playback speed and quality of captured digital video sequences [Ann94c].

## 5.2 Television

Television is the most important application that has driven the development of motion video. Since 1953, television has gone through many changes. In this section we present an overview of the many changes that have occurred, from conventional systems used in black-and-white and color television, to enhanced television systems, which are an intermediate solution, to digital interactive television systems and their coming standards. A summary of the most important characteristics of all television systems is presented in Tables 5.1 and 5.2.

### 5.2.1 Conventional Systems

Black-and-white television and current color television is based on the representation range described in Section 5.1.1. Early on, different video format standards were established in different parts of the world. Conventional television systems employ the following standards:

- *NTSC*

  NTSC *National Television Systems Committee*, developed in the U.S., is the oldest and most widely used television standard. The color carrier is used with approximately 4.429 MHz or with approximately 3.57 MHz. NTSC uses

| System | Total Lines | Active Lines | Vertical Resolution | Optimal Viewing Distance (m) | Aspect Ratio | Horizontal Resolution | Total Picture Elements |
|---|---|---|---|---|---|---|---|
| HDTV-p USA | 1050 | 960 | 675 | 2.5 | 16/9 | 600 | 720,000 |
| HDTV-p Europe | 1250 | 1000 | 700 | 2.4 | 16/9 | 700 | 870,000 |
| HDTV-p NHK | 1125 | 1080 | 540 | 3.3 | 16/9 | 600 | 575,000 |
| NTSC-i | 525 | 484 | 242 | 7.0 | 4/3 | 330 | 106,000 |
| NTSC-p | 625 | 484 | 340 | 5.0 | 4/3 | 330 | 149,000 |
| PAL-i | 625 | 575 | 290 | 6.0 | 4/3 | 425 | 165,000 |
| PAL-p | 625 | 575 | 400 | 4.3 | 4/3 | 425 | 233,000 |
| SECAM-i | 625 | 575 | 290 | 6.0 | 4/3 | 465 | 180,000 |
| SECAM-p | 625 | 575 | 400 | 4.3 | 4/3 | 465 | 248,000 |

Table 5.1: *Spatial characteristics of television systems [BF91].*

a quadrature amplitude modulation with a suppressed color carrier and works with a motion frequency of approximately 30 Hz. A picture consists of 525 lines.

For NTSC television, 4.2 MHz can be used for luminance and 1.5 MHz for each of the two chrominance channels. Home television and VCRs employ only 0.5 MHz for chrominance channels.

- *SECAM*

  SECAM (*SEquential Couleur Avec Memoire*) is a standard used in France and Eastern Europe. In contrast to NTSC and PAL, it is based on frequency modulation. It uses a motion frequency of 25 Hz, and each picture has 625 lines.

- *PAL*

  PAL(*Phase Alternating Line*) was invented by W. Bruch (Telefunken) in 1963. It is used in parts of Western Europe. The basic principle of PAL is a quadrature amplitude modulation similar to NTSC, but the color carrier is not sup-

| System | Total Channel Width (MHz) | Video Basebands (MHz) Y | R-Y | B-Y | Scanning Rates (Hz) Camera | HDTV Display | Conventional Display |
|---|---|---|---|---|---|---|---|
| HDTV USA | 9.0 | 10.0 | 5.0 | 5.0 | 59.94-p | 59.94-p | 59.94-i |
| HDTV Europe | 12.0 | 14.0 | 7.0 | 7.0 | 50-p | 100-p | 50-i |
| HDTV Japan | 30.0 | 20.0 | 7.0 | 3.0 | 60-i | 60-i | NA |
| NTSC | 6.0 | 4.2 | 1.0 | 0.6 | 59.94-i | NA | 59.94-i |
| PAL | 8.0 | 5.5 | 1.8 | 1.8 | 50-i | NA | 50-i |
| SECAM | 8.0 | 6.0 | 2.0 | 2.0 | 50-i | NA | 50-i |

Table 5.2: *Temporal characteristics of television systems [BF91] (NA - Not Available, i-interlaced, p-progressive [non-interlaced]).*

pressed. The color carrier is computed as follows: first, the color carrier is multiplied directly by the color difference of the signal *U*; the color carrier is shifted at 90 degrees, and then multiplied by the color difference of the signal *V*; both results are added together (these three steps represent the regular quadrature amplitude modulation); and one phase of the modulated *V* signal is added to each second line for the purpose of phase errors reduction.

### 5.2.2 Enhanced Definition Systems

*Enhanced Definition Television Systems* (EDTV) are conventional systems modified to offer improved vertical and/or horizontal resolution.

Comb filters are one means for improving horizontal resolution. Used in NTSC broadcasts, they essentially make full use of the 4.2 MHz bandwidth of luminance, producing better than 30% improvement in horizontal resolution. Another improvement in horizontal resolution has been offered in VCRs [BF91].

Vertical resolution improvements were achieved by introducing progressive scanning into receivers designed for NTSC, PAL and SECAM services. For example, in the progressively scanned mode intended for the NTSC service, there are 525 lines in each field versus the 265.5 lines per field as broadcast. An extra "blank" line is presented in the display between each pair of "active" lines. The blank line may be filled in by interpolation of the video information from the active lines above and below it, plus that from the corresponding line of the previous field.

We briefly describe intermediate television systems emerging in the USA and Europe, which offer improvements on their conventional system components (NTSC and PAL).

- *IDTV*

  In the U.S., the intermediate step between NTSC television and HDTV (see Section 5.2.3) is known as IDTV (*Improved-Definition Television*). IDTV is not a new television standard but an attempt to improve NTSC image by using digital memory to double the scanning lines from 525 to 1,050 (the same number as two proposed digital HDTV formats). The pictures are only slightly more detailed than NTSC images because the signal does not contain any new information. Vertical resolution is enhanced, because 1,050-line IDTV images are displayed at once, in 1/60 of a second. Normally, 525-line TV pictures are presented in two interlaced half pictures, each 1/60 second apart. The double lines on IDTV sets, however, are small enough to disappear, at least to the naked eye. In addition, line-doubling helps to eliminate the interline flicker caused by standard interlaced scanning. By separating the chrominance and luminance parts of the video signal, and thus preventing the former from leaking into the latter, IDTV zaps the crawling dots. The improved digital separation of signals also helps cross-color interference.

  An example of improved and advanced television systems is the ACTV-I (Advanced Compatible Television, First System). The channel occupancy of the ACTV-I system is shown in Figure 5.6.

- *D2-MAC*

  D2-MAC (*Duobinary Multiplexed Analogue Components*) is envisioned as the intermediate level between current television and European HDTV. This intermediate solution is already introduced, for example, in Germany as a successor of the PAL standard. D2-MAC uses a time-multiplexing mechanism for component transmission. Figure 5.7 shows the time split for one line of a motion

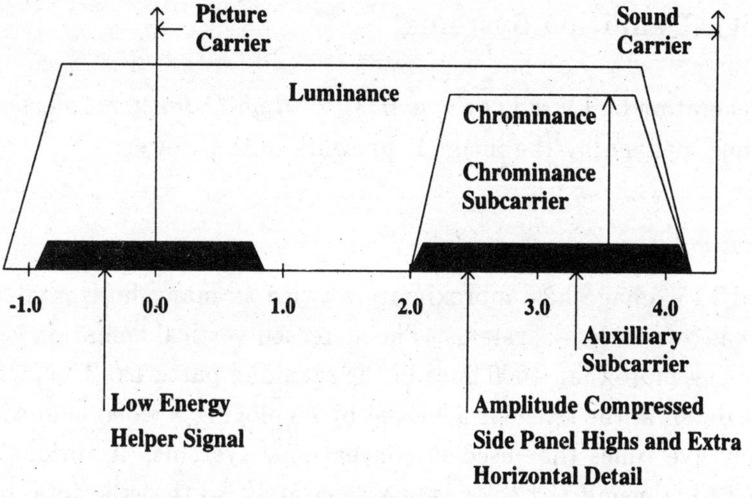


Figure 5.6: *Bandwidth of ACTV-I systems.*

picture. It means that the 64 $\mu s$ time interval is divided, so that 34.4 $\mu s$ are

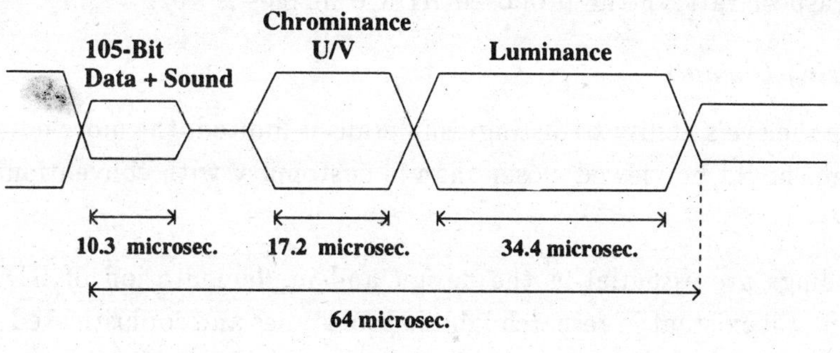


Figure 5.7: *D2-MAC – time multiplexing.*

used for the luminance signal, 17.2 $\mu s$ for chrominance signals and 10.3 $\mu s$ for voice and data.

Further characteristics of the D2-MAC system are: 625 lines are transmitted, but only 574 lines are visible. The width to height ratios of 4:3 and 16:9 are supported. The audio and further data are transmitted in a duobinary coding (D2 using together approximately 105 bits/64 $\mu s$ = 1.64 Mbits/s). Audio channels can be coded as two high-quality stereo signal channels, or up to eight channels of lower audio quality.

### 5.2.3 High-Definition Systems

The next generation of TV is known as HDTV (*High-Definition Television*). HDTV is, in principle, defined by the image it presents to the viewer:

- *Resolution*

  The HDTV image has approximately twice as many horizontal and vertical pixels as conventional systems. The increased vertical definition is achieved by employing more than 1000 lines in the scanning patterns. The increased luminance detail in the image is achieved by employing a video bandwidth approximately five times that used in conventional systems. Additional bandwidth is used to transmit the color values separately, so that the total bandwidth is from five to eight times that used in existing color television services.

- *Aspect Ratio*

  The aspect ratio of the proposed HDTV images is *16/9=1.777*.

- *Viewing Distance*

  Since the eye's ability to distinguish details is limited, the more detailed HDTV image should be viewed closer than is customary with conventional systems.

Digital codings are essential in the design and implementation of HDTV. Digital television is still existent in research labs as prototypes and sophisticated professional studios, although an international digital television standard was already specified by the CCIR (Consultative Committee International Radio) in 1982. This standard describes specific resolution sampling and coding. There are two kinds of possible digital codings: *composite coding* and *component coding*.

#### Composite Coding

The simplest possibility for digitizing video signal is to sample the composite analog video signal. Here, all signal components are converted together into a digital representation. Composite coding of the whole video signal is in principle easier than a digitalization of separate signal components (luminance and two chrominance signals), but there are also severe problems with this approach:

- There is often disturbing cross-talk between the luminance and chrominance information.
- The composite coding of the color television signal depends on the television standard. Therefore, there would exist, besides the different number of lines and motion frequencies, another difference among the various standards. Even using multiplex techniques for further signal transmission, the standard difference would be disturbing because we would then have to apply different transmission techniques to digital television systems of different standards.
- Since luminance information is more important than chrominance, this information should be allocated more bandwidth. The sampling frequency in composite coding cannot be adapted to the bandwidth requirements of individual components; hence, data reduction cannot be adapted to the properties of the individual components.
- Using component coding, the sampling frequency is not coupled with the color carrier frequency.

All the above described disadvantages of composite coding require closer consideration of component coding.

### Component Coding

The principle of component coding consists of separate digitization of various image components or planes; for example, coding of luminance and color difference (chrominance) signals. These digital signals can be transmitted together using multiplexing. The luminance signal is sampled with 13.5 MHz as it is more important than the chrominance signal. These chrominance signals ($R$-$Y$, $B$-$Y$) are sampled with 6.75 MHz. The digitized luminance and chrominance signals are then quantized uniformly with eight bits. Because of the component bandwidth ratio (4:2:2), we get 864 sample values per line for the luminance (720 samples are visible) and 432 for each chrominance component (360 samples are visible).

In PAL, for example, a picture consists of 575 lines with 25 frames per second. The high data rate and the fact that these signals do not fit into the European PCM-hierarchy (139.264 MBits/s, 34.368 MBits/s, etc.) causes problems. Therefore, different *substandards* were introduced and lower data rates defined. These substandards were derived from the bandwidth of the components. We describe some of these substandards in Section 5.2.4.

### HDTV Systems

Worldwide, three different HDTV systems have and are being developed:

- *United States*

  HDTV will be the follower of IDTV. The effort goes toward compatibility with the NTSC format, but several changes will be visible as the width-to-height ratio of the HDTV image will be 16 to 9 with 1,025 lines and a 59.94 motion frequency. The HDTV format will be a full-digital solution. The compatibility with NTSC will be achieved through using IDTV. Parameter characteristics of the U.S. HDTV service are shown in Tables 5.1 and 5.2.

- *Europe*

  The transmission method of the European HDTV system is known as HD-MAC (*High Definition Multiplexed Analog Components*) [VHC89]. The parameters of this HDTV service are shown in Figure 5.6.

  For compatibility with PAL and D2-MAC, the HD-MAC will use a two-level sampling scheme. The particular high-resolution HDTV motion pictures will be transmitted to each of the 625 lines with reduced full-picture motion. Full resolution and full-picture motion can be shown in the HD-MAC receiver using digital image storage. This reduction of the number of lines and halving fo the full-picture motion allows a simpler conversion of this signal into current PAL or D2-MAC signals. The HD-MAC method was specified in Eureka Project EU 95. This project began in 1986 and includes 35 European producers, television studios and research institutes. However, since 1993, Europe tends to follow the North American approach leading to a fully digital system.

- *Japan*

  The first HDTV service available to the public was the NHK (Japan Broadcasting Company) system, known as MUSE, which began operation in late 1989. MUSE is a Direct-Broadcast-from-Satellite (DBS) system that employs a 1125-line image at its input. It converts these lines to the narrow channel required by the satellite transponders. This conversion retains the full detail of the 1125 line image, but only when the scene is stationary. When motion occurs, the definition is reduced by approximately 50%. The spatial and temporal characteristics of HDTV are shown in Tables 5.1 and 5.2.

### 5.2.4 Transmission

For multimedia systems, the *data rates* created by motion video are important. We discuss the U.S. HDTV format first and then the European HDTV format, followed by data rates of the substandards for digital television.

For the U.S. HDTV image we assume 720,000 total pixels per frame (Table 5.1). To compute the data rate for HDTV motion video, we need further parameters such as the number of bits/pixel and number of frames/second. If the quantization is 24 bits/pixel, and the frame rate is approximately 60 frames/second, then the data rate for HDTV will be $1.296 \times 10^8$ bytes/second or $1.0368 \times 10^9$ bits/second (1036.8 Mbits/second). Using a compression method, data rate reduction to 34 Mbits/second is possible without noticeable quality loss.

In the case of European HDTV, the data rate is $1.152 \times 10^9$ bits/second, in general.

To *digital television*, different *substandards* and data reductions can be applied, and hence the data rate can be calculated as follows:

- *Substandard 1*

  Substandard 1 works with a luminance sampling frequency of 11.25 MHz (5/6 of the standard) and with a chrominance sampling frequency of 5.625 MHz

(5/6 of the standard). The data rate is $180 \times 10^6$ bits/second or $22.5 \times 10^6$ bytes/second.

- *Substandard 2*

  Substandard 2 specifies a luminance sampling frequency of 10.125 MHz (3/4 of the standard) and a chrominance sampling frequency of 3.375 MHz (1/2 of the standard). This rate fits into the 140 Mbits/second transmission channels and it is a good compromise. The data rate is $125 \times 10^6$bits/second or $16.875 \times 10^6$ bytes/second.

- *Substandard 3*

  Substandard 3 specifies a luminance sampling frequency of 9.0 MHz (2/3 of the standard) and a chrominance sampling frequency of 2.25 MHz (1/3 of the standard). The data rate is $108 \times 10^6$ bits/second = $13.5 \times 10^6$ bytes/second.

Further reduction of the data rates is possible: first, the *sampling gaps* can be left out, which means that only the visible areas are coded. For example, the luminance consists of 648 sample values per line, but from this number only 540 are visible. The chrominance is digitized with 216 sample values per line, but only 180 pixels are visible. Hence, if we assume that the picture consists of 575 visible lines, then this coding leads to a data rate of:

- (540 + 180 + 180) sample values/line × 575 visible lines/picture = 517,500 sample values/picture
- 517,500 sample values/picture × 8 bits/sample value × 25 pictures/second = $103.5 \times 10^6$bits/second

Second, *a reduction of vertical chrominance resolution* can be performed. In this case, only the chrominance difference signals of each second line are transmitted. Alternating lines of both chrominance components are digitized (*R-Y, B-Y, R-Y, etc.*). Therefore, using Substandard 2, the following data rate can be computed:

- (540 + 90 + 90) sample values/line × 575 visible lines/picture = 414,000 sample values/picture

- 414,000 sample values/picture × 8 bits/sample value × 25 pictures/s = 82.8 × $10^6$ bits/second

Third, different kinds of *source coding* can be applied to the components. For further information, see Chapter 6. Here we present only one result: with an intra-frame working ADPCM, a data reduction of 3 bits/sample (instead of 8 bits/sample) for luminance and chrominance can be achieved. Using Substandard 2, the following data rate can be computed:

- (540 + 90 + 90) sample values/line × 575 visible lines/picture = 414,000 sample values/picture

- 414,000 sample values/picture × 3 bits/sample value × 25 pictures/s = 31.050 × $10^6$ bits/s

## 5.3 Computer-based Animation

To *animate* something is, literally, to bring it to life. An animation covers all changes that have a visual effect. Visual effects can be of different nature. They might include time-varying positions (*motion dynamics*), shape, color, transparency, structure and texture of an object (*update dynamics*), and changes in lighting, camera position, orientation and focus.

A computer-based animation is an animation performed by a computer using graphical tools to provide visual effects. We concentrate in this section on computer-based animation because this kind of animation will become part of multimedia systems, although traditional (non-computer) animation is a discipline itself and exerts considerable influence over computer-based animation. Conversely, many stages of conventional animation seem ideally suited to computer assistance.

### 5.3.1 Basic Concepts

#### Input Process

Before the computer can be used, drawings must be digitized because *key frames*, meaning frames in which the entities being animated are at extreme or characteristic positions, must be drawn. This can be done through optical scanning, tracing the drawings with a data tablet or producing the original drawings with a drawing program in the first place. The drawings may need to be post-processed (e.g., filtered) to clean up any glitches arising from the input process.

#### Composition Stage

The *composition stage*, in which foreground and background figures are combined to generate the individual frames for the final animation, can be performed with *image-composition techniques* [FDFH92]. By placing several low-resolution frames of an animation in a rectangular array, a trail film (*pencil test*) can be generated using the pan-zoom feature available in some frame buffers. The frame buffer can take a particular portion of such an image (*pan*) and then enlarge it to fill the entire screen (*zoom*). This process can be repeated on several frames of the animation stored in the single image. If it is done fast enough, it gives the effect of continuity. Since each frame of the animation is reduced to a very small part of the total image (1/25 or 1/36), and then expanded to fill the screen, the display device's resolution is effectively lowered.

#### Inbetween Process

The animation of movement from one position to another needs a composition of frames with intermediate positions (*intermediate frames*) inbetween the key frames. This is called the *inbetween process.* The process of *inbetweening* is performed in computer-based animation through *interpolation.* The system gets only the starting and ending positions. The easiest interpolation in such a situation is linear interpolation (sometimes called *lerping* – Linear intERPolation), but it has many limitations. For instance, if *lerping* is used to compute intermediate positions of a ball that is thrown in the air using the sequence of three key frames shown in Figure 5.8 (a), the resulting track of the ball shown in Figure 5.8 (b) is entirely unrealistic. Because of the drawbacks of lerping, *splines* are often used instead to

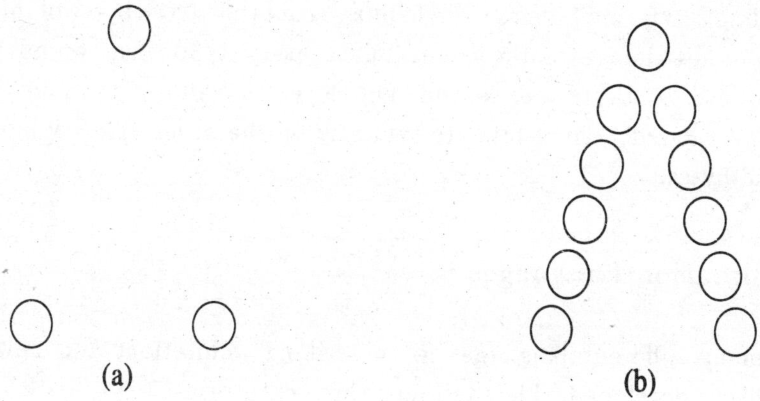

Figure 5.8: *Linear interpolation of the motion of a ball.*

smooth out the interpolation between key frames. Splines can be used to vary any parameter smoothly as a function of time. Splines can make an individual point (or individual objects) move smoothly in space and time, but do not entirely solve the inbetweening problem.

Inbetweening also involves interpolating the shapes of objects in intermediate frames. Several approaches to this have been developed, including one by Burtnyk and Wein [BW76]. They made a *skeleton* for a motion by choosing a polygonal arc describing the basic shape of a 2D figure (or portion of a figure) and a neighborhood of this arc. The figure is represented in a coordinate system based on this skeleton. Inbetweening is performed by interpolating the characteristics of the skeleton between the key frames. A similar technique can be developed for 3D, but generally interpolation between key frames is a difficult problem.

### Changing Colors

For changing colors, computer-based animation uses CLUT (lut) in a frame buffer and the process of double buffering. The lut animation is generated by manipulating the lut. The simplest method is to cycle the colors in the lut, thus changing the colors of the various pieces of the image. Using lut animation is faster than sending an entire new pixmap to the frame buffer for each frame. Assuming 8 color bits per pixel in a $640 \times 512$ frame buffer, a single image contains 320 Kbytes of information. Transferring a new image to the frame buffer every 1/30 of a second requires a bandwidth of over 9 Mbytes per second. On the other hand, new values for the lut can be sent very rapidly, since luts are typically on the order of a few hundred to a few thousand bytes.

## 5.3.2 Animation Languages

There are many different languages for describing animation, and new ones are constantly being developed. They fall into three categories:

- *Linear-list Notations*

  In linear-list notations for animation each event in the animation is described by a starting and ending frame number and an action that is to take place (*event*). The actions typically take parameters, so a statement such as

  ```
  42, 53, B, ROTATE ''PALM'',1,30
  ```

  means "between frames 42 and 53, rotate the object called PALM about axis 1 by 30 degrees, determining the amount of rotation at each frame from table B" [FDFH92]. Many other linear-list notations have been developed, and many are supersets of the basic linear-list idea. An example is *Scefo (SCEne FOrmat)* [Str88], which also includes the notion of groups and object hierarchy and supports abstractions of changes (called *actions*) using higher-level programming language constructs.

- *General-purpose Languages*

Another way to describe animation is to embed an animation capability within a general-purpose programming language. The values of variables in the language can be used as parameters to the routines, which perform the animation.

*ASAS* is an example of such a language [Rei82]. It is built on top of LISP, and its primitive entities include vectors, colors, polygons, solids, groups, points of view, subworlds and lights. *ASAS* also includes a wide range of geometric transformations that operate on objects. The *ASAS* program fragment below describes an animated sequence in which an object called my-cube is spun while the camera pans. This fragment is evaluated at each frame to generate the entire sequence.

(**grasp** my-cube) ; The cube becomes the current object

(**cw** 0.05) ; Spin it clockwise by a small amount

(**grasp** camera) ; Make the camera the current object

(**right** panning-speed) ; Move it to the right

- *Graphical Languages*

One problem with textual languages is inability to visualize the action by looking at the script. If a real-time previewer for textual animation languages were available, this would not be a problem; unfortunately the production of real-time animation is still beyond the power of most computer hardware.

Graphical animation languages describe animation in a more visual way. These languages are used for expressing, editing and comprehending the simultaneous changes taking place in an animation. The principal notion in such languages is substitution of a visual paradigm for a textual one. Rather than explicitly writing out descriptions of actions, the animator provides a picture of the action.

Examples of such systems and languages are *GENESYS*™[Bae69], *DIAL* [FSB82] and *S-Dynamics System* [Inc85].

### 5.3.3 Methods of Controlling Animation

Controlling animation is independent of the language used for describing it. Animation control mechanisms can employ different techniques.

#### Full Explicit Control

Explicit control is the simplest type of animation control. Here, the animator provides a description of everything that occurs in the animation, either by specifying simple changes, such as scaling, translation, and rotation, or by providing key frame information and interpolation methods to use between key frames. This interpolation may be given explicitly or (in an interactive system) by direct manipulation with a mouse, joystick, data glove or other input device. An example of this type of control is the *BBOP* system [Ste83].

#### Procedural Control

Procedural control is based on communication between various objects to determine their properties. Procedural control is a significant part of several other control mechanisms. In particular, in *physically-based systems,* the position of one object may influence the motion of another (e.g., balls cannot pass through walls); in *actor-based systems,* the individual actors may pass their positions to other actors to affect the other actors' behaviors.

#### Constraint-based Systems

Some objects in the physical world move in straight lines, but many objects move in a manner determined by other objects with which they are in contact, and this compound motion may not be linear at all. Such motion can be modeled by constraints. Specifying an animated sequence using constraints is often much easier to do than using explicit control. Systems using this type of control are Sutherland's *Sketchpad* [Sut63] or Borning's *ThingLab* [Bor79].

The extension of constraint-based animation systems to support a hierarchy of constraints and to provide motion where constraints are specified by the dynamics of physical bodies and structural characteristics of materials is a subject of active research.

### Tracking Live Action

Trajectories of objects in the course of an animation can also be generated by tracking live action. Traditional animation uses *rotoscoping*. A film is made in which people/animals act out the parts of the characters in the animation, then animators draw over the film, enhancing the background and replacing the human actors with their animated equivalents.

Another live-action technique is to attach some sort of indicator to key points on a person's body. By tracking the positions of the indicators, one can get locations for corresponding key points in an animated model. An example of this sort of interaction mechanism is the data glove, which measures the position and orientation of the wearer's hand, as well as the flexion and hyperextension of each finger point.

### Kinematics and Dynamics

*Kinematics* refers to the position and velocity of points. A kinematic description of a scene, for example, might say, "The cube is at the origin at time $t = 0$. It moves with a constant acceleration in the direction (1,1,5) thereafter."

By contrast, *dynamics* takes into account the physical laws that govern kinematics (e.g., Newton's laws of motion for large bodies, the Euler-Lagrange equations for fluids, etc.). A particle moves with an acceleration proportional to the forces acting on it, and the proportionality constant is the mass of the particle. Thus, a dynamic description of a scene might be, "At time $t = 0$ seconds, the cube is at position (0 meters, 100 meters, 0 meters). The cube has a mass of 100 grams. The force of gravity acts on the cube." Naturally, the result of a dynamic simulation of such a model is that the cube falls.

### 5.3.4 Display of Animation

To display animations with raster systems, animated objects (which may consist of graphical primitives such as lines, polygons, and so on) must be *scan-converted* into their pixmap in the frame buffer. To show a rotating object, we can scan-convert into the pixmap successive views from slightly different locations, one after another. This scan-conversion must be done at least 10 (preferably 15 to 20) times per second to give a reasonably smooth effect; hence a new image must be created in no more than 100 milliseconds. From these 100 milliseconds, scan-converting should take only a small portion of time. For example, if scan-converting of an object takes 75 milliseconds, only 25 milliseconds remain to erase and redraw the complete object on the display, which is not enough, and a distracting effect occurs. Double-buffering is used to avoid this problem. The frame buffer is divided into two images, each with half of the bits per pixel of the overall frame buffer. As an example, we describe the display of the rotation animation [FDFH92]. Let us assume that the two halves of the pixmap are $image_0$ and $image_1$.

Load look-up table to display values as background color

Scan-convert object into $image_0$

Load look-up table to display only $image_0$

**Repeat**

> Scan-convert object into $image_1$
>
> Load look-up table to display only $image_1$
>
> Rotate object data structure description
>
> Scan-convert object into $image_0$
>
> Load look-up table to display only $image_0$
>
> Rotate object data structure description

**Until** (termination condition).

If rotating and scan-converting the object takes longer than 100 milliseconds, the animation is quite slow, but the transition from one image to the next appears to be instantaneous. Loading the look-up table typically takes less than one millisecond [FDFH92].

### 5.3.5 Transmission of Animation

As described above, animated objects may be represented symbolically using graphical objects or scan-converted pixmap images. Hence, the transmission of animation over computer networks may be performed using one of two approaches:

- The symbolic representation (e.g., circle) of animation objects (e.g., ball) is transmitted together with the operation commands (e.g., roll the ball) performed on the object, and at the receiver side the animation is displayed as described in Section 5.3.4. In this case, the transmission time is short because the symbolic representation of an animated object is smaller in byte size than its pixmap representation, but the display time at the receiver takes longer because the scan-converting operation has to be performed at the receiver side.

  In this approach, the transmission rate (bits/second or bytes/second) of animated objects depends (1) on the size of the symbolic representation structure, where the animated object is encoded, and (2) on the size of the structure, where the operation command is encoded, and (3) on the number of animated objects and operation commands sent per second.

- The pixmap representation of the animated objects is transmitted and displayed on the receiver side. In this case, the transmission time is longer in comparison to the previous approach because of the size of the pixmap representation, but the display time is shorter because the scan-conversion of the animated objects is avoided at the receiver side. It is performed at the sender side where animation objects and operation commands are generated.

  In this approach, the transmission rate of the animation is equal to the size of the pixmap representation of an animated object (graphical image) multiplied by the number of graphical images per second.

### 5.3.6 Comments

The current development of workstations toward support of motion video and animation is progressing very quickly. Silicon Graphics™ workstations (e.g., Indigo™ XS24A, Indigo Elan, and others) provide high-quality color graphics displays, as well as video boards for capturing motion video. The major emphasis in hardware (e.g., cameras, video boards, workstations) is on achieving real-time motion video and computer-based animation. This allows researchers to achieve better results in areas such as "human facial animation based on speech intonation, emotion, and dialogue models" (a research project in the Center for Human Modeling and Simulation at the University of Pennsylvania), "3-dimensional tracking, focus ranging, and precision measurements of objects from a 2-axis camera" (a research project in the GRASP Laboratory at the University of Pennsylvania) and others.

# Chapter 6

# Data Compression

## 6.1 Storage Space

Uncompressed graphics, audio and video data require considerable storage capacity which in the case of uncompressed video is often not even feasible given today's CD technology. The same is true for multimedia communications. Data transfer of uncompressed video data over digital networks requires very high bandwidth to be provided for a single point-to-point communication. To provide feasible and cost-effective solutions, most multimedia systems handle compressed digital video and audio data streams. Note that in this chapter the terms *coding* and *compression* are treated as synonyms.

As shown in [ACM89, ACM91, JSA92a, JSA92b, Lu93, ACD+93] there already exist many compression techniques that are in part competitive and in part complementary. Most of them are already used in today's products, while other methods are still undergoing development or are only partly realized (see also [SPI94]). Whereas *fractal image compression* [BH93] might someday be relevant, today and in the near future, the most important compression techniques are JPEG (for single pictures [Org93, PM93, Wal91]), H.261 (px64, for video [Le 91, ISO93a]), MPEG (for video and audio [Lio91, ITUC90]) and proprietary developments including HQ Learn's DVI (for still images, audio and video [HKL+91]), Intel's *Indeo*, Microsoft's *Video for Windows*, IBM's *Ultimotion Matinee*, Apple's *QuickTime* or *DigiCipher II* developed by General Instruments Corp. and AT&T.

In their daily work, developers and multimedia experts often need a good understanding of the most popular techniques. Most of today's literature, however, is either superficial or dedicated to one of the above mentioned compression techniques, which is then described from a very narrow point of view. In this chapter we compare the most relevant techniques (JPEG, H.261, MPEG, DVI) to provide understanding of their advantages and disadvantages, their common abilities and differences and their suitability for today's multimedia systems. First, a short motivation for the need of compression is given. Subsequently, some requirements for these techniques are derived. In Section 6.4, source, entropy and hybrid coding techniques are explained in detail, while Sections 6.5 through 6.8 provide details on JPEG, H.261, MPEG and DVI, respectively.

## 6.2 Coding Requirements

Images have considerably higher storage requirements than text; audio and video have even more demanding properties for data storage. Not only is a huge amount of storage required, but the data rates for the communication of continuous media are also significant. With the below specified numbers we want to clarify the qualitative transition from simple text to full-motion video data and derive the need for compression. To compare data storage and bandwidth requirements of different visual media (text, graphics, image), the following specifications are based on a typical window size of $640 \times 480$ pixels on a screen:

- For the representation of text, two bytes are used for each character, allowing for some Asian language variants. Each character is displayed using $8 \times 8$ pixels, which is sufficient for the display of ASCII characters.

- For the presentation of vector-graphics, a typical still image is composed of 500 lines [BHS91]. Each line is defined by its horizontal position, vertical position and an 8-bit attribute field. The horizontal axis is represented using 10 bits (log2(640)), and the vertical axis is coded using 9 bits (log2(480)).

- In very simple color display modes, a single pixel of a bitmap can be represented by 256 different colors; therefore, one byte per pixel is needed.

The next examples specify continuous media and derive the amount of storage required for one second of playback:

- An uncompressed audio signal of telephone quality is sampled at 8 kHz and quantized with 8 bits per sample. This leads to a bandwidth requirement of 64 kbits/second and storage requirement of 64 kbits to store one second of playback.

- An uncompressed stereo audio signal of CD quality is sampled at a rate of 44.1 kHz and is quantized with 16 bits per sample; hence, the storage requirement is (44.1 kHz x 16 bits) = 705.6 x $10^3$ bits to store one second of playback and the bandwidth (throughput) requirement is 705.5 x $10^3$ bits/second.

- According to the European PAL standard, video is defined by 625 lines and 25 frames per second. The luminance and color difference signals are encoded separately. The resulting digital data streams are transformed using a multiplexing technique (4:2:2). Corresponding to CCIR 601 (a studio standard for digital video), a sampling rate of 13.5 MHz is used for luminance $Y$. The sampling rate for chrominance ($R$-$Y$ and $B$-$Y$) is 6.75 MHz. If the result is a uniform 8-bit coding of each sample, the bandwidth requirement is (13.5 MHz + 6.75 MHz + 6.75 MHz) x 8 bits = 216 x $10^6$ bits/second. HDTV doubles the number of lines and uses an aspect ratio of 16/9. This leads to a data rate which increases by a factor of 5.33 compared to today's TV rate.

  To determine storage requirements for the PAL standard, we assume the same image resolution as used before (640 × 480 pixels) and 3 bytes/pixel to encode the luminance and chrominance components. Hence, the storage requirement for one image (frame) is (640 pixels x 480 pixels X 3 bytes) = 921,600 bytes or 7,372,800 bits. To store 25 frames/second, the storage requirement is 230.4 x $10^5$ bytes or 184.32 x $10^6$ bits.

The storage and throughput requirements of a computer system that processes still images and in particular continuous media are illustrated by these few examples.

In the case of video, processing uncompressed data streams in an integrated multimedia system leads to secondary storage requirements in the range of at least giga-bytes, and in the range of mega-bytes for buffer storage. The throughput in a multimedia system can be as high as 140 Mbits/second, which must be transferred between different systems. This kind of data transfer rate is not realizable with today's technology, or in the near future with reasonably priced hardware. However, the use of appropriate compression techniques considerably reduces the data transfer rates [NH88, RJ91], and fortunately research, development and standardization have rapidly progressed in this area during the last few years [ACM91]. Some compression techniques for different media are often mentioned in the literature and product descriptions: JPEG for still image compression and H.261 (px64) for video conferencing. Additionally, some audio coding techniques, developed for ISDN and mobile communications, could also be used for compression of speech and music. MPEG is used for video and audio compression, while DVI can be used for still images, as well as for continuous media. DVI consists of two different modes for video coding: Presentation-Level Video (PLV) and Real-Time Video (RTV).

Compression in multimedia systems is subject to certain constraints. The quality of the coded, and later on, decoded data should be as good as possible. To make a cost-effective implementation possible, the complexity of the technique used should be minimal. The processing of the algorithm must not exceed certain time spans.

For each compression technique, there are requirements that differ from those of other techniques (see, for example, the requirements of [ISO93a]). One can distinguish between requirements of an application running in a "dialogue" mode and in a "retrieval" mode, where a dialogue mode means an interaction among human users via multimedia information and a retrieval mode means a retrieval of multimedia information by a human user from a multimedia database. Some compression techniques like px64 are more suitable for dialogue mode applications. Other techniques, like the DVI PLV mode, are optimized for use in retrieval mode applications.

In a *dialogue mode application*, the following requirement, based on human perception characteristics, must be considered: the *end-to-end delay* should not exceed 150 milliseconds (for compression and decompression). A delay in the range of 50 milliseconds should be achieved to support "face-to-face" dialogue applications. The number 50 milliseconds relates to the delay introduced by compression and decompression only. The overall end-to-end delay additionally comprises any delay in the network, in the involved communication protocol processing at the end system and in the data transfer from and to the respective input and output devices.

In a *retrieval mode application*, the following demands arise:

- *Fast forward and backward data retrieval* with simultaneous display should be possible. This implies a fast search for information in multimedia databases.
- *Random access* to single images and audio frames of a data stream should be possible, making the access time less than 0.5 second. This access should be faster than a conventional CD audio system to maintain the interactive character of the application.
- Decompression of images, video or audio should be possible *without a link to other data units*. This allows random access and editing.

For both dialogue and retrieval mode, the following requirements apply:

- To support scalable video in different systems, it is necessary to define a format independent of frame size and video frame rate.
- Various audio and video data rates should be supported; usually this leads to different qualities. Thus, depending on specific system conditions, the data rates can be adjusted.
- It must be possible to synchronize audio with video data, as well as with other media.
- To make an economical solution possible, coding should be realized using software (for a cheap and low-quality solution) or VLSI chips (for a high-quality solution).
- It should be possible to generate data on one multimedia system and reproduce these data on another system. The compression technique should be compatible. This compatibility is relevant in the case of tutoring programs available on a CD for example; it allows different users to read the data on different

systems, thus being independent of the manufacturers. As many applications exchange multimedia data using communication networks, the compatibility of compression techniques is required. Standards like CCITT, ISO and ECMA and/or defacto standards are used to achieve this compatibility.

This set of requirements is taken into account to a varying extent by the various compression schemes.

## 6.3 Source, Entropy and Hybrid Coding

Compression techniques fit into different categories, as shown in Table 6.1. For their use in multimedia systems, we can distinguish among *entropy*, *source* and *hybrid encoding*. Entropy encoding is a *lossless* process, while source encoding is a *lossy* process. Most multimedia systems use hybrid techniques, which are a combination of the two.

*Entropy coding* is used regardless of the media's specific characteristics. The data stream to be compressed is considered to be a simple digital sequence and the semantics of the data is ignored. Entropy encoding is an example of lossless encoding as the decompression process regenerates the data completely. Run-length coding is an example of entropy encoding that is used for data compression in file systems.

*Source coding* takes into account the semantics of the data. The degree of compression that can be reached by source encoding depends on the data contents. In the case of lossy compression techniques, a one-way relation between the original data stream and the encoded data stream exists; the data streams are similar but not identical. Different source encoding techniques make extensive use of the characteristics of the specific medium. An example is the sound source coding, where sound is transformed from time-dependent to frequency-dependent sound concatenations, followed by the encoding of the formants (see Chapter 3 – Speech Generation). This transformation substantially reduces the amount of data. *Formants* are defined as being the maxima of the voice spectrum. In most cases, three to five formants are sufficient to reconstruct the original signal in the time domain. The major problem is the correct reproduction of the transitions between individual voice units in the

| | | |
|---|---|---|
| Entropy Encoding | Run-length Coding | |
| | Huffman Coding | |
| | Arithmetic Coding | |
| Source Coding | Prediction | DPCM |
| | | DM |
| | Transformation | FFT |
| | | DCT |
| | Layered Coding | Bit Position |
| | | Subsampling |
| | | Sub-band Coding |
| | Vector Quantization | |
| Hybrid Coding | JPEG | |
| | MPEG | |
| | H.261 | |
| | DVI RTV, DVI PLV | |

Table 6.1: *A rough classification of coding/compression techniques in multimedia systems.*

time domain.

A content prediction technique can make use, for example, of spatial redundancies within still images. Other techniques perform a transformation of the spatial domain into the two-dimensional frequency domain by using the *Discrete Cosine Transformation* (DCT). Low frequencies define the average color, and the information of high frequencies contains the sharp edges. Hence, low frequencies are much more important than the higher ones, which is a key feature used in DCT-based compression.

Table 6.1 shows examples of coding and compression techniques that are applicable to multimedia applications in relation to the entropy, source and hybrid coding classification. For a better and clearer understanding of *hybrid schemes* we will identify in all schemes (entropy, source and hybrid) a set of typical processing steps.

Figure 6.1 shows this typical sequence of operations performed in the compression of still images, video and audio data streams. The following four steps describe one

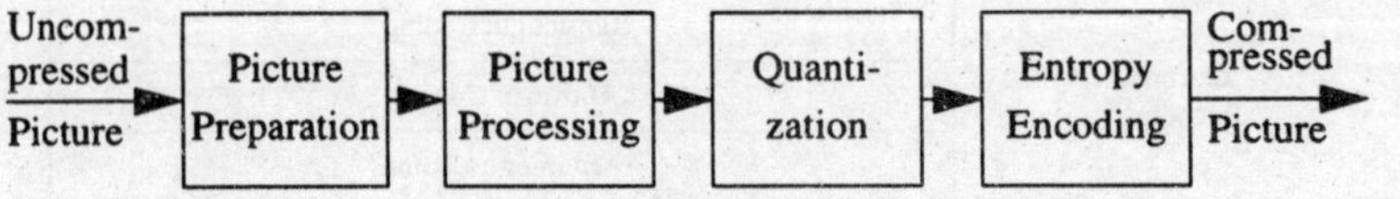


Figure 6.1: *Major steps of data compression.*

image compression.

1. *Preparation* includes analog-to-digital conversion and generating an appropriate digital representation of the information. An image is divided into blocks of 8 × 8 pixels, and represented by a fixed number of bits per pixel.

2. *Processing* is actually the first step of the compression process which makes use of sophisticated algorithms. A transformation from the time to the frequency domain can be performed using DCT. In the case of motion video compression, interframe coding uses a motion vector for each 8 × 8 block.

3. *Quantization* processes the results of the previous step. It specifies the granularity of the mapping of real numbers into integers. This process results in a reduction of precision. This can also be considered as the equivalence of the $\mu$-law and $A$-law, which apply to audio data [JN84]. In the transformed domain, the coefficients are distinguished according to their significance. For example, they could be quantized using a different number of bits per coefficient.

4. *Entropy encoding* is usually the last step. It compresses a sequential digital data stream without loss. For example, a sequence of zeroes in a data stream can be compressed by specifying the number of occurrences followed by the zero itself.

Processing and quantization can be repeated iteratively several times in feedback loops, such as in the case of *Adaptive Differential Pulse Code Modulation* (ADPCM). After compression, the compressed video builds a data stream, where a specification of the image starting point and an identification of the compression technique may be part of this data stream; the error correction code may also be added to the stream. Figure 6.1 shows the compression process applied to an image; the same principle can be applied to video and audio data.

*Decompression* is the inverse process of *compression.* The specific encoders and decoders can function in various ways. Symmetric applications, e.g., dialogue applications, should be characterized by more or less the same costs for encoding and decoding. In the case of asymmetric techniques, the decoding process is less costly than the encoding process. This is used for applications in which: (1) the compression process is performed only once and sample time is available, and (2) the decompression is performed frequently and needs to be done quickly. For example, an *audio-visual tutoring program* will be produced once but it will be used by many students; therefore, it will be decoded many times. In this case, real-time decoding is a fundamental requirement, whereas encoding need not be performed in real-time. This asymmetric processing can be exploited to increase the quality of the images.

## 6.4 Some Basic Compression Techniques

Hybrid compression techniques are a combination of well-known algorithms and transformation techniques that can be applied to multimedia systems. For example, all hybrid techniques shown in Table 6.1 use entropy encoding (in the form of run-length encoding and/or a statistical compression).

The simplest compression techniques are based on *interpolation* and *subsampling.* Here, it is possible to make use of the specific physiological characteristics of the human eye or ear. The human eye is more sensitive to changes in brightness than to color changes. Therefore, it is reasonable to divide the image into YUV components instead of RGB components (see Chapter 5 on YUV and RGB encodings).

Sampled images, audio and video data streams often contain sequences of the same bytes. By replacing these repeated byte sequences with the number of occurrences, a substantial reduction of data can be achieved. This is called *run-length coding,* which is indicated by a special flag that does not occur as a part of the data stream itself. This flag byte can also be realized by using any other of the 255 different bytes in the compressed data stream. To illustrate such a *byte-stuffing,* we define the exclamation mark "!" as a special flag. A single occurrence of this exclamation flag is interpreted as a special flag during decompression. Two consecutive exclamation flags are interpreted as an exclamation mark occurring within the data. The overall run-length coding procedure can be described as follows: if a byte occurs at least four consecutive times, the number of occurrences is counted. The compressed data contains this byte followed by the special flag and the number of its occurrences. This allows the compression of between 4 and 259 bytes into three bytes only. Remembering that we are compressing at least 4 consecutive bytes, and the number of occurrences can start with an offset of -4. Depending on the algorithm, one or more bytes can be used to indicate the length. In the following example, the character "C" occurs 8 consecutive times and is "compressed" to 3 characters "C!8":

Uncompressed data: ABCCCCCCCCDEFGGG

Run-length coded: ABC!8DEFGGG

Run-length encoding is a generalization of *zero suppression,* which assumes that just one symbol appears particularly often in sequences. The blank (null character – space) in text is such a symbol; single blanks or pairs of blanks are ignored. Starting with a sequence of three blanks, they are replaced by an M-byte (M-byte has the same function as the exclamation mark before) and a byte that specifies the number of blanks of this sequence. Sequences of three, to a maximum of 258 bytes, can be reduced to two bytes. The number of occurrences can be indicated with an offset of -3 (because three blanks are being suppressed). Further variations are *tabulators* used to substitute a specific number of zeros (or blanks). The substitution depends on the relative position within a line and the definition of different M-bytes to specify a different number of zero bytes (or blanks). The flag M4-byte could replace 8 zero bytes, and another M5-byte could substitute a sequence of 16 zero bytes. An M5-byte followed by an M4-byte would represent 24 zero bytes.

In the case of vector quantization, a data stream is divided into blocks of $n$ bytes each ($n > 1$). A predefined table contains a set of patterns. For each block, a table entry with the most similar pattern is identified. Each pattern in the table is associated with an index. Such a table can be multi-dimensional; in this case, the index will be a vector. A decoder uses the same table to generate an approximation of the original data stream. For further details and refinements see, e.g., [Gra84].

A technique that can be used for text compression substitutes single bytes for patterns that occur frequently. This pattern substitution replaces, for instance, the terminal symbols of high-level languages ("Begin," "End," "If"). Using an escape-byte, a larger number of patterns can be considered; this escape-byte indicates that an encoded pattern will follow. The next byte is an index used as a reference to one of 256 words. The same technique can be applied to still images, video and audio. In these media, it is not easy to identify small sets of frequently occurring patterns. It is often better to perform an approximation that looks for the most similar pattern instead of searching for the same pattern, in either case leading to the above described vector quantization.

*Diatomic encoding* is a variation of run-length encoding based on a combination of two data bytes. This technique determines the most frequently occurring pairs of bytes. According to an analysis of the English language, the most frequently occurring pairs are the following (note, there are blanks included in the pairs "e " "t ", " a" and "s "): "E ", "T ", "TH", " A", "S ", "RE", "IN" and "HE". Replacement of these pairs by special single bytes that do not occur anywhere else in the text leads to a data reduction of more than 10%.

Different characters do not have to be coded with a fixed number of bits. The Morse alphabet is based on this idea. Frequently-occurring characters are coded with shorter strings and seldom-occurring characters are coded with longer strings. Such statistical encoding depends on the occurrence frequency of single characters or sequences of data bytes. There are different techniques that are based on these statistical methods, the most prominent of which are *Huffman* and *Arithmetic encoding.*

Given the characters that must be encoded, together with the probability of their occurrences, the Huffman coding algorithm determines the optimal code using the minimum number of bits [Huf52]. Hence, the length (number of bits) of the coded characters will differ. In text, the shortest code is assigned to those characters that occur most frequently. To determine a Huffman code, it is useful to construct a binary tree. The leaves (node) of this tree represent the characters that are to be encoded. Every node contains the *occurrence probability* of one of the characters belonging to this subtree. 0 and 1 are assigned to the branches (edges) of the tree.

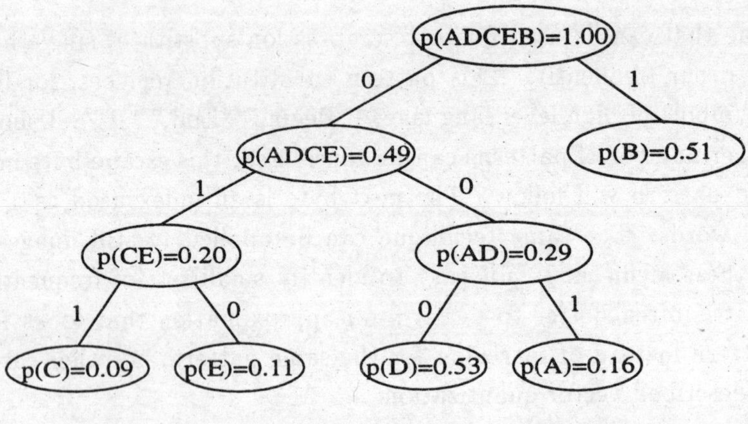


Figure 6.2: *Huffman encoding – an example.*

The following example illustrates this process:

- In Figure 6.2, characters *A, B, C, D* and *E* have the following probability of occurrence:

  $p\ (A) = 0.16,\ p\ (B) = 0.51,\ p\ (C) = 0.09,\ p\ (D) = 0.13,\ p\ (E) = 0.11$

- Characters with the lowest probabilities are combined in the first binary tree, thus *C* and *E* are the leaves. The combined probability of their root node *CE* is 0.20. The edge from node *CE* to node *C* is assigned a 1 and the edge from *CE* to *E* becomes a 0. This is an arbitrary assignment; therefore, with the same data one can get different Huffman codes.

- The following nodes remain:

  $p\ (A) = 0.16,\ p\ (B) = 0.51,\ p\ (CE) = 0.20,\ p\ (D) = 0.13$

  Again, the two nodes with the lowest probabilities are combined into a **binary** subtree; the nodes *A* and *D* are such leaves and the combined probability of their root *AD* is 0.29. The edge from *AD* to *A* is assigned a 1 and the edge from *AD* to *D* a 0. Note, if there are root nodes of different subtrees with the same probabilities, the trees with the shortest maximal path between their roots and their nodes should be combined. This keeps the code length more constant.

- The following nodes remain:

  $p\ (AD) = 0.29,\ p\ (B) = 0.51,\ p\ (CE) = 0.20$

  The nodes with the smallest probabilities are *AD* and *CE*. They are combined into a binary tree; the combined probability of their root node *ADCE* is 0.49. The edge from *ADCE* to *AD* is assigned a 0 and the edge from *ADCE* to *CE* a 1.

- Two nodes remain:

  $p\ (ADCE) = 0.49,\ p\ (B) = 0.51$

  They are combined to a binary tree with the root *ADCEB*. The edge from *ADCEB* to *B* is assigned a 1, and the edge from *ADCEB* to *CEAD* is assigned a 0.

- Figure 6.2 shows the resulting Huffman code in the form of a binary tree. The result is the following code that is stored in a table:

  $w(A) = 001,\ w(B) = 1,\ w(C) = 011,\ w(D) = 000,\ w(E) = 010$

If the information of an image can be transformed into a bit stream, such a table can be used to compress the data without any loss. The most simple way to generate a bit stream is to code the pixels individually and read them line by line. Note that usually more sophisticated methods are applied, as described in the remainder of this chapter. Such a stream can be determined for each image or for a set of images. For videos, a Huffman table can be used for a single sequence of images, for a set of scenes or even for an entire film clip. The same Huffman table must be available for both encoding and decoding.

If we consider run-length coding and all the other methods described so far, which produced the same consecutive symbols (bytes) quite often, it is certainly a major objective to transform images and videos into a bit stream.

From the information theory point of view, arithmetic encoding [Lan84, PMJA88], like Huffman encoding, is optimal. Therefore, the length of the encoded data stream is also minimal. Unlike Huffman coding, arithmetic coding does not encode each symbol separately; each symbol is instead coded by considering the prior data. Therefore, an encoded data stream must always be read from the beginning. Consequently, random access is not possible. In practice, the average compression rates achieved by arithmetic and Huffman coding are similar [Sto88].

*Transformation encoding* pursues a different approach. Data is transformed into another mathematical domain which is more suitable for compression. The inverse transformation must exist and is known to the encoding process. The most widely known example is the Fourier transformation, which transforms data from the time into the frequency domain. The most effective transformations for image compression are the *Discrete Cosine Transformation* (DCT) (see also Section 6.5.2) and to some extent, the *Fast-Fourier-Transformation* (FFT).

Unlike transformation encoding that transforms all data into another domain, selective frequency transformation sub-band coding considers a spectral selection of the signal in predefined frequency bands. The number of bands is an important criterion for quality. This technique is well-suited for the compression of speech and often makes use of FFT for spectral filtering.

Instead of compressing single bytes or sequences of bytes, *differential encoding* can be used. This is also known as *prediction* or *relative encoding.* Let us consider an example of a sequence of characters whose values are clearly different from zero, but which do not differ much. In this case, the calculation of the difference from previous values could be profitable for compression. The following examples explain this technique for different media:

- For still images, during the calculation of differences between nearby pixels or pixel groups, the edges are represented by large values, whereas areas with similar luminance and chrominance are characterized by small values. A homogeneous area is characterized by a large number of zeros which could be further compressed using run-length encoding.

- For video, the use of relative coding in the time domain can lead to encoding of the differences from the previous image only. For newscast and video telephone applications, the background often remains the same for a long time; therefore, the *difference* between subsequent images is very small, leading to a large set of zeros. Another very popular technique is motion compensation (see, for example, [PA91]). Blocks of $8 \times 8$ or $16 \times 16$ pixels in subsequent pictures are compared. For example, let us consider a car moving from left to right. An area further left in a previous picture would be very similar to the same area of the current picture, here this 'motion' can be identified by a motion vector.

- Audio techniques often apply *Differential Pulse Code Modulation* (DPCM) to a sequence of *Pulse Code Modulation* (PCM)-coded samples (see e.g., [JN84]). It is not necessary to store the whole number of bits of each sample. It is sufficient to represent only the first PCM-coded sample as a whole and all following samples as the difference from the previous one.

- *Delta Modulation (DM)* is a modification of DPCM (see [JN84]). When coding the differences, it uses exactly one bit, which indicates whether the signal increases or decreases. This leads to an inaccurate coding of steep edges. This technique is particularly profitable if the coding does not depend on 8-bit grid units. If the differences are small, a smaller number of bits is sufficient.

Difference encoding is an important feature of techniques used in multimedia systems. Further "delta" methods applied to images are described in Section 6.5.2.

Most of the compression techniques described so far are based on already known characteristics of the data, e.g., sequences of bytes occurring frequently or the probability of the occurrence of certain bytes. A non-typical sequence of characters will not be compressed using these methods.

Some compression techniques adapt a particular compression technique to the particular data to be compressed on the fly. This adaptation can be implemented in different ways:

- For each symbol to be encoded, there is a predefined coding table, e.g., as invented by Huffman, containing the corresponding code and a counter in an additional column. This counter is reset to zero at the beginning; for the first symbol to be encoded, the coder determines the code according to the table. Additionally, the counter of the corresponding table entry is increased by one. To reduce access to individual entries, table entries are sorted according to the values of the counters. The most frequently-occurring characters are at the beginning of the table with the higher values of the counters. This procedure leads to encoding symbols with the highest values by using the shortest codes.

- A prominent adaptive compression technique is *Adaptive DPCM* (ADPCM). It is a successive development of DPCM. Here, differences are encoded using a small number of bits only (e.g., 4 bits). Therefore, either rough transitions are coded correctly (these bits represent bits with a higher significance) or small changes are coded exactly (DPCM-encoded values are the less-significant bits). In the first case, the resolution of low audio signals would not be sufficient, and in the second case, a loss of high frequencies would occur. ADPCM adapts to this "significance" for a particular data stream as follows: the coder divides the value of DPCM samples by a suitable coefficient and the decoder multiplies the compressed data by the same coefficient, i.e., the step size of the signal changes.

  The value of the coefficient is adapted to the DPCM-encoded signal by the coder. In the case of a high-frequency signal, very high DPCM coefficient values occur. The coder determines a high value for the coefficient. The result is a very rough quantization of the DPCM signal in passages with steep edges. Low-frequency portions of such passages are hardly considered at all. For a signal with permanently relatively low DPCM values, i.e., with few portions of high frequencies, the coder will determine a small coefficient. Thereby, a good resolution of the dominant low frequency signal portions is guaranteed. If high-frequency portions of the signal suddenly occur in such a passage, a signal distortion in the form of a slope-overload arises. Considering the actually defined step size, the greatest possible change using the existing number of bits will not be large enough to represent the DPCM value with an ADPCM value. The transition of the PCM signal will be faded.

It is possible to explicitly change the coefficient that is adaptively adjusted to the data during compression. Alternatively, the decoder is able to calculate the coefficients itself from an ADPCM-encoded data stream. An audio signal with frequently changing frequency portions of extreme high or low frequencies turns out not to be very suitable for such an ADPCM encoding. In the G.700 series of standards, CCITT has standardized a version of the ADPCM technique using 32 kbits/s for telephone applications that is based on 4 bits per sample and an 8-kHz sampling rate.

Apart from the whole set of basic compression techniques described in this section, some additional well-known techniques are being used today, namely:

- Video compression techniques often use Color Look-Up Tables (CLUT) to achieve data reduction. For instance, this technique is used in distributed multimedia systems [LE91, LEM92].

- A simple technique for audio is silence suppression; in this case, data are only encoded if the volume level exceeds a certain threshold. This can be seen as a special case of run-length encoding.

CCITT incorporates some of the basic audio coding schemes into the G.700 series of standards: G.721 defines PCM coding for 3.4 kHz quality over 64 kbits/second channels; G.728 defines 3.4 kHz quality over 16 kbits/second channels. [ACG93] provides a more detailed description of various audio coding techniques.

In the following sections the most relevant work in the standardization bodies concerning image and video coding is outlined. In the framework of ISO/IECJTC1/SC2/WG8, four subgroups were established in May 1988: *JPEG* (*Joint Photographic Experts Group* working on coding algorithms for still images); *JBIG* (*Joint Bi-Level Expert Group* working on the progressive processing of bi-level coding algorithms); *CGEG* (*Computer Graphics Expert Group* working on coding principles); and *MPEG* (*Moving Pictures Experts Group* working on the coded representation of motion video). The next section presents the results of the JPEG activities.

## 6.5 JPEG

Since June 1982, WG8 (Working Group 8) of ISO (International Standard Organization) has been working on the standardization of compression and decompression for still images [HYS88]. In June 1987, ten different techniques for still color and gray-scaled images were presented. These techniques were compared, and three of them were analyzed further. An adaptive transformation coding technique based on the DCT achieved the best (subjective) results and, therefore, was adopted for JPEG [LMY88, WVP88]. JPEG is a joint project of ISO/IECJTC1/SC2/WG10 and the commission Q.16 of CCITT SGVIII. In 1992, JPEG became an ISO International Standard (IS) [Org93].

JPEG applies to color and gray-scaled still images [LOW91, MP91, Wal91]. A fast coding and decoding of still images is also used for video sequences known as *Motion JPEG*. Today, parts of JPEG are already available as software-only packages or together with specific hardware support. It should be taken into consideration that in most cases, only the very basic JPEG algorithms, with limited spatial resolution, are supported by these products.

In addition to the requirements described in Section 6.2, JPEG fulfills the following requirements to guarantee further distribution and application [Wal91]:

- The JPEG implementation should be independent of image size.
- The JPEG implementation should be applicable to any image and pixel aspect ratio.
- Color representation itself should be independent of the special implementation.
- Image content may be of any complexity, with any statistical characteristics.
- The JPEG standard specification should be state-of-the-art (or near) regarding the compression factor and achieved image quality.
- Processing complexity must permit a software solution to run on as many available standard processors as possible. Additionally, the use of specialized hardware should substantially enhance image quality.

- Sequential decoding (line-by-line) and progressive decoding (refinement of the whole image) should be possible. A lossless, hierarchical coding of the same image with different resolutions similar to Photo-CD images should be supported.

The user can select the quality of the reproduced image, the compression processing time and the size of the compressed image by choosing appropriate individual parameters.

Applications do not have to include both an encoder and a decoder. In many applications only one of them is needed. The encoded data stream has a fixed interchange format that includes encoded image data, as well as the chosen parameters and tables of the coding process. If the compression and decompression process agree on a common set of coding tables to be used, for example, their data of the respective table need not be included in the data stream. There exists a common context between coding and decoding. The interchange format can have an abbreviated format which does not guarantee inclusion of the necessary tables; however, some may be provided (see Appendix B of [Org93]). The interchange format in regular mode (i.e., the non-abbreviated format) includes all of the information necessary for decoding without any previous knowledge of the coding process.

Figure 6.3 outlines the steps of JPEG compression in accordance with the overall scheme shown in Figure 6.1. Four different variants of image compression can be

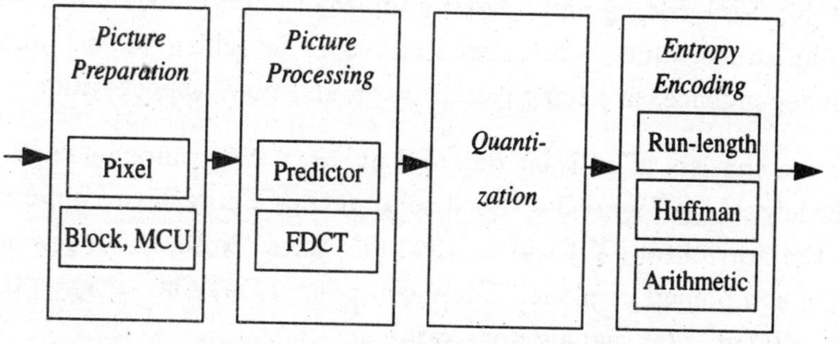


Figure 6.3: *Steps of the JPEG compression process.*

determined that lead to four modes. Each mode itself includes further combinations:

- The lossy sequential DCT-based mode (baseline process) must be supported by every JPEG implementation.
- The expanded lossy DCT-based mode provides a set of further enhancements to the baseline process.
- The lossless mode has a low compression ratio that allows perfect reconstruction of the original image.
- The hierarchical mode accommodates images of different resolutions and selects its algorithms from the three modes defined above.

The *baseline process* takes the following techniques: *Block, MCU, FDCT, Run-length* and *Huffman,* which are explained with the other modes in more detail in this section. In the next section, image preparation for all modes is presented; the remaining steps of image processing, quantization and entropy encoding are described.

### 6.5.1 Image Preparation

For the first step of image preparation, JPEG specifies a very general image model. With this model it is possible to describe most of the well-known two-dimensional image representations. For instance, the model is not based on three image components with 9-bit *YUV* coding and a fixed number of lines and columns. Mapping of encoded chrominance values is not coded either. This fulfills the demand of image parameter independence, like image size, image and pixel aspect ratio.

A source image consists of at least one and at most 255 components or planes, as shown on the left side of Figure 6.4. Each component $C_i$ may have a different number of pixels in the horizontal ($X_i$) and vertical ($Y_i$) axes. Note, the index denotes the number of the component or plane. These components may be assigned to the three colors *RGB*, *YIQ* or *YUV* signals, for example.

Figure 6.5 shows three components of an image, each with the same resolution, and each having a rectangular array $C_i$ of $X_i \times Y_i$ pixels. The three $X_i$ values and three $Y_i$ values are the same.

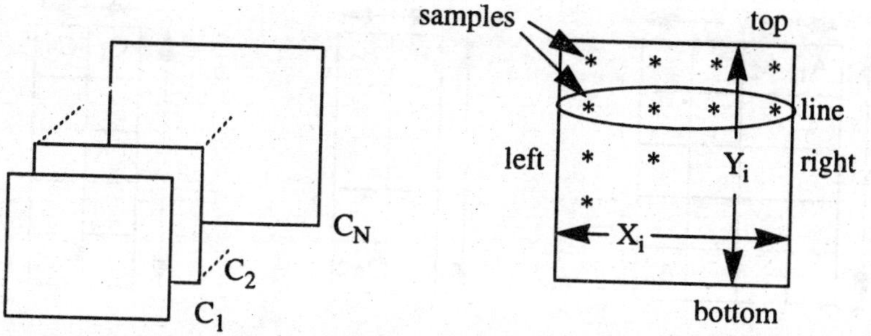


Figure 6.4: *Digital uncompressed still image with the definition of the respective image components according to the JPEG standard.*

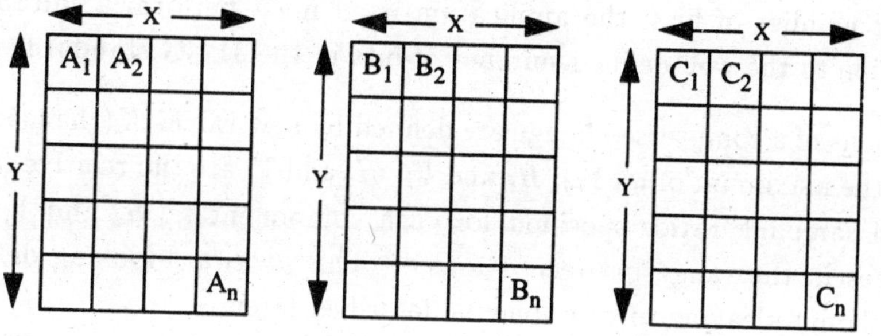


Figure 6.5: *Example of JPEG image preparation with three components having the same resolution.*

The resolution of the individual components may be different. Figure 6.6 shows an image with half the number of columns (i.e., half the number of horizontal samples) in the second and third planes as compared to the first plane: $Y_1 = Y_2 = Y_3$, and $X_1 = 2X_2 = 2X_3$.

A gray-scale image will, in most cases, consist of a single component. An *RGB* color representation has three components with equal resolution (i.e., the same number of lines $Y_1 = Y_2 = Y_3$, and same number of columns $X_1 = X_2 = X_3$). For JPEG, YUV color image processing uses $Y_1 = 4Y_2 = 4Y_3$ and $X_1{=}4X_2{=}4X_3$.

Each pixel is represented by $p$ bits with values in the range of *0* to $2^p - 1$. All pixels of all components within the same image are coded with the same number of bits. The lossy modes of JPEG use a precision of either 8 or 12 bits per pixel. Lossless modes use a precision of 2 up to 12 bits per pixel. If a JPEG application makes use

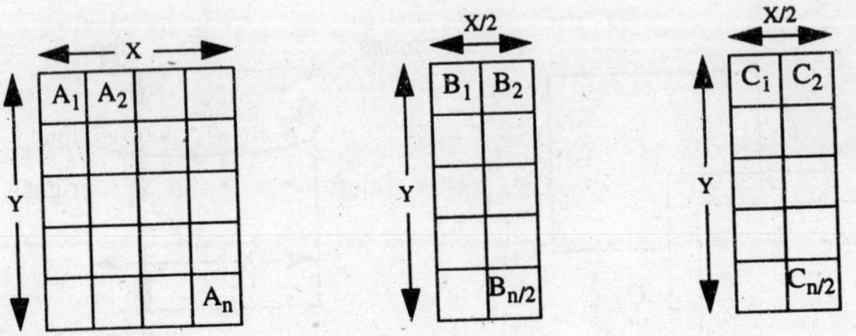


Figure 6.6: *Example of JPEG image preparation with three components having different resolution.*

of any other number of bits, the application itself must perform a suitable image transformation to the well-defined number of bits in the JPEG standard.

The dimensions of a compressed image are defined by new values $X$ (the maximum of all $X_i$), $Y$ (the maximum of all $Y_i$), $H_i$ and $V_i$. $H_i$ and $V_i$ are the relative horizontal and vertical sampling ratios specified for each component $i$. $H_i$ and $V_i$ must be integer values in the range between 1 and 4. This awkward-looking definition is needed for the interleaving of components described later.

Let us consider the following example, also shown in [Org93]. A picture is given with the maximum horizontal and vertical resolution of 512 pixels and the following sampling factors:

Level 0: $H_0 = 4, V_0 = 1$

Level 1: $H_1 = 2, V_1 = 2$

Level 2: $H_2 = 1, V_2 = 1$

Assuming X = 512, Y = 512, $H_{max} = 4$ and $V_{max} = 2$, this leads to

Level 0: $X_0 = 512, Y_0 = 256$

Level 1: $X_1 = 256, Y_1 = 512$

Level 2: $X_2 = 128, Y_2 = 256$

With the given ceiling functions, $X_i$ and $Y_i$ are calculated as follows: for the use of compression, the image is divided in data units. The lossless mode uses one pixel as one data unit. The lossy mode uses blocks of $8 \times 8$ pixels. This definition of data units is a result of DCT, which always transforms connected blocks. In most cases, the data units are processed component by component, and passed on, as shown in Figure 6.3, for the image processing step. As shown in Figure 6.7, for one component, the processing order of data units is left-to-right and top-to-bottom, one component after the other. This is known as *non-interleaved data ordering.* Using

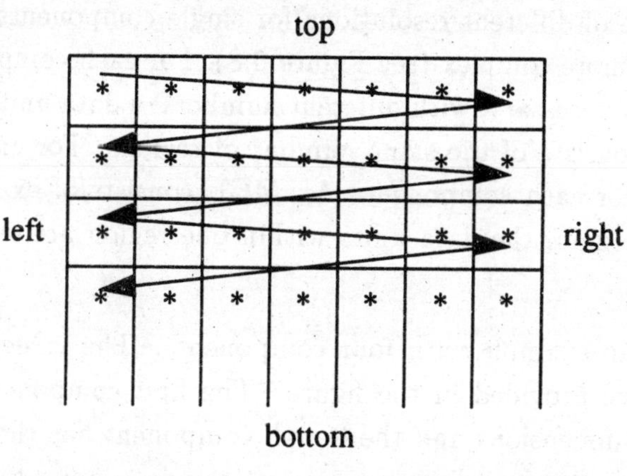


Figure 6.7: *Non-interleaved order of data units, orthe processing of one component according to the JPEG standard.*

this non-interleaved mode for an *RGB*-encoded image with very high resolution, the display would initially present only the red component, then, in turn, the blue and green would be drawn resulting in the original image colors being reconstructed. Due to the finite processing speed of the JPEG decoder, it is therefore often more suitable to interleave the data units as shown in Figure 6.8.

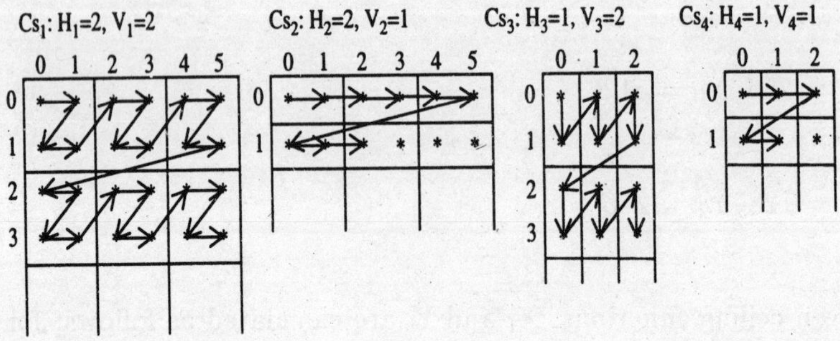


Figure 6.8: *Interleaved data units: an example with four components as derived from the JPEG standard.*

Interleaved data units of different components are combined into *Minimum Coded Units* (MCUs). If all components have the same resolution ($X_i \times Y_i$), an MCU consists of exactly one data unit for each component. The decoder displays the image MCU by MCU. This allows for correct color presentation, even for partly decoded images. In the case of different resolutions for single components, the construction of MCUs becomes more complex (see Figure 6.8). For each component, the *regions* of the data units (if necessary, with different numbers of data units) are determined. Each component consists of the same number of regions. For example, Figure 6.8 shows six regions for each component. An MCU consists of exactly one region in each component. Again, the data units within one region are ordered left-to-right and top-to-bottom.

Figure 6.8 shows an example with four components. The values of $H_i$ and $V_i$ for each component are provided in the figure. The first component has the highest resolution in both dimensions and the fourth component has the lowest resolution. The arrows indicate the sampling direction of the data units for each component. The MCUs are built in the following order:

$$MCU_1 = d^1_{00} d^1_{01} d^1_{10} d^1_{11} d^2_{00} d^2_{01} d^3_{00} d^3_{10} d^4_{00}$$

$$MCU_2 = d^1_{02} d^1_{03} d^1_{12} d^1_{13} d^2_{02} d^2_{03} d^3_{01} d^3_{11} d^4_{01}$$

$$MCU_3 = d^1_{04}d^1_{05}d^1_{14}d^1_{15}d^2_{04}d^2_{05}d^3_{02}d^3_{12}d^4_{02}$$

$$MCU_4 = d^1_{20}d^1_{21}d^1_{30}d^1_{31}d^2_{10}d^2_{11}d^3_{20}d^3_{30}d^4_{10}$$

The data units of the first component are $C_{s1} : d^1_{00}...d^1_{31}$

The data units of the second component are $C_{s2} : d^2_{00}...d^2_{11}$

The data units of the third component are $C_{s3} : d^3_{00}...d^3_{30}$

The data units of the fourth component are $C_{s4} : d^4_{00}...d^4_{10}$

According to the JPEG standard, up to four components can be encoded using the interleaved mode. Each MCU consists of at most ten data units. Within an image, some components can be encoded in the interleaved mode and others in the non-interleaved mode.

### 6.5.2 Lossy Sequential DCT-based Mode

#### Image Processing

After image preparation, the uncompressed image samples are grouped into data units of $8 \times 8$ pixels and passed to the encoder; the order of these data units is defined by the MCUs. In this baseline mode, single samples are encoded using $p =$ 8 bits. Each pixel is an integer in the range of 0 to 255.

The first step of image processing in the baseline mode (baseline process), as shown in Figure 6.9, is a transformation performed by DCT [ANR74, NP78]. The pixel values are shifted into the range [-128,127], with zero as the center. These data units of $8 \times 8$ shifted pixel values are defined by $S_{yx}$, where $x$ and $y$ are in the range of zero to seven. Each of these values is then transformed using *Forward DCT* (FDCT):

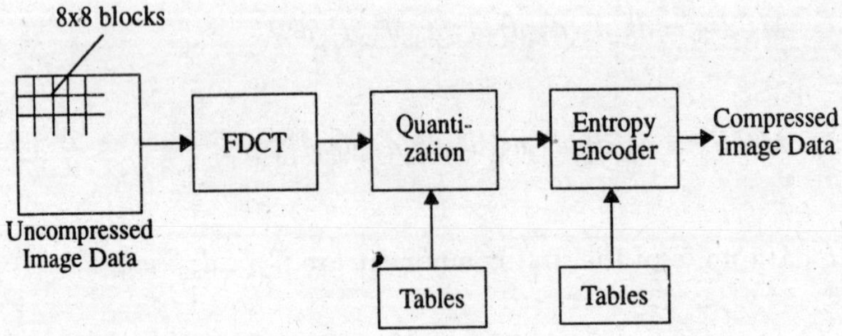


Figure 6.9: *Steps of the lossy sequential DCT-based coding mode.*

$$S_{vu} = \frac{1}{4} c_u c_v \sum_{x=0}^{7} \sum_{y=0}^{7} S_{yx} \cos \frac{(2x+1)u\pi}{16} \cos \frac{(2y+1)}{v\pi}$$

$$\text{where } c_u,\ c_v = \frac{1}{\sqrt{2}} \text{ for u, v} = 0; \text{ otherwise } c_u,\ c_v = 1$$

altogether this transformation must be carried out 64 times per data unit. The result is 64 coefficients of $S_{vu}$.

DCT is similar to *Discrete Fourier Transformation* (DFT); it maps the values from the time to the frequency domain. Therefore, each coefficient can be regarded as a two-dimensional frequency.

The coefficient $S_{00}$ corresponds to the lowest frequency in both dimensions. It is known as the DC-coefficient, which determines the fundamental color of the data unit of 64 pixels. The DC-coefficient is the DCT-coefficient for which the frequency is zero in both dimensions. The other coefficients are called AC-coefficients. AC-coefficients are DCT-coefficients for which the frequency in one or both dimensions is non-zero. For instance, $S_{70}$ represents the highest frequency that occurs in the horizontal direction, which is the closest possible separation of vertical lines in the 8× 8 data unit. $S_{07}$ represents the highest frequency in the vertical dimension, i.e., the closest separation of horizontal lines. $S_{77}$ indicates the highest frequency appearing equally in both dimensions. The absolute value of $S_{77}$ is greatest if the source $8 \times 8$ data unit consists of a full matrix, i.e., with as many $1 \times 1$ components as possible. One or both dimensions are non-zero. Accordingly, for example, $S_{44}$ will be greatest if the block consists of 16 squares of $4 \times 4$ pixels. Taking a closer look at the above FDCT formula, we recognize that the cosine expressions only depend upon $x$ and $u$,

$y$ and $v$ respectively, but do not depend on $S_{yx}$. Therefore, these cosine expressions represent constants that do not have to be calculated over and over again. There are many effective techniques and implementations of DCT. Important contributions can be found in [DG90, Fei90, Hou88, Lee84, LF91, SH86, VN84, Vet85].

For reconstruction of the image, the decoder uses the *Inverse DCT* (IDCT). The coefficients $S_{vu}$ must be used for the calculation:

$$S_{xy} = \frac{1}{4} \sum_{x=0}^{7} \sum_{y=0}^{7} c_u c_v S_{vu} \cos \frac{(2x+1)u\pi}{16} \cos \frac{(2y+1)}{v\pi}$$

$$\text{where } c_u,\ c_v = \frac{1}{\sqrt{2}} \text{ for u, v} = 0\text{; otherwise } c_u,\ c_v = 1$$

If the FDCT, as well as the IDCT, could be calculated with full precision, it would be possible to reproduce the 64 source pixels exactly. From a theoretical point of view, DCT would be lossless in this case. In practice, precision is restricted and DCT is lossy; however, the JPEG standard does not define any precision. For this reason, two different implementations of a JPEG decoder could generate different images as output of the same compressed image. JPEG merely defines the maximum tolerance.

Most of the areas of a typical image consist of large regions of a single color which, after applying DCT, are represented by many coefficients with very low values. The edges, however, are transformed into coefficients which represent high frequencies. Images of average complexity consist of many AC-coefficients with a value of almost zero. Therefore, entropy encoding is used to achieve considerable data reduction.

### Quantization

Following the steps in Figure 6.3, the quantization of all DCT-coefficients is performed. This is a lossy transformation. For this step, the JPEG application provides a table with 64 entries. Each entry will be used for the quantization of one of the 64 DCT-coefficients. Thereby, each of the 64 coefficients can be adjusted separately. The application has the possibility to affect the relative significance of the different coefficients and specific frequencies can be given more importance than others. These coefficients should be determined according to the characteristics of the source image. The possible compression is influenced at the expense of the achievable image quality.

Each table entry is an 8-bit integer value called $Q_{vu}$. The quantization process becomes less accurate as the size of the table entries increases. Quantization and

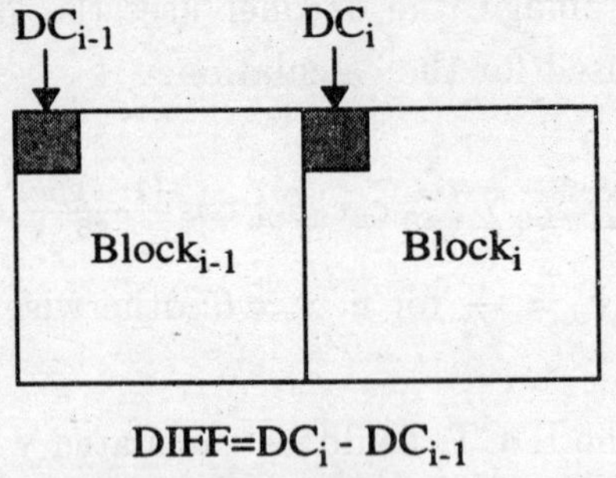


Figure 6.10: *Preparation of DCT DC-coefficients for entropy encoding, including the calculation of the difference between neighboring values.*

de-quantization must use the same tables. No default values for quantization tables are specified in JPEG; applications may specify values which customize the desired picture quality according to the particular image characteristics.

### Entropy Encoding

During the initial step of entropy encoding, the quantized DC-coefficients are treated separately from the quantized AC-coefficients. The processing order of the whole set of coefficients is specified by the *zig-zag sequence* as shown in Figure 6.11.

- The DC-coefficients determine the basic color of the data units. Between adjacent data units the variation of color is fairly small. Therefore, a DC-coefficient is encoded as the difference between the current DC-coefficient and the previous one. Only the differences are subsequently processed (see Figure 6.10).
- The DCT processing order of the AC-coefficients using the zig-zag sequence illustrates that coefficients with lower frequencies (typically with higher values)

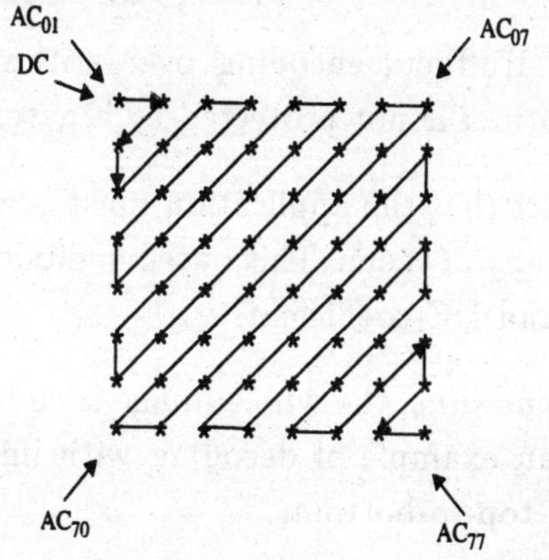


Figure 6.11: *Preparation of DCT AC-coefficient for entropy encoding, in order by increasing frequency.*

> are encoded first, followed by the higher frequencies (with typically small, almost zero values). The result is an extended sequence of similar data bytes, permitting very efficient entropy encoding. Note that the arrow between the DC-coefficient and the first AC-coefficient denotes that this DC value has the lowest frequency.

JPEG specifies Huffman and arithmetic encoding as entropy encoding methods. For the lossy sequential DCT-based mode, discussed in this section, only Huffman encoding is allowed. In both methods, a run-length encoding of zero values of the quantized AC-coefficients is applied first. Additionally, non-zero AC-coefficients, as well as the DC-coefficients, are transformed into a spectral representation to compress the data even more. The number of required bits depends on the coefficient's value. A non-zero AC-coefficient will be represented using between 1 and 10 bits. For the representation of DC-coefficients, a higher resolution of 1 bit to a maximum of 11 bits is used. The result is a representation according to the *ISO Intermediate Symbol Sequence* format, which specifies the following information:

- The number of subsequent coefficients with the value zero.
- The number of bits used for the representation of the coefficient that follows.
- The value of the coefficient represented using the specified number of bits.

The major advantage of Huffman encoding over arithmetic encoding is the free implementation, as the former is not protected by a patent.

Disadvantageous is the fact that the application must provide encoding tables since JPEG does not predefine any of them. This baseline mode allows the use of different Huffman tables for AC- and DC-coefficients.

In the case of *sequential encoding*, the whole image is coded and decoded in a single run. Figure 6.12 shows an example of decoding with immediate presentation; the picture is presented from top-to-bottom.

Figure 6.12: *Sequential picture presentation used in the lossy DCT-based mode.*

### 6.5.3 Expanded Lossy DCT-based Mode

Image preprocessing in this mode differs from the previously described mode in terms of the number of bits per sample. Specifically, a sample precision of 12 bits per sample, in addition to 8 bits per sample, can be used. The image processing is DCT-based and follows rules analogous to the baseline DCT mode.

For the expanded lossy DCT-based mode, JPEG specifies *progressive encoding* in addition to sequential encoding. In the first run, a very rough representation of the image appears which looks out of focus and is refined during successive steps. A schematic example is shown in Figure 6.13.

Progressive image representation is achieved by an expansion of quantization. This is also known as *layered coding*. For this expansion, a buffer is added at the output of the quantizer that temporarily stores all coefficients of the quantized DCT. Progressiveness is achieved in two different ways:

Figure 6.13: *Progressive picture presentation used in the expanded lossy DCT-based mode.*

- By using a *spectral selection* in the first run only, the quantized DCT-coefficients of low frequencies of each data unit are passed to the entropy encoding. In successive runs, the coefficients of higher frequencies are processed.

- *Successive approximation* transfers all of the quantized coefficients in each run, but single bits are differentiated according to their significance. The most-significant bits are encoded first, then the less-significant bits.

Besides Huffman encoding, arithmetic entropy encoding can be used in this mode. The arithmetic encoding requires no tables for the application as it is automatically adapted to the statistical characteristics of an image. According to several publications, the compression achieved by arithmetic coding is sometimes between 5% and 10% better than that achieved by Huffman encoding. Other authors assume a similar compression rate. Arithmetic coding is slightly more complex and its protection by patents must be considered (see [Org93], Appendix L).

Four coding tables for the transformation of DC- and AC-coefficients can be defined by the JPEG application. In a simpler mode, a choice of only two Huffman tables each for the DC- and AC-coefficients of one image is allowed. For this reason, twelve alternative types of processing can be used in this mode (see Table 6.2). The most widely-used display mode is the sequential display mode with 8 bits per sample and Huffman encoding.

| Image Display | Bits per Sample | Entropy Coding |
|---|---|---|
| sequential | 8 | Huffman Coding |
| sequential | 8 | Arithmetic Coding |
| sequential | 12 | Huffman Coding |
| sequential | 12 | Arithmetic Coding |
| progressive successive | 8 | Huffman Coding |
| progressive spectral | 8 | Huffman Coding |
| progressive successive | 8 | Arithmetic Coding |
| progressive spectral | 8 | Arithmetic Coding |
| progressive successive | 12 | Huffman Coding |
| progressive spectral | 12 | Huffman Coding |
| progressive successive | 12 | Arithmetic Coding |
| progressive spectral | 12 | Arithmetic Coding |

Table 6.2: *Types of image processing in the extended lossy DCT-based mode.*

### 6.5.4 Lossless Mode

The lossless mode shown in Figure 6.14 uses data units of single pixels for image preparation. Any precision between 2 and 16 bits per pixel can be used.

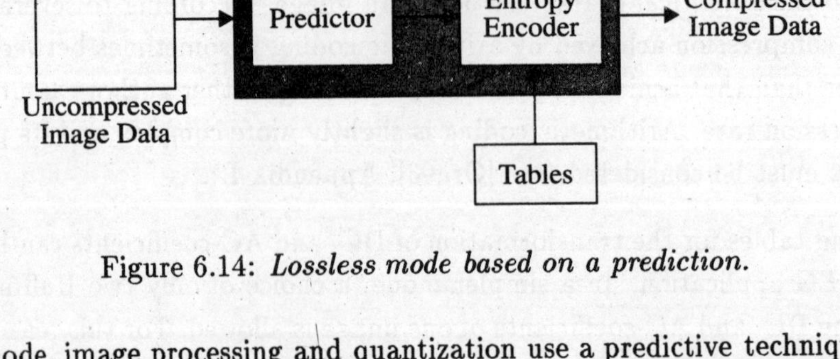


Figure 6.14: *Lossless mode based on a prediction.*

In this mode, image processing and quantization use a predictive technique instead of a transformation encoding technique. As shown in Figure 6.15, for each pixel $X$, one of eight possible predictors is selected. The selection criterion is a prediction

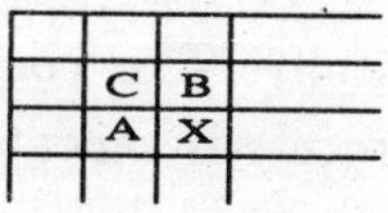


Figure 6.15: *Principle of the prediction in the lossless mode.*

| Selection Value | Prediction |
|---|---|
| 0 | No Prediction |
| 1 | X=A |
| 2 | X=B |
| 3 | X=C |
| 4 | X=A+B-C |
| 5 | X=A+(B-C)/2 |
| 6 | X=B+(A-C)/2 |
| 7 | X=(A+B)/2 |

Table 6.3: *Predictors for lossless coding.*

that is as good as possible of the value of $X$ from the already known adjacent samples $A$, $B$ and $C$. The specified predictors are listed in Table 6.3.

The number of the chosen predictor, as well as the difference of the prediction to the actual value, is passed to the subsequent entropy encoding. Entropy encoding can use either Huffman or arithmetic encoding techniques.

### 6.5.5 Hierarchical Mode

The hierarchical mode uses either the lossy DCT-based algorithms described above or alternatively the lossless compression technique. The main feature of this mode is the encoding of an image at different resolutions, i.e., the encoded data contains images at several resolutions. The prepared image is initially sampled at a lower resolution (reduced by the factor $2^n$). Subsequently, the resolution is reduced by a factor $2^{n-1}$ vertically and horizontally. This compressed image is then subtracted from the previous result. The process is repeated until the full resolution of the image is compressed.

Hierarchical encoding requires considerably more storage capacity, but the compressed image is immediately available at different resolutions. Therefore, applications working with lower resolutions do not have to decode the whole image and subsequently apply image processing algorithms to reduce the resolution – in other words, scaling becomes cheap. According to the authors' experiences with scaled images in the context of DVI, any scaling performed by the application consumes considerable time. It takes less CPU processing time to display an image with full resolution than to process a scaled-down image and display it with a reduced number of pixels. Yet, in the case of images coded according to the JPEG hierarchical mode, the display of a reduced size picture consumes less processing power than any higher resolution.

## 6.6 H.261 (px64)

The driving force behind the H.261 (px64) video coding standard is ISDN. The two B-channels of an ISDN connection (or part of them) can be used to transfer video in addition to audio data. This implies that both users connected via the B-channel have to use the same codec for video signals. Note that *codec* means encoder and decoder, i.e., encoding and decoding, compression and decompression. In the case of an ISDN connection, exactly two B-channels and one D-channel are available at the user interface. The European ISDN hierarchy allows a connection with 30 B-channels, which were originally intended for PABX. Here, we use *B-channels* to specify one or more ISDN channels. The prime considered ISDN applications were videophone and video conferencing systems. For these *dialogue applications*, coding and decoding must be carried out in real-time. In 1984, study group XV of CCITT established a committee that worked on this standard for the compression of moving pictures [Lio91].

First, a compressed data stream with a data rate of $m \times 384$ kbits/second (m = 1, 2, ..., 5) was foreseen. Later, a demand for standardization with $n \times 64$ kbits/second (n = 1, 2, ..., 5) arose. Due to advances in video-coding technology and the necessary support of narrowband ISDN, a decision was made in favor of video compression with a data rate of $p \times 64$ Kbits/second (p = 1, 2,..., 30). After five years, CCITT Recommendation H.261 *Video Codec* for Audiovisual Services at $p \times 64$ kbits/second was finalized in December 1990 [ITUC90]. This recommendation is also known as *px64*, because of the compressed data rate of $p \times 64$ kbits/second. North America adopted the recommendation with slight modifications.

The CCITT recommendation H.261 was developed for real-time processing of encoding and decoding. The maximum signal delay of both compression and decompression must not exceed 150 milliseconds. If the end-to-end delay is too long, an application using this technology will be affected considerably.

### 6.6.1 Image Preparation

Unlike JPEG, H.261 defines a very precise image format. The image refresh frequency at the input must be 29.97 frames per second. During encoding, it is possible to generate a compressed image sequence with a lower frame rate of, for example, 10 or 15 still images per second. Only non-interleaved images are allowed at the input of the coder. The image is encoded as luminance signal ($Y$) and chrominance difference signals $C_b$, $C_r$, according to the CCIR 601 subsampling scheme (2:1:1). Later this was also adopted by MPEG.

Two resolution formats each with an aspect ratio of 4:3 are specified. The so-called *Common Intermediate Format* (CIF) defines a luminance component of 288 lines, each with 352 pixels. The chrominance components have a resolution with a rate of 144 lines and 176 pixels per line to fulfill the 2:1:1 requirement. *Quarter-CIF* (QCIF) has exactly half of the CIF resolution, i.e., 176 × 144 pixels for the luminance and 88 × 72 pixels for the other components. All H.261 implementations must be able to encode and decode QCIF; CIF is optional.

The necessary compression ratio for images with the low QCIF resolution (determined by the bandwidth of an ISDN B-channel) is illustrated by means of the following example. The uncompressed QCIF is composed of a data stream with 29.97 frames per second and a data rate of about 9.115 Mbits/second; for CIF (with the same number of images per second), an uncompressed data rate of about 36.45 Mbits/second is produced. The image should be reduced to a frame rate of 10 pictures per second. This leads to a compression ratio of about 1:47.5, which can be supported with today's technology. Using a CIF format with the same compression ratio a reduction to about the bandwidth of six ISDN B-channels is possible.

In H.261, data units of the size $8 \times 8$ pixels are used for the representation of the $Y$, as well as the $C_b$ and $C_r$ components. A macro block is the result of combining four blocks of the Y-matrix each with one block of the $C_b$ and $C_r$ components. A *group of blocks* is defined to consist of 33 macro blocks. Therefore, a QCIF-image consists of three groups of blocks, and a CIF-image comprises twelve groups of blocks.

### 6.6.2 Coding Algorithms

The H.261 standard uses two different methods of coding: *intraframe* and *interframe*. In the case of intraframe coding, no advantage is taken from the redundancy between frames. This coding technique corresponds to the I-frame coding of MPEG (see Section 6.7.1). For interframe coding, information from previous or subsequent frames is used; this corresponds to the P-frame encoding of MPEG (see Section 6.7.1). The H.261 standard does not provide any criteria for mode choice. The decision must be made during the coding process, depending on the specific implementation.

Similar to JPEG, for intraframe encoding, each block of $8 \times 8$ pixels is transformed into 64 coefficients using DCT. The quantization of DC-coefficients differs from the quantization of AC-coefficients. The next step is to apply entropy encoding to the AC- and DC-parameters, resulting in a variable-length encoded word. *Interframe coding* is based on a prediction for each macro block of an image. This is determined by a comparison of macro blocks from previous images and the current image. The motion vector is defined by the relative position of the previous macro block with respect to the current macro block. Note that according to H.261, the coder need not be able to determine a motion vector. Therefore, a simple H.261 implementation considers only the differences between macro blocks located at the same position of subsequent images. In such cases, the motion vector is always a zero vector.

Subsequently, the motion vector and DPCM-coded macro block are processed. The DPCM-coded macro block is transformed by DCT if and only if its value exceeds a certain threshold. If the difference is less than this threshold, the corresponding macro block is not encoded any further – only the respective motion vector is processed. The components of the motion vector are entropy encoded using a lossless variable-length coding system. All of the transformed coefficients are quantized linearly and variable-length encoded.

Additionally, an optical low pass filter can operate between the DCT and entropy encoding process. This filter deletes any remaining high-frequency noise. Note, such a filter is optional and few implementations actually incorporate it.

For H.261, quantization is a linear function and the step size is adjusted according to the amount of data in the transformation buffer. This mechanism enforces a constant data rate at the output of the coder. Therefore, the quality of the encoded video data depends on the contents of individual images, as well as on the motion within the respective video scene.

### 6.6.3 Data Stream

According to H.261, a data stream has a hierarchical structure composed of several layers, the bottom layer containing the compressed picture. H.261 has the following characteristics (for further details, see [ITUC90]):

- The data stream of an image includes information for error correction.
- For each image, a 5-bit image number is used as a temporal reference.
- If a certain command is passed from the application to the decoder, the image displayed last is *frozen* as a still image. This allows the application at the decoding station to stop/freeze and start/play a video scene without any additional effort.
- Using further commands sent by the encoder (and not by the application), it is also possible to switch between still images and moving images. Alternatively, a time-out signal can also be used instead of this explicit command.

H.261 was designed for conferencing systems and video telephony.

## 6.7 MPEG

The MPEG standard was developed by ISO/IEC JTC1/SC 29/WG11 to cover motion video as well as audio coding according to the ISO/IEC standardization process. Considering the state of the art in CD-technology digital mass storage, MPEG strives for a data stream compression rate of about 1.2 Mbits/second, which is today's typical CD-ROM data transfer rate. MPEG can deliver a data rate of at most 1856000 bits/second, which should not be exceeded [ISO93a]. Data rates for audio are between 32 and 448 Kbits/second; this data rate enables video and audio compression of acceptable quality. In 1993, MPEG was accepted as the International Standard (IS) [ISO93a] and the first commercially available MPEG products entered the market.

The MPEG standard explicitly considers functionalities of other standards::

- *JPEG.* Since a video sequence can be regarded as a sequence of still images, and the JPEG standard development was always ahead of the MPEG standard, the MPEG standard makes use of JPEG.

- *H.261.* Since the H.261 standard was already available during the work on the MPEG standard, the working group strived for compatibility (at least in some areas) with this standard. Implementations that are capable of H.261, as well as of MPEG, may arise, however, MPEG is the more advanced technique.

MPEG is suitable for symmetric as well as asymmetric compression. Asymmetric compression requires more effort for coding than for decoding. Compression is carried out once, whereas decompression is performed many times. A typical application area is retrieval systems. Symmetric compression is known to expect equal effort for the compression and decompression processes. Interactive dialogue applications make use of this encoding technique, where a restricted end-to-end delay is required.

Besides the specification of video [Le 91, VG91] and audio coding, the MPEG standard provides a *system definition*, which specifies the combination of several individual data streams.

### 6.7.1 Video Encoding

In contrast to JPEG, but similar to H.261, the image preparation phase of MPEG, according to our reference scheme shown in Figure 6.1, exactly defines the format of an image. Each image consists of three components (similar to the *YUV* format); the luminance component has twice as many samples in the horizontal and vertical axes as the other two components – this is known as *color-subsampling.* The resolution of the luminance component should not exceed 768 x 576 pixels; for each component, a pixel is coded with eight bits.

The MPEG data stream includes more information than a data stream compressed according to the JPEG standard. For example, the aspect ratio of a pixel is included. MPEG provides 14 different image aspect ratios per pixel. The most important are:

- A square pixel (1:1) is suitable for most computer graphics systems.
- For an image with 702 × 575 pixels, an aspect ratio of 4:3 is defined.
- For an image of 711 × 487 pixels, an aspect ratio of 4:3 is defined.
- For an image with 625 lines, an aspect ratio of 16:9 is defined, the ratio required for European HDTV.
- For an image with 525 lines, an aspect ratio of 16:9 is defined, the ratio required for U.S. HDTV.

The image refresh frequency is also encoded in the data stream. Eight frequencies are defined: 23.976 Hz, 24 Hz, 25 Hz, 29.97 Hz, 30 Hz, 50 Hz, 59.94 Hz and 60 Hz.

A temporal prediction of still images leads to a considerable compression ratio. Moving images often contain non-translational moving patterns such as rotations or waves at the seaside. Areas in an image with these irregular patterns of strong motion can only be reduced by a ratio similar to that of intraframe encoding. The use of temporal predictors requires the storage of a great amount of information and image data. There is a need to balance this required storage capacity and the achievable compression rate. In most cases, predictive encoding only makes sense for parts of images and not for the whole image. Therefore, each image is divided into areas called *macro blocks.* Each macro block is partitioned into $16 \times 16$ pixels for the luminance component and $8 \times 8$ pixels for each of the two chrominance components. These macro blocks turn out to be quite suitable for compression based on motion estimation. This is a compromise of costs for prediction and the resulting data reduction.

Due to the required frame rate, each image must be built up within a maximum of 41.7 milliseconds. From the user's perspective there are no advantages to progressive image display over sequential display. The user has neither the need nor possibility to define the MCUs (Minimum Coded Units) in MPEG (in contrast to JPEG).

MPEG distinguishes four types of image coding for processing, as shown Figure 6.16. The reasons behind this are the contradictory demands for an efficient coding scheme and fast random access. To achieve a high compression ratio, temporal redundancies of subsequent pictures must be exploited (interframe), whereas the demand for fast random access requires intraframe coding. The following types of images are distinguished (*image* is used as a synonym for *still image* or *frame*):

- *I-frames* (*Intra-coded images*) are self contained, i.e., coded without any reference to other images. An I-frame is treated as a still image. MPEG makes use of JPEG for I-frames. However, contrary to JPEG, compression must often be executed in real-time. The compression rate of I-frames is the lowest within MPEG. I-frames are points for random access in MPEG streams.

  I-frames use $8 \times 8$ blocks defined within a macro block, on which a DCT is performed. The DC-coefficients are then DPCM coded; differences of successive blocks of one component are computed and transformed using variable-length coding. MPEG distinguishes two types of macro blocks – the first type includes only the encoded data and the second covers a parameter used for scaling by adjustment of the quantization characteristics.

- *P-frames* (*Predictive-coded frames*) require information of the previous I-frame

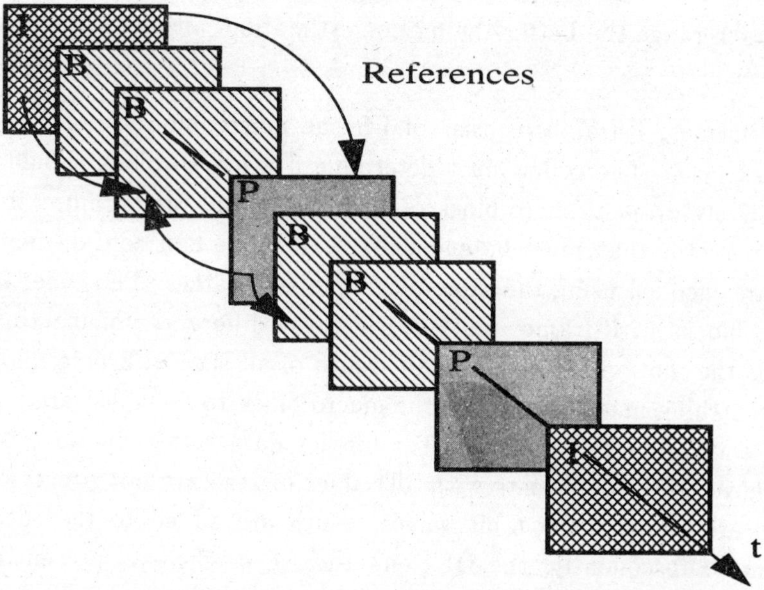


Figure 6.16: *Types of images in MPEG.*

and/or all previous P-frames for encoding and decoding.

The coding of P-frames is based on the fact that, by successive images, their areas often do not change at all but instead, the whole area is shifted. In this case of *temporal redundancy*, the block of the last P- or I-frame that is most similar to the block under consideration is determined. Several methods for motion estimation are available to the encoder. The most processing-intensive methods tend to give better results, so the following trade-offs must be made in the encoder: computational power, and hence cost, versus video quality [ISO93a]. Several matching criteria are available, e.g., the differences of all absolute values of the luminance component are computed. The minimal number of the sum of all differences indicates the best matching macro block. Thereby, MPEG does not provide a certain algorithm for motion estimation, but instead specifies the coding of the result. Only the motion vector (the difference between the spatial location of the macro blocks) and the small difference in content of these macro blocks are left to be encoded. The search range, i.e., the maximum size of the motion vector, is not defined in the standard, but it is constrained by the definable motion vector range. The larger the search range the better the motion estimation, although the computation is slower.

Like I-frames, P-frames consist of I-frame macro blocks and six predictive macro blocks. The coder must determine if a macro block should be coded predictively or as a macro block of an I-frame, and furthermore, if there is a motion vector that must be encoded. A P-frame can contain macro blocks that are encoded using the same technique as I-frames. The coder for specific macro blocks of P-frames must consider the differences of macro blocks, as well as the motion vector. The difference of all six $8 \times 8$ pixel blocks of the best matching macro block and the macro block to be coded are transformed using a two-dimensional DCT. For further data rate reduction, blocks that only have DCT-coefficients with all values of zero are not processed further. These are stored using 6-bit values, which are added to the encoded data stream. Subsequently, the DC- and the AC-coefficients are encoded using the same technique. Note that this differs from JPEG and from the coding of macro blocks of I-frames. In the next step, a run-length encoding and the determination of a variable-length code (not according to Huffman, but similar) is applied. Since the motion vectors of adjacent macro blocks often differ only slightly, DPCM encoding is used. The result is again transformed using a table leading to a variable-length encoded word.

- *B-frames* (*Bi-directionally predictive-coded frames*) require information of the previous and following I- and/or P-frame for encoding and decoding. The highest compression ratio is attainable by using these frames. A B-frame is defined as the difference of a prediction of the past image and the following P- or I-frame. B-frames can never be directly accessed in a random fashion.

  For the prediction of B-frames, the previous as well as the following P- or I-frames are taken into account. The following example illustrates the advantages of a *bi-directional prediction.* In a video scene, a ball moves from left to right in front of a static background. In the left area of the scene, parts of the image appear that in the former image were covered by the ball. A prediction of these areas can be derived from the following but not from the previous image. A macro block may be derived from the previous or the next macro block of P- or I-frames. Apart from a motion vector from the previous to the next image, a motion vector in the other direction can also be used. *Interpolative* motion compensation that uses both matching macro blocks is allowed. In this case, two motion vectors are encoded. The difference of the macro block to be encoded and the interpolated macro block is determined. Further quantization and entropy encoding are performed like P-frame specific macro blocks. B-frames must not be stored in the decoder as a reference for subsequent decoding of images.

- *D-frames* (*DC-coded frames*) are intraframe-encoded. They can be used for fast forward or fast rewind modes. The DC-parameters are DCT-coded; the AC-coefficients are neglected.

  D-frames consist only of the lowest frequencies of an image. They only use one type of macro block and only the DC-coefficients are encoded. D-frames are used for display in fast-forward or fast-rewind modes. This could also be realized by a suitable order of I-frames. For this purpose, I-frames must occur periodically in data stream. Slow-rewind playback requires huge storage capacity. Therefore, all images that were combined in a group must be decoded in the forward mode and stored, after which a rewind playback is possible. This is known as the *group of pictures* in MPEG.

Figure 6.16 shows a sequence of I-, P- and B-frames. For example, the prediction for the first P-frames and a bi-directional prediction for a B-frame is shown. Note that by using B-frames the order of the images in a MPEG-coded data stream often differs from the actual decoding order. A P-frame to be displayed after the related B-frame must be decoded before the B-frame because its data is required for the decompression of the B-frame. This fact introduces an additional end-to-end delay.

The regularity of a sequence of I-, P- and B-frames is determined by the MPEG application. For fast random access, the best resolution would be achieved by coding the whole data stream as I-frames. On the other hand, the highest degree of compression is attained by using as many B-frames as possible. For practical applications, the following sequence has proved to be useful, "IBBPBBPBB IBBPBBPBB ..." In this case, random access would have a resolution of nine still images (i.e., about 330 milliseconds), and it still provides a very good compression ratio.

Concerning quantization, it should be mentioned that AC-coefficients of B- and P-frames are usually large values, whereas those of I-frames are smaller values. Thus, the MPEG quantization is adjusted respectively. If the data rate increases over a certain threshold, the quantization enlarges the step size. In the opposite case, the step size is reduced and the quantization is performed with finer granularity.

### 6.7.2 Audio Encoding

MPEG audio coding uses the same sampling frequencies as Compact Disc Digital Audio (CD-DA) and Digital Audio Tape (DAT), i.e., 44.1 kHz and 48 kHz, and additionally, 32 kHz is available, all at 16 bits.

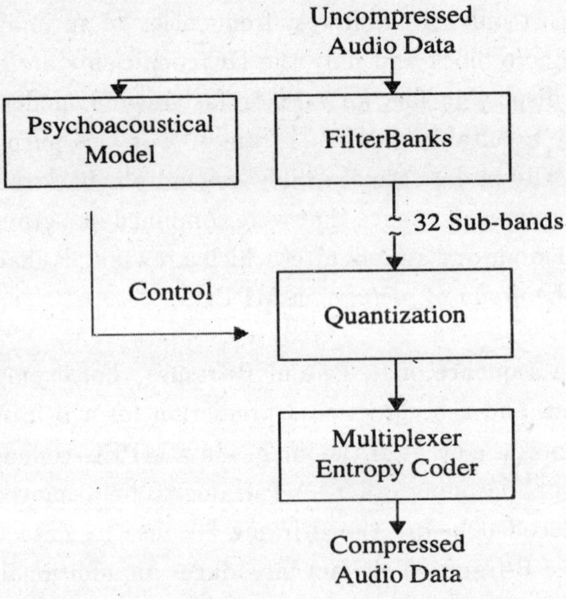


Figure 6.17: *MPEG basic steps of audio encoding.*

Three different layers (Figure 6.17) of encoder and decoder complexity and performance are defined. An implementation of a higher layer must be able to decode the MPEG audio signals of lower layers [Mus90]. Similar to two-dimensional DCT for video, a transformation into the frequency domain is applied for audio. *Fast Fourier Transformation* (FFT) is suitable for this coding, and the spectrum is split into 32 non-interleaved subbands. For each subband, the amplitude of the audio signal is calculated. Also for each subband, the noise level is determined simultaneously to the actual FFT by using a *psychoacoustic model.* At a higher noise level, a rough quantization is performed, and at a lower noise level, a finer quantization is applied. The quantized spectral portions of layers one and two are PCM-encoded and those of layer three are Huffman-encoded. The audio coding can be performed with a single channel, two independent channels or one stereo signal. In the definition of MPEG, there are two different stereo modes: two channels that are processed either independently or as *joint stereo.* In the case of joint stereo, MPEG exploits redundancy of both channels and achieves a higher compression ratio.

Each layer defines 14 fixed bit rates for the encoded audio data stream, which in MPEG are addressed by a bit rate index. The minimal value is always 32 Kbits/second. These layers support different maximal bit rates: layer 1 allows for a maximal bit rate of 448 Kbits/second, layer 2 for 384 Kbits/second and layer 3 for 320 Kbits/s. For layers 1 and 2, a decoder is not required to support a variable bit rate. In layer 3, a variable bit rate is specified by switching the bit rate index. For layer 2, not all combinations of bit rate and mode are allowed:

- 32 Kbits/second, 48 Kbits/second, 56 Kbits/second and 80 Kbits/second are only allowed for a single channel.
- 64 Kbits/second, 96 Kbits/second, 112 Kbits/second, 128 Kbits/second, 160 Kbits/second and 192 Kbits/second are allowed for all modes.
- 224 Kbits/second, 256 Kbits/second, 320 Kbits/second, 384 Kbits/second are allowed for the modes *stereo*, *joint stereo* and *dual channel* modes.

### 6.7.3 Data Stream

#### Audio Stream

MPEG specifies a syntax for the interleaved audio and video data streams. An audio data stream consists of frames, which are divided into audio access units. Each audio access unit is composed of slots. At the lowest complexity (layer 1), a slot consists of four bytes. In any other layer, it consists of one byte. A frame always consists of a fixed number of samples. Most important is the *audio access unit*, which is the smallest possible audio sequence of compressed data that can be completely decoded independent of all other data. The audio access units of one frame lead to a playing time of 8 milliseconds at 48 kHz, of 8.7 milliseconds at 44.1 kHz, and 12 milliseconds at 32 kHz. In the case of stereo signals, data from both channels are merged into one frame.

### Video Stream

A video data stream is comprised of six layers:

1. At the highest level, the *sequence layer*, data buffering is handled. A data stream should have low requirements in terms of storage capacity. For this reason, at the beginning of the *sequence layer* there are the following two entries: the constant bit rate of the sequence and the storage capacity that is needed for decoding. In the processing scheme, a *video-buffer-verifier* is inserted after the quantizer. The resulting data rate is used to verify the delay caused by decoding. The *video-buffer-verifier* influences the quantizer and forms a kind of control loop. Several successive sequences could have a varying data rate. During decoding of several immediately following sequences there is no direct relationship between the end of one sequence and the beginning of the next one. The basic parameters of the decoder are set again and an initialization is executed at this time.

2. The *group of pictures layer* is the next layer. This layer consists of a minimum of one I-frame, which is the first frame. Random access to this image is always possible. At this layer, it is possible to distinguish the order of images in a data stream and during display. The first image of a data stream always has to be an I-frame. Therefore, the decoder decodes and stores the reference frame first. In the order of display, a B-frame can occur before an I-frame.

   Display Order:

   | Type of Frame | B | B | I | B | B | P | B | B | P | B | B | P |
   |---|---|---|---|---|---|---|---|---|---|---|---|---|
   | Number of Frame | 0 | 1 | 2 | 3 | 4 | 5 | 6 | 7 | 8 | 9 | 10 | 11 |

Decoding order:

| Type of Frame | I | B | B | P | B | B | P | B | B | P | B | B |
|---|---|---|---|---|---|---|---|---|---|---|---|---|
| Number of Frame | 2 | 0 | 1 | 5 | 3 | 4 | 8 | 6 | 7 | 11 | 9 | 10 |

3. The *picture layer* contains a whole picture. The temporal reference is defined by an image number. Note that there are data fields defined in this layer which are not yet used in MPEG. The decoder is not allowed to use these data fields, as they are designated for future extensions.

4. The next layer is the *slice layer*. Each slice consists of a number of macro blocks that may vary from one image to the next. Additionally, the DCT quantization of each macro block of a slice is specified.

5. The fifth layer is the *macro block layer*. It contains the sum of the features of each macro block as described above.

6. The lowest layer is the *block layer* (described above).

The MPEG standard also specifies the combination of data streams into a single data stream in the system definition. The same idea was pursued in DVI to define the AVSS (Audio/Video Support System) data format. The most important task of this process is the actual multiplexing. It includes the coordination of input data streams and output data streams, the adjustment of clocks and buffer management. Therefore, the data stream defined by ISO 11172 is divided into single *packs*. The decoder gets the information necessary for its resource reservation from this multiplexed data stream. The maximal data rate is included in the first pack at the beginning of each ISO 11172 data stream. The definition of this data stream makes the following implicit assumption: for data stored on a secondary storage medium, it is possible to read such a header first (if necessary, by random access). In dialogue services like telephone or videophone applications using communication networks, the user will always get the header information first. In a conferencing application, using an MPEG stream might be inconvenient because a new user might like to join an existing conference after the data streams have already been setup. Therefore, the necessary header information would not be directly available to her/him.

For a data stream generated according to ISO 11172, MPEG provides time stamps that are necessary for synchronization. They refer to the relationship between multiplexed data streams, but not between other existing ISO 11172 data streams.

It should be mentioned that MPEG does not prescribe compression in real-time. MPEG defines the process of decoding, but not the decoder itself.

### 6.7.4 MPEG-2

The quality of a video sequence compressed according to the MPEG standard is near the target maximum data rate of about 1.5 Mbits/second. This optimum is in quality and not in performance. Further developments in the area of video coding techniques are based on a target rate of up to 40 Mbits/second; this is known as *MPEG-2* [ISO93b]. MPEG-2 strives for a higher resolution, similar to the digital video studio standard CCIR 601 and leading towards the video quality needed in HDTV. Note that most of the following information on MPEG-2 and MPEG-4 was gleaned by the authors from press releases and many personal communications with members of the MPEG expert group [Liu93].

To ensure that a harmonized solution to the widest range of applications is achieved, the ISO/IEC working group designated ISO/IEC JTC1/SC29/WG11, has been working jointly with ITU-TS Study Group 15 *Experts Group for ATM Video Coding*. MPEG-2 also collaborates with representatives from other parts of ITU-TS, EBU, ITU-RS, SMPTE and the North American HDTV community.

The MPEG group developed the *MPEG-2 Video Standard*, which specifies the coded bit stream for high-quality digital video. As a compatible extension, MPEG-2 Video builds upon the completed MPEG-1 standard by supporting interlaced video formats and a number of other advanced features, including those to support HDTV.

As a generic international standard, MPEG-2 Video was defined in terms of extensible profiles, each of which will support the features needed by an important class of applications. The *MPEG-2 Main Profile* was defined to support digital video transmission in the range of about 2 to 80 Mbits/s over cable, satellite and other broadcast channels, as well as to support digital storage and other communications applications. Parameters of the *Main Profile* and *High Profile* are suitable for supporting HDTV formats.

| | | | | | |
|---|---|---|---|---|---|
| **High Level**<br>1920 pixels/line<br>1152 lines | | $\leq$ 80 Mbit/s | | | $\leq$ 100 Mbit/s |
| **High-1440 Level**<br>1440 pixels/line<br>1152 lines | | $\leq$ 60 Mbit/s | | $\leq$ 60 Mbit/s | $\leq$ 80 Mbit/s |
| **Main Level**<br>720 pixels/line<br>576 lines | $\leq$ 15 Mbit/s | $\leq$ 15 Mbit/s | $\leq$ 15 Mbit/s | | $\leq$ 20 Mbit/s |
| **Low Level**<br>352 pixels/line<br>288 lines | | $\leq$ 4 Mbit/s | $\leq$ 4 Mbit/s | | |
| **LAYERS and PROFILES** | **Simple Profile**<br>No B-frames<br>4:2:0<br>Not Scalable | **Main Profile**<br>B-frames<br>4:2:0<br>Not Scalable | **SNR Scalable Profile**<br>B-frames<br>4:2:0<br>SNR Scala-ble | **Spatially Scalable Profile**<br>B-frames<br>4:2:0<br>SNR Scalable or Spatial Scalable | **High Profile**<br>B-frames<br>4:2:0 or 4:2:2<br>SNR Scalable or Spatial Scalable |

Table 6.4: *MPEG-2 profiles and levels with their most important characteristics. Note that cells in the table without entries are not defined as compliance points (adapted from [Scha93]).*

The MPEG experts also extended the features of the Main Profile by defining a hierarchical/scalable profile. This profile aims to support applications such as compatible terrestrial TV/HDTV, packet-network video systems, backward-compatibility with existing standards (MPEG-1 and H.261) and other applications for which multilevel coding is required. For example, such a system could give the consumer the option of using either a small portable receiver to decode standard definition TV, or a larger fixed receiver to decode HDTV from the same broadcast signal.

All profiles are arranged in a $5 \times 4$ matrix as shown in Table 6.4. The horizontal axis denotes profiles with an increasing number of functionalities to be supported. The vertical axis indicates levels with increased parameters, such as smaller and larger frame sizes. For example, the *Main Profile* in the *Low Level* specifies 352 pixels/line, 288 lines/frame and 30 frames/second, in which B-frames are allowed to occur and a data rate not to exceed 4 Mbits/second; the *Main Profile* in the *High Level* specifies 1920 pixels/line, 1152 lines/frame and 60 frames/second with a data rate not to exceed 80 Mbits/s.

MPEG-2 considers a structure similar to that of the hierarchical mode of JPEG. The hierarchy consists of the compressed motion images scaling, i.e., video is encoded at different *qualities* [Lip91, GV92]. The scaling may act on the following different parameters:

- Spatial scaling facilitates decompression of image sequences with dissimilar horizontal and vertical resolutions. A single data stream could include, for example, images with $352 \times 288$ pixels (H.261 CIF format), $360 \times 240$ pixels, $704 \times 576$ pixels (a format according to CCIR 601) and, for example, 1250 lines at an aspect ratio of 16:9 (European HDTV). These resolutions refer to the luminance component; the chrominance components are subsampled with ratio 1:2. This can be implemented using a pyramid for the level of the DCT-coefficients [GV92]. Thereby, an $8 \times 8$ DCT, $7 \times 7$ DCT, $6 \times 6$ DCT and other transformations can be performed. From the technical point of view, only steps with a factor of two are useful.

- Scaling the data rate allows for playback at a lower frame rate or for fast-forward at a constant frame rate. In MPEG-1 this is defined by using D-frames. D-frames are not allowed in MPEG-2. Hence, fast-forward can be realized using I-frames if there is a suitable distribution of them within the data stream of the entire video clip and not only a group of pictures.

- Scaling in amplitude can be interpreted as a different resolution of different pixels or a different quantization of the DCT-coefficients. This leads to layered coding and to the possibility of progressive image presentation. Progressive coding is not at all important for the presentation of video data. However, it should be possible to extract certain images out of a sequence as a still image from the data stream, in which case progressive coding may be of interest. Layered coding can also be used for data partitioning to transmit more important data with better error correction than less important data.

Scaling is an essential extension from MPEG-1 to MPEG-2. Additionally, MPEG-2 considers current developments in the broadband ISDN world. *Asynchronous Transfer Mode* (ATM) is the realization of B-ISDN, based on the transfer of small packets known as cells. The potential loss of single ATM cells, containing MPEG-2 encoded data, is taken into account in MPEG-2 development. In this case, effects on other images and parts of the video data stream must be minimized. It should also be possible to define sequences of different types of images (I-,P-,B-frames) that minimize the end-to-end delay for a given target data rate.

MPEG group developed the *MPEG-2 Audio Standard* for low bit rate coding of multichannel audio. MPEG-2 audio coding supplies up to five full bandwidth channels (left, right, center and two surround channels), plus an additional low frequency enhancement channel, and/or up to seven commentary/multilingual channels. The MPEG-2 Audio Standard also extends *stereo and mono coding* of the MPEG-1 Audio Standard to half sampling-rates (16 kHz, 22.05 kHz and 24 kHz) to improve quality for bit rates at or below 64 kbits/second per channel.

The *MPEG-2 Audio Multichannel Coding Standard* provides backward-compatibility with the existing MPEG-1 Audio Standard. MPEG organized formal subjective testing of the proposed MPEG-2 multichannel audio codecs and up to three non-backward-compatible codecs. These codecs work with rates ranging from 256 to 448 Kbits/second.

Note that to provide a very accurate description, in following text, the notation and terminology according to the original MPEG-2 specification is used. MPEG-2 addresses video as well as associated audio; it provides the MPEG-2 system with a definition of how audio, video and other data are combined into single or multiple streams which are suitable for storage and transmission. Therefore, it imposes syntactical and semantical rules which are necessary and sufficient to synchronize the decoding and presentation of the video and audio information, while ensuring that coded data buffers in the decoder do not overflow or underflow. The streams include time stamps concerning the decoding, presentation and delivery of these data.

In the first step, the basic multiplexing approach adds to each individual stream system-level information and each individual stream is packetized to produce the *Packetized Elementary Stream* (PES). In the subsequent step, the PESs are combined to form a Program or Transport Stream. Both streams are designed to support a large number of known and anticipated applications, and they retain a significant amount of flexibility as may be required, while providing interoperability between different device implementations.

- The *Program Stream* is similar to the MPEG-1 stream. It is aimed at a relatively error-free environment. The Program Stream's packets may be of variable length. The timing information in this stream can be used to implement a constant end-to-end delay (covering the path from the input of the encoder to the output of the decoder).
- The *Transport Stream* combines the PESs and one or several independent time bases into a single stream. The Transport Stream is designed for use in lossy or noisy media. The respective packets are 188 bytes long, including the 4-byte header. The Transport Stream is well-suited for transmission of digital television and video telephony over fiber, satellite, cable, ISDN, ATM and other networks, and also for storage on digital video tape and other devices.

A conversion between the Program and Transport Stream is possible and reasonable. Note that the MPEG-2 specification of its buffer management constrains the end-to-end delay to below one second for audio and video data, a value which is too high (i.e., not humanly acceptable) for applications in the dialogue mode.

A typical MPEG-2 video stream has a variable bit rate. With the use of a video buffer as specified in this standard, it is possible to also enforce a constant bit rate leading to varying quality.

MPEG-2 standard, at the CD (Committee Draft) status in late 1993, required 3 months to become a DIS (Draft International Standard) and then required a six-month ballot period before becoming an IS (International Standard). Originally, there were plans to specify a MPEG-3 standard approaching HDTV. However, during the development of the MPEG-2 standard, it was found scaling up could adequately meet HDTV requirements. Subsequently, MPEG-3 was dropped.

### 6.7.5 MPEG-4

Work on another MPEG initiative for very low bit rate coding of audio-visual programs started in September 1993 at ISO/IEC JTC1. It is scheduled to achieve CD status in 1995 or 1996.

This work will require the development of fundamentally new algorithmic techniques, including model-based image coding of human interaction with multimedia environments, and low-bit rate speech coding for use in environments like the European Mobile Telephony System (GSM).

## 6.8 DVI

*Digital Video Interactive* (DVI) is a technology that includes coding algorithms. The fundamental components are a VLSI chip set for the video subsystem, a well-specified data format for audio and video files, an application user interface to the audio-visual kernel (AVK, the kernel software interface to the DVI hardware) and compression, as well as decompression, algorithms [HKL+91, Lut91, Rip89]. In this section, we will concentrate mainly on compression and decompression. DVI can process *data, text, graphics, still images, video* and *audio*. The original essential characteristic was the asymmetric technique of video compression and decompression known as Presentation-Level Video (PLV).

DVI has a very interesting history, an understanding of which helps to explain some of its current features. DVI stated as a project at the David Sarnoff Research Center of the RCA company in Princeton in 1984. At that time, the major goals – to compress video and audio at the data rate appropriate for a CD, and to decompress it in real-time – were defined. In 1986, the first draft of a DVI-specific chip using a *silicon compiler* was developed. Also in 1986, General Electrics (GE) took over this technology. The DVI development team became employees of GE and the project continued. The first public presentation took place at the second *Microsoft CD-ROM Conference* in Seattle in March 1987. For the first time, the real-time play-back of video stored on a CD-ROM was demonstrated. In 1989 at the fourth *Microsoft CD-ROM Conference*, IBM and Intel announced their cooperation concerning DVI. The DVI team was later taken over by Intel. The first generation of PS/2 boards were introduced as *ActionMedia 750.* In April 1992, the second generation of these boards for Microchannel and ISA bus machines (*ActionMedia II*) became available. In 1993, the software-only decoder became available as the product Indeo.

Concerning audio, the demand for a hardware solution that can be implemented at a reasonable price is met by using a standard signal processor. Processing of still images and video is performed by a video processor. The video hardware of a DVI board is shown in Figure 6.18. It consists of two VLSI chips containing more than

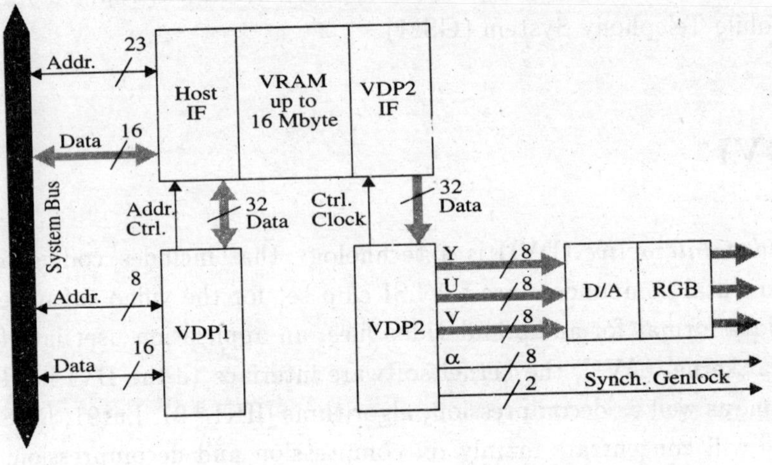


Figure 6.18: *DVI video processing according to [Rip89].*

265,000 transistors each. This Video Display Processor (VDP) consists of the pixel processor VDP1 and the display processor VDP2. VDP1 processes bitmaps and is programmed in microcode; VDP2 generates analog *RGB* signals out of the different bitmap formats and its configuration is also programmable. The coupling of the processors is carried out by the Video-RAM (VRAM). An important characteristic is the capability for microprogramming. It allows one to change and adapt the compression and decompression algorithms to new developments without investing in new hardware.

### 6.8.1 Audio and Still Image Encoding

Audio signals are digitized using 16 bits per sample and are either PCM-encoded or compressed using the Adaptive Differential Pulse Code Modulation (ADPCM) technique. Thereby, a reduction to about four bits per sample is achieved at a quality corresponding to stereo broadcasting. Different sampling frequencies are supported (11025 Hz, 22050 Hz and 44100 Hz for one or two PCM-coded channels; 8268 Hz, 31129 Hz and 33075 Hz for ADPCM for one channel).

When encoding still images, different video input formats can be used. These can be composite, as well as component video signals like *RGB*. In the case of an *RGB* signal, the color of each pixel is split into portions of the three colors of the spectrum – red, green and blue – and each color is processed separately.

For image preparation, DVI assumes an internal digital *YUV* format, i.e., any video input signal must first be transformed into this format. Note, by DVI we refer to the *Action Media II* version. The color of each pixel is split into a luminance component *Y* and the two chrominance components *U* and *V*. The luminance represents a gray scale image. White is not a basic color but a mixture of colors. In the case of an *RGB* signal, a pure white pixel consists of about 30% red, 59% green and 11% blue.

Starting with an *RGB* signal, DVI computes the *YUV* signal using the following relationship:

$$Y = 0.30\ R + 0.59\ G + 0.11\ B,\ U = B - Y,\ V = R - Y$$

leading to:

$U = -0.30\ R - 0.59\ G + 0.89\ B$

$V = 0.70\ R - 0.59\ G - 0.11\ B$

Therefore, DVI determines the components *YUV* according to the following relation:

$Y = 0.299\ R + 0.587\ G + 0.144\ B + 16$

$U = 0.577\ B - 0.577\ Y + 137.23$

$V = 0.730\ R - 0.730\ Y + 139.67$

This is realized in software using fixed-point arithmetic based on the following:

$109\ Y = 32\ R + 64\ G + 16\ B + 1744$ *with* $0\ R,G,B\ 255$

$111\ U = 64\ B - 64\ Y + 15216$ *with* $16\ Y\ 235$

*88 V = 64 R - 64 Y + 12253 with 16 U, V 240*

DVI always combines all chrominance components of $4 \times 4$ pixel blocks into a single value. The chrominance component of the top left pixel of such a block is used as the reference value for the 16 pixels. Therefore, each pixel has an 8-bit value for the luminance *Y*, and for 16 related pixels, a single 8-bit chrominance value *U*, and another 8 bits defining the value for *V*. The result is a 9-bit *YUV* format.

To increase image quality during presentation, an interpolation technique is applied to the chrominance values of adjacent blocks. Note that this is the reason for the recognizable color distortion at the right and at the bottom edges of the images. Additionally, DVI is able to process images in the 16-bit YUV format and the 24-bit *YUV* format. The 24-bit format uses 8 bits for each component. The 16-bit *YUV* format codes the *Y* component of each pixel with 6 bits and the color difference components with 5 bits each. This is the reason for two different bitmap formats, *planar* and *packed.* For the planar format, all data of the *Y* component are stored first, followed by all *U* component values and then all *V* values (9-bit *YUV* format or 24-bit *YUV* format). For the packed bitmap format, the *Y, U* and *V* information of each pixel is stored together followed by the data of the next pixel (16-bit *YUV* format).

Single images in the 24-bit format can be stored immediately or transmitted. Images in the 16-bit format can be compressed using a lossless algorithm which is known as *PIC 1.0.* In 9-bit format, there is a choice between a lossy algorithm and JPEG baseline mode. For backward compatibility to previous DVI algorithms, two additional compression schemes can be applied.

### 6.8.2 Video Encoding

For motion video encoding DVI distinguishes two techniques with different resolutions and dissimilar goals:

- *Presentation-Level Video (PLV)* is characterized by its better quality. This is achieved at the expense of a very time-consuming asymmetric compression performed by specialized compression facilities. In the early stages of DVI technology, PLV compression required, for example, a *Meico Transputer System* with more than 60 transputers to compress one image in three seconds, which corresponds to a 90-fold increase in the time needed for such an operation compared to real-time constraints. PLV is suitable for applications distributed on CD-ROMs. The development of such DVI applications using PLV mode follows the process shown in Figure 6.19.

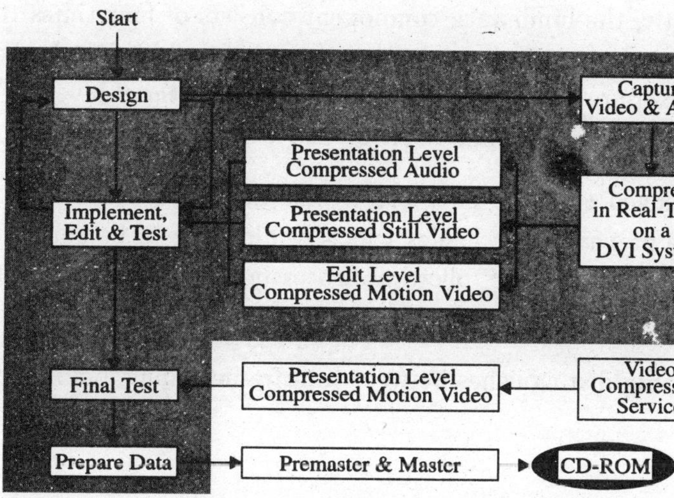


Figure 6.19: *DVI generation process of a PLV-coded video sequence as shown in [Rip89].*

- *Real-Time Video (RTV)* is a symmetric compression technique that works with hardware and software and can be performed in real-time (RTV version 2.0 uses the i750PB chip). Known as *Indeo,* it can also run in real-time on processors such as the Intel 386/486, with certain limitations such as reduced image quality. In previous versions, RTV was known as *Edit-Level Video (ELV).* ELV was conceived to enable the developers of DVI applications to see their video sequences with reduced quality during the construction phase. Afterwards, they would send the videotapes to a DVI compression facility to be compressed in the PLV mode, and would get in return compressed video sequences of higher quality than RTV. Today, RTV is most often used for interactive communication in the same manner as px64.

With respect to the compression steps shown in Figure 6.1, we can again distinguish the various steps:

The image preparation phase of RTV distinguishes three components of an image, in which all pixels are coded with eight bits each. As subsampling is used, the luminance has a higher resolution than the chrominance components. For each 16 pixels of luminance, there is one pixel in each of the chrominance components $U$ and $V$. Consequently, the luminance component consists of four times the number of lines and columns as the other two components. In a block of 16 $Y$ pixels, one $U$ pixel and one $V$ pixel are encoded together. The result is the 9-bit $YUV$ format of RTV (for each 8 $Y$ bits, there is one $U$ bit or one $V$ bit).

It should be mentioned that the RTV algorithms described below may also make use of other image preparation schemes which would have to be supported by the *AVK (Audio Video Kernel)*. The following processing in the RTV algorithm treats all three components under the same scheme.

RTV image processing distinguishes between interframe coding and intraframe coding as follows:

- *Intraframe coding* is based on individual images. The difference between the value of each pixel and the adjacent pixel above is calculated. For the first line, a fictitious line above is used, which has a constant value. This calculation is performed for all components, and it results in many zero values, which is excellent for the consecutive entropy coding steps.

- *Interframe coding* determines the difference between the value of a pixel in the current image and the value of the pixel located at the same place in the preceding image. This is performed for all three components – normally the differences also consist of many zero values.

A quantization is not necessary because of the simple subtraction operations mentioned above. The entropy encoding is based on a linear data stream. It immediately follows the calculation of differences, and is used for both interframe and intraframe coding. A distinction between run-length encoded data bytes (zero bytes) and the remaining vector is made:

- Sequences of existing zero bytes are compressed using run-length coding.
- All other bytes are compressed using a two-dimensional vector-encoding technique. An index into one of the eight available tables is determined that corresponds to two adjacent pixels to be compressed. The different components of an image are typically encoded using different tables.

In a last step, the run-length encoded values and the indices previously determined are transformed according to another table and subsequently Huffman encoded. It is possible to select a new Huffman table that is adapted to the specific content of each image.

PLV is an asymmetric compression technique that is proprietary to Intel and not published in detail [HKL+91]; however, its fundamental principles are well-known. Each picture is divided into rectangular blocks and processed using motion compensation. For each block, a prediction in the form of a block of the previous image is determined. If its position has changed, its motion is recorded in a motion vector. An exceptional feature should be mentioned: the motion vector is measured in terms of pixels, but its values can be real numbers. The interpolation between the values of pixels can result in a motion vector with values of fractions of pixel widths and heights, leading to better resolution. However, the disadvantage is the penalty (computational cost) caused by processing real numbers instead of integers.

The coding of the difference of the predicted block and the actual block of the previous picture is performed as previously described (i.e., two-dimensional vector encoding and Huffman encoding).

### 6.8.3 Data Stream

Besides the actual compression technique, DVI defines a data stream. For example, when a data stream including audio and PLV-encoded video is used, a subdivision into single images is the first step. In addition to the actual image data, the following information is included:

- Version label.

- Information on the choice of interframe or intraframe encoding.
- Height and width of the image (number of pixels).
- Information on which of the eight tables must be used for the two-dimensional vector encoding of this image.
- Huffman tables.
- Information if half resolution in vertical and/or horizontal dimension is used.

Additionally, PCM- or ADPCM-encoded audio data are included in the stream.

## 6.9 Comments

All of the important compression techniques used in multimedia systems turn out to be combinations of different known algorithms.

JPEG must be considered the future standard for the coding of still images. It incorporates a remarkable variety of alternative modes with a high degree of freedom. For example, there could be up to 255 components or planes, an image may comprise up to 65535 lines and each line can have up to 65525 pixels. As a measure of efficiency, the required bits per pixel can be composed, i.e., the average value determined by the ratio of the number of encoded bits and the number of pixels of the image. The following statements apply to DCT-encoded still images [Wal91]:

- 0.25 to 0.50 bits/pixel – moderate to good quality; sufficient for some applications.
- 0.50 to 0.75 bits/pixel – good to very good quality; sufficient for many applications.
- 0.75 to 1.50 bits/pixel – excellent quality suitable for most applications.
- 1,50 to 2.00 bits/pixel – in most cases, not distinguishable from the original; sufficient for almost all applications, even for highest quality requirements.

In lossless mode, a compression ratio of 2:1 is achieved despite the remarkable simplicity of the technique. Today, JPEG is available as a software, as well as hardware solution. However, in most cases, only the baseline mode and predefined image formats are supported. JPEG is often used in multimedia applications which require high quality. The primary goal is to compress an image. However, it is also used as *Motion JPEG* for video compression in applications such as medical imaging.

H.261 is an established standard strongly supported by telecommunication operators. Due to the very restricted resolution in the QCIF format and reduced frame rates, the implementation of H.261 coders and decoders is possible with few, if any technical problems. This is certainly true if motion compensation and the optical low-pass filter are not components of the implementation, though the quality is not always satisfactory in this case. If the image is encoded in CIF format at 25 or 30 images per second using motion compensation, the quality is acceptable. H.261 is mostly used in applications with the dialog mode in a networked environment: video telephony and conferencing. The resulting continuous bit rate is eminently suitable for today's wide area networks operating with ISDN and leased lines.

MPEG is the most promising standard for future compressed digital video and audio. While the JPEG group has a system that can also be used for video, it is too oriented towards *animating* stills rather than using the properties of motion pictures. Currently, the quality of MPEG video can be compared to VHS video recordings, i.e., a data rate of 1.2 Mbits/second, appropriate for CD-ROM drives. The compression algorithm is very good for a resolution of $360 \times 240$ pixels. Obviously, higher resolutions can also be decoded (e.g., a resolution of 625 lines), but the quality is affected. The future of MPEG points towards MPEG-2, which defines a data stream compatible with MPEG-1, but provides data rates up to 40 Mbits/second. This substantially improves the currently available quality of MPEG-coded data. MPEG also defines an audio stream, with various sampling rates, up to DAT quality of 16 bits/sample. One other important part of the MPEG group's work is the definition of a data stream syntax, which has proved to be relatively successful for DVI technology. Further, MPEG was optimized by making use of the retrieval model in application areas such as tutoring systems based on CD-ROMs and interactive TV. This optimization embedded in MPEG-2 will allow TV and HDTV quality at the expense of a higher data rate. MPEG-4 will provide a very high compression ratio coding of video and associated audio.

DVI, as opposed to the other systems, is a proprietary invention now under development by Intel. It defines two quality encoding variants: one for real-time compression given the appropriate hardware, and another that must be compressed off-line, but allows for decompression with the same hardware. The resolutions are 512 × 480 (interpolated from 256 × 240) and 256 × 240 respectively. As mentioned above, DVI also features a file syntax known as AVSS. Due to the standardization of the other formats mentioned, as well as the demand for interchangeable formats, it can be expected that RTV, PLV or both will incorporate more features from these standards to provide compatibility. DVI also specifies high-quality audio and still image compression. For still images, a certain configuration of the JPEG format is supported. The video quality in PLV mode is very good and allows for use in retrieval mode applications similar to MPEG. The RTV mode is good and quite convincing for many applications. As described in this chapter, RTV allows dialogue mode applications. However, many available implementations suffer from considerable compression/decompression delay above 150 milliseconds.

JPEG, H.261, MPEG and DVI are not alternative techniques for data compression. Their goals are different and partly complementary. Most of the algorithms used are very similar but not the same. Technical quality, as well as market availability, determine which techniques will be used in future multimedia systems. This will lead to a *cooperation* and *convergence* of techniques. For example, a future multimedia computer could generate still images in JPEG, use H.261 for a video conference and MPEG-2, as well as DVI PLV, for retrieval of stored multimedia information.

# Chapter 7

# Optical Storage Media

Current magnetic data storage carriers take the form of floppy disks or hard disks and are used as secondary storage media. Here, low average access time and adequate capacity can be offered for a reasonable price. However, since audio and video, either in compressed or uncompressed form, require higher storage capacity than other media, the storage cost for such continuous media data using traditional storage carriers is essentially higher.

Optical storage media offer a higher storage density at a lower cost. The *Audio Compact Disk*, the successor to *Long Play Disks* (LPs), is a commercially successful product in the entertainment industry. The computer industry has profited from this development, especially when audio and video should be stored digitally in the computer. This technology has been *the* main catalyst for the whole development of multimedia in computing because it is used in multimedia external devices. For example, external devices such as video recorders and DAT recorders (Digital Audio Tape) can be used for multimedia systems. The actual integration into the system is difficult, but not impossible [HS91, RSSS90, SHRS90]. For this reason we will discuss the optical storage medium in more detail in this chapter. Other data storage media will not be considered here because they do not have the special properties which should be taken into account with respect to integrated multimedia systems.

This chapter provides an overview of the fundamentals for optical storage media.

Moreover, some analog and WORM (Write Once Read Many) systems will be briefly discussed. The CD-ROM and CD-ROM/XA are explained as they are derived from the CD-DA. Further developments with respect to multimedia such as CD-I, Photo-CD and DVI are presented. In addition to the *read-only* CD developments, there already exist techniques for writing to CD-WO and CD-MO. At the end of this chapter, the relationships between current CD technologies are shown and further developments are mentioned.

## 7.1 History

The video disk in the form of the *Video Long Play* (VLP) has been available for quite some time and was described in detail by 1973. The read-only video disk has not become a commercial success, although there are several *Write-Once* (WO) optical disks of different sizes and formats available on the market. These initial developments were based on analog techniques with the highest quality requirements at a moderate cost.

Ten years later, towards the end of 1982, the *Compact Disk-Digital Audio* (CD-DA) was introduced. This optical disk allows the digital storage of stereo-audio information at a high level of quality. N.V. Philips, in cooperation with the Sony Corporation, specified the CD-DA and developed the basic technology [MGC82, DG82, HTV82, HS82]. The CD-DA specification was published as the *Red Book* [Phi82] on which all other CD formats are based. In the five years since its introduction, approximately 30 million CD-DA recording devices and over 450 million CD-DA disks were sold.

In 1983, the extension of compact disk technology to storage of computer data was announced by N.V. Phillips and the Sony Corporation, and it was presented for the first time in November 1985. This *Compact Disk-Read Only Memory* (CD-ROM) specification was described in the *Yellow Book* [Phi85] and later became the standard ECMA-119 [ECM88]. The standard ECMA-119 specifies the CD-ROM physical format. The CD-ROM logical format is specified in the ISO Standard 9660 and came from the *High Sierra Proposal* (a proposal of industrial companies). It allows data access over file names and directories.

The *Compact Disk-Interactive* (CD-I) was announced by N.V. Phillips and the Sony Corporation in 1986. The CD-I specification is described in the *Green Book* and includes, besides the standard CD technology, a complete system description [Phi88]. In 1987, the *Digital Video Interactive* (DVI) was publicly presented. Here, the algorithms for compression and decompression of audio and video data stored on a CD-ROM are of importance.

In 1988, the *Compact Disk-Read Only Memory / Extended Architecture* (CD-ROM/X. was announced. N.V. Phillips, the Sony Corporation and Microsoft specified the digital optical data carrier for several media and published the specification at the CD-ROM conference in Anaheim, California (USA) in 1989 [Phi89].

Since the beginning of 1990, developments in *Compact Disk-Write Once* (CD-WO) technology, as well as *Compact Disk-Magneto Optical* (CD-MO), have been well-known. The specifications of CD-WO and CD-MO are covered in the *Orange Book* [Phi91].

## 7.2 Basic Technology

In principle, optical storage media use the intensity of reflected laser light as an information source. A laser beam of approximately 780 nm wave length can be focused at approximately 1 $\mu$m. In a polycarbonate *substrate layer* we encounter holes, corresponding to the coded data, which are called *pits*. The areas between these pits are called *lands*. Figure 7.1 shows a cut through an optical disk along a track. In the middle of the figure, the lands and pits are schematically presented.

The *substrate layer* is covered with a thin *reflective layer*. The laser beam is focused on the reflective layer from the substrate layer. Therefore, the reflected beam has a strong intensity at the lands. The pits have a depth of 0.12 $\mu$m (from the substrate surface). The laser beam is lightly scattered at the pits, meaning it is reflected with a weak intensity. The signal, shown in Figure 7.1, denotes schematically the intensity of the reflected beam – a horizontal line is drawn as the threshold value. Hence, according to Figure 7.1, a compact disk consists of:

- The label.

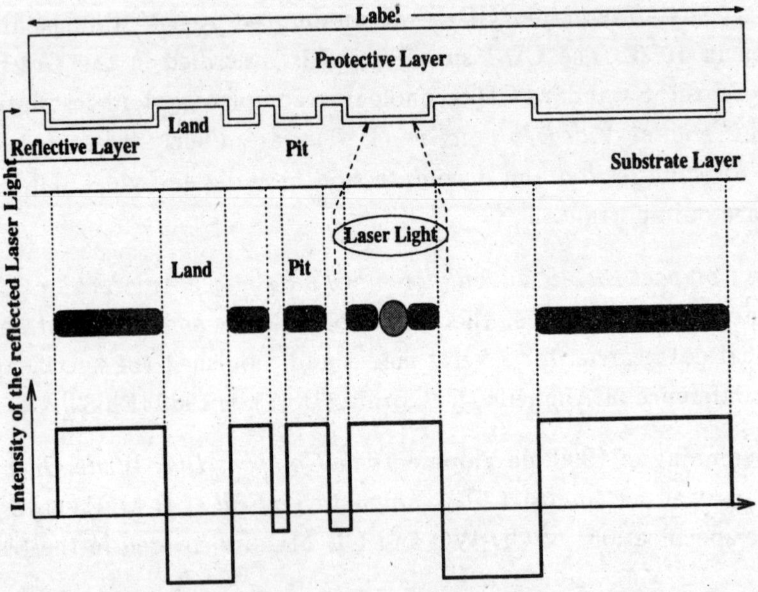


Figure 7.1: *Cut through an optical disk along the data trace. A schematic presentation with the layers (above), the "lands" and the "pits" (in the middle), and the signal (below).*

- The protective layer.
- The reflective layer.
- The substrate layer.

An optical disk consists of a sequential order of these pits and lands allocated in one track. Figure 7.2 shows an enlarged cut of such a structure.

In contrast to floppy disks and other conventional secondary storage media, the entire optical disk information is stored in one track. Thus, the stored information can be easily played back at a continuous data rate. This has advantages for audio and video data, as they are continuous data streams.

The track is a spiral. In the case of a CD, the distance between the tracks is 1.6 $\mu$m. The track width of each pit is 0.6 $\mu$m. The pits themselves have different lengths. Using these measurements, the main advantage of the optical disk in comparison

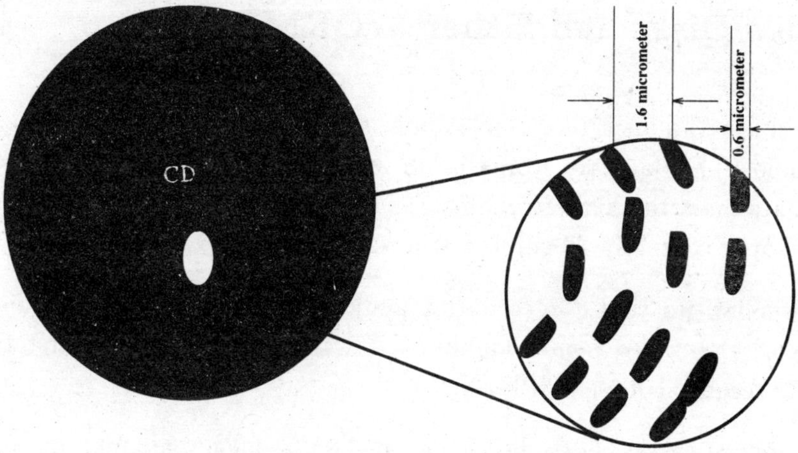


Figure 7.2: *Data on a CD as an example of an optical disk (track with "lands" and "pits").*

to magnetic disks is that on the former 1.66 data bits per $\mu$m can be stored. This results in a data density of 1,000,000 bits per $mm^2$, which implies 16,000 tracks per inch. In comparison, a floppy disk has 96 tracks per inch.

While magnetization can decrease over time and in the case of tapes, for example, cross talk can occur, these effects are unknown in optical disks. Hence, this medium is very good for long-term storage. Only a decomposition or change of the material can cause irreparable damage. According to current knowledge, such effects will not occur.

The light source of the laser can be positioned at a distance of approximately one millimeter from the disk surface, and hence, it does not have to be positioned directly on the disk, respectively near the surface, as is the case with magnetic hard disks. This approach reduces friction and increases the life span of the involved components.

## 7.3 Video Disks and Other WORMs

The video disk, in the form of *Laser Vision*, serves as the output of motion pictures and audio. The data are stored in an analog-coded format on the disk; the reproduced data meet the highest quality requirements. The Laser Vision disk has a diameter of approximately 30 cm and stores approximately 2.6 Gigabytes.

Due to the similarities to LP records for audio information, the video disk was originally called the *Video Long Play* disk. It was described for the first time in Phillips' 1973 Technical Review [Phi73].

The motion picture on the video disk is encoded as frequency modulation, and the audio signal is mixed with the video signal. Figure 7.1 shows the principle of the recorded data. The main information of the mixed audio-video signal is the time at which the signal has the value zero. Hence, each zero cross-point corresponds to a change between a pit and a land on the disk. Such a change can occur at any time, and is written to the disk in a non-quantized form, i.e., the pit length is not quantized. Therefore, this method is time-continuous and *analog*.

Since the video disk was designed as *Read Only Memory* (ROM), many different write-once optical storage systems have come out, known as the *Write Once Read Many (WORM)* disk. An example is the *Interactive Video Disk*. This disk is played at a *Constant Angular Velocity (CAV)*. On each side, 36 minutes of audio and video at a rate of 30 frames per second can be stored and retrieved. One can also store around 54,000 studio quality images per side.

Write-once storage media have a capacity between 600 MBytes and approximately 8 Gigabytes. The diameter of the disks is between 3.5 and 14 inches. The main advantage of a WORM disk, compared to other mass storage media, is the ability to store large amounts of data which may not be changed later, i.e., an archive which is secure. To increase capacity, *juke-boxes* are available, which allow the stocking of several disks and lead to capacities of over 20 Gigabytes.

The following interesting peculiarities occur when using a WORM disk:

- *Media Overflow* can occur when a WORM disk is nearly full. Prior to writing data to a WORM disk, it must be determined if the recorded data can fit onto the disk and/or if the data should be stored on different disks. Further, it is required that if the data need to be stored on more than one physical disk, the time point at which data should be written to another physical disk must be determined. This approach is especially important for continuous media because these media streams can only be interrupted at certain points.

- *Packaging* refers to the problem of fixed-block structures in WORMs. Only data sentences of a given size can be written. For example, if the block size is 2,048 bytes, and only one byte is written, 2,047 bytes will be recorded without any information content.

- *Revision* refers to the problem of subsequently marking invalid areas. For example, during changes of a document invalid areas are be created on the disk(s). These areas have to be subsequently rewritten, which implies a document may be distributed over several WORMs after a while. Here, the distribution of the document over several disks should not disturb the output of the data stream of a continuous medium.

There are also other problems with WORM disks such as the following: besides the number of incompatible WORM disk formats, most multimedia systems lack adequate software support for the WORM disks, which results in a poor integration of WORM technology into the computer environment.

## 7.4 Compact Disk Digital Audio

### 7.4.1 Preliminary Technical Background

The CD has a diameter of 12 cm; the disk is played at a *Constant Linear Velocity* (CLV). Therefore, the number of rotations per time unit depends on the particular radius of the accessed data. The spiral-shaped CD track consists of approximately 20,000 windings. In comparison, an LP disk has only approximately 850 windings.

Information is stored according to the principle shown in Figures 7.1 and 7.3. The length of the pits is always a multiple of 0.3 $\mu$m. The transition from pit to land

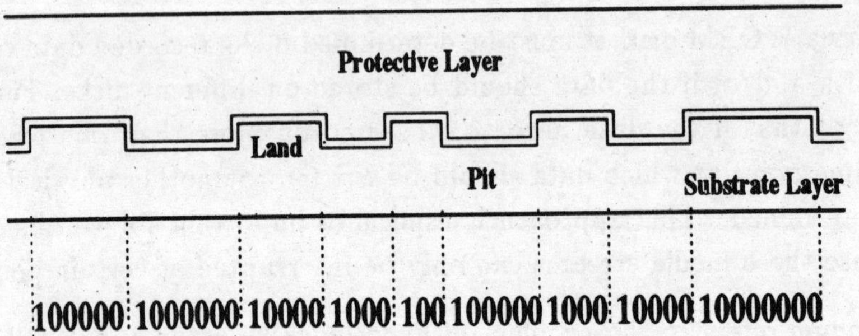


Figure 7.3: *Lands and pits with their related digital data stream.*

and from land to pit corresponds to the coding of a *1* in the data stream. A *0* is coded as no transition. Figure 7.3 shows a data stream as a sequence of lands and pits, and below it is the corresponding digital data stream.

### Audio Data Rate

The audio data rate can be easily derived from the given sample frequency of 44.1 kHz and the 16-bit linear quantization. The stereo-audio signal obeys the pulse-code modulation rules and the following audio data rate is derived:

$$\begin{aligned} \textit{Audio data rate}_{CD-DA} &= 16\frac{bits}{sample} \times 2\ channels \times 44100\frac{samples}{s \times channel} \\ &= 1,411,200\frac{bits}{s} = 1,411,200\frac{bits/s}{8\ bits/byte} \\ &= 176.4\frac{kbytes}{s} \cong 172.3\frac{Kbytes}{s} \end{aligned}$$

Analog LPs and cassette tapes have a signal-to-noise ratio between 50 dB and 60 dB. The quality of the CD-DA is substantially higher. As a first approximation, we can assume 6 dB per bit during the sampling process. Hence, with 16-bit linear sampling, we obtain the following:

$$S/N_{CD-DA} \cong 6\frac{dB}{bit} \times 16\ bits = 96\ dB$$

The signal-to-noise ratio is exactly 98 dB.

**Capacity**

A CD-DA play time is at least 74 minutes. With this value, the capacity of a CD-DA can be easily determined. The following example shows the computation of a capacity for pure audio data without taking into consideration additional information, such as error correction:

$$\begin{aligned} Capacity_{CD-DA} &= 74\ min \times 1,411,200\frac{bits}{s} = 6,265,728,000\ bits \\ &= 6,265,728,000\ bits \times \frac{1}{8\frac{bits}{byte}} \times \frac{1}{1024\frac{bytes}{Kbyte}} \times \frac{1}{\frac{Kbytes}{Mbyte}} \cong 747Mbytes \end{aligned}$$

### 7.4.2 Eight-to-Fourteen Modulation

Each change from pit to land and from land to pit corresponds to the coding of a *1* which is sent across a communication channel as the *channel bit.*

Pits and lands may not follow too closely one after another on a CD-DA since the resolution of the laser is not sufficient to read such direct pit-land-pit-land-pit sequences (i.e., 11111 sequences) correctly. Therefore, an agreement was negotiated that at least two lands and two pits always occur consecutively in a sequence. Hence, between two *1s* there always exist at least two *0s.*

On the other hand, pit or land sequences are not allowed to be too long; they must keep a maximal distance. Otherwise, no phase-correct synchronization signal (clock) can be derived. Hence, the maximal length of the pits and lands is limited. At most, ten *0s* (as the channel bits) can follow one after another.

For these reasons, the bits written on a CD-DA, in the form of pits and lands, do not directly correspond to the actual information; before recording, *Eight-to-Fourteen Modulation* is applied [HS82]. Using this transformation, the regularity of the minimal and maximal distances is met.

Eight-bit words are coded as 14-bit values. Given the minimal and maximal allowable distances, there are 267 valid possibilities. 256 possibilities are used. For example, the code includes the following two entries shown in Table 7.1.

| Audio Bits | Modulation Bits |
|---|---|
| 00000000 | 01001000100000 |
| 00000001 | 10000100000000 |

Table 7.1: *Two values out of the code table.*

| **Audio Bits** | 00000000 | | | | | | 00000001 | | |
|---|---|---|---|---|---|---|---|---|---|
| **Modulation Bits** | | | 0 | 100 | 1000 | 100000 | | 10000 | 100000000 |
| **Filling Bits** | 0 | 10 | | | | | 100 | | |
| **Channel Bits** | 0 | 10 | 0 | 100 | 1000 | 100000 | 100 | 10000 | 100000000 |
| **On the CD-DA** | l | pp | p | lll | pppp | llllll | ppp | lllll | ppppppppp |

Table 7.2: *Integration of the filling bits.*

Through the direct consecutive insert of the modulation bits (14-bit-values), the minimal allowed distance of two bits and the maximal distance of ten bits may still not be followed. Therefore, three additional bits are inserted between two consecutive modulation symbols so that the required regularity can be met. The filling bits are chosen depending on the neighboring bits. Table 7.2 shows an example (the audio bits are taken from Table 7.1) to clarify the integration of the filling bits and the whole transformation process from an 8-bit audio word to its CD-DA representation of lands and pits.

### 7.4.3 Error Handling

The goal of error handling on a CD-DA is the detection and correction of typical error patterns [HTV82]. A typical error, a consequence of a scratch and/or pollution, can be characterized as a *burst error.*

On the first level, a two-stage error correction is implemented according to the Reed-Solomon algorithm: for every 24 audio bytes, at the first stage, individual byte errors are recognized and corrected; at the second stage, double byte errors are recognized and corrected; also, other fault bytes in the sequence can be recognized, but they cannot be corrected using this approach.

On the second level, real consecutive data bytes are distributed over several frames. A *frame* consists of 588 channel bits, which correspond to 24 audio bytes. Therefore, the audio data is stored on the CD-DA in an interleaved form. This means that due to a burst error, only parts of data are modified.

An error rate of $10^{-8}$ is specified. More precisely, the burst errors, which are distributed over a maximal 7 frames, can be recognized and corrected. This corresponds to a track length of 7.7 mm. For example, a 2-mm-diameter hole in a CD-DA means that the audio data can still be played correctly. Nevertheless, experiments have shown that not all devices correct each error according to the given specification. The above described method for error correction is known as *Cross Interleaved Reed-Solomon Code* (CIRSC).

### 7.4.4 Frames, Tracks, Areas and Blocks of a CD-DA

Audio data, error correction, additional control and display-bytes, and a synchronization pattern all constitute *frames*.

- *Audio data* are divided into two groups, each consisting of 12 audio bytes. They contain the high and low bytes of the left and right channels.
- *Error-detection* and *error-correction* bytes (4 bytes per frame) are inserted, according to the above description, at both stages.
- Each frame has a *control* and a *display* byte. It consists of eight bits, which are marked with *P, Q, R, S, T, U, V* and *W* (*subchannel bits*). These subchannel bits are drawn together over 98 frames for each subchannel and used together. Hence, there are eight subchannels, each having 98 bits, of which 72 are used for the actual information. The 98 frames together build a *block*. Unfortunately, sometimes the blocks are also called frames.

  So the *P*-subchannel is used to differentiate between a CD-DA (with audio data) and a CD with other computer data. The *Q*-subchannel is used, for example, in the following:

  - The *lead-in area* for storage of the directory content.

- The rest of the CD-DA for a specification of the relative time inside a track, and for the absolute time specification of the CD-DA.

- The *synchronization pattern* determines the beginning of a frame. The pattern consists of twelve *1s* and twelve *0s* as channel bits, and three filling bits.

Table 7.3 shows an overview of frame components with corresponding bytes and bits.

| | Audio Bits | Modul.Bits | Fil.Bits | Ch.Bits | Together |
|---|---|---|---|---|---|
| Synchronization | | | 3 | + 24 | = 27 bits |
| Control & Display | | i.e. | (14 + 3) | | = 17 bits |
| 12×Data | 12 × 8 | i.e. 12× | (14 + 3) | | = 204 bits |
| 4×Error Handling | | i.e. 4× | (14 + 3) | | = 68 bits |
| 12×Data | 12 × 8 | i.e. 12× | (14 + 3) | | = 204 bits |
| 4×Error Connection | | i.e. 4× | (14 + 3) | | = 68 bits |
| Frames Together | | | | | = 588 bits |

Table 7.3: *Components of a frame.*

Using these data, different data streams with corresponding rates can be recognized [MGC82]:

- The *audio bit stream* (also called the *audio data stream*) carries $1.4112 \times 10^6$ bits/s. Here, only the 16-bit quantized samples are taken.

- The *data bit stream* consists of the audio bit stream, including the control and display bytes, and necessary bytes for error handling. The number of bits can reach the value of $1.94 \times 10^6$ bits/s.

- The channel bit stream includes the data bit streams with the *Eight-to-Fourteen Modulation*, the *filling bits* and the *synchronization bits.* The data rate is approximately $4.32 \times 10^6$ bits/s.

A CD-DA consists of the following three *areas:*

- The *lead-in area* includes the directory of the CD-DA. Here, the beginning of the individual tracks are registered.

- The *program area* includes all tracks of the CD-DA. Here, the actual data are stored.

- At the end of each CD-DA there is a *lead-out area.* This area is used mainly to help the play-recorder when the reader head accidentally goes beyond the program area.

The program area of each CD-DA can consist of 99 *tracks* of different lengths. It includes at least one track and each track incorporates at most one song, or a sentence of a symphony. If the program area is randomly accessed (e.g., access 5th song), the reader head is positioned to the beginning of the particular track (e.g., position to the beginning of the 5th track).

Each track can have (according to the *Red Book*) several *index points.* Therefore, at certain places, direct positioning can occur. Mostly, only two a priori defined *Index Points (IPs)* are used, the $IP_0$ and $IP_1$. $IP_0$ marks the beginning of each track. $IP_1$ defines the beginning of the audio data inside each track. The area between $IP_0$ and $IP_1$ is called *track pregap.* CD-DA disks possess a track pregap of two to three seconds for each piece.

Another structure, called *block* (Figure 7.4), was introduced in addition to frames and tracks, but it does not have a special meaning in CD-DA technology. It is introduced at this point only because of comparability reasons to other CD technologies discussed in the next sections. A CD-DA block includes 32 frames and stores 2,352 bytes.




Figure 7.4: *CD-DA block layout according to the "Red Book."*

### 7.4.5 Advantages of Digital CD-DA Technology

Errors on a CD-DA can be caused by damage or pollution. The CD-DA is not sensitive, with respect to uncompressed audio, to the usual appearance of reading errors. The CD-DA specification, in the form of the *Red Book*, serves as the basis for all optical CD storage media. For example, *Eight-to-Fourteen Modulation* and the *Cross Interleaved Reed-Solomon Code* are always used. Hence, a fundamental specification has been developed which is used in many systems and means compatibility for many systems.

The disadvantage of the CD-DA technology is that its achieved reliability is too low for the storage of computer data. This lead to a further development of the CD technology.

## 7.5 Compact Disk Read Only Memory

The *Compact Disk Read Only Memory* (CD-ROM) was designed as the storage format for general computer data – in addition to uncompressed audio data [Che86, FE88, Hol88, LR86, OC89]. Further, CD-ROM technology has been planned to be the basis for storage of other media (e.g., video) [KSN+87, Wil89]. This was specified in the *Yellow Book* by N.V. Phillips and the Sony Corporation [Phi85]. The *Yellow Book* was later accepted as the ECMA standard [ECM88].

CD-ROM tracks are divided into *audio* (corresponding to the CD-DA) and *data* types. One track itself may either contain audio only or data only. A CD-ROM can contain both types of tracks, tracks with audio and other tracks with data. In such a mixed form, the data tracks are usually located at the beginning of the CD-ROM and then followed by the audio tracks. Such a CD is called a *Mixed Mode Disk* (see Figure 7.11).

### 7.5.1 Blocks

A CD-DA has an error rate of less than $10^{-8}$ and allows random access to individual tracks and index points. The use of a CD-ROM with its general-purpose computer data requires much better error correction and random access to a data unit with a higher resolution than the track.

This data unit is called a *block*, meaning the *physical block*. In the ISO 9660 standard, there also exists the notion of a *logical block*. The logical block has similar properties to the sectors of other media and file systems. A CD-ROM block consists of 2,352 bytes of a CD-DA block. Hence, the de facto CD-DA standard serves as the basis for the de facto CD-ROM standard.

Out of the 2,352 bytes of a block, 2,048 or 2,336 bytes (depending on whether computer data or audio data are stored on CD-ROM) can be used for user data. The remaining bytes are used for the identification of random access, as well as for another error correction layer, thereby lowering the error rate further.

75 blocks per second are played back, each consisting of 32 frames. Each frame is 73.5 bytes (588 bits).

$$Block = 1411200\frac{bits}{s} \times \frac{1}{75}s \times \frac{1}{8bits/byte} = 2352bytes$$

Figure 7.5 shows the data hierarchy of a CD-ROM with audio data.

### 7.5.2 Modes

The CD-ROM was specified with the following goal: it should serve to hold uncompressed CD-DA data and computer data. This goal is achieved by introducing two modes: *mode 1* and *mode 2*.

#### CD-ROM Mode 1

CD-ROM mode 1 serves as the actual storage of computer data (Figure 7.6). The block contains 2,048 bytes for information storage out of the available 2,352 bytes. The 2,352 bytes are split into the following groups:

- 12 bytes for ***synchronization***, i.e., for the detection of the block beginning.

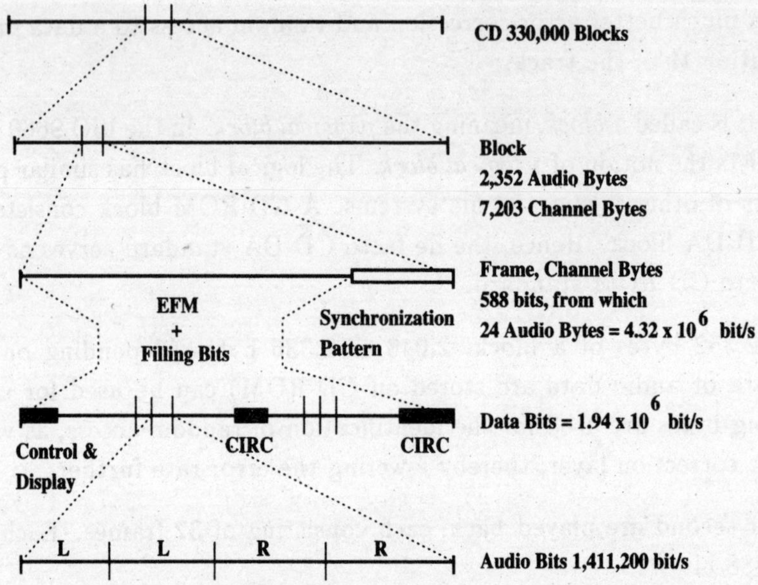


Figure 7.5: *CD-ROM data hierarchy with audio data.*

| Sync | Header | User Data | EDC | Blanks | ECC |
|---|---|---|---|---|---|
| 12 | 4 | 2048 | 4 | 8 | 276 |

← 2,352 bytes →

Figure 7.6: *CD-ROM mode 1 block layout according to the "Yellow Book."*

- 4 bytes for the *header*, which carries an unambiguous specification of the block. The first byte stores minutes, the second byte stores seconds and the third byte contains the block number. The fourth byte includes the mode specification.
- 2,048 bytes for the *user data.*
- 4 bytes for error detection.
- 8 unused bytes.
- 276 bytes for error correction. Hence, an error rate of $10^{-12}$ can be achieved.

A CD-ROM contains 333,000 blocks to be played in 74 minutes. The *capacity* of a CD-ROM with all blocks in mode 1 can be computed as follows:

$$
\begin{aligned}
Capacity_{CD-ROM_{mode1}} &= \\
&= 333,000 blocks \times 2048 \frac{bytes}{block} = 681,984,000 bytes \\
&= 681,984,000 \times \frac{1}{1024 \frac{bytes}{Kbyte}} \times \frac{1}{1024 \frac{Kbytes}{Mbyte}} \approx 660 Mbytes
\end{aligned}
$$

The *data rate* in mode 1 is:

$$
\begin{aligned}
Rate_{CD-ROM_{mode1}} &= \\
&= 2,048 \frac{bytes}{Block} \times 75 \frac{Blocks}{s} = 153.6 \frac{Kbytes}{s} \equiv 150 \frac{Kbytes}{s}
\end{aligned}
$$

### CD-ROM Mode 2

CD-ROM mode 2 holds data of any media. The data layout of a CD-ROM block in mode 2 is shown in Figure 7.7. Here, each block offers 2,336 bytes for information storage. The synchronization and header are processed in the same way as in mode

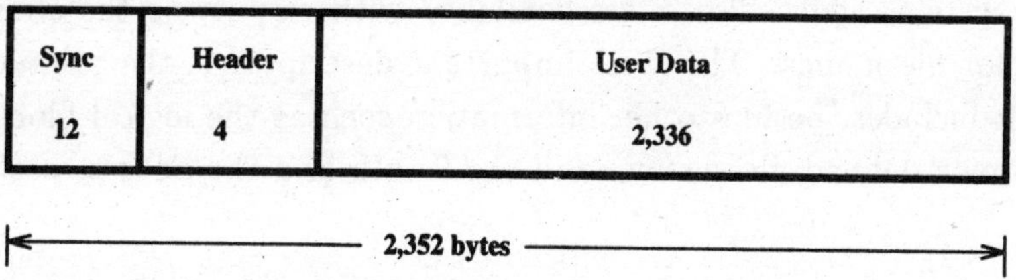


Figure 7.7: *CD-ROM mode 2 block layout according to the "Yellow Book."*

1. Additional error correction does not exist. The capacity and data rate of a CD-ROM with all blocks in mode 2 can be computed as follows:

$$
Capacity_{CD-ROM_{mode2}} = 333,000\ blocks \times 2336 \frac{bytes}{block} \approx 777,888,000\ bytes
$$

$$
Rate_{CD-ROM_{mode2}} = 2336 \frac{bytes}{block} \times 75\ blocks/s \approx 175.2\ Kbytes/s
$$

### 7.5.3 Logical Data Format

At some point, it was recognized that the specification of the blocks in mode 1 was not a sufficient equivalent to the sectors. The logical data format with the directory was missing. Therefore, a group of industry representatives met in Del Webb's High Sierra Hotel & Casino in Nevada and worked out a proposal. It is called the *High Sierra Proposal* and it became the basis for the ISO 9660 standard, which exactly describes this format [KGTM90].

With this standard, a *directory tree* is defined, which includes all the information about the files. Additionally, there is a table in which all the directories are listed in compressed form. This path table – *Table of Contents* – allows direct access to files at any level. The table is loaded into the computer memory while mounting the CD. This static method is efficient because CD-ROM data cannot be changed (read only), yet most implementations use only the actual directory tree.

In the first track, ISO 9660 reserves the first 16 blocks (sectors 0 to 15) as the *system area.* This area can be used for indication of production-specific properties. Starting at sector 16, the *volume descriptor* (primary volume descriptor, supplementary volume descriptor, etc.) is stored. The supplementary volume descriptor can describe another file system, which also offers flexibility with respect to the allowed character string for file names. The most important descriptor is the primary volume descriptor. It includes, besides other information such as the logical block size, the length of its own defined file system, and the length and the addresses of the path tables.

Each volume descriptor is stored in a block with 2,048 bytes. A CD-ROM can include any number of volume descriptors. Mostly, individual volume descriptors are repeated as copies to provide increased access reliability. The volume descriptor area is closed with *volume descriptor terminators*, which are also implemented as a special block.

ISO 9660 uses the logical block size, which is equal to the power of two of a number beginning with 512 bytes. It is not allowed to have a logical block size greater than the size of the actual block (sector). The maximal logical block size is 2,048 bytes (de facto), although ISO 9660 does not strictly require this size.

If the underlying technology offers another physical block size, with ISO 9660, other logical block sizes are possible. Therefore, current block sizes of 512 bytes, 1,024 bytes and 2,048 bytes exist. The logical block size is the same for the entire file system. Files start at the beginning of logical blocks. While files can start and end inside of physical blocks (sector), directories always start at sector boundaries.

### 7.5.4 Limitations of the CD-ROM Technology

Any CD has a high storage capacity and constant data transfer rate. Random access to a CD track of approximately up to one second can be tolerated for audio playback. This access time, on one hand, still has important advantages in comparison to LPs, cassettes and DATs. On the other hand, these access times for a CD-ROM mean a significant disadvantage as a data carrier in comparison to magnetic disks (with a mean access time of under 10 milliseconds). The following effects contribute to the CD-ROM access time:

- *Synchronization time* occurs because the internal clock must be adjusted to be in phase with the signal reading the CD. Here, delays are in the range of milliseconds.

- Due to the Constant Linear Velocity (CLV) playback of a CD, reading the inner part of the CD requires around 200 rotations per second, and reading the outer part of the CD requires around 530 rotations per second. The *rotation delay* is specified as the maximal duration to position the laser above the desired sector within one rotation, and to correctly adjust the rotation speed. Hence, depending on the particular device, rotation delay can be up to 200 milliseconds.

- The *seek time* refers to the adjustment of the correct radius, in which the laser also must first locate the track and adjust itself. The seek time is at most one second.

These partially overlapping effects contribute to the highest maximal time of up to approximately one second for the worst case. However, the real values can be very different, depending on the actual and desired position of the information. Using cache-hierarchies, the access time for very good disk drives can be lowered to 200 milliseconds.

A constant audio stream on a CD-ROM block needs to be stored sequentially. We cannot, for example, play an audio track and the data of a CD-ROM mode 1 track simultaneously. Although very important for many multimedia systems, simultaneous playback of audio and other data is not possible.

## 7.6 CD-ROM Extended Architecture

The *Compact Disk Read Only Memory/Extended Architecture* (CD-ROM/XA) standard was established by N.V.Phillips and the Sony and Microsoft Corporations and is based on the CD-ROM specification [Fri92, GC89, Phi89]. The main motivation for this additional development was the concurrent output of several media, which was insufficiently considered in previous approaches. Before this standard specification, other definitions and systems could produce simultaneous output, such as CD-I (*Compact Disk Interactive*) and DVI (*Digital Video Interactive*). The experiences of CD-I were taken into account during the development of the CD-ROM/XA because of the tight connection of N.V. Phillips and the Sony Corporation to CD-I. Hence, many properties are identical.

The *Red Book* specifies a track for uncompressed audio data (Figure 7.4). The *Yellow Book* describes tracks for computer data with CD-ROM mode 1 (Figure 7.6) and tracks for compressed media with CD-ROM mode 2 (Figure 7.7). CD-ROM/XA uses CD-ROM mode 2 to define actual blocks. CD-ROM/XA defines, in addition to CD-ROM mode 2, a *subheader*, which describes the particular block (sector) as shown in Figures 7.8 and 7.9. This makes it possible to interleave different media using only mode 2 blocks. During playback, individual CD-ROM/XA data streams are separated.

### 7.6.1 Form 1 and Form 2

CD-ROM/XA differentiates blocks with form 1 and form 2 formats. This is similar to the CD-ROM modes:

- *Form 1*

  This CD-ROM mode 2 XA format provides improved error detection and correction. Analogous to the CD-ROM mode 1, four bytes are needed for detection and 276 bytes for correction. Contrary to CD-ROM mode 1, the unused eight bytes of mode 1 are used for subheaders. Figure 7.8 shows a block where 2,048 bytes are used as data.

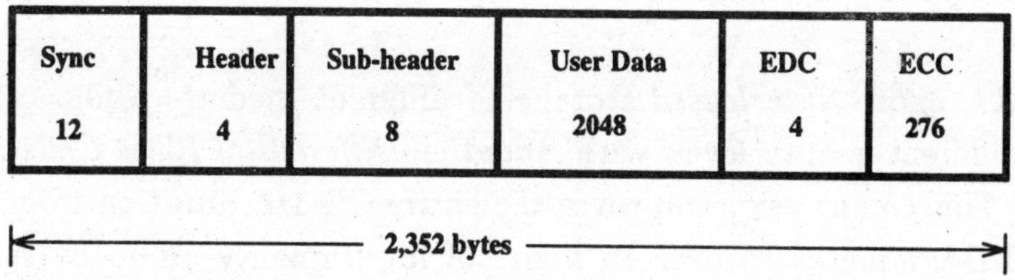


Figure 7.8: *CD-ROM/XA block layout according to the "Green Book" – layout of a CD-ROM block in mode 2, form 1.*

- *Form 2*

  This CD-ROM mode 2 XA format (Figure 7.9) allows 13% more storage capacity out of the entire block size (2,352 bytes) for user data, which means 2,324 bytes for user data. This is gained at the expense of worse error handling. In these form 2 blocks, compressed data of different media, including audio and video, can be stored.

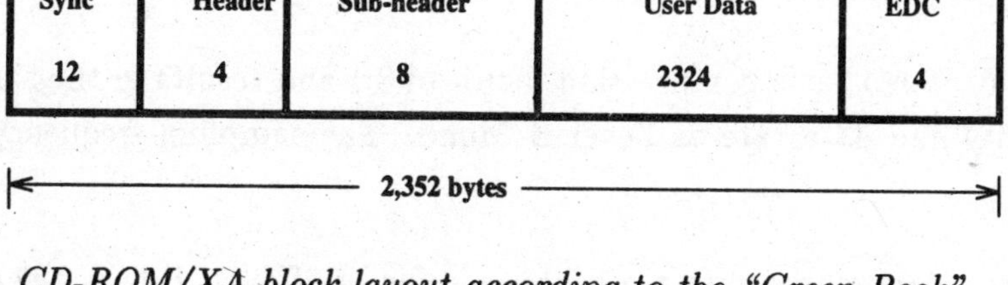


Figure 7.9: *CD-ROM/XA block layout according to the "Green Book" – layout of a CD-ROM block in mode 2, form 2.*

In the case of a CD-DA, CD-ROM or Mixed Mode Disk, a track always consists of homogeneous data, meaning either audio or computer data. The computer cannot, for example, concurrently retrieve uncompressed audio data and traditional computer data. The main advantage of the CD-ROM/XA is that within one track, blocks of different media can be stored, yet all are coded in CD-ROM mode 2. Therefore, it follows that CD-ROM/XA makes interleaved storage and retrieval possible.

### 7.6.2 Compressed Data of Different Media

CD-ROM/XA allows *interleaved* storage of different media. Audio can be compressed in different quality levels with *Adaptive Differential Pluse Code Modulation* (ADPCM). This compression improves the entire CD-DA duration from 74 uncompressed CD-DA minutes to over 19 hours of lower-quality audio by reducing the audio signal to four bits per sample. Further, this compression is necessary for simultaneous retrieval of other media. The following variants are possible:

- *Level B Stereo* has a compression factor of 4:1 in comparison to a CD-DA audio signal. The sample frequency of Level B is 37,800 Hz. This compression provides a CD-DA with a playback time capacity of 4 hours and 48 minutes, in comparison to 74 minutes when no compression at all is used. The data rate is around 43 Kbytes/s.

- *Level B Mono* has a compression factor of 8:1 in comparison to a CD-DA audio signal. This allows storage of 9 hours and 36 minutes of audio data. The data rate is approximately 22 Kbytes/s.

- *Level C Stereo* has a compression factor of 8:1 and results in the same storage capacity and data rate as Level B Mono. The sampling frequency is 18,900 Hz.

- *Level C Mono* works with a compression factor of 16:1. Hence, the storage capacity is a maximal 19 hours and 12 minutes with a data rate of approximately 11 Kbytes/s.

MPEG audio does not use ADPCM coding and therefore is not compatible with the CD-ROM/XA specification. But it can be assumed that in the future, compatibility will be designed into the specification. This media-specific encoding and decoding is not a part of the CD technology.

For implementations of the CD-ROM/XA format, the choice of medium and its corresponding quality can only be done by considering the maximal data rate. The same is applicable to other CD-based applications and formats, such as CD-I and DVI.

The logical format of a CD-ROM/XA uses the ISO 9660 specification. The ISO 9660 standard specifies *interleaved files*, i.e., several files are interleaved. *Channel interleaving* of audio, video and other data inside of one file is not specified in the ISO 9660 standard. Further, this standard does not prescribe any mandatory file content. Unfortunately, the notion of *file interleaving* is often used for interleaved files, as well as for channel interleaving.

## 7.7 Further CD-ROM-based Developments

The coexistence of different technologies is shown in Figure 7.10. It is important to point out that the CD-DA, CD-ROM and CD-ROM/XA specifications can be thought of as the layers in the communication systems. Basically, the CD-DA specification is valid for all layers. Although because of further developments, not all fundamental facts are summarized in the *Red Book*. For example, the *Mixed Mode Disk* is not defined there.

Based on these fundamental technologies, other CD-based developments which handle several media, or special media and application areas, have appeared or will soon appear. In the long run, we can see that further CD technologies will be based on CD-DA, CD-ROM and CD-ROM/XA.

### 7.7.1 Compact Disk Interactive

The *Compact Disk Interactive* (CD-I) was developed by N.V. Phillips and the Sony Corporation [vLZ89] prior to the specification of CD-ROM/XA. In 1986, CD-I was announced and in 1988 specified in the *Green Book* [Phi88] (based on the *Red Book*

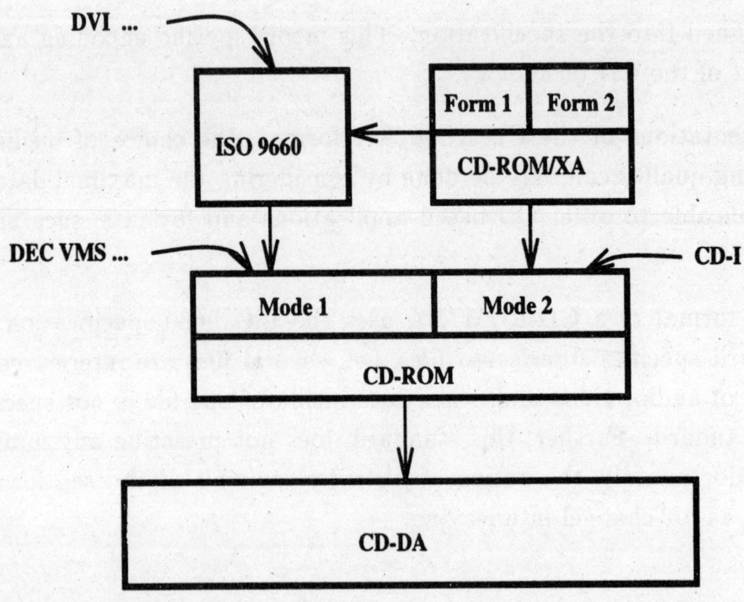


Figure 7.10: *CD Read Only technologies as layers.*

[Bas90, Int89, SvdM91]). CD-I was conceptually designed only for consumer electronics as an addition to a TV. Since October 1991, corresponding devices have been on the market.

CD-I represents an entire system. It contains a CD-ROM-based (not CD-ROM/XA) format with interleaving of different media and a definition of compression for different media. Further, CD-I defines a system software with CD-RTOS (Real-Time Operating System), which is an OS-9 derivation with extensions for real-time processing, and the output hardware for multimedia data.

The CD-I hardware is called the *Decoder.* Its size is comparable with the size of a current VCR. It consists of a main processor from the Motorola 68000 family and special video and audio elements. It also contains the CD player with a controller, joystick and mouse interface. Besides these components, an interface to an *RGB* monitor or TV is planned. CD-I devices are considered to be a replacement and/or extension of the CD-DA devices in the consumer environment.

| | CD-DA | CD-I Level A | CD-I Level B | CD-I Level C |
|---|---|---|---|---|
| Sampling Frequency | 44.1 | 37.8 | 37.8 | 18.9 |
| Bandwidth (kHz) | 20 | 17 | 17 | 8.5 |
| Coding | 16 bit PCM | 8 bit ADPCM | 4 bit ADPCM | 4 bit ADPCM |
| Max. Recording Duration in Hours (Stereo/Mono) | 74 min/- | 4.8/2.4 | 9.6/4.8 | 19.2/9.6 |
| Max. Number on Concurrent Channels (Stereo/Mono) | 1/- | 2/4 | 4/8 | 8/16 |
| Portion (in %) of Entire Stream(Stereo/Mono) | 100/ | 50/25 | 25/12.5 | 12.5/6.25 |
| Signal-to-Noise Ratio (S/M) in dB | 98 | 70 | 60 | 50 |
| Quality | Audio CD | LP | FM Radio | AM Radio |

Table 7.4: *CD-I audio coding (standards).*

### Audio Encoding

Audio coding includes several quality levels differing in capacity and data rate, as shown in Table 7.4. The CD-I audio coding standard specifies quality levels, such as Level A, Level B and Level C, using ADPCM in the same way as CD-ROM/XA. The close relationship between CD-I and CD-ROM/XA is there because CD-I was the basis for the CD-ROM/XA specification. The low data rates can be used in combination with images or motion pictures. Several channels of lower quality can also be used for different languages.

### Image Encoding

For coding of images using CD-I, different quality levels and resolutions can be used. The following overview shows that different size and data rates are also possible:

- *YUV* encoding serves for reproduction of natural pictures with many colors. The luminance component *Y* and the chrominance components *U, V* are coded with 360 × 240 pixels and 18 bits/pixel. There are 262,144 colors per image possible. These parameters lead to an image size of:

$$\frac{Data\ Size}{Image} = 360 \times 240 \times 18 \times \frac{1\ bit}{8\ bits/byte} = 194,400\ bytes$$

- CD-I can work with four bits per pixel using the *Color Look-Up Table* (CLUT). As an alternative, another 3.7 or 8 bits per pixel are available. This is suitable for simple graphics with fast access to a preloaded color table. Using the four bits per pixel, at most 16 colors can be presented. For example, with a resolution of 720 × 240 pixels and four bits/pixel, the image size is:

$$\frac{Data\ Size}{Image} = 720 \times 240 \times 4 \times \frac{1\ bit}{8\ bits/bytes} = 86,400\ bytes$$

- *RGB* encoding is used for high-quality image output. Here, each of the *R, G* and *B* components is coded with five bits/pixel. Using an additional bit, the colors are coded with 16 bits/pixel; hence, 65,538 colors per image can be presented. With the resolution of 36 × 240 pixels, the image size is:

$$\frac{Data\ Size}{Image} = 360 \times 240 \times 16 \times \frac{1\ bit}{8\ bits/byte} = 172,800\ bytes$$

### Animation Encoding

Animation consists of motion pictures with few colors. The coding of animation is implemented with run-length coding and approximately 10,000 to 20,000 bytes per image. In the future, CD-I will use MPEG coding for video compression. The data format is similar to the ISO 9660 standard specification, but not quite compatible.

Although CD-I technology was actually designed by the consumer industry, today systems exist as parts of computers in commercial areas. CD-I is important in the context of CD technology because it provides the basis for CD-ROM/XA.

### 7.7.2 Compact Disk Interactive Ready Format

All CD formats are based on the same CD-DA standard, but it is not always possible to play a CD-I disk on a CD-DA device. It is also not correct to assume that all CD-DA devices will be replaced, for example, by CD-I devices. Therefore, there is a need for a format specification of an optical disk which can be played by CD-DA devices, as well as by CD-I devices – namely, the *Compact Disk Interactive Ready Format* [Fri92].

For this purpose, the *track pregap* area between the index points $IP_0$ and $IP_1$ at the beginning of a track is enlarged from 2-3 seconds to at least 182 seconds. The information specific to CD-I is stored in this area. This information can contain details about a particular piece of music, images or the biography of the composer and the conductor. A CD-I Ready Disk can be played in three different ways:

- Using the usual CD-DA media, the CD information in the track pregap area is ignored and only the audio is played.
- Using the second mode, only the CD-I data in the track pregap area is used. Data of all media are stored there and can be read, presented and interpreted.
- Using the third mode, the CD-I data from the track pregap area are presented simultaneously during audio output. This method is similar to the Mixed Mode Disk (see Section 7.5). For this purpose, the CD-I data are read and stored first. The next step is the output of the audio and corresponding CD-I data. Hence, a simultaneous presentation of the data is achieved.

### 7.7.3 Compact Disk Bridge Disk

The *Compact Disk Bridge Disk* (CD Bridge Disk) has a goal similar to the CD-I Ready Disk of being a format specification for an output device compatible with different CD formats. The CD-I Ready Disk has a fixed disk format for CD-DA and CD-I devices, whereas the CD Bridge Disk has a fixed disk format for CD-ROM/XA and CD-I devices [Fri92]. Figure 7.11 shows the placement of the CD Bridge Disk format among the different CD formats.

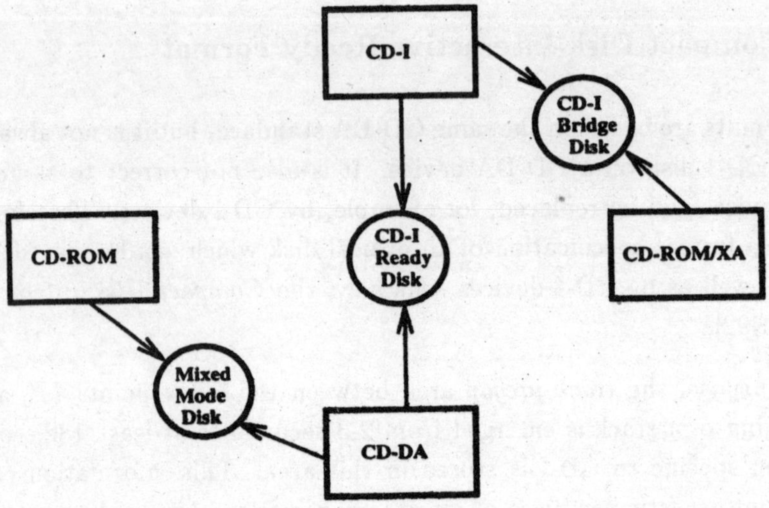


Figure 7.11: *CDs with several compatible formats: Mixed Mode Disk, CD-I Ready Disk and CD Bridge Disk.*

A CD Bridge Disk must satisfy the CD-I and CD-ROM/XA specifications. A common subset is defined which holds for both formats:

- All tracks with computer data (which are not uncompressed audio, CD-DA) must be written in CD-ROM mode 2. No CD-ROM mode 1 blocks are allowed to exist on the disk. All tracks with computer data can be followed by all audio tracks (CD-DA).
- Another example of compatibility with respect to both specifications is the track entry in the table of contents at the beginning of the CD. The reference to the CD-I tracks is not given in this area. All tracks with data are marked as CD-ROM/XA tracks.

### 7.7.4 Photo Compact Disk

The *Photo Compact Disk* (Photo-CD) from Eastman Kodak and N.V. Phillips Company is an example of a CD Bridge Disk [Fri92]. It was announced as the *Kodak Photo-CD System* in 1990 and will be, according to the press announcement, li-

| Picture Name | compressed/uncompressed | line number | column number |
|---|---|---|---|
| Base/16 | uncompressed | 128 | 192 |
| Base/4 | uncompressed | 256 | 384 |
| Base | uncompressed | 512 | 768 |
| 4Base | compressed | 1024 | 1536 |
| 16Base | compressed | 2048 | 3072 |

Table 7.5: *Image resolution of a Photo-CD [Klee92].*

censed from Agfa-Gevaert. Here, photographs of a high quality are stored. The Photo-CD is based on mechanisms described in Section 7 8, i.e., it has "write once" characteristics. The Photo-CD can be read as a CD Bridge Disk from CD-I and CD-ROM/XA devices. Additionally, it can be read and written as CD-WO (see Section 7.8) on special Photo-CD devices.

The Photo-CD is based on the following process: first, photographs are created conventionally using cameras and film; after film development, the pictures are digitalized with 8-bit luminance resolution and $2 \times 8$ bits chrominance resolution (each pixel is coded in 24 bits); subsequently, each picture is coded with one to five resolutions as shown in Table 7.5.

The integration of photos into digital computers and TVs brings many new applications to the home and business. Pictures can be retrieved by a computer or a TV extension. Using different resolutions, a digital zoom can be easily implemented. Using low resolutions, several pictures can be shown concurrently during an overview presentation. The pictures can be modified and inserted into documents.

### 7.7.5 Digital Video Interactive

*Digital Video Interactive* (DVI) describes – similar to CD-I – different components of a system. An overview of DVI, focusing on compression formats, is presented in Section 6.8. DVI consists of compression and decompression algorithms, highly integrated dedicated hardware components for compression and decompression of motion pictures in real-time, an application programming interface (to the Audio-Visual Kernel = AVK) and a fixed data format. In contrast to CD-I, the emphasis is not on CD-technology, but on compression algorithms [HKL+91, Lut91, Rip89].

DVI uses the CD-ROM mode 1 shown in Figure 7.6. In addition to this format, the ISO 9660 format for CD-ROM is used as the basis for the AVSS (Audio/Video Support System) interleaved file format. For example, Commodore uses the CD-ROM mode 1, as well as ISO 9660 format with the CDTV (Commodore Dynamic Total Vision). Yet, it is worth-while to mention that the ISO 9660 distinguishes among different *Interchange Levels*. DVI uses the basic mode (Interchange Level 1) with file names consisting of at most 8-Point-3-Characters (eight characters for filename prefix and three characters for filename suffix, prefix and suffix are separated by point) from a specific pre-defined character set. CDTV uses up to 30 characters from the Interchange Level 2, leading to larger file names.

## 7.8 Compact Disk Write Once

So far, all of the CD technologies considered (the sole exception being the Photo-CD described in Section 7.7.4) do not allow the user to write to the disk. Thus, the application scope is limited. This has led research laboratories to develop, besides the *Read Only Storage Media*, compact disks that can be recorded once or several times.

The *Compact Disk Write Once* (CD-WO), like WORM (Write Once Read Many), allows the user to write once to a CD and afterwards to read it many times [AFN90]. CD-WO is specified in the second part of the *Orange Book* [Phi91].

### 7.8.1 Principle of the CD-WO

The following section briefly explains the principle of CD-WO [Kle92]. Figure 7.12 shows a cross-section of a CD-WO, vertical to the disk surface and data track. In the case of read-only CDs, the substrate (a polycarbonate) lies directly next to the reflection layer. In the case of a CD-WO, an *absorption layer* exists between the substrate and the reflection layer. This layer can be irreversibly modified through strong thermal influence, which changes the reflection properties of the laser beams.

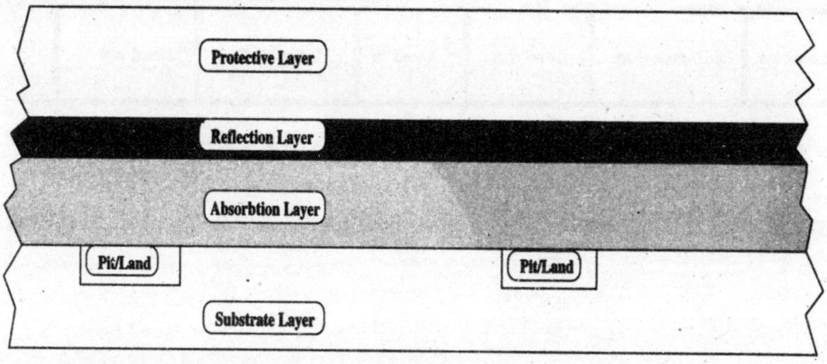


Figure 7.12: *Cross-section of a CD-WO disk.*

In its original state, a CD-WO player recognizes a track consisting of lands. The absorption layer in the pre-grooved track is heated to above $250^0$C with a laser three to four times the intensity of a reading player. Hence, the absorption layer changes such that the reflection of the laser light now corresponds to a pit. This method determines the most remarkable property of the CD-WO: its data can be played by any devices which are meant only for read-only CDs.

### 7.8.2 Sessions

All CD systems described so far assume that a *lead-in* area exists before the actual data area of a CD, and a *lead-out* area exists after the actual data of a CD (see Section 7.4.4). The content is written in a *table of contents* in the lead-in area. Each player needs this table of contents to position the player correctly. In the case of writing to a CD-WO, this lead-in area with the table of contents can be overwritten only after the entire write activity is complete. This means that the actual data of a CD-WO must be written before the table of contents is created. This further means that, in the meantime, the disk cannot be accessed and played by any other device.

Therefore, the principle of *several sessions* was introduced, as shown in Figure 7.13. Each session has its own lead-in area and lead-out area. During one write activity, all data for a session are written together with their table of contents, after which the disk can be played on other devices. Thereby the structure of a CD can be

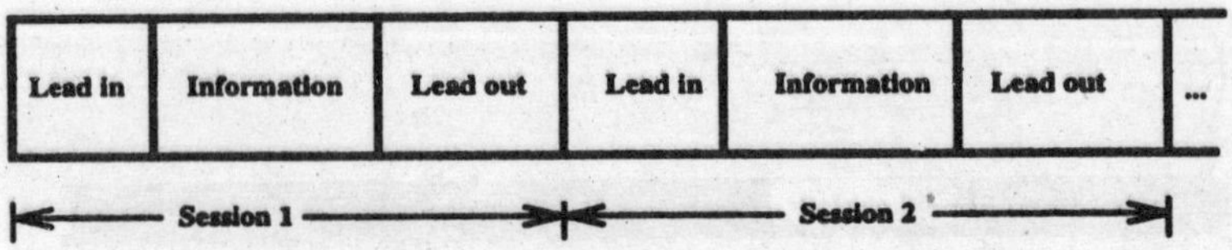


Figure 7.13: *Disk layout of a "hybrid disk" with several sessions.*

extended up to a maximal 99 sessions. However, because of the space requirement for lead-in and lead-out areas, at most 46 sessions can be stored. Each session consists again of its lead-in area, the data area and lead-out area. Until 1992, all available devices could read only one session. CD-WOs with only one session are called *regular CD-WOs.* A CD-WO with more than one session is called a *hybrid CD-WO.*

The *CD-WO recorder* typically works at a data rate double that of the player. This decreases the time for recording (write) by half the time for playing (read), but increases the requirements on the computer and its necessary software for installing and running a CD-WO. The reason is that this data rate must be sustained during the entire write activity. Simpler programs therefore produce an image (a one-to-one copy) of the CD-WO on a hard disk. In the second step, the data are transferred to the CD-WO. A storage-saving approach produces the data in the correct order and transfers them (without intermediate storage of the entire CD-WO information) at the necessary rate to the CD-WO.

The above description of CD-WO devices shows that a CD-WO disk could be a substitution, for example, for the CD-DA disk if it would have the same cost as CD-DA disk. However, the production process of the CD-WO is and will continue to be more expensive than the process for original CDs. Hence, CD-WO is only used in special application areas such as when huge data sets, because of technical or legal reasons, must be stored in an irreversible way. CD-WO also has application in the area of CD publishing because the production of an expensive and time-consuming master may be omitted. Fewer circulations with higher update (actual facts) can be produced.

## 7.9 Compact Disk Magneto Optical

The *Compact Disk Magneto Optical (CD-MO)* has a high storage capacity and allows one to write multiple times to the CD. CD-MO is specified in the first part of the *Orange Book* [Phi91].

### 7.9.1 Principle of the Magnetic-Optical Method

The magnetic-optical method is based on the polarization of the magnetic field where the polarization is caused by a heat.

To be written, the block (sector) is heated to above $150^0$C. Simultaneously, a magnetic field approximately 10 times the strength of the earth's magnetic field is created. The individual dipoles in the material are then polarized according to this magnetic field. Hereby, a pit corresponds to a low value of the magnetic field. A land is coded through a high value of the magnetic field.

After the CD is irradiated with a laser beam, the polarization of the light changes corresponding to the existing magnetization. Using this process, the read operation is executed.

For a delete activity, a constant magnetic field is created in the area of a block and the sector is simultaneously heated.

### 7.9.2 Areas of the CD-MO

A CD-MO consists of an optional *read-only* area and a *write-many* (recordable) area.

The read-only area (the premastered area in Figure 7.14) includes data which were written in a specified format onto the disk. Figure 7.14 shows the relationship between the premastered area of a CD-MO and read-only technologies. Therefore, only the CD-MO read-only area can be read by available playback devices.

The recordable area of a CD-MO cannot be played because the CD-MO read/write technology is fundamentally different from any CD-DA, CD-ROM, CD-ROM/XA

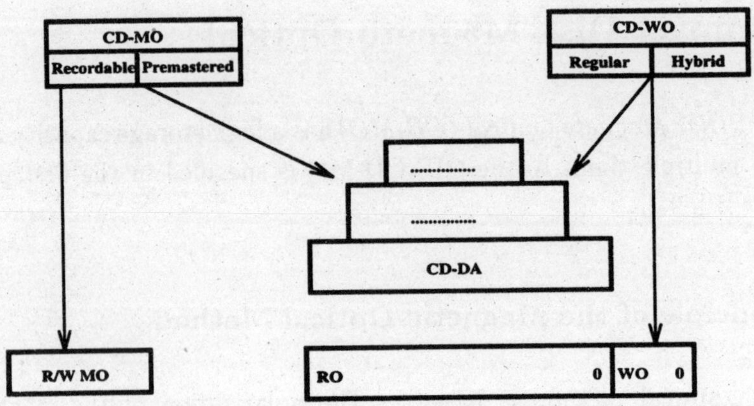


Figure 7.14: *CD-WO and CD-MO in relation to other CD technologies.*

or CD-WO device. Figure 7.14 shows the relationship between this recordable area and the fundamental magnetic-optical technology. Hence, this technology is unfortunately incompatible with all other CD systems, even though the same system parameters as in the other approaches were specified. For example, the dimensions and rotation speed are the same.

## 7.10 The Prospects of CD Technologies

Compact disk technology will remain the optical storage technology for all kinds of media. The relationship between different standards, shown in Figure 7.15, allows for a broad field of applications. Except for the CD-MO, the CD-DA with its optical technology still serves as the basis. A closer view and comparison of the formats show how the specification of CD technology has progressed. CD-ROM mode 1 defines improved error handling for computer data. In CD-ROM/XA form 1, based on CD-ROM mode 2, the same improved error handling is offered as in CD-ROM mode 1. This may mean that, for example, CD-ROM mode 1 could be omitted if so many applications did not already exist. The compression methods of CD-ROM/XA should use the JPEG, MPEG and CCITT ADPCM standards, and not limit themselves to the other coding methods for which cheaper integrated elements on the CD-ROM/XA controller boards already exist.

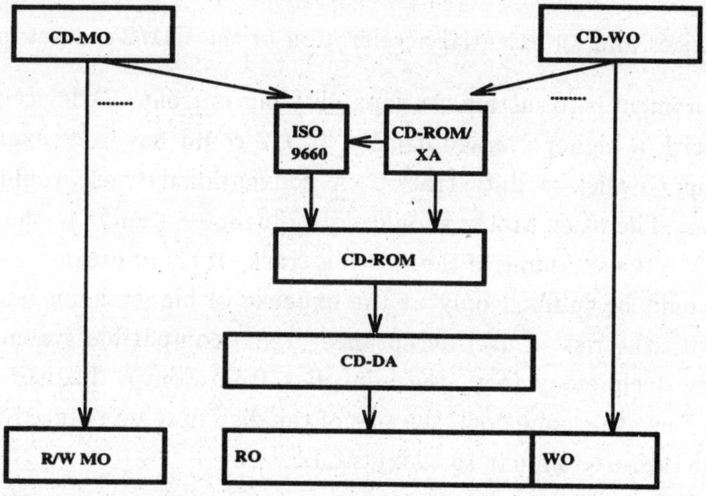


Figure 7.15: *The most important CD technologies and their mutual relations as a hierarchical structure.*

The disadvantage of all CDs is still the relatively high duration of the approximately 200 ms mean access. This property will not be improved substantially in the future. Unfortunately, there is also the incompatibility of the CD-MO to be considered.

The storage capacity of CDs is sufficient for many current systems. In research labs there are already optical storage media which work with a blue – instead of red – laser. One can envision, given the current pace of storage density increases, that in a few years there may exist a CD/2 which will have a capacity at least 16 times greater than today's CDs. Note that CD/2 is a fiction, standing for no ongoing research or development project.

Existing data rates require and determine efficient compression methods for audio, images and especially video. Analogous to the steps from TV to HDTV, from ISDN to B-ISDN and from MPEG to MPEG-2, one can also envision a CD/2 data transfer speed increase of up to factor 16. Indeed, today some CD-ROM built-in devices can continuously transfer above 600 Kbytes/s.

CD/2 devices should have the capability to also use current CDs as a storage medium. The difference would be that CD/2 disks would provide the aforementioned improved properties. This would allow a successive replacement of CD devices with new CD/2 devices and an essential acceleration of the CD/2 market introduction.

A harder requirement is to sustain the capability of a current CD device to play CD/2 disks. Even with a higher storage density, CD/2 could have, for example, several spirals running parallel as data tracks. A conventional track would be used by current devices. The other tracks should not influence – similar to the introduction of the color TV – the sampling of the existing track. It is important to note that this requirement could be fulfilled only at the expense of higher financial investments. Conversely, with the risk of user acceptance, a non-compatible system could make use of any new technology (e.g., the mini disk from Sony). Instead of increasing capacity to achieve the same goal, the size of the disk may be reduced to a Mini-CD with a storage capacity similar to today's CD.

# Chapter 8

# Computer Technology

A multimedia system is comprised of both hardware and software components, but the major driving force behind a multimedia development is research and development in hardware capabilities. For example, *Compact Disks* with their high storage capacity at a relatively low price provided the first step toward multimedia storage capabilities. Note that multimedia computer technology is a necessary but not sufficient pre-condition for *multimedia.* Unfortunately, computer hardware technology advances faster than the equivalent software. For example, many powerful computers with several signal-processors and RISC-processors have been built, but the capabilities of these processors are supported only very rarely by the current operating systems. Indeed, many operating systems cannot even fully use the capabilities of the processors in traditional workstations – they were designed for older generation of processors.

Besides the multimedia hardware capabilities of current personal computers (PCs) and workstations, computer networks with their increasing throughput and speed start to offer services which support multimedia communication systems. Also in this area, computer networking technology advances faster than the software. Today there are commercially-available computer networks with a throughput of over 100 Mbit/s, but full integration of high-speed networks and multimedia PCs or workstations are either missing or available only in research laboratories.

Many research projects are working toward solutions of the problems described above. Examples are European initiatives such as RACE, especially the German BERKOM project, and American high-speed network testbeds such as the AURORA, Blanca, Nectar, VISTAnet and CASA testbeds, and others [Par94].

We discuss in this chapter multimedia hardware components and their integration with the networks to support multimedia communication systems because without the necessary hardware, data storage capacity and continuous high data throughput, multimedia implementations would be impossible. The starting point for multimedia communication systems was the hybrid system where digital and analog components were integrated. The goal is a fully digital multimedia communication system [HS91].

Further, we give an overview of computer technology contributing to the development of multimedia workstations.

## 8.1 Communication Architecture

Local multimedia systems (i.e., multimedia workstations) frequently include a network interface (e.g., Ethernet card) through which they can communicate with each other. However, the transmission of audio and video cannot be carried out with only the conventional communication infrastructure and network adapters.

Until now, the solution was that continuous and discrete media have been considered in different environments, independently of each other. It means that fully different systems were built. For example, on the one hand, the *analog telephone system* provides audio transmission services using its original dial devices connected by copper wires to the telephone company's nearest *end office*. The end offices are connected to switching centers, called *toll offices*, and these centers are connected through high bandwidth intertoll trunks to *intermediate switching offices*. This hierarchical structure allows for reliable audio communication. On the other hand, *digital computer networks* provide data transmission services at lower data rates using network adapters connected by copper wires to switches and routers.

Even today, professional radio and television studios transmit audio and video streams in the form of analog signals, although most network components (e.g., switches), over which these signals are transmitted, work internally in a digital mode. Figure 8.1 shows an analog and a digital environment without any interaction.

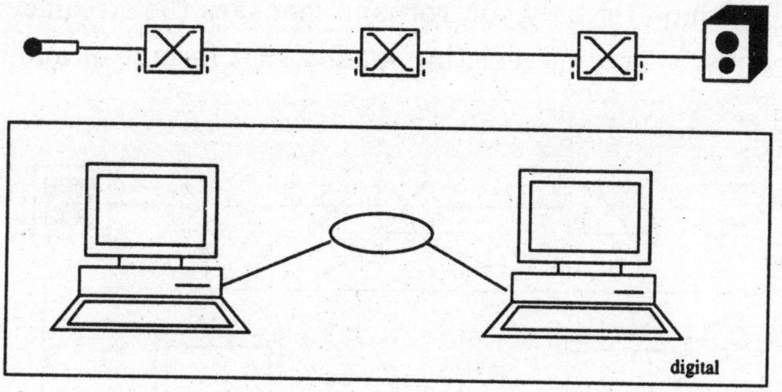


Figure 8.1: ***Analog and digital environments without interaction.***

### 8.1.1 Hybrid Systems

By using existing technologies, integration and interaction between analog and digital environments can be implemented. This integration approach is called the *hybrid approach.*

The main advantage of this approach is the high quality of audio and video and all the necessary devices for input, output, storage and transfer that are available. The hybrid approach is used for studying application user interfaces, application programming interfaces or application scenarios. The transmission techniques used in these cases are less important, although to meet the goal of full digital integration, this approach is not satisfactory.

#### Integrated Device Control

One possible integration approach is to provide a control of analog input/output audio-video components in the digital environment. Moreover, the connection between the sources (e.g., CD player, camera, microphone) and destinations (e.g., video recorder, write-able CD), or the switching of audio-video signals can be controlled digitally.

Figure 8.2 shows a possible computer control and management of external analog components. The computer only controls and manages the streams, but it does not process the streams; hence, the existing quality and format of audio and/or video are not changed.

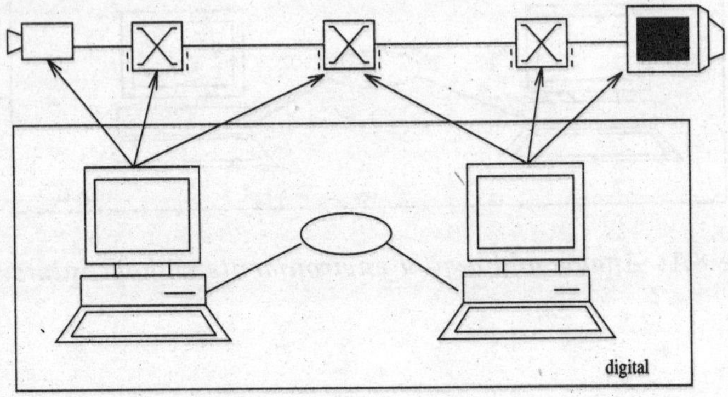


Figure 8.2: *Computer control of all audio-video components.*

Based on this hybrid approach, the Bell Communication Research Laboratory implemented the *Integrated Media Architecture Laboratory* (IMAL) in 1987. The IMAL project integrated a number of analog and digital networks [LD87]. The purpose of IMAL was to understand multimedia communication and to develop the necessary corresponding services.

Another example is the *Touring Machine System*™ from the Bellcore Information Networking Research Laboratory. A primary goal of the Touring Machine project is to provide a hybrid network infrastructure on which applications requiring complex multimedia communications can be developed, independent of the actual network fabric used to provide transport.

A third example is *Media Space*, created at the Xerox Palo Alto Research Center (PARC) in the mid-1980s. It provides an environment for collaborative work among the geographically separate research laboratories at Xerox PARC [BBI93].

### Integrated Transmission Control

A second possibility to integrate digital and analog components is to provide a common transmission control. This approach implies that analog audio-video sources and destinations are connected to the computers for control purposes to transmit continuous data over digital networks, such as a cable network. Figure 8.3 show a possible system configuration.

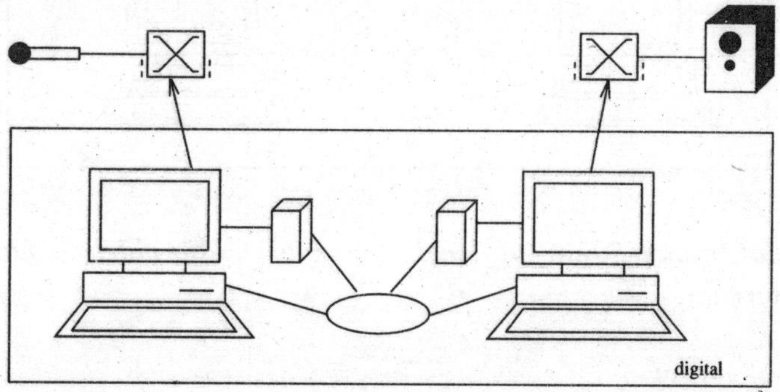


Figure 8.3: *Continuous data input into a digital network under computer control.*

For example, the video services of the *MIT Muse and Pygmalion Project* [CGR90, HS93, MTA+89] are based on such an approach: each computer is connected to the Ethernet for data communication, as well as to the cable network. The audio-video sources and destinations are connected to the computers through a Parallax family of adapters [Par87].

For both approaches above, the computer always controls the devices for processing and transmitting audio-video data. These data are not transferred through the computer but outside of it. Hence, in a very clever way, the problem of processing audio-video data under real-time conditions is avoided.

### Integrated Transmission

The next possibility to integrated digital and analog components is to provide a common transmission network. This implies that external analog audio-video devices are connected to computers using A/D (D/A) converters outside of the computer, not only for control, but also for processing purposes. Continuous data are transmitted over shared data networks. Figure 8.4 shows a possible system configuration. This system structure implies several issues:

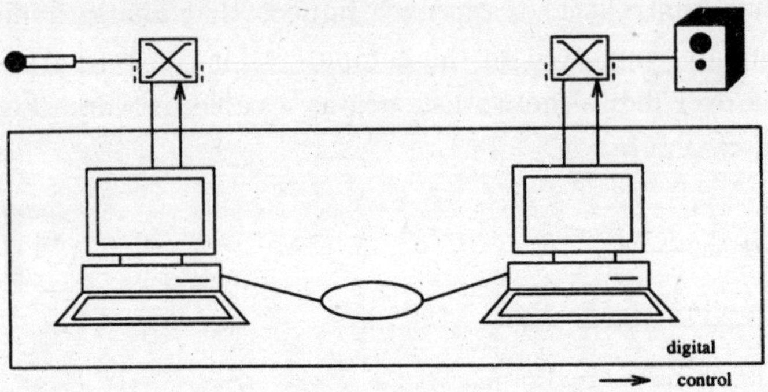


Figure 8.4: *Continuous data of local, external audio-video devices transmitted through the computer.*

- Computers control external devices.
- The continuous data are processed externally, as well as in the computer. This leads to diminished functionality and additional system software complexity because continuous data transferred between external audio-video-devices have a different processing environment than continuous data transferred, for example, from the hard disk to a video window.
- Before communication between different computers occurs, audio-video signals are digitized, coded and compressed (if possible).
- Synchronization of different media within a digital environment causes problems (see Chapter 15 on synchronization).

An example of this approach is the DIME project [RSSS90] of the IBM European Networking Center. Here, audio-video devices are connected to PS/2 computers through audio and video cards [Moo90] and transmitted over the data network.

Another example is the *Boulder Project* from US West, Colorado [CSA+89]. The research department is geographically split into two locations and between them a data connection of 45 Mbit/s is installed. Both places have a configuration of audio-video devices similar to IMAL. Between both laboratories, data of different media are transmitted.

### 8.1.2 Digital Systems

#### Connection to Workstations

In digital systems, audio-video devices can be connected directly to the computers (workstations) and digitized audio-video data are transmitted over shared data networks, Audio-video devices in these systems can be either analog or digital. Figure 8.5 shows an integrated system structure with analog devices and A/D and D/A interfaces. Figure 8.6 shows an integrated system structure with digital end-system devices and interfaces.

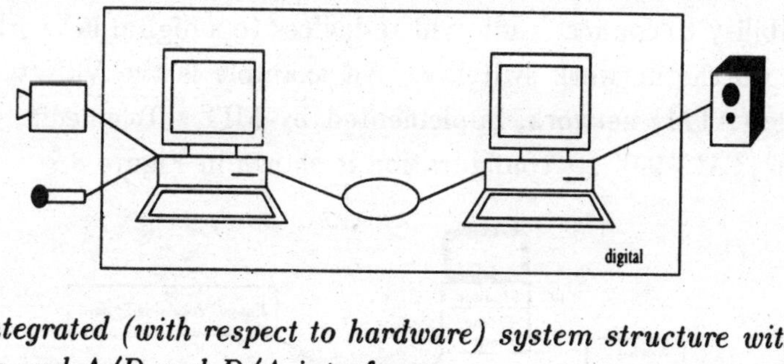


Figure 8.5: *Integrated (with respect to hardware) system structure with analog end-system devices and A/D and D/A interfaces.*

An example of a digital system is the *Etherphone* system from Xerox PARC [Swi87]. A digital audio communication was demonstrated over an Ethernet, although not in a fully integrated form, i.e., the audio was not processed in the main memory.

Another example is an early project by AT&T in Naporville, which considered a similar system architecture to a Etherphone [LL89, LBH+90]. Here, a computer was directly connected to a *Fast Packet Switching* network. The processing of continuous media in the computer was allowed through extensions of the UNIX operating

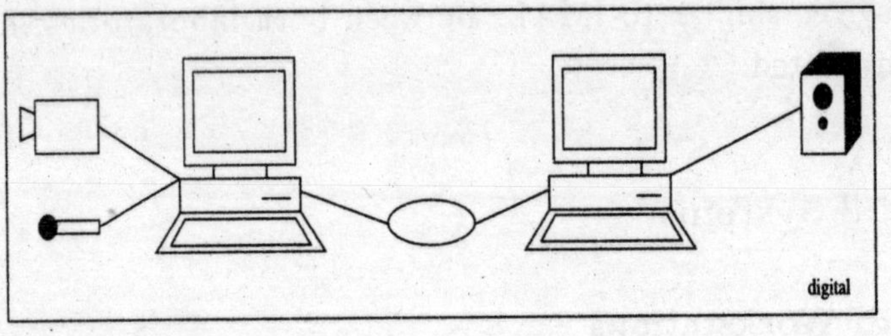


Figure 8.6: *Integrated (with respect to hardware) system structure with digital end-system devices and interfaces.*

system.

#### Connection to Switches

Another possibility to connect audio-video devices to a digital network is to connect them directly to the network switches. An example is the VuNet Asynchronous Transfer Mode (ATM) network, implemented by MIT's Telemedia, Networks and System Group [TAC+94]. Its configuration is shown in Figure 8.7.

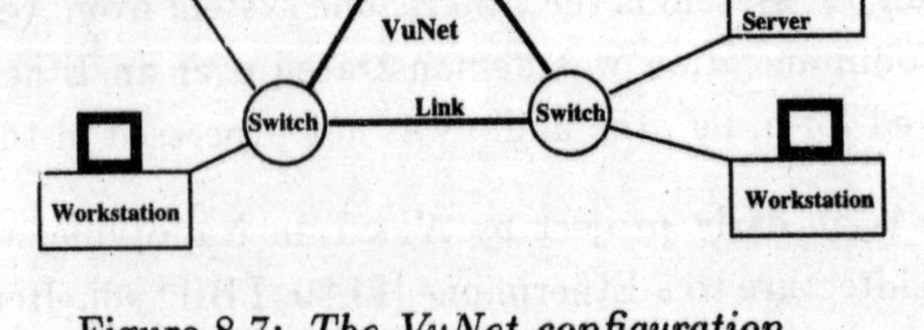


Figure 8.7: *The VuNet configuration.*

## 8.2 Multimedia Workstation

*Current workstations* are designed for the manipulation of discrete media information. The data should be exchanged as quickly as possible between the involved components, often interconnected by a common bus. Computationally intensive and dedicated processing requirements lead to dedicated hardware, firmware and additional boards. Examples of these components are hard disk controllers and FDDI-adapters.

A *multimedia workstation* is designed for the simultaneous manipulation of discrete and continuous media information. The main components of a multimedia workstation are:

- *Standard Processor(s)* for the processing of discrete media information.
- *Main Memory* and *Secondary Storage* with corresponding autonomous controllers.
- *Universal Processor(s)* for processing of data in real-time (signal processors).
- *Special-Purpose Processors* designed for graphics, audio and video media (containing, for example, a micro code decompression method for DVI processors) [Rip89, Tin89, Lut91].
- *Graphics and Video Adapters.*
- *Communications Adapters* (for example, the Asynchronous Transfer Mode Host Interface [TS93].
- Further *special-purpose adapters.*

The Silicon Graphics workstation, running IRIX with $REACT^{TM}$ [Ska94] (shown in Figure 8.8), is very close to a multimedia workstation with the above-mentioned components.

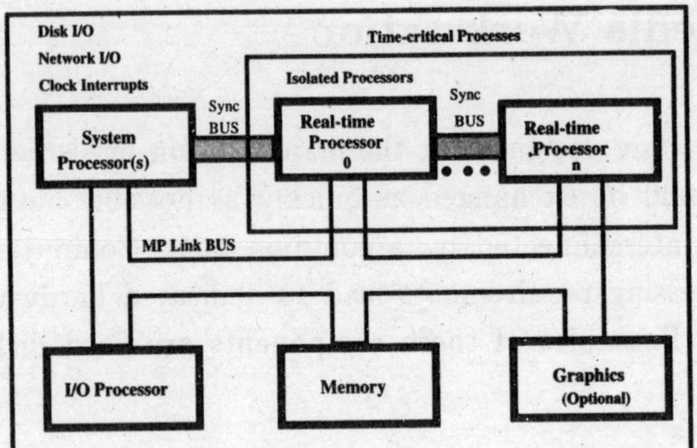


Figure 8.8: *Silicon Graphics workstation architecture (POWER Lock Processor Isolation).*

### Bus

Within current workstations, data are transmitted over the traditional asynchronous *bus*, meaning that if audio-video devices are connected to a workstation, continuous data are processed in a workstation, and the data transfer is done over this bus, which provides low and unpredictable time guarantees. In multimedia workstations, in addition to this bus, the data will be transmitted over a second bus which can keep time guarantees. In later technical implementations, a bus may be developed which transmits two kinds of data according to their requirements (this is known as a *multi-bus system*).

The notion of a bus has to be divided into *system bus* and *periphery bus*. In their current versions, system busses such as ISA, EISA, Microchannel, Q-bus and VME-bus support only limited transfer of continuous data. The further development of periphery busses, such as SCSI, is aimed at the development of data transfer for continuous media.

### Multimedia Devices

The main peripheral components are the necessary input and output multimedia devices. Most of these devices were developed for or by consumer electronics, resulting in the relative low cost of the devices. Microphones, headphones, as well as passive and active speakers, are examples. For the most part, active speakers and headphones are connected to the computer because it, generally, does not contain an amplifier. The camera for video input is also taken from consumer electronics. Hence, a video interface in a computer must accommodate the most commonly used video techniques/standards, i.e., NTSC, PAL, SECAM with FBAS, RGB, YUV and YIQ modes. A monitor serves for video output. Besides Cathode Ray Tube (CRT) monitors (e.g., current workstation terminals), more and more terminals use the color-LCD technique (e.g., a projection TV monitor uses the LCD technique). Further, to display video, monitor characteristics, such as *color*, *high resolution*, and *flat and large shape*, are important.

### Primary Storage

Audio and video data are copied among different system components in a digital system. An example of tasks, where copying of data is necessary, is a segmentation of the LDUs or the appending of a *Header* and *Trailer*. The copying operation uses system software-specific memory management designed for continuous media. This kind of memory management needs sufficient main memory (primary storage). Besides ROMs, PROMs, EPROMs and partially static memory elements, low-cost dynamic memory modules are especially needed. The steadily decreasing cost of these modules, together with steadily increasing storage capacities, profits the multimedia world.

The copying of data in a workstation can be performed using either the bus master method or the Central Processing Unit (CPU), although it is not always possible to use the former method. In most cases, the copying operation is performed by the CPU.

### Secondary Storage

The main requirements put on secondary storage and the corresponding controller are a high storage density and low access time, respectively.

On the one hand, to achieve a high storage density, for example, a Constant Linear Velocity (CLV) technique was defined for the CD-DA (Compact Disc Digital Audio) (see Section 7.4). CLV guarantees that the data density is kept constant for the entire optical disk at the expense of a higher mean access time. On the other hand, to achieve time guarantees, i.e., lower mean access time, a Constant Angle Velocity (CAV) technique could be used. Because the time requirement is more important, the systems with a CAV. are more suitable for multimedia than the systems with a CLV.

Further requirements put on secondary storage are a high capacity at a low price and a storage of discrete and continuous media together.

### Processor

In a multimedia workstation, the necessary work is distributed among different processors. Although currently, and for the near future, this does not mean that all multimedia workstations must be multi-processor systems. The processors are designed for different tasks. For example, a *Dedicated Signal Processor (DSP)* allows compression and decompression of audio in real-time. Moreover, there can be special-purpose processors employed for video. Figure 8.9 shows an example of a multi-processor for multimedia workstations envisioned for the future (Intel '786 [Pre90]).

As a future development, a multimedia system could consist of multi-universal processors, which would have DSP properties unified with CPU properties. According to the application, these elements could be configured for exclusive processing of discrete or continuous media. Hence, this would provide the possibility of a multimedia workstation which supports customization of processors according to an application specification.

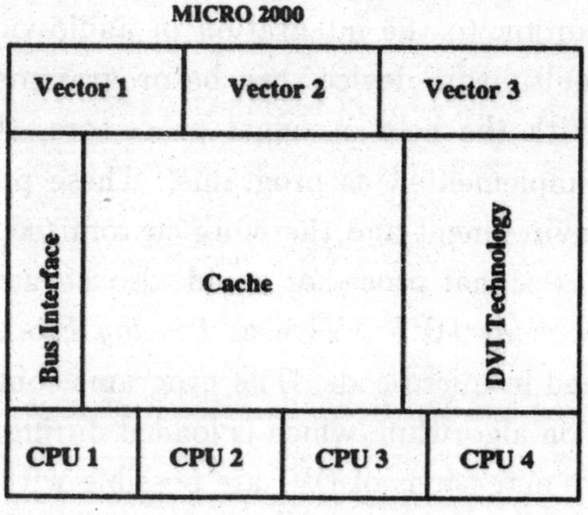


Figure 8.9: *Multi-processor system, Intel '786 [Pre90].*

**Operating System**

Another possible variant to provide computation of discrete and continuous data in a multimedia workstation could be distinguishing between *processes* for discrete data computation and for continuous data processing. These processes could run on separate processors. Given an adequate operating system, perhaps even one processor could be shared according to the requirements between processes for discrete and continuous data. The further development of multimedia operating systems is likely to go in this direction.

## 8.3 Comments

Digital systems consist, for most existing research and development projects, of traditional computers *enhanced* with hardware for multimedia functions. Examples of such enhancements are adapters connecting audio-video sources and destinations with the system bus in a workstation. These adapters do not place the data in the main memory during continuous media transfer, which would slow down the processing. Further improvements of traditional computers can be achieved by using compression methods. These methods considerably reduce the data rate of video, as well as that of audio (see Chapter 6).

Digital systems allow, in addition to the integration of audio-video devices, *high flexibility* because different multimedia devices can be programmed. For example, consider an audio mixer. With the help of signal processors, the mix functions are a set of filter functions implemented as programs. These programs could be modified easily in a digital environment and therefore customized according to any application requirements. The signal processor could also be used for other purposes. Another example represents DVI. DVI uses *Display Processor* VDP (Pixel Process), which is programmed in micro-code. The programs contain a part of the compression and decompression algorithm, which is loaded during the initialization phase. Therefore, some future extensions of DVI are possible without changing the underlying hardware.

Requirements, with respect to the performance capability of digital systems, do not always allow the use of software solutions in a digital environment. A hardware implementation mostly increases performance capability, but flexibility decreases. This boundary between dedicated hardware and general-purpose software components is dependent on technology, application and cost. Using a multimedia workstation architecture with a multimedia operating system, this boundary can be flexibly modified.

# Chapter 9

# Multimedia Operating Systems

## 9.1 Introduction

The operating system is the shield of the computer hardware against all software components. It provides a comfortable environment for the execution of programs, and it ensures effective utilization of the computer hardware. The operating system offers various services related to the essential resources of a computer: CPU, main memory, storage and all input and output devices.

For the processing of audio and video, multimedia application demands that humans perceive these media in a natural, error-free way. These continuous media data originate at sources like microphones, cameras and files. From these sources, the data are transferred to destinations like loudspeakers, video windows and files located at the same computer or at a remote station. On the way from source to sink, the digital data are processed by at least some type of move, copy or transmit operation. In this data manipulation process there are always many resources which are under the control of the operating system. The integration of discrete and continuous multimedia data demands additional services from many operating system components.

The major aspect in this context is real-time processing of continuous media data. Process management must take into account the timing requirements imposed by the handling of multimedia data. Appropriate scheduling methods should be applied. In contrast to the traditional real-time operating systems, multimedia operating systems also have to consider tasks without hard timing restrictions under the aspect of fairness.

To obey timing requirements, single components are conceived as resources that are reserved prior to execution. This concept of *resource reservation* has to cover all resources on a data path, i.e., all resources that deal with continuous media. It also may affect parts of the application that process continuous media data. In distributed systems, for example, resource management also comprises network capacity [HVWW94].

The *communication* and *synchronization* between single processes must meet the restrictions of real-time requirements and timing relations among different media. The main memory is available as a shared resource to single processes.

In multimedia systems, *memory management* has to provide access to data with a guaranteed timing delay and efficient data manipulation functions. For instance, physical data copy operations must be avoided due to their negative impact on performance; buffer management operations (such as are known from communication systems) should be used.

Database management is an important component in multimedia systems. However, database management abstracts the details of storing data on secondary media storage. Therefore, database management should rely on file management services provided by the multimedia operating system to access single files and file systems. For example, the incorporation of a CD-ROM XA file system as an integral part of a multimedia *file system* allows transparent and guaranteed continuous retrieval of audio and video data to any application using the file system; the database system is one of those applications. However, database systems often implement their own access to stored data.

Since the operating system shields devices from applications programs, it must provide services for *device management* too. In multimedia systems, the important issue is the integration of audio and video devices in a similar way to any other input/output device. The addressing of a camera can be performed similar to the addressing of a keyboard in the same system, although most current systems do not apply this technique.

Product information dealing with operating system extensions for the integration of multimedia [IBM92c, Win91, DM92, IBM92e, IBM92d] typically provide a detailed description of application interfaces. In this chapter we will concentrate on the basic concepts and internal tasks of a multimedia operating system.

As the essential aspect of any multimedia operating system is the notion of *real-time*, the following section details this idea in its relationship to multimedia. Subsequently, the concept of resource management is discussed. The section on process management contains a brief presentation of traditional real-time scheduling algorithms. Further, their suitability and adaptability toward continuous media processing is examined. The section on file systems outlines disk access algorithms, data placement and structuring. The subsequent sections illustrate interprocess communication and synchronization, memory management and device management. This chapter concludes with a discussion of typical system architectures which comprise real-time and non-real-time environments.

## 9.2 Real Time

Since the notion of *real-time* developed independently from research in continuous media processing, the next section starts with a general definition of real-time. Later, it shows the relevance of real-time for multimedia data and processes.

### 9.2.1 The Notion of "Real-Time"

The German National Institute for Standardization, DIN, similar to the American ANSI, defines a real-time process in a computer system as follows:

> *A real-time process is a process which delivers the results of the processing in a given time-span.*

Programs for the processing of data must be available during the entire run-time of the system. The data may require processing at an a priori known point in time, or it may be demanded without any previous knowledge [Ger85]. The system must enforce externally-defined time constraints. Internal dependencies and their related time limits are implicitly considered. External events occur – depending on the application – deterministically (at a predetermined instant) or stochastically (randomly). The real-time system has the permanent task of receiving information from the environment, occurring spontaneously or in periodic time intervals, and/or delivering it to the environment given certain time constraints.

The main characteristic of real-time systems is the correctness of the computation. This correctness does not only apply to errorless computation, but also on the time in which the result is presented [SR89]. Hence, a real-time system can fail not only if massive hardware or software failures occur, but also if the system is unable to execute its critical workload in time [KL91]. Deterministic behavior of the system refers to the adherence of time spans defined in advance for the manipulation of data, i.e., meeting a guaranteed response time. Speed and efficiency are not – as is often mistakenly assumed – the main characteristics of a real-time system. In a petrochemical plant, for example, the result is not only unacceptable when the engine of a vent responds too quickly, but also when it responds with a large delay. Another example is the playback of a video sequence in a multimedia system. The result is only acceptable when the video is presented neither too quickly nor too slowly. Timing and logical dependencies among different related tasks, processed at the same time, also must be considered. These dependencies refer to both internal and external restrictions. In the context of multimedia data streams, this refers to the processing of synchronized audio and video data where the relation between the two media must be considered.

### Deadlines

A deadline represents the latest acceptable time for the presentation of a processing result. It marks the border between normal (correct) and anomalous (failing) behavior. A real-time system has both hard and soft deadlines.

The term *soft deadline* is often used for a deadline which cannot be exactly determined and which failing to meet does not produce an unacceptable result. We understand a soft deadline as a deadline which in some cases is missed and may yet be tolerated as long as (1) not too many deadlines are missed and/or (2) the deadlines are not missed by much. Such soft deadlines are only reference points with a certain acceptable tolerance. For example, the start and arrival times of planes or trains, where deadlines can vary by about ten minutes, can be considered as soft deadlines.

Whereas soft deadlines may be violated, *hard deadlines* should never be violated. A hard deadline violation is a system failure. Hard deadlines are determined by the physical characteristics of real-time processes. Failing such a deadline results in costs that can be measured in terms of money (e.g., inefficient use of raw materials in a process control system), or human and environmental terms (e.g., accidents due to untimely control in a nuclear power plant or fly-by-wire avionics systems) [Jef90].

### Characteristics of Real Time Systems

The necessity of deterministic and predictable behavior of real-time systems requires processing guarantees for time-critical tasks. Such guarantees cannot be assured for events that occur at random intervals with unknown arrival times, processing requirements or deadlines. Further, all guarantees are valid only under the premise that no processing machine collapses during the run-time of real-time processes. A real-time system is distinguished by the following features (c.f. [SR89]):

- Predictably fast response to time-critical events and accurate timing information. For example, in the control system of a nuclear power plant, the response to a malfunction must occur within a well-defined period to avoid a potential disaster.
- A high degree of schedulability. Schedulability refers to the degree of resource utilization at which, or below which, the deadline of each time-critical task can be taken into account.
- Stability under transient overload. Under system overload, the processing of critical tasks must be ensured. These critical tasks are vital to the basic

functionality provided by the system.

Management of manufacturing processes and the control of military systems are the main application areas for real-time systems. Such process control systems are responsible for real-time monitoring and control. Real-time systems are also used as command and control systems in fly-by-wire aircraft, automobile anti-lock braking systems and the control of nuclear power plants [KL91]. New application areas for real-time systems include computer conferencing and multimedia in general, the topic of our work.

### 9.2.2 Real Time and Multimedia

Audio and video data streams consist of single, periodically changing values of continuous media data, e.g., audio samples or video frames. Each Logical Data Unit (LDU) must be presented by a well-determined deadline. Jitter is only allowed *before* the final presentation to the user. A piece of music, for example, must be played back at a constant speed. To fulfill the timing requirements of continuous media, the operating system must use real-time scheduling techniques. These techniques must be applied to all system resources involved in the continuous media data processing, i.e., the entire end-to-end data path is involved. The CPU is just one of these resources – all components must be considered including main memory, storage, I/O devices and networks.

The *real-time requirements* of traditional real-time scheduling techniques (used for command and control systems in application areas such as factory automation or aircraft piloting) have a high demand for security and fault-tolerance. The requirements derived from these demands somehow counteract real-time scheduling efforts applied to continuous media. Multimedia systems which are not used in traditional real-time scenarios have different (in fact, more favorable) real-time requirements:

- The *fault-tolerance* requirements of multimedia systems are usually less strict than those of real-time systems that have a direct physical impact. The short time failure of a continuous media system will not directly lead to the destruction of technical equipment or constitute a threat to human life. Please note that this is a general statement which does not always apply. For example, the support of remote surgery by video and audio has stringent delay and correctness requirements.

- For many multimedia system applications, missing a deadline is not a severe failure, although it should be avoided. It may even go unnoticed, e.g., if an uncompressed video frame (or parts of it) is not available on time it can simply be omitted. The viewer will hardly notice this omission, assuming it does not happen for a contiguous sequence of frames. Audio requirements are more stringent because the human ear is more sensitive to audio gaps than the human eye is to video jitter.

- A sequence of digital continuous media data is the result of periodically sampling a sound or image signal. Hence, in processing the data units of such a data sequence, all time-critical operations are periodic. Schedulability considerations for periodic tasks are much easier than for sporadic ones [Mok84].

- The bandwidth demand of continuous media is not always that stringent; it must not be a priori fixed, but it may eventually be lowered. As some compression algorithms are capable of using different compression ratios – leading to different qualities – the required bandwidth can be negotiated. If not enough bandwidth is available for full quality, the application may also accept reduced quality (instead of no service at all). The quality may also be adjusted dynamically to the available bandwidth, e.g., by changing encoding parameters. This is known as scalable video.

In a traditional real-time system, timing requirements result from the physical characteristics of the technical process to be controlled, i.e., they are provided externally. Some applications must meet external requirements too. A distributed music rehearsal is a futuristic example: music played by one musician on an instrument connected to his/her workstation must be made available to all other members of the orchestra within a few milliseconds, otherwise the underlying knowledge of a global unique time is disturbed. If human users are involved in just the input or only the output of continuous media, delay bounds are more flexible. Consider the playback of a video from a remote disk. The actual delay of a single video frame to be transferred from the disk to the monitor is unimportant. Frames must only arrive in a regular fashion. The user will only notice any difference in delay as start delay (i.e., for the first video frame to be displayed).

## 9.3 Resource Management

Multimedia systems with integrated audio and video processing are at the limit of their capacity, even with data compression and utilization of new technologies. Current computers do not allow *processing* of data according to their deadlines without any resource reservation and real-time process management. *Processing* in this context refers to any kind of manipulation and communication of data. This stage of development is known as *the window of insufficient resources* (see Figure 9.1) [ATW+90]. With CD-DA (Compact Disc Digital Audio) quality, the highest

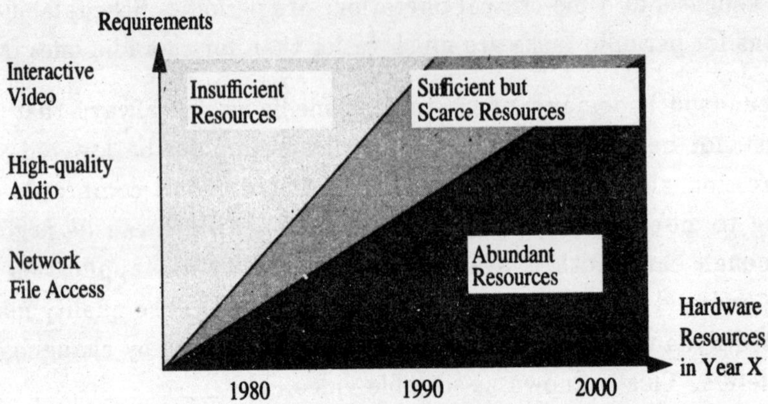


Figure 9.1: *Window of insufficient resources.*

audio requirements are satisfied. In video technology, the required data transfer rate will go up with the development of digital HDTV and larger TV screens. Therefore, no redundancy of resource capacity can be expected in the near future.

In a multimedia system, the given timing guarantees for the processing of continuous media must be adhered to by every hardware and software system component along the data path. The actual requirements depend on the type of media and the nature of the applications supported[SM92a]. For example, a video image should not be presented late because the communication system has been busy with a transaction from a database management system. In any realistic scenario we encounter several multimedia applications which concurrently make use of shared resources. Hence, even high bandwidth networks and huge processing capabilities require the use of real-time mechanisms to provide guaranteed data delivery. Further, the concept of integration does not allow solving this problem just by a slight modification of the system for traditional applications.

Thus, in an integrated distributed multimedia system, several applications compete for system resources. This shortage of resources requires careful allocation. The system management must employ adequate scheduling algorithms to serve the requirements of the applications. Thereby, the resource is first allocated and then managed.

Resource management in distributed multimedia systems covers several computers and the involved communication networks. It allocates all resources involved in the data transfer process between sources and sinks. For instance, a CD-ROM/XA device must be allocated exclusively, each CPU on the data path must provide 20% of its capacity, the network must allocate a certain amount of its bandwidth and the graphic processor must be reserved up to 50% for such a process. The required throughput and a certain delay is guaranteed. At the connection establishment phase, the resource management ensures that the new "connection" does not violate performance guarantees already provided to existing connections. Applied to operating systems, this model covers the CPU (including process management), memory management, the file system and device management. Therefore, we chose to detail this issue for all resources in a generic notion of resources in the following paragraphs. The resource reservation is identical for all resources, whereas the management is different for each.

### 9.3.1 Resources

A resource is a system entity required by tasks for manipulating data. Each resource has a set of distinguishing characteristics classified using the following scheme:

- A resource can be active or passive. An active resource is the CPU or a network adapter for protocol processing; it provides a service. A passive resource is the main memory, communication bandwidth or a file system (whenever we do not take care of the processing of the adapter); it denotes some system capability required by active resources.

- A resource can be either used exclusively by one process at a time or shared between various processes. Active resources are often exclusive; passive resources can usually be shared among processes.

- A resource that exists only once in the system is known as a single, otherwise it is a multiple resource. In a transputer-based multiprocessor system, the individual CPU is a multiple resource.

Each resource has a capacity which results from the ability of a certain task to perform using the resource in a given time-span. In this context, capacity refers to CPU capacity, frequency range or, for example, the amount of storage. For real-time scheduling, only the temporal division of resource capacity among real-time processes is of interest. Process management belongs to the category of active, shared, and most often single resources. A file system on an optical disk with CD-ROM XA format is a passive, shared, single resource.

### 9.3.2 Requirements

The requirements of multimedia applications and data streams must be served by the single components of a multimedia system. The resource management maps these requirements onto the respective capacity. The transmission and processing requirements of local and distributed multimedia applications can be specified according to the following characteristics:

1. The throughput is determined by the needed data rate of a connection to satisfy the application requirements. It also depends on the size of the data units.

2. We distinguish between local and global (end-to-end) delay:

   (a) The delay "at the resource" is the maximum time span for the completion of a certain task at this resource.

(b) The end-to-end delay is the total delay for a data unit to be transmitted from the source to its destination. For example, the source of a video telephone is the camera, the destination is the video window on the screen of the partner.

3. The jitter (or delay jitter) determines the maximum allowed variance in the arrival of data at the destination.

4. The reliability defines error detection and correction mechanisms used for the transmission and processing of multimedia tasks. Errors can be ignored, indicated and/or corrected. It is important to notice that error correction through re-transmission is rarely appropriate for time-critical data because the re-transmitted data will usually arrive late. Forward error correction mechanisms are more useful. In terms of reliability, we also mean the CPU errors due to unwanted delays in processing a task which exceed the demanded deadlines.

In accordance with communication systems, these requirements are also known as *Quality of Service parameters (QoS)*.

### 9.3.3 Components and Phases

One possible realization of resource allocation and management is based on the interaction between clients and their respective resource managers. The client selects the resource and requests a resource allocation by specifying its requirements through a QoS specification. This is equivalent to a workload request. First, the resource manager checks its own resource utilization and decides if the reservation request can be served or not. All existing reservations are stored. This way, their share in terms of the respective resource capacity is guaranteed. Moreover, this component negotiates the reservation request with other resource managers, if necessary.

The following example of a distributed multimedia system illustrates this generic scheme. During the connection establishment phase, the QoS parameters are usually negotiated between the requester (client application) and the addressed resource manager. The negotiation starts in the simplest case with specification of the QoS parameters by the application. The resource manager checks whether these requests can be guaranteed or not. A more elaborate method is to optimize single parameters. In this case, two parameters are determined by the application (e.g., throughput and reliability), and the resource manager calculates the best achievable value for the third parameter (e.g., delay). To negotiate the parameters for end-to-end connections over one or more computer networks, resource reservation protocols like ST-II are employed [Top90]. Here, resource managers of the single components of the distributed system allocate the necessary resources.

In the case shown in Figure 9.2, two computers are connected over a LAN. The transmission of video data between a camera connected to a computer server and the screen of the computer user involves, for all depicted components, a resource manager.

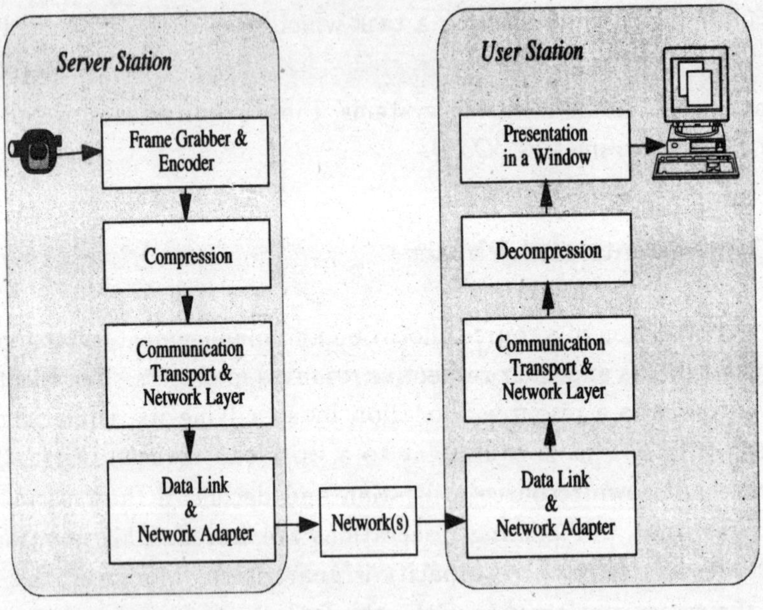


Figure 9.2: *Components grouped for the purpose of video data transmission.*

This example illustrates that, in addition to the individual resource managers, there must exist a protocol for coordination between these services, such as ST-II.

**Phases of the Resource Reservation and Management Process**

A resource manager provides components for the different phases of the allocation and management process:

1. *Schedulability Test*

   The resource manager checks with the given QoS parameters (e.g., throughput and reliability) to determine if there is enough remaining resource capacity available to handle this additional request.

2. *Quality of Service Calculation*

   After the schedulability test, the resource manager calculates the best possible performance (e.g., delay) the resource can guarantee for the new request.

3. *Resource Reservation*

   The resource manager allocates the required capacity to meet the QoS guarantees for each request.

4. *Resource Scheduling*

   Incoming messages from connections are scheduled according to the given QoS guarantees. For process management, for instance, the allocation of the resource is done by the scheduler at the moment the data arrive for processing.

With respect to the last phase, for each resource a scheduling algorithm is defined. The schedulability test, QoS calculation and resource reservation depend on this algorithm used by the scheduler.

### 9.3.4 Allocation Scheme

Reservation of resources can be made either in a pessimistic or optimistic way:

- The *pessimistic approach* avoids resource conflicts by making reservations for the worst case, i.e., resource bandwidth for the longest processing time and the highest rate which might ever be needed by a task is reserved. Resource conflicts are therefore avoided. This leads potentially to an underutilization of resources. In a multimedia system, the remaining processor time (i.e., the time reserved for traffic but not used) can be used by discrete media tasks. This method results in a guaranteed QoS.

- With the *optimistic approach,* resources are reserved according to an average workload only. This means that the CPU is only reserved for the average processing time. This approach may overbook resources with the possibility of unpredictable packet delays. QoS parameters are met as far as possible. Resources are highly utilized, though an overload situation may result in failure. To detect an overload situation and to handle it accordingly a monitor can be implemented. The monitor may, for instance, preempt processes according to their importance.

The optimistic approach is considered to be an extension of the pessimistic approach. It requires that additional mechanisms to detect and solve resource conflicts be implemented.

### 9.3.5 Continuous Media Resource Model

This section specifies a model frequently adopted to define QoS parameters and hence, the characteristics of the data stream. It is based on the model of Linear Bounded Arrival Processes (LBAP), as described in [And93]. In this model a distributed system is decomposed into a chain of resources traversed by the messages on their end-to-end path. Examples of such resources are single schedulable devices (such as CPU) or combined entities (such as networks).

The data stream consists of LDUs. In this context, we call them messages. In a first step, the data stream itself is characterized as strictly periodic, irregular with a definite maximum message size. Various data streams are independent of each other.

A closer inspection shows a possible variance of the message rate, the maximum rate is well-defined. This variance of the data rate results in an accumulation of messages (burst), where the maximal range is defined by the maximum allowed number of messages.

In the LBAP model, a burst of messages consists of messages that arrived ahead of schedule. LBAP is a message arrival process at a resource defined by three parameters:

- $M$ = Maximum message size (byte/message).
- $R$ = Maximum message rate (message/second).
- $B$ = Maximum Burstiness (message).

**Example**

The LBAP model is discussed in terms of a specific example: two workstations are interconnected by a LAN. A CD player is attached to one workstation. Single channel audio data are transferred from the CD player of this workstation over the network to the other computer. At this remote station, the audio data are delivered to a speaker. The audio signal is sampled with the frequency of 44.1 kHz. Each sample is coded with 16 bits. This results in a data rate of:

$$R_{byte} = 44100Hz \times \frac{16bits}{8bits/byte} = 88200bytes/s$$

The samples on a CD are assembled into frames. These frames are the audio messages to be transmitted. Seventy-five of these audio messages are transmitted per second ($R$) according to the CD-format standard. Therefore, we encounter a maximum message size of:

$$M = \frac{88200bytes/s}{75messages/s} = 1176bytes/message$$

Up to 12000 bytes are assembled into one packet and transmitted over the LAN. In a packet of 12000 bytes transmitted over the LAN, we will never encounter more messages than:

$$\frac{12000bytes}{1176bytes/message} \geq 10messages = B$$

It obviously follows that:

- $M$ = 1176 bytes/message.
- $R$ = 75 messages/s.
- $B$ = 10 messages.

### Burst

In the calculation below it is assumed that, because of lower adjacent data rate, a burst never exceeds a maximum data rate. Hence, bursts do not succeed one another. During a time interval of length $t$, the maximum number of messages arriving at a resource must not exceed:

$$\bar{M} = B + R \times t(message)$$

For example, assume $t = 1s$.

$$\bar{M} = (10messages + 75messages/s \times 1s = 85messages$$

The introduction of Burstiness $B$ allows for short time violations of the rate constraint. This way, programs and devices that generate bursts of messages can be modeled. Bursts are generated, e.g., when data is transferred from disks in a bulk transfer mode or, in our example, when messages are assembled into larger packets.

**Maximum Average Data Rate**

The maximum average data rate of the LBAP is:

$\bar{R} = M \times R(bytes/s)$

For example:

$\bar{R} = (1176bytes/message \times 75messages/s = 88200bytes/s)$

**Maximum Buffer Size**

Messages are processed according to their rate. Messages which arrive "ahead of schedule" must be queued. For delay period, the buffer size is:

$S = M \times (B + 1)(bytes)$

For example:

$S = (1176bytes/message \times 11message = 12936bytes$

**Logical Backlog**

The function $b(m)$ represents the logical backlog of messages. This is the number of messages which have already arrived "ahead of schedule" at the arrival of message $m$. Let $a_i$ be the actual arrival time of message $m_i$; $0 \leq i \leq n$. Then $b(i)$ is defined by:

$b(m_0) = 0$ messages

$b(m_i) = max(0 \text{ messages}, b(m_{i-1}) - (a_i - a_{i-1})R + 1 \text{ message})$

For example:

$a_{i-1} = 1.00s; a_i = 1.01\bar{3}s; b(m_{i-1}) = 4$ messages

$b(m_i) = max(0 \text{ messages}, 4 \text{ messages} - (1.01\bar{3}s - 1.00s) \times 75 \text{ messages}/s + 1 \text{ message}) =$ 4 messages

**Logical Arrival Time**

The logical arrival time defines the earliest time a message $m_i$ can arrive at a resource when all messages arrive according to their rate. The logical arrival time of a message can then be defined as:

$l(m_i) = a(n_i) + \frac{b(m_i)}{R}$

For example:

$l(m_i) = 1.01\bar{3}s + \frac{4 \text{ messages}}{75 \text{ messages}/s} = 1.0\bar{6}$

Equivalently, it can be computed as:

$l(m_0) = a_0$

$l(m_i) = max(a_i, l(m_{i-1}) + \frac{1}{R})$

For example:

$$l(m_{i-1}) = 1.05\bar{3}s$$

$$l(m_i) = max(1.01\bar{3}s, 1.05\bar{3}s + \frac{1\ messsage}{75\ messages/s}) = 1.0\bar{6}$$

**Guaranteed Logical Delay**

The *guaranteed logical delay* of a message m denotes the maximum time between the logical arrival time of $m$ and its latest valid completion time. It results from the processing time of the messages and the competition among different sessions for resources, i.e., the waiting time of the message. If a message arrives "ahead of schedule" the actual delay is the sum of the logical delay and the time by which it arrives too early. It is then larger than the guaranteed logical delay. It can also be smaller than the logical delay when it is completed "ahead of schedule." The *deadline* $d(m)$ is derived from the delay for the processing of a message $m$ at a resource. The deadline is the sum of the logical arrival time and its logical delay.

**Workahead Messages**

If a message arrives "ahead of schedule" and the resource is in an idle state, the message can be processed immediately. The message is then called a *workahead message*; the process is a workahead process. A maximum *workahead time A* can be specified (e.g., from the application) for each process. This results in a maximum *workahead limit W*:

$$W = A \times R$$

For example:

$A = 0.04s$

$0.04s \times 75\ messages/s = 3\ messages$

If a message is processed "ahead of schedule" the logical backlog is greater than the actual backlog. A message is critical if its logical arrival time has passed. Throughout the rest of the chapter the LBAP model is assumed to apply to the arrival processes at each resource. The resource must ensure that the arrival processes at the output interface obeys the LBAP parameters.

## 9.4 Process Management

Process management deals with the resource main processor. The capacity of this resource is specified as processor capacity. The process manager maps single processes onto resources according to a specified scheduling policy such that all processes meet their requirements. In most systems, a process under control of the process manager can adopt one of the following states:

- In the initial state, no process is assigned to the program. The process is in the idle state.
- If a process is waiting for an event, i.e., the process lacks one of the necessary resources for processing, it is in the blocked state.
- If all necessary resources are assigned to the process, it is ready to run. The process only needs the processor for the execution of the program.
- A process is running as long as the system processor is assigned to it.

The process manager is the *scheduler*. This component transfers a process into the ready-to-run state by assigning it a position in the respective queue of the dispatcher, which is the essential part of the operating system kernel. The dispatcher manages the transition from ready-to-run to run. In most operating systems, the next process to run is chosen according to a priority policy. Between processes with the same priority, the one with the longest ready time is chosen.

Today and in the near future existing operating systems must be considered to be the basis of continuous media processing on workstations and personal computers. In the next four years, there will certainly be no newly developed multimedia operating systems which will be accepted in the market; therefore, existing multitasking systems must cope with multimedia data handling. The next paragraph provides a brief description of real-time support typically available in such systems.

### 9.4.1 Real Time Process Management in Conventional Operating Systems: An Example

UNIX and its variants, Microsoft's Windows-NT, Apple's System 7 and IBM's OS/2™, are, and will be, the most widely installed operating systems with multitasking capabilities on personal computers (including the Power PC) and workstations. Although some of them are enhanced with special priority classes for real-time processes, this is not sufficient for multimedia applications. In [NHNW93], for example, the SVR4 UNIX scheduler which provides a real-time static priority scheduler in addition to a standard UNIX timesharing scheduler is analyzed. For this investigation three applications have been chosen to run concurrently; "typing" as an interactive application, "video" as a continuous media application and a batch program. The result was that only through trial and error a particular combination of priorities and scheduling class assignments might be found that works for a specific application set, i.e., additional features must be provided for the scheduling of multimedia data processing. To be more specific, let us have a deeper look into real-time capabilities of one of these systems, namely OS/2. On the basis of this system, the available real-time support is demonstrated.

#### Threads

OS/2 was designed as a time-sharing operating system without taking serious real-time applications into account. An OS/2 thread can be considered as a light-weight process: it is the dispatchable unit of execution in the operating system. A thread belongs to exactly one address space (called process in OS/2 terminology). All threads share the resources allocated by the respective address space. Each thread has its own execution stack, register values and dispatch state (either executing or ready-to-run). Each thread belongs to one of the following priority classes:

- The time-critical class is reserved for threads that require immediate attention.
- The fixed-high class is intended for applications that require good responsiveness without being time-critical.
- The regular class is used for the executing of normal tasks.
- The idle-time class contains threads with the lowest priorities. Any thread in this class is only dispatched if no thread of any other class is ready to execute.

### Priorities

Within each class, 32 different priorities (0, ... , 31) exist. Through time-slicing, threads of equal priority have equal chances to execute. A context switch occurs whenever a thread tries to access an otherwise allocated resource. The thread with the highest priority is dispatched and the time-slice is started again. At the expiration of the time slice, OS/2 can preempt the dispatched thread if other threads of equal or higher priority are ready to execute. The time slice can be varied between 32 msec and 65536 msec. The goal at the determination of the time slice duration is to keep the number of context switches low and to get a fair and efficient schedule for the whole run-time of the system. Threads of the regular class may be subject to a dynamic rise of priority as a function of the waiting time.

Threads are preemptive, i.e., if a higher-priority thread becomes ready to execute, the scheduler preempts the lower-priority thread and assigns the CPU to the higher-priority thread. The state of the preempted thread is recorded so that execution can be resumed later.

### Physical Device Driver as Process Manager

In OS/2, applications with real-time requirements can run as *Physical Device Drivers (PDD)* at ring 0 (kernel mode). These PDDs can be made non-preemptable. An interrupt that occurs on a device (e.g., packets arriving at the network adapter) can be serviced from the PDD immediately. As soon as an interrupt happens on a device, the PDD gets control and does all the work to handle the interrupt. This may also include tasks which could be done by application processes running in ring 3 (user mode). The task running at ring 0 should (but must not) leave the kernel mode after 4 msec.

PDD programming is complicated mainly due to difficult testing and debugging. PDD is bound to its device; it only handles requests from its device regardless of any other events happening in the system. Different streams that request real-time scheduling can only be served by their PDDs. They run in competition with each other without the possibility of coordinating or managing them by any higher instance. This is insufficient for a multimedia system where messages can arrive at different adapter cards. Internal time-critical system activities cannot be controlled and managed through PDDs. Therefore, they cannot be considered and accounted for during scheduling decisions. The execution of real-time processes with PDDs is only a reasonable solution for a system where streams arrive at only one device and no other activity in the system has to be considered.

Operating system extensions for continuous media processing can be implemented as PDDs. In this approach, a real-time scheduler and the process management run as a PDD being activated by a high resolution timer. In principle, this is the implementation scheme of the OS/2 Multimedia Presentation Manager™, which represents the multimedia extension to OS/2.

### Enhanced System Scheduler as Process Manager

Time-critical tasks can also be processed together with normal applications running in ring 3, the user level. The critical tasks can be implemented by threads running in the priority class time-critical with one of the 32 priorities within this class. Each real-time task is assigned to one thread. A thread is interrupted if another thread with higher priority requires processing. Non-time-critical applications run as threads in the regular class. They are dispatched by the operating system scheduler according to their priority.

The main advantage of this approach is the control and coordination of all time-critical threads through a higher instance, the system scheduler. This instance, running with a higher priority than all other threads, controls and coordinates threads according to the adapted scheduling algorithm and the respective processing requirements. It can observe the run-time behavior of single threads. Another entity, the resource manager, determines feasible schedules, takes care of QoS calculating and resource reservation. The competition for the CPU is regulated. The employment of an internal scheduling strategy and resource management allows the provision of processing guarantees. Yet it requires that the native scheduler be enhanced.

#### Meta-scheduler as Process Manager

The normally priority-driven system scheduler is used to schedule all tasks. A meta-scheduler is employed to assign priorities to real-time tasks, i.e., this meta-scheduler considers only tasks with real-time requirements. Non-time-critical tasks are processed when no time-critical task is ready for execution. In an integrated system the process management of continuous data processes will not be realized as a meta-scheduler; it rather will be part of the system process manager itself. This meta-scheduler approach is also applied in many UNIX systems.

### 9.4.2 Real-time Processing Requirements

Continuous media data processing must occur in exactly predetermined – usually periodic – intervals. Operations on these data recur over and over and must be completed at certain deadlines. The real-time process manager determines a schedule for the resource CPU that allows it to make reservations and to give processing guarantees. The problem is to find a feasible scheduler which schedules all time-critical continuous media tasks in a way that each of them can meet its deadlines. This must be guaranteed for all tasks in every period for the whole run-time of the system. In a multimedia system, continuous and discrete media data are processed concurrently.

For scheduling of multimedia tasks, two conflicting goals must be considered:

- An uncritical process should not suffer from starvation because time-critical processes are executed. Multimedia applications rely as much on text and graphics as on audio and video. Therefore, not all resources should be occupied by the time-critical processes and their management processes.
- On the other hand, a time-critical process must never be subject to priority inversion. The scheduler must ensure that any priority inversion (also between time-critical processes with different priorities) is avoided or reduced as much as possible.

Apart from the overhead caused by the schedulability test and the connection establishment, the costs for the scheduling of every message must be minimized. They are more critical because they occur periodically with every message during the processing of real-time tasks. The overhead generated by the scheduling and operating system is part of the processing time and therefore must be added to the processing time of the real-time tasks. Thus, it is favorable to keep them low. It is particularly difficult to observe the timing behavior of the operating system and its influence on the scheduling and the processing of time-critical data. It can lead to time garbling of application programs. Therefore, operating systems in real-time systems cannot be viewed as detached from the application programs and vice versa.

### 9.4.3 Traditional Real-time Scheduling

The problem of real-time processing is widely known in computer science [HS89, Lev89, SG90, TK91]. Some real-time scheduling methods are employed in operations research. They differ from computer science real-time scheduling because they operate in a static environment where no adaptation to changes of the workload is necessary [WC87].

The goal of traditional scheduling on time-sharing computers is optimal throughput, optimal resource utilization and fair queuing. In contrast, the main goal of real-time tasks is to provide a schedule that allows all, respectively, as many time-critical processes as possible, to be processed in time, according to their deadline. The scheduling algorithm must map tasks onto resources such that all tasks meet their time requirements. Therefore, it must be possible to show, or to proove, that a scheduling algorithm applied to real-time systems fulfills the timing requirements of the task.

There are several attempts to solve real-time scheduling problems. Many of them are just variations of basic algorithms. To find the best solutions for multimedia systems, two basic algorithms are analyzed, *Earliest Deadline First Algorithm* and *Rate Monotonic Scheduling*, and their advantages and disadvantages are elaborated. In the next section, a system model is introduced, and the relevant expressions are explained.

### 9.4.4 Real-time Scheduling: System Model

All scheduling algorithms to be introduced are based on the following system model for the scheduling of real-time tasks. Their essential components are the resources (as discussed previously), tasks and scheduling goals.

A task is a schedulable entity of the system, and it corresponds to the notion of a thread in the previous description. In a hard real-time system, a task is characterized by its timing constraints, as well as by its resource requirements. In the considered case, only periodic tasks without precedence constraints are discussed, i.e., the processing of two tasks is mutually independent. For multimedia systems, this can be assumed without any major restriction. Synchronized data, for example, can be processed by a single process.

The time constraints of the periodic task $T$ are characterized by the following parameters ($s$, $e$, $d$, $p$) as described in [LM80]:

- $s$: Starting point
- $e$: Processing time of $T$
- $d$: Deadline of $T$

- $p$: Period of $T$
- $r$: Rate of $T(r = \frac{1}{p})$

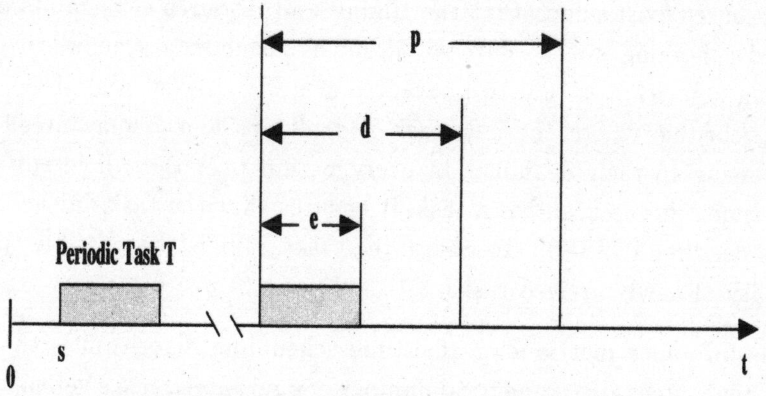


Figure 9.3: *Characterization of periodic tasks.*

whereby $0 \leq e \leq d \leq p$ (see Figure 9.3). The starting point $s$ is the first time when the periodic task requires processing. Afterwards, it requires processing in every period with a processing time of $e$. At $s + (k-1)p$, the task $T$ is ready for $k$-processing. The processing of $T$ in period $k$ must be finished at $s + (k-1)p + d$. For continuous media tasks, it is assumed that the deadline of the period $(k-1)$ is the ready time of period $k$. This is known as *congestion avoiding deadlines*: the deadline for each message ($d$) coincides with the period of the respective periodic task ($p$).

Tasks can be preemptive or non-preemptive. A preemptive task can be interrupted by the request of any task with a higher priority. Processing is continued in the same state later on. A non-preemptive task cannot be interrupted until it voluntarily yields the processor. Any high-priority task must wait until the low-priority task is finished. The high-priority task is then subject to priority inversion. In the following, all tasks processed on the CPU are considered as preemptive unless otherwise stated.

In a real-time system, the scheduling algorithm must determine a schedule for an exclusive, limited resource that is used by different processes concurrently such that all of them can be processed without violating any deadlines. This notion can be extended to a model with multiple resources (e.g., CPU) of the same type. It can also be extended to cover different resources such as memory and bandwidth for communication, i.e., the function of a scheduling algorithm is to determine, for a given task set, whether or not a schedule for executing the tasks on an exclusive bounded resource exists, such that the timing and resource constraints of all tasks are satisfied (planning goal). Further, it must calculate a schedule if one exists. A scheduling algorithm is said to guarantee a newly arrived task if the algorithm can find a schedule where the new task and all previously guaranteed tasks can finish processing to their deadlines in every period over the whole run-time. If a scheduling algorithm guarantees a task, it ensures that the task finishes processing prior to its deadline [CSR88]. To guarantee tasks, it must be possible to check the schedulability of newly arrived tasks.

A major performance metric for a real-time scheduling algorithm is the guarantee ratio. The guarantee ratio is the total number of guaranteed tasks versus the number of tasks which could be processed.

Another performance metric is the processor utilization. This is the amount of processing time used by guaranteed tasks versus the total amount of processing time [LL73]:

$$U = \sum_{i=1}^{n} \frac{e_i}{p_i}$$

### 9.4.5 Earliest Deadline First Algorithm

The *Earliest Deadline First (EDF) algorithm* is one of the best-known algorithms for real-time processing. At every new ready state, the scheduler selects the task with the earliest deadline among the tasks that are ready and not fully processed. The requested resource is assigned to the selected task. At any arrival of a new task (according to the LBAP model), EDF must be computed immediately leading to a new order, i.e., the running task is preempted and the new task is scheduled according to its deadline. The new task is processed immediately if its deadline is earlier than that of the interrupted task. The processing of the interrupted task is continued according to the EDF algorithm later on. EDF is not only an algorithm for periodic tasks, but also for tasks with arbitrary requests, deadlines and service execution times [Der74]. In this case, no guarantee about the processing of any task can be given.

EDF is an *optimal, dynamic* algorithm, i.e., it produces a valid schedule whenever one exists. A dynamic algorithm schedules every instance of each incoming task according to its specific demands. Tasks of periodic processes must be scheduled in each period again. With $n$ tasks which have arbitrary ready-times and deadlines, the complexity is $\Theta(n^2)$.

For a dynamic algorithm like EDF, the upper bound of the processor utilization is 100%. Compared with any static priority assignment, EDF is optimal in the sense that if a set of tasks can be scheduled by any static priority assignment it also can be scheduled by EDF. With a priority-driven system scheduler, each task is assigned a priority according to its deadline. The highest priority is assigned to the task with the earliest deadline; the lowest to the one with the furthest. With every arriving task, priorities might have to be adjusted.

Applying EDF to the scheduling of continuous media data on a single processor machine with priority scheduling, process priorities are likely to be rearranged quite often. A priority is assigned to each task ready for processing according to its deadline. Common systems usually provide only a restricted number of priorities. If the computed priority of a new process is not available, the priorities of other processes must be rearranged until the required priority is free. In the worst case, the priorities of all processes must be rearranged. This may cause considerable overhead. The EDF scheduling algorithm itself makes no use of the previously known occurrence of periodic tasks.

EDF is used by different models as a basic algorithm. An extension of EDF is the *Time-Driven Scheduler* (TDS). Tasks are scheduled according to their deadlines. Further, the TDS is able to handle overload situations. If an overload situation occurs the scheduler aborts tasks which cannot meet their deadlines anymore. If there is still an overload situation, the scheduler removes tasks which have a low "value density." The value density corresponds to the importance of a task for the system.

In [LLSY91] another priority-driven EDF scheduling algorithm is introduced. Here, every task is divided into a *mandatory* and an *optional* part. A task is terminated according to the deadline of the mandatory part, even if it is not completed at this time. Tasks are scheduled with respect to the deadline of the mandatory parts. A set of tasks is said to be schedulable if all tasks can meet the deadlines of their mandatory parts. The optional parts are processed if the resource capacity is not fully utilized. Applying this to continuous media data, the method can be used in combination with the encoding of data according to their importance. Take, for example, a single uncompressed picture in a bitmap format. Each pixel of this monochrome picture is coded with 16 bits. The processing of the eight most significant bits is mandatory, whereas the processing of the least-significant bits can be considered optional. With this method, more processes can be scheduled. In an overload situation, the optional parts are aborted. This implementation leads to decreased quality by media scaling. During QoS requirement specification, the tasks were accepted or informed that scaling may occur. In such a case, scaling QoS parameters can be introduced which reflect the respective implementation. Therefore, this approach avoids errors and improves system performance at the expense of media quality.

### 9.4.6 Rate Monotonic Algorithm

The *rate monotonic scheduling* principle was introduced by Liu and Layland in 1973 [LL73]. It is an optimal, static, priority-driven algorithm for preemptive, periodic jobs. Optimal in this context means that there is no other static algorithm that is able to schedule a task set which cannot be scheduled by the rate monotonic algorithm. A process is scheduled by a static algorithm at the beginning of the processing. Subsequently, each task is processed with the priority calculated at the beginning. No further scheduling is required. The following five assumptions are necessary prerequisites to apply the rate monotonic algorithm:

1. The requests for all tasks with deadlines are periodic, i.e., have constant intervals between consecutive requests.

2. The processing of a single task must be finished before the next task of the same data stream becomes ready for execution. Deadlines consist of runability constraints only, i.e., each task must be completed before the next request occurs.

3. All tasks are independent. This means that the requests for a certain task do not depend on the initiation or completion of requests for any other task.

4. Run-time for each request of a task is constant. Run-time denotes the maximum time which is required by a processor to execute the task without interruption.

5. Any non-periodic task in the system has no required deadline. Typically, they initiate periodic tasks or are tasks for failure recovery. They usually displace periodic tasks.

Further work has shown that not all of these assumptions are mandatory to employ the rate monotonic algorithm [LSST91, SKG91]. Static priorities are assigned to tasks, once at the connection set-up phase, according to their request rates. The priority corresponds to the importance of a task relative to other tasks. Tasks with higher request rates will have higher priorities. The task with the shortest period gets the highest priority and the task with the longest period gets the lowest priority.

The rate monotonic algorithm is a simple method to schedule time-critical, periodic tasks on the respective resource. A task will always meet its deadline, if this can be proven to be true for the longest response time. The *response time* is the time span between the request and the end of processing the task. This time span is maximal when all processes with a higher priority request to be processed at the same time. This case is known as the *critical instant* (see Figure 9.4). In this figure, the priority of $a$ is, according to the rate monotonic algorithm, higher than $b$, and $b$ is higher than $c$. The *critical time zone* is the time interval between the critical instant and the completion of a task.

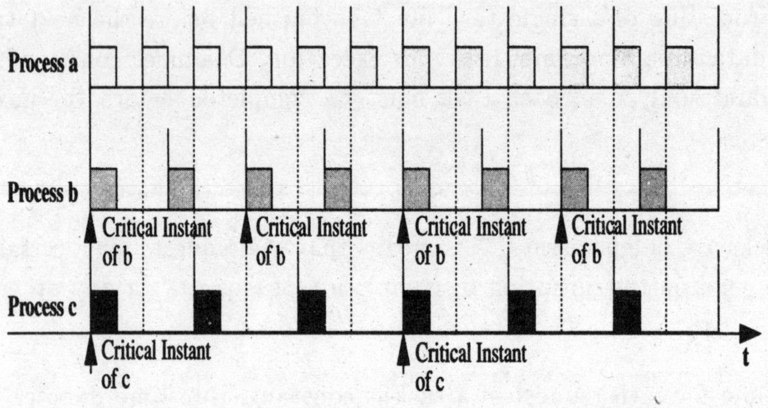


Figure 9.4: *An example of critical instants.*

### 9.4.7 EDF and Rate Monotonic: Context switches

Consider an audio and a video stream scheduled according to the rate monotonic algorithm. Let the audio stream have a rate of 1/75 s/sample and the video stream a rate of 1/25 s/frame. The priority assigned to the audio stream is then higher than the priority assigned to the video stream. The arrival of messages from the audio stream will interrupt the processing of the video stream. If it is possible to complete the processing of a video message that requests processing at the critical instant before its deadline, the processing of all video messages to their deadlines is ensured, thus a feasible schedule exists.

If more than one stream is processed concurrently in a system, it is very likely that there might be more context switches with a scheduler using the rate monotonic algorithm than one using EDF. Figure 9.5 shows an example.

### 9.4.8 EDF and Rate Monotonic: Processor Utilizations

The processor utilization of the rate monotonic algorithm is upper bounded. It depends on the number of tasks which are scheduled, their processing times and their periods. There are two issues to be considered:

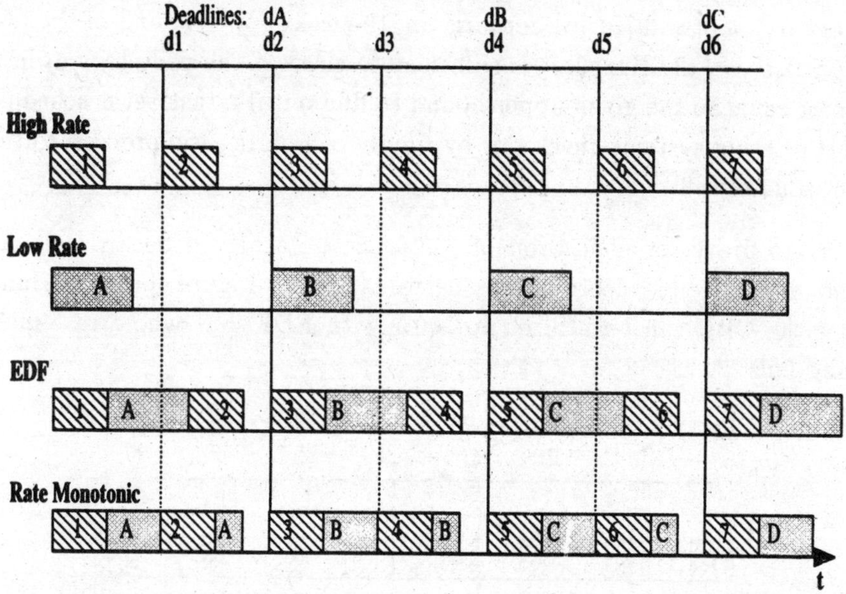


Figure 9.5: *Rate monotonic versus EDF: context switches in preemptive systems.*

1. The upper bound of the processor utilization which is determined by the critical instant.

2. For each number $n$ of independent tasks $t(j)$, a constellation can be found where the maximum possible processor utilization is minimal. The least upper bound of the processor utilization is the minimum of all processor utilizations over all sets of tasks $t(j)$; $j \in (1, ..., n)$ that fully utilize the CPU. A task set fully utilizes the CPU when it is not possible to raise the processing time of one task without violating the schedule.

Following this assumption, [LL73] gives an estimation of the maximal processor utilization where the processing of each task to its deadline is guaranteed for any constellation. A set of $m$ independent, periodic tasks with fixed priority will always meet its deadline if:

$$U(m) = m \times \left(2^{\frac{1}{m}} - 1\right) \geq \frac{e_1}{p_1} + \ldots + \frac{e_m}{p_m}$$

According to [LS86] and [LL73], for large $m$, the least upper bound of the processor utilization is $U = ln2$. Hence, it is sufficient to check if the processor utilization is less than or equal to the given upper bound to find out if a task set is schedulable or not. Most existing systems check this by simply comparing the processor utilization with the value of $ln2$.

With EDF, a processor utilization of 100% can be achieved because all tasks are scheduled dynamically according to their deadlines. Figure 9.6 shows an example where the CPU can be utilized to 100% with EDF, but where rate monotonic scheduling fails.

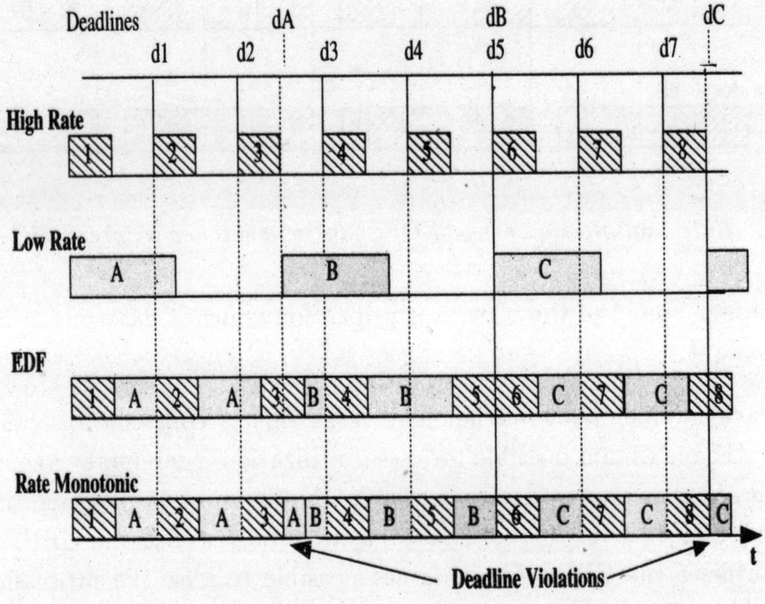


Figure 9.6: *Rate monotonic versus EDF: processor utilization.*

The problem of underutilizing the processor is aggregated by the fact that, in most cases, the average task execution time is considerably lower than the worst case execution time. Therefore, scheduling algorithms should be able to handle transient processor overload. The rate monotonic algorithm on average ensures that all deadlines will be met even if the bottleneck utilization is well above 80%. With one deadline postponement, the deadlines on average are met when the utilization is over 90%. [SSL89] mentions an achieved utilization bound for the Nowy's Inertial

Navigation System of 88%.

As described above, a static algorithm schedules a process once at the beginning of processing. Single tasks are not explicitly scheduled afterwards. A dynamic algorithm schedules every incoming task according to its specific demands. Since the rate monotonic algorithm is an optimal static algorithm, no other static algorithm can achieve a higher processor utilization.

### 9.4.9 Extensions to Rate Monotonic Scheduling

There are several extensions to this algorithm. One of them divides a task into a mandatory and an optional part. The processing of the mandatory part delivers a result which can be accepted by the user. The optional part only refines the result. The mandatory part is scheduled according to the rate monotonic algorithm. For the scheduling of the optional part, other, different policies are suggested [CL88, LLN87, CL89].

In some systems there are aperiodic tasks next to periodic ones. To meet the requirements of periodic tasks and the response time requirements of aperiodic requests, it must be possible to schedule both aperiodic and periodic tasks. If the aperiodic request is an aperiodic continuous stream (e.g., video images as part of a slide show), we have the possibility to transform it into a periodic stream. Every timed data item can be substituted by $n$ items. The new items have the duration of the minimal life span. The number of streams is increased, but since the life span is decreased, the semantic remains unchanged. The stream is now periodical because every item has the same life span [Her90]. If the stream is not continuous, we can apply a sporadic server to respond to aperiodic requests. The server is provided with a computation budget. This budget is refreshed $t$ units of time after it has been exhausted. Earlier refreshing is also possible. The budget represents the computation time reserved for aperiodic tasks. The server is only allowed to preempt the execution of periodic tasks as long as the computation budget is not exhausted. Afterwards, it can only continue the execution with a background priority. After refreshing the budget, the execution can resume at the server's assigned priority. The sporadic server is especially suitable for events that occur rarely, but must be handled quickly (e.g., a telepointer in a CSCW application) [SG90, SSL89, Spr90].

The rate monotonic algorithm is, for example, applied in real-time systems and real-time operating systems by NASA and the European Space Agency [SR89]. It is particularly suitable for continuous media data processing because it makes optimal use of their periodicity. Since it is a static algorithm, there is nearly no rearrangement of priorities and hence – in contrast to EDF – no scheduling overhead to determine the next task with the highest priority. Problems emerge with data streams which have no constant processing time per message, as specified in MPEG-2 (e.g., a compressed video stream where one of five pictures is a full picture and all others are updates of a reference picture). The simplest solution is to schedule these tasks according to their maximum data rate. In this case, the processor utilization is decreasing. The idle time of the CPU can be used to process non-time-critical tasks. In multimedia systems, for example, this is the processing of discrete media.

### 9.4.10 Other Approaches for In-Time Scheduling

Apart from the two methods previously discussed, further scheduling algorithms have been evaluated regarding their suitability for the processing of continuous media data. In the following paragraphs, the most significant approaches are briefly described and the reasons for their non-suitability, compared to EDF and rate-monotonic, are enumerated.

*Least Laxity First (LLF).* The task with the shortest remaining laxity is scheduled first [CW90, LS86]. The laxity is the time between the actual time $t$ and the deadline minus the remaining processing time. The laxity in period $k$ is:

$$l_k = (s + (k-1)p + d) - (t + e)$$

LLF is an *optimal, dynamic* algorithm for *exclusive resources.* Furthermore, it is an optimal algorithm for multiple resources if the ready-times of the real-time tasks are the same. The *laxity* is a function of a deadline, the processing time and the current time. Thereby, the processing time cannot be exactly specified in advance. When calculating the laxity, the worst case is assumed. Therefore, the determination of the laxity is inexact. The laxity of waiting processes dynamically changes over time.

During the run-time of a task, another task may get a lower laxity. This task must then preempt the running task. Consequently, tasks can preempt each other several times without dispatching a new task. This may cause numerous context switches. At each scheduling point (when a process becomes ready-to-run or at the end of a time slice), the laxity of each task must be newly determined. This leads to an additional overhead compared with EDF. Since we have only a single resource to schedule, there is no advantage in the employment of LLF compared with EDF. Future multimedia systems might be multiprocessor systems; here, LLF might be of advantage.

*Deadline Monotone Algorithm.* If the deadlines of tasks are less than their period ($d_i < p_i$), the prerequisites of the rate monotonic algorithm are violated. In this case, a fixed priority assignment according to the deadlines of the tasks is optimal. A task $T_i$ gets a higher priority than a task $T_j$ if $d_i < d_j$. No effective schedulability test for the deadline monotone algorithm exists. To determine the schedulability of a task set, each task must be checked if it meets its deadline in the worst case. In this case, all tasks require execution to their critical instant [LW82, LSST91]. Tasks with a deadline shorter than their period, for example, arise during the measurements of temperature or pressure in control systems. In multimedia systems, deadlines equal to period lengths can be assumed.

*Shortest Job First (SJF).* The task with the shortest remaining computation time is chosen for execution [CW90, Fre82]. This algorithm guarantees that as many tasks as possible meet their deadlines under an overload situation if all of them have the same deadline. In multimedia systems where the resource management allows overload situations this might be a suitable algorithm.

Apart from the most important real-time scheduling methods discussed above, others might be employed for the processing of continuous media data (an on-line scheduler for tasks with unknown ready-times is introduced by [HL88]; in [HS89], a real-time monitoring system is presented where all necessary data to calculate an optimal schedule are available). In most multimedia systems with preemptive tasks, the rate monotonic algorithm in different variations is employed. So far, no other scheduling technique has been proven to be at least as suitable for multimedia data handling as the EDF and rate monotonic approaches.

### 9.4.11 Preemptive versus Non-preemptive Task Scheduling

Real-time tasks can be distinguished into *preemptive* and *non-preemptive* tasks. If a task is *non-preemptive*, it is processed and not interrupted until it is finished or requires further resources. The contrary of non-preemptive tasks are *preemptive tasks.* The processing of a preemptive task is interrupted immediately by a request of any higher-priority task. In most cases where tasks are treated as non-preemptive, the arrival times, processing times and deadlines are arbitrary and unknown to the scheduler until the task actually arrives. The best algorithm is the one which maximizes the number of completed tasks. In this case, it is not possible to provide any processing guarantees or to do resource management.

To guarantee the processing of periodic processes and to get a feasible schedule for a periodic task set, tasks are usually treated as preemptive. One reason is that high preemptability minimizes priority inversion. Another reason is that for some non-preemptive task sets, no feasible schedule can be found; whereas for preemptive scheduling, it is possible. Figure 9.7 shows an example where the scheduling of preemptive tasks is possible, but non-preemptive tasks cannot be scheduled.

Liu and Layland [LL73] show that a task set of $m$ periodic, preemptive tasks with processing times $e_i$ and request periods $p_i$ $\forall i \in (1, ..., m)$ is schedulable:

- With fixed priority assignment if:

  $\sum \frac{e_i}{p_i} \leq \ln 2$

- And for deadline driven scheduling if:

  $\sum \frac{e_i}{p_i} \leq 1$

Here, the preemptiveness of tasks is a necessary prerequisite to check their schedulability.

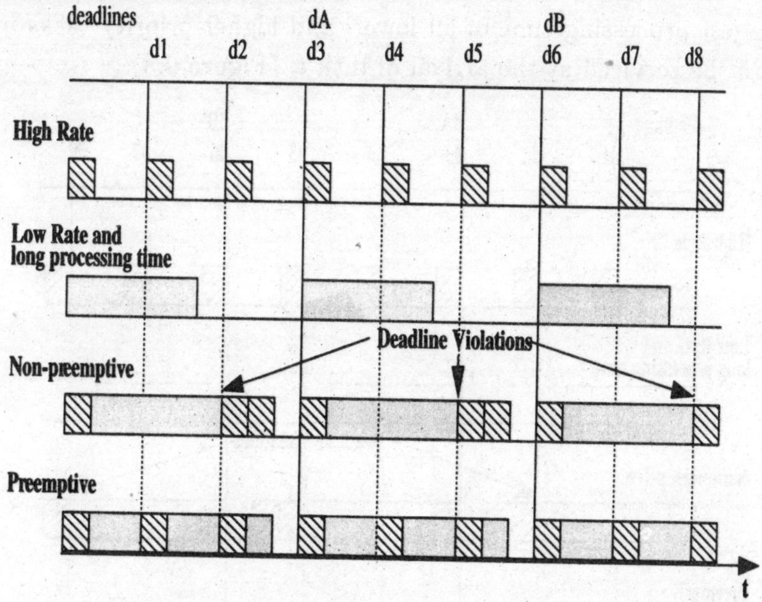


Figure 9.7: *Preemptive vs. non-preemptive scheduling.*

The first schedulability test for the scheduling of *non-preemptive tasks* was introduced by Nagarajan and Vogt in [NV92]. Assume, without loss of generality, that task $m$ has highest priority and task 1 the lowest. They proove that a set of $m$ periodic streams with periods $p_i$, deadlines $d_i$, processing times $e_i$ and $d_i \leq p_i \forall i \in (1, ..., m)$ is schedulable with the non-preemptive fixed priority scheme if:

$$d_m \geq e_m + max_{(1 \leq i \leq m)} e_i$$

$$d_i \geq e_i + max_{(1 \leq j \leq m)} e_j + \sum_{j=i+1}^{m} e_j F(d_i - e_j, p_j)$$

where $F(x, y) = ceil(\frac{x}{y}) + 1$

This means that the time between the logical arrival time and the deadline of a task $t_i$ has to be larger or equal to the sum of its processing time $e_i$ and the processing time of any higher-priority task that requires execution during that time interval, plus the longest processing time of all lower- and higher-priority tasks $max_{(1\leq j\leq m)}$ $e_j$ that might be serviced at the arrival of task $t_i$ (Figure 9.8).

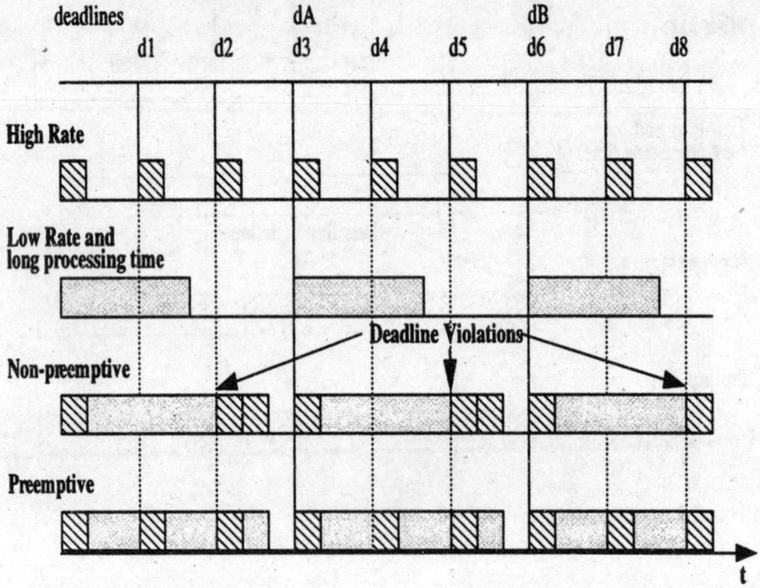


Figure 9.8: *Deadline requirements for non-preemptive scheduling.*

The schedulability test is an extension of Liu's and Layland's. Given $m$ periodic tasks with periods $p_i$ and the same processing time $E$ per message, let $d_i = p_i + E$ be the deadline for task $t_i$. Then, the streams are schedulable:

- With the non-preemptive rate monotonic scheme with:

$$\sum \frac{1}{p_i} \times E \leq \ln 2$$

- With deadline-based scheduling, the same holds with:

$$\sum \frac{1}{p_i} \times E \leq 1$$

Consequently, non-preemptive continuous media tasks can also be scheduled. However, the scheduling of non-preemptive tasks is less favorable because the number of schedulable task sets is smaller compared to preemptive tasks.

### 9.4.12 Scheduling of Continuous Media Tasks: Prototype Operating Systems

Most multimedia operating systems apply one of the previously discussed methods. In some systems, the scheduler is replaced by a real-time scheduler. Therefore, these systems can be viewed as new operating systems. They are usually not compatible with existing systems and applications. Other systems apply a meta-scheduler based on an existing process manager. Only these systems will have a commercial impact in the short and medium terms because they allow existing applications to run.

**ARTS**

The *Advanced Real Time Technology Operating System* is a real-time operating system for a distributed environment with one real-time process manager. It was developed on SUN3 workstations and connected with a real-time network based on the IEEE.802.5 Token Ring and Ethernet by the Computer Science department of Carnegie Mellon University. To solve the scheduling problems, the Time-Driven Scheduler (TDS) with a priority inheritance protocol was adopted. This priority inheritance protocol was used to prevent unbounded priority inversion among communication tasks. Tasks with hard deadlines are scheduled according to the rate monotonic algorithm. The system is also provided with other scheduling methods for experimental reasons [MT90].

**YARTOS**

*Yet Another Real Time Operating System* was developed at the University of North Carolina at Chapel Hill as an operating system kernel to support conferencing applications [JSP91]. An optimal, preemptive algorithm to schedule tasks on a single processor was developed. The scheduling algorithm results from the integration of a synchronization scheme to access shared resources with the EDF algorithm. Here, a task has two notions of deadline, one for the initial acquisition of the processor, and one for the execution of operations on resources. To avoid priority inversion, tasks are provided with separate deadlines for performing operations on shared resources. It is guaranteed that no shared resource is accessed simultaneously by more than one task. Further, a shared resource is not occupied by a single task longer than absolutely necessary.

### Split-level Scheduling

The *split-level scheduler* was developed within the DASH project at the University of California at Berkeley. Its main goal was to provide a better support for multimedia applications [And93]. The applied scheduling policy is deadline/workahead scheduling. The LBAP-model is used to describe arrival processes. Critical processes have priority over all other processes and they are scheduled according to the EDF algorithm preemptively. Interactive processes have priority over workahead processes as long as they do not become critical. The scheduling policy for workahead processes is unspecified, but may be chosen to minimize context switching. For non-real-time processes, a scheduling strategy like UNIX time-slicing is chosen.

### Three Class Scheduler

This scheduler was developed as part of a video-on-demand file servicer at DEC, Littleton. The design of the scheduler is based on a combination of weighted round-robin and rate monotonic scheduling [RVG+93]. Three classes of schedulable tasks are supported. The isochronous class with the highest priority applies the rate monotonic algorithm, the real-time and the general-purpose classes use the weighted round-robin scheme. A general-purpose task is preemptive and runs with a low priority. The real-time class is suitable for tasks that require guaranteed throughput and bounded delay. The isochronous class supports real-time periodic tasks that require performance guarantees for throughput, bounded latency and low jitter. Real-time and isochronous tasks can only be preempted in "preemption windows."

The scheduler executes tasks from a ready queue in which all isochronous tasks are arranged according to their priority. At the arrival of a task, the scheduler determines whether the currently running task must be preempted. General-purpose tasks are immediately preempted, real-time tasks are preempted in the next preemption window and isochronous tasks are preempted in the next preemption window if their priority is lower than the one of the new task. Whenever the queue is empty, the scheduler alternates between the real-time and general-purpose classes using a weighted round-robin scheme.

### Meta-scheduler

To support real-time processing of continuous media, a meta-scheduler for the operating systems AIX™[WBV92] and OS/2 [MSS92] was developed at the European Networking Center of IBM in Heidelberg. Both are based on the LBAP model. According to the rate monotonic algorithm, rates are mapped onto system priorities.

### Experience with the Meta-scheduler Approach

In this paragraph, the employment of the OS/2 meta-scheduler is discussed [MSS92]. Experience shows the limits of this approach. For example, each process in the system is able to run with a priority initially intended for real-time tasks. These processes are not scheduled by the resource manager and therefore violate the calculated schedule. A malicious process can block the whole system by simply running with the highest priority without giving up control.

The management of scheduling algorithms requires exact time measurement. In OS/2, for example, it is not possible to measure the exact time a thread is using the CPU. Any measurement of the processing time includes interrupts. If a process is interrupted by another process, it also includes the time needed for the context switch. The granularity of the OS/2 system timers is insufficient for the processing of real-time tasks. Hence, the rate control is inaccurate because it is determined by the granularity of the system timer.

To achieve full real-time capabilities, at least the native scheduler of the operating system would must be extended. The operating system should be enhanced by a class of fast, non-preemptive threads and the ability to mask interrupts for a short period of time. Priorities in this thread class should only be assigned to threads that are already registered by the resource manager. This class should be reserved exclusively for selected threads and monitored by a system component with extensive control facilities. Performance enhancement of the scheduler itself, incorporating some mechanisms of real-time scheduling like EDF, would be another solution. The operating system should, in any case, provide a time measurement tool that allows the measurement of pure CPU time and a timer with a finer granularity. This may be achieved through a timer chip.

## 9.5 File Systems

The *file system* is said to be the most visible part of an operating system. Most programs write or read files. Their program code, as well as user data, are stored in files. The organization of the file system is an important factor for the usability and convenience of the operating system. A file is a sequence of information held as a unit for storage and use in a computer system [Kra88].

Files are stored in secondary storage, so they can be used by different applications. The life-span of files is usually longer than the execution of a program. In traditional file systems, the information types stored in files are sources, objects, libraries and executables of programs, numeric data, text, payroll records, etc. [PS83]. In multimedia systems, the stored information also covers digitized video and audio with their related real-time "read" and "write" demands. Therefore, additional requirements in the design and implementation of file systems must be considered.

The file system provides access and control functions for the storage and retrieval of files. From the user's viewpoint, it is important how the file system allows file organization and structure. The internals, which are more important in our context, i.e., the organization of the file system, deal with the representation of information in files, their structure and organization in secondary storage. Because of its importance for multimedia, disk scheduling is also presented in this context.

The next section starts with a brief characterization of traditional file systems and disk scheduling algorithms. Subsequently, different approaches to organize multimedia files and disk scheduling algorithms for the use in multimedia systems are discussed.

## 9.5.1 Traditional File Systems

The two main goals of traditional files systems are: (1) to provide a comfortable interface for file access to the user, and (2) to make efficient use of storage media. Whereas the first goal is still an area of interest for research (e.g., indexing for file systems [Sal91] and intelligent file systems for the content-based associative access to file system data [GO91]), the structure, organization and access of data stored on disk have been extensively discussed and investigated over the last decades. To understand the specific multimedia developments in this area, this section gives a brief overview on files, file system organizations and file access mechanisms. Later, disk scheduling algorithms for file retrieval are discussed.

### File Structure

We commonly distinguish between two methods of file organization. In sequential storage, each file is organized as a simple sequence of bytes or records. Files are stored consecutively on the secondary storage media as shown in Figure 9.9 . They

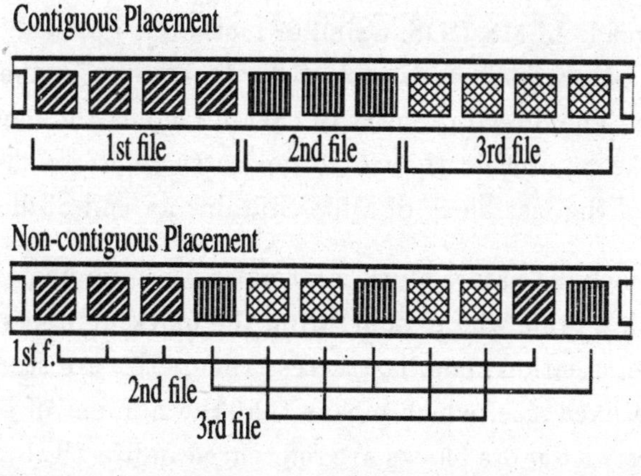


Figure 9.9: Contiguous and non-contiguous storage.

are separated from each other by a well defined "end of file" bit pattern, character or character sequence. A file descriptor is usually placed at the beginning of the file and is, in some systems, repeated at the end of the file. Sequential storage is the only possible way to organize the storage on tape, but it can also be used on disks. The main advantage is its efficiency for sequential access, as well as for direct access [Kra88]. Disk access time for reading and writing is minimized.

Additionally, for further improvement of performance with caching, the file can be read ahead of the user program [Jan85]. In systems where file creation, deletion and size modification occur frequently, sequential storage has major disadvantages. Secondary storage is split and fragmented, through creation and deletion operations, and files cannot be extended without copying the whole files into a larger space. The files may be copied such that all files are adjacently located, i.e., without any "holes" between them.

In non-sequential storage, the data items are stored in a non-contiguous order. There exist mainly two approaches:

- One way is to use linked blocks, where physical blocks containing consecutive logical locations are linked using pointers. The file descriptor must contain the number of blocks occupied by the file, the pointer to the first block and it may also have the pointer to the last block. A serious disadvantage of this method is the cost of the implementation for random access because all prior data must be read. In MS-DOS, a similar method is applied. A *File Allocation Table (FAT)* is associated with each disk. One entry in the table represents one disk block. The directory entry of each file holds the block number of the first block. The number in the slot of an entry refers to the next block of a file. The slot of the last block of a file contains an end-of-file mark [Tan87].
- Another approach is to store block information in mapping tables. Each file is associated with a table where, apart from the block numbers, information like owner, file size, creation time, last access time, etc., are stored. Those tables usually have a fixed size, which means that the number of block references is bounded. Files with more blocks are referenced indirectly by additional tables assigned to the files. In UNIX, a small table (on disk) called an i-node is associated with each file (see Figure 9.10). The indexed sequential approach is an example for multi-level mapping; here, logical and physical organization

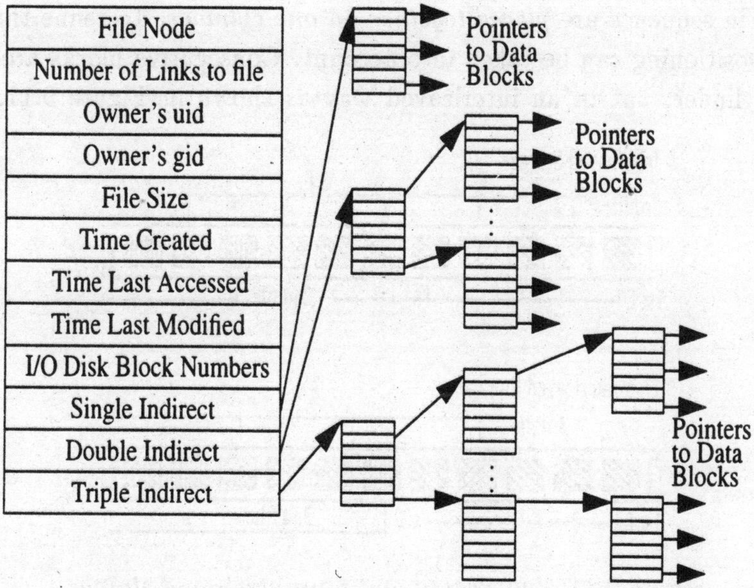


Figure 9.10: *The UNIX i-node [Tane87].*

are not clearly separated [Kra88].

### Directory Structure

Files are usually organized in *directories.* Most of today's operating systems provide tree-structured directories where the user can organize the files according to his/her personal needs. In multimedia systems, it is important to organize the files in a way that allows easy, fast, and contiguous data access.

### Disk Management

Disk access is a slow and costly transaction. In traditional systems, a common technique to reduce disk access are *block caches.* Using a block cache, blocks are kept in memory because it is expected that future read or write operations access these data again. Thus, performance is enhanced due to shorter access time. Another way to enhance performance is to reduce disk arm motion. Blocks that are likely to be accessed in sequence are *placed together on one cylinder*. To refine this method, rotational positioning can be taken into account. Consecutive blocks are placed on the same cylinder, but in an interleaved way as shown in Figure 9.11. Another

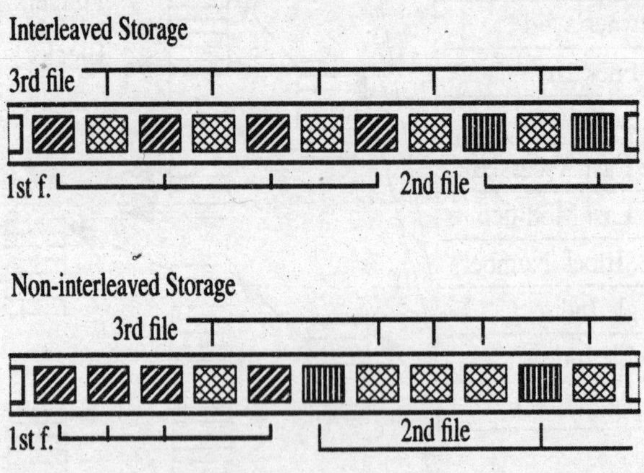


Figure 9.11: *Interleaved and non-interleaved storage.*

important issue is the placement of the mapping tables (e.g., I-nodes in UNIX) on the disk. If they are placed near the beginning of the disk, the distance between them and the blocks will be, on average, half the number of cylinders. To improve this, they can be placed in the middle of the disk. Hence, the average seek time is roughly reduced by a factor of two. In the same way, consecutive blocks should be placed on the same cylinder. The use of the same cylinder for the storage of mapping tables and referred blocks also improves performance.

### Disk Scheduling

Whereas strictly sequential storage devices (e.g., tapes) do not have a scheduling problem, for random access storage devices, every file operation may require movements of the read/write head. This operation, known as "to seek," is very time consuming, i.e., a *seek time* in the order of 250 ms for CDs is still state-of-the-art. The actual time to read or write a disk block is determined by:

- The seek time (the time required for the movement of the read/write head).

- The latency time or rotational delay (the time during which the transfer cannot proceed until the right block or sector rotates under the read/write head).
- The actual data transfer time needed for the data to copy from disk into main memory.

Usually the seek time is the largest factor of the actual transfer time. Most systems try to keep the cost of seeking low by applying special algorithms to the scheduling of disk read/write operations. The access of the storage device is a problem greatly influenced by the file allocation method. For instance, a program reading a contiguously allocated file generates requests which are located close together on a disk. Thus head movement is limited. Linked or indexed files with blocks, which are widely scattered, cause many head movements. In multi-programming systems, where the disk queue may often be non-empty, fairness is also a criterion for scheduling. Most systems apply one of the following scheduling algorithms:

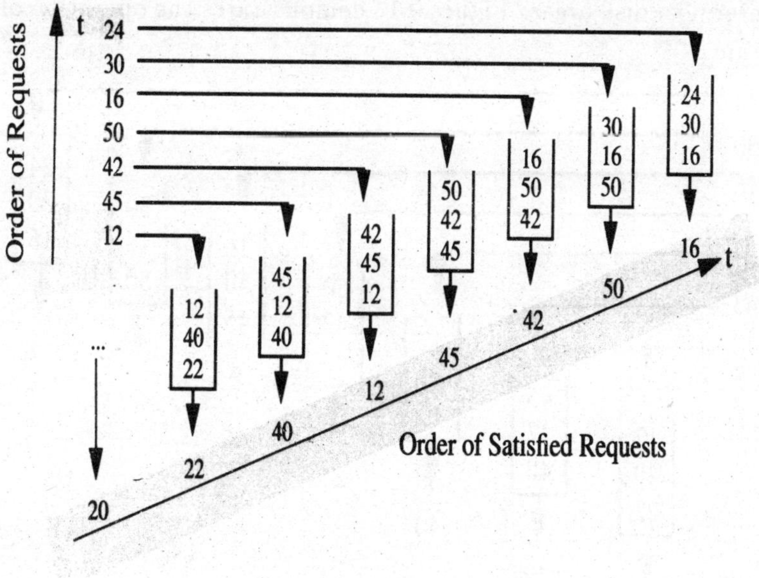


Figure 9.12: *FCFS disk scheduling.*

- *First-Come-First-Served (FCFS)*

With this algorithm, the disk driver accepts requests one-at-a-time and serves them in incoming order. This is easy to program and an intrinsically fair algorithm. However, it is not optimal with respect to head movement because it does not consider the location of the other queued requests. This results in a high average seek time. Figure 9.12 shows an example of the application of FCFS to a request of three queued blocks.

- *Shortest-Seek-Time First (SSTF)*

At every point in time, when a data transfer is requested, SSTF selects among all requests the one with the minimum seek time from the current head position. Therefore, the head is moved to the closest track in the request queue. This algorithm was developed to minimize seek time and it is in this sense optimal. SSTF is a modification of Shortest Job First (SJF), and like SJF, it may cause starvation of some requests. Request targets in the middle of the disk will get immediate service at the expense of requests in the innermost and outermost disk areas. Figure 9.13 demonstrates the operation of the SSTF algorithm.

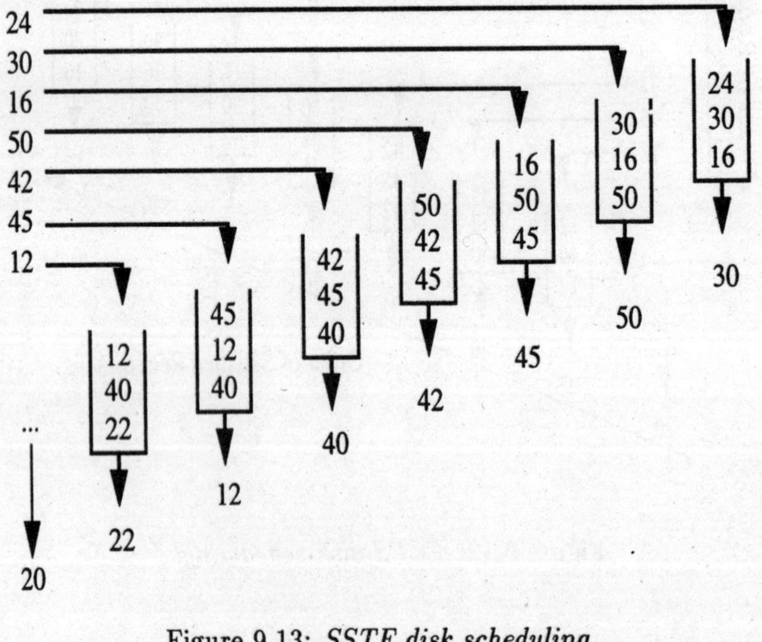


Figure 9.13: *SSTF disk scheduling.*

- *SCAN*

  Like SSTF, SCAN orders requests to minimize seek time. In contrast to SSTF, it takes the direction of the current disk movement into account. It first serves all requests in one direction until it does not have any requests in this direction anymore. The head movement is then reversed and service is continued. SCAN provides a very good seek time because the edge tracks get better service times. Note that middle tracks still get a better service then edge tracks. When the head movement is reversed, it first serves tracks that have recently been serviced, where the heaviest density of requests, assuming a uniform distribution, is at the other end of the disk. Figure 9.14 shows an example of the SCAN algorithm.

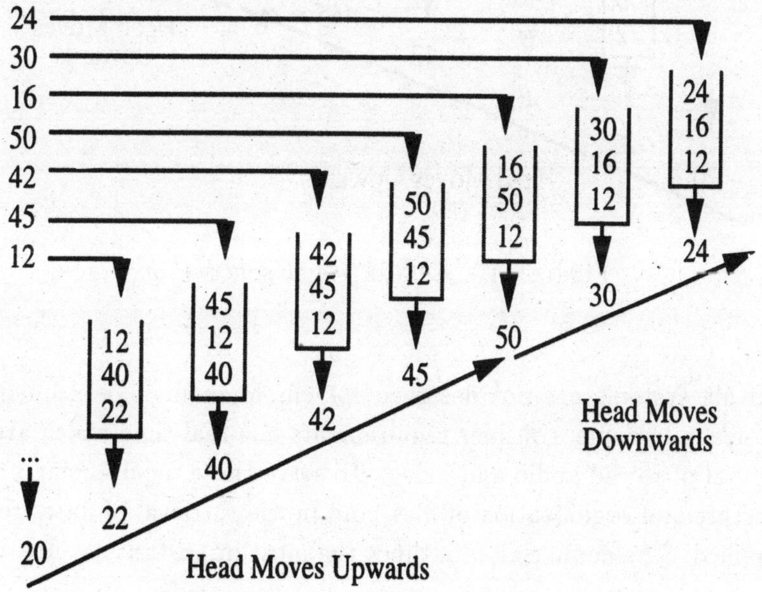


Figure 9.14: *SCAN disk scheduling.*

- *C-SCAN*

  C-SCAN also moves the head in one direction, but it offers fairer service with more uniform waiting times. It does not alter the direction, as in SCAN. Instead, it scans in cycles, always increasing or decreasing, with one idle head movement from one edge to the other between two consecutive scans. The performance of C-SCAN is somewhat less than SCAN. Figure 9.15 shows the operation of the C-SCAN algorithm.

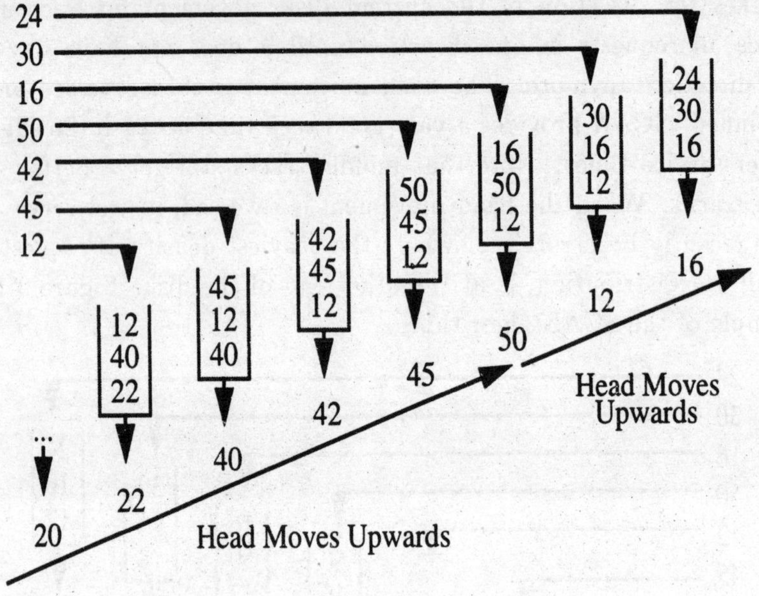


Figure 9.15: *C-SCAN disk scheduling.*

Traditional file systems are not designed for employment in multimedia systems. They do not, for example, consider requirements like real-time which are important to the retrieval of stored audio and video. To serve these requirements, new policies in the structure and organization of files, and in the retrieval of data from the disk, must be applied. The next section outlines the most important developments in this area.

### 9.5.2 Multimedia File Systems

Compared to the increased performance of processors and networks, storage devices have become only marginally faster [Mul91]. The effect of this increasing speed mismatch is the search for new storage structures, and storage and retrieval mechanisms with respect to the file system. Continuous media data are different from discrete data in:

- *Real Time Characteristics*

  As mentioned previously, the retrieval, computation and presentation of continuous media is time-dependent. The data must be presented (read) before a well-defined deadline with small jitter only. Thus, algorithms for the storage and retrieval of such data must consider time constraints, and additional buffers to smooth the data stream must be provided.

- *File Size*

  Compared to text and graphics, video and audio have very large storage space requirements. Since the file system has to store information ranging from small, unstructured units like text files to large, highly structured data units like video and associated audio, it must organize the data on disk in a way that efficiently uses the limited storage. For example, the storage requirements of uncompressed CD-quality stereo audio are 1.4 Mbits/s; low but acceptable quality compressed video still requires about 1Mbit/s using, e.g., MPEG-1.

- *Multiple Data Streams*

  A multimedia system must support different media at one time. It does not only have to ensure that all of them get a sufficient share of the resources, it also must consider tight relations between different streams arriving from different sources. The retrieval of a movie, for example, requires the processing and synchronization of audio and video.

There are different ways to support continuous media in file systems. Basically there are two approaches. With the first approach, the organization of files on disk remains as is. The necessary real-time support is provided through special disk scheduling algorithms and sufficient buffer to avoid jitter. In the second approach, the organization of audio and video files on disk is optimized for their use in multimedia systems. Scheduling of multiple data streams still remains an issue of research.

In this section, the different approaches are discussed and examples of existing prototypes are introduced. First, a brief introduction of the different storage devices employed in multimedia systems is given. Then, the organization of files on disks is discussed. Subsequently, different disk scheduling algorithms for the retrieval of continuous media are introduced.

### Storage Devices

The storage subsystem is a major component of any information system. Due to the immense storage space requirements of continuous media, conventional magnetic storage devices are often not sufficient. Tapes, still in use in some traditional systems, are inadequate for multimedia systems because they cannot provide independent accessible streams, and random access is slow and expensive.

Apart from common disks with large capacity, some multimedia applications, such as kiosk systems, use CD-ROMs to store data. In general, disks can be characterized in two different ways:

- First, how information is stored on them. There are re-writeable (magnetic and optical) disks, write-once (WORM) disks and read-only disks like CD-ROMs.
- The second distinctive feature is the method of recording. It is distinguished between magnetic and optical disks. The main differences between them are the access time and track capacity. The seek time on magnetic disks is typically above 10 ms, whereas on optical disks, 200 ms is a common lower bound. Magnetic disks have a constant rotation speed (Constant Angular Velocity, CAV). Thus, while the density varies, the storage capacity is the same on inner and outer tracks. Optical disks have varying rotation speed (Constant Linear Velocity, CLV) and hence, the storage density is the same on the whole disk.

Therefore, different algorithms for magnetic and optical disks are necessary. File systems on CD-ROMs are defined in ISO 9660. They are considered to be closely related to CD-ROMs and CD-ROM-XA. Very few variations are possible. Hence, we will focus the description on algorithms applicable to magnetic storage devices.

### File Structure and Placement on Disk

In conventional file systems, the main goal of the file organization is to make efficient use of the storage capacity (i.e., to reduce internal and external fragmentation) and to allow arbitrary deletion and extension of files. In multimedia systems, the main goal is to *provide a constant and timely retrieval of data.* Internal fragmentation occurs when blocks of data are not entirely filled. On average, the last block of a file is only half utilized. The use of large blocks leads to a larger waste of storage due to this internal fragmentation. External fragmentation mainly occurs when files are stored in a contiguous way. After the deletion of a file, the gap can only be filled by a file with the same or a smaller size. Therefore, there are usually small fractions between two files that are not used, storage space for continuous media is wasted.

As mentioned above, the goals for multimedia file systems can be achieved through providing enough buffer for each data stream and the employment of disk scheduling algorithms, especially optimized for real-time storage and retrieval of data. The advantage of this approach (where data blocks of single files are scattered) is flexibility. External fragmentation is avoided and the same data can be used by several streams (via references). Even using only one stream might be of advantage; for instance, it is possible to access one block twice, e.g., when a phrase in a sonata is repeated. However, due to the large seek operations during playback, even with optimized disk scheduling, large buffers must be provided to smooth jitter at the data retrieval phase. Therefore, there are also long initial delays at the retrieval of continuous media.

Another problem in this context is the *restricted transfer rate.* With upcoming disk arrays, which might have 100 and more parallel heads, the projected seek and latency times of less than 10 ms and a block size of 4 Kbytes at a transfer rate of 0.32 Gigabit/s will be achieved. But this is, for example, not sufficient for the simultaneous retrieval of four or more production-level MPEG-2 videos compressed in HDTV-quality that may require transfer rates of up to 100 Mbit/s. [Ste94a].

Approaches which use specific disk layout take the specialized nature of continuous media data into account to minimize the cost of retrieving and storing streams. The much greater size of continuous media files and the fact that they will usually be retrieved sequentially because of the nature of the operation performed on them (such as play, pause, fast forward, etc.) are reasons for an optimization of the disk layout. Our own application-related experience has shown that continuous media streams predominantly belong to the write-once-read-many nature, and streams that are recorded at the same time are likely to be played back at the same time (e.g., audio and video of a movie) [LS93]. Hence, it seems to be reasonable to store continuous media data in large data blocks contiguously on disk. Files that are likely to be retrieved together are grouped together on the disk. Thus, interference due to concurrent access of these files is minimized. With such a disk layout, the buffer requirements and seek times decrease.

The disadvantage of the contiguous approach is external fragmentation and copying overhead during insertion and deletion. To avoid this without scattering blocks in a random manner over the disk, a multimedia file system can provide constrained block allocation of the continuous media. In [GC92], different placement strategies were compared. The size of the blocks ($M$) and the size of the gaps ($G$) between them can be derived from the requirement of continuity. The size is measured in terms of sectors. We assume that the data transfer rate $r_{dt}$ is the same as the disk rotation rate ($sectors/s$). The continuity requirement in this case is met if the time to skip over a gap and to read the next media block does not exceed the duration of its playback $T_{play}(s)$ [RKV92]:

$$T_{play}(s) \geq \frac{M(sectors)+G(sectors)}{r_{dt}(sectors/s)}$$

Since there are two variables in the equation, the storage pattern ($M$, $G$) is not unique. There are several combinations possible to satisfy the above equation. Problems occur if the disk is not sufficiently empty, so that single data streams cannot be stored exactly according to their storage pattern. In this case, the continuity requirements for each block are not strictly maintained. To serve the continuity requirements, read-ahead and buffering of a determined number of blocks must be introduced. See, for example, [RV91, RKV92, VR93] for a detailed description of this storage method.

Some systems using scattered storage make use of a special disk space allocation mechanism to allow fast and efficient access. Abbott performed the pioneer work in this field [Abb84]. He was especially concerned about the size of single blocks and their positions on disk. Another topic to be considered is the placement of different streams. With interleaved placement, all $n$'th blocks of each stream are in close physical proximity on disk. A contiguous interleaved placement is possible, as well as a scattered interleaved placement. With interleaved data streams, synchronization is much easier to handle. On the other hand, the insertion and deletion of single parts of data streams become more complicated.

In [KWY94], a layout algorithm was developed and analyzed which provides a uniform distribution of media blocks on the disk after copying or writing audio and video files. It takes into account that further files will be merged. Therefore, a set of non-filled gaps is left. This uniform distribution is achieved by storing new blocks at the center of existing – so far – non-filled gaps. With this "central merging method" gaps are successively split into two new equal gaps. It was shown that the mean efficiency of the secondary storage usage with this algorithm was about 75% without violation of any real-time constraint [KWY94].

### Disk Scheduling Algorithms

The main goals of traditional disk scheduling algorithms are to reduce the cost of seek operations, to achieve a high throughput and to provide fair disk access for every process. The additional real-time requirements introduced by multimedia systems make traditional disk scheduling algorithms, such as described previously, inconvenient for multimedia systems. Systems without any optimized disk layout for the storage of continuous media depend far more on reliable and efficient disk scheduling algorithms than others. In the case of contiguous storage, scheduling is only needed to serve requests from multiple streams concurrently. In [LS93], a round-robin scheduler is employed that is able to serve hard real-time tasks. Here, additional optimization is provided through the close physical placement of streams that are likely to be accessed together.

The overall goal of disk scheduling in multimedia systems is to meet the deadlines of all time-critical tasks. Closely related is the goal of keeping the necessary buffer space requirements low. As many streams as possible should be served concurrently, but aperiodic requests should also be schedulable without delaying their service for an infinite amount of time. The scheduling algorithm must find a balance between time constraints and efficiency.

### Earliest Deadline First

Let us first look at the EDF scheduling strategy as described for CPU scheduling, but used for the file system issue as well. Here the block of the stream with the nearest deadline would be read first. The employment of EDF, as shown in Figure 9.16, in the strict sense results in poor throughput and excessive seek time. Further,

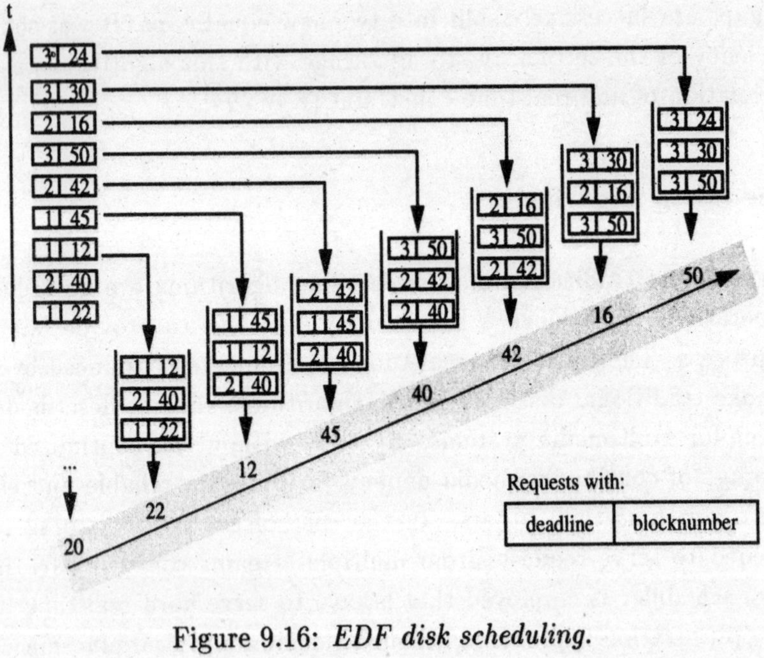


Figure 9.16: *EDF disk scheduling.*

as EDF is most often applied as a preemptive scheduling scheme, the costs for preemption of a task and scheduling of another task are considerably high. The overhead caused by this is in the same order of magnitude as at least one disk seek. Hence, EDF must be adapted or combined with file system strategies.

### SCAN-Earliest Deadline First

The SCAN-EDF strategy is a combination of the SCAN and EDF mechanisms [RW93]. The seek optimization of SCAN and the real-time guarantees of EDF are combined in the following way: like in EDF, the request with the earliest deadline is always served first; among requests with the same deadline, the specific one that is first according to the scan direction is served first; among the remaining requests, this principle is repeated until no request with this deadline is left.

Since the optimization only applies for requests with the same deadline, its efficiency depends on how often it can be applied (i.e., how many requests have the same or a similar deadline). To increase this probability, the following tricky technique can be used: all requests have release times that are multiples of the period $p$. Hence, all requests have deadlines that are multiples of the period $p$. Therefore, the requests can be grouped together and be served accordingly. For requests with different data rate requirements, in addition to SCAN-EDF, the employment of a periodic fill policy is proposed [YV92] to let all requests have the same deadline. With this policy, all requests are served in cycles. In every cycle, each request gets an amount of service time that is proportional to its required data rate. The cycle length is equal to the sum of the service times of all requests. Thus, in every cycle, all requests can be given a deadline at the end of the cycle.

SCAN-EDF can be easily implemented. Therefore, EDF must be modified slightly. If $D_i$ is the deadline of task i and $N_i$ is the track position, the deadline can be modified to be $D_i + f(N_i)$. Thus the deadline is deferred. The function $f()$ converts the track number of $i$ into a small perturbation of the deadline, as shown in the example of Figure 9.17. It must be small enough so that $D_i + f(N_i) \leq D_j + f(N_j)$ holds for all $D_i \leq D_j$. For $f(N_i)$, it was proposed to choose the following function [RW93]:

$$f(N_i) = \frac{N_i}{N_{max}}$$

where $N_{max}$ is the maximum track number on disk. Other functions might also be appropriate.

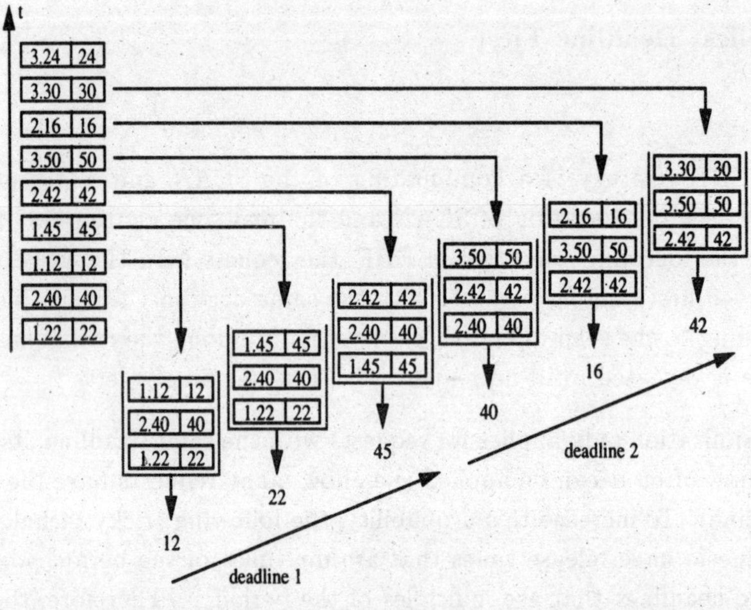


Figure 9.17: *SCAN-EDF disk scheduling with* $N_{max} = 100$ *and* $f(N_i) = N_i/N_{max}$.

We enhanced this mechanism by proposing a more accurate perturbation of the deadline which takes into account the actual position of the head ($N$). This position is measured in terms of block numbers and the current direction of the head movement (see also Figures 9.18 and 9.19):

1. If the head moves toward $N_{max}$, i.e., upward, then

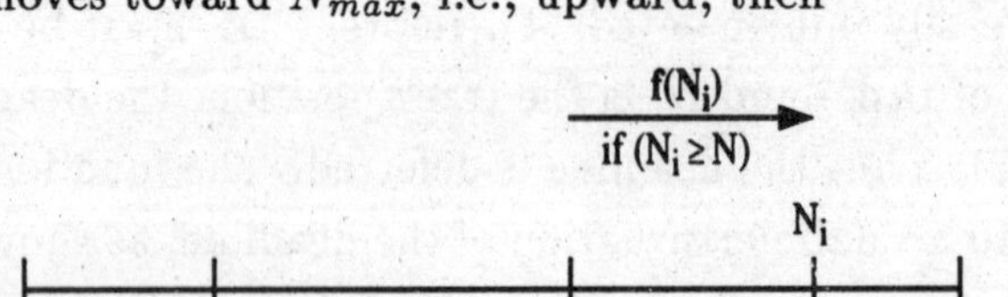


Figure 9.18: *Accurate EDF-SCAN algorithm, head moves upward.*

   (a) for all blocks $N_i$ located between the actual position N and $N_{max}$, the perturbation of the deadline is:

$$f(N_i) = \frac{N_i - N}{N_{max}} \; for \; all \; N_i \geq N$$

(b) for all blocks $N_i$ located between the actual position and the first block (no. 0):

$$f(N_i) = \frac{N_{max} - N_i}{N_{max}} \; for \; all \; N_i < N$$

2. If the head moves downward towards the first blocks, then

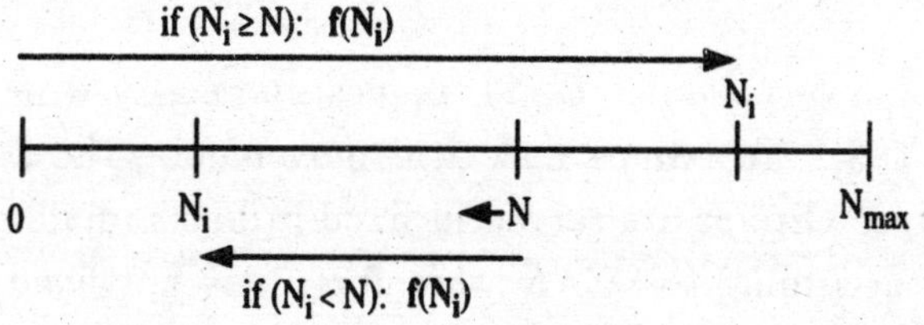


Figure 9.19: *Accurate EDF-SCAN algorithm, head moves downward.*

(a) for all blocks located between the actual position and $N_{max}$:

$$f(N_i) = \frac{N_i}{N_{max}} \; for \; all \; N_i > N$$

(b) for all blocks located between this first block with the block number 0 and the actual position:

$$f(N_i) = \frac{N - N_i}{N_{max}} \; for \; all \; N_i \leq N$$

Our algorithm is more computing-intensive than those with the simple calculation of [RW93]. In cases with only a few equal deadlines, our algorithm provides improvements and the expenses of the calculations can be tolerated. In situations with many, i.e., typically more than five equal deadlines, the simple calculation provides sufficient optimization and additional calculations should be avoided. SCAN-EDF was compared with pure EDF and different variations of SCAN. It was shown that SCAN-EDF with deferred deadlines performed well in multimedia environments [RW93].

### Group Sweeping Scheduling

With *Group Sweeping Scheduling (GSS)*, requests are served in cycles, in round-robin manner [CKY93]. To reduce disk arm movements, the set of $n$ streams is divided into $g$ groups. Groups are served in fixed order. Individual streams within a group are served according to SCAN; therefore, it is not fixed at which time or order individual streams within a group are served. In one cycle, a specific stream may be the first to be served; in another cycle, it may be the last in the same group. A smoothing buffer which is sized according to the cycle time and data rate of the stream assures continuity. If the SCAN scheduling strategy is applied to all streams of a cycle without any grouping, the playout of a stream cannot be started until the end of the cycle of its first retrieval (where all requests are served once) because the next service may be in the last slot of the following cycle. As the data must be buffered in GSS, the playout can be started at the end of the group in which the first retrieval takes place. Whereas SCAN requires buffers for all streams, in GSS, the buffer can be reused for each group. Further optimizations of this scheme are proposed in [CKY93]. In this method, it is ensured that each stream is served once in each cycle. GSS is a trade-off between the optimization of buffer space and arm movements. To provide the requested guarantees for continuous media data, we propose here to introduce a "joint deadline" mechanism: we assign to each group of streams one deadline, the "joint deadline." This deadline is specified as being the earliest one out of the deadlines of all streams in the respective group. Streams are grouped in such a way that all of them comprise similar deadlines. Figure 9.20 shows an example of GSS.

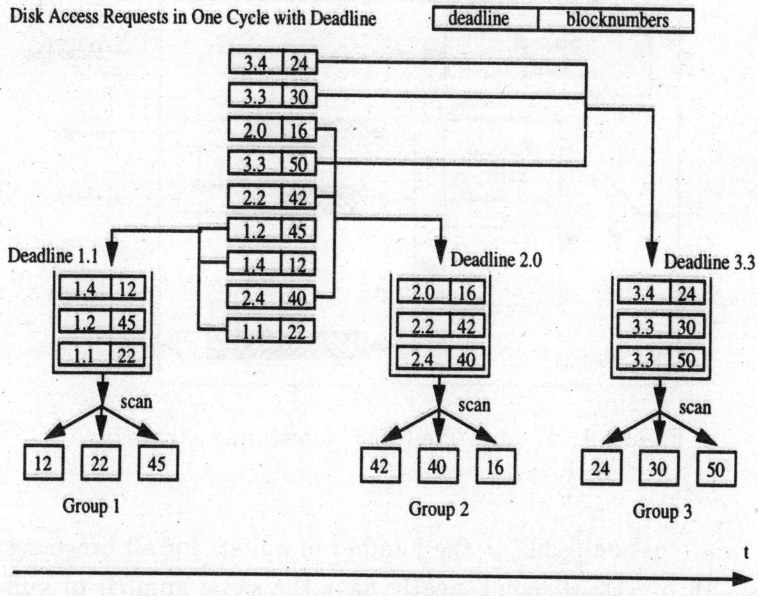


Figure 9.20: *Group sweeping scheduling as a disk access strategy.*

### Mixed Strategy

In [Abb84], a *mixed strategy* was introduced based on the *shortest seek* (also called greedy strategy) and the *balanced strategy.* As shown in Figure 9.21, every time data are retrieved from disk they are transferred into buffer memory allocated for the respective data stream. From there, the application process removes them one at a time. The goal of the scheduling algorithm is:

- To maximize transfer efficiency by minimizing seek time and latency.
- To serve process requirements with a limited buffer space.

With shortest seek, the first goal is served, i.e., the process of which data block is closest is served first. The balanced strategy chooses the process which has the least amount of buffered data for service because this process is likely to run out of data. The crucial part of this algorithm is the decision of which of the two strategies must be applied (shortest seek or balanced strategy). For the employment of shortest,

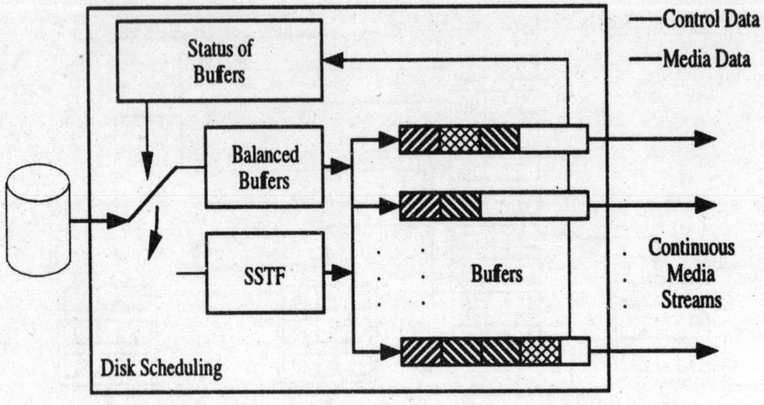


Figure 9.21: em Mixed disk scheduling strategy.

seek two criteria must be fulfilled: the number of buffers for all processes should be balanced (i.e., all processes should nearly have the same number of buffered data) and the overall required bandwidth should be sufficient for the number of active processes, so that none of them will try to immediately read data out of an empty buffer. In [Abb84], the urgency is introduced as an attempt to measure both. The urgency is the sum of the reciprocals of the current "fullness" (amount of buffered data). This number measures both the relative balance of all read processes and the number of read processes. If the urgency is large, the balance strategy will be used; if it is small, it is safe to apply the shortest seek algorithm.

### Continuous Media File System

*CMFS Disk Scheduling* is a non-preemptive disk scheduling scheme designed for the Continuous Media File System (CMFS) at UC-Berkeley [AOG91]. Different policies can be applied in this scheme. Here the notion of the slack time $H$ is introduced. The slack time is the time during which CMFS is free to do non-real-time operations or workahead for real-time processes, because the current workahead of each process is sufficient so that no process would starve, even if it would not be served for $H$ seconds. The considered real-time scheduling policies are:

- The *Static/Minimal policy* is based on the minimal *Workahead Augmenting Set (WAS)*. A process $p_i$ reads a file at a determined rate $R_i$. To each process, a positive integer $M_i$ is assigned which denotes the time overhead required to read a block covering, for example, the seek time. The CMFS performs a set of operations (i.e., disk operations required by all processes) by seeking the next block of a file and reading $M_i$ blocks of this file. Note, we consider only read operations; the same also holds, with minor modifications, for write operations. This seek is done for every process in the system. The data read by a process during this operation "last" $\frac{M_i \times A}{R_i}$, where $A$ is the block size in bytes. The WAS is a set of operations where the data read for each process "last longer" than the worst-case time to perform the operations (i.e., the sum of the read operations of all processes is less than the time read data last for a process). A schedule is derived from the set that is workahead-augmenting and feasible (i.e., the requests are served in the order given by the WAS). The *Minimal Policy,* the minimal WAS, is the schedule where the worst-case elapsed time needed to serve an operation set is the least (i.e., the set is ordered in a way that reduces time needed to perform the operations, for example, by reducing seek times). The *Minimal Policy* does not consider buffer requirements. If there is not enough buffer, this algorithm causes a buffer overflow. The *Static Policy* modifies this schedule such that no block is read if this would cause a buffer overflow for that process. With this approach, starvation is avoided, but its use of short operations causes high seek overhead.

- With the *Greedy Policy,* a process is served as long as possible. Therefore, it computes at each iteration the slack time $H$. The process with the smallest workahead is served. The maximum number $n$ of blocks for this process is read; $n$ is determined by $H$ (the time needed to read $n$ blocks must be less than or equal to $H$) and the currently available buffer space.

- The *Cyclical Plan Policy* distributes the slack time among processes to maximize the slack time. It calculates $H$ and increases the minimal WAS with $H$ milliseconds of additional reads; an additional read for each process is done immediately after the regular read determined by the minimal WAS. This policy distributes workahead by identifying the process with the smallest slack time and schedules an extra block for it; this is done until $H$ is exhausted. The number of block reads for the least workahead is determined. This procedure is repeated every time the read has completed.

The *Aggressive* version of the Greedy and the Cyclical Plan Policy calculates $H$ of all processes except the least workahead process that is immediately served by both policies. If the buffer size limit of a process is reached, all policies skip to the next process. Non-real-time operations are served if there is enough slack time. Performance measurements of the above introduced strategy showed that Cyclical Plan increases system slack faster at low values of the slack time (which is likely to be the case at system setup). With a higher system slack time, apart of the Static/Minimal Policy, all policies perform about the same.

All of the disk scheduling strategies described above have been implemented and tested in prototype file systems for continuous media. Their efficiency depends on the design of the entire file system, the disk layout, tightness of deadlines, and last but not least, on the application that is behaving. It is not yet common sense which algorithm is the "best" method for the storage and retrieval of continuous media files. Further research must show which algorithm serves the timing requirements of continuous media best and ensures that aperiodic and non-real-time requests are efficiently served.

### Data Structuring

Continuous media data are characterized by consecutive, time-dependent logical data units. The basic data unit of a motion video is a frame. The basic unit of audio is a sample. Frames contain the data associated with a single video image, a sample represents the amplitude of the analog audio signal at a given instance. Further structuring of multimedia data was suggested in the following way [RV91, Ran93, SF92]: a strand is defined as an immutable sequence of continuously recorded video frames, audio samples, or both. It means that it consists of a sequence of blocks which contain either video frames, audio samples or both. Most often it includes headers and further information related to the type of compression used. The file system holds primary indices in a sequence of *Primary Blocks.* They contain mapping from media block numbers to their disk addresses. In *Secondary Blocks* pointers to all primary blocks are stored. The *Header Block* contains pointers to all secondary blocks of a strand. General information about the strand like, recording rate, length, etc., is also included in the header block.

Media strands that together constitute a logical entity of information (e.g., video and associated audio of a movie) are tied together by synchronization to form a multimedia rope. A rope contains the name of its creator, its length and access rights. For each media strand in this rope, the strand ID, rate of recording, granularity of storage and corresponding block-level are stored (information for the synchronization of the playback start for all media at the strand interval boundaries). Editing operations on ropes manipulate pointers to strands only. Strands are regarded as immutable objects because editing operations like insert or delete may require substantial copying which can consume significant amounts of time and space. Intervals of strands can be shared by different ropes. Strands that are not referenced by any rope can be deleted, and storage can be reclaimed [RV91]. The following interfaces are the operations that file systems provide for the manipulation of ropes:

- RECORD [media] [requestID, mmRopeID]

  A multimedia rope, represented by mmRopeID and consisting of media strands, is recorded until a STOP operation is issued.

- PLAY [mmRopeID, interval, media] requestID

  This operation plays a multimedia rope consisting of one or more media strands.

- STOP [requestID]

  This operation stops the retrieval or storage of the corresponding multimedia rope.

- Additionally, the following operations are supported:

  - INSERT [baseRope, position, media, withRope, withInterval]
  - REPLACE [baseRope, media, baseInterval, withRope, withInterval]
  - SUBSTRING [baseRope, media, interval]
  - CONCATE [mmRopeID1, mmRopeID2]

– DELETE [baseRope, media, interval]

Figure 9.22 provides an example of the INSERT operation, whereas Figure 9.23 shows the REPLACE operation.

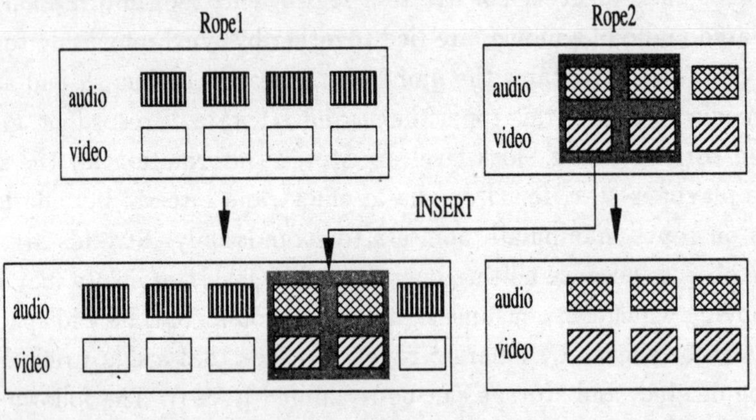


Figure 9.22: *INSERT operation.*

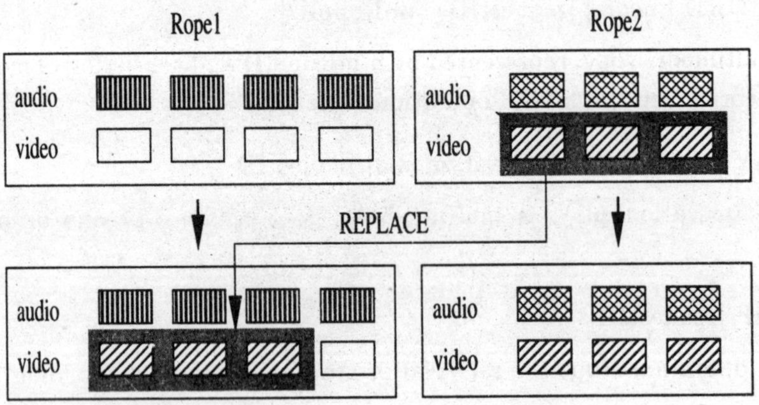


Figure 9.23: *REPLACE operation.*

The storage system is divided into two layers:

- The *rope server* is responsible for the manipulation of multimedia ropes. It communicates with applications, allows the manipulation of ropes and communicates with the underlying *storage manager* to record and play back multimedia strands. It provides the rope abstraction to the application. The rope access methods were designed similarly to UNIX file access routines. Status messages about the state of the play or record operation are passed to the application.

- The *storage manager* is responsible for the manipulation of strands. It places the strands on disk to ensure continuous recording and playback. The interface to the rope server includes four primitives for manipulating strands:

  1. "PlayStrandSequence" takes a sequence of strand intervals and displays the given time interval of each strand in sequence.
  2. "RecordStrand" creates a new strand and records the continuous media data either for a given duration or until StopStrand is called.
  3. "StopStrand" terminates a previous PlayStrandSequence or RecordStrand instance.
  4. "DeleteStrand" removes a strand from storage.

The experimental Video File Server introduced in [Ran93] supports integrated storage and retrieval of video. The "Video Rope Server" presents a device-independent directory interface to users (Video Rope). A Video Rope is characterized as a hierarchical directory structure constructed upon stored video frames. The "Video Disk Manager" manages a frame-oriented motion video storage on disk, including audio and video components.

## 9.6 Additional Operating System Issues

### 9.6.1 Interprocess Communication and Synchronization

In multimedia systems, *interprocess communication* refers to the exchange of different data between processes. This data transfer must be very efficient because continuous media require the transfer of a large amount of data in a given time span. For the exchange of discrete media data, the same mechanisms are used as in traditional operating systems. Data interchange of continuous media is closely related to memory management and is discussed in the respective section.

*Synchronization* guarantees timing requirements between different processes. In the context of multimedia, this is an especially interesting aspect. Different data streams, database entries, document portions, positions, processes, etc., must be synchronized. Thus, synchronization is important for various components of a multimedia system and therefore is not included in this discussion on operating systems.

### 9.6.2 Memory Management

The memory manager assigns physical resource *memory* to a single process. Virtual memory is mapped onto memory that is actually available. With *paging,* less frequently used data is swapped between main memory and external storage. Pages are transferred back into the main memory when data on them is required by a process. Note, continuous media data must not be swapped out of the main memory. If a page of virtual memory containing code or data required by a real-time process is not in real memory when it is accessed by the process, a page fault occurs, meaning that the page must be read from disk. Page faults affect the real-time performance very seriously, so they must be avoided. A possible approach is to lock code and/or data into real memory. However, care should be taken when locking code and/or data into real memory. Real memory is a very scarce resource to the system. Committing real memory by pinning (locking) will decrease overall system performance. The typical AIX kernel will not allow more than about 70% of real memory to be committed to pinned pages [IBM91].

The transmission and processing of continuous data streams by several components require very efficient data transfer restricted by time constraints. Memory allocation and release functions provide well-defined access to shared memory areas. In most cases, no real processing of data, but only a data transfer, is necessary. For example, the camera with a digitalization process is the source and the presentation process is the sink. The essential task of the other components is the *exchange* of continuous media data with relatively high data rates in real-time. Processing involves computing, adding, interpreting and stripping headers. This is well-known in communications [MR93b]. The actual implementation can either be with external devices and dedicated hardware in the computer, or it can be realized with software components.

Early prototypes of multimedia systems incorporate audio and video based on external data paths only. Memory management, in this case, has a switching function only, i.e., to control an external switch.

A first step toward integration was the incorporation of the external switch function into the computer. Therefore, some dedicated adapter cards that are able to switch data streams with varying data rates were employed.

A complete integration can be achieved with a full digital approach within the computer, i.e., to offer a pure software solution. Data are transmitted between single components in real-time. Copy operations are – as far as possible – reduced to the exchange of pointers and the check of access rights. This requires the access of a shared address space. Data can also be directly transferred between different adapter cards. The transfer of continuous media data takes place in a real-time environment. This exchange is controlled, but not necessarily executed, by the application. The data transfer must be performed by processes running in a real-time environment. The application running in a non-real-time environment generates, manipulates and consumes these data streams at an operating system interface.

### 9.6.3 Device Management

Device management and the actual access to a device allows the operating system to integrate all hardware components. The physical device is represented by an abstract device driver. The physical characteristics of devices are hidden. In a conventional system, such devices include a graphics adapter card, disk, keyboard and mouse. In multimedia systems, additional devices like cameras, microphones, speakers and dedicated storage devices for audio and video must be considered. In most existing multimedia systems, such devices are not often integrated by device management and the respective device drivers.

Existing operating system extensions for multimedia usually provide one common system-wide interface for the control and management of data streams and devices. In Microsoft Windows and OS/2 this interface is known as the Media Control Interface (MCI). The multimedia extensions of Microsoft Windows, for example, provide the following classes of function calls:

- *System commands* are not forwarded to the single device driver (MCI driver); they are served by a central instance. An example of such a command is the query concerning all devices connected to the system (Sysinfo).
- Each device driver must be able to process *compulsory commands.* For instance, the query for specific characteristics (capability info) and the opening of a device (open) are such commands.
- Basic commands refer to characteristics that all devices have in common. They can be supported by drivers. If a device driver processes such a command, it must consider all variants and parameters of the command. A data transmission is typically started by the basic command "play."
- Extended commands may refer to both device types and special single devices. The "seek" command for the positioning on an audio CD is an example. On the basis of a controllable camera, the required concepts are explained in more detail. A camera has functions to adjust the focal length, focus and position. An abstraction of the functionality provided by the physical camera as an video input device covers the following layers, which relate to different components in a multimedia system:
  - The application has access to a logical camera without knowledge about the specific control functions of the camera. The focal length is adjusted in millimeters. The driver translates a specific "set focal length command" into a sequence of camera hardware control commands and passes them to the control logic. The provision of such an abstract interface and the transformation into hardware-dependent commands is a task of the device management of a multimedia operating system.
  - Different input device classes have similar characteristics. The zoom operation of a camera can be applied in a similar way to the presentation of a still image. The still image could be zoomed. For example, consider an image stored on a Photo-CD with a given resolution. The zoom operation could result in the presentation either of the image with its specified

resolution, or of a particular section of the image. This kind of abstraction is part of the programming environment of a multimedia system and not a task of an operating system, although in some cases it is performed by the operating system. The basic commands define several operations supported by different devices. The basic command used for the start of a data transmission between the camera and the video window of an application – called the play command in this context – can be used in a second realization for file transfer – as a kind of copy command.

To complete the description of the camera control, the positioning of the camera is discussed. To change the position of the camera, the application specifies the target coordinates in a polar coordinate system. Yet, a concrete camera control can only execute commands like "move swivel slope head in a specific direction with a defined speed." The direction can be "left" or "right," respectively "up" or "down." Eight different speed levels are given, but it is only possible to change the speed in steps of the maximum two levels. During acceleration, consecutive commands with speed levels 2, 4, 6, 8 must be executed. It is the task of the camera driver to perform the mapping of coordinates into this positioning controlled by time and speed.

To define the required application interface, the selectable control class can be subdivided into four function categories [RSSS90]:

1. Defined, compulsory and generic: all operations that must be provided for each device driver, regardless of its specific functionality, belong to this category. This corresponds to the above-mentioned commands of the MCI.

2. Defined, compulsory and device specific: all functions and parameters specified in this category must be provided by the device driver. Therefore, there exists a defined interface in the respective operating system. For example, a camera driver must be able to answer an inquiry for an eventual existing auto focus mechanism.

3. Defined but not compulsory: for each device type, a set of functions is defined which covers all known possibilities. The functions cannot be provided by all different devices and drivers. In the case of the camera, such functions are, for example, to position and adjust the focal length, because not every camera

has these facilities. The interface is defined keeping in mind what is possible and meaningful. If such a function is employed, although it is not supported by the implementation, a well-defined error handling mechanism applies. The application can handle these errors, and therefore it is independent of the connected physical devices.

4. Not defined and not compulsory: we must be aware that there will always be unpredictable new devices and special developments. Hence, the operating system provides a fourth category of functions to cover all these calls.

An unambiguous definition of these categories allows easier integration of devices into the programming environment. The multimedia extensions of today's operating systems incorporate device management with a first step of functional distinction toward the above outlined categories.

## 9.7 System Architecture

The employment of continuous media in multimedia systems also imposes additional, new requirements to the system architecture. A typical multimedia application does not require processing of audio and video to be performed by the application itself. Usually, data are obtained from a source (e.g., microphone, camera, disk, network) and are forwarded to a sink (e.g., speaker, display, network). In such a case, the requirements of continuous media data are satisfied best if they take "the shortest possible path" through the system, i.e., to copy data directly from adapter to adapter. The program then merely sets the correct switches for the data flow by connecting sources to sinks. Hence, the application itself never really touches the data as is the case in traditional processing. A problem with direct copying from adapter to adapter is the control and the change of quality of service parameters. In multimedia systems, such an adapter to adapter connection is defined by the capabilities of the two involved adapters and the bus performance. In today's systems, this connection is static. This architecture of low-level data streaming corresponds with proposals for using additional new busses for audio and video transfer within a computer. It also enables a switch-based rather than a bus-based data transfer architecture [Fin91, HM91]. Note, in practice we encounter headers and trailers surrounding continuous media data coming from devices and being delivered to devices. In the case of compressed video data, e.g., MPEG-2, the program stream contains several layers of headers compared with the actual group of pictures to be displayed.

Most of today's multimedia systems must coexist with conventional data processing. They share hardware and software components. For instance, the traditional way of protocol processing is slow and complicated. In high-speed networks, protocol processing is the bottleneck because it cannot provide the necessary throughput. Protocols like VMTP, NETBLT and XTP try to overcome this ' awback, but research in this area has shown that throughput in most communication systems is not bounded by protocol mechanisms, but by the way they are implemented [CJRS89]. A time-intensive operation is, for example, physical buffer copying. Since the memory on the adapter is not very large and it may not store all related compressed images, data must be copied at least once from adapter into main memory. Further copying should be avoided. Appropriate buffer management allows operations on data without performing any physical copying. In operating systems like UNIX, the buffer management must be available in both the user and the kernel space. The data need to be stored in shared memory to avoid copying between user and kernel space. For further performance improvement, protocol processing should be done in threads with upcalls, i.e., the protocol processing for an incoming message is done by a single thread. A development to support such a protocol process management is, for example, the x-Kernel.

The architecture of the protocol processing system is just one issue to be considered in the system architecture of multimedia supporting operating systems. Multimedia data should be delivered from the input device (e.g., CD-ROM) to an output device (e.g., a video decompression board) across the fastest possible path. The paradigm of streaming from source to sink is an appropriate way of doing this. Hence, the multimedia application opens devices, establishes a connection between them, starts the data flow and returns to other duties.

As stated above, the most dominant characteristic of multimedia applications is to preserve the temporal requirement at the presentation time. Therefore, multimedia data is handled in a *Real-Time Environment (RTE)*, i.e., its processing is scheduled according to the inherent timing requirements of multimedia data. On a multimedia computer, the RTE will usually coexist with a *Non-Real-Time Environment (NRTE)*. The NRTE deals with all data that have no timing requirements. Figure 9.24 shows the approached architecture. Multimedia I/O devices are, in gen-

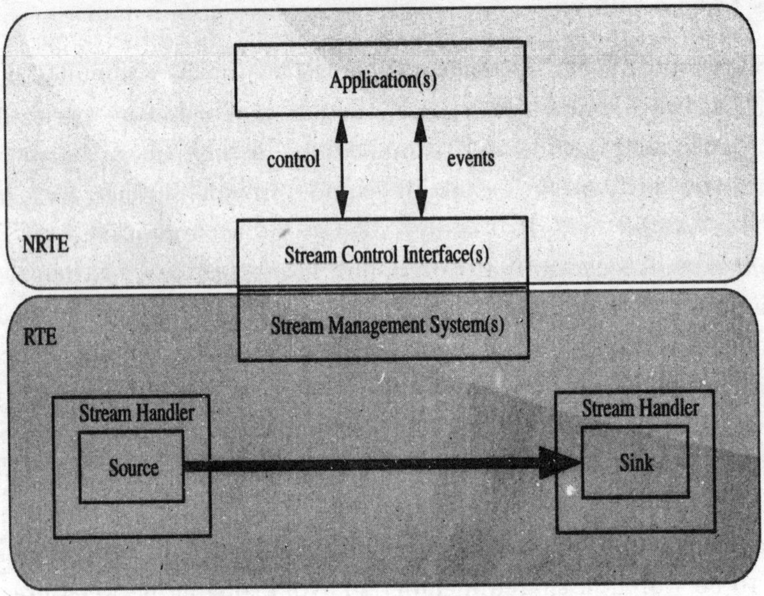


Figure 9.24: *Real-time and non-real-time environments.*

eral, accessed from both environments. Data such as a video frame, for example, is passed from the RTE to the display. The RTE is controlled by related functions in the NRTE. The establishment of communication connections at the start of a stream must not obey timing requirements, but the data processing for established connections is compelled. All control functions are performed in the NRTE. The application usually calls only these control functions and is not involved in active continuous media data handling. Therefore, the multimedia application itself typically runs in the NRTE and is shielded from the RTE. In some scenarios, users may want applications to "process" continuous media data in an application-specific way. In our model, such an application comprises a module running as stream handler in the RTE. The rest of the applications run in the NRTE, using the available stream control interfaces. System programs, such as communication protocol processing and database data transfer programs, make use of this programming in the RTE. Whereas applications like authoring tools and media presentation programs are relieved from the burden of programming in the RTE, they just interface and control the RTE services. Applications determine processing paths which are needed for their data processing, as well as the control devices and paths.

To reduce data copying, buffer management functions are employed in the RTE. This buffer management is located "between" the stream handlers. Stream handlers are entities in the RTE which are in charge of multimedia data. Typical stream handlers are filter and mixing functions, but they are also parts of the communication subsystem described above and can be treated in the same way. Each stream handler has endpoints for input and output through which data units flow. The stream handler consumes data units from one or more input endpoints and generates data units through one or more output endpoints.

Multimedia data usually "enters" the computer through an input device, a source, and "leaves" it through an output device, a sink (where storage can serve as an I/O device in both cases). Sources and sinks are implemented by a device driver. Applications access stream handlers by establishing sessions with them. A session constitutes a virtual stream handler for exclusive use by the application which has created it. Depending on the required QoS of a session, an underlying resource management subsystem multiplexes the capacity of the underlying physical resources among the sessions. To manage the RTE data flow through the stream handlers, control operations are used which belong to the NRTE. These functions make up the stream management system in the multimedia architecture. Operations are provided by all stream handlers (e.g., operations to establish sessions and connect their endpoints) and operations specific to individual stream handlers usually determine the content of a multimedia stream and apply to particular I/O devices.

Some applications which are all in the NRTE have the need to correlate discrete data such as text and graphics with continuous streams, or to post-process multimedia data (e.g., to display the time stamps of a video stream like a VCR). These applications need to obtain segments of multimedia at the stream handler interface. With a grab function, the segments are copied to the application as if stream duplication took place. Due to this operation, the data units lose their temporal properties because they enter the NRTE. Applications that must generate or transform multimedia data keeping real-time characteristics must use a stream handler included in the RTE, which performs the required processing.

The synchronization of streams is a function that is provided by the stream management subsystem. Synchronization is specified on a connection basis and can be expressed using the notions of a clock or logical time systems. It determines points in time at which the processing of data units shall start. For regular streams, the stream rates can be used to relate data units to synchronization points. Sequence numbers can accomplish the same task. Time stamps are a more versatile means for synchronization as they can also be used for non-periodic traffic. Synchronization is often implemented by delaying the execution of a thread or by delaying the receive operation on a buffer exchanged between stream handlers.

Many operating systems already provide extensions to support multimedia applications. In the next paragraphs, three of these multimedia extensions are presented.

### 9.7.1 UNIX-based Systems

In the UNIX operating system, the applications in the user space generally make use of system calls in the NRTE. Either the whole operating system or a part of it is also located in the NRTE and in the kernel space. Extensions to the operating system providing real-time capabilities make up the RTE part of the kernel space (see Figure 9.25).

The actual implementation of the RTE varies substantially:

- SUN OS does not yet provide an RTE.
- AIX includes real-time priorities. This feature provides the basis for the RTE in the AIX-based Ultimedia™ server.
- The IRIX operating system on Silicon Graphics Workstations has real-time capabilities, i.e., it includes an RTE.

### 9.7.2 QuickTime

QuickTime is a software extension to the Macintosh System. It provides the capability to capture, store, manage, synchronize and display continuous media data.

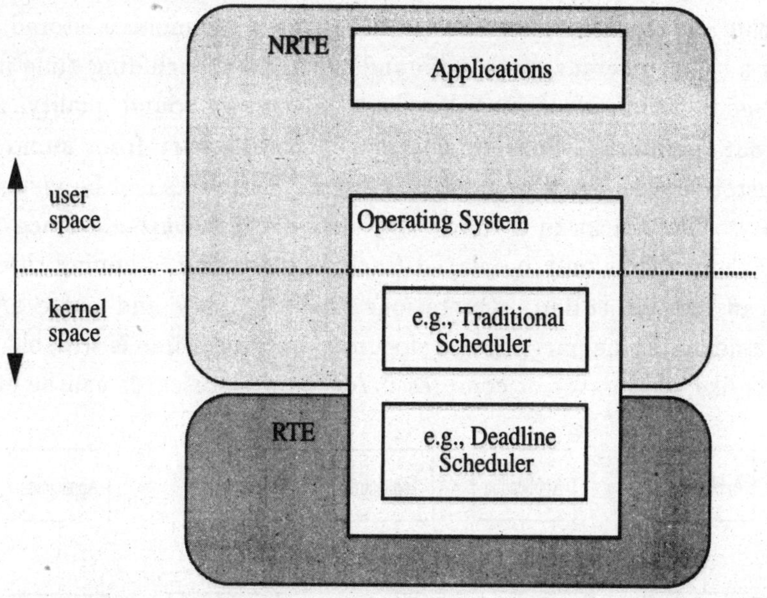


Figure 9.25: *NRTE and RTE in UNIX systems.*

A more detailed description can be found in [DM92]. It introduces digitized video as standard data type into the system, and it allows an easier handling of other continuous media like audio and animation. Standard applications are enhanced by multimedia capabilities. Apple has announced QuickTime to be available for other operating systems like Windows and UNIX as well. An integration of future hardware and software developments is possible.

The standard data type of QuickTime is a movie. All kinds of continuous media data are stored in movie documents. Additionally, time information like the creation and modification date, duration, etc., are also kept in the movie document. With each movie, a poster frame is associated that appears in the dialog box. Other information like current editing selection, spatial characteristics (transformation matrix, clipping region) and a list of one or more tracks are associated with the movie. A track represents a stream of information (audio or video data) that flows in parallel to every other track. With each track, information like creation and modification data, duration, track number, spatial characteristics (transformation matrix, display window, clipping region), a list of related tracks, volume and start time, duration, playback rate and a data reference for each media segment is stored. A media segment is a set of references to audio and video data, including time information (creation, modification, duration), language, display or sound quality, media data type and data pointers. Future releases will have, apart from audio and video tracks, "custom tracks" such as a subtitle track. All tracks can be viewed or heard concurrently. The tracks of a movie are always synchronized. Since movies are documents they cannot only be played (including pausing, stepping through, etc.), but they can also be edited. Operations like cut, copy and paste are possible. Movie documents can be part of other documents. QuickTime is scalable. Hardware components like accelerator or compressor/decompressor cards can be employed.

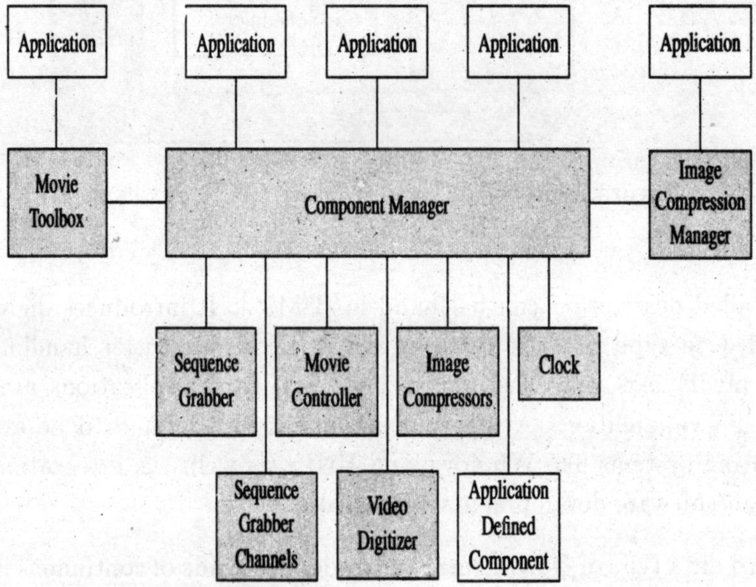


Figure 9.26: *QuickTime architecture.*

The QuickTime architecture comprises three major components (see Figure 9.26): the *Movie Toolbox* offers a set of services to the user that allows him/her to incorporate movies into applications. These applications may directly manipulate characteristics of audio and video data of movies. The movie is integrated in the desktop environment. Movie data can be imported and exported with the system clipboard and a movie can be edited within the Movie Toolbox.

The second component, known as the *Image Compression Manager,* provides a common interface for compression and decompression of data, independent of the implementation, to and from hard disk, CD-ROM and floppy. It offers a directory service to select the correct compression component. Different interface levels for different application requirements are available. The compression techniques are a proprietary image compression scheme, a JPEG implementation and a proprietary video compressor for digitized video data (leading to a compression ratio of 8:1, and if temporal redundancies are also removed, to a ratio of 25:1). An animation compressor can compress digital data in lossy and lossless (error-free) modes. A graphics compressor is also available. The pixel depth conversion in bits per pixel can be used as a filter to be applied in addition to other compressors.

The *Component Manager* provides a directory service related to the components. It is the interface between the application and various system components. It shields developers from having to deal with the details of interfacing with specific hardware. In the Component Manager, object-oriented concepts (e.g., hierarchical structure, extensible class libraries, inheritance of component functionality, instance-based client/server model) are applied. Thus, applications are independent of implementations, can easily integrate new hardware and software and can adapt to the available resources. The components managed by the Component Manager are the Clock, the Image Compressor and Image Decompressor, the Movie Controller, the Sequence Grabber, Sequence Grabber Channel and the Video Digitizer. Furthermore, application-defined components can be added.

There is a simple resource management scheme applied to the local environment only: in the case of scarce resources, audio is prioritized over video, i.e., audio playback is maintained (if possible) whereas single video frames might be skipped. If an application calls the Movie Toolbox during playback, there are the following possibilities to handle these calls:

- The commonly used mode is a preemptive calling sequence, where the application returns to the system after each update. This might cause jerky movie output.
- With a non-preemptive calling sequence, the application does not return to the system while a movie is played. This counteracts the multitasking capability.

- The high-performance controlled preemptive calling sequence is a compromise, where the application gives up control to the Movie Toolbox for a specified time period (e.g., 50 ms).

As an additional resource management scheme for better performance, it is recommended to turn off the virtual memory while playing QuickTime movies. If it is on, it will cause the sound to skip and it will lower the frame rate during the playback of a movie. However, no RTE exists.

The concept of components in QuickTime allows for easy extension without affecting applications. It attempts to form a hierarchical structure of functionality by components. The movie controller component eases user interface programming. A disadvantage of QuickTime is that there is no clear layering of abstractions for programmers and that the functionality of managers and components sometimes overlaps.

### 9.7.3 Windows Multimedia Extensions

The Microsoft *Windows Multimedia Extensions (WME)* are an enhancement to the Windows programming environment. They provide high-level and low-level services for the development of multimedia applications for application developers, using the extended capabilities of a multimedia personal computer [Win91].

The following services for multimedia applications are provided by the WME:

- A *Media Control Interface (MCI)* for the control of media services. It comprises an extensible string-based and message-based interface for communication with MCI device drivers. The MCI device drivers are designed to support the playing and recording of waveform audio, the playing of MIDI (Musical Instrument Digital Interface) files, the playing of compact disk audio from a CD-ROM disk drive and the control of some video disk players.
- A *Low-level API (Application Programming Interface)* provides access to multimedia-related services like playing and recording audio with waveform and MIDI audio devices. It also supports the handling of input data from joysticks and precise timer services.

- A *multimedia file I/O service* provides buffered and unbuffered file I/O. It also supports the standard IBM/Microsoft Resource Interchange File Format (RIFF) files. These services are extensible with custom I/O procedures that can be shared among applications.

- The most important *device drivers* available for multimedia applications are:

  - An *enhanced high-resolution video display driver* for Video 7 and Paradise VGA cards providing 256 colors, improved performance, and other new features.

  - A *high-resolution VGA video display driver* allowing the use of a custom 16-color palette as well as the standard palette.

  - A *low resolution VGA video display driver* providing 320-by-320 resolution with 256 colors.

  - The *Control Panel Applets* that allow the user to change display drivers, to set up a screen saver, to install multimedia device drivers, to assign waveform sounds to system alerts, to configure the MIDI Mapper and to calibrate joysticks. A MIDI Mapper supports the MIDI patch service that allows MIDI files to be authored independently of end-user MIDI synthesizer setups.

Figure 9.27 shows the rough architecture of MS Windows Multimedia Extensions: MMSYSTEM library provides the Media Control Interface services and low-level multimedia support functions. The communication between the low-level MMSYSTEM functions and multimedia devices, such as waveform, MIDI, joystick and timer, is provided by the multimedia device drivers. The high-level control of media devices is provided by the drivers for the Media Control Interface.

The main concepts of the architecture of the Multimedia Extensions are extensibility and device-independence. They are provided by a translation layer (MMSYSTEM) that isolates applications from device drivers and centralizes device-independent code, run-time linking that allows the MMSYSTEM translation layer to link to the drivers it needs and a well-defined and consistent driver interface that minimizes the development of specialized code and makes the installation and upgrade processes easier.

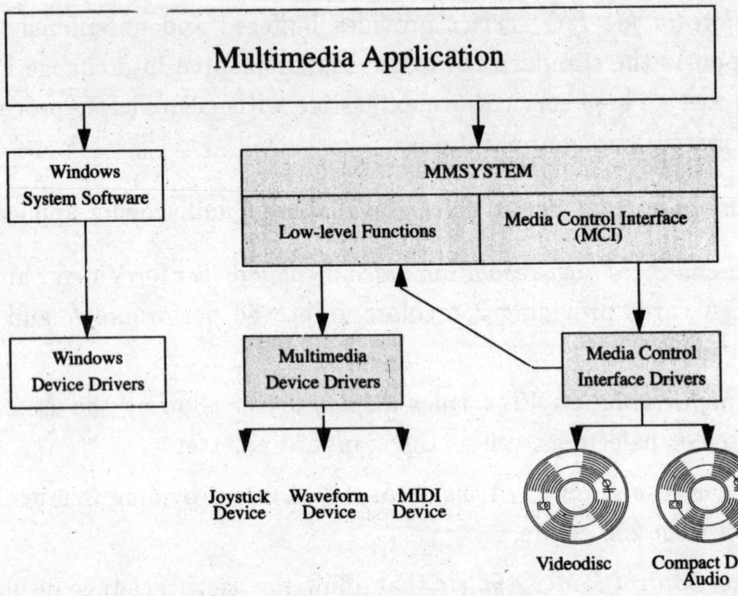


Figure 9.27: *MS Windows Multimedia Extensions architecture.*

### 9.7.4 OS/2 Multimedia Presentation Manager/2

The Multimedia Presentation Manager/2 (MMPM/2) is part of IBM's Operating System/2 (OS/2). OS/2 is a platform well-suited for multimedia because it supports, e.g., preemptive multitasking, priority scheduling, overlapped I/O and demand-paged virtual memory storage. Figure 9.28 provides an overview of the architecture.

The *Media Control Interface (MCI)* is a device-independent programming interface that offers commands similar to an entertainment system. The following list comprises a selection of typical MCI-commands:

- "Open," "close," and "status of a device" are provided for all devices.
- For playback and recording device-dependent "play," "record," "resume," "stop," "cue" and "seek" commands exist.
- "Set cue point" allows for synchronization.

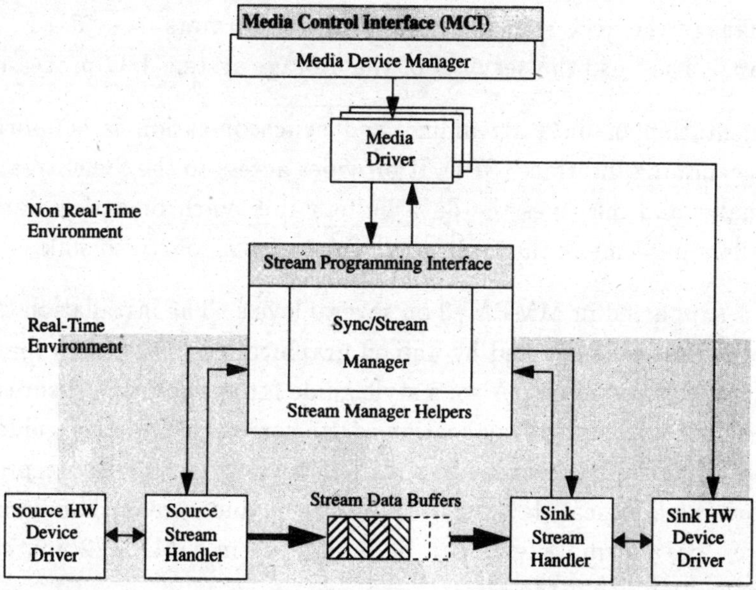


Figure 9.28: *The architecture of the OS/2 Multimedia Presentation Manager/2.*

- "Get table of contents of a CD-ROM" is an example of a device-specific command.

A logical device in MMPM/2 is a logical representation of the functions available from either a hardware device, a hardware device with software emulation or a software emulation only. The actual implementation is not relevant to an application because the MCI provides this device independence.

Examples of logical devices are an "Amplifier-Mixer Device," similar to a home stereo amplifier-mixer, a "Waveform Audio Device" to record and play digital audio, a sequencer device for MIDI-sounds, a "CD Audio Device" that provides access to audio compact disks (CD-DA), a "CD-XA Device" to support CD-ROM/XA disks and a "Videodisk Device" to control video disk players which deliver analog video and audio signals.

The multimedia I/O functions enable media drivers and applications to access and manipulate data objects that are stored in memory or on a file system. Storage system I/O processes handle the access to specific storage devices. File format I/O processes manage the access to data stored in file formats like "RIFF Waveform" and "BitMap." They use the services of the storage system I/O processes.

The implementation of data streaming and synchronization is supported by the Stream Programming Interface (SPI). It provides access to the SyncStream Manager that coordinates and manages the data buffers and synchronization data. Pairs of stream handlers implement the transport of data from source to sink.

Ease of use is supported in MMPM/2 on several levels. The installation of programs and setup of devices is supported by unified graphical user interfaces that centralize these functions for easy access. Also, a style guide for applications ensures that there is a common look and feel of applications that correspond to this guide. There is a high degree of flexibility because application developers and device providers can integrate their own logical devices, I/O processes and stream handlers. So, new media devices, data formats, etc. can be integrated in MMPM/2 and can be used by every application using the MCI.

OS/2 with MMPM/2 is a platform that has some basic operating mechanisms to support the processing and presentation of multimedia information as it is needed in multimedia application scenarios. It incorporates an RTE, implemented as a set of device drivers. MMPM/2 is an advanced platform for the development of these multimedia applications, providing the media and stream abstractions.

Finally it should be pointed out that MMPM/2 and WME look very similar and have many concepts in common.

## 9.8 Concluding Remarks

In this chapter we addressed the major issues of operating systems related to multimedia data processing, namely, resource management, scheduling and file systems. This discussion includes the most relevant existing architectures of such systems.

The concepts employed by current multimedia operating systems have been initially used in real-time systems and were adapted to the requirements of multimedia data. Today's operating systems incorporate these functions either as device drivers or as extensions based on the existing operating system scheduler and file systems. As a next step, an integration of real-time processing and non-real-time processing in the native system kernel can be expected.

# Chapter 10

# Networking Systems

A *multimedia networking system* allows for the data exchange of discrete and continuous media among computers. This communication requires proper services and protocols for data transmission.

## 10.1 Layers, Protocols and Services

- A *service* provides a set of operations to the requesting application. Logically related services are grouped into *layers* according to the OSI reference model. Therefore, each layer is a *service provider* to the layer lying above. The services describe the behavior of the *layer* and its *service elements* (Service Data Units = SDUs). A proper service specification contains no information concerning any aspects of the implementation.

- A *protocol* consists of a set of rules which must be followed by peer layer instances during any communication between these two peers. It is comprised of the *format* (syntax) and the *meaning* (semantics) of the *exchanged data units* (Protocol Data Units = PDUs). The peer instances of different computers cooperate together to provide a service.

Multimedia communication puts several *requirements* on services and protocols, which are independent from the layer in the network architecture. In general, this set of requirements depends to a large extent on the respective application. However, without defining a precise value for individual parameters, the following requirements must be taken into account:

- Audio and video data processing need to be bounded by deadlines or even defined by a time interval. The data transmission – both between applications and transport layer interfaces of the involved components – must follow within the demands concerning the time domains.

- End-to-end jitter must be bounded. This is especially important for interactive applications such as the telephone. Large jitter values would mean large buffers and higher end-to-end delays.

- All guarantees necessary for achieving the data transfer within the required time span must be met. This includes the required processor performance, as well as the data transfer over a bus and the available storage for protocol processing.

- Cooperative work scenarios using multimedia conference systems are the main application areas of multimedia communication systems. These systems should support multicast connections to save resources. The sender instance may often change during a single session. Further, a user should be able to join or leave a multicast group without having to request a new connection setup, which needs to be handled by all other members of this group.

- The services should provide mechanisms for synchronizing different data streams, or alternatively perform the synchronization using available primitives implemented in another system component.

- The multimedia communication must be compatible with the most widely used communication protocols and must make use of existing, as well as future networks. *Communication compatibility* means that different protocols at least coexist and run on the same machine simultaneously. The relevance of envisaged protocols can only be achieved if the same protocols are widely used.

Many of the current multimedia communication systems are, unfortunately, proprietary experimental systems.

- The communication of discrete data should not starve because of preferred or guaranteed video/audio transmission. Discrete data must be transmitted without any penalty.

- The fairness principle among different applications, users and workstations must be enforced.

- The actual audio/video data rate varies strongly. This leads to fluctuations of the data rate, which needs to be handled by the services. Figure 10.1 shows data rates of three different situations: we distinguish among uncorrelated pictures, persons in a room and a news speaker. In spite of the high fluctuation

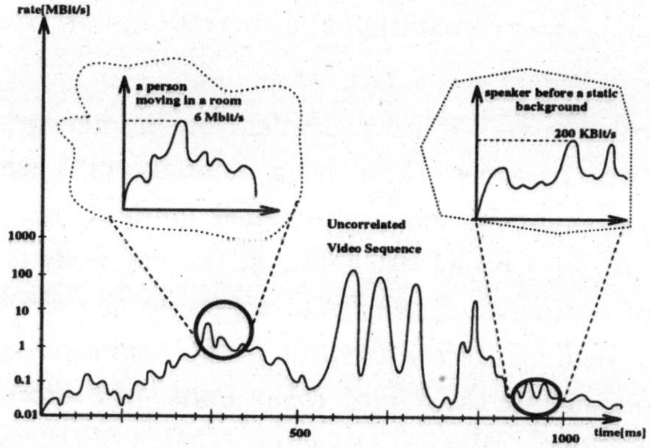


Figure 10.1: *Examples of rates in three situations.*

of the actual values (the peaks), the average values are relatively low. The information rate, shown in Figure 10.1, is based on a coding according to CCIR 601. Note that many compression schemes enforce a constant data rate, leading to a quality of video that depends on the content.

The above described requirements apply to different components of a communication system. By way of describing multimedia communication systems, let us consider the individual layers of the *ISO-OSI Reference Model* [Tan88], which provides at least the conceptual basis for any communication system:

1. *Physical Layer*

   The physical layer defines the transmission method of individual bits over the physical medium, such as fiber optics.

   For example, the type of modulation and bit-synchronization are important issues. With respect to the particular modulation, delays during the data transmission arise due to the propagation speed of the transmission medium and the electrical circuits used. They determine the maximal possible bandwidth of this communication channel. For audio/video data in general, the delays must be minimized and a relatively high bandwidth should be achieved.

2. *Data Link Layer*

   The data link layer provides the transmission of information blocks known as *data frames.* Further, this layer is responsible for access protocols to the physical medium, error recognition and correction, flow control and block synchronization.

   Access protocols are very much dependent on the network. Networks can be divided into two categories: those using point-to-point connections and those using broadcast channels, sometimes called *multi-access channels* or *random access channels.* In a broadcast network, the key issue is how to determine, in the case of competition, who gets access to the channel. To solve this problem, the *Medium Access Control (MAC)* sublayer was introduced and MAC protocols, such as the *Timed Token Rotation Protocol* and *Carrier Sense Multiple Access with Collision Detection (CSMA/CD)*, were developed. The MAC sublayer is especially important in Local Area Networks (LANs), nearly all of which use multi-access channels as the basis for their communication.

   Continuous data streams require *reservation* and *throughput guarantees* over a line. To avoid larger delays, the error control for multimedia transmission needs a different mechanism than retransmission because a late frame is a lost frame. However, because of the new high-speed networks based on fiber optics, there may not be a need for any error control at this layer. These networks favor multimedia transmission because of their very low transmission error rate. Further, a fixed-size information block (cell), such as in Asynchronous Transfer Mode (ATM) networks, allows for an efficient protocol implementation providing, reservations and guaranteed throughput.

3. *Network Layer*

The network layer transports information blocks, called *packets*, from one station to another. The transport may involve several networks. Therefore, this layer provides services such as addressing, internetworking, error handling, network management with congestion control and sequencing of packets.

Again, continuous media require *resource reservation* and *guarantees* for transmission at this layer. A request for reservation for later resource guarantees is defined through *Quality of Service (QoS) parameters*, which correspond to the requirements for continuous data stream transmission. The reservation must be done along the path between the communicating stations. For this purpose, connection-oriented behavior is needed where the reservation is made during the connection setup. Through this approach, end-to-end delay with small jitter and correct packet ordering can be enforced. If internetworking is included, for different communication structures in multicasting or broadcasting connections, duplication of packets can follow, which may introduce further complexity into the reservation process. The network QoS for a connection should be negotiated at this layer.

4. *Transport Layer*

The transport layer provides a process-to-process connection. At this layer, the QoS, which is provided by the network layer, is enhanced, meaning that if the network service is poor, the transport layer has to bridge the gap between what the transport users want and what the network layer provides. Large packets are segmented at this layer and reassembled into their original size at the receiver. Error handling is based on process-to-process communication.

With respect to continuous data streams, the QoS parameters must match their requirements. Again, the error handling does not include retransmission because this mechanism would introduce high end-to-end delays and strong jitter. Also, synchronization, which allows time relations between two LDUs (Logical Data Unit) of one connection, and between SDUs (Session Data Unit) of different connections, is often said to be a function of this layer.

5. *Session Layer*

The session layer guarantees the existence of a connection during a session. Types of sessions include point-to-point sessions, multicast sessions (a connection to many destinations) and multidrop sessions (a connection from many sources).

In the case of continuous media, *multimedia sessions* which reside over one or more transport connections, must be established. This introduces a more complex view on connection reconstruction in the case of transport problems. Another aspect is data coding. It is important for the presentation layer to know when an LDU is ready for presentation, especially if, for example, an intraframe was compressed.

6. *Presentation Layer*

   The presentation layer abstracts from different formats (the local syntax) and provides common formats (transfer syntax). Therefore, this layer must provide services for transformation between the application-specific formats and the agreed-upon format. An example is the different representation of a number for Intel or Motorola processors.

   The multitude of audio and video formats also require conversion between formats. This problem also comes up outside of the communication components during exchange between data carriers, such as CD-ROMs, which store continuous data. Thus, format conversion is often discussed in other contexts.

7. *Application Layer*

   The application layer considers all application-specific services, such as *file transfer service* embedded in the file transfer protocol (ftp) and the *electronic mail service.*

   With respect to audio and video, special services for support of real-time access and transmission must be provided. For example, in the case of an application such as video-on-demand, special services on the video server side for support of real-time database access and transmission must be developed [RVG+93].

The following section describes the principles of different networks according to the ISO-OSI Reference Model (i.e., physical layer, data link layer and their sublayers).

The other layers (i.e. network, transport, session, presentation and application layers) are discussed in Chapter 11. The presentation mainly includes issues regarding audio and video data transmission and the analysis of networks with respect to their multimedia capabilities. We will assume a fundamental understanding of networks, outlined in network textbooks such as [Tan88, Sta92, BG87, Pry93, Par94], ISO standards and many technical product descriptions.

## 10.2 Networks

The main goal of distributed multimedia communication systems is to transmit all their media over the same network. We will examine in the remainder of this chapter different networks with respect to their multimedia transmission capabilities.

Depending mainly on the distance between end-points (stations/computers), networks are divided into three categories: *Local Area Networks (LANs)*, *Metropolitan Area Networks (MANs)*, and *Wide Area Networks (WANs)*.

## 10.3 Local Area Networks (LANs)

A LAN is characterized by (1) its extension over a few kilometers at most, (2) a total data rate of at least several Mbps, and (3) its complete ownership by a single organization. Further, the number of stations connected to a LAN is typically limited to 100. However, the interconnection of several LANs allows the number of connected stations to be increased. The basis of LAN communication is *broadcasting* using *broadcast channel* (multi-access channel). Therefore, the MAC sublayer is of crucial importance in these networks.

### 10.3.1 High-speed Ethernet

Ethernet is the most widely used LAN. Currently available Ethernet offers bandwidth of at least 10 Mbps, but new fast LAN technologies for Ethernet with bandwidths in the range of 100 Mbps are starting to come on the market. This bus-based network uses the *CSMA/CD protocol* for resolution of multiple access to the broadcast channel in the MAC sublayer – before data transmission begins, the network state is checked by the sender station. Each station may try to send its data only if, at that moment, no other station transmits data. Therefore, each station can simultaneously *listen* and *send*. If multiple stations start to transmit data at the same time, the sending stations detect the collision by recognizing errors in their own data. Subsequently, stations try again to transmit the data after a randomly computed time, assuming that no other station has begun transmitting in the meantime.

The difficulty in building any CSMA/CD high-speed Ethernet on top of fiber optics is getting the collision detection to work. Several methods (e.g., power sensing, directional coupling) are possible using the passive star configuration [RJ85]. Fibernet II from Xerox [SRN+83] uses the active star configuration for collision detection.

The communication of continuous data requires guarantees of a maximal end-to-end delay and a minimal jitter. In principle, Ethernet cannot guarantee these requirements. However, there are several possibilities for using this type of LAN for audio and video transmission.

#### Handling of Continuous Data as any Other Data

In the first variant, continuous data are handled in the same way as other data. If the maximal utilization of the network is bounded, the number of errors due to delays is extremely small. This approach is currently the most used solution, but it is not satisfactory if the network load is high.

#### Dynamic Adaptation

To avoid the errors due to a high network load, continuous data transmission can be dynamically adapted to the network load. This means that if the network load is high, the data rate of continuous media can be reduced dynamically. This is possible with the help of scalable coding (see Section 6.7.4), but here again, transmission errors are possible.

### Dedicated Ethernet

Another possibility for the transmission of audio/video data is to dedicate a separate Ethernet LAN to the transmission of continuous data. This solution requires compliance with a proper additional protocol. Further, end-users need at least two separate networks for their communications: one for continuous data and another for discrete data. This approach makes sense for experimental systems, but means additional expense in the end-systems and cabling.

A similar solution is comprised of one LAN as a digital network for transmission of control and discrete data and another LAN as an analog network for transmission of video and audio. This approach can be found in *Media Spaces*, created at Xerox PARC [BBI93] and in the *Cruiser Environment*, developed at Bellcore [FKRR93].

### Hub

A very pragmatic solution can be achieved by exploiting an installed network configuration. Most of the Ethernet cables are not installed in the form of a bus system. They make up a star (i.e., cables radiate from the central room to each station). In this central room, each cable is attached to its own Ethernet interface.

Instead of configuring a bus, each station is connected via its own Ethernet to a *hub*. Hence, each station has the full Ethernet bandwidth available, and a new network for multimedia transmission is not necessary. Additional cost is created by the usage of the hub. In this solution, it is assumed that each Ethernet provides enough bandwidth to each station, but a file transfer may interfere with the audio and video transmission.

### Fast Ethernet

Fast Ethernet, known as *100Base-T* offers throughput speed of up to 100 Mbits/s, and it permits users to move gradually into the world of high-speed LANs.

The Fast Ethernet Alliance, an industry group with more than 60 member companies, began work on the *100-Mbits/s 100 Base-TX* specification in the early 1990s. The alliance submitted the proposed standard to the IEEE and it was approved. During the standardization process, the alliance and the IEEE also defined a *Media-Independent Interface (MII)* for fast Ethernet, which enables it to support various cabling types on the same Ethernet network. Therefore, fast Ethernet offers three media options: 100 Base-T4 for half-duplex operation on four pairs of UTP (Unshielded Twisted Pair cable), 100 Base-TX for half- or full-duplex operation on two pairs of UTP or STP (Shielded Twisted Pair cable), and 100 Base-FX for half- and full-duplex transmission over fiber optic cable.

Like 10 Mbits/s Ethernet, 100 Mbits/s fast Ethernet can be configured in switched or shared-media implementations. Full-duplex operation requires a switch, which allows individual nodes to transmit and receive data simultaneously. Full-duplex fast Ethernet switches will effectively increase network throughput speeds to 200 Mbits/s [Mel94].

Fast Ethernet requires new workstation adapter cards, as well as new hubs or switches equipped with 100 Mbits/s transceivers. Not required are changes to existing Ethernet applications. Another of Fast Ethernet's strengths is that it can be added easily to shared-media and switched 10 Base-T (10 Mbits/s Ethernet, connected with TPC) networks.

### 10.3.2 Token Ring

The Token Ring is a LAN with 4 or 16 Mbits/s throughput. All stations are connected to a logical ring. In a Token Ring, a special bit pattern (3-byte), called a *token*, circulates around the ring whenever all stations are idle. When a station wants to transmit a frame, it must get the token and remove it from the ring before transmitting. Ring interfaces have two operating modes: *listen* and *transmit*. In the *listen* mode, input bits are simply copied to the output. In the *transmit* mode, which is entered only after the token has been seized, the interface breaks the connection between the input and the output, entering its own data onto the ring. As the bits that were inserted and subsequently propagated around the ring come back, they are removed from the ring by the sender. After a station has finished transmitting the last bit of its last frame, it must regenerate the token. When the last bit of the frame has gone around and returned, it must be removed, and the interface must immediately switch back into the *listen* mode to avoid a duplicate transmission of the data.

Each station receives, reads and sends frames circulating in the ring according to the *Token Ring MAC Sublayer Protocol* (IEEE standard 802.5). Each frame includes a *Sender Address* (SA) and a *Destination Address* (DA). When the sending station drains the frame from the ring, a *Frame Status* field is updated, i.e., the A and C bits of the field are examined. Three combinations are allowed:

- A=0, C=0 : destination not present or not powered up.
- A=1, C=0 : destination present but frame not accepted.
- A=1, C=1 : destination present and frame copied.

Most of the time, after reading a frame, the station sends the frame to a neighboring station because the DA of the received packet is not the same as the station's own address. If the DA is identical to the owner's address, this packet is stored in the local storage (as long as there is enough buffer space). If a frame is rejected at the receiver station due to a lack of a buffer space or some other reason, the sender has the option to try again (in a while).

The IEEE Standard 802.5 protocol includes an elaborate scheme for handling *multiple priority schemes.* The token contains a field which reflects the priority of the token. In a frame, a priority is indicated in the *Access Control (AC)* field of the frame header. When a frame is transmitted, it inherits the priority from the token that was captured, and the priority is stored in the AC field.

The *priority operation* works as follows: a station can transmit a frame at a given priority using any available token with a priority less than or equal to that of the frame. If an appropriate token is not available, the station may reserve a token of the required priority in a passing token or frames as follows:

- If another station has reserved an equal or higher priority in a passing token or frame, the station cannot make any reservation in this frame or token.

| Priority | Application |
|---|---|
| 0 | Free usable; used by most applications |
| 1-3 | Free usable |
| 4 | Used by bridges |
| 5-6 | Reserved but not used |
| 7 | Used by ring management |

Table 10.1: *Priorities used in Token Ring.*

- If the reservation bits have not been set, or if they have been set to a lower priority than that required by the station, it sets the reservation bits to its required priority.

When a station removes one of its frames from the Token Ring and finds nonzero values in the reservation bits, it must originate a priority token equal to the reservation bits. To prevent a station from continuously transmitting priority frames, the Token Ring provides a *fairness* scheme. Although a priority can be preempted at any time by the request of a higher priority, once the highest priority has been satisfied, the priority reverts to a lower priority, and eventually to a normal priority. Priorities are ordered according to their importance, as shown in the Table 10.1.

The *priority scheme*, together with the *fixed maximal propagation delay* of a frame, makes it possible to support a guaranteed data transmission of continuous media. The principal strength of this purpose is the *predictable* nature of a station's opportunity to transmit. The worst case, or the longest period of time that a station must wait until it gets a token, is deterministic and can be calculated. For example [BPSWL93], given a ring of *N* stations, the *token rotation time* $t_{trt}$ can be characterized as

$$t_{irt} = \tau_l + \sum_{i=0}^{N-1} \tau_i$$

where $\tau_l$ is the *ring latency* (the fixed delay due to attachment delays and the physical ring length) and $\tau_i$ is the *token holding time* of station *i* for a given rotation of the token. The largest allowable frame size is 16 K bytes and the maximal token holding time $\tau_{max}$ is 10 ms. (In today's attachments, we usually encounter

$\tau_{max} = 2ms.$) Hence, in the worst case, a station may have to wait $(N-1)\times\tau_{max}+\tau_l$ seconds between consecutive opportunities to transmit data. Note that typically, $\tau_l$ is negligible compared to $(N-1)\times\tau_{max}$.

A reservation mechanism is useful for bounding the access delay of high-priority traffic. For example [BPSWL93], if at a given time there is only one station wishing to transmit a high-priority packet, the worst access delay is bounded by

$$t_{access} \leq 2 \star \tau_{max}$$

The upper bound is higher if there are multiple high-priority frames to transmit from different stations. Given *M* stations transmitting high-priority data, the worst case delay is bounded by

$$t_{access} \leq (M-1)\tau_{mm} + 2\tau_{max}$$

where $\tau_{mm}$ is the transmission time of high-priority multimedia data. The component $2\tau_{max}$ in the above expression means that the high priority frame may wait one round ($\tau_{max}$) to reserve the token if the token's priority field is free, and then wait another round ($\tau_{max}$) to grasp the token. The component $(M-1)\tau_{mm}$ means that, in the worst case, the *M-th* high-priority station must wait (*M-1*) rounds to reserve the priority token.

In this LAN, there are – similar to Ethernet – different possibilities for supporting a *continuous media transmission*. Some variants, described in the Ethernet section, can be adopted to the Token Ring. For example, scaling of media can be used in exactly the same manner. The following approaches can also be considered for continuous media transmission:

### Using the Existing Priority Mechanism

The existing priority mechanism, without modification of any communication components, allows for the use of these LANs for continuous media transmission. The continuous data streams all get the same higher priority than discrete media streams.

However, with a high share of continuous media in the Token Ring traffic, undesirable delays of data frames occur. To achieve good performance, a simple form of bandwidth management is to limit the number of active multimedia sessions on a Token Ring segment. For example, when DVI-PLV multimedia data are transmitted with a high priority in a client/server application, it is possible to run at most 13 multimedia sessions independently of the data traffic on one Token Ring [ACT93].

Other results show that using the existing priority mechanism with allocation of separate queues at the end-point stations for different priority frames reduces the delay of multimedia traffic. Under heavy load, when the delay is most critical, the provision of multiple queues is essential to reduce the delay. Additionally, priority access mechanisms help to reduce the delay, particularly under light load conditions [BPSWL93].

### Using Various Priorities for Continuous Media Streams

Within continuous media streams, priorities can be assigned according to the *importance* of the particular stream. For example, all audio streams are assigned a higher priority level than any other continuous media streams. For this approach, two higher priority levels are needed, for example, priorities 5 and 6 can be used. This approach obtains good results, although by many audio streams, failures can also occur.

### Resource Reservation

It is possible to admit audio and video traffic of multiple streams at the same higher priority levels, but a resource reservation for these connections will also have to be performed. This can be done in at least three ways:

- *Static Resource Reservation*

  Resource reservation can be done *statically* by a predefined distribution of resources according a rule like "the 8 multimedia-capable stations can each send up to maximum of 1.2 Mbits/s of continuous media data". Only a small environment and applications with well-known throughput requirements can use this approach.

- *Dynamic Central Resource Reservation*

  As an alternative, each station can "talk" during connection establishment to central management to get an agreement and an assignment of tight resources. Finally, the data are transmitted according to this agreement.

  This central management can be, for example, a *bandwidth manager* which has all the necessary information to distribute the requested resource capacity (i.e., the required bandwidth). There are already suitable protocols for such a central bandwidth management. They might also allow for network resource reservation across LAN boundaries in the future, although the connection establishment phase will take a much longer time than it does in a LAN setup.

  The problem of resource reservation also touches on operating system resources. This area is discussed in Chapter 8 on multimedia operating systems. The reservation tests for non-interruptive planning methods with respect to the Token Ring are presented in [NV92]. They are applicable toward reservation of the operating system resources, as well as toward reservation of the network bandwidth.

- *Dynamic Distributed Resource Reservation*

  Distributed bandwidth management can allocate a required resource to the connection faster than a central solution. In the following paragraphs, a *time-optimized* mechanism is briefly described [Ste93a].

  Each multimedia station contains an internal table *Available Resource Table "art"*. This table includes records about the available network bandwidth, together with the bandwidth, already in use, for the ongoing audio and video connections. Hence, during the initialization of the Token Ring we can reduce the common available bandwidth to 80% of the real bandwidth (i.e., 3.2 Mbits/s for the 4 Mbits/s, respectively 12.8 Mbits/s for the 16 Mbits/s, early Token Ring release version). The remaining 20% includes the control traffic for the ring management (typically, this is around 3%), which has the highest priority (7) in the priority scale of traffic in the ring. This principle leads to sufficient capacity for other media. The 80% bound is an experience value, which can be adjusted according to the application and configuration scenario.

The *resource managers* of all multimedia stations belong to a group with a common address in the Token Ring. Therefore, each resource manager can send messages to all other managers using this address. Hereby, the *functional addresses* in Token Ring can be used.

In the first phase of a connection setup, the local resource manager compares the required capacity with the currently available capacity. If the bandwidth, recorded in *art* and actually available, is less than the required bandwidth, the connection request is immediately rejected. In the case of having sufficient bandwidth, which is recorded in the local *art*, at the own station, the resource request is delegated to the group of all other resource managers. For example, consider a bandwidth requirement (wish) of 1.41 Mbits/s. This requirement is sent to all members of the group. Let the available bandwidth at that moment be 10 Mbits/s. In the first step, the requesting station compares the required bandwidth with its own available bandwidth value (recorded in the local *art*). The required bandwidth can be provided and the value is modified in *art* from 10 Mbits/s to 8.59 Mbits/s. In the next step, the requesting station sends the resource reservation request with bandwidth value -1,410,000 (bits) to the group. This information is used by all other stations for comparison and modification of the locally stored bandwidth values in their *arts*.

After all other resource managers check their capacity, the frame with the resource request comes back to the requesting station, also including a response. If the response is positive, the required station knows that all members of the group are informed and their local *arts* are adjusted. In the case of a negative response of at least one station in the group, the resource request is rejected and all members of the group are informed. The possibility of rejection can occur because of a collision of simultaneous connection requests, issued by various stations attached to the early token release Token Ring. To avoid such an access collision concerning the available bandwidth, Ethernet-similar access methods should be used. For example, only three access trials are allowed, and they are distributed according to a particular statistic. Hence, the probability of collisions decreases dramatically. The protocol was optimized for establishment of a high-speed connection with the assumption that few collisions occur.

During the *connection close up*, all stations must be informed, and the values in their *arts* must be reset. In the example mentioned above, the value 1,410,000 is sent to the whole group.

The initialization of a new station in a ring happens through a query sent to all available *arts* of all other participants. If all other stations respond and send their *art* bandwidth values, and the values are all the same, the new station initializes its own *art* with this value. Inconsistences will be handled through an additional management protocol.

This method can be used for streams with a variable bit rate also. For the reservation, the maximal values are given. Yet, the resources will not be wasted because the gaps can be used by discrete data traffic.

Further, the distributed resource reservation method can be used not only for bandwidth reservation, but also for reservation of other resources within a ring. For example, the limited number of available *Functional Addresses* in Token Ring can be handled in a similar way.

The distributed resource reservation method assumes that each station is handled according to the bandwidth agreement. For violation cases, a separate control and monitoring component needs to be implemented.

The most important network resource to be managed is the *bandwidth*, which can be distributed using the above described methods. An increase in bandwidth allows a higher number of concurrent continuous media streams. Yet, a main criterion for the effectivity of the access protocol is the *bit length* compared to the size of the physical network. The following example shows: with bandwidth of 100 Mbits/s, a *bit* in fiber optics has the following "size":

$$Length = \frac{propagation\ speed\ in\ fiber\ optics}{data\ rate}$$

$$Length \approx \frac{2 \times 10^8 m/s}{100 \times 10^6 bits/s} = 2m/bit$$

On the other hand, a bit in a copper cable with 64 kbits/s bandwidth has the following "size":

$$Length = \frac{propagation\ speed\ in\ copper}{data\ rate}$$

$$Length \approx \frac{2.5 \times 10^8 m/s}{64 \times 10^3 bits/s} = 3.9km/bit$$

In the Token Ring, the data are always read, written and sometimes copied and changed from and to the cable. Therefore, some bits are not "on" the cable, but "in" the attachment. Here, each station buffers at least 64 bits of the forwarded data. Therefore, with a higher data rate, several frames could be simultaneously on the Token Ring. The transition toward higher rates led to the introduction of the *Early-Token-Release-Principle.* This method allows stations to release the token before receiving their frame back. It means that after sending data, the sending station immediately releases the token again. Here, several frames may be on the ring. Due to the *Early Release* policy, the priority reservation mechanism may be less effective [BPSWL93]. In most cases, however, at a physical ring speed of 5 μsec/km, the ring must be very large to accommodate an entire frame. For example, for a 4 km ring of 20 stations, the ring latency $\tau_l$ is approximately 20 μsec, and can hold to 320 bits (at the 16 Mbps rate). Hence, in the worst case, a station wishing to transmit a priority frame may have to wait $N \times \tau_l$ seconds to gain access to the ring. This may only occur if all stations are sending frames which are smaller than the ring size and the reservation requests are essentially chasing the token around the ring. This, however, may be only a problem in very large rings with many stations.

### 10.3.3 FDDI

The *Fiber Distributed Data Interface (FDDI)* is a high-performance fiber optic LAN, which is configured as a ring. It is often seen as the successor of the Token Ring IEEE 802.5 protocol. The standardization began in the *American Standards Institute (ANSI)* in the group X3T9.5 in 1982. Early implementations appeared in 1988.

Compared to the Token Ring, FDDI is more a backbone than a LAN only because it runs at 100 Mbps over distances up to 100 km with up to 500 stations. The Token Ring supports typically between 50-250 stations. The distance of neighboring stations is less than 2 km in FDDI.

The FDDI design specification calls for no more than one error in $2.5 \times 10^{10}$ bits. Many implementations will do much better. The FDDI cabling consists of two fiber rings, one transmitting clockwise and the other transmitting counter-clockwise. If either one breaks, the other can be used as a backup.

FDDI supports different transmission modes which are important for the communication of multimedia data (see Figure 10.2). The *synchronous mode* allows a

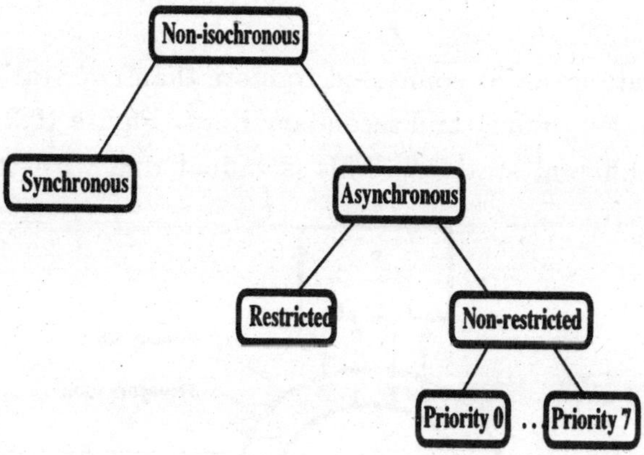


Figure 10.2: *Communication possibilities in FDDI: an overview of data transmission modes.*

bandwidth reservation; the *asynchronous mode* behaves similar to the Token Ring protocol. Many current implementations support only the asynchronous mode. Before diving into a discussion of the different modes, we will briefly describe the topologies and FDDI system components. The details are described in standard documents, as well as, for example, in [MK93]

## Topology

The main *topology* features of FDDI are the two fiber rings, which operate in opposite directions (*dual ring topology*). The *primary ring* provides the data transmission, the *secondary ring* improves the fault tolerance. Individual stations can be - but do not have to be - connected to both rings. FDDI defines two classes of stations, A and B:

- Any class A station (*Dual Attachment Station*) connects to both rings. It is connected either directly to a primary ring and secondary ring or via a concentrator to a primary and secondary ring (see Figure 10.3).
- The class B station (*Single Attachment Station*) only connects to one of the rings. It is connected via a concentrator to the primary ring.

The concentrator-station can be connected to more than two stations. Further, it is always connected to the primary and secondary rings. Figure 10.3 shows a complete configuration with different stations. This is a dual ring with trees. In case of a

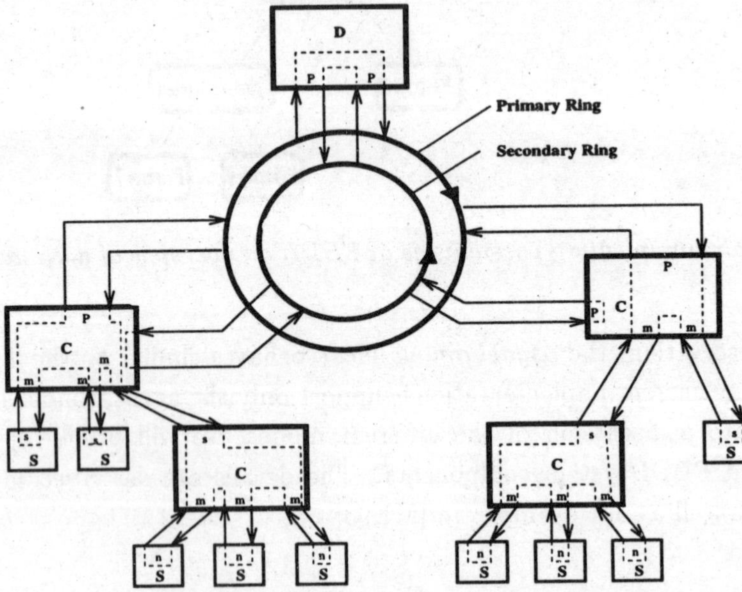


Figure 10.3: *A possible connection of different FDDI stations: a dual ring with several trees.*

failure, the FDDI ring will be newly reconfigured.

### Reliability

In addition to the fault tolerance level provided by the dual rings (secondary ring), the *reliability* of an FDDI network is enhanced by the use of *station bypass switches* or *concentrators (CON)*. A station equipped with a bypass switch is "extracted" from the ring when the station experiences a power failure. A CON facilitates the connection of stations to the ring and it extracts from the ring any faulty station connected to it. The use of reliable CONs to interconnect stations is the heart of the *dual homing configuration.* In most cases, dual homing is more reliable than dual ring; however, the dual homing technique is beneficial only if the following conditions are met [Ngu93]:

- The number of dual attachment stations must be at least four.
- The link reliability should be at least $\sqrt{2}/2$, where the link reliability is defined as the difference probability: (1 - link error probability).
- The primary ring comprising CONs must be reliable.
- The number of CON pairs on the primary ring should be as small as possible.

Another approach to make complex FDDI networks more reliable is to use *creative topologies*, which means to set up configurations that reduce link vulnerability and/or to use redundant resources. Such a configuration approach is *a concentrator tree.* A concentrator tree is a method of interconnecting concentrators such that the A and B ports of each concentrator in the tree connect to M ports of the same concentrator higher in the tree. The concentrator tree alone is no more reliable than approaches such as dual-homing because damage to any set of links still results in isolation. Mechanisms which can survive more than two link failures are of interest to some applications. One technique involves a concentrator tree with connections between the top and bottom of the tree. This configuration is called the *concentrator tree with loop-back* [HM93].

### FDDI Architecture

FDDI includes the following components which are shown in Figure 10.4:

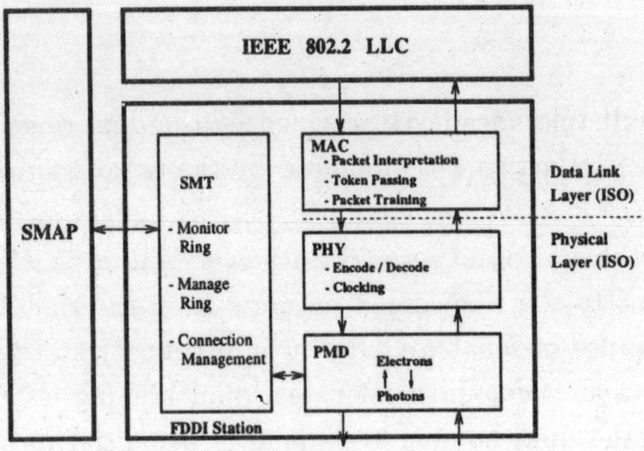


Figure 10.4: *FDDI reference model*

- *PHYsical Layer Protocol (PHY)*

  is defined in the standard *ISO 9314-1 Information Processing Systems: Fiber Distributed Data Interface - Part 1: Token Ring Physical Protocol.*

- *Physical Layer Medium-Dependent (PMD)*

  is defined in the standard *ISO 9314-3 Information Processing Systems: Fiber Distributed Data Interface - Part 1: Token Ring Physical Layer, Medium Dependent.*

- *Station ManagemenT (SMT)*

  defines the management functions of the ring according to *ANSI Preliminary Draft Proposal American National Standard X3T9.5/84-49 Revision 6.2, FDDI Station Management.*

- *Media Access Control (MAC)*

  defines the network access according to *ISO 9314-2 Information Processing Systems: Fiber Distributed Data Interface - Part 2: Token Ring Media Access Control.*

Hence, the physical layers *PMD* and *PHY* provide the transmission over fiber optics. FDDI uses multimode fibers with a diameter of 62.5$\mu$m because the additional expense of single mode fibers is not needed for networks running at only 100 Mbps.

However, it is also possible to take monomode fiber with a diameter of 125 $\mu$m. Further, it uses LEDs with wavelength of 1.320 nm, rather than lasers, not only due to lower cost, but also because FDDI may sometimes be used to connect directly to end systems. The physical layer uses for encoding a scheme known as *"4 out of 5"*: each group of four MAC symbols (0s, 1s and certain nondata symbols such as start-of-frame) are encoded as a group of five bits (four bits for encoding of the four MAC symbols, plus an additional *Non Return to Zero Inverted (NRZI)* bit). Therefore, the physical data rate increases to 125 Mbits/s.

The *SMT* functions are the *control*, *supervision* and *management* of the connected stations and the network itself. Here with respect to the stations, the initialization, activation and supervision of the performance and error handling activities are meant. With respect to the network, the main functions are addressing, reservation of the bandwidth and configuration.

The LAN access component, *MAC*, decides which station may access the ring. It provides address recognition functions and repeats, removes or inserts frames from/to the network. The length of the frame varies, but it is never longer than 4,500 bytes. The addressing allows, besides point-to-point communication, also *multicast* and *broadcast* communications.

### FDDI Timed Token Rotation Protocol

The FDDI-specific access protocol is the *Timed Token Rotation Protocol.* This protocol provides support for two types of service: *synchronous* and *asynchronous.* Each station may be allocated a portion of the network bandwidth for its synchronous traffic. If a station receives the token, it can transmit messages in the synchronous mode for at least its preallocated time (called *synchronous capacity*) before releasing the token to its downstream neighbor. Messages in the asynchronous mode are transmitted only if certain time constraints are valid.

For the protocol, a *Target Token Rotation Time (TTRT)* is introduced. This value represents a typical and desired time for a ring round-trip of a packet. This value is set up during the initialization of the ring through a query to the SMT components of all stations. Each station stores this value. The TTRT must be, according to the

FDDI specification, more than 4ms and less than 165ms. A typical TTRT value is around 50ms. Such values are met, for example, in networks with high utilization and 75 connected stations using approximately 30 km of fiber optics.

Each station measures continuously the *real round-trip time* of a token and stores this time as the *Token Rotation Time (TRT)*. The TRT represents the last measured duration which, with respect to a particular station, a token needed for its last round trip. With respect to the asynchronous and synchronous traffics, the following considerations apply:

- *Asynchronous Traffic*

  The *asynchronous* traffic can be sent only if the network has free capacity. The criterion for this free capacity is the comparison between the last measured TRT and the preassigned TTRT. A station can always send asynchronous data if the following condition is true: $TRT < TTRT$. Hence, asynchronous traffic occurs in the network at most up to the time duration of TTRT.

  Some other approaches, describing how asynchronous traffic can coexist with synchronous traffic without too much delay penalty, are:

  - To transmit the non-real-time messages ahead of real-time messages, unless it is absolutely necessary to transmit real-time messages first to meet their deadlines [HR93]. The determination by a station, if it can defer the transmission of its real-time messages to a later time and still guarantee timely delivery of the real-time messages, is essential in this case.
  - To use a *Restricted Token* according to Figure 10.2. In this case, the total asynchronous bandwidth is reserved for dialogues between two stations as follows: the sending station informs the receiving station about a dialogue wish. This happens through normal (*non-restricted*) asynchronous traffic. The next step is the transmission of the corresponding packets from the sending station as additional packets together with the *restricted token*. At this moment, no other station is allowed to use the asynchronous bandwidth. The receiving station can continue the ongoing dialogue. This dialogue ends when the sending station removes the *restricted token* and places a *non-restricted token* on the network. The asynchronous

traffic with the *non-restricted token* distinguishes among eight priorities, which is similar to Token Ring.

- *Synchronous Traffic*

  To guarantee that the deadlines of synchronous messages are met, network parameters such as *synchronous bandwidth*, the *TTRT* and the *buffer size* must be chosen carefully [MZ93]:

  - The *synchronous bandwidth* is the most critical parameter in determining whether message deadlines are met. Through the SMT procedures, bandwidth for synchronous traffic is allocated to each station. The bandwidth allocation is called *Synchronous Allocation (SA)*.

    If the synchronous bandwidth is too small, the node may not have enough network access time to transmit messages to meet their deadlines. Conversely, large synchronous bandwidths can result in a long TRT, which can also cause message deadlines to be missed.

  - Proper selection of *TTRT* is also important because the time duration for all synchronous connections in their sum cannot cross the TTRT value. A smaller TTRT results in less available utilization and limits network capacity. On the other hand, if TTRT is too large, the token may not arrive often enough at a node to meet message deadlines.

  - Each node has a *buffer* for outgoing synchronous messages. The size of this buffer also affects the real-time performance of the network. The size of the buffer for incoming messages also affects the real-time network performance. The receiving node should be able to keep pace with incoming messages. A buffer that is too small can result in messages being lost due to buffer overflow. A buffer that is too large wastes memory.

The TRT value is maximally double the value of TTRT [SJ87]. For example, with a TTRT value of 50 ms, the maximal round-trip time is limited to 100 ms. The TRT is therefore a metric for the current utilization of the ring.

### FDDI Audio and Video Transmission

For audio and video transmission in FDDI, the synchronous mode is very adequate. Yet the time spent on bandwidth reservation cannot be neglected. Dependent on the relation between TRT and TTRT during data transmission, we distinguish between the following cases:

1. *TRT < TTRT*

   Figure 10.5 shows this relation. The station can send data as long as the local

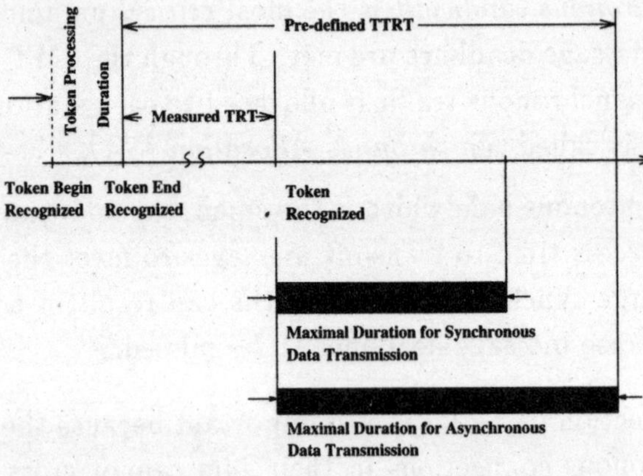


Figure 10.5: *Synchronous and asynchronous traffic on an FDDI with* $TRT < TTRT$.

   TRT counter does not cross the TTRT value.

2. *TRT > TTRT*

   Figure 10.6 shows this relation. The station can transmit yet only its syn-

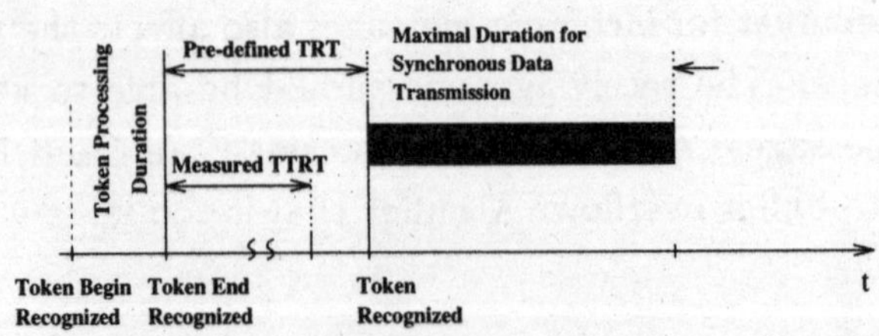


Figure 10.6: *Synchronous traffic on an FDDI with* $TRT > TTRT$.

   chronous traffic.

Next, an example of the *Timed Token Rotation Protocol* is presented. Let us assume that the TTRT takes eight time units and there are three stations connected to the FDDI ring. Each station has reserved one time unit (SA) for the synchronous traffic and sends according to the reservation. All stations would like to transmit as much non-restricted asynchronous traffic as the network admits. Table 10.2 shows the values of the corresponding TRT counters per station together with the transmitting units. After Station 1, Station 2 receives data, after that. Station 3 receives data and then again Station 1. Before the system is balanced, the measured TRT time units are of different values (e.g., 0, 9, 10). At each station, the decision concerning which data to send is determined as shown in Figures 10.5 and 10.6. It means that if $TRT < TTRT$, synchronous and asynchronous traffic can be sent. If $TRT \geq TTRT$, only synchronous data units are sent to the other station. This process repeats until the system is balanced. For example, at the beginning, where measured TRT is 0 time units and pre-defined TTRT is 8 time units, 1 synchronous data unit and 8 asynchronous data units can be sent. After the system is balanced, the behavior from Figures 10.5 and 10.6 is applied further, i.e., Station 1 sends 1 synchronous data unit to Station 2, where TRT is 8 time units ($TRT = TTRT$), Station 2 sends 1 synchronous data unit to Station 3, where TRT is 8 time units, and Station 3 sends 5 asynchronous data units and 1 synchronous data unit to Station 1, where TRT is 3 time units ($TRT < TTRT$), and so on. The joined relations, which also demonstrate the proper distribution of the asynchronous traffic, are the result (Table 10.2).

### Further Properties of FDDI

- *Multicasting*

  The multicasting service became one of the important networking services to support multimedia applications, such as cooperative applications. It is very advantageous to have multicasting as part of the network lower layers, such as the data link layer or the MAC layer, because the higher layers do not have to spend any time and resources for multiplying (making copies) data to be sent. Therefore, overhead transmission delays are avoided.

  FDDI supports *group addressing*, hence multicasting is part of the network. We discucs the multicasting service in Chapter 11, where communication sys-

| Station 1 | | | Station 2 | | | Station 3 | | |
|---|---|---|---|---|---|---|---|---|
| *TRT* | *syn* | *asyn* | *TRT* | *syn* | *asyn* | *TRT* | *syn* | *asyn* |
| 0 | 1 | 8 | 9 | 1 | | 10 | 1 | |
| 11 | 1 | | 3 | 1 | 5 | 8 | 1 | |
| *System is balanced, first cycle starts:* | | | | | | | | |
| 8 | 1 | | 8 | 1 | | 3 | 1 | 5 |
| 3 | 1 | 5 | 8 | 1 | | 8 | 1 | |
| 8 | 1 | | 3 | 1 | 5 | 8 | 1 | |
| *Cycle starts again:* | | | | | | | | |
| 8 | 1 | | 8 | 1 | | 3 | 1 | 5 |

Table 10.2: *Example: TRT values per Station*

tems above the data link layer are described. In this case, the multicasting service is not part of the lower layers of the network, hence other solutions must be implemented.

- *Synchronization*

  The synchronization among different data streams is not part of the network, therefore it must be solved separately. Here, the relation between synchronous and asynchronous data is of interest. A tight time relationship, existing at the sender, does not have necessarily to exist at the receiver side because of the Timed Token Rotation Protocol.

- *Packet Size*

  The size of the used packets can directly influence the data delay in applications. For example, in the case of speech/audio transmission with an 8KHz sampling rate and a data rate of 64 kbits/s, the audio packets must be collected until an FDDI frame is complete. Here, the desirable FDDI frame size would be very small.

- *Implementations*

  Unfortunately, many FDDI implementations do not support the synchronous mode, which is very useful for the transmission of continuous media. In asynchronous mode additionally, the same methods can be used as described previously by Token Ring. In the case of an available synchronous mode, the continuity of the asynchronous traffic can be disrupted. Therefore, guarantees, as described by Token Ring, can be given only if no station uses the synchronous mode.

- *Restricted Token*

  If only two stations interact by transmitting continuous media data, then one can also use the asynchronous mode with *Restricted Token.* This leads to small end-to-end delays, but it inhibits any other asynchronous traffic on the LAN. Hence, this mode should be only used for the transmission of continuous media, if no other station requests such a service.

### FDDI-II

The *synchronous mode*, in general, requires non-negligible times for the reservation of the synchronous bandwidth. Further, the synchronous mode guarantees a bandwidth with a maximal delay. This delay does not exceed double of TTRT value. Of course, data in the synchronous mode can arrive much earlier at the receiver also. The jitter depends heavily on the utilization of the ring. Therefore, the delay is bounded by a maximal value, which can reach 100 ms, and may play an important role in dialogue applications. It means, additionally, that the early arrived data must be stored. For this purpose, a buffer for the duration of at least one TTRT is needed. This argument led to the introduction of an additional *isochronous mode* in *FDDI-II* (see Figure 10.7).

The design of FDDI-II started in 1984 and was planned as an addition to the original FDDI. FDDI-II is a hybrid High-Speed Local Area Network (HSLAN). It integrates *circuit switched services* (isochronous services) for delay-sensitive applications, such as voice and video, and *packet services* (synchronous and asynchronous services), as available in basic FDDI on the same physical medium. Although the packet switched service remains connection-less, the circuit switched service is connection-oriented. Figure 10.8 illustrates the relationship between FDDI-II and the OSI reference model.

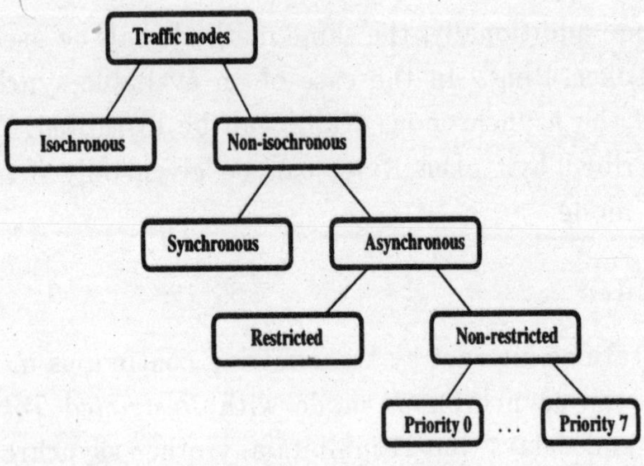


Figure 10.7: *Communication possibilities in FDDI-II: overview of the transmission mode.*

The *FDDI-II Hybrid Ring Control (HRC)* protocol integrates isochronous and asynchronous packet data by carrying both in special fixed-length, fixed-duration frames called *cycles.* The HRC consists of two additional data link layer entities, the *Hybrid MUltipleXer (HMUX)*, and the *Isochronous MAC*, in addition to the MAC entity of FDDI.

FDDI-II networks have two major modes of operation: *basic* and *hybrid.* The basic mode provides packet data services and is "compatible" with the FDDI protocol. Note, "compatible" does not mean that FDDI and FDDI-II stations can simultaneously operate on the same ring. Following initialization in the basic mode, FDDI-II networks may switch to hybrid mode operation, where packet and isochronous services are both provided within the FDDI-II cycle structure. In steady-state hybrid mode operation, one station is designed to be the *cycle master*, which is responsible for generating all cycles on the ring, and for maintaining cycle timing. All other stations, called *slaves*, repeat incoming cycles for a transmission onto the ring after inserting their own packet and isochronous data into the cycles. A station which is capable of becoming the cycle master and generating the cycles, is classified as the *monitor station.* Otherwise, the stations are classified as *non-monitor stations.* In hybrid mode, a new cycle is generated by the cycle master every 125$\mu$s with the cycle length of 125 $\mu$s[BK93]. Cycles circulate around the ring and return to the cycle master. Multiple cycles can be present on the ring at the same time.

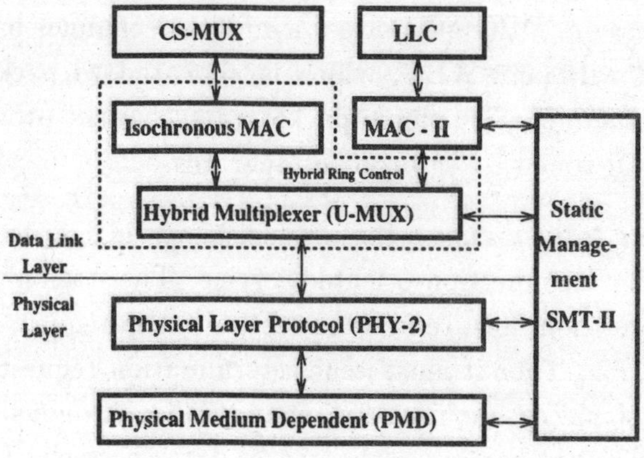


Figure 10.8: *FDDI-II reference model.*

A cycle is composed of four parts: a *preamble*, a *cycle header*, a *Dedicated Packet Group (DPG)*, and 96 *cyclic groups*. Collectively, the DPG and cyclic groups are referred to as the *cycle body*. The cycle header contains all of the peer-to-peer information. Sixteen time slots, known as *Wide Band Channels (WBCs)*, are available in each cycle. These slots are byte-interleaved across the 96 cyclic groups. A single WBC allows data transfer at 6.144 Mbps. This value (6.144 Mbps) is the smallest common multiple of the American (four times) and European (three times) primary rate of the Narrowband ISDN (American Narrowband ISDN rate is 1.536 Mbps, European Narrowband ISDN rate is 2.048 Mbps.)[TG90]. WBCs can be allocated *individually* or *combined*, and they can be used between two or more stations as the transmission channel for duplex connections.

Each WBC can be dynamically allocated for either the packet or isochronous data by the cycle master through updating the *Programming Template*, which is transmitted in each cycle according to the WBC request from SMT. An isochronous WBC can split the available bandwidth into multiples of 8 kbits/s as virtual connections. Therefore, different channels can be implemented, for example, 16 kbits/s, 64 kbits/s, 128 kbits/s, 1,536 kbits/s, 2,048 kbits/s. The maximum number of WBCs for isochronous traffic is set up during the initiatization phase. If all WBCs are used for isochronous data in the 100 Mbps bandwidth range, 98.304 Mbps bandwidth would be available for this class of traffic [KJ93].

For *packet transmission*, DPG guarantees a minimal channel bandwidth. It is, in turn, concatenated with any WBC, which is allocated to packet data to form a *single packet data channel.* The single packet data channel provides a virtual ring over which the FDDI timed token protocol operates.

For *isochronous data transmissions*, the channel bandwidth is centrally allocated on a demand basis, using a connection-oriented service. The station wishing to establish an isochronous connection must send a connection setup request to the cycle master prior to a conversation. Then it must issue a termination request upon finishing the conversation. The signaling, required for setting up isochronous connections, would normally be carried out in-band over the packet data channels. Consequently, using such a connection-oriented and centralized access control, FDDI-II is able to fairly and accurately provide bandwidth access and control. However, it reveals several performance weaknesses, such as bandwidth waste in HSLAN, degradation of packet data transmission performance, and finally, upon finishing conversations, the freed channels remain idle and unused for an average of half the propagation delay of the ring before being reassigned by the cycle master [YH93].

The alternative would be to provide distributed control and access of bandwidth using a connectionless service for both packet and isochronous data transmission. This access scheme is implemented in $FDDI - II^*$ [YH93].

FDDI-II is very good for the transmission of continuous data because of the isochronous service. The commercial relevance of FDDI-II as opposed to the original FDDI is still doubtful. One reason may involve the incompatibility of both systems. Existing FDDI systems cannot be connected to an FDDI-II, they must be replaced.

### 10.3.4 Local ATM Networks

In this section we first briefly discuss ATM characteristics and the ATM architecture, and then we present local ATM network issues. In Section 10.5 we discuss the switching properties of WAN ATM networks.

### ATM Characteristics

The *Asynchronous Transfer Mode (ATM)* is a cell (packet) switching concept with minimal function in network. The ATM concept uses a *fixed length packet (cell)* of size 53 bytes - 48 bytes of user data and a 5 bytes header (see Figure 10.9). ATM

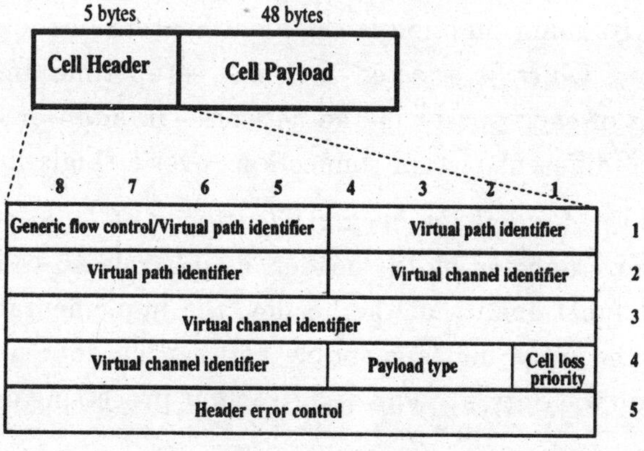


Figure 10.9: *ATM cell.*

allows the systems to operate at a much *higher rate* than usual packet switching systems. The high rate is achieved because of the following characteristics:

1. *No error protection or flow control on a link-to-link basis.*

   If a link of the connection, either the user-to-network link or a link between two ATM switches, introduces an error during transmission, or is temporarily overloaded thereby causing the loss of packets, no special action is taken on that link (e.g., no request for retransmission is made on that link, as is common in packet switching). It means nothing is done to correct errors inside the network. The ATM network relies on end-to-end protocols.

2. *ATM operates in a connection-oriented mode.*

   Before data are transferred from a multimedia terminal to the network, a logical/virtual connection setup phase must allow the network to perform a reservation of the necessary resources. If no sufficient resources are available, the connection is refused and the requesting terminal is notified. After the end of the data transfer phase, the allocated resources are released. This connection-oriented mode allows the network to provide (in all cases) a minimal packet loss ratio.

3. *The header functionality is reduced.*

   To guarantee fast processing in the network, the ATM header has a very limited function. Its main function is the identification of the *virtual connection* by an identifier, which is selected at a call setup time and is guaranteed a proper routing of each packet in the network. In addition, it allows an easy multiplexing of different virtual connections over a single link.

   In addition to the *Virtual Connection Identifier (VCI)*, a very limited number of functions are supported by the header, mainly related to maintenance. Due to the limited functionality of the header, the implementation of the header processing in the ATM nodes is simple and can be done at very high speeds (150 Mbits/s up to Gbits/s). This results in low processing and queuing delays.

4. *The information field length is relatively small.*

   To reduce the internal buffers in the switching nodes, and to limit the queuing delays in those buffers, the information field length is kept relatively small. This assures a small end-to-end delay caused by the packetization of audio and video data into ATM cells.

The ATM concept guarantees the possibility of transporting any data independent of its characteristics such as the bit rate, its quality requirements or its bursty nature. This means that the ATM networks are suitable, with their speed and bandwidth characteristics, to offer a transmission service for the multimedia traffic with different quality requirements. This capability was one of the main motivations for CCITT to decide that ATM will be the transfer mode of the future *Broadband-ISDN*, which represents the concept for high-speed WANs.

### ATM Architecture

The same logical hierarchical architecture as used in OSI is used for ATM B-ISDN network in the CCITT Standard I.321 (see Figure 10.10). Only lower layers of ATM

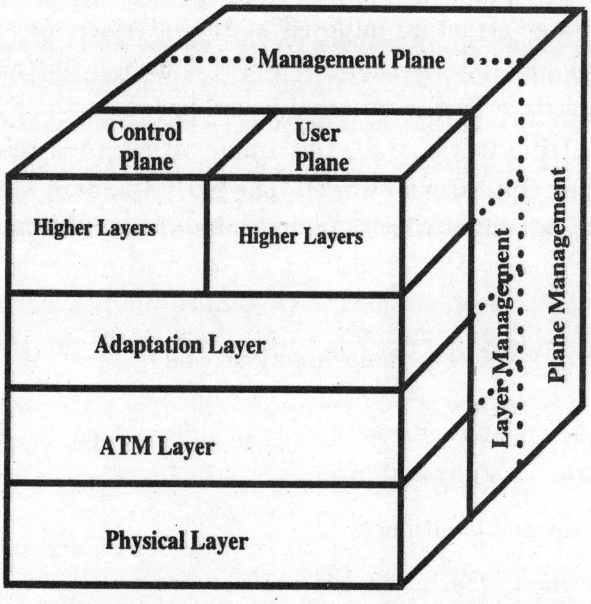


Figure 10.10: *B-ISDN ATM protocol reference model.*

B-ISDN are specified by CCITT. The B-ISDN protocol model for ATM contains three planes: *a user plane* to transport user information, *a control plane* mainly composed of signaling information and *a management plane*, used to maintain the network and to perform operational functions. For each plane, a layered approach is used with an independence between the layers. According to CCITT, there are three lower layers:

- *The PHYsical Layer (PHY)*

  carries data (bits/cells). It is composed of two sublayers: *the Physical Medium (PM)* sublayer which supports pure medium-dependent bit functions, and *the Transmission Convergence (TC)* sublayer, which converts the ATM cell stream into bits to be transported over the physical medium.

  The preferred medium for the full-duplex 155.52 Mbps service, as well as 622.08 Mbps service, is the *optical fiber*.

  The transmission structure (for 155.52 Mbps data rate) used to multiplex cells from various virtual channels can be either a *continuous stream of cells* with no multiplex frame structure imposed at the interface, or a *placement of cells in a synchronous time-division multiplex envelope.* In this case, the bit stream at the interface has an external frame based on the Synchronous Digital Hierarchy (SDH). In the U.S., this frame structure is referred to as SONET (Synchronous Optical NETwork). The SDH standard G.709 defines a hierarchy of data rates, all of which are multiples of 51.84 Mbps.

- *The ATM Layer*

  is fully independent of PHY. The main functions are:

  - *Multiplexing* and *demultiplexing* of cells of different connections into a single cell stream on a physical layer.
  - *Translation* of the cell identifier.
  - *Provision with one of the service classes.*
  - *Management functions.*
  - *Extraction (addition)* of the cell header.
  - *Implementation of a flow control mechanism* at the user-network interface.

- *The ATM Adaptation Layer (AAL)*

  enhances the service provided by the ATM layer. It performs functions for the user, control and management planes and supports the mapping between the ATM layer and the next higher layer. AAL consists of a *Segmentation And Reassembly (SAR)* sublayer, where the higher layer information is segmented into ATM cell size stream at the sender, and the cell stream is reassembled into the higher layer data units at the receiver. AAL further includes the *Convergence* Sublayer (CS) with functions like message identification, time/clock recovery, etc.

  To accommodate various services (e.g., voice, video, data, ...), several types of AAL have been defined. Up to now, five AALs have been defined, which include support for connection-oriented, connectionless, Variable Bit Rate (VBR) and Constant Bit Rate (CBR) services:

- *AAL1* supports CBR services after a virtual connection is established. This service class is advantageous for high-quality constant bit rate audio and video.
- *AAL2* offers a transfer of data with a VBR. In addition, timing information is transferred between source and destination. In the CS sublayer, the following functions are performed: *clock recovery* (e.g., time stamps), *handling of lost or misdelivered cells* and *Forward Error Correction (FEC)* for audio and video services.
- *AAL3/4* should be used for transfer of data which are sensitive to loss, but not to delay. This AAL may be used for connection-oriented, as well as for connectionless, data communication (e.g., multimedia file transfer, multimedia e-mail).
- The ATM Forum defined a different AAL for high-speed data transfer (e.g., transaction transmission), called *AAL5*. An AAL5 packet has far less overhead than AAL3/4. Further, this layer minimizes the computer's cost in handling cells and behaves like data communications interfaces for Ethernet and FDDI (LAN emulation), so that existing data communication software can easily be ported to support ATM.

### ATM Cell Information

ATM services and capabilities are achieved using the information in the ATM cell header. Hence, we describe some header information which is important for the support of multimedia data transmission:

- *Virtual Connections*

  Functions such as the source, destination address and sequence number are not required to be part of an ATM cell. Every virtual connection is identified by a number, which has only a local significance (per link). The virtual connection is identified by two subfields of the header: *Virtual Channel Identifier (VCI)* and *Virtual Path Identifier (VPI)*.

- *Virtual Channels*

Since the ATM network is connection-oriented, a VCI is assigned to each connection during the connection setup procedure . A VCI has only a local significance at the link between two ATM nodes. In each ATM node along the path between the sender and the receiver, the VCI is translated. If the connection is released, the VCI values of the involved path are released and can be reused by other connections.

An interesting advantage of this VCI principle is the use of multiple VCI values for multicomponent services (e.g., video telephony, TV etc.). For example, a video telephone call may use three communication streams: voice, video and data, each of which will be transported over a separate VCI. It allows the network to add or remove streams during transmission. This means that the video telephony service can start with voice only (single VCI) and the video stream can be added (and removed) over a separate VCI later on. The signaling for managing the particular connections is transported over a separate VCI. This VCI principle has an implication to call establishment and management in the higher layers, where a video telephone call between sender and receiver (one logical call connection) can be mapped to three virtual connections, dependent on which media the sender or receiver wants to use for communication

- *Virtual Path*

  Future broadband networks will support semi-permanent connections between end-points. This concept is known as a *virtual path* or a *virtual network.* To perform this virtual network, another field is defined in the header *Virtual Path Identifier.*

- *Priorities*

  The ATM header supports a differentiation of logical connections through different priorities. Two types of priorities exist: *time priority* and *semantic priority.* In the time priority system, it is assumed that some cells may remain longer in the network than others. In a semantic priority system, some cells have a higher probability of being lost, giving rise to a higher cell loss ratio.

  Priorities can either be assigned on a per connection basis (per VPI or per VCI), or on a per cell basis. In the first option, all cells in the virtual channel/path have the same priority. In the second case, cells within a virtual channel/path may have different priorities. No priorities at all lead to the best sharing of resources, but do not allow a differentiation between services with different quality requirements. With priorities applied to continuous media streams, guarantees are provided on a statistical basis with a very high probability.

- *Maintenance*

  To maintain the overall network and to provide performance monitoring (which implies a monitoring of the media quality) of the ATM connections, some additional bits are useful. The *Payload Type Identification (PTI)* distinguishes, using the PTI information field, which type of data (e.g., video, data, control, ...) is carried in the ATM cell.

- *Multiple Access*

  In addition, to allow multiple terminals (users) to be connected to the same physical link, a point-to-multipoint protocol is specified. This protocol is useful, for example, for video-conferencing applications. To perform this point-to-multipoint function, the *Generic Flow Control (GFC)* field in the ATM header is used. GFC provides the possibility to negotiate shared access to the network at the *User-Network Interface (UNI)*, i.e., how to multiplex the shared network among the cells of the various ATM connections.

- *Header Error Protection*

  The header of the ATM cell is the most sensitive part to be protected against corruption. Therefore, it should be protected against single bit errors and, if possible, also against burst errors. To protect the header, a coding principle based on a generalization of Hamming codes is very suitable, namely the BCH codes (Bose-Chadhuri-Hocquenghem) [Pry93].

### ATM Connectivity between Traditional LANs and ATM Networks

The ATM WANs will enforce the LANs to provide for an *ATM connectivity* if they want to internetwork over long distances.

There are several possibilities to have an ATM connectivity of a traditional LAN (e.g., Ethernet, FDDI, Token Ring) to the ATM networks:

- to introduce additional functionality at the gateways between LAN and ATM WAN and at the *ATM hubs* (bridges) between traditional LANs and ATM LAN, Figure 10.11 shows a possible topology. ATM intelligent hubs support

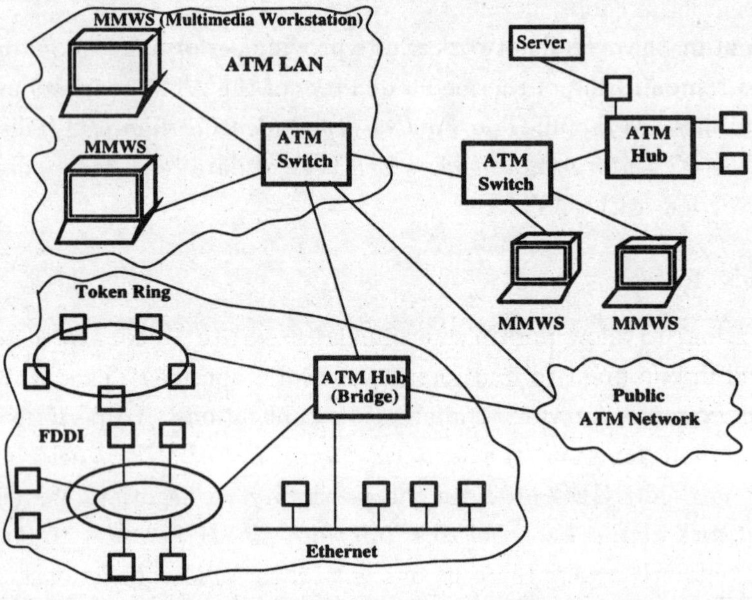


Figure 10.11: *ATM connectivity of traditional LANs and an ATM LAN.*

  multiple LAN segments of multiple LAN types (e.g., Ethernet, Token Ring and FDDI) and provide bridge and routing functionalities. Further, they give every terminal the full capacity by relying on the high switching capabilities of the hubs.

- To implement additional ATM software at the end-points above the traditional LAN protocol stack [AA93].

  For example, between two Ethernet interfaces, the ATM concept can be emulated. The ATM cells are encapsulated inside the Ethernet packets. A network architecture, consisting of at least one LAN/fiber switch node whose job is to switch cells between in-house physical LAN links and an external B-ISDN fiber, is proposed in [AA93]. A possible structure of an ATM/Ethernet interface at a multimedia end-user workstation is shown in Figure 10.12. There

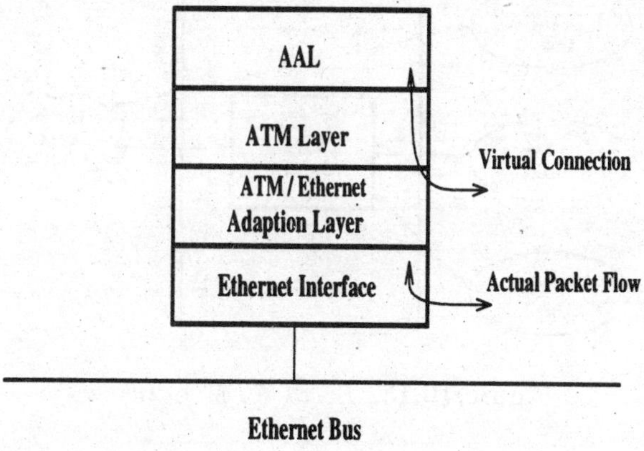


Figure 10.12: *Example: ATM connectivity in Ethernet.*

may be a decrease in throughput, but considering the connectivity to a wide range of multimedia services over the WAN, it is certainly worthy to take into account this "speed penalty".

### Local ATM Network

An ATM LAN connects ATM multimedia terminals, i.e., workstations or servers with an ATM host interface, either via a private UNI (User Network Interface) with a private ATM switch, or via a public UNI with a public ATM network, as shown in Figure 10.13. A simple star configuration is used; hence, no MAC protocol must be defined, as is done in other HSLAN systems. Hence , for this star architecture, only a point-to-point interface is defined.

An ATM LAN can be used to cover a small geographical area as well as a large one. It can have a small number of terminals or a large number of terminals just by dimensioning the size of the ATM LAN switch, and by using interfaces with short or long distances. There are some differences in the service requirements between ATM LAN switches and ATM switches for B-ISDN:

- An ATM LAN switch may provide only a limited number of ports (typically

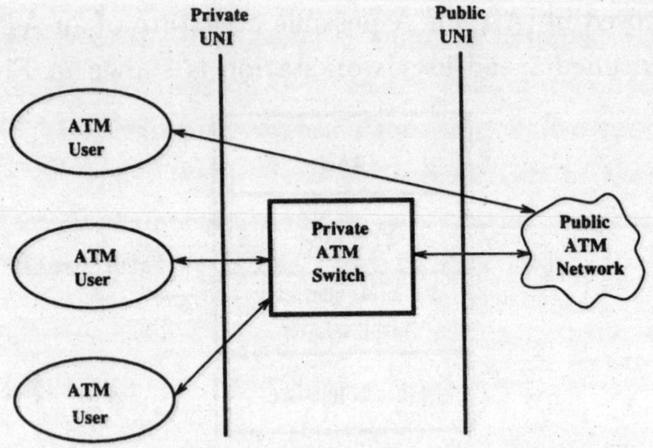


Figure 10.13: *Local ATM network.*

below 1024 ports) due to the fact that the amount of attached stations in a LAN environment is limited.

- Delays inside the switches themselves will dominate the link delays. To provide a total delay comparable to traditional LANs, such switches must minimize this value. Therefore, switching delay is much more important in ATM LANs than in comparable WANs.

- Several LAN applications rely on data to be exchanged between all or a set of stations. Therefore, an ATM LAN switch must provide capabilities for both multicasting and broadcasting.

- Reliability is crucial for WANs which carry voice data. In ATM LANs, we may not encounter the same stringent requirements.

- The connection establishment in a WAN is similar to the telephone paradigm where we are accustomed to wait for some time. This is difficult in LANs. There, we encounter an immediate data transmission. Hence, ATM LANs should have a very short connection establishment.

A high-performance, self-routing ATM LAN switch is proposed in [TYL93]. We discuss ATM switching, routing, and multicasting properties in Section 10.5. because these properties are common for ATM LANs and ATM WANs.

The end-points of ATM LANs require high-performance end-to-end protocols because the delays in the end-points will dominate link and ATM LAN switch delays. As mentioned above, it is proposed to use the AAL5 to carry signaling data. For user data, the AAL1/2 should be used for voice/video services, AAL3/4 for the other services.

## 10.4 Metropolitan Area Networks (MANs)

Between LAN and WAN we have the *Metropolitan Area Network (MAN)*, which covers an entire city, but uses LAN technology. MAN uses a shared medium with distributed switching and Medium Access Control (MAC). MANs have generally higher data rates than LANs, i.e., more than 100 Mbits/s. The administration can be either public or private. The number of stations connected in a MAN is mostly around thousands. A MAN's services include:

- *The interconnection of different LANs.*

  For *LAN interconnection*, a gateway/bridge performs functions such as protocol conversion, address mapping, access control, etc. depending on the compatibility of the interconnected LANs. Since most LANs operate in connectionless mode, it is appropriate that the MAN also interconnects these LANs in a connectionless way. This means that no resources are usually allocated in the MAN. However, continuous media transmission requires guarantees which can easily be provided by a resource allocation.

- *Host-to-host computer internetworking.*

  MAN host-to-host networking can be supported by [Pry93]:

  1. Providing a semi-permanent point-to-point connection with high throughput and high reliability. In this case, a connection is established at installation time, and ensures that enough resources are available on the MAN. Therefore, the mode of operation is connection-oriented, and resources are assigned semi-permanently.
  2. Offering a number of isochronous slots, requested on demand by signaling. This solution is more comparable to a circuit switched solution, where a

TDM (Time Division Multiplexing) approach is taken. This functionality may not be available in all MANs.

3. Offering a number of non-isochronous slots. In this case, resources of the MAN are only occupied when data must be transported (on-demand). This type of service is provided in the connectionless mode.

- *Voice and video communication.*

  For voice and video services, the three alternatives described in host-to-host internetworking can be used depending on the quality of requirements. If voice and video are offered via alternatives 1 or 3, the jitter must be removed at the receiving terminal.

In addition to these services, functions like broadcasting and multicasting, etc. can be offered.

There are two main proposals for MAN standards: (1) *FDDI* from ANSI, which was initially proposed as a high-speed LAN but achieved a span of up to 100 km, and (2) *Distributed Queue Dual Bus (DQDB)* from the group IEEE 802.6. In Europe, an additional MAN mechanism, called *Orwell*, has been considered and developed by researchers of British Telecom. However, it has not been retained by a standards body. We described the FDDI mechanisms already in Section 10.3.3, therefore in this section we concentrate on the DQDB and Orwell mechanisms, as well as on MAN connectivity to ATM B-ISDN.

### 10.4.1 Distributed Queue Dual Bus (DQDB)

The MAC mechanism using a token is not effective anymore in the data rate range above 100 Mbits/s and a geographic range of a network above 100 km [RB90]. The reason is the ring or bus latency, which requires the token to circulate to the next active station and along the entire ring or bus. Therefore, if the geographic range of a network is large, it takes a long time until the token comes back to the sending station, and a release of a token occurs. If the packet is large, the sending station does not release the token until it sends all the data which may occupy several frames, hence the latency is equal to multiple TRTs.

This argument supported a development of a further network which originally became known as *Queued Packet Synchronous Exchange (QPSX)* [NBH88]. This network was a cooperative effort of the company QPSX, the University of West Australia and Telecom Australia. Because of the naming collision between the standard name and the company name, this network was renamed and is now the *Distributed Queue Dual Bus (DQDB)*.

This IEEE 802.6 MAN standard is characterized by a bus with a data rate of $2 \times 150$ Mbits/s. It uses different kinds of cables. DQDB is based on two counter rotating symmetric bus-systems as shown in Figure 10.14. In contrast to FDDI,

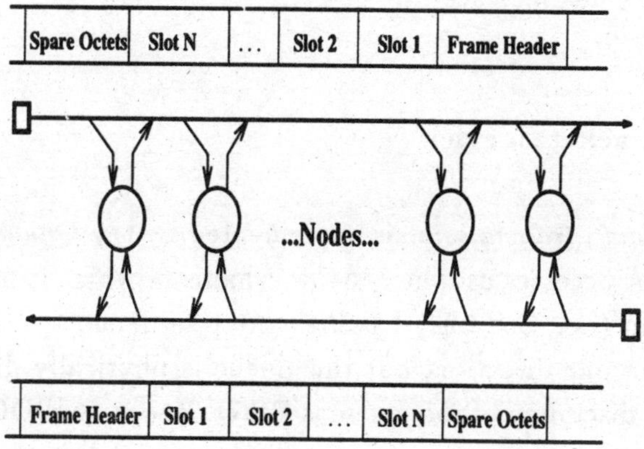


Figure 10.14: *Distributed Queue Dual Bus - principal topology with standard names.*

both busses carry data and therefore, are not only used for fault tolerance. The data are transmitted on the bus - analog to FDDI-II - in 125 $\mu$s frames. Each frame includes further time slots of fixed length, called *segments*. The time slot transports the data between the nodes. It means that the bus capacity is allocated in slots of 53 bytes to *Access Units (AUs)* via which user terminals gain access to the network. Slots are generated at the *head* of each bus.

The DQDB MAC mechanism is fundamentally different from most of the other LAN/MAN protocols with shared access. In these other protocols, there is no continuous record kept of the network state in the nodes. In those networks, state information must be derived from the medium first before accessing it. This feature makes these systems' performance very sensitive to the size of the network. For example, in FDDI, the performance is negatively influenced by the length of the ring. DQDB is based on the *distributed queuing algorithm*, where the current state information of the network is stored in each node; namely every node knows the exact number of segments still waiting to be put on the bus. If a node has a segment to transmit, it uses this local information (stored in a counter) to determine the position of the segment.

The DQDB standard includes one complete specification of the *connectionless packet service* for asynchronous data transmission. The *isochronous service* is nearly completed. Work on the so-called *Guaranteed Bandwidth (GBW) protocol* for *connection-oriented data service* has just begun.

### Connectionless Packet Service

The *asynchronous data transmission* is implemented by the *Queued Arbitrated (QA) Access* function. QA accesses use the MAC mechanism, which is based on *distributed queues*. The system (i.e., one bus) has logically one queue for the storage of data to be transmitted in one direction, but this queue is physically distributed over the nodes. The service discipline of the queue is FIFO. Hence, in a DQDB system, there are two logical queues available, one for the traffic in each direction. One bus is used to coordinate the queuing discipline of the segments to be transferred over the other bus, and vice versa. This coordination is achieved by collecting requests from the nodes when these nodes have segments to transmit. The following four steps explain this process taking the upper bus, shown in Figure 10.14, as an example for data to be transmitted:

1. Each *listening station* (node in Figure 10.14) counts all, from the right, requests coming in on the lower bus. These requests are stored in the internal queue. Now, if from the left on the upper bus, a free time slot arrives, the oldest request in the queue is satisfied. Hence, the request entry can be deleted from the queue. Afterwards, the queue contains all, further right, open "send requests" which must be transmitted on the upper bus. The same principle is applicable to the lower bus with left-ordered stations and with a second queue.

2. A *station, willing to send, issues a "send request"*. To perform this action, the station waits for a free request field at the lower bus. If such a free request field arrives at the lower bus, the station makes its request by marking the *Request Field* on the lower bus and it queues its own "send request" in the internal queue for the upper bus.

3. The *station, willing to send, waits to send data.* It can always store, at most, one of its own requests, according to the above described principle, in the queue. Further, it must continuously trace the bus and take away the requests from the internal queue, corresponding to the free time slots arriving at the upper bus. Additionally, it registers further requests from the lower bus.

4. The *station sends the data.* The station's own "send request" has the highest preference in the queue. Now, at the first free time slot occurring at the upper bus, the data are transmitted and the request entry is removed from the queue. The free time slot is marked as *busy.* Further, the incoming "send requests" are queued and processed as described above.

In summary, the DQDB protocol is based on counters keeping track of requests by different stations and making sure that a station refrains from transmission until reservations made prior to its own request have been satisfied.

The standard states that *priorities* of transmission requests are distinguished by the use of different request bits to be queued in different priority queues. It also states that the connectionless service is restricted to low priority. It means that the connectionless traffic may only be transmitted if the high-priority queues are empty. Unfortunately, not all implementations follow this approach with multiple priority queues.

### Isochronous Service

For continuous data, *isochronous data transmission* is essential. This kind of transmission is implemented by the *pre-arbitrated function.* Certain time slots of this particular type, known as SLT, are marked at the head stations. The slot type *SLT* gets the value 1. The SLT slots can only be used according to the reservation previously done. The SLT slots arrive every 125 $\mu$s and therefore the slot frequency corresponds to 8 kHz. Hence, the isochronous mode of the DQDB can be connected with the PCM hierarchy to the WANs. Further, the 8 kHz frequency allows integration of audio and video data, which are often sampled in multiples of 8 kHz.

### Connection-oriented Data Transmission

The connection-oriented data transmission is provided by the *Guaranteed Bandwidth Protocol (GBW)*. GBW represents an enhancement of the basic DQDB protocol and it is tailored to the requirements of the Variable Bit Rate (VBR) traffic requiring bandwidth guarantees. Hence, GBW is, using the priority mechanism, compatible with the basic DQDB protocol at the lowest priority and is able to allocate a required bandwidth for connection-oriented data service at higher priorities 1 or 2.

According to the GBW protocol, the queues for each priority include all segments not yet transmitted but "accepted" for immediate transmission. In this context, accepted means that the segment has passed the *traffic shaper* described in the next paragraph. The GBW protocol also uses a distributed queuing algorithm as follows: Each queue can be described as a linked list of 0's and 1's where a "1" represents a segment enqueued by the station itself and a "0" represents a request by a downstream station. The queue is updated each time a segment is transmitted, a segment is admitted by the traffic shaper or a request is received. By this kind of distributed queue, GBW allows multiple outstanding requests.

GBW *shapes the traffic* by limiting the rate of enqueuing segments for a specific connection according to the bandwidth accepted at call setup. Hence, to shape the traffic, a variable *credit* and the system parameters *income*, *slotcost* and *creditmax* are used. For each slot passing on the bus to be used for transmission, the parameter *income* is added to the current value of *credit*. A connection is allowed to enqueue a segment if the value of credit exceeds the parameter *slotcost* indicating the amount of "money" to be spent for the transmission of one segment. At the time of enqueuing the segment, the current value of credit is immediately reduced by *slotcost*. To reduce burstiness, the *credit* value is upper bounded by *creditmax*. The parameters of GBW are determined by the network management. During the enabling of high priorities, the fairness scheme "Bandwidth Balancing" must be disabled. Otherwise, high-priority transmission does not work [As90].

Low-priority traffic is controlled in a different way. GBW allows connectionless traffic to be transmitted at priority 0 with a mechanism fully compatible to the DQDB protocol, i.e., with dynamic bandwidth sharing without bandwidth guarantees.

### Reachability and Fairness

Several critical issues of the basic DQDB protocol are subjects for improvement. One of these is the *reachability problem.* The solution to this problem is: each station must know which bus is reachable to other stations. Besides the reachability problem, the location of the station with respect to the *head stations* has an impact on the *fairness.* The stations, which are located closer to the *head end*, can transmit earlier data in the direction of this *head end* than other stations. For the proper operation of the protocol, it is important to transport the data until the *head ends* are reached, although utilization is lowered and it is not necessary for the actual data transmission.

Several solutions have been devised to counteract the potential unfairness of DQDB. One prominent example is *Bandwidth Balancing (BWB)*, which was incorporated into the IEEE 802.6 draft standard for MANs. This scheme attempts to prevent unfair allocation of bus capacity by artificially forcing an Access Unit (AU) to forego a certain fraction of its bus access entitlement. The scheme is such that the greater the fraction, the smaller the potential for unfairness. In general, this technique achieves fairness but at the expense of a wasted bandwidth.

Another approach for fairness improvement is *Reactive DQDB protocol (R-DQDB)*, where more status information about the bus activity is collected via special control slots dedicated to this purpose. This additional information allows an AU to discover if it is experiencing unfairness relative to other users. If this is the case, the reactive protocol allows the disadvantaged AU to issue additional requests for capacity, which has the effect of immediately establishing fairness. The overhead of R-DQDB consists of periodically collecting bus status information to determine the number of active AUs. A bus sampling rate of one per 100 slots was found to be very adequate [OF93].

The isochronous mode of DQDB fits the requirements for the transmission of continuous data very well. However, most implementations do not support this mode yet. The simultaneous access of several stations to the network data also allows an effective and high data rate for the networks with larger spatial expansion.

All networks considered so far offer their services to the higher·component of the data link layer, the *logical link control*, according to the IEEE Standard 802.2. This layer must not have specific properties to support multimedia transport. It must provide only an effective access to all, with the required parameters corresponding MAC services.

### 10.4.2 Orwell

The *Orwell mechanism* for MANs is based on the *slotted ring* approach. The use of fixed slots allows an easy synchronization mechanism, whereas high performance is achievable at very high rates. This scheme allows the integration of asynchronous (packet-like) and isochronous traffic (continuous-like).

The basic principle of the slotted ring is as follows: the ring is partitioned into slots of equal length; every slot has bits on the transmission line and in the node(s); to ensure that an integer number of slots is present on the ring, a latency register, located in a monitor node, is introduced to virtually lengthen the ring to a multiple number of slots; these slots circulate around the ring and are either empty or full, indicated by a single bit; if the content of a slot arrives at the destination node, it will be read; in the case of a node wanting to send data, writing of data can be performed if an empty slot is passing by.

In general, the deletion of a filled slot can be done either in the source or destination node, which provides two different access methods (source releasing approach/destination releasing approach). Orwell defines the *destination releasing approach.* This results in better performance since the released slot can already be used by another node between the destination and source node. To ensure fairness on the ring and to prevent a node from monopolizing the ring, the access is organized in *cycles*, also called *reset intervals.* Each node on the ring has a counter indicating how many slots may be occupied by that node during a cycle.

Two classes of services are defined: *class 1 for isochronous traffic* and *class 2 for asynchronous traffic*. Four priority levels are provided, implemented by four queues in each node. This is also reflected in the Orwell slot header. To increase the bandwidth of the Orwell ring, several rings can be assembled in parallel. This configuration allows a flexible increase of the network capacity, as well as providing higher network reliability. The slot structure was lined up close to the ATM structure. Therefore, ATM cells can be completely transported by the Orwell ring.

The performance of the Orwell ring is very good because of the destination releasing approach. The ring can be loaded with up to 240 Mbits/s; however, at these high loads, the delay on the ring becomes rather large (more than 1ms) [Pry93].

### 10.4.3 MAN Connectivity to ATM Networks

The physical limitations of a MAN prevent it from being used as a wide-area solution, so ATM B-ISDN (ATM WAN) systems must provide internetworking among different MANs. The B-ISDN can function as a higher hierarchical level of switching, interconnecting different MANs.

In the case of a FDDI MAN, there is a large incompatibility between ATM and FDDI, requiring additional adaptation functions in the gateways or bridges. For example, the cell size of ATM and the frame size of FDDI are incompatible. This requires a permanent segmentation and reassembly at the internetworking unit, which influences the end-to-end delays. It also requires additional substantial processing capabilities to maintain the throughput. The segmentation and reassembly can be achieved, for example, by the AAL4 layer.

The specification of DQDB and Orwell was performed in parallel with the ATM specification, therefore it will become easier to interconnect them. The DQDB protocol uses slot-based transmission where the slot size (53 bytes) was adopted from ATM. Sometimes, DQDB is called the "Shared Medium ATM", but the similarity between the ATM and DQDB is limited to the payload field length.

The future and relevance of DQDB depends highly on availability of gateways between DQDB and ATM B-ISDN. Internetworking means mapping DQDB slots to ATM cells and vice versa, as well as service internetworking. Some internetworking solutions, such as *cell-to-slot internetworking* and *frame internetworking* were tested for DQDB connection-oriented mode through simulations. The cell-to-slot internetworking modifies ATM cells to DQDB slots and vice versa. The frame internetworking reassembles cells/slots and modifies AAL frames to DQDB initial MAC PDU and vice versa. Both modes were compared, receiving aggregated traffic from B-ISDN and using high-priority transmission controlled by GBW protocol for access to DQDB. The cell-to-slot mode performed better and showed to be more advantageous [MR93a].

More generally, ATM connectivity of MANs may be provided as follows:

- *Semi-permanent Basis*

  As described in Section 10.4.1, the DQDB standard up to now only covers the *connectionless packet service.* The final specification of the *isochronous service* and the *connection-oriented data service* are still in progress.

  For the connectionless mode, some precautions must be taken due to the connection-oriented nature of the ATM concept. Solutions may be:

  - The installation of semi-permanent connections, using *virtual paths* and transporting different *virtual channels* between all MANs to be interconnected. This may result in a *virtually meshed network* [TP90].
  - The provision of special Message IDentification (MID) values in the AAL.
  - The provision of very fast call setup [Pry89], also called *fast reservation protocol* [TBR92].

- *Connectionless Servers*

  Because of the connectionless transport in MANs, instead of virtual linking all the MANs, the linking one or more servers that are capable of serving connectionless data is possible. A connectionless server based on the *Switched Multimegabit Data Service (SMDS)* or the *Connectionless Broadband Data Services (CBDS)* might be appropriate [HL90].

- *Direct ATM Connection via an ATM LAN*

  Traffic increase may continue until the final solution is that each device within the user's premises will have its own direct connection to the B-ISDN via an

ATM LAN. This would result in a full star-like topology with every subscriber directly connected to the ATM network, with the maximal functions expressed in terms of B-ISDN traffic.

In principle, DQDB as a whole turns out to be well-suited for continuous media traffic. However, the required modes are not fully specified and only connectionless packet service is available, which is not suitable to transport audio and video data. Orwell is an experimental MAN which so far is well-designed for multimedia data transport. However, it is questionable if Orwell will receive wide attention in the real world. Whereas a few years ago, the necessity to have MANs was well-accepted, today's high-speed LANs on the one side and the ATM LANs on the other side show that we might encounter LANs and WANs only in the future.

## 10.5 Wide Area Networks (WANs)

WANs typically span entire countries. The data rates of current WANs (e.g., Internet's T3 NFSNET backbone has a data rate of 45 Mbits/s) are lower than those of LANs and MANs, but this changes with the up-coming Broadband ISDN and its new technologies for high-speed networking. The ownership is split among multiple organizations (the carrier owns the communications subnet and numerous clients own the hosts). The basis of a WAN's communication is point-to-point connection, except for satellite networks.

Currently we see two main wide area networks which are/will be used for multimedia transmission: *traditional networks*, such as Internet, and *ATM B-ISDN* We describe in this section the basic mechanisms and principles of these WAN systems below the network layer which are relevant to multimedia transmission. With respect to traditional WAN systems, we present the connectivity issues and a brief overview of the Internet network. Internet functions, such as *multicasting* and *routing* at the network layer, are crucial for multimedia applications, such as collaborative computing. These issues will be discussed in Chapter 11. In the case of ATM B-ISDN, we discuss *switching* functions, *routing* and *host interfacing* issues important for multimedia transmission.

### 10.5.1 Traditional WAN's

#### Connectivity

Connectivity of different local networks over a wide area is an important and crucial feature for WANs. This function allows users to execute multimedia networked applications which provide for remote project collaborations. The connectivity of the systems can be described in terms of three levels:

- *Basic Level*

  At the first level, basic *link connectivity* is provided. This is commonly provided either through the use of leased lines or by using the available public packet data network infrastructure, which is commonly X.25-based.

  In 1990, the principal backbone networks for the Internet in the USA became NSFNET (National Science Foundation Network) and other agency networks such as NASA's NSI and Department of Energy networks. NSFNET is organized to interconnect regional and local networks that serve the academic community. NSI connectivity reflects the networking needs of NASA science and research projects.

  The link interconnectivity between USA and Europe is based on:

  - *Specific lines*, which mostly operate at approximately 64 kbits/s or below and tend to serve a specific need. An example is the line between Oslo and College Park, which connects NORDUNET and the US research network infrastructure.
  - *Fat pipes* in which larger bandwidth (typically a fraction of T1) is purchased and shared among several networks. An example is a T1 link (1.5 Mbps) for the *Multicast Backbone (MBone)* service connectivity [MB94]. MBone is a virtual network that shares the same physical media as the Internet. For multimedia traffic in this basic level, Internet (MBone) can make use of switched lines which have a guaranteed bandwidth. Also, experiments showed [MB94] that bandwidth capacities lower than T1 are unsuitable for MBone video, although some users, even sometimes entire

countries, have managed on special configured networks to use MBone applications at 54 and 64 kbps.

- *Network Level*

  The next level of connectivity provides *network connection* so that an end-to-end connectivity may be established. This level of connection is typically provided through the use of a single protocol suite, or by sharing link or physical connectivity between networks using multiple protocol suites.

  The focus of international internetworking in addressing multiple protocol suites is to find a method for coexistence and interoperability. In our context, we see the need for this to be provided for continuous streams. An example is Internet's research to develop mechanisms for an *integration of multiple protocol suites* within the Internet that maximizes the functionality and performance of the end-to-end systems for different quality of media.

  Another challenge is to provide *multicasting* functions in the Internet routers when continuous media are transmitted. Currently, MBone can support multicast using a network of routers (mrouters) which can support multicasting. The reason for the need of the multicasting functions, when continuous media are transmitted, is the bandwidth. A multicast stream is *bandwidth-efficient* because one packet can touch all workstations on a network. Thus, a 128 kbits/s video stream (typically 1-4 frames per second) uses the same bandwidth, whether it is received by one workstation or 20.

- *Application Level*

  In the upper level, user network services are provided, such as electronic mail, conferencing and application sharing, by providing the connection of similar networking services between different protocol suites. This often takes the form, for example, of application gateways (packet format translations) between OSI and Transmission Control Protocol/Internet Protocol (TCP/IP) services and translations of media qualities from one end-point to another.

  An example where application-to-application connectivity is visible is the set of MBone applications which connect users all over the world. The Mbone applications, such as *nv* (net video), *vat* (visual audio tool) and *wb* (whiteboard)are based on IP multicast and some are using the *Real-Time Protocol*

*(RTP)* on top of the *User Datagram Protocol (UDP)*/IP. These applications provide connectivity for users who are running MBone tools on workstation architectures, such as Sun, Silicon Graphics, DEC, Hewlett-Packard and PC architecture Macintosh for multimedia conferencing over the WAN.

### Internet

The internetting experiment by DARPA in 1973 led to the evolution of a system of networks, called *Internet*, which is global in scope. There are over 7500 networks interlinked, supporting over 1,000,000 computers, and millions of users in over three dozen countries [LR93].

Internet is layered similar to the OSI reference model shown in Figure 10.15. The

| Layer | Example |
|---|---|
| Application | FTP, Telnet, SMTP, X-Windows |
| Transport | UDP, TCP, TP4, Routing |
| Internet | ICMP, IP, CLNP |
| Subnetwork | Ethernet, X.25, FDDI, Token Ring |
| Link | HDLC, PPP, SLIP |
| Physical | RS 232, V.35, 10 Base T, Fiber optic, etc. |

Figure 10.15: *Internet layering.*

Internet's major backbones currently support transfer rates from T1 (1.5 Mbits/s) to T3 (45 Mbits/s). Internet's transmission mode is based on packet-switching technology. This is implemented by the *Internet Protocol (IP)* environment which provides the *network connectivity.* Its multicasting capability provides a strong support for multimedia collaborative applications.

*Application-to-application connectivity* is provided by the *Transmission Control Protocol (TCP)*, as well as other transport (e.g., UDP) and higher layer protocols (e.g., RTP).

The Internet is a cooperative effort among all the diverse networks that make it up. The Internet essentially provides electronic mail, file transfer capabilities and remote login. Special electronic mail procedures are also used to support news distribution applications and bulletin boards. New Internet applications support audio (e.g., vat) and video (e.g., nv), conferencing capabilities, as well as application sharing tools (e.g., wb).

### Interconnection Devices

In a WAN, the source and destination are connected by a sequence of *interconnection devices* (packet switches). The packet switches must cooperate to calculate a path through the network. They are referred to:

- At the network layer as *routers*.

  Routers are used if LANs or MANs must be connected over longer distance and service like "isolation required to ensure that local problems do not affect other areas" is needed. Routers verify and modify the packets that they forward, and recalculate new checksums. Routers are not end-node transparent. If an end-node needs to send a packet to a node on some other LAN through a router, the packet must be addressed to the router's hardware address. The routers differ from "routing bridges" because they use software that implements a routing protocol. This protocol determines the next node along the path that a particular packet is to take. For multimedia transmission, the routers need to be extended to support *multicasting functions.* Current state-of-the-art in MBone is that *mrouters* support multicasting. *mrouters* are either upgraded commercial routers, or dedicated workstations with modified kernels in parallel with standard routers [MB94].

  The most popular types of routing protocols are

  - *Distance vector* (e.g., ARPANET routing algorithm, DECnet Phases III and IV, AppleTalk's routing algorithm)

    Each router is responsible for keeping track and informing its neighbors of its distance to each destination. The router computes its distance to a destination based on its neighbor's distance to the destination. The only information a router must know a priori is its own ID and the cost of its links to each neighbor.

For multicasting in mrouters, the *Distance Vector Multicast Routing Protocol* is used [WPD88]. Some researchers consider this protocol inadequate for rapidly changing network topologies because the routing information propagates too slowly [Per93].

- *Link state* (e.g., DECnet Phase V and OSPF)

  Each router is responsible for determining the identities of its neighbors and constructing a *Link State Packet (LSP)*, which lists its neighbors and the cost of the link to each. The LSP is transmitted to all of the other routers, which are responsible for storing the most recently generated LSP from each other router. Given this information (the LSP database), it is possible to calculate routes.

  An example of an LSP protocol, which will also be used in mrouters, is the *open shortest path link state protocol* proposed by the *Open Shortest Path Working Group* [MB94]. This link state protocol is based on an algorithm developed by Deering [Moy93]. Note that using this protocol and also the distance vector multicast routing protocol, mrouters dynamically compute a source tree for each participant in a multicast group.

- At the data link layer as *bridges.*

  Bridges are used to connect LANs. They conditionally forward packets from one network port to another. Since bridges operate in store-and-forward mode with packets, they present a much longer processing delay than repeaters. There are three types of bridges:

  - *Transparent bridges* are used in networks like Ethernet and 802.3, and they are completely transparent to the end-nodes on the network and are protocol-independent. The basic mechanism behind a transparent bridge is that it acts as a station on two or more LANs, listens promiscuously to each packet, stores the packet for forwarding and forwards it onto every other LAN to which it is connected when the LAN arbitration protocol for the destination LAN indicates the medium is available. This idea works as long as there are no loops in the topology. To enable people to plug transparent bridges into arbitrary topologies, bridges run a *spanning tree protocol.* The protocol matches the current topology into a spanning tree, i.e., a loop-free subset of the topology that has maximal coverage.

- *Source route bridges* are used in Token Ring networks, and they are protocol-independent and not end-node transparent.

  The mechanism behind source route bridging is that the source end-node puts a route into each data packet's header. The way that the source end-node discovers a route is by issuing an "explorer" packet that makes copies of itself for every possible path, with each copy keeping a diary of where it has been. Then, the destination can choose a route, based on the received explorer packets, or send them back to the source and let the source choose a route.

- *Combination bridges* are used to connect, for example, Token Ring to FDDI.

Bridges for multimedia are easier to implement than routers. One requirement is that they must provide guarantees to the payer if possible.

- At the physical layer as *repeaters.*

  Repeaters unconditionally copy bits of data from one port to another. They do not check or regenerate checksums in the data stream. They are transparent to protocols and are end-node transparent.

  There is no special processing required for multimedia.

### 10.5.2 B-ISDN: ATM

*Broadband Integrated Services Digital Network (B-ISDN)* is a network concept which represents the extension of the *Narrowband ISDN (N-ISDN).* The goal of B-ISDN is to define an application interface and a corresponding WAN with conversational, distributed, messaging and query services of different bandwidth requirements. Further, the goal is to provide connectionless and connection-oriented services for transmission of different media. CCITT Study Group XVIII works on B-ISDN standards.

| Channel | Bandwidth |
|---|---|
| B | 64 kbits/s |
| $H_0$ | 385 kbits/s |
| $H_1$ | 1,920 kbits/s (Europa), 2,048 kbits/s (USA) |
| $H_2$ | 32,768 kbits/s (Europa) |
| $H_4$ | 132,032 - 139,264 kbits/s |

Table 10.3: *Channels and the corresponding data rates.*

### Transfer Modes

Until 1987, the B-ISDN was based on *Synchronous Transfer Mode (SMT)*. Since 1988, the *Asynchronous Transfer Mode* is the basis of B-ISDN [HH91, Sta92].

- *Synchronous Transfer Mode*

  *STM* in the N-ISDN works in a connection-oriented mode with fixed assigned bandwidth according to the time multiplexing method. Therefore, already at the lowest layer, a guaranteed transmission with a determined bandwidth (as in N-ISDN) can be supported. Only small end-to-end delays occur. A time window is called *a slot.* These slots are reserved for the duration of a connection. They lay within periodically repeated structures called *frames*. The assignment of time slots and frames is shown in Figure 10.16. Each slot

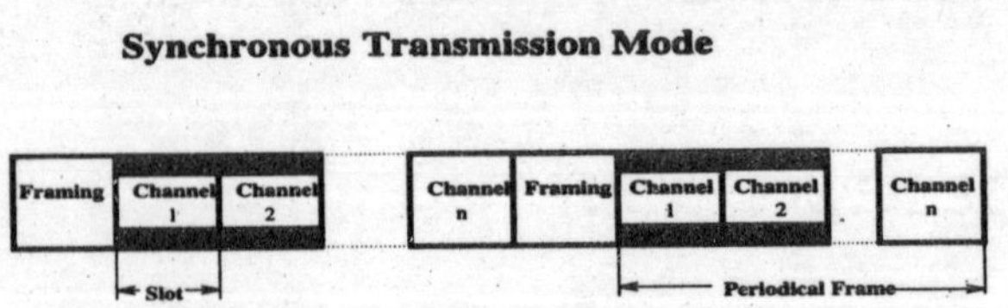


Figure 10.16: *Assignment of time slots in STM (time multiplexing method).*

  has a fixed duration. STM adapts well to the PCM-transmission hierarchies and therefore to the N-ISDN. The channels with correspondent data rates are shown in Table 10.3. This approach is not flexible because of the fixed data rates and the fixed assignment of bandwidth to connections. There are several solutions to improve the flexibility:

- *Compression methods*

  For example, the video compression methods described in Chapter 6, may be used. Many multimedia systems already use compression methods such as JPEG or MPEG.

- *Additional slots*

  One solution is to introduce many slots, for instance, 2,048 8 bit-slots for 15 Mbits/s. The disadvantage of this solution is the increased management overhead by many possible combinations.

- *Container solution*

  As a compromise, a *container* solution was discussed, which allows a limited number of partitions. For example, these can be $H_4 + 4 \times H_1 + n \times B + D$ with containers in $H_1$ and $H_4$ channels. The static STM mechanism remains and the left bandwidth is not continuously used through this partial reservation.

If data with fixed data rates are used, the STM approach is appropriate for the transmission. It means STM is suitable for transmission of continuous media because it utilizes the bandwidth and end-to-end delays are low.

- *Asynchronous Transfer Mode*

  The *Asynchronous Transfer Mode (ATM)* concept was introduced in Section 10.3.4. The ATM approach is more efficient and flexible for a transmission of data streams with variable data rates than the STM approach because the total bandwidth is better utilized.

We will concentrate in the next paragraphs on ATM WAN issues such as *switching* and ATM *host interfacing* to multimedia workstations, which provide the connectivity functionality for multimedia communication systems.

### Switching

In the past, various *switching* architectures were developed for different applications such as voice and data, based on transfer modes like STM and packet switching. The switching architectures developed for STM and packets switches are not applicable to ATM because of (1) the high speed at which the switch must operate (from 150 up to at least 600 Mbits/s today), and (2) the statistical behavior of the ATM streams passing through the ATM switching systems.

Today, ATM switches as products are installed by public operators to offer a public wide broadband service (these systems are called an *ATM Central Office*), and by private users to fulfill internal high-speed communication needs (ATM LAN).

The switching requirements for ATM correspond to the requirements of B-ISDN, which must be capable of transporting all kinds of information, ranging from tele-control over voice to high-quality video. As we described before, these services have different requirements in terms of *bit rate* (from a few kbits/s up to hundreds of Mbits/s), *behavior in time* (constant bit rate or variable bit rate), *semantic transparency* (cell loss rate, bit error rate) and *time transparency* (delay, delay jitter). We describe some of the major service requirements the ATM switches have to cope with:

- *Bandwidth*

  The usual bit rate, which ATM switches are able to switch, is around 150 Mbits/s. This does not mean that ATM switches have to operate internally at 150 Mbits/s. Switching of a single path can be realized in parallel so that a lower speed can be used internally, or several 150 Mbits/s paths can be multiplexed on a single link so that internally higher speeds than 150 Mbits/s are implemented (potentially in the Gbits/s domain).

- *Broadcast/Multicast*

  In classical STM and packet switches, only point-to-point connections are available because data are switched from one logical inlet to another logical outlet. However, the future broadband network requires multicast and broadcast functionality. Therefore, there is a requirement on future ATM switches to provide these functionalities. These functions are required for services, such as conferencing, concurrent video library access and TV distribution.

- *Performance*

In ATM environments, the following performance parameters are important for multimedia applications:

- *Throughput and Bit Error Rate*

  In ATM switches, the *throughput* and *bit error rate* are mainly determined by the high speed hardware technology (CMOS, BICMOS or ECL), where bit rates of hundreds of Mbits/s can easily be achieved with an acceptable bit error rate.

- *Connection Blocking*

  *Connection blocking* is determined as the probability that not enough resources can be found between input and output to guarantee the quality of all existing connections and the new connection. If the switch has enough resources (i.e., bandwidth and header values) on the input and the output of the switch, no connection blocking occurs internally. If the switch does not have enough resources, an explicit check of internal switch resources has to occur. So, a new connection will be accepted, and resources will be allocated only if enough resources are also available on the external links.

- *Cell Loss Probability*

  It is possible that more cells arrive simultaneously and compete for a buffer than a buffer in the switch can store. Hence, some cells will be dropped and therefore lost. Typical values for *cell loss probability* mentioned for ATM switches range between $10^{-8}$ to $10^{-11}$. This is considered to be harmless as the header information of the cell is typically protected by some kind of FEC.

- *Cell Insertion into other Connections*

  It is also possible that ATM cells are internally misrouted in the switch, so they arrive erroneously on another logical connection. The probability of this *cell insertion* must be kept within limits, and values of 1000 times or better than the cell loss rate are typically mentioned in the literature ($10^{-14}$) [Pry93].

- *Switching Delay*

  The time to switch an ATM cell through a switch is of importance for the end-to-end delay. Typical values for the delay of ATM switches are between 10 and 1000 $\mu$s with a jitter of a few 100 $\mu$s or less [Pry93]. For any continuous media applications, an end-to-end delay in the range of 100 ms is acceptable. Hence, the switching delay coming from the switch is a minor portion, even if we encounter, for example, several ATM switches in the data path.

An ATM *switching fabric* is composed of basic ATM switching building blocks, also called *switching elements.* An ATM switching element size can be from two inputs and two outputs at 150 Mbits/s, up to 16 inputs and 16 outputs at 2.4 Gbits/s. A switching fabric, composed of a large number of identical basic switching building blocks, is called *Multi-stage Interconnection Network (MIN).*

The ATM *switching architecture* consists of the *control part* and the *transport part.* The *control part* of the switch controls the cell transport. It decides, for example, which input to connect to which output. The control part uses QoS parameters to control the performance of its own services, such as call setup, as well as the transport ATM services, such as cell transmission. Quality of service parameters for the control network are related to the signaling protocols, e.g., the call setup time, call release time, etc. The *transport part* is responsible for the correct transportation of cells from an ATM input to an ATM output, within the QoS specifications of ATM. Typical QoS parameters for the transport part are the cell loss rate, bit error rate, cell delay, cell delay jitter, etc.

The transportation of data from an incoming logical ATM channel to an outgoing logical ATM channel means selection between a number of outgoing logical channels. A logical ATM channel is characterized by a physical input/output (physical port number) and by a logical channel on the physical port (VCI and/or VPI). To provide the *switching function*, two other functions must be implemented:

- *Routing* (space switching).
  Routing in an ATM switch means to route the cell internally from the input to the output.

- *Queuing* (time switching).

  Queuing cells means to transport a cell from a slot $k$ to a time slot $l$. Since the pre-assigned time slot concept disappears in an ATM system, contention problems arise if two or more logical channels compete for the same time slot. This can be solved by temporarily queuing the ATM cells before sending them out.

We discuss briefly the *routing* of cells in MINs because this function is closely related to the multicasting function which is crucial for multimedia applications.

ATM is based on a connection-oriented approach, therefore, the routes (logical ATM channels) from the source to the destination are determined during the connection setup. The header values (VPI/VCI) are assigned to each section of a connection, and translated when switched from one section to another to get the cell routed. When switching/multiplexing in cells is to be performed, the header/link translation (routing) from the input data (incoming header) to the output data (outgoing header) occurs.

The routing function can be categorized with respect to the *routing decision time* and the *routing information place*: The time parameter decides when the translation decision is made namely, if the routing decision is made once for a connection or every time a cell arrives at a switch. The place parameter specifies where the routing information is stored.

- *Routing Decision Time*

  Routing translation can be performed either once for the complete duration of the connection (*connection-based routing*), or it can be performed for every cell separately (*cell-based routing*). For the first case, it means that the MIN is internally connection-oriented or uses pre-set path routing. This case is more suitable for continuous media transmission because the data arrive at the receiver in order. A problem may occur if a contention occurs along the pre-assigned path, which causes an increase of the end-to-end delay for the media PDUs. This problem can be solved using resource reservation mechanisms at the switches.

  In the second case, the MIN operates internally connectionless. In the first case, all cells of the virtual connection follow the same route/path through the MIN; in the second case, they do not. The cell-based mode of operation should be chosen when data can arrive at the receiver out of order, or the urgency of the transmitted data is high (e.g., transactions). This mode allows each cell to choose a path which has enough resources to handle congestion. This implies functions which report resource availability in the switches.

- *Routing Information Place*

  Routing information can either be transported by each cell itself via a so-called *routing tag*, or it can be stored in *routing tables* in the switching blocks. In the case where a routing table is used, this table must be accessed via an entry. For multimedia transmission, the routing tables are preferable because of multicasting. The routing tables become multicast routing tables. An example of an ATM switch which supports multicasting in the cell-based mode is Roxane [Pry93]. Most of the currently available ATM switches do not support multicasting .

### Host-interfacing to Multimedia Workstations

Another important aspect of ATM B-ISDN is the *impact of ATM at the end-points* (hosts) which are represented through multimedia workstations. We discuss some opportunities of how the end-points can take advantage of the ATM concept for transmission of multimedia:

- *Support of VBR Coding*

  When video signals are encoded in digital format using a simple Pulse Code Modulation (PCM) method, the resulting bit rate is fixed and simply the product of the sampling rate and the number of bits per sample. However, as soon as a compression algorithm is used, the resulting bit rate varies in time. Hence, the bit rate generated by the future video codec will fluctuate in time or will be different for different qualities of video images like in MPEG 1, 2, 4.

  In classical STM networks, this fluctuating rate must be converted into a Constant Bit Rate (CBR), namely that at which this STM network is operating. For example, 64 kbits/s are required for N-ISDN and 139,264 kbits/s are needed for videophone or TV distribution service (Table 10.3). This bit rate equalization can be realized by an output buffer between the encoder and the network and a feedback signal between encoder and buffer.

In ATM networks, the limitation of working at a constant bit rate disappears because of the AAL2, so the output buffer is basically no longer required at the output of the encoder. The output of the encoder can be directly fed into the ATM network, resulting in a *VBR* video encoder.

- *Support of Medium Layered Coding*

In future B-ISDN, we see the new multimedia services to consist of, for example, one or more of the following service components: *audio*, *standard video*, *high-definition video overhead*, *teletext*, and *data*. For example, HDTV is composed of all five different service components. All these individual components can be transported individually over separate virtual channels. However, some restrictions must be taken into account between those different virtual channels, mainly with respect to the relative delay through the network. For example, the lip synchronization between voice sound and video image requires delay (skew) difference $\leq$ 80 ms [SE93]. Therefore, the individual service components can be further divided into *layers*. Every higher layer uses the information of the lower layer to construct the image of that layer with the required quality. In terms of resolution, this is known as *hierarchical encoding*. An example of such a layered model (hierarchical encoding) for a video medium is shown in Figure 10.17. Sound (HIFI) and data (subtitling) represent *non-hierarchical encoding*. This implies that each layer of the medium quality division will be assigned a separate VCI/VPI and different service, which may help in the adaptive behavior of each medium during the transmission.

An important advantage of this layered approach is the compatibility between different services and terminals. An additional advantage of this layered coding principle is its possibility to cope efficiently with the cell loss caused by the ATM network [Pry93]. However, a wide acceptance of a specific layering tends to be difficult to achieve.

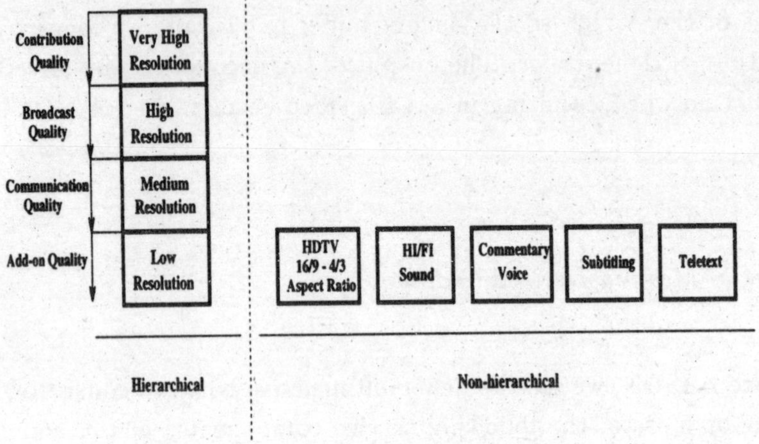


Figure 10.17: *Layered video encoding.*

## 10.6 Conclusion

Most current multimedia network systems are available as commercial products only for single user computers (PCs). Most experimental and research software provides the capabilities of video/audio data transfer on multiuser UNIX machines (e.g., MBone tools). The most popular networked multimedia applications are interactive video retrieval, TV and audio broadcasting, conferencing and electronic mail.

Most cooperative multimedia applications use the underlying networks, for example, Ethernet or Internet, without any specific changes. Video and voice teleconferencing have been demonstrated on the Internet with datagram-based protocol in [TP91, NS92, CCH+93b] and other implementations. Hence, it is not true that multimedia communication systems need at least the bandwidth of 100 Mbits/s to provide acceptable communication. Current usage of MBone (1.5Mbits/s) with the video and audio conferencing software nv/vat supports remote presence at conferences and other technical meetings [Moy93].

Current existing network solutions may work for multimedia traffic if the utilization of the network is low. However, this situation will change as soon as these applications become more widely used. The number of end-users increases, and with it the network traffic. Large quantities of such traffic cannot be supported anymore without handling different types of service at gateways and routers, and in the end-to-end protocols. For example, Internet already faces challenges in routing today:

- Routing tables expanded beyond router capabilities.
- Premature exhaustion of assigned IP network numbers due to inefficient allocation of the IP address space.
- IP's inability to address more than four billion hosts connected to a single Internet.

In the case of end-to-end protocols, TCP's window mechanism, because of its limited window size, does not effectively utilize the potential transmitting capacity of high-speed networks. The already installed base of networks will not be replaced just for providing multimedia capabilities everywhere. These networks, especially in the LAN domain, will remain and here we can exploit their properties for carrying continuous media traffic as was outlined in this chapter.

New commercial services, such as SONET fiber links and gigabit ATM LANs and WANs, together with new workstation capabilities including sound and video, produce demanding requirements in terms of multiple types of service. Hence, existing networks will have to change/expand towards supporting multiple types of service and/or new high-speed networks, such as ATM LANs and ATM WANs, will have to be installed. For example, the new challenges in Internet already lead to modifications of its current protocol suite. Several methods and modifications are described in [JBZ90, JB88, BCS93, ZDE$^{+}$93].

Several new protocols at the network/transport layers in Internet (e.g., ST-II) and higher layers in B-ISDN are currently centers of research to support more efficient transmission of multimedia and multiple types of service. We discuss the changes in the transport system toward accommodation of integrated services, as well as new protocols in higher layers, in Chapter 11.

# Chapter 11

# Multimedia Communication Systems

The consideration of multimedia applications supports the view that local systems expand toward distributed solutions. Applications such as kiosks, multimedia mail, collaborative work systems, virtual reality applications and others require high-speed networks with a high transfer rate and communication systems with adaptive, lightweight transmission protocols on top of the networks.

In Chapter 10, high-speed network requirements, such as low latency for interactive operations, high bandwidth above 10 Mbps, and low error-bit rate were discussed. Several networks were described that support transmission of multimedia, such as FDDI, High-Speed Ethernet, Priority Token Ring (PRT) or ATM networks with bandwidth of 100 Mbps and above.

In this chapter we discuss important issues related to multimedia communication systems above the data link layer. From the communication perspective, we divide the higher layers of the Multimedia Communication System (MCS) into two architectural subsystems: an *application subsystem* and a *transport subsystem*.

In the section on application subsystems, management and service issues for group collaboration and session orchestration are presented. Group collaboration and session management provide support for a large group of multimedia applications, such as tele-collaboration. The section on transport subsystems includes a presentation of transport and network layer protocols that are used for the standardized support of networked multimedia applications. The third section of this chapter consists of a discussion about *Quality of Service* (QoS) and resource management in MCSs.

## 11.1 Application Subsystem

### 11.1.1 Collaborative Computing

The current infrastructure of networked workstations and PCs, and the availability of audio and video at these end-points, makes it easier for people to cooperate and bridge *space and time*. In this way, network connectivity and end-point integration of multimedia provides users with a *collaborative computing* environment. Collaborative computing is generally known as *Computer-Supported Cooperative Work* (CSCW).

There are many tools for collaborative computing, such as *electronic mail*, *bulletin boards* (e.g., Usenet news), *screen sharing tools* (e.g., ShowMe from SunSoft), *text-based conferencing systems* (e.g., Internet Relay Chat, CompuServe, American Online), *telephone conference systems*, *conference rooms* (e.g., VideoWindow from Bellcore), and *video conference systems* (e.g., MBone tools nv, vat). Further, there are many implemented CSCW systems that unify several tools, such as Rapport from AT&T, MERMAID from NEC and others.

In this section we present a framework for collaborative computing and general related issues exemplified by different systems and tools.

#### Collaborative Dimensions

Electronic collaboration can be categorized according to three main parameters: *time, user scale* and *control* [WSM+91]. Therefore, the collaboration space can be partitioned into a three-dimensional space (shown in Figure 11.1).

- *Time*

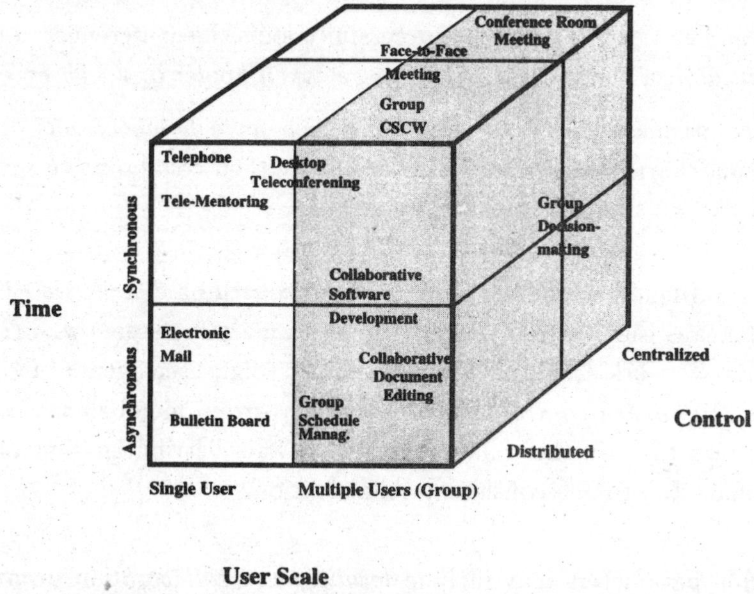


Figure 11.1: *Dimensions of collaborative computing.*

With respect to time, there are two modes of cooperative work: *asynchronous* and *synchronous*. *Asynchronous cooperative work* specifies processing activities that do not happen at the same time; the *synchronous cooperative work* happens at the same time.

- *User Scale*

  The user scale parameter specifies whether a *single user* collaborates with another user or a *group* of more than two users collaborate together. Groups can be further classified as follows [Stu94]:

  - A group may be *static* or *dynamic* during its lifetime. A group is *static* if its participating members are pre-determined and membership does not change during the activity. A group is *dynamic* if the number of group members varies during the collaborative activity, i.e., group members can join or leave the activity at any time.
  - Group members may have different roles in the CSCW, e.g., a *member* of a group (if he or she is listed in the group definition), a *participant* of a

group activity (if he or she successfully joins the conference), a *conference initiator*, a *conference chairman* , a *token holder* or an *observer.*

- Groups may consist of members which have *homogeneous* or *heterogeneous* characteristics and requirements of their collaborative environment.

- *Control*

  Control during a collaboration can be *centralized* or *distributed. Centralized control* means that there is a chairman (e.g., main manager) who controls the collaborative work and every group member (e.g., user agent) reports to him or her. *Distributed control* means that every group member has control over his/her own tasks in the collaborative work and distributed control protocols are in place to provide consistent collaboration.

Other partition parameters may include *locality, and collaboration awareness. Locality* partition means that a collaboration can occur either in the *same place* (e.g., a group meeting in an office or conference room) or among users located in *different places* through *tele-collaboration.* With respect to this parameter, we assume in this section tele-collaboration.

*Collaboration awareness* divides group communication systems into *collaboration-transparent*, and *collaboration-aware* systems. The collaboration-transparent system is an existing application (e.g., a favorite text processor/spreadsheet) extended for collaboration. For example, some new *document editing* systems are collaboration-transparent because single user document editors were expanded for simultaneous editing of a shared document among several users. The collaborative-aware system is a dedicated software application for CSCW. For example, a conferencing system is a collaborative-aware system.

Group communication systems can be further categorized into *computer-augmented collaboration* systems, where *collaboration* is emphasized, and *collaboration-augmented computing* systems, where the concentration is on *computing* [MR94]. Computer-augmented collaboration is centered around a social activity, for instance discussion, or decision-making, where the computers and networks help to improve this activity. Collaboration-augmented computing is centered around tools that accommodate multiple users.

### Group Communication Architecture

*Group communication* (GC) involves the communication of multiple users in a synchronous or an asynchronous mode with centralized or distributed control (the gray area in Figure 11.1).

A group communication architecture consists of a *support model, system model* and *interface model* [WSM+91]. The GC *support model* includes *group communication agents* that communicate via a multi-point multicast communication network as shown in Figure 11.2. Group communication agents may use the following for their

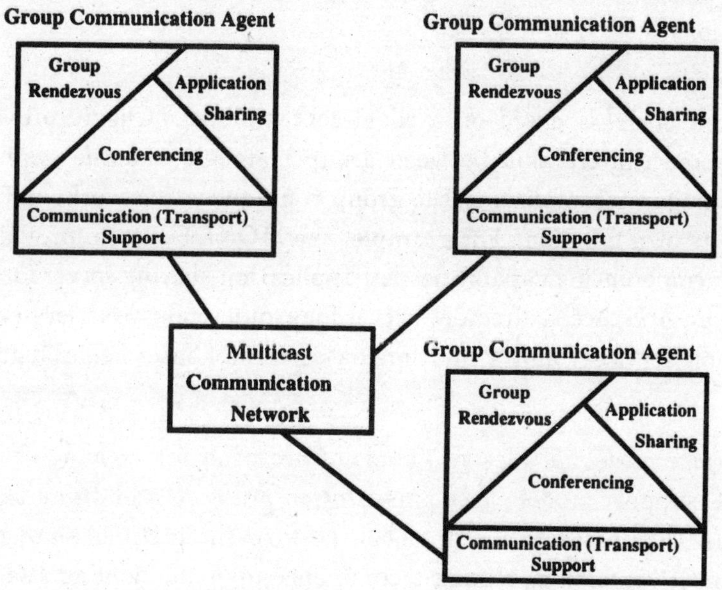


Figure 11.2: *Group communication support model.*

collaboration:

- *Group Rendezvous*

  *Group rendezvous* denotes a method which allows one to organize meetings, and to get information about the group, ongoing meetings and other static and dynamic information.

- *Shared Applications*

*Application sharing* denotes techniques which allow one to replicate information to multiple users simultaneously. The remote users may point to interesting aspects (e.g., via tele-pointing) of the information and modify it so that all users can immediately see the updated information (e.g., joint editing). Shared applications mostly belong to collaboration-transparent applications.

- *Conferencing*

  *Conferencing* is a simple form of collaborative computing. This service provides the management of multiple users for communicating with each other using multiple media. Conferencing applications belong to collaboration-aware applications.

The GC *system model* is based on a client-server model. Clients provide user interfaces for smooth interaction between group members and the system. Servers supply functions for accomplishing the group communication work, and each server specializes in its own function. For example, the MONET system provides a conference server for conferencing capabilities, an application sharing server for providing a *shared or group workspace*, a directory server for group rendezvous services (directory and registration services) and a multimedia server for intermedia synchronization [SRB+92].

The GC *interface model* includes two kinds of protocols for exchanging information within the GC support model: *user presentation protocols* and *group work management protocols.* User presentation protocols perform interactions among the clients, such as opening a conference, closing a conference, dynamic joining and leaving of a meeting and floor passing. Group work management protocols specify the communication between the clients and the servers. Services such as registration of active conferences and queries for further conference information are supported by these protocols.

### Group Rendezvous

*Group rendezvous methods* allow for setting up collaborative group meetings and providing other static and dynamic information about groups and ongoing or future meetings. The group rendezvous tools provide a single set of session (e.g., conference) and activity information at the user interface. There are *synchronous* and *asynchronous methods* for group rendezvous:

- *Synchronous Rendezvous Methods*

  Synchronous rendezvous methods use *directory services* and *explicit invitations. Directory services* (e.g., X.500) access information stored in a knowledge base about the conference, such as the name of the conference, registered participants, authorized users and name and role of the participants. Examples of conferencing systems which use the directory method for group rendezvous are:

  - MBone's session directory tool, *sd*

    *sd* may be used as a guide to announce open conferences [JM93a]. *sd* resides at a known address and port on each user's workstation and both listen for announcements and post their own sessions.
  - Touring machine's *name server query*

    The name server acts as a central repository of both static and dynamic information, such as authorized users, registered clients and ongoing sessions [Lab93]. A client can query for all interesting sessions to join or all clients in a particular session.
  - MONET's *directory service*

    The directory server provides directory and registration services. A catalog of various resources such as people, machines and tools across the network is available to the directory service. A registration service deals with registering participants and groups for conferences [SRB+92].

  The *explicit invitations* method sends invitations either point-to-point or point-to-multipoint to conference participants. The problem here is that calling others requires the initiator of the conference to know where users reside. An example of group rendezvous supported via explicit invitations, is ISI's (USC Information Sciences Institute) session orchestration tool, *mmcc* [SW94a].

- *Asynchronous Rendezvous Methods*

Asynchronous rendezvous methods may be implemented through *e-mail* or *bulletin boards.* Borenstein suggests *e-mail* as a platform for group rendezvous, embedded in synchronous conferencing applications [Bor92]. The e-mail-based mechanism encapsulates in the body message enough information about a group session establishment. This scheme builds on the already existing e-mail infrastructure for both distributing information and addressing end-users.

*Bulletin boards* are used to support asynchronous rendezvous. Local bulletin boards on the Internet already announce seminars, classes, conferences and other open meetings of a school or institution. The *World Wide Web* (WWW) offers new possibility for global group rendezvous offers. The WWW infrastructure is beginning to be used to announce and dynamically update public sessions or upcoming open conferences [IET94].

### Application Sharing Approach

Sharing applications is recognized as a vital mechanism for supporting group communication activities. Sharing applications means that when a shared application program (e.g., editor) executes any input from a participant, all execution results performed on the *shared object* (e.g., document text) are distributed among all the participants. Shared objects are displayed, generally, in *shared windows* [HTM92].

Application sharing is most often implemented in collaboration-transparent systems, but can also be developed through collaboration-aware, special-purpose applications. An example of a software toolkit that assists in development of shared computer applications is Bellcore's *Rendezvous* system (language and architecture) [HBP+93]. Shared applications may be used as conversational props in tele-conferencing situations for collaborative document editing and collaborative software development.

An important issue in application sharing is *shared control.* The primary design decision in sharing applications is to determine whether they should be *centralized* or *replicated* [OMS+92, SW94a]:

- *Centralized Architecture*

  In a centralized architecture, a single copy of the shared application runs at one site. All participants' input to the application is forwarded to the local site and the application's output (shared object) is then distributed to all sites. Figure 11.3 (a) shows the centralized architecture.

The advantage of the centralized approach is *easy maintenance* because there is only one copy of the application that updates the shared object. The disadvantage is *high network traffic* because the output of the application needs to be distributed every time. In the case of images, the output data traffic may be significant. This means that a *high-bandwidth network* is needed.

- *Replicated Architecture*

  In a replicated architecture, a copy of the shared application runs locally at each site. Input events to each application are distributed to all sites and each copy of the shared application is executed locally at each site. Figure 11.3 (b) shows the replicated architecture.

  The advantages of this architecture are *low network traffic*, because only input events are distributed among the sites, and *low response times*, since all participants get their output from local copies of the application. The disadvantages are the requirement of *the same execution environment* for the application at each site, and the *difficulty in maintaining consistency*. The problem is discussed below.

As stated above, one important problem with shared applications in a replicated architecture is maintaining the *consistency of shared objects*. A variety of mechanisms exist to maintain data consistency among group members. Examples include *centralized locks, floor passing schemes, and dependency detections*. Here, we discuss *floor passing control* because this kind of control is the most relevant to group communication.

The notion of a *floor* is used to maintain the consistency of shared object *data* (multimedia documents) or *applications* (programs) shared among participants. The group member who holds the floor (the *floor holder*) has the right to manipulate shared objects in shared windows. Hence, the floor holder can perform operations such as opening and closing shared windows, loading documents into a shared window and issuing an input event to the shared application to manipulate shared data.

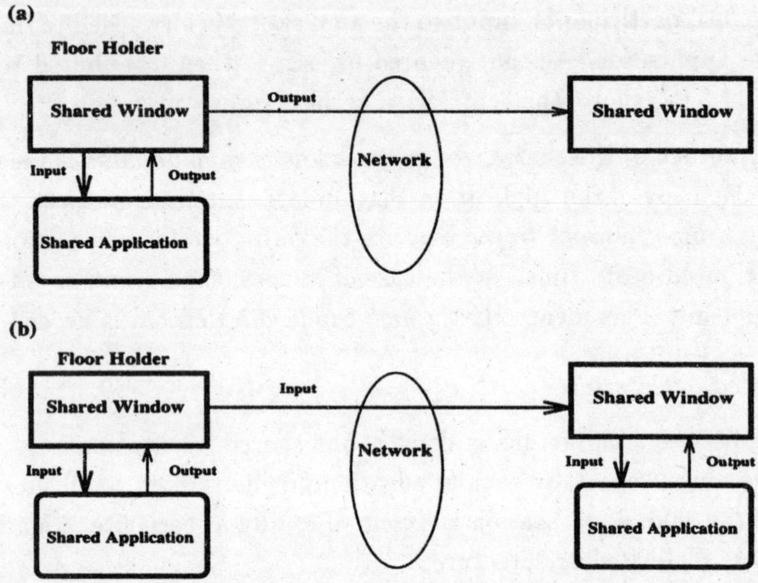


Figure 11.3: *Sharing application architectures: (a) centralized architecture, (b) replicated architecture.*

A possible shared data manipulation architecture is shown in Figure 11.4. A CSCW control component resides at every site and dispatches input events coming from an *input* device (e.g., keyboard). It checks if the active site is a floor holder. If the site is a floor holder, it accepts and processes the input event as well as distributes the input event to other sites. If the site is not a floor holder, the CSCW control discards its own input and accepts input events coming from another site.

A replicated shared control architecture is used in CSCW systems such as MERMAID (Multimedia Environment for Remote Multiple Attendee Interactive Decision-making) from NEC [OMS+92], the broadband ISDN group tele-working system from Hitachi [HTM92] and others.

### Conferencing

Conferencing supports collaborative computing and is also called *synchronous tele-collaboration.* Conferencing is a *management service* that controls the communica-

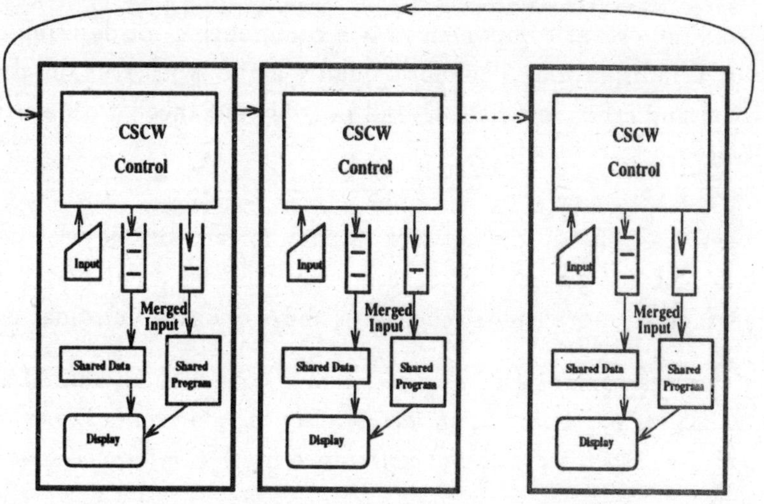


Figure 11.4: *Shared data manipulation architecture.*

tion among multiple users via multiple media, such as video and audio, to achieve simultaneous face-to-face communication. More precisely, video and audio have the following purposes in a tele-conferencing system:

- *Video* is used in technical discussions to display view-graphs and to indicate how many users are still physically present at a conference. For visual support, workstations, PCs or *video walls* can be used.

  For conferences with more than three or four participants, the screen resources on a PC or workstation run out quickly, particularly if other applications, such as shared editors or drawing spaces, are used. Hence, mechanisms which quickly resize individual images should be used.

  This situation also implies that large *video walls* in conference rooms with multiple, high-resolution screens (e.g., Bellcore's VideoWindow [FKRR93]) may continue to be necessary even after workstations are video-equipped everywhere. The systems supporting conference rooms with video walls attempt to provide the richness of human communication situations, such as unplanned hallway encounters (e.g., Cruiser from Bellcore), drop-in seminars, panel discussions (e.g., Media Space from Xerox PARC), jury trials and lectures.

- *Audio* is an important component in tele-conferencing for describing and clarifying visual information. Therefore, quality audio, with true full-duplex communication and echo cancellation, and possibly enhanced with spatial queues, is necessary.

Conferencing services rely on low network latency for acceptable user interactivity and high bandwidth for potentially data-intensive media. Further, they rely on *distributed messaging* for transmission of data and/or control information.

Conferencing services control a *conference* (i.e., a collection of shared state information such as *who is participating in the conference, conference name, start of the conference, policies associated with the conference*, etc.) *Conference control* includes several functions:

- *Establishing* a conference, where the conference participants agree upon a common state, such as identity of a chairman (moderator), access rights (floor control) and audio encoding. Conference systems may perform *registration, admission*, and *negotiation* services during the conference establishment phase, but they must be flexible and allow participants to join and leave individual media sessions or the whole conference. The flexibility depends on the control model.
- *Closing* a conference.
- *Adding* new users and *removing* users who leave the conference.

Conference control utilizes and cooperates with per-media session management components (see Section 11.1.2.) to tie together several streams.

Conference states can be stored (located) either on a central machine (*centralized control*), where a central application acts as the repository for all information related to the conference, or in a *distributed* fashion. The control model follows from the location of the conference state. Accordingly, the control model may be either *centralized* or *distributed.*

- *Centralized Conference Control*

Centralized conference control provides the establishment of a conference. First, the initiator (e.g., chairman) starts a conference by selecting an initial group of invited conference members (explicit invitation for group rendezvous). This implies that the chairman knows the addresses of all conference participants. The knowledge of the conference state is inquired from a central directory server, which implies that the client has registered his/her location.

Second, each invited client *responds* to the invitation so that the initiator is informed of who will participate in the conference. After this step, a *negotiation* of conference policies and an *admission* of resources is performed among the conference participants. During the negotiation, the shared conference state is distributed using a *reliable messaging* service to all conference participants. All information related to the conference is stored on a central machine.

This *static control*, implemented through explicit exchange of the conference state, guarantees the consistency of the state space to every participant, and works well for small conferences.

The advantage of the centralized conference control is the guaranteed *consistency* of the conference state. The disadvantage is that when a new participant (outside of the invited group) wants to join, explicit exchange of the conference state must be performed among all participants, which causes large delays. Furthermore, if a conference participant has a link failure, it is more difficult to re-establish the conference state.

- *Distributed Conference Control*

  Distributed conference control is based on a *distributed conference state*. This is achieved as follows: the initiator of the conference establishes a multicast space (e.g., multicast tunnel in MBone) with multicast entries for distribution of information to the conference participants and the conference is established; the conference participants join the conference by tuning into a particular multicast entry (e.g., multicast address), announced through group rendezvous means (e.g., sd).

  Each site distributes its own participation status to other conference participants, but there is no global notion of a group membership, and no guarantees that all users will have the same view of the state space. Hence, this *loose control* is implemented through retransmitting the state periodically for eventual consistency. The periodical retransmission is done using an *unreliable messaging* service. The loose control works well for large conferences. This loose control is provided by sessions called *lightweight sessions* [JMF93], which are used on the *Multicast Backbone (MBone)* [MB94]. MBone is a multicast-capable segment of Internet which has been used for a number of applications including multimedia (audio, video and shared workspace) conferencing. These applications include *vat* (LBL's Visual Audio Tool) [JM92], *ivs* (INRIA Videoconferencing System) [INR93], *nv* (Xerox's Network Video tool) [Fre92] and *wb* (LBL's shared whiteboard) [JM93b].

Advantages of distributed conference control are: *inherent fault tolerance*, which means that if a network connection breaks down in the middle of a conference and it is repaired, it is easier to re-establish the shared conference state since there is no strict consistency requirement; and *scaling* properties, although at some point refresh periodicity needs to adapt to the size and scope of the conference, otherwise, the conference may be in danger of flooding itself with session reports. The disadvantage is that the conference participants may not have the same view of the state space.

Given the wide diversity of *collaboration styles*, it appears difficult to derive a canonical conference control protocol, although there are some attempts to achieve this goal with the *Conference Control Channel Protocol (CCCP)*[HW94].

It is promising to develop common, underlying control functions and allow the combination of these in appropriate ways [Sch94a]. Further, *state agreement protocols* might be invoked to agree on the shared state, also called the *ephemeral teleconferencing state* [SW94b]. The state is *ephemeral* because the importance of the state is valid only during the duration of the conference. Agreement Protocols with distributed control involve a *policy* to control the session state. In [SW94b], three aspects of policies are identified: *initiator of policies*, *voting policies* and *consistency policies.* The first aspect specifies which members may initiate certain change operations. The voting policy specifies the decision about the change of the shared state which was issued by a group member. Modification of the shared state is based on *voting rules.* To achieve consistency, the state agreement covers the functionality of the floor and access control, media negotiation, directory services for conferences, invitation services, user location services, etc.

### 11.1.2 Session Management

*Session management* is an important part of the multimedia communication architecture. It is the core part which separates the control, needed during the transport, from the actual transport. Session management is extensively studied in the collaborative computing area, therefore we concentrate on architectural and management issues in this area.

#### Architecture

A session management architecture is built around an entity – *session manager* – which separates the control from the transport [SC92]. By creating a reusable session manager, which is separated from the user-interface, conference-oriented tools avoid a duplication of their effort. A possible session control architecture is shown in Figure 11.5. The session control architecture consists of the following components:

- *Session Manager*

  Session manager includes *local* and *remote* functionalities. Local functionalities may include (1) *membership control management*, such as participant authentication or presentation of coordinated user interfaces; (2) control management for shared workspace, such as *floor control*; (3) *media control management*, such as intercommunication among media agents or synchronization; (4) *configuration management*, such as exchange of interrelated QoS parameters or selection of appropriate services according to QoS; and (5) *conference control management*, such as an establishment, modification and a closing of a conference. Remotely, the session manager communicates with other session managers to exchange session state information which may include the floor information, configuration information, etc. It is important to note that in different conferencing systems, the conference control and floor control can be embedded either in the application layer (e.g., Group Tele-Working System from Hitatchi labs) or in the session layer (e.g., Touring machine from

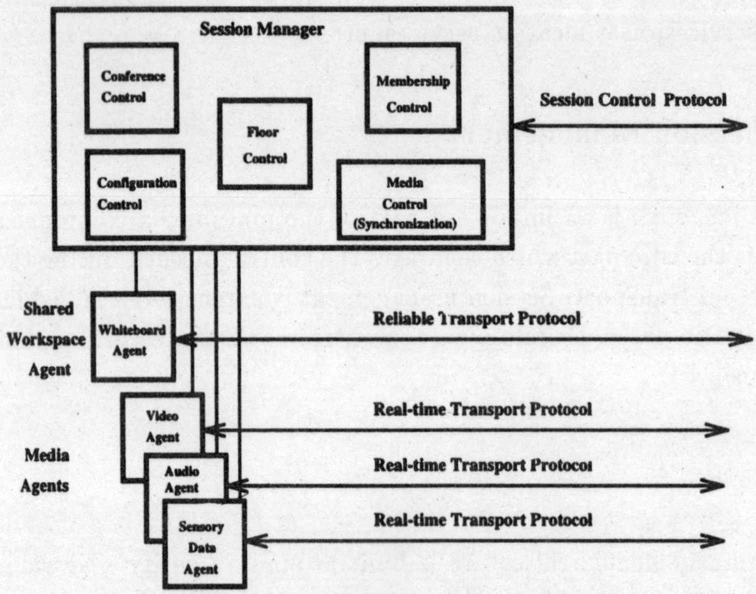


Figure 11.5: *Session control architecture.*

Bellcore).

- *Media Agents*

  Media agents are separate from the session manager and they are responsible for decisions specific to each type of media. This modularity allows a replacement of agents. Each agent performs its own control mechanism over the particular medium, such as mute, unmute, change video quality, start sending, stop sending, etc.

- *Shared Workspace Agent*

  The shared workspace agent transmits shared objects (e.g., telepointer coordinate, graphical or textual object ) among the shared applications.

### Control

Each session is described through its *session state.* This state information (start time of session, policies associated with the session, session name) is either *pri-*

*vate* (e.g., local resources) or *shared* among all session participants (e.g., conference participants).

*Session management* includes two steps to process the session state: an *establishment* and a *modification* of the session. During the establishment, the session manager negotiates, agrees, and sets the logical state of its own session. Further, it negotiates, agrees and sets billing policy and other policies with other session managers. Further, it permits "publishing" a session (e.g., using group rendezvous service), allowing others to locate and joint a session. It negotiates and defines the transport topology with the transport subsystem.

Dependent on the functions, which an application requires and a session control provides, several control mechanisms are embedded in session management:

- *Floor Control*

  Within shared workspaces, the *floor control* is employed to provide access to the shared workspace. Further, the floor control in shared applications (Section 11.1.1) is often used to maintain data consistency (social protocol). Each system makes decisions, such as the level of *simultaneity* and *granularity* at which to enforce access control. In the simplest form of floor control, applications use a *floor-passing mechanism* (gavel-passing [SW94a], chalk-passing [Sch94a]). The floor-passing mechanism means that at any time, only one participant has the floor. The floor is handed off to another participant when requested. To obtain the floor, the participant must explicitly take action to signal a floor change.

  With real-time audio, there is no notion of data consistency, instead, the floor control is typically used in more formal settings to promote turn-taking (e.g., distributed classroom). For more life-like audio interaction, no floor control is optimal.

  Floor control for real-time video is frequently used to control bandwidth usage.

  The floor control mechanisms are low-level means used to implement *floor policies* [RSV94]. A floor policy describes how participants request the floor and how the floor is assigned and released. Typically, a session-wide floor holder is selected by a chairman, although it is desirable to have flexible floor control policies.

- *Conference Control*

  For conferencing applications, conference control is employed. We discussed a possible conference control (the centralized approach with static control versus the distributed approach with loose control) in Section 11.1.1).

- *Media Control*

  Media control mainly includes a functionality, such as the synchronization of media streams, which is broadly discussed in Chapter 15.

- *Configuration Control*

  Configuration control includes a control of media quality, QoS handling, resource availability and other system components to provide a session according to users requirements. QoS handling and corresponding resource management are discussed in Section 11.3. This control may embed services, such as the negotiation and renegotiation of media quality.

- *Membership Control*

  Membership control may include services, for example, *invitation* to a session, *registration* into a session, *modification* of the membership during the session, etc.

For distribution of the shared session control information among the session managers, *reliable messaging services* or *unreliable messaging services* with periodic refreshment can be used. The goal is to provide a *distributed messaging* service with different degrees of reliable delivery. For example, periodic update messages may not require reliable delivery at all. On the other hand, for floor exchange, it may be critical to know that the update was received by all participants, since if not, multiple video channels may, for example, result and may overextend the capacity of the network. There may even be conference participants who value the delivery of the same message type differently [HW94].

## 11.2 Transport Subsystem

We present in this section a brief overview of transport and network protocols and their functionalities, which are used for multimedia transmissions. We evaluate them with respect to their suitability for this task.

### 11.2.1 Requirements

Distributed multimedia applications put new requirements on application designers, as well as network protocol and system designers. We analyze the most important enforced requirements with respect to the multimedia transmission:

#### User and Application Requirements

Networked multimedia applications by themselves impose new requirements onto data handling in computing and communications because they need (1) substantial data throughput, (2) fast data forwarding, (3) service guarantees, and (4) multicasting.

- *Data Throughput*

  Audio and video data resemble a stream-like behavior, and they demand, even in a compressed mode, high *data throughput.* In a workstation or network, several of those streams may exist concurrently demanding a high throughput. Further, the data movement requirements on the local end-system translate into terms of manipulation of large quantities of data in real-time where, for example, data copying can create a bottleneck in the system.

- *Fast Data Forwarding*

  *Fast data forwarding* imposes a problem on end-systems where different applications exist in the same end-system, and they each require data movement ranging from normal, error-free data transmission to new time-constraint traffic types traffic. But generally, the faster a communication system can transfer a data packet, the fewer packets need to be buffered. This requirement leads to a careful spatial and temporal resource management in the end-systems and routers/switches. The application imposes constraints on the total maximal end-to-end delay. In a retrieval-like application, such as video-on-demand, a delay of up to one second may be easily tolerated. In an opposite dialogue application, such as a videophone or videoconference, demand end-to-end delays lower than typically 200 msec inhibit a natural communication between the users.

- *Service Guarantees*

  Distributed multimedia applications need *service guarantees*, otherwise their acceptance does not come through as these systems, working with continuous media, compete against radio and television services. To achieve services guarantees, resource management must be used. Without resource management in end-systems and switches/routers, multimedia systems cannot provide reliable QoS to their users because transmission over unreserved resources leads to dropped or delayed packets [DHVW93].

- *Multicasting*

  *Multicast* is important for multimedia-distributed applications in terms of sharing resources like the network bandwidth and the communication protocol processing at end-systems.

### Processing and Protocol Constraints

Communication protocols have, on the contrary, some constraints which need to be considered when we want to match application requirements to system platforms.

A typical multimedia application does not require processing of audio and video to be performed by the application itself. Usually the data are obtained from a source (e.g., microphone, camera, disk, network) and are forwarded to a sink (e.g., speaker, display, network). In such a case, the requirements of continuous-media data are satisfied best if they take "the shortest possible path" through the system, i.e., to copy data directly from adapter-to-adapter, and the program merely sets the correct switches for the data flow by connecting sources to sinks. Hence, the application itself never really touches the data as is the case in traditional processing.

A problem with direct copying from adapter-to-adapter is the control and the change of QoS parameters. In multimedia systems, such an adapter-to-adapter connection is defined by the capabilities of the two involved adapters and the bus performance. In today's systems, this connection is static. This architecture of low-level data streaming corresponds to proposals for using additional new busses for audio and video transfer within a computer. It also enables a switch-based rather than a bus-based data transfer architecture [Fin91, HM91]. Note, in practice we encounter headers and trailers surrounding continuous-media data coming from devices and being delivered to devices. In the case of compressed video data, e.g., MPEG-2, the program stream contains several layers of headers compared with the actual group of pictures to be displayed.

Protocols involve a lot of *data movement* because of the layered structure of the communication architecture. But copying of data is expensive and has become a bottleneck, hence other mechanisms for buffer management must be found.

Different layers of the communication system may have different PDU sizes, therefore, a *segmentation* and *reassembly* occur. This phase has to be done fast, and efficient. Hence, this portion of a protocol stack, at least in the lower layers, is done in hardware, or through efficient mechanisms in software.

Some parts of protocols may use *retransmission error-recovery* mechanism which imposes requirements on buffer space for queues at the expense of larger end-to-end delays.

The new underlying packet/cell networks which work in an *asynchronous transfer mode* (most of them, although, for example, FDDI offers also an isochronous transfer mode which is best suited for multimedia transmission) put requirements on the protocol design for continuous media. What has to happen is that the higher protocols must provide a synchronous behavior to the application, but they rely on an asynchronous behavior of the service provider at the packet/cell level. This means introduction of connection-oriented protocols (e.g., ST-II) where, during the connection establishment, preparation for "synchronous transmission" of continuous media has to occur, or some connection-like behavior has to be enforced to provide service guarantees (e.g., RSVP with IP).

### 11.2.2 Transport Layer

Transport protocols, to support multimedia transmission, need to have new features and provide the following functions: *timing information*, *semi-reliability*, *multicasting*, *NAK (None-AcKnowledgment)-based error recovery mechanism* and *rate control*.

First, we present transport protocols, such as TCP and UDP, which are used in the Internet protocol stack for multimedia transmission, and secondly we analyze new emerging transport protocols, such as RTP, XTP and other protocols, which are suitable for multimedia.

#### Internet Transport Protocols

The Internet protocol stack includes two types of transport protocols:

- *Transmission Control Protocol (TCP)*

  Early implementations of video conferencing applications were implemented on top of the TCP protocol. TCP provides a reliable, serial communication path, or virtual circuit, between processes exchanging a full-duplex stream of bytes. Each process is assumed to reside in an Internet host that is identified by an IP address. Each process has a number of logical, full-duplex ports through which it can set up and use as *full-duplex TCP connections*.

  Multimedia applications do not always require full-duplex connections for the transport of continuous media. An example is a TV broadcast over LAN, which requires a full-duplex control connection, but often a simplex continuous media connection is sufficient.

  During the *data transmission* over the TCP connection, TCP must achieve *reliable, sequenced delivery* of a stream of bytes by means of an underlying, unreliable datagram service. To achieve this, TCP makes use of retransmission on timeouts and positive acknowledgments upon receipt of information. Because retransmission can cause both out-of-order arrival and duplication of data, sequence numbering is crucial. Flow control in TCP makes use of a window technique in which the receiving side of the connection reports to the sending side the sequence numbers it may transmit at any time and those it has received contiguously thus far.

For multimedia, the positive acknowledgment causes substantial overhead as all packets are sent with a fixed rate. Negative acknowledgment would be a better strategy. Further, TCP is not suitable for real-time video and audio transmission because its retransmission mechanism may cause a violation of deadlines which disrupt the continuity of the continuous media streams. TCP was designed as a transport protocol suitable for non-real-time reliable applications, such as file transfer, where it performs the best.

- *User Datagram Protocol (UDP)*

  UDP is a simple extension to the Internet network protocol IP that supports multiplexing of datagrams exchanged between pairs of Internet hosts. It offers only multiplexing and checksumming, nothing else. Higher-level protocols using UDP must provide their own retransmission, packetization, reassembly, flow control, congestion avoidance, etc.

  Many multimedia applications use this protocol because it provides to some degree the real-time transport property, although loss of PDUs may occur. For experimental purposes, UDP above IP can be used as a simple, unreliable connection for medium transport.

  In general, UDP is not suitable for continuous media streams because it does not provide the notion of connections, at least at the transport layer; therefore, different service guarantees cannot be provided.

Several extensions are proposed to increase the performance of both UDP and TCP protocols so that a larger group of applications (i.e., also multimedia applications) can use them. Large windows and time stamps are now draft standards. Also, selective acknowledgments might be taken in, although this mechanism provides a win when the packet loss rate approaches one per round-trip time [Bin93].

### Real-time Transport Protocol (RTP)

RTP is an end-to-end protocol providing network transport functions suitable for applications transmitting real-time data, such as audio, video or simulation data over multicast or unicast network services. It is specified and still augmented by the Audio/Video Transport Working Group [SCFJ94]. RTP is primarily designed to satisfy the needs of multi-party multimedia conferences, but it is not limited to that particular application.

RTP has a companion protocol RTCP (RTP-Control Protocol) to convey information about the participants of a conference. RTP provides functions, such as *determination of media encoding, synchronization, framing, error detection, encryption, timing* and *source identification.* RTCP is used for the *monitoring of QoS* and for *conveying* information about the participants in an ongoing session. The first aspect of RTCP, the monitoring, is done by an application called a QoS monitor, which receives the RTCP messages. This monitor estimates the current QoS for monitoring, fault diagnosis and long-term statistics. The second aspect of RTCP is used for "loosely controlled" sessions. RTP and RTCP information is transmitted through separate ports.

RTP does not address resource reservation and does not guarantee QoS for real-time services. This means that it does not provide mechanisms to ensure timely delivery of data or guaranteed delivery, but relies on lower-layer services to do so. Further, it does not guarantee delivery or prevent out-of-order delivery, nor does it assume that the underlying network is reliable and delivers packets in sequence. The RTP header carries sequence numbers to allow the end system to reconstruct the sender's packet sequence, but also they can be used to properly place the packet, for example, in video decoding.

RTP makes use of the network protocol ST-II or UDP/IP for the delivery of data. It relies on the underlying protocol(s) to provide demultiplexing.

Profiles are used to specify certain parts of the header for particular sets of applications. This means that particular media information is stored in an *audio/video profile*, such as a set of formats (e.g., media encodings) and a default mapping of those formats.

RTP is used in some of the MBone tools, for example, *nv*. The program *nv* is a packet video program used to support visual interaction in tele-conferencing over MBone. *nv* does all the network I/O, RTP the processing and the X window system does the interaction.

### Xpress Transport Protocol (XTP)

XTP was designed to be an efficient protocol, taking into account the low error ratios and higher speeds of current networks [SDW92]. It is still in the process of augmentation by the XTP Forum to provide a better platform for the incoming variety of applications. XTP integrates transport and network protocol functionalities to have more control over the environment in which it operates [Che92]. XTP is intended to be useful in a wide variety of environments, from real-time control systems to remote procedure calls in distributed operating systems and distributed databases to bulk data transfer. It defines for this purpose six service types: *connection, transaction, unacknowledged data gram, acknowledged datagram, isochronous stream* and *bulk data*.

In XTP, the end-user is represented by a *context* becoming active within an XTP implementation. Two contexts (or several in multicast mode) are joined together to form an *association*. The path between two XTP sites is called a *route*. There are two types of XTP packets: information packets which carry user data, and control packets which are used for protocol management.

For *flow control*, XTP uses sliding window, or rate-based flow control. If window-based control is selected, the window size is negotiated during the connection setup. To advance the flow-control window, XTP uses a *combined mechanism* between a cumulative acknowledgment (e.g., TCP also uses a cumulative acknowledgement mechanism) and a selective acknowledgment, with a run-length encoding.

Data packet *retransmissions* are triggered by the arrival of status reports showing missing data. Status reports are requested and a certain timer controls the duration of the response to the request. After the timer expires and a status report was not received, a new status report is issued, and XTP enters a *synchronizing handshake*, where all further data transmission are halted until the correct status is received.

Therefore, XTP will never retransmit a data packet without positive indication that it has not been received.

The error management is different for each of these service types. Therefore, XTP error control is primary a set of building blocks, known as *mechanisms*, from which a variety of error control *policies* can be constructed. Therefore, error control features can be tailored to the needs of the user.

There are some features which meet the requirements for multimedia communication, such as [Mil93b]:

- XTP provides a connection-oriented transport and network transmission, hence it gives the benefit to map XTP on ATM networks and to use the possibilities of bandwidth reservation of ATM networks.
- Different transport services are provided: connection-mode, connectionless-mode and transaction-mode. Very important is the fast-connect-establishment for tele-transaction service.
- Flexible error management allows the turning off of the retransmission mechanism, which is useful for multimedia applications.
- XTP has rate-based flow control which allows it to provide a convenient mechanism for throughput and bandwidth reservation when QoS request is issued.

There are some problems with XTP in regard to supporting continuous media transmission:

1. XTP was designed to be implemented in VLSI to achieve high performance, because it is too complex. However, most current implementations of XTP are done in software and their performance is too slow for transmission of continuous media streams [SGC94].
2. If the round rotation time of the underlying network (e.g., Ethernet) frequently fluctuates, XTP constantly enters the synchronizing handshake which is very undesirable in high-speed networks and for continuous media transmission [AC93].

3. XTP has a *large header*, which creates an overhead of 44 bytes regardless of mode. For example, if an audio stream, with 160-bytes packet size (or less for compressed audio coding) is being transmitted, the header overhead represents 27% of the body content which is more than just a nuisance.

4. Source identification and discrimination are missing in XTP. Source discrimination refers to the necessity to discriminate among several sync and content sources, all arriving through the same network transport association. This feature is important for security and authentication reasons.

5. Internetworking with other protocols is not worked out to provide QoS handling and resource reservation.

### Other Transport Protocols

Some other designed transport protocols which are used for multimedia transmission are:

- *Tenet Transport Protocols*

  The Tenet protocol suite for support of multimedia transmission was developed by the Tenet Group at the University of California at Berkeley. The transport protocols in this protocol stack are the *Real-time Message Transport Protocol* (RMTP) and *Continuous Media Transport Protocol* (CMTP). They run above the *Real-Time Internet Protocol* (RTIP).

  The RMTP provides connection-oriented, performance-guaranteed, unreliable delivery of messages. This transport layer is quite lightweight. Two features frequently associated with transport layers, connection management and reliable delivery through retransmission, are absent from this protocol. Thus, the main functions of this transport layer are *flow control* (accomplished by rate control) and the fragmentation and reassembly of messages.

  CMTP is designed to support the transport of periodic network traffic with performance guarantees.

  The RMTP and CMTP provide data and continuous media (periodic network traffic) transmission, but they obey the resource administration done by the

*Real-time Channel Administration Protocol (RCAP)* which provides resource reservation, admission and QoS handling. Therefore, together the protocol stack also provides guaranteed services with deterministic and statistical QoS bounds [Gup94, BM91].

- *Heidelberg Transport System (HeiTS)*

  The Heidelberg Transport System (HeiTS) is a transport system for multimedia communication. It was developed at the IBM European Networking Center (ENC), Heidelberg. HeiTS provides the raw transport of multimedia over networks. It uses the *Heidelberg Continuous media Realm* (HeiCoRe), which is a real-time environment for handling multimedia data within workstations. The central issue of HeiCoRe and HeiTS together is to provide guaranteed services during multimedia transmission. HeiCoRe includes the *Heidelberg Resource Administration Technique* (HeiRAT), a resource management subsystem that addresses these issues [VHN92].

- *METS: A Multimedia Enhanced Transport Service*

  METS is the multimedia transport service developed at the University of Lancaster [CCH93a]. It runs on top of ATM networks.

  The transport protocol provides an ordered, but non-assured, connection-oriented communication service and features resource allocation based on the user's QoS specification. It allows the user to select upcalls for the notification of corrupt and lost data at the receiver, and also allows the user to re-negotiate QoS levels. The protocol incorporates buffer sharing, rate regulation, scheduling, and basic flow monitoring modules to provide different services, such as guaranteed services with deterministic QoS, statistical QoS bounds and best effort services.

### 11.2.3 Network Layer

The requirements on the network layer for multimedia transmission are a provision of *high bandwidth*, *multicasting*, *resource reservation and QoS guarantees*, *new routing protocols* with support for streaming capabilities and *new higher-capacity routers* with support of intergated services.

### Internet Services and Protocols

Internet is currently going through major changes and extensions to meet the growing need for real-time services from multimedia applications.

There are several protocols which are changing to provide *integrated services*, such as best effort service, real-time service and controlled link sharing. The new service, *controlled link sharing*, is requested by the network operators. They need the ability to control the sharing of bandwidth on a particular link among different traffic classes. They want to be able to divide traffic into few administration classes and assign to each a minimal percentage to the link bandwidth under conditions of overload, while allowing 'unused' bandwidth to be available at other times [BCS93].

- *Internet Protocol (IP)*

  IP provides for the unreliable carriage of datagrams from source host to destination hosts, possibly passing through one or more gateways (routers) and networks in the process. We examine some of the IP properties which are relevant to multimedia transmission requirements:

  - *Type of Service*: IP includes identification of the service quality through the *Type of Service (TOS)* specification. TOS specifies (1) precedence relation and (2) services such as *minimize delay*, *maximize throughput*, *maximize reliability*, *minimize monetary cost* and normal service. Any assertion of TOS can only be used if the network into which an IP packet is injected has a class of service that matches the particular combination of TOS markings selected. The assumption is that different networks offer varying classes of service. Different classes may support different media requirements. For example, multimedia conferencing would need service class which supports low delay, high throughput and intermediate reliability. Precedence handling would support priority schemes in a wide area network and therefore support real-time network traffic. Unfortunately, at present, few commercial routers implement precedence handling in a way that affects the forwarding of packets. In general, no guarantees are provided.

    The TOS capability of IP becomes increasingly important as networks emerge that have the ability to deliver specific classes of services and offer certain service guarantees. The changes, which may need to be specified, are: for multimedia, we may not need a precedence relation but an *AND* relation; instead of having services, such as *minimize, maximize delay*, etc., lower and upper bounds of a delay should be introduced.

- *Addressing and Multicasting*: One of the most critical functions of the IP is the *addressing*, i.e., to establish a global address space that allows every network in the Internet to be uniquely identified. The IP addressing structure is shown in Figure 11.6. The network addressing structure was

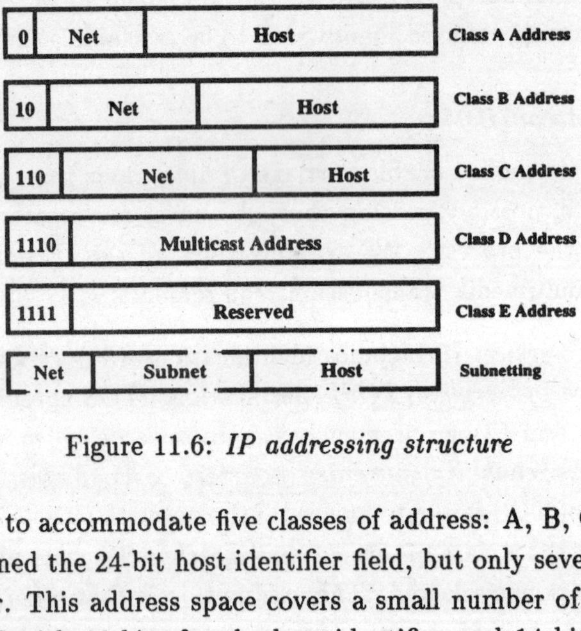


Figure 11.6: *IP addressing structure*

revised to accommodate five classes of address: A, B, C, D and E. *Class A* retained the 24-bit host identifier field, but only seven bits for network number. This address space covers a small number of class A networks. *Class B* with 16 bits for the host identifier and 14 bits for the network number allows a larger number of Class B networks. *Class C* allocates 21 bits for network number and eight bits for host identifier, therefore many more Class C networks are available. A common practice is to assign a class B network address to a collection of LANs.

The LAN technology brought the concept of convenient *broadcasting* to all end-points on the LAN. LANs also introduced the concept of *multicasting*, in which only a subset of the end-points on the LAN are targeted to receive a particular transmission. This capability allows an application to send a single message to the network and have it delivered to multiple recipients. This service is attractive in a variety of distributed applications, including multi-side audio/video conferencing and distributed database maintenance. This concept is captured in the Internet architecture through special Internet *Class D* addresses, in which multicast-addressed packets are routed (and duplicated at routers when necessary) to all targets that are part of the multicast group.

The realization of multicasting in a WAN environment is a nontrivial undertaking. The routing system must be made aware of which networks have hosts participating in each multicast group, so that the arrival of a multicast-addressed packet can trigger proper forwarding to the destination networks. To avoid duplicative replications of multicast packets by multiple routers, a spanning tree of routers is constructed as part of the multicasting algorithm, to route and duplicate multicast packets.

The worldwide Internet has been providing an IP multicast routing service for some time now, through an Internet segment called *MBone* (Multicast Backbone). The MBone is a collection of UNIX workstations running a routing daemon called "mrouted", which is an implementation of the *Distance Vector Multicast Routing Protocol (DVMRP)* [WPD88]. The MBone is layered on top of the Internet's unicast topology. Connection between the MBone's UNIX workstations is provided by the same Internet links that are used for the usual applications. As multicast datagrams are forwarded from one MBone router to another, they are "tunneled", so that to intervening non-multicast routers they look like regular unicast traffic. Using the MBone, conference sessions from IETF and other Internet technical meetings can be multicast and the remote users can listen to the technical talks and ask the speaker questions.

*Class E* addresses have been reserved for future extensions.

– *Interconnectivity Between Internet Protocol and Underlying Networks*: The Internet family of protocols is one of today's most widespread protocol stacks in computer networking. There is a strong interest in transporting the IP datagrams, which may carry multimedia traffic, over different networks, for example, an Ethernet or an ATM B-ISDN. Hence, the mapping between the Internet protocol and the underlying layers is of importance. Another important function in this task is the *binding* of IP addresses to lower-level network addresses. For example, in the case of Ethernet LANs, routers need to encapsulate IP packets in a properly addressed Ethernet packet. Ethernet uses 48-bit addressing. The router learns the binding of the IP to the 48-bit LAN address through the *Address Resolution Protocol* (ARP). This protocol allows a router (or any host) to broadcast a query containing an IP address, and receive back the associated LAN address. A related protocol, *reverse ARP*, can be used to ask which IP address is bound to a given LAN address.

Analogously, in the case of ATM LANs, routers need to encapsulate IP packets in properly addressed cells, and vice versa. Through the ARP protocol, respectively reverse ARP, a mapping between the IP address and VPI/VCI occurs [OG93].

- *Routing*: A major subject in Internet architecture is the *routing* of IP packets because the basic model of Internet consists of networks connected by routers. To create an opportunity for further experimental exploration of different routing protocols for global networking, the concept of *Autonomous Systems (AS)* was developed. ASs are collections of routers falling under a common administrative authority. In theory, the routers commonly use the same routing protocol - *Interior Gateway Protocol (IGP)*, within the AS. AS of gateways (routers) exchange reachability information by means of an *Exterior Gateway Protocol (EGP)*. As the common IGP for the Internet, the *Open Shortest Path First (OSPF)* link-state routing algorithm has been adopted. For EGP , the *Border Gateway Protocol (BGP)* was developed. For routing of OSI connectionless packets the *Inter-Domain Routing Protocol (IDRP)* was standardized in the OSI community.

  For multimedia, the best performance would be achieved if a fixed path (static route) could be allocated, because along this path, guarantees can be met and no or little jitter is experienced. The problem with this extension is that the IP protocol would lose the ability to bypass link-layer failures, which is a fundamental property of the Internet architecture, and should be retained for integrated services. Further, in the case of a static route, if no resource reservation would be performed along the fixed path, the flexibility of changing a route (in the case of congestion) on a packet basis would be lost, which would decrease the performance of the *best effort* service. Hence, it is very difficult to achieve.

- *Internet Group Management Protocol (IGMP)*

  Internet Group Management protocol (IGMP) is a protocol for managing Internet multicasting groups. It is used by conferencing applications to join and leave particular multicast group. The basic service permits a source to send datagrams to all members of a multicast group. There are no guarantees of the delivery to any or all targets in the group.

  Multicast routers periodically send queries (*Host Membership Query messages*) to refresh their knowledge of memberships present on a particular network. If no reports are received for a particular group after some number of queries, the routers assume the group has no local members, and that they need not forward remotely originated multicasts for that group onto the local network. Otherwise, hosts respond to a query by generating reports (*Host Membership Reports*), reporting each host group to which they belong on the network interface from which the query was received. To avoid an "impulsion" of concurrent reports there are two possibilities: either a host, rather than sending reports immediately, delays for a D-second interval the generation of the report; or, a report is sent with an IP destination address equal to the host group address being reported. This causes other members of the same group on the network to overhear the report and only one report per group is presented on the network.

  Queries are normally sent infrequently, so as to keep the IGMP overhead on host and routers very low. However, when a multicast router starts up, it may issue several queries to quickly build up its knowledge of local membership.

  When a host joins a new group, it should immediately transmit a report for that group, rather than waiting for a query, in case it is the first member of the group.

  IGMP is specified in RFC 1112 and uses an IP packet format with additional IGMP fields such as IGMP type (Host Membership Query, Host Membership Report), checksum, or group address [Dee89].

In a multimedia scenario, IGMP must loosely cooperate with an appropriate resource management protocol, such as RSVP, to provide a resource reservation for a member who wants to join a group during a conference.

- *Resource reSerVation Protocol (RSVP)*

RSVP is a protocol which transfers reservations and keeps a state at the intermediate nodes. It does not have a data transfer component. RSVP messages are sent as IP datagrams, and the router keeps "soft state", which is refreshed by periodic reservation messages. In the absence of the refresh messages, the routers delete the reservation after a certain timeout.

This protocol was specified by IETF to provide one of the components for integrated services on the Internet. To implement integrated services, four components need to be implemented: the *packet scheduler*, *admission control routine*, *classifier*, and the *reservation setup protocol*. The RSVP protocol was designed to satisfy requirements, such as [BCS93]:

  - It must accommodate heterogeneous service needs.
  - It must give flexible control over the manner in which reservations can be shared along the branches of the multicast delivery tree.
  - It must accommodate elementary actions such as adding one sender and/or receiver to an existing set, or deleting one.
  - It must be robust enough to scale well to large multicasting groups.
  - It must provide for advance reservation of resources, and for the preemption that this implies.

A *reservation* specifies the amount of resources to be reserved for all, or some subset of the packets in a particular session. A resource reservation requires adding a *flow* specification control state in the routers which represents an important and fundamental change to the Internet model because the Internet architecture was founded on the concept that all flow-related states should be in the end-systems [BCS93].

Hence, the resource quantity is specified by the *flow-spec*, which parameterizes the packet scheduling mechanism. The packet subset to receive those resources is specified by a *filter-spec.* A filter-spec defines a packet filter that is instantiated in the classifier.

The RSVP protocol mechanism provides a very general facility for creating and maintaining a distributed reservation state across the mesh of a multicast delivery path.

RSVP reservations are receiver-oriented, which means that the sender starts, but the actual reservation of resources is performed by the receiver. This is done to support heterogeneous receivers in a multicast group.

### STream Protocol, Version 2 (ST-II)

ST-II provides a connection-oriented, guaranteed service for data transport based on the stream model [Top90]. The connections between the sender and several receivers are setup as uni-directional connections, although also duplex connections can be setup.

ST-II is an extension of the original ST protocol [For79]. It consists of two components: the *ST Control Message Protocol (SCMP)*, which is a reliable, connectionless transport for the protocol messages and the *ST* protocol itself, which is an unreliable transport for the data.

ST-II provides a resource reservation during the connection setup. The reservation is originated from the source. It sends a SCMP message with a *flow specification*, which describes the stream requirements (QoS) in terms of packet size, data rate, etc. If the destination accepts the call, it returns the final flow specification to the source. The resource reservation scheme is presented in more detail in Section 11.3.3.

To perform processing in the nodes, ST data packets do not carry complete addressing information. They have a *HOP IDentifier (HIP)*, similar to a virtual circuit number, which is negotiated for each hop during the setup phase.

ST-II is suitable for multimedia transmission because of its resource reservation along the path between the sender and receiver.

#### Real-Time Internet Protocol (RTIP)

In the Tenet scheme, the services of RTIP (Real-Time Internet Protocol) are used. RTIP provides for connection-oriented, performance-guaranteed, unreliable delivery of packets [VZ91]. It occupies an analogous place in the Tenet protocol stack as the IP in the Internet protocol suite. It communicates with RCAP for resource reservation, therefore it provides guaranteed service [Mah93].

The Tenet protocol suite was designed for real-time communication, with particular emphasis on multimedia transmission.

## 11.3 Quality of Service and Resource Management

The user/application requirements on the Multimedia Communication System (MCS) are mapped into communication services which make the effort to satisfy the requirements. Because of the heterogeneity of the requirements, coming from different distributed multimedia applications, the services in the multimedia systems need to be parametrized. Parameterization allows for flexibility and customization of the services, so that each application does not result in implementing of a new set of service providers.

### 11.3.1 Basic Concepts

Parameterization of the services is defined in ISO (International Standard Organization) standards through the notion of *Quality of Service (QoS)*. The ISO standard defines QoS as a concept for specifying how "good" the offered networking services are. QoS can be characterized by a number of specific parameters. There are several important issues which need to be considered with respect to QoS:

#### QoS Layering

Traditional QoS (ISO standards) was provided by the network layer of the communication system. An enhancement of QoS was achieved through inducing QoS into transport services. For MCS, the QoS notion must be extended because many other services contribute to the end-to-end service quality. To discuss further QoS and resource management, we need a *layered* model of the MCS with respect to QoS. We assume throughout this section the model shown in Figure 11.7. The MCS consists of three layers: *application, system* (including communication services and operating system services), and *devices* (network and MultiMedia (MM) devices). Above the application may or may not reside a human user. This implies the in-

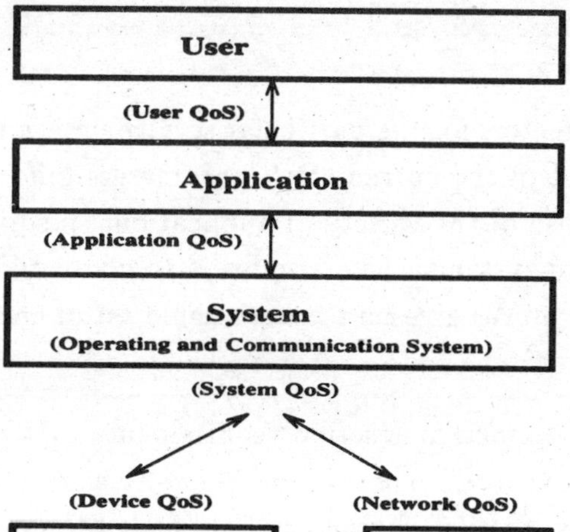


Figure 11.7: *QoS-layered model for the MCS.*

troduction of QoS in the *application* (application QoS), in the *system* (system QoS) and in the *network* (network QoS). In the case of having a human user, the MCS may also have a user QoS specification. We concentrate in the network layer on the network device and its QoS because it is of interest to us in the MCS. The MM devices find their representation (partially) in application QoS.

### Service Objects

Services are performed on different objects, for example, media sources, media sinks, connections and Virtual Circuits (VCs), hence the QoS parameterization specifies these *service objects.* In ISO standards, the QoS description is meant to be for services, processing a *transport/network connection.* In Tenet protocol suite, the services operate over a *"real-time" channel* of a packet switched network [FV90]. In METS, a QoS parameter specification is given for *call, connection and VC* objects [CCH93a]. In RSVP (Resource Reservation Protocol), a flow specification is given for parameterization of the *packet scheduling mechanism in the routers or hosts* [ZDE+93]. At higher layers in communication systems, the service objects, for example *media* [NS95a] or *streams* [SE93], may be specified.

### QoS Description

The set of chosen parameters for the particular service determines what will be measured as the QoS. Most of the current QoS parameters differ from the parameters described in ISO because of the variety of applications, media sent and the quality of the networks and end-systems. This also leads to many different QoS parameterizations in the literature. We give here one possible set of QoS parameters for each layer of MCS.

The *application QoS parameters* describe requirements for the application services possibly specified in terms of (1) *media quality*, which includes the media characteristics and their transmission characteristics, such as end-to-end delay, and (2) *media relations*, which specify the relations among media, such as media conversion or inter/intra stream synchronization [NS95a].

*System QoS parameters* describe requirements on the communication services and OS services resulting from the application QoS. They may be specified in terms of both *quantitative* and *qualitative criteria*. Quantitative criteria are those which can be evaluated in terms of certain measures, such as bits per second, number of errors, task processing time, PDU size, etc. The QoS parameters include throughput, delay, response time, rate, data corruption at the system level and task and buffer specification. Qualitative criteria specify the expected services needed for provision of QoS, such as interstream synchronization, ordered delivery of data, error-recovery mechanism, scheduling mechanism, etc. The expected services can be associated with specific parameters. For example, the interstream synchronization can be defined through an acceptable skew within the particular data stream [SE93]. Qualitative criteria can be used by the *coordination control* (see Section 11.1.2) to invoke proper services for particular applications.

*Network QoS parameters* describe requirements on network services. They may be specified in terms of: (1) *network load*, describing the ongoing network traffic and characterized through *average/minimal interarrival* time on the network connection, *packet/cell size* and *service time* in the node for the connection's packet/cell [FV90]; and (2) *network performance*, describing the requirements which the network services must guarantee. Performance might be expressed through a *source-to-destination delay* bound for the connection's packet and packet loss rate [FV90]. Generally, performance bounds are chosen for QoS parameters, such as latency, bandwidth, or delay-jitter, where delay jitter is the maximum difference between end-to-end delays experienced by any two packets [ZK91], but also other parameters for control of QoS (e.g., priority). Note that network services depend on a *traffic model* (arrival of connections requests) and perform according to *traffic parameters*, such as peak data rate or burst length. Hence, calculated traffic parameters are dependent on network QoS parameters and specified in a *traffic contract*.

*Device QoS parameters* typically specify timing and throughput demands for media data units.

### QoS Parameter Values and Types of Service

The specification of QoS parameter values determines the types of service. There are at least three types of service distinguished: *guaranteed, predictive* and *best-effort* services.

*Guaranteed services* provide QoS guarantees, as specified through the QoS parameter values (bounds) either in *deterministic* or *statistical* representation. The deterministic bounds can be given through a *single value* (e.g., average value, contractual value, threshold value, target value), a *pair of values* (e.g., minimum and average value, lowest quality and target quality) or an *interval of values* (lower bound is the minimum value and upper bound is the maximum value). Guaranteed services may also deal with statistical bounds of QoS parameters [FV90], such as statistical bound on error rate etc.

A *predictable service* (historical service) is based on past network behavior, hence the QoS parameters are estimates of past behavior which the service tries to match

[CSZ92].

*Best-effort services* are services based on either no guarantees, or on partial guarantees. There is either no specification of QoS parameters required, or some bounds in deterministic or statistical forms are given. Most of the current network protocols have best effort services.

Note that various systems may provide different classifications of services. An example is the classification of integrated services in the current proposal of the modified Internet architecture [BCS93]. In addition to *best-effort* and *real-time services* (guaranteed service), a service such as *controlled link sharing* is part of the service model (see Section 11.2.2.)

### Resource

A *resource* is a system entity required by tasks for manipulating data. Each resource has a set of distinguishing characteristics [Ste94b]:

- There are *active* and *passive* resources. An active resource is, for example, the CPU or a network adapter for protocol processing; it provides a service. A passive resource is, for example, the main memory (buffer space) or bandwidth (link throughput); it denotes some system capabilities required by active resources.
- A resource can be either used *exclusively* by one process or *shared* between various processes. For example, a loudspeaker is an exclusive resource, whereas bandwidth is a shared resource.
- A resource that exists only once in the system is known as a *single resource*, otherwise it is a *multiple resource*. In a transputer-based multiprocessor system, the individual CPU is a multiple resource.

Services for multimedia networked applications need resources to perform their functions. Of special interest are resources which are shared among application, system and network, such as CPU cycles or network bandwidth. It is important to point out that all shared resources in each layer of MCS can be mapped into three main system resources: *bandwidth of communication channels*, *buffer space* and *CPU processing power*.

## Resource Management Architecture

Resources are managed by various components of a resource management subsystem in a networked multimedia system (Figure 11.8). The main goal of resource

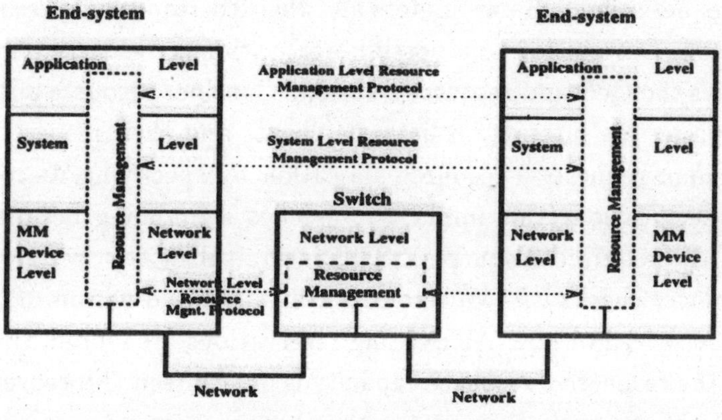


Figure 11.8: *Resource management in MCSs.*

management is to provide guaranteed delivery of multimedia data. This goal implies three main actions: (1) to *reserve* and *allocate* resources (end-to-end) during multimedia call establishment so that traffic can flow according to the QoS specification, which means distribution and negotiation of the QoS specification for system components involved in the data transfer from the source(s) to the sink(s); (2) to *provide* resources according to the QoS specification, which means adhering to resource allocation during multimedia delivery using proper service disciplines; and (3) to *adapt* to resource changes during on-going multimedia data processing.

The resource management subsystem includes *resource managers* at the hosts as well as the network nodes. *Resource management protocols* are used to exchange information about resources among the resource management. The specific tasks of both resource managers and their protocols are discussed in the next subsections.

### Relation between QoS and Resources

QoS parameters specify the resource quantity allocated to the services, as well as the service disciplines managing the shared resource in MCS. For example, the end-to-end delay QoS parameter determines the behavior of transmission services along the path between media source and sink with respect to packet scheduling (bandwidth allocation), queuing (buffer allocation) and task scheduling (CPU processing time allocation).

The above described relation between QoS and resources is embedded in the form of different mappings between QoS parameters and their corresponding resources in resource management. Description of a possible realization of resource allocation and management shows the QoS and resource relation. Consider resource allocation and management based on the interaction between clients and their respective resource managers. The *client* requests a resource allocation by specifying its requirements through a QoS specification (this implicitly includes a mapping between the QoS specification and the required resources). This is equivalent to a workload request. The *resource manager* checks its own resource utilization and decides if the reservation request can be served or not. All existing reservations are stored, this way their share in terms of the respective resource capacity is guaranteed. Moreover, this component negotiates the reservation request with other resource managers if necessary. Applying the generic scheme on a case, as shown in Figure 11.9, the transmission of video data between a camera, connected to a computer server, and the screen of the computer user involves a resource manager for all depicted components.

## 11.3.2 Establishment and Closing of the Multimedia Call

Before any transmission with QoS guarantees in MCS can be performed, several steps must be executed: (1) the application (or user) defines the required QoS; (2) QoS parameters must be distributed and negotiated; (3) QoS parameters between different layers must be translated if their representation is different; (4) QoS parameters must be mapped to the resource requirements; and (5) required resources must be admitted/reserved/allocated along the path between sender(s) and receiver(s). These steps are performed during multimedia call establishment. The close-down

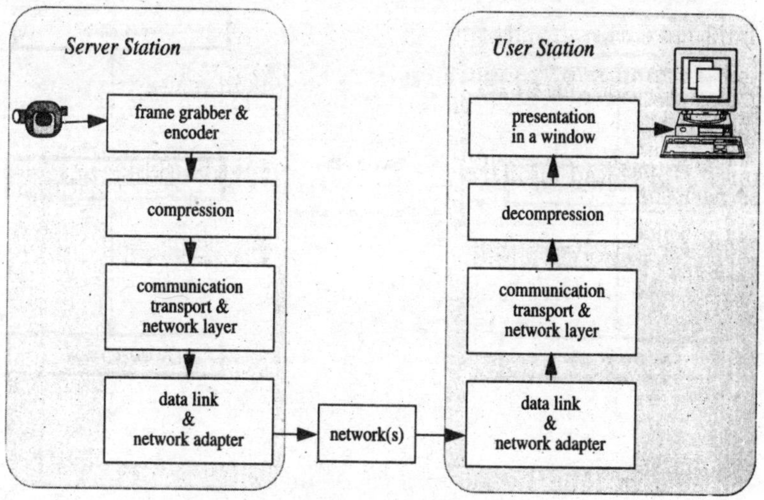


Figure 11.9: *Components grouped for the purpose of video data transmission.*

procedure, from the resource management point of view, concerns resource deallocation.

### QoS Negotiation

If we assume that the user has defined the multimedia application requirements, these requirements must be distributed to the resource management entities of all involved system components. The distribution of QoS parameters requires two services: *negotiation of QoS parameters* and *translation of QoS parameters* (if different QoS specification of system components occurs). To characterize an actual negotiation, we ask *who are the parties?* and *how do the parties negotiate?* There are really two parties to any QoS negotiation. We will consider *peer-to-peer negotiation*, which can be, for example, application-to-application negotiation, and *layer-to-layer communication*, which might be, for example, application-to-system negotiation or human-user-to-application negotiation.

In ISO terminology, peer-to-peer negotiation is also called caller-to-callee negotiation, and layer-to-layer negotiation is called service-user-to-service-provider negotiation (see Figure 11.10).

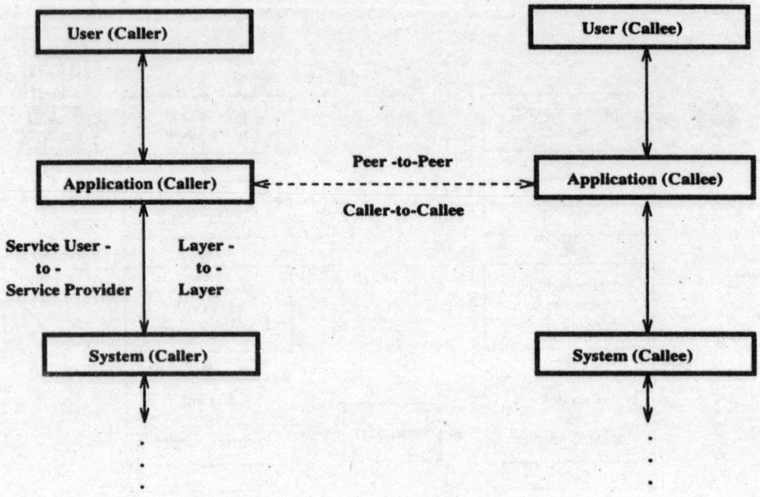


Figure 11.10: *Negotiation.*

The purpose of the negotiation is to establish common QoS parameter values among the services users (peers) and service providers (underlying layers). We further assume negotiation of QoS parameters where the QoS parameter values are specified with deterministic bounds (minimal value and average value). There are several possibilities of negotiation among the peers (caller, callee) and the service provider:

- *Bilateral Peer-to-Peer Negotiation*

  This type of negotiation takes place between the two service users (peers), and the service provider is not allowed to modify the value proposed by the service user (Figure 11.11).

- *Bilateral Layer-to-Layer Negotiation*

  This type of negotiation takes place only between the service user and service provider. This negotiation covers two possible communications: (1) between local service users and providers, for example, between application requirements and OS service guarantees, and (2) between host-sender and the network, for example, when the sender wants to broadcast multimedia streams.

- *Unilateral Negotiation*

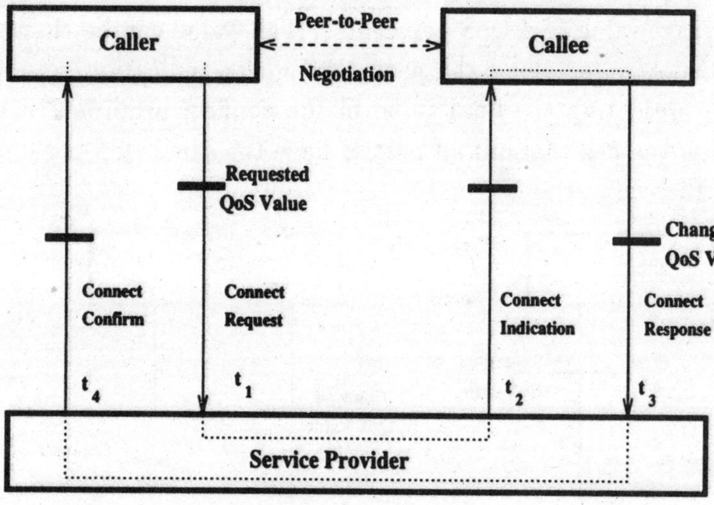


Figure 11.11: *Bilateral peer-to-peer negotiation.*

In this negotiation, the service provider, as well as the called service user, are not allowed to change the QoS proposed by the calling user. This negotiation is reduced to "take it or leave it" [DBB+93]. Further, this negotiation also allows the case in which the receiver may take the proposed QoS and, although may not have the capability to accommodate the QoS parameters, can modify the host-receiver and participate with lower quality on the communication. A similar case occurs in TV broadcasting. The color TV signal is broadcast uniformly to every user, but users with black and white TVs can still watch the TV program, i.e., the control of the quality is done at the receiver device.

- *Hybrid Negotiation*

  In the case of broadcast/multicast communication, every participating host-receiver may have different capabilities from the host-sender, but still wants to participate in the communication (e.g., conference). Hence, between host-sender and network, the QoS parameter values can be negotiated using bilateral layer-to-layer negotiation and unilateral negotiation between network and host-receiver as described above.

- *Triangular Negotiation for Information Exchange*

  In this type of negotiation, the calling user introduces into the request primitive the average value of a QoS parameter. This value can be changed by the service provider/callee along the path through an indication/response primitive before presenting the final value in the confirm primitive to the caller. At the end of the negotiation, all parties have the same QoS parameter value (Figure 11.12).

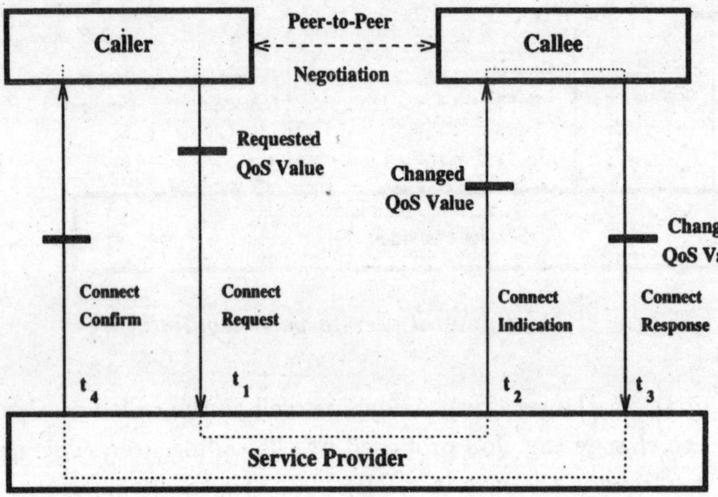


Figure 11.12: *Triangular negotiation for information exchange.*

- *Triangular Negotiation for a Bounded Target*

  This is the same type of negotiation as the previous one, only the values of a QoS parameter are represented through two bounds: target (average value), and the lowest quality acceptable (minimal value). The goal is to negotiate the target value, i.e., the service provider is not allowed to change the value of the lowest quality (if it cannot provide at least the lowest quality, the connection request is immediately rejected), but it is free to modify the target value. The callee will make the final decision concerning the selected value of the target. This selected value of the QoS will be returned to the caller by the confirm primitive (Figure 11.13) [DBB+93].

- *Triangular Negotiation for a Contractual Value*

  In this case, the QoS parameters are specified through a minimal requested value and bound of strengthening. The goal of this negotiation is to agree on

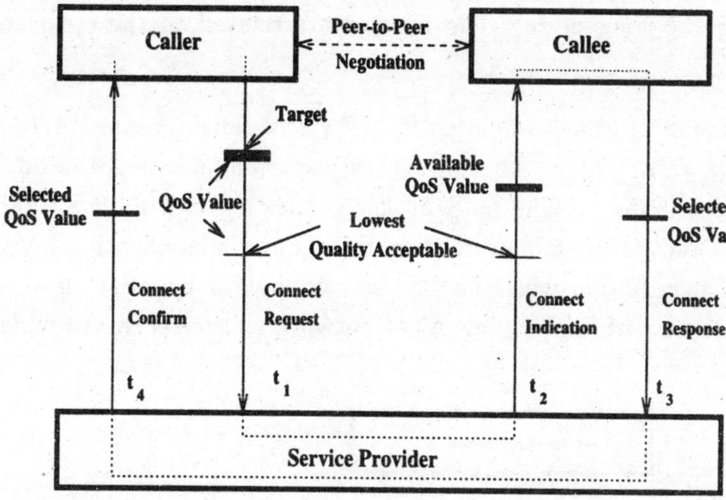


Figure 11.13: *Triangular negotiation for bounded target.*

a contractual value, which in this case is the minimal request QoS parameter value. The service provider can modify the minimal request value towards the strengthening bound value. The callee makes the final decision and reports with a response/confirm primitive to the caller. The contractual value can also be the maximal QoS parameter value, or threshold [DBB+93] values, which the service user wants to achieve as a contract value.

There are still very few call establishment protocols which have negotiation mechanisms built in. We present some examples which have some notion of negotiation in them.

The *ST-II protocol* provides end-to-end guaranteed service across the Internet network [WH94]. The parameters related to the throughput are negotiated with a triangular negotiation for a bounded target. For parameters related to delay, there is no negotiation. The calling user specifies the maximum transit delay in the connect request. During the establishment of the connection, each ST-agent participating in the stream will have to estimate the average transit delay that it will provide for this stream and the average variance of this delay. The provider presents in the connect indication the total estimated average delay and average variance of delay. The called user decides if the (expected) average delay and delay jitter are sufficient before accepting the connection. The parameters related to the error control are not negotiated.

Other establishment protocols such as *RCAP (Real-time Channel Administration Protocol* [BM91], *RSVP* [ZDE+93] and others use triangular negotiation for different QoS parameter values. The QoS broker is another end-to-end establishment protocol [NS95a] and includes bilateral negotiation at the application layer between peers, unilateral negotiation with the OS, and triangular negotiation at the transport subsystem layer with underlying ATM network as the service provider (Figure 11.14).

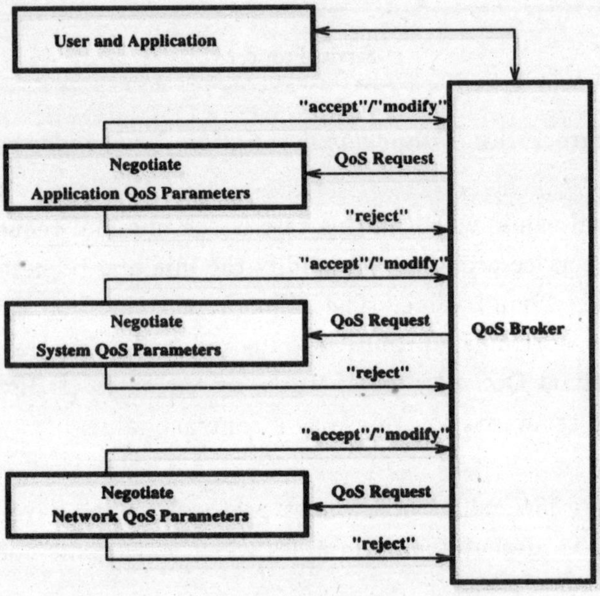


Figure 11.14: *Negotiation in QoS broker.*

### Translation

It is widely accepted that different MCS components require different QoS parameters, for example, the mean loss rate, known from packet networks, has no meaning as a QoS video capture device. Likewise, frame quality is of little use to a link layer service provider because the frame quality in terms of number of pixels in both axes is a QoS value to initialize frame capture buffers.

We always distinguish between user and application, system and network with different QoS parameters. However, in future systems, there may be even more "layers" or there may be a hierarchy of layers, where some QoS values are inherited and others are specific to certain components. In any case, it must always be possible to derive all QoS values from the user and application QoS values. This derivation –known as *translation*– may require "additional knowledge" stored together with the specific component. Hence, translation is an additional service for layer-to-layer communication during the call establishment phase. The split of parameters, shown in Figure 11.7, requires translation functions as follows:

- *Human Interface – Application QoS*

  The service which may implement the translation between a human user and application QoS parameters is called a *tuning service*. A tuning service provides a user with a Graphical User Interface (GUI) for input of application QoS, as well as output of the negotiated application QoS. The translation is represented through video and audio clips (in the case of audio-visual media), which will run at the negotiated quality corresponding to, for example, the video frame resolution that end-system and the network can support. Example of such a GUI is shown in Figure 11.15 [NS95b].

- *Application QoS – System QoS*

  Here, the translation must map the application requirements into the system QoS parameters, which may lead to translation such as from "high quality" synchronization user requirement to a small (milliseconds) synchronization skew QoS parameter [SE93], or from video frame size to transport packet size. It may also be connected with possible segmentation/reassembly functions.

- *System QoS – Network QoS*

  This translation maps the system QoS (e.g., transport packet end-to-end delay) into the underlying network QoS parameters (e.g., in ATM, the end-to-end delay of cells) and vice versa.

The important property of the translation service is that it be *bidirectional trans-*

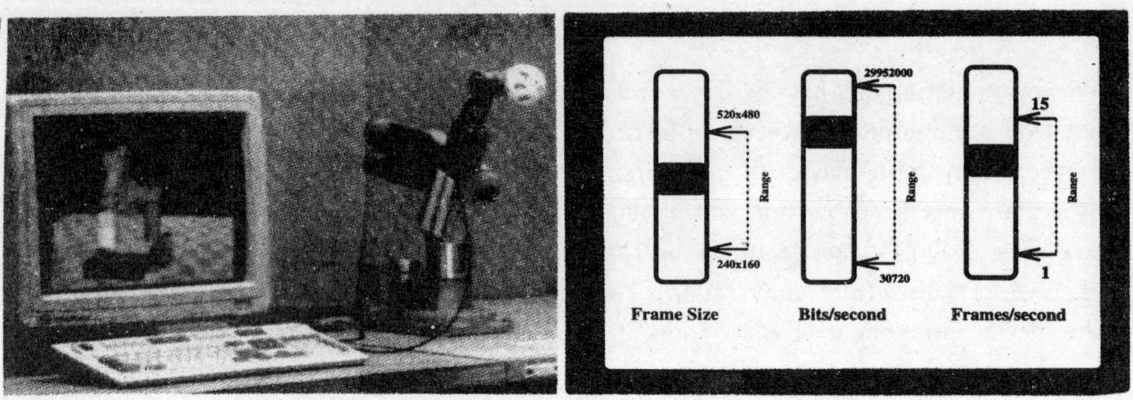


Figure 11.15: *Graphical user interface.*

*lation* [NS95a]. This can cause problems because, for example, the video rate and video frame size together give the throughput parameter for the network. Now, if the throughput bound has to be relaxed, the new throughput value may translate into either lowering the quality of the image or lowering the video frame rate.

At this point, using the previously mentioned "additional knowledge", a bidirectional translation is possible. In the above mentioned example, such a rule may be: (1) to reduce the frame size (always keeping the same ratio between horizontal and vertical resolution) until we encounter 112 pixels in the horizontal direction; (2) to reduce the frame rate until we have one frame per second; and, (3) to provide an indication that no further reduction is possible and the connection must be closed.

The reverse translation results in *media scaling.* In general, media scaling methods perform different degrees of media quality degradation if resources are not available. The dynamic QoS change (translation, negotiation, renegotiation of QoS) is used in conjunction with scaling techniques [TTCM92].

### Scaling

*Scaling* means to subsample a data stream and only present a fraction of its original contents. In general, scaling can be done either at the source or at the receiver.

Scaling methods, used in an MCS, can be classified as follows [DHH+93]:

- *Transparent scaling* methods can be applied independently from the upper protocol and application layers. This means that the transport system scales the media down. Transparent scaling is usually achieved by dropping some portions of the data stream. These portions need to be identifiable by the transport system.
- *Non-transparent scaling* methods require an interaction of the transport system with the upper layers. This kind of scaling implies a modification of the media stream before it is presented to the transport layer. Non-transparent scaling typically requires modification of some parameters in the coding algorithms, or even recoding of a stream that was previously encoded in a different format.

In an MCS, scaling can be applied to both audio and video data:

- For *audio*, transparent scaling is difficult because presenting a fraction of the original data is easily noticed by the human listener. Dropping a channel of a stereo stream is an example. Hence, non-transparent scaling must be used for audio streams. For example, a change of the sampling rate at the stream source achieves an audio scaling.
- For *video* streams, the applicability of a specific scaling method depends strongly on the underlying compression technique. There are several domains to which scaling can be applied [DHH+93]:
  - *Temporal scaling* reduces the resolution of the video stream in the time domain. This means that the number of video frames transmitted within a time interval decreases. Temporal scaling is best suited for video streams in which individual frames are self-contained and can be accessed independently.
  - *Spatial scaling* reduces the number of pixels of each image in a video stream. For spatial scaling, hierarchical arrangement is ideal because it has the advantage that the compressed video is immediately available in various resolutions.

- *Frequency scaling* reduces the number of DCT coefficients applied to the compression of an image.
- *Amplitude scaling* reduces the color depth for each image pixel. This can be achieved by introducing a coarser quantization of the DCT coefficients, hence requiring a control of the scaling algorithm over the compression procedure.
- *Color space scaling* reduces the number of entries in the color space. One way to realize color space scaling is to switch from color to gray-scale presentation.

A combination of these scaling methods is possible. In the case of non-transparent scaling, frequency, amplitude and color space scaling are applied at the source during the encoding of the video. Transparent scaling may use temporal scaling or spatial scaling.

### Resource Admission

The next step, after every layer inquires or gets its own QoS specification through negotiation and translation, is resource admission. The admission service is an important service at every node along the path between source (sender) and sink (receiver) to check resources for availability. In networks, it is the mechanism used to accept or reject new connections. The admission service checks availability of shared resources using availability tests. The resource availability tests are called *admission tests.* Based on the results of the admission tests, the reservation protocol creates either a "reserve" message with admitted QoS values or a "reject" message when the minimal bound of QoS values cannot be satisfied. The admitted QoS values may be lower than the target value, but they may still be above the minimal value as shown in Figures 11.12 and 11.13.

There are three types of tests which admission should perform: (1) a *schedulability test* of shared resources such as CPU schedulability, packet schedulability at the entrance to the network and at each network node for delay, jitter, throughput and reliability guarantees; (2) a *spatial test* for buffer allocation for delay and reliability guarantees; and, (3) a *link bandwidth test* for throughput guarantees.

The admission tests, as mentioned above, depend on the implementation of control (e.g., rate control) mechanisms in the multimedia transmission protocols. There is extensive research into admission control [HLG93], [Kes92], etc. At this point, it is important to emphasize that any QoS negotiation, and therefore resource admission must be closely related to a *cost function*, for example, *accounting*.

As one example, let us assume we have a *video-on-demand* service running in a community. We can save resources if we allow the video clip to be moved to a server "nearby" the respective client. This can be done more easily if we have prior knowledge of the required demand. Hence, a user who "orders" a video clip for a certain future time (e.g., 1 hour ahead) may pay less than another user who chooses some video clip and immediately wants to access it. If the client is not forced to pay, he/she will always demand the best available QoS. In this case, some other clients may end up with a reduction in quality or not using this service at all because this is the only result they get through any QoS negotiation. With the introduction of appropriate accounting, QoS negotiation may well become a real negotiation.

### Resource Reservation/Allocation

For the provision of guaranteed QoS in MCS, *reservation and allocation of resources* is necessary. Without resource reservation and management in end-systems and routers/switches, transmission of multimedia data leads to dropped or delayed packets. The reservation and allocation of resources in most systems is *simplex*, i.e., the resources are reserved only in one direction on a link, which implies that the senders are logically distinct from receivers.

Reservation/allocation of resources can be made either in a *pessimistic* or in an *optimistic* way:

- The *pessimistic approach* avoids resource conflicts by making reservations for the worst case, for example, a reservation for the longest processing time of the CPU or the highest bandwidth needed by a task. Resource conflicts are therefore avoided. This leads potentially to an underutilization of resources. This method results in a guaranteed QoS.

- The *optimistic approach* reserves resources according to an average workload. In the case of the above-mentioned example, CPU is only allocated for the average processing time. This approach may overload resources when unpredictable behavior occurs. QoS parameters are met as far as possible. Resources are highly utilized, though an overload situation may result in failure. A *monitor function* to detect overload and to solve the problem should be implemented. The monitor function then preempts processes according to their importance.

Both approaches represent points in a continuum because the process requires a resource in a stochastic fashion. This requirement has both an average and a peak value. One can assign to it any value between the average and the peak value. The closer the assignment is to the peak value, the lower the probability that the process will be denied the use of the resource at a certain time. Hence, the assignment represents a tradeoff between the peak rate multiplexing (pessimistic approach) and the statistical multiplexing (optimistic approach).

Additional mechanisms to detect and solve resource conflicts must be implemented. The resource managers (e.g., in HeiRAT [WH94]) may provide the following data structures and functions for resource reservation:

- *Resource Table*: A resource table contains information about the managed resources. This includes static information like the total resource capacity available, the maximum allowable message size, the scheduling algorithm used, dynamic information like pointers to the connections currently using the resource, and the total capacity currently reserved.

- *Reservation Table*: A reservation table provides information about the connections for which portions of the managed resources are currently reserved. This information includes the QoS guarantees given to the connections and the fractions of resource capacities reserved for these connections.

- *Reservation Function*: A reservation function, used during the call establishment phase, calculates the QoS guarantees that can be given to the new connection and reserves the corresponding resource capacities.

The reservation and allocation of resources depends on the *reservation model*, its *protocols* and a set of *resource administration functions*, such as admission, allocation, monitoring and deallocation, for individual resources.

- **Reservation Model**

  There are three types of reservation models: (1) *Single Sender/Single Receiver* (e.g., RCAP); (2) *Single Sender/Multiple Receivers* (e.g., ST-II); and (3) *Multiple Senders/Multiple Receivers* (e.g., RSVP).

  The reservation model is determined by its *reservation direction and style* [ZDE+93]. The reservation direction can be *sender-oriented* (e.g., ST-II) or *receiver-oriented* (e.g., RSVP). Sender-oriented reservation means that the sender transmits a QoS specification (e.g., flow specification) to the targets. The intermediate routers and targets may adjust the QoS specification with respect to available resources before the QoS specification is transmitted to the sender. Receiver-oriented reservation means that the receiver describes its resource requirements in a QoS specification and sends it to the sender in a "reservation" message [ZDE+93]. It is assumed that a sender has issued a "path" message before, providing information about outgoing data.

  The *reservation style* represents a creation of a path reservation and time when the senders and receivers perform the QoS negotiation and resource reservation. The style for sender-oriented reservation may be either that the sender creates a *single reservation* along the link to the receiver, or the sender creates a *multicast reservation* to several targets. The reservation style for receiver-oriented reservation is defined in RSVP as follows [ZDE+93]:

  - *Wildcard-Filter* style – a receiver creates a single reservation, or resource "pipe", along each link, shared among all senders for the given session.
  - *Fixed Filter* style – each receiver selects the particular sender whose data packets it wants to receive.
  - *Dynamic Filter (DF)* – each receiver creates N distinct reservations to carry flows from up to N different senders. A later DF reservation from the same receiver may specify the same value of N and the same common flowspec, but a different selection of particular senders, without a new admission control check. This is known as *channel switching*, which is

analogous to a television set. If a receiver, using DF reservation style, changes the number of distinct reservations N or the common flow specification, this is treated as a new reservation that is subject to admission control and may fail.

The reservation style can also be divided with respect to time when actual resource allocation occurs: (1) *immediate reservation*, and (2) *advanced reservation.* The advanced reservation service is essential in multi-party multimedia applications. There are two possible approaches to the advanced reservation: (1) a *centralized* approach, where an advanced reservation server exists, and (2) a *distributed* approach, where each node on the channel's path "remembers" the reservations.

- **Resource Reservation/Allocation Protocols**

  A resource reservation protocol performs no reservation or allocation of required resources itself; it is only a vehicle to transfer information about resource requirements and to negotiate QoS values, which users desire for their end-to-end applications. Resource reservation protocols are control protocols embedded in a multimedia call establishment protocol. The resource reservation protocol implies that every node and host has a *resource manager* which is responsible for sending and receiving the control messages, and invoking the resource administration functions (such as admission control, QoS translation, mapping between QoS and resources, routing and other management services) needed to make the proper decision for establishing a multimedia call between senders and receivers with QoS guarantees. It means that the resource manager works closely with network management agents for proper reservation and administration decisions.

  The resource reservation protocols work generally as follows: the initiator of the connection (e.g., sender) sends QoS specifications in a "reservation" message (connect request); at each router/switch along the path, the reservation protocol passes a new resource reservation request to the resource manager, which may consist of several components (for example, in RSVP, this kind of manager is called a "traffic controller" and consists of an admission control routine, packet scheduler and packet classifier); after the admission decision, the resource manager reserves the resources and updates the particular service information for QoS provision (e.g., packet scheduler in RSVP). Figure 11.16 shows sender-initiated resource reservation/allocation protocol with "accept" response.

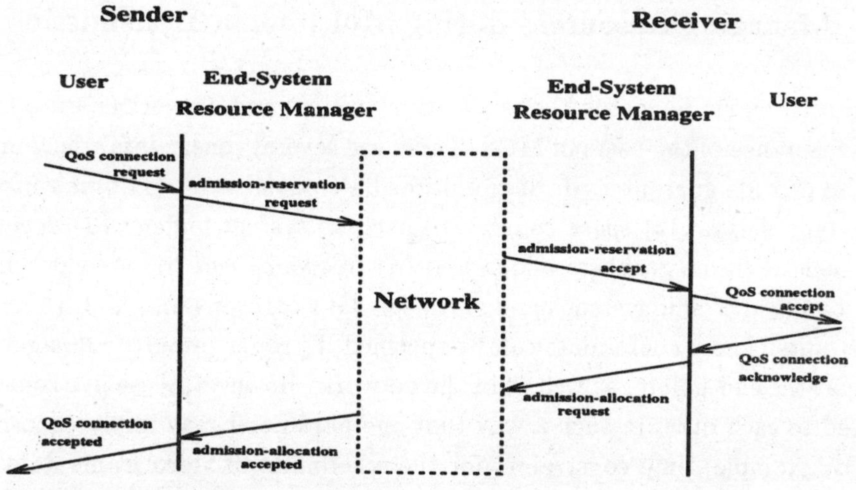


Figure 11.16: *Resource reservation/allocation protocol with "accept" response*

## Resource Deallocation

After the transmission of media, resources must be deallocated, which means, the CPU, network bandwidth and buffer space must be freed and the connections through which the media flow must be torn down. The tear down process must be done without disruption of other flows in the network. Further, the tear down process implies updating the resource availability by the resource manager. The resource deallocation is divided with respect to the direction of the request. (1) *Sender* requests closing of the multimedia call. This implies that the resources for all connections corresponding to the multimedia call along the path between sender and receiver(s) must be deallocated and the resource availability must be updated at every node; (2) *Receiver* requests closing of the multimedia call. This request is sent to the sender and during the traversing of the path, the resources are deallocated.

Deallocation depends on the mechanisms of resource management at the nodes and on the tear down protocols.

### 11.3.3 Managing Resources during Multimedia Transmission

*QoS guarantees* must be met in the application, system and network (Figure 11.7) to get the acceptance of the users of MCS. There are several constraints which must be satisfied to provide guarantees during multimedia transmission: (1) *time constraints* which include delays; (2) *space constraints* such as system buffers; (3) *device constraints* such as frame grabbers allocation; (4) *frequency constraints* which include network bandwidth and system bandwidth for data transmission; and, (5) *reliability constraints*. These constraints can be specified if proper resource management is available at the end-points, as well as in the network. However, these five constraints are related to each other in such a way that one parameter may imply choosing another. For example, time constraints for the scheduling of video frame data imply a corresponding bandwidth allocation. We discuss in the following subsection rate control mechanisms for delay, delay-jitter and throughput (bandwidth) provision, as well as error control for reliability provision. Process and buffer management are presented in Chapter 9 (Operating Systems).

We assume at this point that proper resource reservation and allocation has occurred as described in the previous subsections.

#### Rate Control

If we assume an MCS to be a tightly coupled system, which has a central process managing all system components, then this central instance can impose a synchronous data handling over all resources; in effect we encounter a fixed, imposed data rate. However, an MCS usually comprises loosely coupled end-systems which communicate over networks. In such a setup, rates must be imposed. Here, we make use of all available strategies in the communications environment.

High speed networking provides opportunities for multimedia applications to have stringent performance requirements in terms of throughput, delay, delay-jitter and loss rate. Conventional packet switching data networks with window-based flow control and FCFS cannot provide services with strict performance guarantees. Hence, for MCS, new *rate-based flow control* and *rate-based service disciplines* are being introduced. These control mechanisms are connected with a connection-oriented network architecture which supports explicit resource allocation and admission control policies.

A *rate-based service discipline* is one that provides a client with a minimum service rate independent of the traffic characteristics of other clients. Such a discipline, operating at a switch, manages the following resources: *bandwidth*, *service time (priority)* and *buffer space*. Together with proper admission policies, such disciplines provide throughput, delay, delay-jitter and loss rate guarantees. Several rate-based scheduling disciplines have been developed [ZK91]:

- *Fair Queuing*

  If *N* channels share an output trunk, then each one should get *1/Nth* of the bandwidth. If any channel uses less bandwidth than its share, then this portion is shared among the rest equally. This mechanism can be achieved by the *Bit-by-bit Round Robin (BR)* service among the channels. The BR discipline serves *n* queues in the round robin service, sending one bit from each queue that has a packet in it. Clearly, this scheme is not efficient; hence, fair queuing emulates BR as follows: each packet is given a finish number, which is the round number at which the packet would have received service, if the server had been doing BR. The packets are served in the order of the finish number. Channels can be given different fractions of the bandwidth by assigning them weights, where weight corresponds to the number of bits of service the channel receives per round of BR service.

- *Virtual.Clock*

  This discipline emulates *Time Division Multiplexing (TDM)*. A virtual transmission time is allocated to each packet. It is the time at which the packet would have been transmitted, if the server would actually be doing TDM.

- *Delay Earliest-Due-Date (Delay EDD)*

  Delay EDD [FV90] is an extension of EDF scheduling (Earliest Deadline First) where the server negotiates a service contract with each source. The contract states that if a source obeys a peak and average sending rate, then the server provides bounded delay. The key then lies in the assignment of deadlines to packets. The server sets a packet's deadline to the time at which it should be sent, if it had been received according to the contract. This actually is the expected arrival time added to the delay bound at the server. By reserving bandwidth at the peak rate, Delay EDD can assure each channel a guaranteed delay bound.

- *Jitter Earliest-Due-Date (Jitter EDD)*

  Jitter EDD extends Delay EDD to provide delay-jitter bounds. After a packet has been served at each server, it is stamped with the difference between its deadline and actual finishing time. A regulator at the entrance of the next switch holds the packet for this period before it is made eligible to be scheduled. This provides the minimum and maximum delay guarantees.

- *Stop-and-Go*

  This discipline preserves the "smoothness" property of the traffic as it traverses through the network. The main idea is to treat all traffic as frames of length $T$ bits, meaning the time is divided into frames. At each frame time, only packets that have arrived at the server in the previous frame time are sent. It can be shown that the delay and delay-jitter are bounded, although the jitter bound does not come free. The reason is that under Stop-and-Go rules, packets arriving at the start of an incoming frame must be held by full time $T$ before being forwarded. So, all the packets that would arrive quickly are instead being delayed. Further, since the delay and delay-jitter bounds are linked to the length of the frame time, improvement of Stop-and-Go can be achieved using multiple frame sizes, which means it may operate with various frame sizes.

- *Hierarchical Round Robin (HRR)*

  An HRR server has several service levels where each level provides round robin service to a fixed number of slots. Some number of slots at a selected level are allocated to a channel and the server cycles through the slots at each level. The time a server takes to service all the slots at a level is called the *frame time* at the level. The key of HRR is that it gives each level a constant share of the bandwidth. "Higher" levels get more bandwidth than "lower" levels, so the frame time at a higher level is smaller than the frame time at a lower level. Since a server always completes one round through its slots once every frame time, it can provide a maximum delay bound to the channels allocated to that level.

Some other disciplines. suitable for providing guaranteed services, are schemes such as the *Weighted Fair Queueing (WFQ)* algorithm [CSZ92]. In WFQ, each packet is stamped with a time-stamp as it arrives and then it is transmitted in increasing order of the time-stamps.

To bound the delays in rate-based disciplines, *traffic shaping* schemes can be applied at the sending host, for example, *Leaky Bucket* and its variations (e.g., *Token Bucket*) [CSZ92]. In Leaky Bucket, the sending host places the data into a bucket and the data drain out the bottom of the bucket, being sent on the network at a certain rate. The rate is enforced by a regulator at the bottom of the bucket. The bucket size limits how much data may build up waiting for the network.

Rate-based disciplines are divided depending on the policy they adopt: (1) the *work-conserving discipline* serves packets at the higher rate as long as it does not affect the performance guarantees of other channels which also means a server is never idle when there is a packet to be sent (e.g., Delay EDD, Virtual Clock, Fair Queuing); and (2) the *non-work-conserving discipline* does not serve packets at a higher rate under any circumstances, which also means that each packet is assigned, explicitly or implicitly, an *eligibility time*. Even when the server is idle, if no packets are eligible, none will be transmitted (e.g., Stop-and-Go, HRR, Jitter EDD).

Rate-based service disciplines need to allocate resources per client, hence the clients need to specify their traffic (using QoS parameters). The traffic specification for Virtual Clock, HRR and Stop-and-Go are : a *transmission rate* averaged over an *interval.* Delay EDD and Jitter EDD have three parameters: *minimal packet inter-arrival time*, *average packet inter-arrival time* and *interval* over which the average packet inter-arrival time was computed. Fair Queuing was described for datagram networks, so no traffic specification was proposed.

The buffer space requirements for the three non-work-conserving disciplines are almost constant for each node traversed by the channel [ZK91]. The buffer space requirement for work-conserving Delay EDD increases linearly for each node along the path. Throughput guarantees are provided by all rate-based services. Delay guarantees are provided only by Delay EDD and all non-work-conserving services (also by Weighted Fair Queueing). Jitter guarantees are provided by Stop-and-Go and Jitter EDD.

### End-to-End Error Control

Multimedia extensions to existing operating systems provide a fast and efficient data transport between sources and destinations located at the same computer. Glitches on video streams may (but should not) occur, but audio is always conveyed in a reliable way. The solution becomes different if we take into account networks. In the past, several multimedia communication systems have been proposed which usually offer unreliable transport. For example, the UDP/IP protocol was used for experiments to transmit digital audio over the Internet. Other examples are the Tenet protocol suite's transport protocols RMPT (Real-time Message Transport Protocol) and CMTP (Continuous Media Transport Protocol) which provide unreliable but timely delivery for multimedia communication.

A substantive degree of reliability in MCSs is necessary because of the following:

1. *Decompression Technology*

   Most audio and video compression schemes cannot tolerate loss; they are unable to resynchronize themselves after a packet loss or at least visible or/and other perceptual errors are introduced.

2. *Human Perception*

   Loss of digital audio, for example, is detected by a human ear very quickly and results in lower acceptance of the multimedia system.

3. *Data Integrity*

   For example, in a recording application, one cannot recover from an error that is induced in the first recording of data. Fortunately, in this type of application, where multimedia data is written to disk, there are often less stringent real-time requirements for the receiver.

To ensure required reliability of MCSs, end-to-end error control consists of two steps *error detection* and *error correction*.

- *Error Detection*

  Reliability should be enforced, although there is some error tolerance in the multimedia systems. This works only if the *application* is able to isolate the errors. For example, some wrong colors within a video frame may not matter because they are hardly visible to the human user as they appear for only a short fraction of a second, but if the frame boundaries are destroyed, there is no way to recover from the error. This means that structural information within a data stream needs to be protected, but not always content. This also implies that existing error detection mechanisms, such as *checksumming* and *PDU sequencing*, must be extended toward conveying further information. These existing mechanisms allow detection of data corruption, loss, duplication and misorder at the lower levels (e.g., packets in the transport layer), but on the application PDU level, where the decision should actually be made, if the packet is lost or not, error detection is left out.

  Another example for enforcing error detection at a higher layer (above the transport layer) is MPEG-2 encoded video. This compression produces three type of frames in the video streams. The most important frame type is the I-frame, which contains the structural information of the video stream for a certain time interval. The two other types of video frames (P-frame and B-frame) follow the I-frame with supporting information. Hence, it is important for the multimedia communication system not to lose the I-frame (strict reliability requirements on the sequence of I-frames), but there is a certain tolerance towards losses of P-frames or B-frames.

  In the transport and lower layers the error detection mechanisms must be extended too because of the "lateness" concept. It means that if a PDU arrives too late at the receiver, this information is useless for an application and should be detected as an error. To identify late data it is necessary to determine the lifetime of PDUs and compare their actual arrival time with their latest-expected arrival time. The latest expected arrival time can be derived from the traffic model (throughput and rate) associated with a connection. This means that for continuous streams, the expiration time can be calculated from the PDU rate. Therefore, only the first PDU has to carry a time stamp, although this is not an ideal solution because error detection is forced to start with the first PDU, and no interruption of the service is possible. With a time stamp in every PDU the error detection can start at any point during the media transmission. This mechanism requires a synchronized system clock at the sender and receiver to allow an accurate determination of the end-to-end delay. A possible protocol for this kind of synchronization is Mill's *Network Time Protocol (NTP)*[Mil93a].

- *Error Correction*

  The traditional mechanism for reliability provision is *retransmission* (e.g., TCP protocol uses this mechanism), which uses an acknowledgment principle after receiving data or window-based flow control. If the acknowledgment is negative, the data are re-sent by the sender. The traditional reliable transfer strategies are not suitable for multimedia communication because: (1) with explicit acknowledgment the amount of data to be stored at the sender for potential retransmission can become very large (e.g., in the case of video); (2) with the traditional window-based flow control, the sender may be forced to suspend transmission while a continuous data flow is required; (3) the retransmitted data might be received "too late" to be consumed in real-time; and, (4) traditional mechanisms also do not scale to multiple-target communication – they are not designed for multicasting communication, only for point-to-point communication. We will outline some error correction schemes for MCS currently discussed in the research:

  - *Go-back-N Retransmission*

    This method is the most rigid error correction scheme. The mechanism is as follows: if PDU $i$ is lost, the sender will go back to $i$ and restart transmission from $i$. The successive PDUs after $i$ are dropped at the receiver. The lost PDU is recovered only if $i \leq n$, where $n$ is specified at the beginning of the transmission. This means it is specified ($n$) how far back the data should be retransmitted if a packet is lost. This is a simple protocol where no buffering or resequencing of the PDUs at the receiver are necessary. The receiver only sends a negative acknowledgment if PDU $i$ is lost. The problem is that if after that $i$'th PDU the packets were transmitted successfully, they are dropped too, which may lead to several implications: (1) *gap introduction* (Figure 11.17); and (2) *violation of throughput guarantees.* The retransmission introduces gaps because the receiver has to wait at least $2 \times end - to - end\ delay$ to get the proper PDU $i$. Also, for a multimedia connection where throughput guarantees are provided through rate control, the retransmitted data must be sent either "on top" of the guaranteed throughput or the retransmitted PDU will fall under the rate control. This again leads to a gap in the stream presentation which needs to be handled properly through a mechanism such as freezing the video, or turning down the audio.

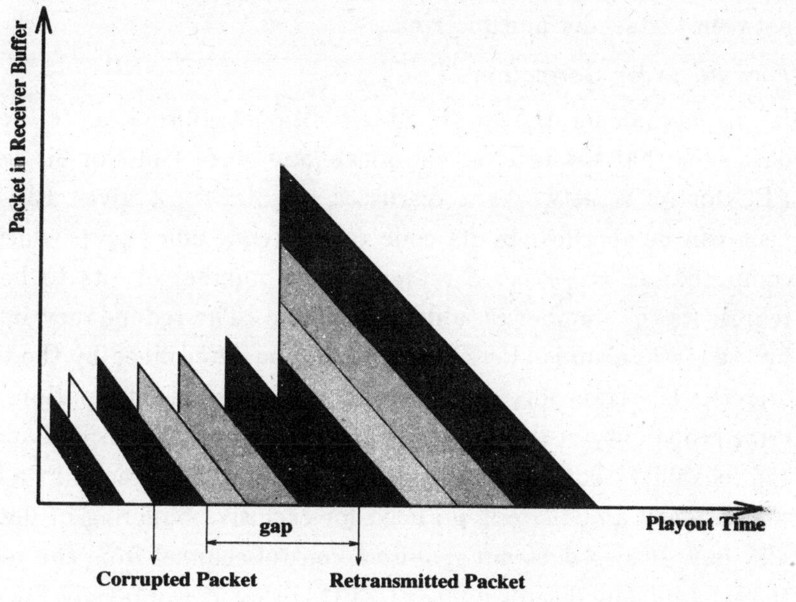


Figure 11.17: *Gaps in Go-back-N retransmission.*

– *Selective Retransmission*

Selective retransmission provides better channel utilization. The receiver sends a negative acknowledgment to the sender if PDU $i \leq n$ is lost. The sender retransmits only those PDUs which have been reported missing, not the consecutive packets too. The disadvantage of this mechanism is its complicated implementation. At the receiver, every successfully received PDU must be stored until all previous PDUs have been received correctly. It has been shown that this resequencing is worthwhile only if the receiver is able to store at least two times the data corresponding to the bandwidth-delay product.

– *Partially Reliable Streams*

Partially reliable streams introduce a weak concept of reliability. This mechanism limits the number of packets to be retransmitted. Only the last $n$ packets of the stream in a certain time interval will be retransmitted. The value $n$ can be calculated from the timing constraint of the multimedia application, taking into account the reliability of the underlying network. The possible $n$ can be negotiated during the call setup between the sender and receiver.

– *Forward Error Correction (FEC)*

In this mechanism, the sender adds additional information to the original data such that the receiver can locate and correct bits or bit sequences. FEC for ATM networks is discussed in [Bie93]. A given FEC mechanism can be specified by its code rate $C$ (code efficiency), which can be computed: $C = \frac{S}{(S+E)}$; $S$ represents the number of bits to be sent, $E$ represents the number of added check bits. The redundancy introduced by the mechanism is $(1 - C)$ and it must be determined by the transport system. The transport system needs two pieces of informations: (1) the error probability of the network between the sender and receiver; and (2) the reliability required from the application. FEC results in a low end-to-end delay and there is no need for exclusive buffering of data before play-out. It also does not require a control channel from the receiver to the sender. The disadvantage of FEC is that it works only for error detection and correction within a packet but not for complete packet loss, i.e., FEC cannot guarantee that corrupted or lost packets can always be recovered. Further, FEC increases the demand on throughput significantly. The negative effects of added congestion on a network due to FEC overhead can more than offset the benefits of FEC recovery [Bie93].

Also, FEC requires hardware support at end-systems to encode and decode the redundant information with sufficient speed. FEC is also used for storing audio data at Compact Disc (CD) devices.

– *Priority Channel Coding*

Priority channel coding refers to a class of approaches that separates the medium (e.g., voice) into multiple data streams with different priorities. These priorities are then used to tag voice packets so that during periods of congestion, the network is more likely to discard low-priority packets which carry information less important for reconstructing the original media stream. This scheme enables multiple priority channels to maintain a higher QoS over larger loss ranges than channels using a single priority for all voice packets. Channel coding requires that the network be able to control packet loss during congestion through a priority mechanism. The use of different streams for different priorities requires synchronization at a per-packet granularity to reconstruct the voice signal. Another example where prioritized transmission can be used is for MPEG-2 encoded video. Here, I and P frames could be sent at high priority and B frames could be sent at low priority. Network switches drop lower-priority cells or provide a lower grade of service during periods of network congestion.

– *Slack Automatic Repeat ReQuest (S-ARQ)*

S-ARQ is an error control scheme based on retransmission of lost voice packets in high-speed LANs. The packets are subject to delay-jitter, hence the receiver observes *gaps*, which result in interruptions of continuous playback of the voice stream. Delay-jitter in packetized voice transmission is commonly addressed through a control time at the receiver. The first packet is artificially delayed at the receiver for the period of the control time to buffer sufficient packets to provide for continuous playback in the presence of jitter. The voice data consist of talk spurts and periods of silence. Since talk spurts are generally isolated from each other by relatively long silence periods, voice protocols typically impose the control time on the first packet of each talk spurt. The *slack time* of a packet is defined as the difference between its arrival time at the receiver and its playback time, which is the point in time at which playback of the packet must begin at the receiver to achieve a zero-gap playback schedule for the talk spurt. Due to delay-jitter, a packet may arrive before or after its playback time. In the former case, the packet is placed in a *packet voice receiver* queue until it is due for playback. In the latter case, a gap has occurred and the packet is played immediately. The principle of S-ARQ is to extend the control time at the beginning of a talk spurt and to use it so that the slack time of arriving packets is lengthened. An example is shown in Figure 11.18 [DLW93].

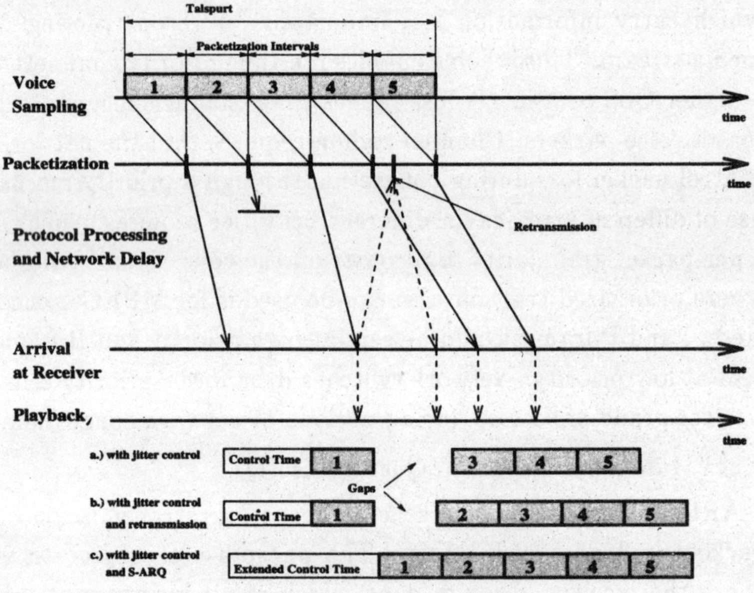


Figure 11.18: *S-ARQ.*

The error control/correction schemes for multimedia communication systems, as described above, can be divided into two classes: (1) *partial retransmission mechanisms* (e.g., Go-Back-N, Selective Retransmission, Partially Reliable streams, S-ARQ); and (2) *preventive mechanisms* (e.g., FEC, Priority Channel Coding). All partial retransmission schemes lack the possibility of introducing a discontinuity or of working properly if we introduce large end-to-end delays with large buffers. Hence, preventive schemes should be used.

### Resource Monitoring

Resource monitoring is an important part of resource management in networks, as well as at end-points. Resource monitoring functionality is embedded in the resource manager and is closely connected to the network management agent. Network management works with *agents* at every intermediate network node (routers/switches), which are concerned with: (1) the information which can be exchanged among the intermediate network nodes; and the structure of this information stored in the *Management Information Base* (MIB); and, (2) the protocol used to exchange information between the network agent and the managed component (e.g., resource manager). The Management Information Base (MIB) may also be used for resource admission. To use network management for resource management, the MIBs of the network management must be extended for multimedia communication with the QoS parameters. Further, network management may be enhanced with functionalities for QoS supervision and problem resolving functions.

*Monitoring in networks* can add overhead during multimedia transmission, which should not cause a violation of QoS guarantees. Hence, monitoring should be flexible, which means that: (1) most of the monitoring variables should be optional; and, (2) monitoring should be able to be turned on and off [WH94]. There are two possible modes to operate resource monitoring: *end-user mode* and *network mode*. The former requests a status report about the resources; the latter reports regularly the resource status on different nodes along the path between communicating end-users.

*Monitoring at end-systems* includes a *supervisor function* to continuously observe that the processed QoS parameters do not exceed their negotiated values. As an example, a compression component may allow delivery at a peak rate of 6 Mbits/s over a duration of at most three frame lengths. However, at some point in time the system starts to deliver a continuous bit rate of 6 Mbits/s. The monitoring function will detect this behavior by being called from an exception handler of the rate control component: a buffer overflow occurred at the sender – something which should never happen. The monitoring function finds out that the origin of the exceeded QoS value is an erroneous compressing component. It should be pointed out that the design and implementation of such a monitoring function is a non-trivial task and that a clearly defined notion of the QoS is a prerequisite.

*Resource Administration Protocols* provide communication about resources between individual resource managers at the intermediate nodes and end-points during multimedia transmission. They can be implemented either as part of the *network management protocols* or as separate *resource management protocols.* In the former, the resource administration protocols may be embedded in the following currently standard network management protocols: (1) *CMIS/CMIP (Common Management Information Services and Protocol)*, OSI family standards which are applied in wide area network environments; and, (2) *SNMP (Simple Network Management Protocol)*, a protocol currently prevalent in local area networks. SNMP is based on the Internet protocol. An example of a separate resource administration protocol is RCAP in the Tenet protocol stack.

Another classification of administration protocols can be done according to the criteria: is the administration protocol part of the transmission protocol, or not. An example for coupling the establishment, transmission and management phases is the ST-II protocol. ST-II is further coupled to SNMP-MIB for management. An example where the administration protocol is decoupled from transmission protocols, is RCAP [BM91]. RCAP is decoupled from the RTIP (Real-time Internet Protocol), RMTP (Real-time Message Transport Protocol) and CMTP (Continuous Media Transport Protocol). The user can request status from RCAP about the resources, but the transport/network protocols do not interact during the transmission with RCAP.

**Resource Adaptation**

In continuous media communication, it is important to support a framework capable of dynamically changing the network capacity of each session. Hence, it is important for the MCS architecture to support dynamic change of QoS parameters so that they can be balanced to reach an optimal value for all sessions in a predictable manner.

There are two important factors which must be provided to achieve this goal: (1) notification and renegotiation of QoS parameters , i.e., a protocol for reporting the QoS changes and modifying QoS parameters of existing connections (may be done by resource administration protocols); and, (2) adaptive resource schemes to respond to and accommodate the changes either in the network, the hosts or both.

During multimedia transmission, change of QoS parameters and associated resources can occur. If such changes occur, *renegotiation of QoS parameters* must begin. Hence, renegotiation is a process of QoS negotiation when a call is already setup. The renegotiation request can come either from the user, who wants to change the quality of service, from the host system due to overload of the workstation (multi-user, multi-process environment) or from the network due to overload and congestion. The renegotiation request is sent to the resource manager. A possible signaling paradigm for renegotiation at the end-point is shown in Figure 11.19.

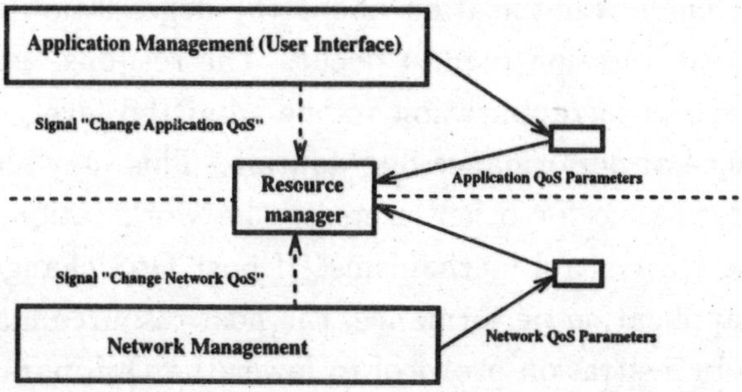


Figure 11.19: *Signaling paradigm for renegotiation at the end-point.*

- *User Request for Renegotiation*

  If the user-sender requires a change of QoS, this may imply adaptation of multimedia sources and local host resources, as well as network resources. The resource manager must check if local resources are available. We assume that the renegotiation request can be accommodated at the multimedia source, meaning, that, for example, the user does not require 30 frames/second if the video encoder can provide only 10 frames/second. Further, the resource administration protocol must be invoked to check the availability of network resources if the change of QoS requires change of network resources. If resources are available, resource reservation and allocation is performed.

  If the user-receiver requires change of QoS for the receiving media, first the resource manager checks the local resource and reserves it. Then, the sender is notified via a resource administration protocol and the same admission procedure follows as in the case of a user-sender requiring QoS changes. At the end, the receiver must be notified to change the local resource allocation. In a broadcast or multicast communication structure, different QoS values may be applied for the same connection to different end-systems.

- *Host System Request for Renegotiation/Change*

  This request may come from the operating system, if such a capability is provided, in a multi-user environment. In this case, several users are admitted and some of the users (misbehaved users) violate their admitted application requirements. Then, a notification about the degradation of the QoS performance and a renegotiation request occur. The response is either adaptation of the misbehaved user/application to the admitted level, or the misbehaved user's acceptance of performance degradation. This may also result in degradation of performance for other users of the workstation, which should be omitted by the OS control mechanisms. If host QoS changes result in degradation of the application performance, the host resource manager may invoke the resource administration protocol to lower the QoS parameters in the network between the sender and receiver.

- *Network Request for Renegotiation/Change*

  Overload of the network at some nodes can cause a renegotiation request for QoS change. This request comes as a notification from the resource administration protocol to the host reporting that the allocation of resources must change. There are two possibilities: (1) the network can adapt to the overload; or, (2) the network cannot adapt to the overload. In the former case, the network still needs to notify the host because some degradation may occur during the modification of resources (e.g., if the network tears down a connection and establishes a new connection). This actually may interrupt the media flow, so the host must react to this change. In the latter case, the source (host) must adapt.

We describe several mechanisms for resource adaptation when the renegotiation request comes from the network due to network overload. The adaptation mechanisms implicitly offer partial solutions for cases when the renegotiation request comes from the user or the host system.

- *Network Adaptation*

  The fixed routing and resource reservation for each conversation, combined with load fluctuations, introduce problems of network unavailability and loss of network management. Thus, a proper balancing of the network load is desirable and necessary to: (1) increase network availability; (2) allow network administrators to reclaim resources; and, (3) reduce the impact of unscheduled, run-time maintenance on clients with guaranteed services. Efficient routing and resource allocation decisions, made for previous clients which made requests for QoS guarantees, reduce the probability that a new client's request will be refused by the admission scheme. The more efficient the routing and resource allocation, the MORE guaranteed connection requests are accepted.

  One possibility for implementing a *load balancing policy* is to employ the following mechanisms: *routing*, *performance monitoring* (detecting load changes), *dynamic re-routing* (changing the route) and *load balancing control* (making a decision to re-route a channel) [PZF92]. The routing mechanism implements the routing algorithm which selects a route in adherence to certain routing constraints. The performance monitoring mechanism monitors the appropriate network performance and reports it to the load balancing control. The dynamic re-routing mechanism is needed to establish the alternative route and to perform a transparent transition from the primary route to the alternative route. The load balancing control mechanism receives information from the performance monitoring mechanism and determines whether load balancing can be attempted using a load balancing algorithm defined by the policy. If load balancing can be attempted, the routing mechanism provides an alternative route and the transition from the primary route to the alternative route is accomplished using the dynamic re-routing mechanism.

  The adaptive resource scheme in this protocol is the *dynamic re-routing mechanism.* When channel $i$ is to be re-routed, the source tries to establish a new channel that has the same traffic and performance parameters and shares the same source and destination as channel $i$, but takes a different route. The new channel is called *a shadow channel* [PZF92] of channel $i$. After the shadow channel has been established, the source can switch from channel $i$ to the shadow channel and start sending packets on it. After waiting for the maximum end-to-end delay time of channel $i$, the source initiates a tear-down message for channel *i*. If the shadow channel shares part of the route with the old channel, it is desirable to let the two channels share resources. This further implies that the establishment and tear-down procedures are aware of this situation, so that the establishment does not request the new resource and the tear-down procedure does not free the old resource.

- *Source Adaptation*

  Another alternative reaction to changes in the network load is to adapt the source rate according to the currently available network resources. This approach requires *feedback* information from the network to the source which results in graceful degradation in the media quality during periods of congestion. For example, in [KMR93], the feedback control mechanism is based on predicting the evolution of the system state over time. The predicted system state is used to compute the target sending rate for each frame of video data. The adaptation policy strives to keep the bottleneck queue size for each connection at a constant level. Each switch monitors the buffer occupancy and service rate per connection. The buffer occupancy information is a count of the number of queued packets for the connection at the instant when the feedback message is sent. The rate information is the number of packets transmitted for the connection in the time interval between two feedback messages. There are two possibilities to implement the feedback transmission mechanism. (1) The per-connection state information is periodically appended to a data packet for the corresponding connection. At the destination, this information is extracted and sent back to the source. A switch updates the information fields in a packet only if the local service rate is lower than that reported by a previous switch along the path. (2) The feedback message is sent in a separate control packet which is sent back along the path of the connection towards the source.

  Other source adaptation schemes (for video traffic) may control overload.

  - *Rate Control using Network Feedback*

    In this approach, each source adapts to changes in network conditions caused by an increase or decrease in the number of connections or by sudden changes in the sending rates of existing connections. Changes in the traffic conditions are detected by explicit or implicit feedback from the network. Explicit feedback is in the form of information about the traffic loads or buffer occupancy levels. Implicit feedback information about packet losses and round robin delay is available from acknowledgments.

- *Traffic Shaping at Source*

  Another way to control congestion is to smooth out traffic at the source. Typically, most of the burstiness reduction can be obtained by smoothing over an interval of 1-4 frames [KMR93].

- *Hierarchical Coding*

  Hierarchical coding describes algorithms which produce two or more types of cells describing the same block of pixels with different degrees of detail. However, these coders are more complex and use a greater amount of bandwidth to transmit images than single-layer coders [KMR93].

### 11.3.4 Architectural Issues

Networked multimedia systems work in *connection-oriented mode*, although the Internet is an example of a connectionless network where QoS is introduced on a packet basis (every IP packet carries type of service parameters because the Internet does not have a service notion). MCS, based on that Internet protocol stack, uses RSVP, the new control reservation protocol, which accompanies the IP protocol and provides some kind of "connection" along the path where resources are allocated.

QoS description, distribution, provision and connected resource admission, reservation, allocation and provision must be embedded in different components of the multimedia communication architecture. This means that proper services and protocols in the end-points and the underlying network architectures must be provided.

The *end-point architectures* need to incorporate components like resource managers for end-point resources and service agents for communication with network management. Resource managers need to include translation services, admission control, resource reservation and management for the end-point. Further, resource managers and service agents need access to MIBs with QoS specifications, which can be used by the resource administration (for status reporting) of the resources. Especially, the system domain needs to have QoS and resource management. Several important issues, as described in detail in previous sections, must be considered in the end-point architectures: (1) QoS specification, negotiation and provision; (2) resource admission and reservation for end-to-end QoS; and, (3) QoS configurable transport systems.

*Network routers/switches* need to employ MIBs, resource managers and network management to provide connections/VCIs/channels with QoS guarantees. Further, resource managers must consist of several components, such as packet classifier and packet scheduler for QoS provision, as well as admission controller for admission of resource. The network management includes traffic monitors in the form of agents, which communicate to have a global view on network resources.

Some examples of architectural choices where QoS and resource management are designed and implemented include the following:

1. The OSI architecture provides QoS in the network layer and some enhancements in the transport layer. The OSI 95 project considers integrated QoS specification and negotiation in the transport protocols [DBB+93].

2. Lancaster's QoS-Architecture (QoS-A) [CCH93a] offers a framework to specify and implement the required performance properties of multimedia applications over high-performance ATM-based networks. QoS-A incorporates the notions of *flow*, *service contract* and *flow management*. The *Multimedia Enhanced Transport Service (METS)* provides the functionality to contract QoS.

3. The Heidelberg Transport System (HeiTS) [WH94], based on ST-II network protocol, provides continuous-media exchange with QoS guarantees, upcall structure, resource management and real-time mechanisms. HeiTS transfers continuous media data streams from one origin to one or multiple targets via multicast. HeiTS nodes negotiate QoS values by exchanging flow specification to determine the resources required - delay, jitter, throughput and reliability.

4. The UC Berkeley's Tenet Protocol Suite with protocol set RCAP, RTIP, RMTP and CMTP provides network QoS negotiation, reservation and resource administration through the RCAP control and management protocol.

5. The Internet protocol stack, based on IP protocol, provides resource reserva-

tion if the RSVP control protocol [ZDE+93] is used.

6. QoS handling and management is provided in UPenn's end-point architecture (OMEGA Architecture) at the application and transport subsystems [NS95a], where the *QoS Broker*, as the end-to-end control and management protocol, implements QoS handling over both subsystems and relies on control and management in ATM networks.

7. The *Native-Mode ATM Protocol Stack* [KS95], developed in the IDLInet (IIT Delhi Low-cost Integrated Network) testbed at the Indian Institute of technology provides network QoS guarantees.

Resource management, based on QoS requirements. has become an important part of multimedia communication systems across all system components because of the requests for resource guarantees. These requests are introduced because of: (1) increasing application varieties and requirements; and, (2) incoming new media transmitted over the high-speed networks.

## 11.4 Comments

### 11.4.1 Trends in Collaborative Computing

New application disciplines place new demands on the collaboration infrastructure and new tele-services are emerging. Only conferencing and application sharing is not enough. Multimedia networked applications, such as tele-medicine, tele-working, virtual collaborative space, distributed simulations and tele-action require sophisticated handling at the level of an application subsystem. We discuss these application more in detail in Chapter 17.

Future collaborative computing will incorporate a (possibly unknown) number of people at geographically distributed sites, using a variety of applications from different application domains. With the *heterogeneity* of collaborative multimedia applications, interoperability issues need to be satisfied.

### Simplification of Groupware Development

The development process for groupware needs to be simplified through re-usable components. Groupware should have a plug-and-play architecture [SW94a]. Also, collaborative development support during software engineering should be at much higher level.

### Shared Abstractions and Standard Interfaces

Shared abstractions and standard interfaces need to be developed to accommodate heterogeneity. The *Rendezvous* architecture from Bellcore provides already a partial solution for graphical shared abstractions [HBP+93]. The Rendezvous architecture is based on a centralized *abstraction* that collects information common to all users into a single space. Each user has his/her own *personal view* to this information. There is a link between each view and the abstraction. The links are responsible for maintaining consistency between each view and the abstraction. Figure 11.20 shows the shared abstraction of different personal views on a graph.

Standard interfaces are strongly supported by the industry. In March 1993, the Hewlett-Packard Company, IBM Corp., SCO (Santa Cruz Operation, Inc.), Sun Microsystems, Inc., Univel and UNIX System Laboratories, Inc. announced their intent to deliver a common open software environment across their UNIX system platforms. They have defined a specification for a common desktop environment that gives end-users a consistent look and feel. They have defined a consistent set of Application Programming Interfaces (APIs) for the desktop that will run across all of their systems, opening up a larger opportunity for software developers [UNI93].

### Standard Protocols

Standard protocols will need to incorporate communication mechanisms which support collaborative computing, such as *multicast* or *protocol abstractions*.

Multicast is needed to provide efficient multiway communication (1-to-N, N-to-1, N-to-N). Protocol abstractions, such as *distributed session control*, are needed to

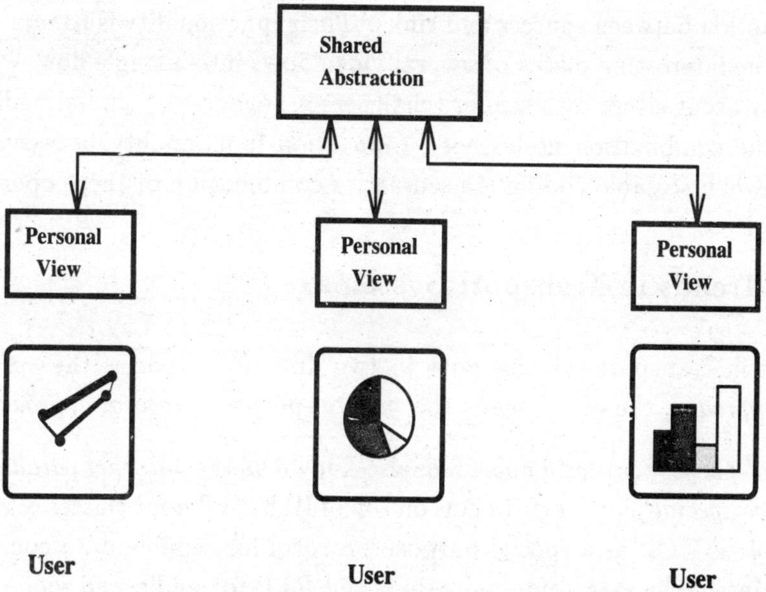


Figure 11.20: *Shared abstraction.*

shield users from the complexity of multipart multimedia coordination. Several abstractions have emerged to describe streams, connections and other objects in communication systems. In the Internet draft [BCS93], the *flow* abstraction was specified to describe the object which is processed by the *integrated services* in the Internet architecture.

### Self-describing Media Agents

Descriptive languages are required to characterize varied groupware capabilities and requirements.

### Translations

Translations among different CSCW sites are needed to overcome hardware and software heterogeneity, for example, to bridge different media encoding schemes. *Combination nodes* [Luk94], [Sch93] have been proposed to provide translation at the conjunction between sources and sinks. Their functionality is to *mix*, *compose* an *assemble* the interesting pieces of several video flows into a single flow, where the *selection* may occur either by a sender (chairperson) or receiver (individually tailored). Further, the combination nodes need *translation* functionality between encodings, *reduction* when scalable coding is used and a combination of these operations.

### 11.4.2 Trends in Transport Systems

The trend in transport systems goes in two directions: one is the *special-purpose protocol approach*, the other one is the *general-purpose protocol approach* [Cha93].

The *special-purpose protocol approach*, also known as the *Internet paradigm*, is to design various *special-purpose* protocols on top of IP for different classes of applications. An example is TCP as a special-purpose protocol for reliable data communication, UDP for unreliable data communication, and RTP for audio and video transport.

The *general-purpose protocol approach* is to provide a general set of services that the user can pick and use. An example is XTP, where the user can select one-way, two-way or three-way handshaking for connection setup and release, etc.

It is hard to predict which paradigm is the right one for the future. More and more special application types are coming. Whether to keep designing and supporting growing protocols in a machine, or use a general protocol to let user pick is a question to answer.

A more realistic and flexible approach may be to develop *application-tailored* protocols that are customized for specific types of services, such as transferring voice, video, text and image data [SP90], [SSS+93], [Nah93]. In our opinion, the transport subsystems move more and more towards a provision of several service classes. Therefore, a transport system may offer, for example, a class of guaranteed services and a class of best-effort services. Within each service class, the services are customized through QoS specification, and accordingly, services inside of the class are selected and customized toward applications.

# Chapter 12

# Database Systems

Multimedia database systems are database systems where, besides text and other discrete data, audio and video information will also be stored, manipulated and retrieved. To provide this functionality, multimedia database systems require a proper storage technology and file system.

Current storage technology allows for the possibility of reading, storing and writing audio and video information in real-time. This can happen either through dedicated external devices, which have long been available, or through system integrated secondary storage. The external devices were developed for studio and electronic entertainment applications; they were *not* developed for storage of discrete media. An example is a video recorder controlled through a digital interface. On the other hand, the integrated secondary storage for audio and video is often based on optical technology (see Chapter 7). The system integration of secondary storage is performed by the operating system through the device drivers. ross@systems.seas.upenn.edu Further, multimedia databases need proper file systems (see Chapter 9) because external devices can be accessed easier through a file directory. The same applies to the integrated secondary storage.

## 12.1 Multimedia Database Management System

Multimedia applications often address file management interfaces at different levels of abstraction. Consider the following three applications: a *hypertext application* can manipulate nodes and edges; an *audio editor* can read, write and manipulate audio data (sentences); an *audio-video distribution service* can distribute stored video information.

At first, it appears that these three applications do not have much in common, but in all three their functions can uniformly be performed using a *Multimedia DataBase Management System (MDBMS)*. The reason is that in general, the main task of a *DataBase Management System (DBMS)* is to abstract from the details of the storage access and its management. As shown in Figure 1.1 (architectural overview of all multimedia system components), MDBMS is embedded in the multimedia system domain, located between the application domain (applications, documents) and the device domain (storage, compression and computer technology). The MDBMS is integrated into the system domain through the operating system and communication components. Therefore, all three applications can be put on the same abstraction level with respect to DBMS. Further, a DBMS provides other properties in addition to storage abstraction:

- *Persistence of Data*

  The data may outlive processing programs, technologies, etc. For example, insurance companies must keep data in databases for several decades. During this time, computer technology advances and with these changes operating systems and other programs advance. This implies that a DBMS should be able to manipulate data even after the changes of the surrounding programs.

- *Consistent View of Data*

  In multi-user systems it is important to provide a consistent view of data during processing database requests at certain points. This property is achieved using *time synchronization protocols.*

- *Security of Data*

Security of data and integrity protection in databases in case of system failure is one of the most important requirements DBMS. This property is provided using the *transaction concept.*

- *Query and Retrieval of Data*

  Different information (entries) is stored in databases, which later can be retrieved through database queries. Database queries are formulated with *query languages* such as SQL. Further, every entry in a database includes its own state information (e.g., entry was modified), which needs to be retrieved correctly to provide correct information about the entry.

The inclusion of multimedia functionalities entails database management of very large amounts of data distributed over different secondary storage media. For example, in the case of a relational database, a vector of attributes representing a video clip with sound can require a storage capacity of several megabytes. Besides the need for a large storage capacity, real-time requirements are also demanded of DBMS processing of continuous data. The design of an MDBMS must comply with these requirements. It is important to point out that if external devices are used, the real-time requirements are outside of the DBMS scope and the connected devices implicitly meet them. In an integrated system, real-time requirements need to be considered inside of the DBMS scope. A more detailed consideration of MDBMSs and multimedia systems is given in [Mey91].

In the following sections, the tasks of a database system with respect to multimedia and an overview of system architecture are presented. Further, a description of multimedia data formats and their related operations follows. Final comments of this chapter concentrate on the expected research results in this area.

## 12.2 Characteristics of an MDBMS

An MDBMS can be characterized by its objectives when handling multimedia data:

1. *Corresponding Storage Media*

Multimedia data must be stored and managed according to the specific characteristics of the available storage media. Here, the storage media can be both computer integrated components and external devices. Additionally, read-only (such as a CD-ROM), write-once and write-many storage media can be used.

2. *Descriptive Search Methods*

   During a search in a database, an entry, given in the form of text or a graphical image, is found using different queries and the corresponding search methods. A query of multimedia data should be based on a *descriptive, content-oriented search* in the form, for example, of "The picture of the woman with a red scarf". This kind of search relates to all media, including video and audio.

3. *Device-independent Interface*

   The interface to a database application should be device-independent. For example, a parameter could specify that the following audio and video data will not change in the future. Hence, the MDBMS will know that the storage media is a *CD-WO*.

4. *Format-independent Interface*

   Database queries should be independent from the underlying media format, meaning that the interfaces should be format-independent. The programming itself should also be format-independent, although in some cases, it should be possible to access details of the concrete formats. Hence, the application programmer determines the level of format abstraction with its advantages and disadvantages. This leads to the development of applications which may also make use of future formats. MDBMS device-independence and format-independence allow for new storage technologies to be used without changing the current multimedia database applications.

5. *View-specific and Simultaneous Data Access*

   The same multimedia data can be accessed (even simultaneously) through different queries by several applications. Hence, consistent access to shared data (e.g., shared editing of a multimedia document among several users) can be implemented.

6. *Management of Large Amounts of Data*

   The DBMS must be capable of handling and managing large amounts of data and satisfying queries for individual relations among data or attributes of relations [Fel90].

7. *Relational Consistency of Data Management*

   Relations among data of one or different media must stay consistent corresponding to their specification. The MDBMS manages these relations and can use them for queries and data output. Therefore, for example, *navigation* through a document is supported by managing relations among individual parts of a document. There are several different relations [Mey91]:

   - The *attribute relation* provides different descriptions or presentations of the same object. For example, consider a "bird" entry in an ornithological lexicon. Here, the voice for each bird is recorded as an audio signal, the flight of each bird is presented as a motion video and additional images and text accompany the bird description. From the viewpoint of a relational database, an attribute vector is assigned to each bird, including the different representations as attributes.
   - The *component relation* includes all the parts belonging to a data object. A catalogue of the components of a car and a book, consisting of chapter, section and subsection components, are examples of this relation.
   - The *substitution relation* defines different kinds of presentation of the same information. For example, the results of an equation can be presented as tables, graphs or animation.
   - A *synchronization relation* describes the temporal relations between data units. Lip synchronization between audio and video is one example of this relation.

8. *Real-time Data Transfer*

   The read and write operations of continuous data must be done in real-time. The data transfer of continuous data has a higher priority than other database management actions. Hence, the primitives of a multimedia operating system should be used to support the real-time transfer of continuous data.

9. *Long Transactions*

   The performance of a transaction in a MDBMS means that transfer of a large amount of data will take a long time and must be done in a reliable fashion. An example of a long transaction is the retrieval of a movie.

Most of the current prototypes of an MDBMS include the management of storage, local multimedia devices and adapters. This pragmatic approach has the advantage that a multimedia system is fully managed in agreement with the requirements of the considered DBMS. This approach is also often chosen for document and hypertext processing systems. Note that, for example, the results from the network communication (e.g., management of remote devices) are not often taken into account in an MDBMS. However, the remote multimedia devices in MDBMS must be managed too. The current solution is that the device management, as well as the integration of local and remote devices, is often developed in conjunction with the communication system.

In both research areas (MDBMS and communication systems), the development of multimedia primitives as part of the operating system is not sufficiently considered, although the management of multimedia devices should actually be the task of the operating system. In our architecture model, shown in Figure 1.1, the system components around MDBMS and MDBMS itself have the following functions:

- The operating system provides the management interface for MDBMS to all local devices.

- The MDBMS provides an abstraction of the stored data and their equivalent devices, as is the case in DBMS without multimedia.

- The communication system provides for MDBMS abstractions for communication with entities at remote computers. These communication abstractions are specified through interfaces according to, for example, the Open System Interconnection (OSI) architecture.

- A layer above the DBMS, operating system and communication system can unify all these different abstractions and offer them, for example, in an object-oriented environment such as a *toolkit*. Thus, an application should have access to each abstraction at different levels.

This model corresponds, more or less, to the proposed MDBMS architecture presented in [Mey91]. To refine this architecture, for each medium, an individual *management unit* could be implemented, which would be used by the medium-specific server, and the *services* of the management unit could be offered to a common query processor [Loc90]. This query processor is managed by a *database application interface manager*. The application interface manager provides an application interface to the user with a specification of different *views* to a database entry (e.g., entry "bird" can be specified by sound, motion video and/or text views). Another management unit processes the relations between data of different media.

This MDBMS architecture does not imply any implementation with the same partition of the components.

## 12.3 Data Analysis

Meyer-Wegener performed a detailed analysis of multimedia data storage and manipulation in a multimedia database system [Mey91]. This section describes the analysis of compressed data and other media. In the analysis, two questions are addressed:

1. **How are these data structured?**

   It is important to specify what kind of information is needed in the entry structure to process the multimedia entry in a MDBMS.

2. **How can these data be accessed?**

   That is to say, how are the proper operations defined to access multimedia entries. One can define media-dependent, as well as media-independent operations. In a next step, a class hierarchy with respect to object-oriented programming may be implemented.

In the following section we will consider the first question. The second question is analyzed in detail in Section 12.5.

## 12.4 Data Structure

In general, data can be stored in databases either in unformatted (unstructured) form or in formatted (structured) form. *Unformatted* or *unstructured* data are presented in a unit where the content cannot be retrieved by accessing any structural detail. For example, a data description such as "Mr. Clemens Engler is a student in the eighth term" cannot be accessed by any structural detail.

*Formatted* or *structured* data are stored in variables, fields or attributes with corresponding values. Here, the particular data parts are characterized according to their properties. For example, a data description such as:

```
A.Student.Surname = Engler
A.Student.GivenName = Clemens
A.Term = 8
```

can be accessed by structural details (student's given name, surname or term).

Additionally, multimedia data can be stored in databases as *raw*, *registering* and *descriptive data types*.

### 12.4.1 Raw Data

An uncompressed image consists of a set of individual pixels. The pixels represent *raw data* in the form of bytes and bits. They create the unformatted information units, which represent a long sequence or set of symbols, pixels, sample values, etc.

### 12.4.2 Registering Data

To retrieve and correctly interpret such an image, the details of the coding and the size of the image must be known. Let us assume that each pixel in an image is encoded with eight bits for the luminance and both chrominance difference signals. The resolution will be $1,024 \times 1,024$ pixels. These registering data are necessary to provide a correct interpretation of the raw data. Traditional DBMSs usually know only numbers and characters, which have fixed semantics; therefore, no additional description is required. Image, audio and video data allow for a number of attributes during coding and structuring. Without this additional description, the multimedia data could only be interpreted with difficulty, or not at all. Many components and applications of a multimedia system assume an implicit knowledge which in individual cases may also be sufficient, but MDBMS should be provided as a generally accessible service for all applications and components. Therefore, it is necessary to also handle all different formats. Moreover the semantics of the registering data can be extended to define existing relations between data objects of one or several media.

### 12.4.3 Descriptive Data

Today, the search for textual and numerical content is very effective. However, the search for image, audio or video information is much more difficult. Therefore, optional description (descriptive data) should be assigned to each multimedia unit. In the case of an image, the particular scene could be described in the form of text. These descriptive data provide additional redundant information and ease data retrieval during later searches. Descriptive data could be presented in unstructured or structured form.

### 12.4.4 Examples of Multimedia Structures

We present examples of raw, registered, and descriptive data for different media such as text, image, video and audio.

In the case of *text*, the individual forms are:

1. Characters represent raw data.
2. The registering data describe the coding (e.g., ASCII). Additionally, a length entry must follow or an end symbol must be defined.
3. The descriptive data may include information for layout and logical structuring of the text or keywords.

*Images* can be stored in databases using the following forms:

1. Pixels (pixel matrix) represent raw data. A compressed image may also consist of a *transformed pixel* set. For example, the coefficients of the discrete cosine transformation in two-dimensional frequency presentation represent a *transformed pixel* set. A further compression of the raw data can include a set of entropy-encoded data.
2. The registering data include the height and width of the picture. Additionally, the details of coding are stored here. For example, in the case of a JPEG compressed image, the mode is entered first. This may be a specific JPEG mode based on a discrete cosine transformation. Additionally, for example, the eight bits per sample value for image processing, the sequential image structure and the entropy encoding scheme are defined. The tables for quantizing process and entropy encoding must also be specified.
3. Examples of descriptive data are individual lines, surfaces and subjects, or situations as a whole scene (e.g., "Birthday and 1995 New Year's Eve celebration at Lisa's favorite restaurant", or

   ```
   B.Reason = New Year's Eve / Birthday
   B.Date = 12/31/95
   B.Place = Favorite Restaurant
   B.Name = Lisa
   B.Keyword1 = New Year's Eve Celebration
   ```

A motion video sequence can have a very different set of characteristics. It consists of the following information:

1. Raw data are defined in the simplest case through a sequence of pixel matrices. Mostly through motion video coding, the redundancies over several images are used for data reduction (intra-frame coding), so that each image does not carry all the necessary data for decompression. Also, a variable-rate data stream can be created.

2. The registering data provide, in addition to other information, the number of images per second (see Chapter 6). A data stream, coded according to the CCITT H.261 standard, is described as being QCIF (Quarter Common Intermediate Format) with a resolution of 177 × 144 pixels for the luminance component and 88 × 72 pixels for the color difference components. The motion video, coded according to MPEG-2, is described by the relation between consecutive images; types are coded (1 I-frame, 2 B-frame, 1 P-frame, 2 P-frame, 1 I-frame, etc.). Random access to each individual image of the motion video must follow.

3. The descriptive data provide a scene description (e.g., "Jan's birthday party with his friends from kindergarten").

Individual *audio* sequences can be classified according to the following scheme:

1. Raw data may be the digital sample values created by a simple PCM coding. The compressed values may also be considered as raw data.

2. The registering data represent the properties of the audio coding. Using a PCM coding, the sample rate, the quantization line and the resolution of the individual samples are the registering data. Compressed audio data can also carry additional information used by a parameterized decoder. Often, the coding information is already included in the raw data (e.g., ADPCM coding).

3. The descriptive data represent the content of the audio passages in a short form. In the case of a music composition, the name of the composition, the composer name and the name of the player can be entered. In the case of speech, a short content description, or the whole text can be written down.

### 12.4.5 Comments on Data Analysis

Audio and video data are often stored in a composed, integrated form (e.g., by using MPEG). This guarantees a continuous data stream during the output process. The recording can also be a combination of individual audio and video data. A hierarchy in the media can be inserted. Hence, DBMS can address combined media in the form of raw, registering and descriptive data.

For the application, a format-independent access is important and should be supported by a DBMS. Therefore, it makes sense to define access to uncompressed data at the application interface, although the data are actually processed (e.g., stored, transmitted) in a compressed form.

The division of data into raw, registering and descriptive data types requires strict management during database manipulation. For this management, system support and generation of context-dependent frames for text description should be implemented. If, for example, a motion video of landscapes is used for a travel catalogue, and some data already exist, the structure of the new descriptive data should be derived from the existing descriptive data of other entries.

## 12.5 Operations on Data

An MDBMS must offer, for all data types presented in Section 12.4, corresponding *operations* for archival and retrieval. The media-related operations will be handled as part of or an extension of query languages (e.g., SQL). In databases, following different classes of operations for each medium are needed: input, output, modification, deletion, comparison and evaluation.

The *input (insert/record)* operation means that data will be written to the database. In this case, the raw and registering data are always needed. The descriptive data can be attached later. If during the input operation of motion video and audio the length of the data is not known a priori, the MDBMS may have problems choosing the proper server or disk.

The *output (play)* operation reads the raw data from the database according to the registering data. Hence, for decoding a JPEG coded image, the Huffman table can be transmitted to the decoder in advance. The transmission of the raw data follows.

*Modification* usually considers the raw data. The modification of image data should be done by an editor. For motion video, cutting with *in/out fading* is usually needed. For audio data, in addition to in/out-fading, the volume, bass, treble and eventually balance can also be modified. The modification attributes are stored in registering data. Here, the attributes are defined as time-dependent functions performed during play of data. Modification can also be understood as a data conversion from one format to another. In this case, the registering data must be modified together with raw data. Another variant of modification is transformation from one medium to another, such as text-to-speech transformation. The conversion function, analogous to an editor, should be implemented outside the MDBMS. Such a transformation is implemented through reading of the data, externally converting it to another medium and recording the transformed data in the database.

During the *delete* operation, the consistency of the data must be preserved, i.e., if raw data of an entry are deleted, all other data types (registering and descriptive data) related to raw data are deleted.

Many queries to the MDBMS consist of a search and retrieval of the stored data. These queries are based on *comparison* information. Here, individual patterns in the particular medium are compared with the stored raw data. This kind of search is not very successful. Another approach uses pattern recognition where a pattern from raw data may be stored as registering data and a comparison is based on this pattern. The current efficiency of this approach is low for MDBMSs and is only used for certain applications. A comparison can also be based on the corresponding format of the descriptive data. Here, each audio sequence can be identified according to its unambiguous name (a maximum of 16 characters) and the creation time.

Other comparisons are based on content-oriented descriptive data. For example, the user enters the nominal phrase with a limited set of words. The MDBMS converts this input into predicates. In this case, synonyms can be used and are managed by the system. This concept allows for a content-related search, which is used for images and can be ported without any difficulties to all types of media [LM89, LM90, Mey91].

The goal of *evaluating* the raw and registering data is to generate the corresponding descriptive data. For example, during the storage of facsimile documents, Optical Character Recognition (OCR) can be used. Otherwise, in most cases, an explicit user input is required. The results in [LM89], [LM90], [Mey91] can be used.

## 12.6 Integration in a Database Model

A main issue for the implementation and usage of an MDBMS is the *database model.* Primarily, the data types (Section 12.4) and operations (Section 12.5) used are important. These data types and operations can be integrated in both a *relational model* and an *object-oriented model* [SZ87].

Abstract data types of all media can be defined with descriptive attributes according to their formats. For example, consider the attributes of *uncompressed video* in Table 12.1. Attributes are stored in a multimedia database and operations can retrieve and modify them.

| Attribute Name | Attribute Type | Attribute Value |
|---|---|---|
| height: | integer; | 480 |
| width: | integer; | 640 |
| encoding: | uncompressed; | YUV |
| stream_encoding: | s_mode; | PAL |
| pixel_depth: | integer; | (8,8,8) |
| rate: | signed integer; | 25 |
| colormap_size: | integer; | |
| colormap: | array; | (...) |
| pixel: | structure(Y,U,V) of bits | |
| image: | array (...) of pixels | |
| video: | timed_list of images | |

Table 12.1: *Attributes of uncompressed video.*

### 12.6.1 Relational Database Model

The simplest possibility to implement a multimedia database is to use the relational database model because the attributes of different media in relational databases are defined in advance. Hence, the attributes can specify not only text (as is done in current database systems), but also, for example, audio or video data types. The main advantage of this approach is its compatibility with current database applications.

In the following paragraphs, we will analyze different types of the relational model using an example. In this example, a relation "student" is given for the admission of a sport institute's students into the obligatory athletics course. A relation's attributes (e.g., picture, exercise devices) can be specified through different media types (e.g., image, motion video). Further, our example database includes other entries such as: "athletics", "swimming" and "analysis".

```
Student   (Admission_Number  Integer,
           Name              String,
           Picture           Image,
           Exercise_Device_1 Video
           Exercise_Device_2 Video)

Athletics (Admission_Number  Integer,
           Qualification     Integer,
           The_High_Jump     Video,
           The_Mile_Run      Video)

Swimming  (Admission_Number  Integer,
           Crawl             Video)

Analysis  (Qualification     Integer,
           Error_Pattern     String,
           Comment           Audio)
```

- *Type 1 Relational Model*

  In the *type 1 relational model*, the value of a certain attribute can be fixed over the particular set of the corresponding attribute types, e.g., the frame rate of motion video can be fixed.

  For our example it means that when attributes such as exercise devices 1 and 2 from entry "student" are retrieved, the video will play at the fixed rate defined by the type 1 specification.

- *Type 2 Relational Model*

  A variable number of entries can be defined through the type 2 relational model.

  In our example, the individual disciplines (such as athletics and swimming) of each admitted student are identified through their admission numbers.

- *Type 3 Relational Model*

  In addition to the fixed values of attributes per relation and the variable number of entries, an entry can simultaneously belong to several relations. This property is called the type 3 relational model.

  In our example, a video entry of a student performing a high jump can be assigned to the relation "athletics" for qualification purposes as well as to the relation "analysis" for an educational application with an analysis of typical errors in the individual sport disciplines.

### 12.6.2 Object-oriented Database Model

In object-oriented databases, instead of defining relations, as is the case in relational databases, classes with objects are defined. These objects can be put in relations via a class hierarchy. Therefore, a semantic specialization of classes and objects can follow. For example, if we consider the above example of students from the sport institute, the sport institute is the main class. Different kinds of sport departments (e.g., athletics, swimming) build subclasses of the sport institute class. Students are the objects of each subclass.

Some MDBMSs use this approach with many different kinds of class hierarchies. As a consequence of these many hierarchies, no generally applicable class hierarchy can be recognized today. These systems offer good information navigation and flexible presentation possibilities. On the other hand, in comparison to the relational model, the important set operations for queries (e.g., get an element from a set, include an element into a set) are incompletely supported.

## 12.7 Comments

MDBMS are still under development. Most MDBS systems are bound very closely to a multimedia application or application area. An example is the current development of MDBMS for multimedia document processing (hypertext, hypermedia). Other application areas, such as conferencing systems, leave any consideration of MDBMS out. Therefore, there are only few application experiences with MDBMS.

If such experiences existed, a *minimal MDBMS* could be defined. According to [Loc90], such a minimal MDBMS is defined as a system which satisfies all requirements put on a MDBMS using the minimal knowledge about the application. This minimal MDBMS has been, until now, unknown.

The database models presented are strongly influenced by the representation of uncompressed images and content-oriented search. Development in data compression techniques and the requirements for higher media quality will bring more frequent use of compressed data.

Attribute types, such as image, video and audio, must be further modified and refined. In this context, the close relation between the data units of one or different media should be integrated.

An implementation of consistency by a transaction [Gra81] and an implementation of composed transactions [Mos82] need to be adapted to the large amounts of data and real-time conditions. These properties would help ensure that a transaction does not have to start again and again. In this case, a predicate with respect to time conditions, as an additional attribute, could be integrated into a transaction.

Research needs to be done in the area of a content-oriented search with respect to continuous media. Queries, such as "Search for the speech probe with the children song about ten small Indians", or "Search for the video clip with Prince Andrew in the Andalusian costume", are difficult to perform. It is still unclear if a solution is actually possible.

With respect to distributed multimedia databases and network access, integration of multimedia communication and database technology is necessary [BCG+90, GCB88, KG89]. An extension of the Remote Database Access (RDA) for continuous data, a distributed MDBMS and a multimedia client-server system need to be implemented. In a client server environment, the concepts of several clients per transaction and/or several servers per transaction should be considered for support of cooperative multimedia applications.

Today, the integration of MDBMS with an operating system is not done in the best way. Most often, time critical data are either processed through separate external devices, or processed with a lower quality through DBMSs. For an integrated MDBMS, harmony with the new operating system extensions must follow.

# Chapter 13

# Documents, Hypertext and MHEG

A *document* consists of a set of structural information that can be in different forms of media, and during presentation can be generated or recorded [App90]. A document is aimed at the perception of a human, and is accessible for computer processing.

## 13.1 Documents

A *multimedia document* is a document which is comprised of information coded in at least one continuous (time-dependent) medium and in one discrete (time-independent) medium. Integration of the different media is given through a close relation between information units. This is also called *synchronization.* A multimedia document is closely related to its environment of tools, data abstractions, basic concepts and document architecture.

Currently, continuous and discrete data are processed differently: text is processed within an editor program as a type of a programming language (namely the Type Character); a motion picture can be manipulated with the same editor program only through library calls. The goal of abstracting multimedia data is to achieve integrated, i.e., uniform, description and processing of all media. This reduces the complexity of program generation and maintenance that process multimedia data. Since Chapter 16 discusses in detail different approaches to programming abstractions, we will not concentrate here on this issue. Abstractions of multimedia data serve as the fundamental building block for programming different multimedia applications, especially editors and other document processing tools.

Basic *system concepts* for document processing use multimedia abstractions and also serve as concepts for the information architecture in a document. Thus, we use the terms *document architecture* and *information architecture* interchangeably.

### 13.1.1 Document Architecture

Exchanging documents entails exchanging the document content as well as the document structure. This requires that both documents have the same *document architecture.* The current standardized, respectively in the progress of standardization, architectures are the *Standard Generalized Markup Language* (SGML) and the *Open Document Architecture* (ODA). There are also proprietary document architectures, such as DEC's *Document Content Architecture* (DCA) and IBM's *Mixed Object Document Content Architecture* (MO:DCA).

Information architectures use their data abstractions and concepts. A document architecture describes the connections among the individual elements represented as *models* (e.g., presentation model, manipulation model). The elements in the document architecture and their relations are shown in Figure 13.1. Figure 13.2 shows a multimedia document architecture including relations between individual discrete media units and continuous media units.

The manipulation model describes all the operations allowed for creation, change and deletion of multimedia information. The representation model defines: (1) the *protocols* for exchanging this information among different computers; and, (2) the *formats* for storing the data. It includes the relations between the individual information elements which need to be considered during presentation. It is important to mention that an architecture may not include all described properties, respectively models.

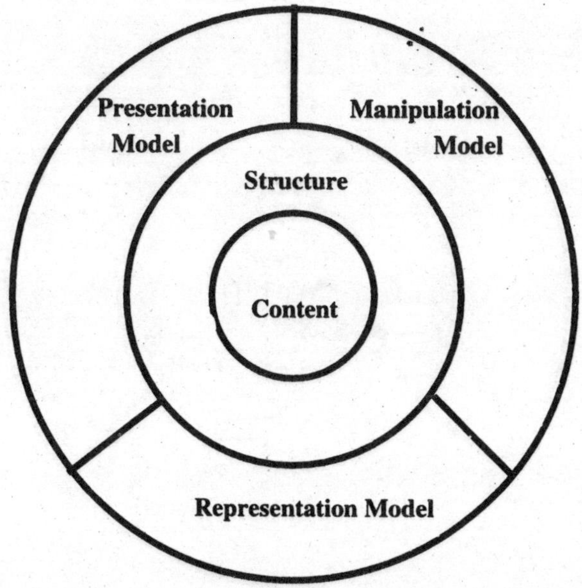


Figure 13.1: *Document architecture and its elements.*

### 13.1.2 Manipulation of Multimedia Data

The user becomes most aware of multimedia documents through tools for *manipulation of multimedia data*, such as *editors, desktop publishing programs* and other *text processing programs.*

A document undergoes the process shown in Figure 13.3. The information included in a document belongs to a certain document type, e.g., a *business letter* or an *internal memorandum.* The same document can belong to other types which mainly influence the final representation. The transformation from the actual information to its final representation behaves according to rules specific to the document architecture.

The processing cycles (Figure 13.3) of a traditional document and an interactive multimedia presentation are analogous, as shown in Figure 13.4. Currently, an author edits a document with a text editor. Thus, he or she uses the system's character set (e.g., ASCII) as the actual content of a document, as well as a hidden language available in most interactive editors for structural description (e.g.,

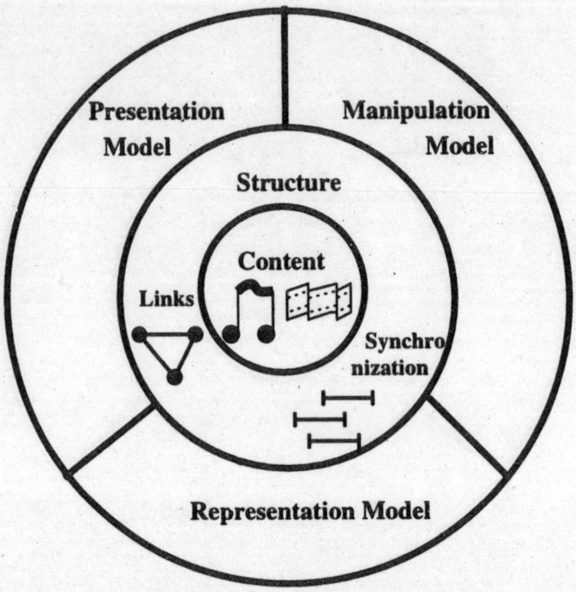


Figure 13.2: *A multimedia document architecture and its constituent elements.*

SGML). At this point, the document exists in a processable representation. The subsequent formatting process determines the layout of the document. The result is a final representation of the document. A typical example of this representation is the typesetting language *PostScript*™. The availability of hypertext and multimedia technology have changed the representation of documents. Although the processing cycle of document generation will remain the same, it is apparent that there will be major changes in how documents are displayed. The output of interactive hypermedia documents will be mostly computer-supported. Therefore, the presentation of a document will have to be not only *final*, but also *executable*. While there are a broad range of processable formats, there are too few final representation formats. It has been internationally recognized that such a final representation (exchange format) is very important, especially in a distributed, heterogeneous system environment. This exchange format for interactive multimedia presentation is called *MHEG (Multimedia and Hypermedia Information Coding Expert Group)*.

Using the main concepts of *hypermedia and hypertext* for multimedia documents, the following sections of this chapter present the document architectures SGML

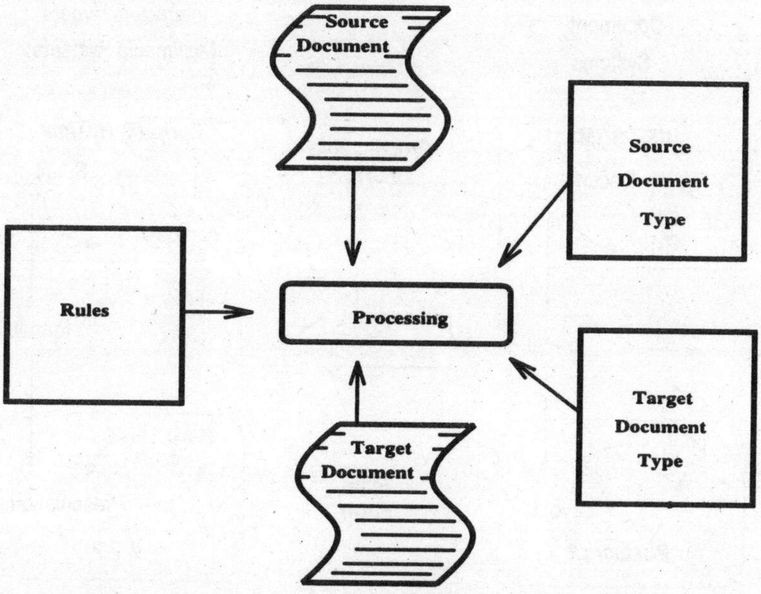


Figure 13.3: *Processing of a document: from the information to the presentation*

and ODA. Finally, MHEG is briefly described.

## 13.2 Hypertext and Hypermedia

Communication reproduces knowledge stored in the human brain via several media. Documents are one method of transmitting information. Reading a document is an act of reconstructing knowledge. In an ideal case, knowledge transmission starts with an author and ends with a reconstruction of the same ideas by a reader. Information loss is minimal. Figure 13.5 shows this communication process between an author and a reader.

Today's ordinary documents (excluding hypermedia), with their linear form, support neither the reconstruction of knowledge, nor simplify its reproduction. Knowledge must be artificially serialized before the actual exchange. Hence, it is transformed into a *linear* document and the structural information is integrated into the actual content. In the case of hypertext and hypermedia, a graphical structure is possible

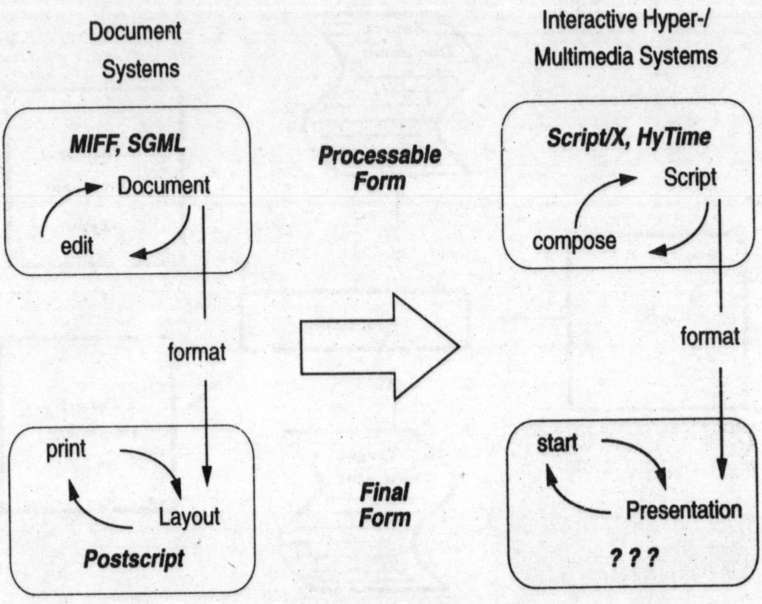


Figure 13.4: *Problem description.*

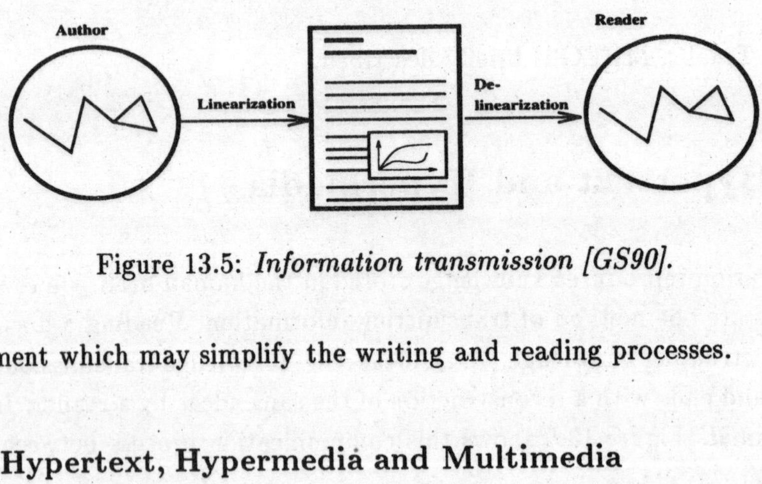


Figure 13.5: *Information transmission [GS90].*

in a document which may simplify the writing and reading processes.

### 13.2.1 Hypertext, Hypermedia and Multimedia

A book or an article on a paper has a given structure and is represented in a sequential form. Although it is possible to read individual paragraphs without reading previous paragraphs, authors mostly assume a sequential reading. Therefore many paragraphs refer to previous learning in the document. Novels, as well as movies, for example, always assume a pure sequential reception. Scientific literature can consist of independent chapters, although mostly a sequential reading is assumed. Technical documentation (e.g., manuals) consists often of a collection of relatively independent information units. A lexicon or reference book about the Airbus, for example, is generated by several authors and always only parts are read sequentially. There also exist many cross references in such documentations which lead to multiple searches at different places for the reader. Here, an electronic help facility, consisting of information links, can be very significant.

Figure 13.6 shows an example of such a link. The arrows point to such a relation

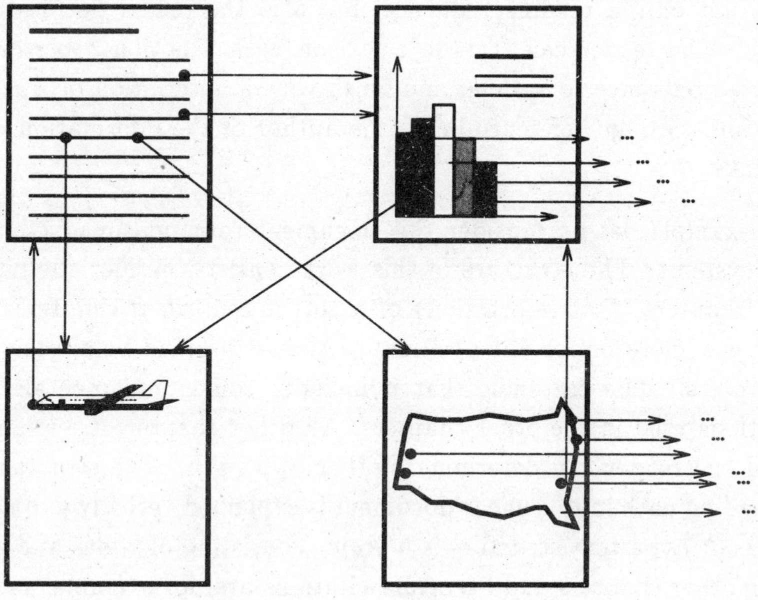

Figure 13.6: *Hypertext data. An example of linking information of different media.*

between the information units (LDUs). In a text (top left in the figure), a reference to the landing properties of aircrafts is given. These properties are demonstrated through a video sequence (bottom left in the figure). At another place in the text, sales of landing rights for the whole USA are shown (this is visualized in the form of a map, using graphics - bottom right in the figure). Further information about the airlines with their landing rights can be made visible graphically through a selection of a particular city. A special information about the number of the different airplanes sold with landing rights in Washington is shown at the top right in the figure with a bar diagram. Internally, the diagram information is presented in table form. The left bar points to the plane, which can be demonstrated with a video clip

### Non-linear Information Chain

Hypertext and hypermedia have as a major property a *non-linear information link*. There exists not only a reading sequence, but also the reader decides on his/her reading path. The reader can start in a lexicon with a notion *hypertext*, then go through a cross reference to *systems* and finish with a description of *AppleTalk*. By this association, through reference links, the author of the information determines the actual links.

As another example, let us consider this document (our multimedia book) about multimedia systems. The structure of this work consists, besides the introductory and closing chapters (first impression) of a set of *equivalent* chapters. Actually, Chapter 2 has a more important position: it should be read before any of the remaining chapters. The reason is that it includes some fundamentals to explain common notions used in the other chapters. All other chapters are relatively independent and the reader can determine his/her own path. The structure is a tree where the reading path in this linear document is explained verbally and not through the structure. A hypertext structure is a *graph*, consisting of nodes and edges. The references to other chapters and literature citations are, for example, such pointers which build a tree-similar document to a graph.

- The *nodes* are the actual *information units*. They are, for example, the text elements, individual graphics, audio or video LDUs. The information units are shown at the user interface mostly in their own windows.

- The *edges* provide links to other information units. They are usually called *pointers* or *links*. A pointer is mostly a directed edge and includes its own information too.

### Anchor

The forward movement in linear sorted documents is called a *navigation* through the graph. At the user interface, the origin of pointers must be marked, so that the user can move to a further information unit. This origin of a pointer is called an *anchor.* A main factor of the user interface is the concept of the anchor: how can the anchor be represented properly?

- A *media-independent representation* can happen through the selection of general graphical elements, such as *buttons.* In such an element, information about the destination node should be included. If the destination node is a text, a short, descriptive text of the content can be represented. In the case of an image, the image content can appear in minimized form on the screen. A visual representation of the video content can follow in form of a *moving icon* (Micon). This is a minimized motion picture which represents a characteristical portion of the video sequence of the destination node (MIT Project Elastic Charles [Bra87]). If the content of the destination node consists of audio information, a visual representation of the audio content must follow. For example, in the case of a music passage, a picture of the composer could be displayed.

- In a *text*, individual words, paragraphs or text sections of different length can be used for representation. The positioning of the pointer to the marked area and double clicking in this area leads to a display of the destination node, connected with the clicked information (e.g., see Figure 13.11).

- In *images*, specific graphical objects or simply areas are defined as selection objects. A specific marking can occur through a color or stripe.

- In a *motion video*, media-independent representations of the anchor are preferred. There can also be time-changing areas used. Mostly, no spatial selection occurs and the particular shown image is conclusive. A timely selection is supported.

- With respect to *audio*, a media-independent solution is used. In this case, a short, descriptive text or an image of the size of an icon is preferably shown.

Figure 13.7 emphasizes the relation among multimedia, hypertext and hypermedia.

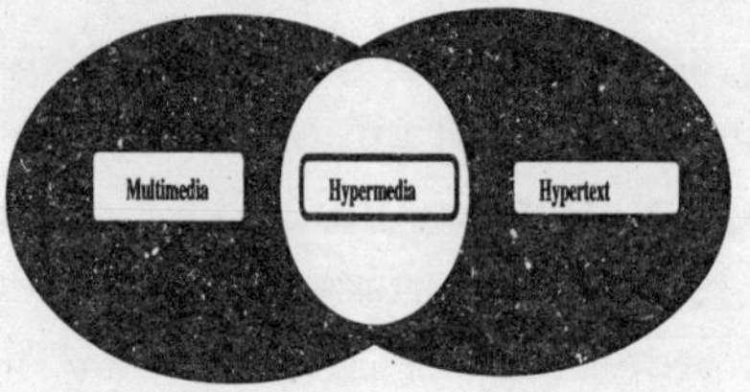


Figure 13.7: *The hypertext, hypermedia and multimedia relationship.*

**Hypertext System**

A *hypertext system* is mainly determined through non-linear links of information. Pointers connect the nodes. The data of different nodes can be represented with one or several media types. In a pure text system, only text parts are connected. We understand *hypertext* as an information object which includes links to several media.

**Multimedia System**

A *multimedia system* contains, according to Section 2.3, information which is coded at least in a continuous and discrete medium.

For example, if only links to text data are present, then this is not a multimedia system. It is a *hypertext.* A video conference, with simultaneous transmission of text and graphics, generated by a document processing program, is a multimedia application. Although it does not have any relation to hypertext and hypermedia.

**Hypermedia System**

As Figure 13.7 shows, a *hypermedia system* includes the non-linear information links of hypertext systems and the continuous and discrete media of multimedia systems.

For example, if a non-linear link consists of text and video data, then this is a hypermedia, multimedia and hypertext system.

As is often the case, we will not use the notion hypermedia in its strongest sense. If not explicitly specified, *hypertext* and *hypermedia* are used interchangeably.

There have been many international conferences covering this area since the late 1980s: Hypertext'87, Hypertext'89, etc. A good overview of articles chosen from the first Hypertext'87 conference is in [ACM88]. ECHT'90 was the first *European Conference on Hypertext* held in Paris. There exists a large number of conferences and workshops, in addition to these main international events, at the regional and national levels.

### 13.2.2 Hypermedia Systems: An Example

Actually, it is not easy to present on paper a real hypermedia system. Therefore, it is urgently recommended to the reader to work with such a system (e.g., the NCSA Mosaic© tool for viewing hypermedia documents written in HTML – an application of SGML) to get a better understanding of the properties and the advantages and disadvantages.

The following example of a *lecture "hypertext"*, as a hypermedia document, is similar to [Nie90b, Nie90a]. It describes the part of a typical manipulation process with a hypermedia system.

#### First Screen

A possibly natural environment is created for the reader of a hypertext to improvise the usual setup (Figure 13.8). Therefore, at the beginning of the lecture, a book is shown, which can be opened by clicking on it. The title of the document appears on the cover.

Additional information can also be shown, such as when the reader last opened the book. The same information (after the book was opened) is only shown with respect to the individual nodes.

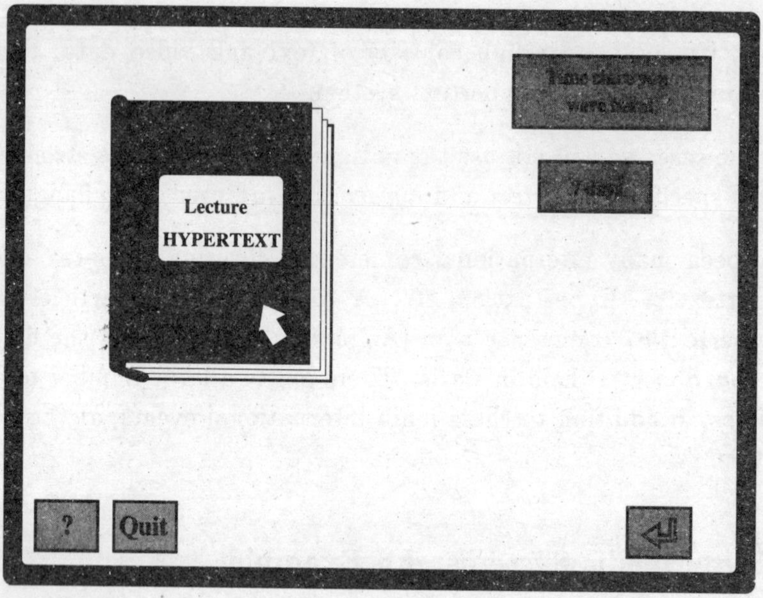


Figure 13.8: *The first screen of a hypermedia lecture.*

A content-sensitive help function (with respect to the particular state of the system) can be made available. The help function describes the actual state and the implications of possible interactions with the user. Further, it allows for the possibility to access general help information. An application of hypertext, which is very popular, consists of such system-wide help functions. Here, the text medium is most often used.

### Second Screen

Upon opening the book (Figure 13.9), the reader is presented with an overview of the document in the form of a two-dimensional content directory. There is no first chapter. Besides the linking nodes with edges (i.e., the information units with pointers), the physical ordering of the nodes among each other can provide additional information. Hence, chapters that are closely related to each other can be presented on the screen near each other. The author can express semantic relations through the layout. For example, if a document describes ODA, SGML and hypertext,

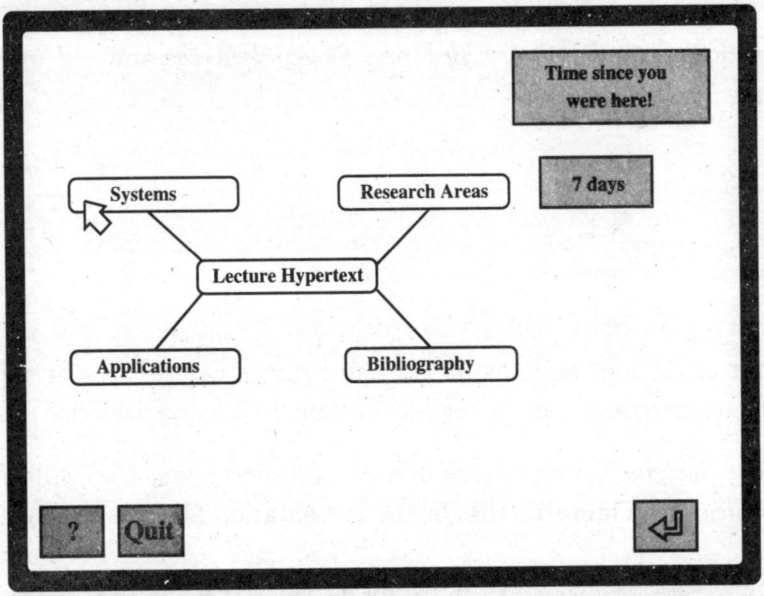


Figure 13.9: *The second screen – first-level content directory.*

(1) ODA and SGML can be placed close together during the presentation of both document architectures, and (2) *hypertext* can be used in both architectures.

The content directory in its most general form is often represented by a tree graph. The nodes that have already been visited can be marked as such, which simplifies navigation. When clicking at a node, only a paragraph is shown because of overview reasons.

On one hand, if too many nodes are linked in the content directory, the reader loses the comprehensive view. Given a 14" screen with VGA resolution and a content directory in form of a tree, a practical number of displayed nodes is 30. It is assumed that all nodes are simultaneously presented. On the other hand, if too few nodes are shown (e.g., only three), then this may lead to a large number of levels which will cause a fragmented perspective. The optimal number of presented nodes depends on the screen size, the number of pointers and the degree of possible levels. Many nodes can be presented as trees, few nodes can be part of complex graphs. Mostly, content directories are trees. The content of the particular destination node refines the content directory. In our example (Figure 13.9), *Lecture Hypertext* is divided into four sections: *Applications*, *Systems*, *Research Areas* and *Bibliography*. The reader selects *Systems* here.

### Third Screen

The structure of the four sections on the third screen can be presented in a refined version. The four sections can be seen as *buttons* which the user can select.

The following *Systems* subtopics are offered: *Requirements*, *User Interface Design* and a *Classification* (Figure 13.10). In the presentation (Figure 13.10), a multilevel

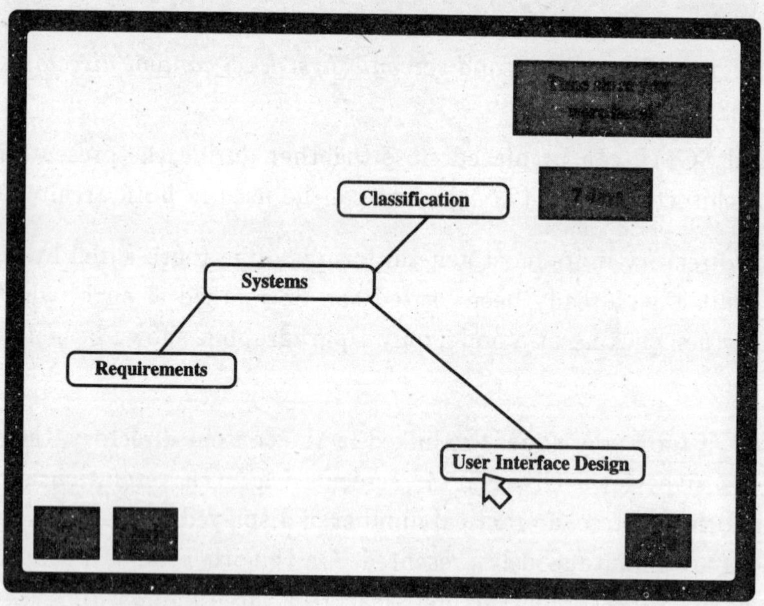


Figure 13.10: *The third screen – second-level content directory.*

content directory could be hidden, but we assume this is not the case. The user may get information about the user interface and select this information unit. Here, the reader selects *User Interface Design*.

### Fourth Screen

Typical information about the medium text, used in *User Interface Design*, is presented on the fourth screen (Figure 13.11). In addition, the book's content directory

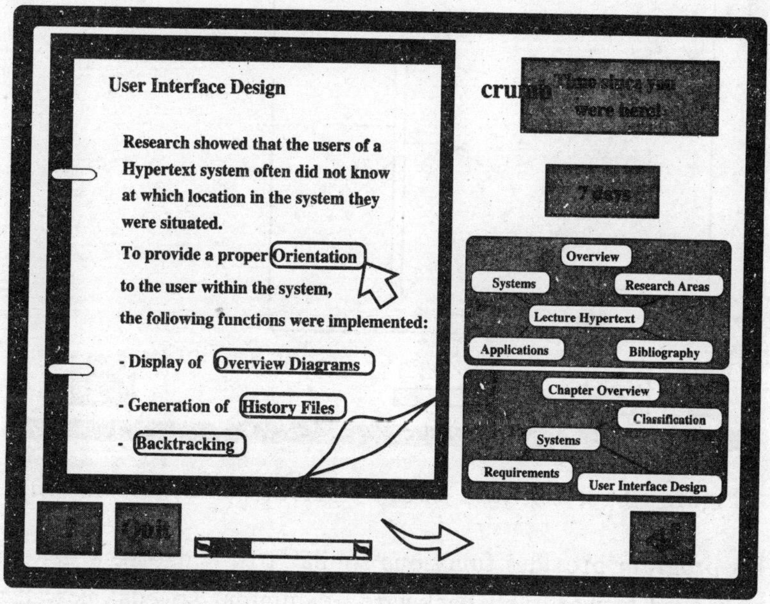


Figure 13.11: *The fourth screen – details about User Interface Design.*

and the second level are visible. The selected path *Systems/User Interface Design* is specially marked. This helps the reader to navigate through the document. Text is displayed on one side of the screen imitating an opened book. Some parts of the screen are marked as anchors: *Orientation, Overview Diagrams, History Files* and *Backtracking.* Each of these anchors points to further information. This can lead to faster pacing without absorbing previous information. Further information about the topic *Orientation* is available as a motion video. The user clicks on the anchor *Orientation* (Figure 13.11) and the screen shown in Figure 13.12 appears.

### Fifth Screen

The fifth screen (Figure 13.12) leads the reader to a video clip showing examples of *Orientation.* Here, there may also be an additional program for motion picture

Figure 13.12: *The fifth screen – details about Orientation.*

control. This program provides functions similar to a video recorder, meaning the video can be moved forward and backward at different speeds, as well as stopped, and a still image can be displayed. Additionally, certain positions in the video clip (e.g., the beginning of the clip) should be made accessible.

The selection of the symbol at the lower right corner leads the reader back to the preceding node, in this case, to the *User Interface Design* screen (Figure 13.13).

### Sixth Screen

The sixth screen is a return to the User Interface Design screen. The user now selects History Files. The cross-bar under the opened book is a scroll-bar. It indicates that the displayed page represents only approximately 25% of all the information stored

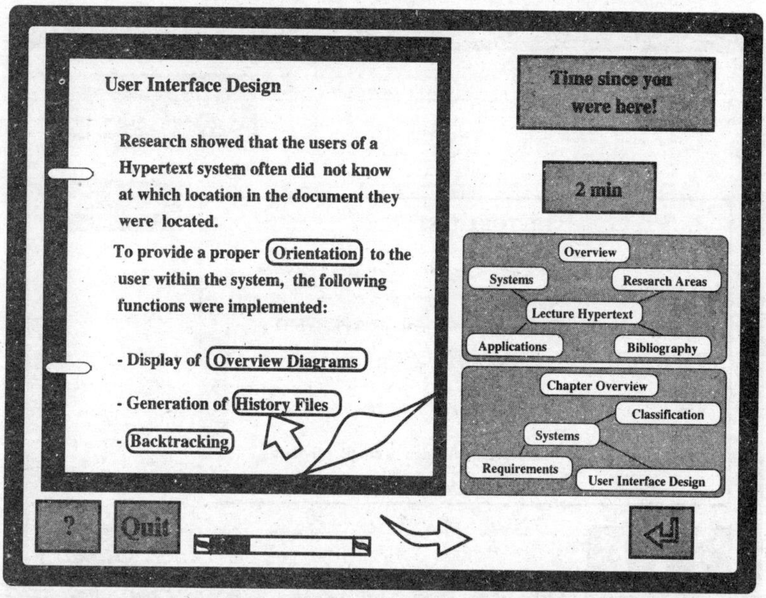


Figure 13.13: *Hypermedia example: sixth screen – details about the user interface.*

in the node about *User Interface Design.* Additional pages can be viewed by rolling the roll-bar or selection of the pointer.

### Seventh Screen

The *History Files* screen (Figure 13.14) shows the particular nodes last read. Specifically, the reader read the *cover page* 5 minutes ago, the overview about the *lecture Hypertext* 2 minutes ago, the chapter *Systems* 4 minutes ago, and the *User Interface Design* in the chapter *systems* 2 minutes ago. This history list shows all of the traversed nodes. Each node can be accessed again by selecting an element in the list.

Often, a graphical assignment is better to keep in mind than a textual description. The user, for example, may remember that there is a picture where a red hat is placed in the upper left corner. Alternatively, a display of the traversed nodes may help the reader to find his/her way through the document. This is not a very good solution, however if many screens have been involved.

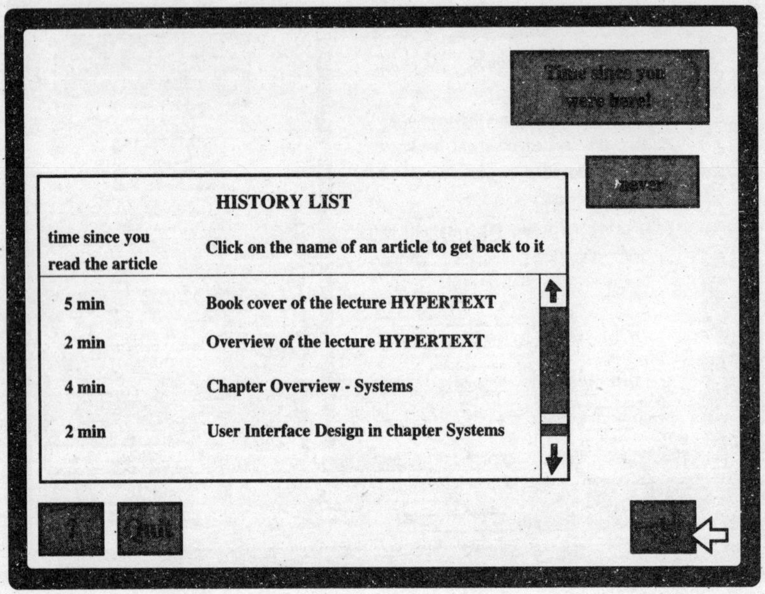


Figure 13.14: *The Seventh screen – history of previously presented information.*

With this short, virtual navigation through a hypertext lecture, some characteristic properties of a hypertext system have been shown. Various systems use different concepts, functions and layout of the user interface.

### Further Application Areas

A lecture is not the only respectively typical application area. The following areas have shown to be useful domains for hypertext systems:

- In some classical computer applications, hypertext is already state-of-the-art; especially, the help function.
- In the area of commercial applications, repair and operational manuals can be found. Here, different media are used. This technology leads to a replacement of a microfilm which can be found by the distribution of replacement parts. A repair instruction can be presented much more flexibly using motion pictures. Here, an interaction in the form of a slow forward and backward rewinding

is expected. Exhibition and product catalogues create, together with other applications from the advertisement branch, the basis for a number of diverse applications.

- The organization of ideas, brainstorming and the generation of scientific documents count, for example, as intellectual applications. Here, the structure of the document is not clear at the beginning of its generation. During the intellectual process of writing a document, the structure gets clarified.

- Education and tutorials can be improved through the input of continuous media. Foreign language education requires the audio medium. In museums, further explanation of exhibition pieces can be offered to visitors using audio and video.

- Tourist information systems and interactive science-fiction movies count on the areas of entertainment and free-time activities. A new generation of computer games is going to become available.

Hypertext provides advantages whenever the document for a specific application does not require strict linear structure. However, the authors' experiences show that hypertext will not replace all conventional print material.

### 13.2.3 History

The history of hypertext goes quite far back, although it has been only recently (in the last couple of years) that hypertext systems came on the market. Also, the integration of continuous media was demonstrated in laboratories several years ago. In the following paragraph, we will give a short overview of hypermedia/hypertext history according to [Nie90b].

Vannever Bush is the originator of the main hypertext concept, the linked information structure. He described the first hypertext system *Memex* (MEMory EXtender). Memex was never implemented, it exists only on the paper. Vannever Bush developed the ideas for this topic in 1932. He published the first descriptive article as *We May Think* in 1945.

Let us imagine all information in the form of microfilm being placed on a table. With proper projectors, areas could be displayed in similar form as using X Window System™. Here, an *associative index* is generated which links the different microfilm areas together (these are the pointers).

Doug Englebart developed a project to augment the human capability *Augment* at the Stanford Research Institute (SRI) 1962-1976. One part of it is *NLS (oN Line System)*, which has hypertext properties. NLS served as joint document storage for all created documents during this project. All scientists working on this project used it with its possibilities of pointers. At the end, there were approximately 100,000 entries.

Ted Nelson used the notion *Hypertext* for the first time in 1965. In his system *Xanadu*, all information which human beings described at any time, was contained. His concepts described the access to local, as well as to remote data. Xanadu was not implemented with his global information content until now.

Since the middle of the 1960s, work on hypertext systems has been going on at Brown University, Providence, RI. In 1967, the *Hypertext Editing System* was developed under the leadership of Andries van Dam. This was the first run-able hypertext system. It needed 120-Kbyte main memory of a small IBM/360 mainframe computer. It was sold and used for the documentation of the Apollo mission. The successor project was *FRESS (File Retrieval and Editing SyStem)* in 1968. Both systems linked documents through pointers, the user interface was implemented through text. At Brown University from this time, successful research in the area of hypertext/hypermedia has continued.

The *Aspen Movie Map* is probably the first important hypermedia system which supports continuous media too. It was developed at the *MIT Architecture Machine Group* under the intensive cooperation of Andrew Lippman. This group was built up later on with other scientists and was known as the *MIT Media Lab* [Bra87]. With this application, a virtual drive through the city Aspen (Colorado) could be followed on the computer screen. The user could move in all four geographical directions as s/he desired. A *joystick* served as an input of the direction. The technique consisted of a large set of individual images which were stored on a video disk. For this purpose, four cameras were installed on a pick-up with the angle of

90° to each other (with the view: front, back, right, left). The car drove through all streets of the city and took one image every three meters. The images were linked through implicit pointers: therefore, a drive through the city could be simulated. The drive was simulated with a maximal two images per second; therefore, a speed of approximately 110 km/h could be achieved. The display occurred through two screens: the first screen displayed the picture of the street and the second screen showed a street map with the actual position.

Successor projects concentrated on the joint usage of video, individual images and text for bike and car repair-manuals.

Until now, all hypertext systems mentioned were not developed as products and seldom were used outside of their research groups. In 1982, Symbolics started development of the *Symbolics Document Examiner*. It was ready as the first hypertext product in 1985. Its main application was the documentation of the Symbolics Workstation, which was comprised of about 8,000 pages. It contained approximately 10,000 nodes and 23,000 pointers. Also, the metaphor *a book on the screen* was used and an emphasis was put on a simple user interface.

Since 1985, many hypertext systems have been announced and established on the market. *NoteCards* from Xerox and *Intermedia* from Brown University started as research projects and ended up as products. The *Guide*, implemented by Office Workstation Limited, started as product development. It was the first product based on mini computers (1986). In 1987, the Apple company presented the *HyperCard*. It was installed for free on all Macintosh computers and was therefore widely available.

### Concepts

Hypertext systems differ from each other in their fundamental concepts:

- *Unspecific systems* were not developed for any specific application. They are determined to be used generally for the generation and reading of hypertext documents. The Apple (HyperCard) product is an example.
- *Application-specific systems* were developed for determined usage. For example, gIBIS gives explanations for political discussions. It is meant to be a

decision help. In gIBIS, three special nodes and nine different pointer types exist [CB88].

### 13.2.4 Systems: Architecture, Nodes and Pointers

#### Architecture

The architecture of a hypertext system can be divided into three layers with different functionalities [CG87]:

- *Presentation Layer*

  At the upper layer, the *presentation layer*, all functions connected to the user interface are embedded. Here, nodes and pointers are mapped to the user interface. At the user interface, one or several parts of the document are visualized. This layer determines, based on the given structure and user's desired display, which data are presented and how they are presented. This layer takes over control of all inputs.

- *Hypertext Abstract Machine*

  The *Hypertext Abstract Machine (HAM)* is placed between the presentation and storage layers. It can expect from the underlying layer database functions for storage of multimedia data in a distributed environment. It does not have to consider input and output of the upper layer. HAM knows the structure of the document, it has the knowledge about the pointers and its attributes. The data structure, respectively a document architecture, is constructed for the management of the document. This layer has the least system dependency in comparison to the other two layers. Therefore, it is the most suitable layer for standardization [Nie90b].

- *Storage Layer*

  The *storage layer* (also called the database layer) is the lowest layer. All functions connected with the storage of data, i.e., secondary storage management, belong to this layer. The specific properties of the different discrete and continuous media need to be considered. Functionalities from traditional database systems are expected, such as persistence (data persist through programs and processes), multi-user operations (synchronization, locks, ...) and the restoration of data after a failure (transaction). The nodes and pointers of a hypertext document are processed as data objects without any special semantics.

Unfortunately, in most current implementation, there is no clear division between the different layers. The reasons are: shorter development time, efficient implementations and currently an incomplete, respectively unavailable general multimedia interface for the lowest layer.

### Nodes

A *node* is an information unit (LDU) in a hypertext document. The main classification criterion of different realizations is the maximal stored data amount in one node:

- The maximal stored *data amount can be limited* and mapped onto the screen size. The metaphor of a note card, respectively a frame, was introduced here (e.g., HyperCard). A video clip and audio passage could be limited to the duration of, for example, 20 seconds.

  An author is forced eventually to distribute logical connected text content to several cards, although it is not desired. Applying it to video clips and audio passages, it would mean that the close interconnection among the distributed sequences could get lost easily. An advantage is the overview.

- Window-based systems with an *unlimited data amount* per node are the alternative. Forward and backward scrolling of pages is offered analogous to other windows at the user interface. *Intermedia* is such a system. Here, at every node the amount of data, coded as continuous media, is not limited (in principle) with respect to its duration.

  Therefore, individual nodes can include a very different length, although at first they may appear equal. Two different methods at the user interface are used for the presentation of further information: Either it is switched between the nodes, or scrolling is used in one node with the usual mechanisms known in window systems.

A secondary criterion applies to the *time point of information generation.* Usually, the author specifies the whole content of the nodes during the generation of the document. Alternatively, the author can generate information according to his/her previous input during the presentation time. This approach allows the author to include, for example, information about a company, also a pointer, to the actual course of the company's stocks on the New York stock exchange. This information can be requested automatically through the *videotext service* and presented as part of the hypertext document.

### Pointers

Pointers are the edges of a hypertext graph. Hypertext systems are classified according to different criteria with respect to edges. As a first question, one can ask: *Which information includes a pointer?*

- *Simple pointers* link two nodes of the graph without containing any further information. They are visible only through the relation between the nodes.

- *Typed pointers* include, in addition to the link between two nodes, further information. Each pointer gets a *label.* Through this label, commentaries to the particular label are possible (e.g., author and creation date).

  One can use further semantics. For example, in the case of an educational unit, the continuation of reading further details could depend on the result of an exam testing the previous details. The pointers then include a formula to activate the further reading. The formula is dependent on the result of the test. Also, access rights can be controlled through pointers. Another possibility consists of assigning types to pointers according to their properties. For example, it can be used to differentiate between the relations *destination node is an example* and *destination node is a detail.* These different semantics can also be expressed through different representations of the anchor at the user interface.

Another property of the pointers is connected to the question: *What does the pointer mean?* Often, pointers with very different meanings are used together. This usage complicates the understanding. The author of a hypertext should know about this problem and use unambiguous pointers. The following relations can be expressed through pointers:

- *To be*: *A* is part of *B*. This sentence represents a set relation.
- *To present*: *A* is an example of *B*, *A* demonstrated *B*.
- *To influence*: *A* causes *B*, *B* is a result of *A*. Consequences from a behavior can be described more closely.
- *To need* or *to be needed*: *A* needs *B*, *B* is needed by *A*. This relation expresses a necessity.
- *To own*: *A* has *B*, *A* is associated with *B*. Here, ownership is expressed.
- *To include*: *A* includes *B*, *A* consists of *B*, *A* occurs in *B*. An inclusion relation is expressed in different meanings.
- *To be similar*: *A* is similar to *B*, *A* is different from *B*, *A* replaces *B*, *A* is the alternative to *B*. Using this relation, similarities can be expressed.

Another basic property of pointers is described with the question: *Who is responsible for the pointer specification?* There are two possibilities:

- *Implicit Pointers*

  A relation between nodes can be established automatically by a hypertext system. The author determines the algorithm according to which pointers are created. The system *Intermedia* automatically generates all pointers which belong to one index. A similar approach can be taken by lexicons. Query references are done automatically using main notions of an entry.

- *Explicit Pointers*

  The author creates all links by him/herself.

A pointer can be created at different times. The question follows: *When is the destination of a pointer specified?*

- In the classical case, the pointer is created during the generation of a hypertext document, and hereby the origin of the destination node is determined. The author determines explicitly the links of the information units during document processing.

- A destination node can be determined first by using the pointer, i.e., during reading. The author specifies an algorithm for the creation of the pointers, but they are determined first during the reading depending on the context. The system computes the destination node.

  An example is a travel plan which shows the trains to one specific destination station. A pointer to the next train depends on actual time. This example comes from the information system to the city Glasgow *Glasgow Online* [Har89].

In the most systems, a pointer has one source and one destination node. One can also ask the questions: *Which direction has a pointer?* and *What is the number of outgoing pointers?*

The direction is mostly unidirectional. *Backtracking* is supported by the system itself. Hence, the path always leads back to the source. The alternative would be to have bidirectional pointers, but then the anchor, as well as the destination node, would have to be specially marked. Introducing bidirectional pointers, it is possible to have multiple references from several nodes to the same destination node. Hence, these kinds of pointers must be marked at the destination node and a further choice criterion must exist. Most systems support unidirectional pointers with only one destination node. It is easier to understand and generate.

The last question is connected to the form of an anchor at the user interface: *How is the pointer represented?* Section 13.2.1 shows different possibilities.

**Tools**

A hypertext system consists of several necessary tools. *Editor(s)* process information represented in different media. Beside this, the generation, management, editing and deletion of pointers are supported.

*Search tools* allow the search of desired information. Also different media need to be considered.

*Browser* allows a shortened but clear representation of the nodes and edges. The nodes are described media-dependently. The structure is presented to the user mostly in a graphical representation. Often, only the previously read text or relevant information can be displayed.

During the *navigation* through a document, a proper support of the phenomena *Getting Lost in the Hyperspace* is needed. A *backtracking* and clear representation of the whole structure with respect to the actual position should be available.

### 13.2.5 Some Final Comments about Hypertext Systems

The *ordering* during a reading of a hypertext document should be pre-specified with respect to the context and reader's interest. Therefore, the structure of the document can change depending on the context [Hof91].

For example, a textbook about the esophagus can offer to a medical student in his/her first semester an overview of the organ's functionality. Only a limited set of nodes are presented. The most pointers build a tree with a suggested path. A navigation through this document turns out to be simple. In the following semesters, the students are lead to specific topics in the surgery area. Using text, graphics, video and audio, different possibilities of surgical procedures can be presented. The hypertext document includes in this context, in addition to the fundamental notions, a detailed description of the surgery. Further sections in this document discuss research aspects. References point to a number of other articles, and also current unsolved research aspects are shown. The user has the possibility of navigating through the whole document.

The most current hypertext systems do not allow any references to nodes outside of their internal data structure. For example, shared electronic letters cannot be stored as documents in one hypertext system, and simultaneously sent through another mailing program. *Open solutions* would be required in this case to support links between information units of different hypertext applications. This requires standardized exchange formats and protocols.

A hypertext document is stored mostly on one computer. In a *distributed environment*, information units can be located on different computers. The pointers go beyond the computer boundaries. According to the presented architecture, the storage layer would be mostly affected.

Further interesting development and research projects refer to the following aspects and questions:

- Size and concept of the information units.

  (What size is the *optimal size*? Which factors does this specification depend on?)

- Support of distributed documents by migration of information and/or the reorganization of networks.

  (How can a document be preserved with respect to its remotely stored content?)

- Version management.

  (Which elements should comply with version management? What should this management look like?)

- Authorization and access rights.

  (Which elements should be subject to an authorization and what should their access rights be?)

- Cooperative work, joint document processing.

  (Which accesses should be locked? How is such a management implemented?)

- Virtual views onto hypermedia documents.

(What does the virtual view determine? How are the virtual views managed?)

Concluding, a short evaluation of the hypertext/hypermedia properties is given. A part of this evaluation is based on personal experiences of the authors, further ideas come from discussion with experts. Many aspects, which are visible at the beginning of working with such systems, are mostly positive. Operation of most systems can be learned quite easily without manual. The user knows quickly and effectively how to find the desired information and how to manipulate all data.

Many of these enumerated properties are system-dependent, but most hypertext systems show the named properties. The hypertext documents themselves are very different in nature. Some are structured clearly and easy to read, others are not structured properly, hence they are difficult to read.

Hypermedia integrates diverse media in a very elegant and simple fashion. Each relation between information units is implemented with pointers. Some systems also support the joint management of information among several persons. This technique has some properties which need to be critically evaluated. The most well-known effect is *Getting Lost in the Hyperspace.* While reading such a document, the perspective and context can get lost. Hypertext documents can easily become so called *spaghetti books* because of many pointers with different meanings. A hypertext document is difficult to bring into paper form without any information loss. Hence, even without audio and video information, the reader needs a computer. Some systems use their own window systems. There is a lack of established standards for information exchange among current hypertext systems.

Different task forces work on standards for hypermedia. Extensions of document architectures ODA and SGML include hypertext techniques. They support a data exchange of hypertext-like documents in a heterogeneous environment.

Further activities are embedded in ISO/IEC JTC1 SC2/WG12 *Multimedia and Hypermedia Information Coding Expert Group (MHEG).* This group works on the *coded representation of multimedia and hypermedia information* [MHE93].

The ANSI group X2V1.8M represents the *Music Information Processing Standards (MIPS) Committee.* This committee works on *HyTime* with respect to hypertext and the *Standard Music Description Language (SMDL).*

In summary, hypertext is not suitable for all kinds of documents and applications. This technique is very good with lexicons. The information units can be linked to each other through references (pointers). In comparison to an access and search in a book, the usage of hypertext system makes finding information faster.

Video and audio can be included in such a lexicon easily. For example, passages from music or animal voices can be stored under a certain entry's explanation. Video allows a short representation of typical movement processes as part of a lexicon entry.

Another area of using hypermedia is education and tutorials. Coursework may be supported by audio-visual means. These means can be used according to the learning behavior of the individual participants. For the instructors, the hypertext research works toward a didactical support for course design. For example, such a system was developed at the University of Karlsruhe [Mue89].

## 13.3 Document Architecture SGML

The *Standard Generalized Markup Language (SGML)* [Gol91b], [Org86] was supported mostly by American publishers. Authors prepare the text, i.e., the content. They specify in a uniform way the title, tables, etc., without a description of the actual representation (e.g., script type and line distance). The publisher specifies the resulting layout.

The basic idea is that the author uses *tags* for marking certain text parts. SGML determines the form of *tags.* but it does not specify their location or meaning. User groups agree on the meaning of the tags. SGML makes a *frame* available with which the user specifies the syntax description in an object-specific system. Here, classes and objects, hierarchies of classes and objects, inheritance and the link to methods (processing instructions) can be used by the specification. SGML specifies the syntax, but not the semantics. For example,

```
<title>Multimedia-Systems</title>

<author>Felix Gatou</author>
```

```
<side>IBM</side>

<summary>This exceptional paper from Peter ...
```

This example shows an application of SGML in a text document.

### 13.3.1 Some Details

Figure 13.15 shows the processing of an SGML document. It is divided into two

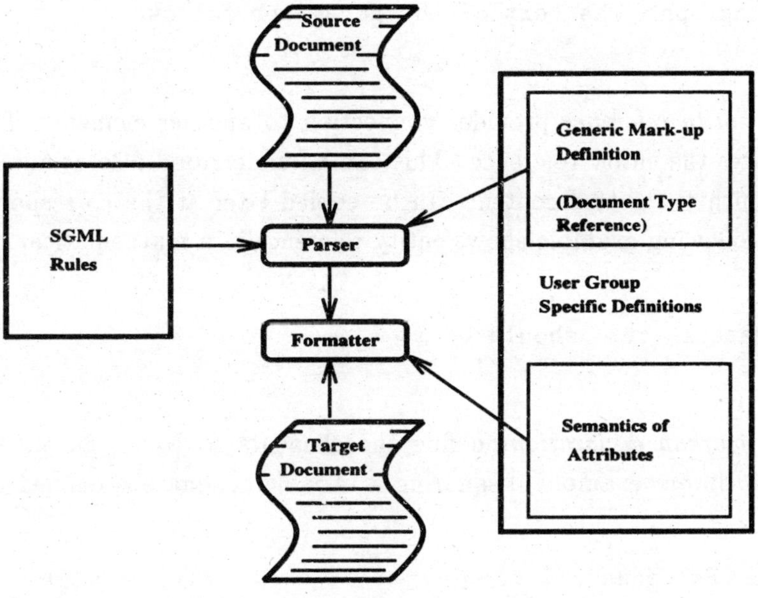


Figure 13.15: *SGML: Document processing – from the information to the presentation.*

processes. Only the *formatter* knows the meaning of the tag and it transforms the document into a formatted document. The parser uses the tags, occurring in the document, in combination with the corresponding document type. Specification of the document structure is done with tags. Here, parts of the layout are linked together. This is based on the joint context between the originator of the document and the formatter process. It is not defined through SGML.

Tags are divided into different categories:

- The *descriptive markup (tags)* describes the actual structure always in the form:

  ```
  <start-tag> respectively also </end-tag>
  ```

  An example is the definition of a paragraph at its beginning:

  ```
  <paragraph> The text of the paragraph follows ..
  ```

- The *entity reference* provides connection to another element. This element replaces the entity reference. This can be understood also as an abbreviation to which the actual content can be copied later at the corresponding place. The following example shows entity reference in a mathematical context:

  **&square x ....** **should be** $x^2$

- The *markup declarations* define the elements to which an entity reference refers. In our example of squaring a variable x, square is defined as:

  ```
  <!ELEMENT square (...)>
  ```

  A markup declaration can be used to define rules for the structure (the classes). The following example illustrates the construction of an article *paper*:

  ```
  <!ELEMENT paper (preamble, body, postamble)>

  <!ELEMENT preamble (title, author, side)>
  ```

```
<!ELEMENT title (#CDATA)> -- character data

<!ELEMENT body (...)>
```

- Instructions for other programs in a text are entered through *processing instructions.* They can be meant, for example, for the formatter. Using processing instructions, different media can be inserted.

SGML defines a syntax for tags through a grammar which needs to be followed. SGML does not define the semantics of these tags.

The *information or document architecture* of SGML is shown in Figure 13.16. SGML

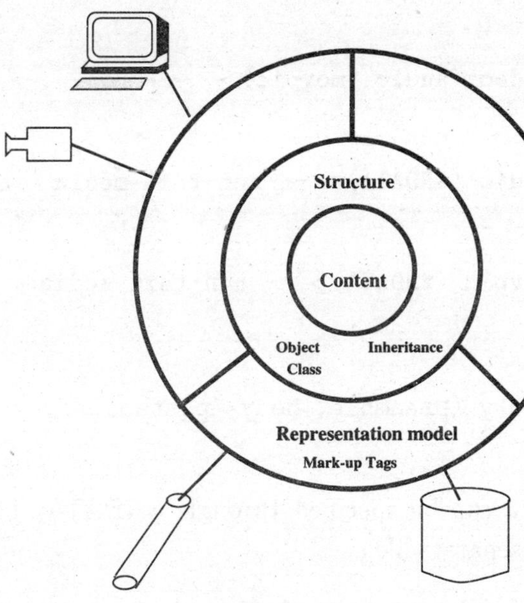


Figure 13.16: *SGML: Document architecture – emphasis on the representation model.*

with its tags possesses a representation model. Objects, classes and inheritance can be used for the definition of the structure.

### 13.3.2 SGML and Multimedia

*Multimedia data* are supported in the SGML standard only in the form of graphics. A graphical image as a CGM (*Computer Graphics Metafile*) is embedded in an SGML document. The standard does not refer to other media [Org86].

```
<!ATTLIST video id ID #IMPLIED>

<!ATTLIST video synch synch #IMPLIED>

<!ELEMENT video (audio, movpic)>

<!ELEMENT audio (#NDATA)> -- non-text media

<!ELEMENT movpic (#NDATA)> -- non-text media
...
<!ELEMENT story (preamble, body, postamble)> :
```

A link to concrete data can be specified through #NDATA. The data are stored mostly externally in a separate file.

The above example shows the definition of video which consists of audio and motion pictures.

Multimedia information units must be presented properly. The synchronization between the components is very important here. HyTime [Gol91a] and MHEG [MHE93] work on these issues.

### 13.3.3 Closing Comments about SGML

A standardized document exchange is necessary with respect to the communication. Sender (writer) and receiver (reader) can be distributed in time, as well as in space. Often, documents are processed automatically. This requires a joint context. The syntax is transmitted and the semantics must be discussed in SGML separately. The *Document Type Definitions* form the basis for these discussion.

SGML as a standard will stay in its current form [Org86], but extensions(additions) are also worked out. A standardized layout semantics is necessary. This will simplify interactions of user groups. The *Document Style Semantics and Specification Language (DSSSL)* is such an extension to the standard. Based on PostScript, a *Standard Page Description Language (SPDL)* is specified.

With respect to multimedia, pointers are included as non-readable. An extension for the description of music represents *Standard Music Description language(SMDL)* and HyTime.

Another application conforming to International Standard ISO 8879 – SGML – is the *HyperText Markup Language (HTML)*. HTML is a mark-up language for hypertext which is understood by all WWW (World Wide Web) clients. HTML is persuaded to become a standard for interchange of hypertext information on the network. It is proposed to be registered as a MIME (RFC1521) content type. HTML can be used to represent:

- Hypertext news, mail, online documentation and collaborative hypermedia.
- Menus of options.
- Database query results.
- Simple structured documents with in-lined graphics.
- Hypertext views of existing bodies of information.

## 13.4 Document Architecture ODA

The *Open Document Architecture (ODA)* [Org89] was initially called the *Office Document Architecture* because it supports mostly office-oriented applications. The main goal of this document architecture is to support the exchange, processing and presentation of documents in open systems. ODA has been endorsed mainly by the computer industry, especially in Europe.

### 13.4.1 Some Details on ODA

The main property of ODA is the distinction among content, logical structure and layout structure. This is in contrast to SGML where only a logical structure and the contents are defined. ODA also defines semantics. Figure 13.17 shows these three aspects linked to a document. One can imagine these aspects as three orthogonal

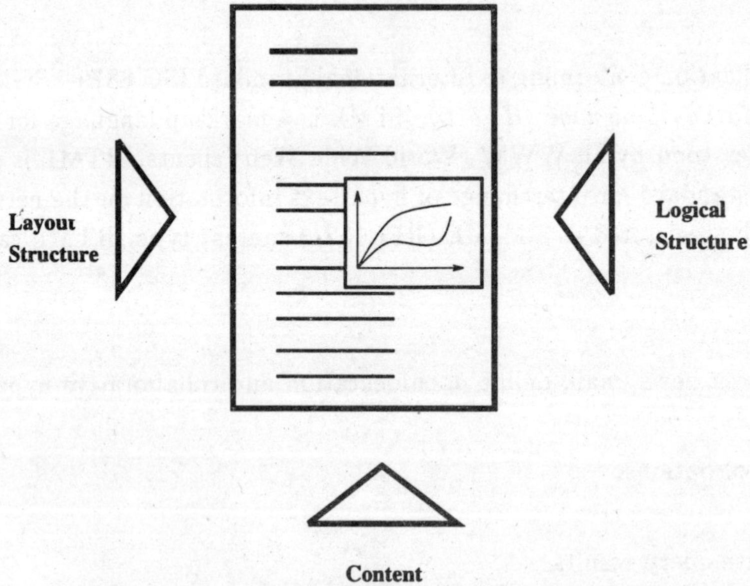


Figure 13.17: *ODA: Content, layout and logical view.*

views of the same document. Each of these views represent one aspect, together we get the actual document.

### Content Portions

The content of the document consists of *Content Portions.* These can be manipulated according to the corresponding medium.

A *content architecture* describes for each medium: (1) the specification of the elements, (2) the possible access functions and, (3) the data coding. Individual elements are the Logical Data Units (LDUs), which are determined for each medium. The access functions serve for the manipulation of individual elements. The coding of the data determines the mapping with respect to bits and bytes.

ODA has content architectures for media *text, geometrical graphics* and *raster graphics.* Contents of the medium *text* are defined through the *Character Content Architecture.* The *Geometric Graphics Content Architecture* allows a content description of still images. It also takes into account individual graphical objects. This is similar to CGM. Pixel-oriented still images are described through *Raster Graphics Content Architecture.* It can be a bitmap as well as a facsimile.

### Layout Structure and Logical Structure

The structure and presentation models describe – according to the information architecture – the *cooperation* of information units. These kinds of meta information distinguish layout and logical structure.

The *layout structure* specifies mainly the representation of a document. It is related to a two dimensional representation with respect to a screen or paper. The presentation model is a tree. Figure 13.18 shows the content of a document together with the layout structure. Using *frames* the position and size of individual layout elements is established. For example, the page size and type style are also determined.

The *logical structure* includes the partitioning of the content as shown in Figure 13.19. Here, paragraphs and individual headings are specified according to the tree structure. Lists with their entries are defined (example) as:

```
paper = preamble body postamble
```

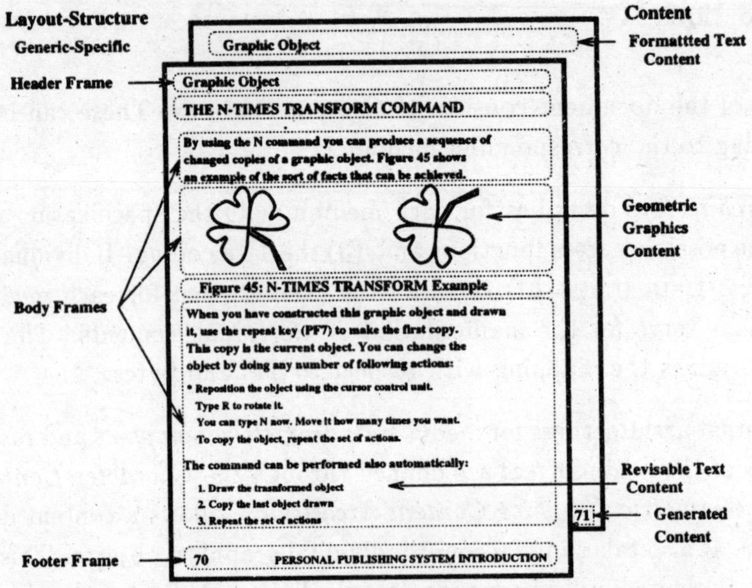


Figure 13.18: *Layout view and content of an ODA document.*

```
body = chapter1 chapter2

chapter1 = heading paragraph ...  picture ...

chapter2 = heading paragraph picture paragraph
```

The above example describes the logical structure of an article. Each article consists of a *preamble*, a *body* and a *postamble*. The body includes two chapters, both of them start with headings. A content is assigned to each element of this logical structure.

An example, shown in Figure 13.20, demonstrates the relation among a content, logical structure and layout structure. Figure 13.21 shows the contents and the logical and layout structures of the document from Figure 13.20. This figure consists of a title, a describing text and a figure. The title and describing text are mapped onto the content architecture *Character Content Architecture*. The figure belongs to the content architecture *Raster Graphics Content Architecture*.

The logical structure of the example dictates for each section at least one title, one paragraph and one figure. This behavior is shown in Figure 13.21.

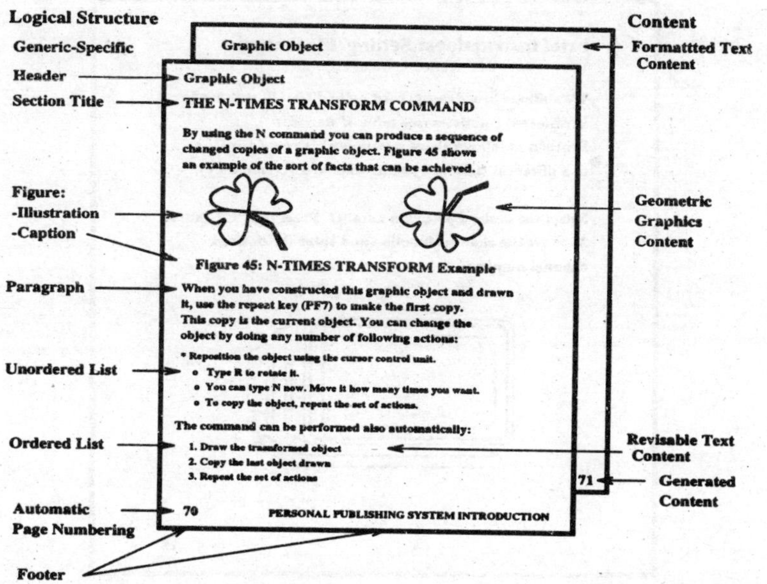


Figure 13.19: *Logical view and content of an ODA document.*

In the upper right paragraph of Figure 13.21, the layout structure of the document is displayed. It consists of several *frames* which are ordered in a certain style on the two-dimensional surface.

The ordering is presented through individual lines between the elements of the different areas. A *content portion* is assigned to each leaf of the logical tree (a basic object) and of the layout tree.

ODA distinguishes the following layout and logical structures:

- The *generic logical* and *generic layout structures* include a set of default values. For example, a paragraph can be specified with *LeftHandOffset = 0.*

- The *specific logical* and *specific layout structure* describe a concrete document. They are linked to the generic structure. For example, a concrete paragraph can be defined with *LeftHandOffset = 1cm.* The following example presents a specific layout object:

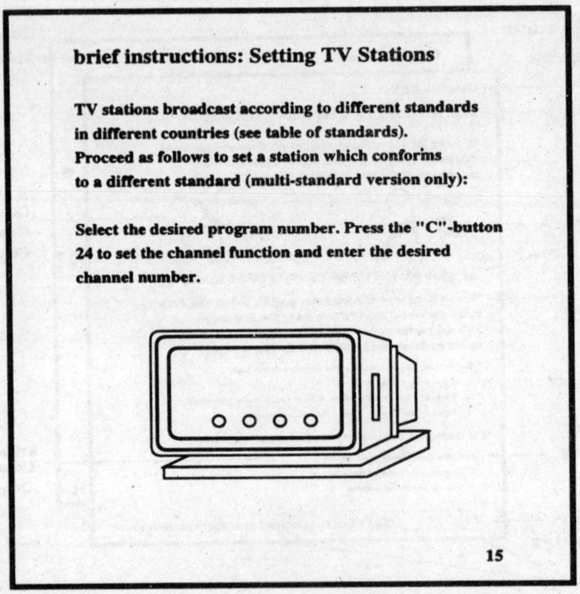

**brief instructions: Setting TV Stations**

**TV stations broadcast according to different standards in different countries (see table of standards). Proceed as follows to set a station which conforms to a different standard (multi-standard version only):**

**Select the desired program number. Press the "C"-button 24 to set the channel function and enter the desired channel number.**

**15**

Figure 13.20: *An ODA document (example).*

| | |
|---|---|
| object type: | block |
| object identifier: | title |
| position: | (x=111, y=222) |
| dimensions: | (height=333 width=444) |
| content architecture class: | formatted character content architecture |
| content portions: | (POINTER TO TEXT) |

The information architecture ODA includes the cooperative models shown in Figure 13.22. The fundamental descriptive means of the structural and presentational models are linked to the individual nodes which build a document. The document is seen as a tree. Each node (also a document) is a *constituent*, or an object. It consists of a set of attributes, which represent the properties of the nodes. A node itself includes a concrete value or it defines relations between other nodes. Hereby, relations and operators, as shown in Table 13-1, are allowed.

If we consider document processing according to Figure 13.3, in ODA it can be presented as shown in Figure 13.23.

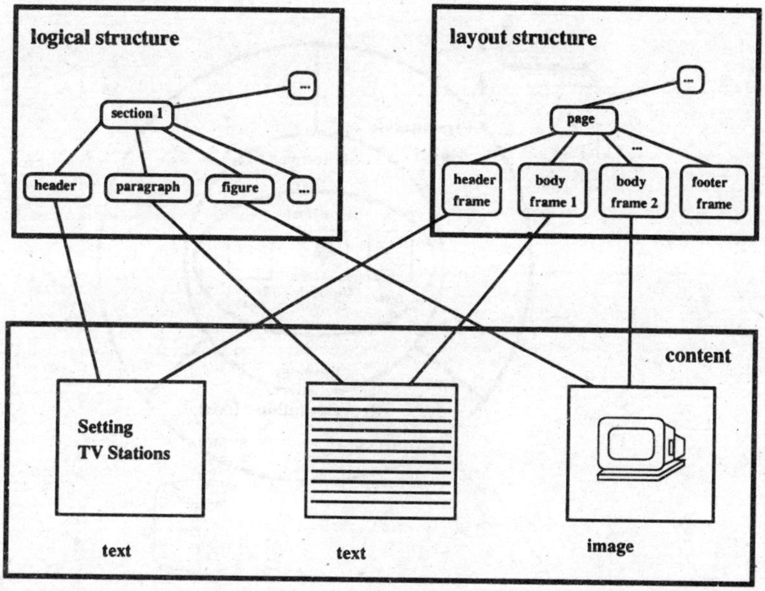


Figure 13.21: *Relations among content and logical and layout structures (example from Figure 13.20).*

The simplified distinction is between the editing, formatting (*Document Layout Process* and *Content Layout Process*) and actual presentation (*Imaging Process*). Current WYSIWYG (What You See Is What You Get) editors include these in one single step. It is important to mention that the processing assumes a linear reproduction. Therefore, this is only partially suitable as a document architecture for a hypertext system. Hence, work is occurring on *Hyper-ODA*. For the document exchange, different *document architecture classes* can be used, as shown in Figure 13.23:

- A *formatted document* includes the specific layout structure, and eventually the generic layout structure. It can be printed directly or displayed, but it cannot be changed.

- A *processable document* consists of the specific logical structure, eventually the generic logical structure, and later of the generic layout structure. The document cannot be printed directly or displayed. Change of content is possible.

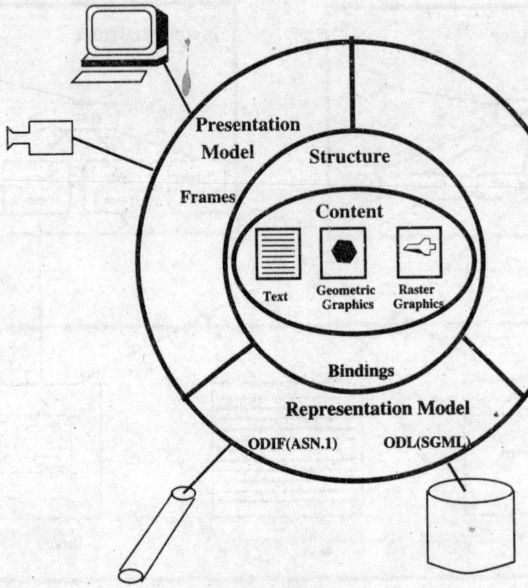


Figure 13.22: *ODA information architecture with structure, content, presentation and representation model.*

- A *formatted processable document* is a mixed form. It can be printed, displayed and the content can be changed.

For the communication of an ODA document, the representation model, shown in Figure 13.22, is used. This can be either the *Open Document Interchange Format (ODIF)* (based on ASN.1), or the *Open Document Language (ODL)* (based on SGML).

The *manipulation model* in ODA, shown in Figure 13.22, makes use of *Document Application Profiles (DAPs)*. These profiles are an ODA extension for document manipulation. Because of the ODA structure, the extension defines three different levels, which represent a subset of ODA (*Text Only, Text + Raster Graphics + Geometric Graphics, Advanced Level*).

| Sequence | all child nodes are ordered sequentially |
|---|---|
| Aggregate | no ordering among the child nodes |
| Choice | one of the child nodes has a successor |
| Optional | one or no (operator) |
| Repeat | one .... any times (operator) |
| Optional Repeat | 0 ... any times (operator) |

Table 13.1: *Relations among nodes.*

### 13.4.2 ODA and Multimedia

Multimedia requires, besides spatial representational dimensions, the *time* as a main part of a document. If ODA should include continuous media, further extensions in the standard are necessary. Currently, multimedia is not part of the standard. All further paragraphs discuss only possible extensions, which formally may or may not be included in ODA in this form.

#### Contents

The *content portions* will change to *timed content portions* [RG90]. Hereby, the duration does not have to be specified *a priori.* These types of content portions are called *Open Timed Content Portions.* Let us consider an example of an animation which is generated during the presentation time depending on external events. The information, which can be included during the presentation time, is images taken from the camera. In the case of a *Closed Timed Content Portion*, the duration is fixed. An example is a song.

#### Structure

Operations between objects must be extended with a time dimension where the time relation is specified in the father node $v$ in proportion to the child nodes $k_1$, $k_2$. The following additional examples and described relations can be found in chapter 15 on

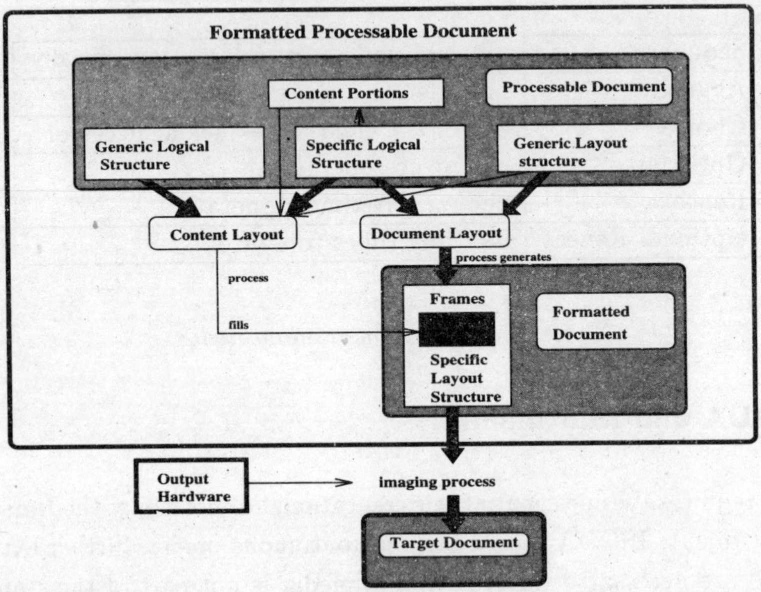


Figure 13.23: *ODA document processing – from the information to the presentation.*

synchronization:

- *before*: $k_1$ before $k_2$, $k_1 + k_2 > v$
- *meets*: $(k_1, k_2), k_1$ exactly before $k_2, k_1 + k_2 = v$
- *overlaps*
- *during*
- *start*
- *end*
- *middle*
- *at*
- *equal*

### Content Architecture

Additional content architectures for audio and video must be defined. Hereby, the corresponding elements, LDUs, must be specified. For the access functions, a set of generally valid functions for the *control* of the media streams needs to be specified. Such functions are, for example, *Start* and *Stop*. Many functions are very often device-dependent. One of the most important aspects is a compatibility provision among different systems implementing ODA.

During data coding, a link to the existing *de-jure* and *de-facto* standards is required. Especially important standards are: JPEG for image compression, MPEG for video and audio, H.261 for video and CD technology. The possibility of an *open architecture* should be considered. With this approach, further developments could be considered today without changing or extending the standard.

### Logical Structures

Extensions for multimedia of the logical structure also need to be considered. For example, a film can include a logical structure. It could be a tree with the following components:

1. Prelude
    - Introductory movie segment
    - Participating actors in the second movie segment
2. Scene 1
3. Scene 2
4. ...
5. Postlude

Such a structure would often be desirable for the user. This would allow one to deterministically skip some areas and to show or play other areas.

A time relation between different objects is also relevant for the definition of the logical structure. This time relation should be specified only to the extent that the user perceives content portions to be *in sync.* A relation can be defined between the subtitles and the scene as a whole, although the exact time cannot be specified by the logical structure. This would rather count the layout structure.

A spatial relation between different objects is defined in the same way as it is done by other discrete media. Instead of a tree structure in an ODA multimedia document, it should be possible to define a graph. This would allow for any kind of hypermedia techniques.

### Layout Structure

The layout structure needs extensions for multimedia. The time relation by a motion picture and audio must be included. Further, questions such as *When will something be played?*, *From which point?* and *With which attributes and dependencies?* must be answered.

The spatial relation can specify, for example, relative and absolute positions by the audio object. Additionally, the volume and all other attributes and dependencies should be determined.

Especially by the continuous media, *interactivity* needs to be considered. The document is not only anymore a paper, the *linear* processing will become the *interactive* processing. In the case of ODA, the *imaging process* should not be left out, as we will discuss in the next section in terms of MHEG.

If all extensions of ODA with respect to the integration of continuous media are summarized, the result is the multimedia document architecture shown in Figure 13.2.

## 13.5 MHEG

The committee ISO/IEC JTC1/SC29 (*Coding of Audio, Picture, Multimedia and Hypermedia Information*) works on the standardization of the exchange format for multimedia systems. The actual standards are developed at the international level in three working groups cooperating with research and industry. Figure 13.24 shows that the three standards deal with the coding and compression of individual media. The results of the working groups: the *Joint Photographic Expert Group (JPEG)*

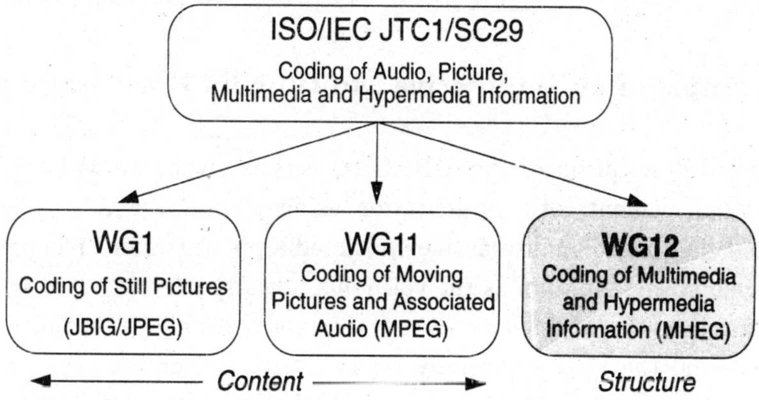


Figure 13.24: *Working Groups within the ISO-SG29.*

and the *Motion Picture Expert Group (MPEG)* are of special importance in the area of multimedia systems (see Chapter 6 on compression).

In a multimedia presentation, the contents, in the form of individual information objects, are described with the help of the above named standards. The structure (e.g., processing in time) is specified first through timely spatial relations between the information objects. The standard of this structure description is the subject of the working group WG12, which is known as the *Multimedia and Hypermedia Information Coding Expert Group (MHEG)*. The name of the developed standard is officially called *Information Technology - Coding of Multimedia and Hypermedia Information (MHEG)*. The final MHEG standard will be described in three documents. The first part will discuss the concepts, as well as the exchange format. The second part describes an alternative, semantically to the first part, isomorph syntax of the exchange format. The third part should present a reference architecture for a linkage to the script languages. The main concepts are covered in the first document, and the last two documents are still in progress; therefore, we will focus on the first document with the basic concepts. Further discussions about MHEG are based mainly on the committee draft version, because: (1) all related experiences have been gained on this basis [ME94]; (2) the basic concepts between the final standard and this committee draft remain to be the same; and, (3) the finalization of this standard is still in progress while printing this book. Note that the following discussion is based on [ME94] designing, implementing and improving the MHEG standard.

### 13.5.1 Example of an Interactive Multimedia Presentation

Before a detailed description of the MHEG objects is given, we will briefly examine the individual elements of a presentation using a small scenario. Figure 13.25 presents a time diagram of an interactive multimedia presentation. The presentation starts with some music. As soon as the voice of a news-speaker is heard in the audio sequence, a graphic should appear on the screen for a couple of seconds. After the graphic disappears, the viewer carefully reads a text. After the text presentation ends, a *Stop button* appears on the screen. With this button the user can abort the audio sequence. Now, using a displayed input field, the user enters the title

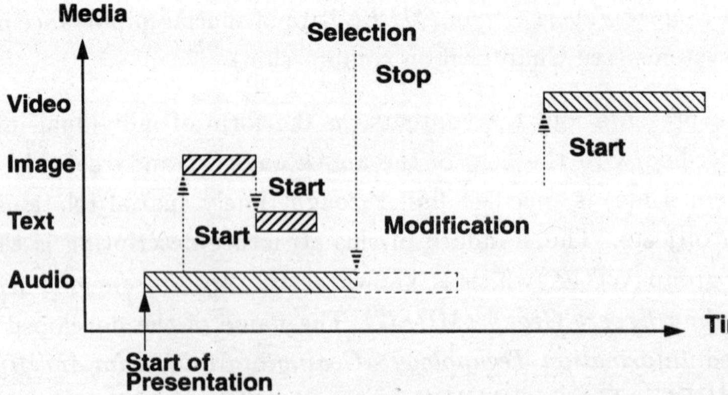


Figure 13.25: *Time diagram of an interactive presentation.*

of a desired video sequence. These video data are displayed immediately after the modification.

### Content

A presentation consists of a sequence of information representations. For the representation of this information, media with very different properties are available. Because of later *reuse*, it is useful to capture each information LDU as an individual object. The contents in our example are: the video sequence, the audio sequence, the graphics and the text.

### Behavior

The notion *behavior* means all information which specifies the representation of the contents as well as defines the run of the presentation. The first part is controlled by the actions *start, set volume, set position*, etc. The last part is generated by the definition of timely, spatial and conditional links between individual elements. If the state of the content's presentation changes, then this may result in further commands on other objects (e.g., the deletion of the graphic causes the display of the text). Another possibility, how the behavior of a presentation can be determined, is when external programs or functions (script) are called.

### User Interaction

In the discussed scenario, the running animation could be aborted by a corresponding user interaction. There can be two kinds of user interactions. The first one is the *simple selection*, which controls the run of the presentation through a prespecified choice (e.g., push the Stop button). The second kind is the more complex *modification*, which gives the user the possibility to enter data during the run of the presentation (e.g., editing of a data input field).

### Container

Merging together several elements as discussed above, a presentation, which progresses in time, can be achieved. To be able to exchange this presentation between the involved systems, a *composite* element is necessary. This element is comparable to a container. It links together all the objects into a unit. With respect to hypertext/hypermedia documents, such containers can be ordered to a complex structure, if they are linked together through so-called hypertext pointers.

## 13.5.2 Derivation of a Class Hierarchy

Figure 13.26 summarizes the individual elements in the MHEG class hierarchy in the form of a tree. Instances can be created from all leaves (roman printed classes). All

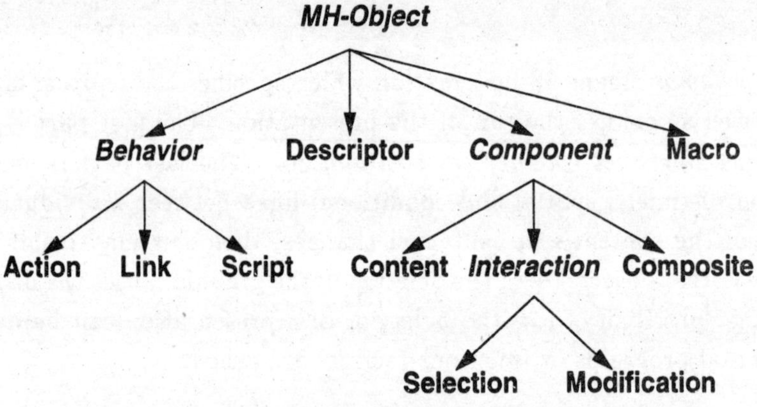


Figure 13.26: *Class hierarchy of MHEG objects.*

internal nodes, including the root (*italic* printed classes), are abstract classes, i.e., no instances can be generated from them. The leaves inherit some attributes from the root of the tree as an abstract basic class. The internal nodes do not include any further functions. Their task is to unify individual classes into meaningful groups. The action, the link and the script classes are grouped under the behavior class, which defines the behavior in a presentation. The interaction class includes the user interaction, which is again modeled through the selection and modification class. All the classes together with the content and composite classes specify the individual components in the presentation and determine the component class. Some properties of the particular MHEG engine can be queried by the descriptor class. The macro class serves as the simplification of the access, respectively reuse of objects. Both classes play a minor role; therefore, they will not be discussed further.

The development of the MHEG standard uses the techniques of object-oriented design. Although a class hierarchy is considered a kernel of this technique, a closer look shows that the MHEG class hierarchy does not have the meaning it is often assigned. Methods of the classes are not specified in the standard, therefore only some attributes of the MH-object class are passed from their derived classes. In this context, a problem of using ASN.1 syntax for MHEG class description becomes obvious. ASN.1 does not support inheritance mechanisms; therefore, the reuse of the attributes in the remaining classes, which are defined in the MH object class, is applied. It needs to be mentioned that the MHEG class hierarchy is used mainly because of didactical reasons. For the implementation of a MHEG run-time environment, it does not have any importance.

### MH-Object-Class

The abstract MH-Object-Class inherits both data structures *MHEG Identifier* and *Descriptor*.

*MHEG Identifier* consists of the attributes *MHEG Identifier* and *Object Number* and it serves as the addressing of MHEG objects. The first attribute identifies a specific application. The *Object Number* is a number which is defined only within the application. The data structure *Descriptor* provides the possibility to characterize more precisely each MHEG object through a number of optional attributes. For example, this can become meaningful if a presentation is decomposed into individual objects and the individual MHEG objects are stored in a database. Any author, supported by proper search functions, can reuse existing MHEG objects.

In the following paragraphs, the MHEG classes are presented and some main mechanisms are discussed. For more technical details, the interested reader should see the committee draft [MHE93].

### 13.5.3 Contents

#### Content Class

The content class differs from the other classes because it provides the link to the actual contents. Through this content class, this information becomes flexible and is linked together in an open way in the system. Each content object represents exactly one information within a presentation.

The type of the particular medium is defined in a content object through the attribute *MHEG Classification* and the coding is specified through the attribute *Hook*. The actual data can be included either in the object (*included data*), or they can be referenced through an unambiguous identifier (*referenced data* ). The included data are meaningful only when a small amount of data is present. The reason is efficiency because the content object itself is transformed, before any exchange occurs, through the encoder/decoder. The referenced data have the advantage that they can be reused outside of MHEG.

At the time of content object processing, it must be guaranteed that the referenced data were requested through proper application services. For the presentation of data, one medium-corresponding representation component is used.

The standard includes a set of codings. Besides the existing standards, future standard (*Non-MHEG Standardized Catalogue*), as well as application-specific coding methods (*Proprietary Catalogue*), are considered. This is done through an open definition of the individual formats.

#### Virtual Coordination Systems

The so-called *Generic Space* defines a virtual coordination system. Content objects can be defined relative in dimension and ordering to each other. There are three axes: X (width), Y (height) and Z (depth). A value from -32768 to 32767 is assigned to each axis. During the run-time, a translation from the virtual MHEG coordinates to the physical coordinate system is performed in the particular presentation service (e.g., the number of pixels which cover a Motif window). Additionally, a time coordinate system exists with its axis T. The defined value set for this axis is an interval from 0 to infinity where the scale unit is a millisecond.

### Virtual Views

Until now we assumed that the presentation of the contents occurs exactly as originated. Actually, MHEG provides a set of possibilities which can control a presentation of the content objects through proper parameters. For example, a movie can be played according to certain time specifications, the volume of an audio sequence can be set or the visual area of a graphic can be specified. The manipulation of these parameters is determined through corresponding commands (see action class) in the coding. The following example of a computer simulated basketball game shows that the same player of each team can occur at different positions of the field at the same time. Instead of storing all possible presentation combinations as separate content objects, the change of the parameter is modeled as a call of an object's method. Using this approach, so-called virtual views (*Presentable*) to each content object are created during run-time. These virtual views are specified at the presentation-composition through unambiguous numbers. During run-time, they fix the parameters according to the representation. Figure 13.27 shows some examples of virtual views and illustrates the reuse possibilities.

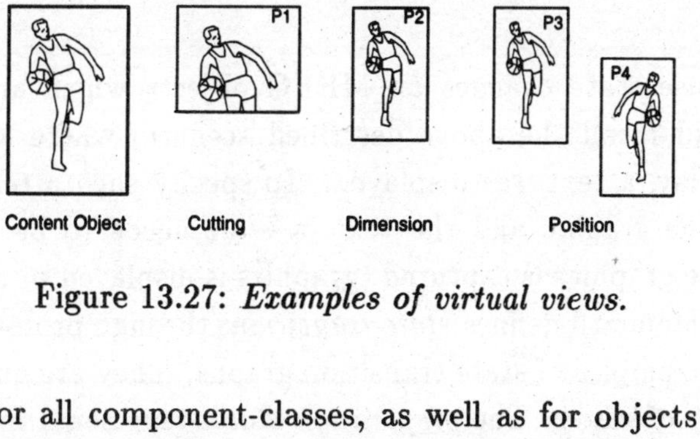


Figure 13.27: *Examples of virtual views.*

Such views exist for all component-classes, as well as for objects of the selection, modification and composite classes. However, they have within each class different specifications. In the next paragraphs, if MHEG objects are addressed, virtual views are meant. Only in the case of a different handling, the exclusion of virtual views will be stated explicitly.

### 13.5.4 Behavior

#### Action Class

The behavior of individual MHEG objects is determined with the *action class*. According to the object-oriented terminology, an action-object is a message which is sent to a MHEG object. By the destination object, a corresponding method is called which performs a change on this object. In an action object, the destination object is not specified. Hence, the action class represents only the interface (set of all public methods) to influence the presentation of individual MHEG objects. The implementation of the individual methods is hidden in the encapsulation of its specifics. Further, the capability of polymorphism is often used. This means that actions with the same name but with different specifications can exist. Altogether this leads to a very homogeneous interface (e.g., the display of objects occurs independently of the medium with the action *run*).

Individual actions can be classified into different groups depending on which method they influence. It is apparent that not each action for each MHEG object, respectively virtual view, is meaningful.

#### States and State Transitions

Some actions cause state changes on MHEG objects which are very important. The reader should recall the above described scenario where after the ending of the graphics display, a text was displayed. To specify such a relation between the presentation of the graphic and the text, a *state* needs to be defined where the virtual view of the graphics is captured (graphics is displayed or not displayed). For this purpose, the standard defines *state transitions* through protocol engines. Figure 13.28 shows two examples of state transition graphs. They are quite simple because of the low number of states. The *preparation status* represents the availability of an MHEG object. An example of a content object explains the status. At the beginning the object is in the *not ready* state. With the action *prepare*, referenced data are eventually localized and the necessary subsystem is initialized for the presentation. If these activities are performed successfully, the state changes to *ready* and the

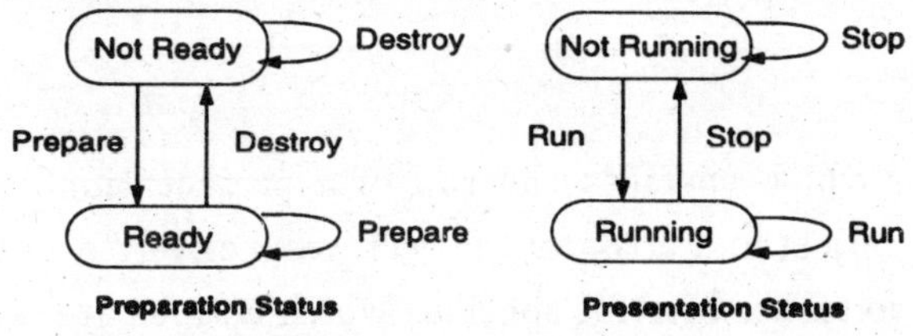


Figure 13.28: *An example of two state transition graphs.*

object can be displayed by a virtual view. With the action *destroy*, the resources, allocated by the object, can be freed. The display of this object depends on the *presentation status* of a corresponding virtual view.

Further state transitions are defined for the *composition status, modification status, time-stone status* and *script activation status.* An exception is the *selection status.* The different statuses are determined first with the modeling of the individual user interactions in a presentation. The previously described actions are basic operations of an MHEG object.

The construction of an action object also includes *complex runs* that are defined by grouping several basic actions. Depending on requirements, single actions can be performed in parallel or sequentially. The data structure of the action class defines for this purpose a *Parallel Action List.* The elements of this list consist again of a list of basic actions. *Delayed Sequential Action* is defined as a *Sequence of Actions.* The basic actions in *Delayed Sequential Action* are processed only sequentially. Figure 13.29 gives a graphical overview of the data structure.

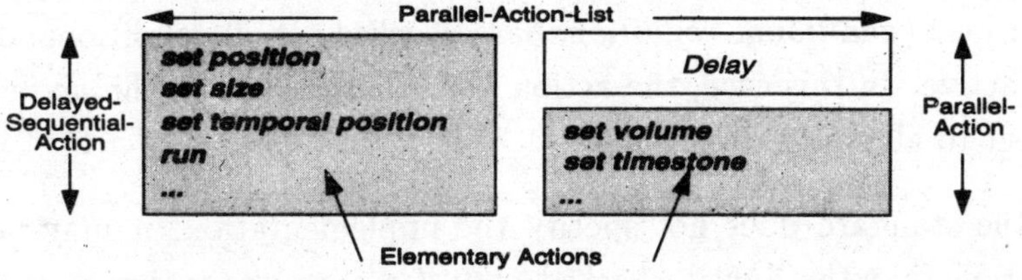


Figure 13.29: *An example of an action object.*

### Link Class

So far, no relation which specifies the run of a presentation could be established between an action object and a content object, respectively a virtual view. The link class must fulfill two tasks. First, it specifies which actions are sent to which MHEG objects. Second, the conditions are specified under which this process occurs. From these tasks, it can be derived that the processing of an MHEG-coded presentation is based on an event-driven processing model. This model is suitable for the mapping of parallel running, synchronized processes which exist often in interactive multimedia presentations. Their sequentialization depends on the performing system.

A link object consists of a set of links. The semantics of a link are shown in Figure 13.30. A link connects a source object with one or several destination objects. The

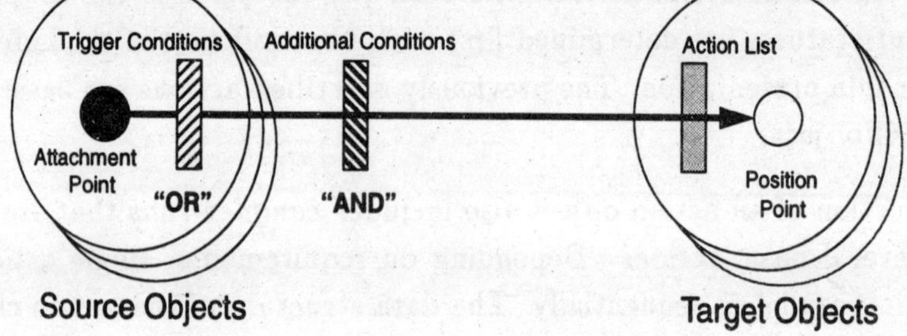


Figure 13.30: *Construction of a link.*

source can be MHEG objects, as well as virtual views. The performance of a link is always dependent on a condition (*trigger condition*), which can be expressed through the possible state transition in the source object. Only if this condition is satisfied, other conditions (*additional conditions*) are checked. If all conditions are satisfied, the link is active. In this case, the action objects, specified in the *action list* of the link, are sent to all destination objects.

Although the standard does not specify the implementation, it may be appropriate to mention that the link is checked only if a state transition of the particular source objects occurred. This implementation is driven by efficiency reasons. The *attachment point* is used to position destination objects relative to the source object. It means that coordinates in an action object express a relative position of the destination object with respect to the source object.

### Script Class

Another possibility to determine the behavior of objects or the run of a presentation is the *script class.* This class was considered to support an MHEG presentation in other run-time environments (e.g., Script/X), external programs (e.g., a C-program) or functions calls. Comparable with the content class, different languages either standardized (MHEG-Catalogue) or non-standardized (Non-MHEG-Catalogue), are supported.

## 13.5.5 User Interaction

Using the previously described classes, the user cannot interact with a running presentation. The introductory scenario has discussed that the MHEG standard distinguishes two kinds of user interactions: selection and modification.

### Selection Class

The selection class provides the possibility to model an interaction as a selection of a value from a pre-defined value set. The explanation of the link class has shown that the run of a presentation is controlled by the occurrence of events which are given by the standard. With a selection object, it is possible to consider user interactions also in the form of such events. A selection object takes over the definition of these application-specific events. A corresponding event value is prepared for the particular selection possibilities. At a certain point in the user interaction, there exists a virtual view on the selection object (similar to a content object). The event of the user interaction is stored in the view. The storage is performed through the assignment of the particular event value onto a *selection status* field, which is predetermined. The change of this status field should lead to the following situation: the condition of a link object is satisfied and therefore actions are sent to other objects.

The change of the status field, as well as the display and control of proper primitives (the following primitives are specified in the standard: *menu, pull-down menu, pop-up menu, button list, key list, device list, scrolling list, switch, item, button, key, device*) at the user interface are suborders of the user interface services. With the coding of a selection object, it is not specified which kind of primitives should be used for the interaction. The primitive and its properties (e.g., text on the knob) are set through actions (see selection style presentability) which are sent to the virtual views of a selection object.

### Modification Class

The second form of user interaction serves as the input and manipulation of data. In contrast to a selection object, no value set is pre-defined by a modification object. The event of an interaction is represented through an entered content object. Its content is represented through the virtual view, which is defined for the content object, and it is modified through the primitive of the user interface. The actual processing state of the content object is captured in these virtual views in a *modification status* field before the modification (*modifiable*), during the modification (*modifying*) and after the modification (*modified*). Hence, it is possible, similar to the selection, to query the status field through a link object, and therefore to control the run of a presentation.

During the international agreement process, it was recognized that the ASN.1 coding is incomplete in the CD-document. Exactly, the deal concerned a variable in the content object. The value of this variable can serve again as a parameter for an action (e.g., volume by *set volume*). In the current ASN.1 coding, a reference to this variable for action objects is not possible. Therefore, so-called *generic values* are included in the later version of the standard. They can contain the event of a modification according to type. The following types have been specified: *Boolean, Character String, Numeric Value, Numeric Vector, Spatial Vector, Temporal* and *Volume.* Further, they can be reused by action objects. In some cases (e.g., fill out a sheet), it will be necessary to return the values to the application. They can be performed by the action *return.*

### 13.5.6 Container

#### Composite Class

The composite class has the task of composing all the necessary objects from the previously described classes into a presentation. Independently, if a single object is included or referenced, each composite object behaves as a *container*. It means that it represents a closed unit for the exchange of presentations among systems. The functionality of a composite object must satisfy some assumptions for the synchronized output through the MHEG engine. Through pointers (compare hypertext links) between different composite objects, any complex presentation can be created. At this point, the meaning of the abstract classes *Behavior* and *Component* (Figure 13.26) should be clear. Figure 13.31 shows graphically the structure of a composite object, including defined virtual views (*Presentables*) and two link objects (*Container-start-up, Presentation-start-up*).

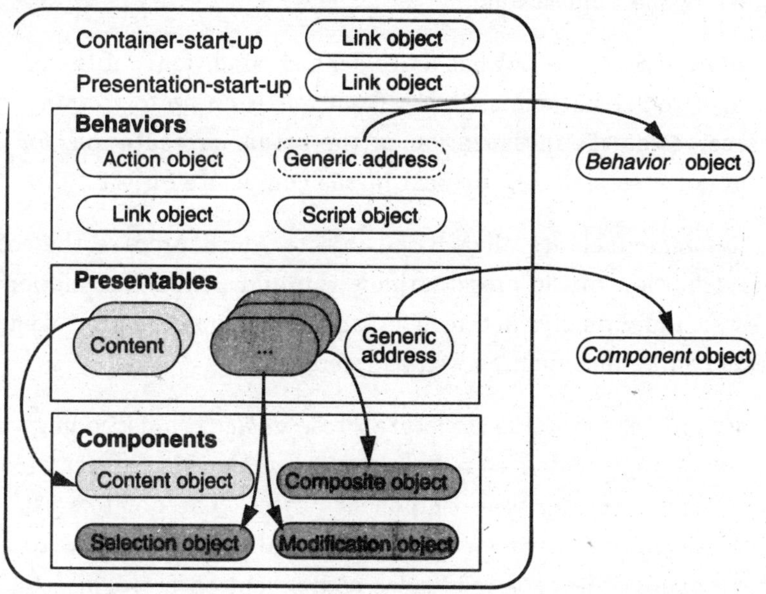


Figure 13.31: *Construction of a composite object.*

Before we describe the individual parts, let us mention that the performance of each composite object, as by all other MHEG objects, runs in two phases. The first phase, started by the action *prepare*, initializes the composite object. It means that the object itself, both start-up-link-objects and the included virtual views, are registered. The second phase is the actual performance of the presentation. It is triggered by the action *run* on a *composite-presentable.*

This *two-phase* processing can also be seen in the construction of a composite object in both start-up-link-objects. The *container start-up-link* serves as the initialization of the *components* included in the composite object. During the initialization, eventually necessary resources for the output are activated, or reserved in the executing system. This is done to prevent, for example, delays which are caused by necessary *loading* of swapped out parts. At the same time, further link objects can be initialized which are necessary for the description of the behavior of the component object and its virtual views. Here, the link object always has the same condition per definition: "if the preparation status of the corresponding composite objects switches from *not ready* to *ready*, then ...". What happens in individual cases is in the responsibility of the application.

Also the *Presentation Start-up-link* has a pre-defined condition: "if the presentation status of a composite-presentable switches from *not running* to *running*, then ...". This condition serves as the initialization of the actual presentation, for example, through the start of a virtual view defined in the composite object.

The structure *behavior* includes all MHEG objects which prepare the component objects for the definition of the presentation's run and define the relations among the virtual views. Individually, action, link and script objects are taken in. The behavior objects can be included, as well as referenced.

The virtual views are defined in the structure *Presentable.* From a coding viewpoint, each virtual view is represented as a pair: an unambiguous integer value in the composite object and a pointer to a component object. The pointers usually point to objects in the structure *Components.* If a virtual view is related to a *generic address*, the component object is a referenced component object. This is meaningful if a hypertext structure should be constructed through the link of several composite objects

All component objects, which are listed in the structure *Components*, are contained physically in the composite object and marked with an unambiguous index.

The MHEG standard does not assume any granularity of the single composite object. A composite object can relate to, for example, single user interaction as part of an application, or it can describe a complete presentation. The granularity is determined at the end by the particular application. For example, in the case of a kiosk application, a typical page-oriented construction of the presentation's run leads to the definition of a composite object per page.

### 13.5.7 Closing Comments

Comparing ODA and SGML, SGML defines only a syntax for text marking, and the semantics are undefined; ODA includes a specified semantics for description of documents.

ODA offers the possibility to implement an open standard with integration of continuous media. This would allow the exchange of multimedia documents in the same way as we exchange text documents through the mailing systems today. But, there are still many missing aspects as described in the previous section.

ODA will have to consider *security* and *color* aspects. Further, backwards compatibility should be preserved. In the future, besides text and graphic, also tables and data will be supported in documents. This will require a data exchange between a document and spreadsheet, as well as a transformation from data to text. The notion of partial documents should be introduced. *Partial documents* are incomplete documents which include external pointers. These documents allow the definition of a document above the computer boundaries. Formulas should be included as part of ODA. A version management should be introduced; further content architectures for others should be defined.

MHEG provides a specification for documents which includes time and user interactions. Pictorial-related formats exist. *ScriptX* from Kaleida is the most prominent example. At this point, it is not clear which architecture/language/format will be widely accepted in the future because, for example, HyTime as an exclusion to SGML has also been developed.

# Chapter 14

# User Interfaces

In computer science, we understand the *user interface* as the interactive input and output of a computer as it is perceived and operated on by users. *Multimedia user interfaces* are computer interfaces that communicate with users using multiple media, sometimes using multiple modes such as written text together with spoken language [May93a].

Multimedia would be without any value if applications did not use the various media at the user interface for input and output. Media determine not only *how* human-computer interaction occurs, but also *how well.* For example, to boot the first computers, the user had to enter a range of addresses through register switches and commands at a mainframe console. Punch cards were used for input and paper was the main form of output. *Text* was the only medium for interaction with terminals. Later, applications were controlled through text menus, which simplified user input. Nevertheless, the user had to adjust to the computer.

*Graphical user interfaces* – using the mouse as the main input device – have greatly simplified human-machine interaction. A large number of graphical commands are hidden to the users through the use of a *Window System* (e.g., *Presentation Manager*™, *GEM, NeWS, MS-Windows* or the *X Window System*™). There are also other software programs which achieve similar user interfaces as an X Window System. The computer has been adapted – at least in part – to the user.

Despite these advances, there are still many well known problems with current user interfaces. One problem is *computer interaction* which is still neither natural nor effective. Speaking is often more suitable for the situation than writing. Changes and commentaries can be made verbally, which is more effective (i.e., faster) than making changes and comments in electronic text. Reading and listening are not alternatives to each other; they complement one another (e.g., audio textbooks).

Another problem is the *specification of object movement.* A specification of movements using graphics or text is often much more difficult and complicated than using a motion video. For example, consider an electronic textbook about tennis. The individual movements and typical errors can be presented much more easily using motion video than graphics images, or even text alone.

The development goes toward more effective human-computer interfaces using new interactive devices, which is an area of research in the field of *virtual reality.* The goal is to provide interactive devices such as *data gloves and body suits* for input, and *holography, head-mounted displays and three-dimensional sound device* for output. These devices help to move objects in a 3D space.

## 14.1 General Design Issues

The main emphasis in the design of multimedia user interfaces is *multimedia presentation.* There are several issues which must be considered:

1. To determine the appropriate information content to be communicated.

2. To represent the essential characteristics of the information.

3. To represent the communicative intent.

4. To chose the proper media for information presentation.

5. To coordinate different media and assembling techniques within a presentation.

6. To provide interactive exploration of the information presented.

The objective of the multimedia presentation system should be the *appropriateness principle* [Nor91]: "The surface representation used by the artifact should allow the person to work with exactlv the information acceptable to the task: neither more nor less."

### 14.1.1 Architectural Issues

An effective presentation design process should not only involve sequential flow of actions, but also parallel and interactive actions [SF91]. This means that there is a requirement for extensive feedback going on between the components making decisions about media and modalities. Additionally, the design includes a number of higher-level concerns, such as goals and focus of the dialogue, the user's context and current task, and media selection to represent this information in a way that corresponds to these concerns. A conceptual architecture with a knowledge base (lower part of the figure), used by an intelligent multimedia presentation system (upper part of the figure - both parts are separated by the black arrow), is shown in Figure 14.1 [RH93].

### 14.1.2 Information Characteristics for Presentation

A complete set of information characteristics makes knowledge definition and representation easier because it allows for appropriate mapping between information and presentation techniques. The information characteristics specify:

- *Types*

  Characterization schemes are based on *ordering information.* There are two types of ordered data: (1) *coordinates versus amount*, which signify points in time, space or other domains; or (2) *intervals versus ratio*, which suggests the types of comparisons meaningful among elements of coordinate and amount data types.

- *Relational Structures*

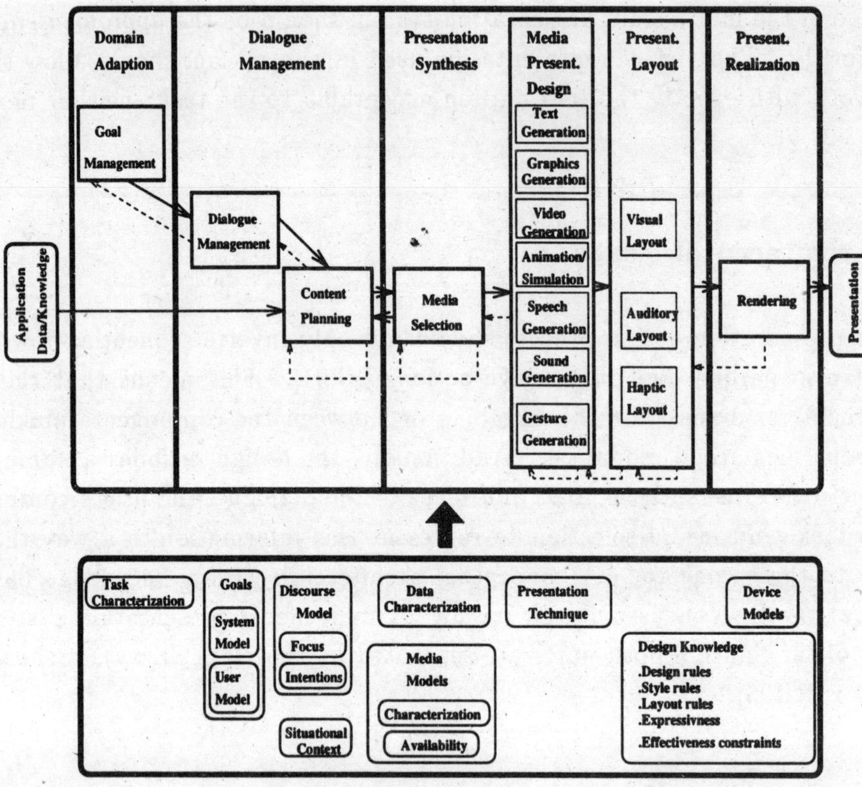


Figure 14.1: *Conceptual architecture of a multimedia presentation system [RH93].*

This group of characteristics refers to the way in which a relation maps among its domain sets (dependency). There are *functional dependencies* and *non-functional dependencies.* An example of a relational structure which expresses functional dependency is a *bar chart.* An example of a relational structure which expresses non-functional dependency is a student entry in a relational database.

- *Multi-domain Relations*

  Relations can be considered across multiple domains, such as: (1) *multiple attributes* of a single object set (e.g., positions, colors, shapes, and/or sizes of a set of objects in a chart); (2) *multiple object sets* (e.g., a cluster of text and graphical symbols on a map); and, (3) *multiple displays.*

- *Large Data Sets*

  Large data sets refer to numerous attributes of collections of heterogeneous objects (e.g., presentations of semantic networks, databases with numerous object types and attributes of technical documents for large systems, etc.).

### 14.1.3 Presentation Function

Presentation function is a program which displays an object (e.g., *printf* for display of a character). It is important to specify the *presentation function* independent from presentation form, style or the information it conveys. Several approaches consider the presentation function from different points of view. For example, one approach views the presentation function as a set of information-seeking goals [RM91], another approach considers it as a hierarchical representation of media-independent presentation goals derived from a plan-based theory of communication [May93b].

### 14.1.4 Presentation Design Knowledge

To design a presentation, issues like *content selection*, *media and presentation technique selection* and *presentation coordination* must be considered.

*Content selection* is the key to convey the information to the user. However, we are not free in the selection of the it because content can be influenced by constraints imposed by the size and complexity of the presentation, the quantity of information, limitations of the display hardware, and the need for presentation completeness and coherence.

*Media selection* determines partly the information characteristics described earlier. For *selecting presentation techniques*, rules can be used. For example, rules for selection methods, i.e., for supporting a user's ability to locate one of the facts in a presentation, may specify a preference for graphical techniques. Media must be chosen to be "adequate". For example, to present a course on how to play tennis, graphics and video are more suitable than text only. On the other hand, it may not be of great help to receive all electronic mail as audio data only because the receiver has very few opportunities to scan over the content; he/she must listen to most of the received information.

*Coordination* can be viewed as a process of composition. Coordination needs mechanisms such as : (1) encoding techniques (e.g., among graphical attributes, sentence forms, audio attributes, or between media); (2) presentation objects that represent facts (e.g., coordination of the spatial and temporal arrangement of points in a chart); and, (3) multiple displays (e.g., windows). Coordination of multimedia employs a set of composition operators for merging, aligning and synthesizing different objects to construct displays that convey multiple attributes of one or more data sets. For example, the user interface shown in Figure 14.2 results from the composition of objects with attributes such as color, position, size and medium specification (text, graphics, image) (user interface taken from the NCSA Mosaic tool).

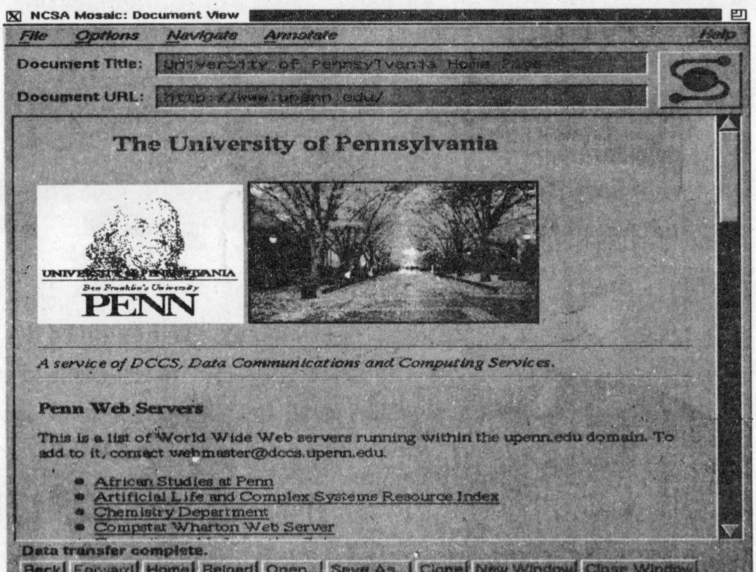


Figure 14.2: *User interface of University of Pennsylvania's Mosaic home page illustrating a result of coordination.*

### 14.1.5 Effective Human-Computer Interaction

One of the most important issues regarding multimedia interfaces is effective human-computer interaction of the interface, i.e., *user-friendliness.* We will discuss this property in detail in Section 14.6.

Here, we will just briefly enumerate the main issues the user interface designer should keep in mind: (1) *context*; (2) *linkage to the world* beyond the presentation display; (3) *evaluation of the interface* with respect to other human-computer interfaces; (4) *interactive capabilities*; and (5), *separability* of the user interface from the application.

## 14.2 Current Work

Although the topic of generating a user interface with several media is crucial for the success of multimedia systems and applications, there is still a lack of serious attention given to this issue. The current literature tends to be either very abstract or problem-specific.

A primary source of information is the *SIGCHI (ACM Special Interest Group for Computer-Human Interaction)* and the annual *Human Factors Society Conference.* A good overview for generating graphical interfaces is given in [FWC84], discussing matters such as classification of the interactions and classification of the actions performed. A joint work in the area of intelligent multimedia interfaces is presented in [May93a]. Issues discussed include presentation design, the communicative act of multi-sentential text in multimedia presentations and a presentation planner that composes different media together at the user interface.

Some authors worked on partial problems in user interfaces such as color mapping [Mur84], the size and position of windows among each other [Gai85, Gai86] and the use of icons in alternative window systems [Mye84]. Other authors consider input interface problems to provide the ability to interpret typed or spoken natural language utterances together with deictic mouse or data-glove gestures to resolve ambiguous references (e.g., "put that there") [NTDS89]. The most work to integrate video and audio at the input interface is done for hypertext/hypermedia applications (for early work see [Fri87, Hyp88, MDR90, Sch87]). Further, relevant work on user interfaces exists at the MIT Media Lab [Bra87].

For output media, the majority of research concentrates on automated generation of single output media. Progress has been made in *graphical design* (e.g., the design of tables and charts [Mac86], network diagrams [Mar91b, Mar91c], business graphics displays [RMM91], three-dimensional explanatory graphics [Fei85]), *linguistic realization* and *text planning*. Temporal media (e.g., animation and speech) and temporal information associated with events (e.g., points in time, duration, ordering relations) are done in the COMET project, using Allen's temporal logic to construct temporal plans [FM93].

Several projects provide problem-specific solutions to design of multimedia presentation systems, such as:

- *WIP* is a multimodal presentation system which presents and understands combinations of graphics, text and pointing gestures, and generates illustrated instructions for technical devices (e.g., it can generate visual instructions on how to operate an espresso machine) [AFG+93]. It can be part of a system which automatically generates multimodal and illustrated documents.

- *COMET (Columbia Operations and Maintenance Explanation Testbed)* automatically designs integrated textual and three dimensional graphical presentations to explain the operation and maintenance of an army field radio [FM93].

- *TEXTPLAN (Textual EXplanation PLanner)* provides narrated, animated directions over an object-oriented map using a collection of multimedia actions (e.g., speech acts, graphical acts) for media integration and control [May93b].

- *AIMI (An Intelligent Multimedia Interface)* has a goal to develop a portable intelligent multimedia/multimodal interface [BM93]. *Portable* means that much of the system processing is independent of any particular back-end system. With this functionality, AIMI can be connected to a new back-end with minimum effort. AIMI reasons in detail about the meaning of user input, using a number of AI (Artificial Intelligence) approaches. Similarly, when presenting information to the user, the system is able to intelligently choose among the presentation alternatives available to it and then design the most appropriate presentation. Currently, AIMI includes natural language, maps, mouse gestures, business charts, specialized interactive inspectors, still images and non-speech audio.

## 14.3 Extension through Video and Audio

Continuous stream audio and video play a significant role in multimedia. The main issue during the presentation of continuous media streams is the continuity in *time*. Hence, time is a new presentation dimension in a user interface. Figure 14.3 shows multimedia at the user interface taking time into account.

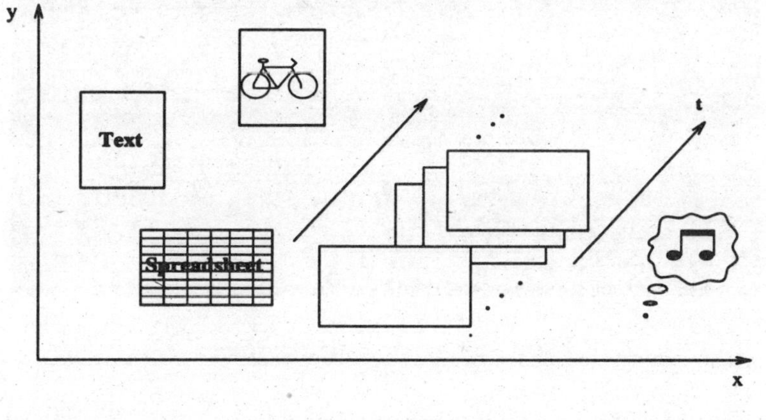


Figure 14.3: *Multimedia at the user interface with the presentation dimension "time".*

An illusion of a *continuity* by the user is created through the presentation of a sequence of static elements In the case of audio, the continuity of data is achieved through reconstruction of an analog signal.

## 14.4 Video at the User Interface

A continuous sequence of, at least, 15 individual images per second gives a rough perception of a continuous motion picture. At the user interface, video is implemented through a continuous sequence of individual images. Hence, video can be manipulated at this interface similar to manipulation of individual still images. An example of a user interface for manipulating images is the software package *xv*, developed by John Bradley of the GRASP Laboratory at the University of Pennsylvania (shown in Figure 14.4).

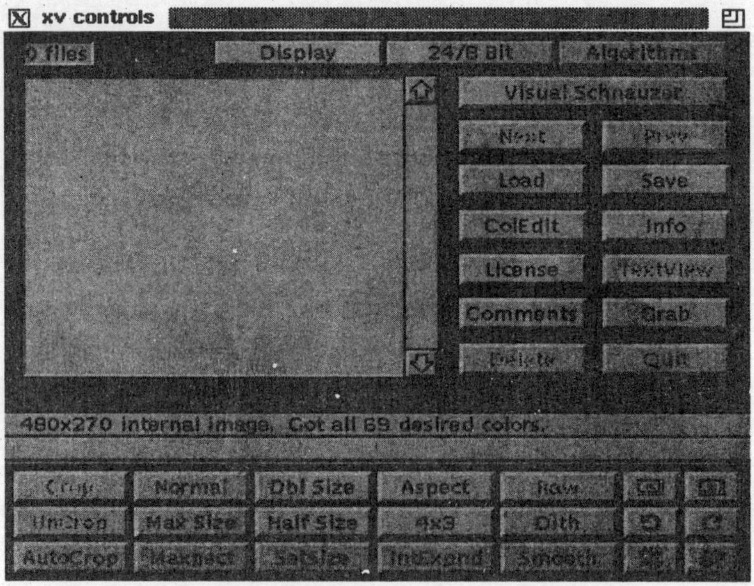


Figure 14.4: *xv user interface.*

When an individual image consisting of pixels (no graphics, consisting of defined objects) can be presented and modified, this should also be possible for video (e.g., to create special effects in a movie). However, the functionalities for video are not as simple to deliver because the high data transfer rate necessary is not guaranteed by most of the hardware in current graphics systems. Also, window systems (software) as the main graphical user interface are a limiting factor. Usually, there can be one to at most four video windows with a quality of 25-30 images per second presented simultaneously because the service of a video window obeys the same rules as any other window.

### 14.4.1 Hardware for Visualization of Motion Pictures

Special hardware for visualization of motion pictures is available today, mostly through additional video cards. Early examples of such additional hardware are IBM-M-Motion and ActionMedia II (Intel/IBM) cards, and the Parallax, Sun and RasterOps cards. Today, these cards have become an integral part of the multimedia system.

Most motion video components integrated in a window system use the chroma-key methods where an application generates a video window with a certain color. Traditionally, this color is a certain blue (coming from a video technique used in the TV). The window system handles, in general, the video window as a monochrome pixel graphic window, but on the device level, there is a switch which allows for the selection of the display between the standard graphics and motion video. This switch usually brings the standard graphics to the screen. If the hardware switch detects motion video, such a video window presents the video signal taken directly from a camera. Using a communication-capable multimedia system, this camera can be controlled remotely. The video data may be transmitted from the camera into a computer network and then displayed.

### 14.4.2 Example: Remote Camera Control Application

Remote camera control is used, for example, in surveillance applications. Another example is a microscope, remotly controlled in a telesurgery environment. We discuss below an application in which an engineer remotely controls a CIM-completion process with the help of a remote-control video camera [WSS94].

### Application Specification

The camera is connected to a computer which serves as a *camera server* through a standardized analog interface. The camera control occurs, for example, through a serial RS-232-C interface. The camera-server sends commands such as *focus*, *zoom* and *position* to the camera through this serial interface. The actual control of the camera is initiated by the camera-client, which can be located remotely. In addition to the data path for camera control, there is also a video data path, i.e., the video data are digitized, compressed and sent by the camera-server to the camera-client where the engineer is located. The video image taken from the camera is displayed.

### User Interface

The simplest decision would have been, in this case, to use the *keyboard*. Fixed control functions could be assigned to individual keys. For example, the keys *left, right, up* and *down* would move the camera in the corresponding directions.

In a window system, individual *buttons* can be programmed to position a camera. In addition to the directions *left, right, up*, and down, other directions, such as *left up* and *left down*, can be specified through other buttons. Pushing the button initiates the positioning process. The particular movement is stopped explicitly with the *stop* button. Another possibility to position a camera is by the pushing and releasing of a button, i.e., continuous movement of the camera follows through several consecutive "push" and "release" button actions.

Instead of using *buttons* in a window system, positioning in different axes can also be done through *scrollbars*. To activate the different graphical elements, a *touch-screen* can be used instead of mouse. A finger or pen can activate the user interface elements. A more natural, simpler, form of camera control could be implemented with a *joystick*. The movement of the joystick is translated into a camera position. Here, additional hardware for support of the joystick is necessary. Another possibility is a *data glove*, and graphical simulation of the camera views and the production line. The movement of the data glove is translated into the camera position in the graphical simulation; if the camera position in the simulated (virtual) environment is correct, it is sent to the camera-server, which moves camera in the real environment.

Note that *graphical simulations* as user interfaces for controlling teleoperation are preferred. The user sees movements in the *virtual environment.* If the movement is correct, the position and possibly other information are transmitted to the real remote site. The input devices to the graphical simulations are mice or data gloves.

### Direct Manipulation of the Video Window

In our setup we decided to use a very user-friendly variant known as direct manipulation of the video window [SS94]. There are two possibilities:

1. *Absolute Positioning*

   Imagine a tree in the upper right corner of the video window. The user positions the cursor on this object and *double-clicks* with the mouse. Now, the camera will be positioned so that the tree is the center of the video window, i.e., the camera moves in the direction of the upper right corner. This method of object pointing and activating a movement of camera is called *absolute positioning.* The camera control algorithm must derive the position command from: (1) the relative position of the pointer during the object activation in the video window; and, (2) the specified focal distance.

2. *Relative Positioning*

   Imagine the pointer to the right of the center of the video window. By pushing the mouse button, the camera moves to the right. The relative position of the pointer with respect to the center of the video window determines the direction of the camera movement. When the mouse button is released, the camera movement stops. This kind of direct manipulation in the video window is called *relative positioning.* A camera can move at different speeds. A speed can be specified through the user interface as follows:

   - If the mouse has several buttons, different speeds can be assigned to each button. For example, the left mouse button could responsible for slow, accurate motion (e.g., for calibration of the camera). The right buttons could be for fast movement of the camera.

- Instead of working with several mouse buttons, the distance of the pointer to the window center could determine the speed; the larger the distance, the faster the movement of the camera.

From the viewpoint of user-friendliness, the best method of camera control is direct manipulation of the video window. More specific, the relative positioning with speed specification, using the distance of the pointer to the window center, is the preferred solution.

## 14.5 Audio at the User Interface

*Audio* can be implemented at the user interface for application control. Thus, speech analysis is necessary.

Speech analysis is either speaker-dependent or speaker-independent. *Speaker-dependent* solutions allow the input of approximately 25,000 different words with a relatively low error rate. Here, an intensive learning phase to train the speech analysis system for speaker-specific characteristics is necessary prior to the speech analysis phase. A *speaker-independent* system can recognize only a limited set of words and no training phase is needed.

During audio output, the additional presentation dimension of *space* can be introduced using two or more separate channels to give a more natural distribution of sound. The best-known example of this technique is *stereo*. Further developments include the mono-subwoofer channel and quadraphony. In the case of stereo, spatial positions are assigned to audio sources.

For example, during a conference with four participants, a fixed place is assigned to each participant. The motion video of participant $L$ is displayed in the upper left corner of the screen. The corresponding sound of this participant is transmitted only through the left speaker. Participant $M$ is visually and acoustically located in the middle. Participant $R$ is positioned to the right. In this example, the conference system always activates the video window with the loudest-speaking participant. The recognition of the loudest acoustic signal can be measured over a duration of five seconds. Therefore, short, unwanted and loud signals can be compensated for. In the active video window, the video is displayed with 25 frames per second. Motion video is displayed only in one video window at one time because of technical reasons. In the video windows of the other (quieter) participants, the last image of the motion video sequence, when they were active, is displayed.

In the case of *monophony*, all audio sources have the same spatial location. A listener can only properly understand the loudest audio signal. The same effect can be simulated by closing one ear. Stereophony allows listeners with bilateral hearing capabilities to hear lower intensity sounds. It is important to mention that the main advantage of bilateral hearing is not the spatial localization of audio sources, but the extraction of less intensive signals in a loud environment.

In a window system, it is possible for a user to position a window on the screen. In [LPC90], this paradigm was applied to medium audio as follows. The sound application opens different audio sources using location identification (e.g., source to the right or left). To each audio source there is assigned an *audio window* which appears on the screen at the location specified (e.g., right or left). The location of the source can be changed by moving the audio window. The number of audio windows is limited. First experiences have shown that a maximum of two audio windows can be opened at the same time. As an extension of this approach, an audio window can offer the user control over the relative volume and depth.

The concept of the audio window allows for application independent control of audio parameters, including spatial positioning. Most current multimedia applications using *audio* determine the spatial positioning themselves and do not allow the user to change it. An example of such an application is the audio tool for SUN workstations. Figure 14.5 shows the user interface of this audio tool.

## 14.6 User-friendliness as the Primary Goal

*User-friendliness* is the main property of a good user interface. As an example, compare a multimedia-integrated telephone service with an ISDN telephone service. Today's telephones consist of a large number of touch keys, each sometimes representing three different functions. It is not an easy task to operate such a telephone.

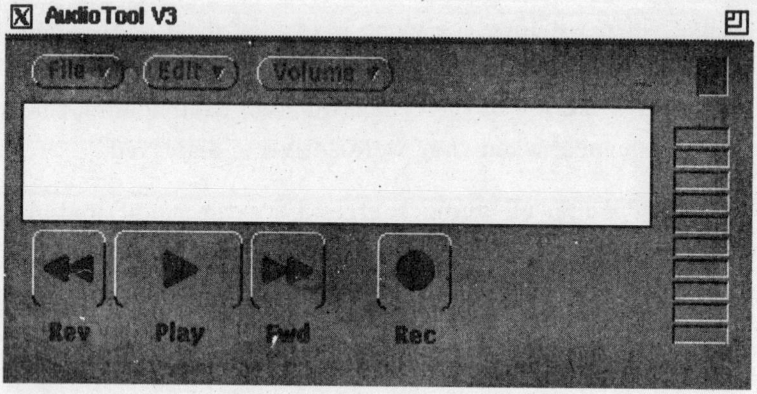


Figure 14.5: *Audio tool user interface.*

Indeed, given sporadic user the user may forget many of these functions. However, with a multimedia-integrated telephone, some of the disadvantages of the current ISDN telephone user interface can be eliminated through use of multimedia data, e.g., through display of some multimedia information on the screen [SG88]. The goal is implementation of a user-friendly human-computer interface.

*What* this user-friendliness means and *how* this property is achieved are not always clear. The design of a user-friendly graphical interface requires the consideration of many conditions. The addition of audio and video to the user interface does not simplify this process. In this section, a number of generally applicable criteria for multimedia user interfaces is presented.

We will restrict the discussion of user-friendliness to multimedia systems in the office or home. The reason is that different applications have different user-friendliness requirements. For example, in the case of a car phone, speech recognition is one important requirement of user-friendliness. By speaking a person's name, that person is called. Loud noise caused by a car, together with reflected sound waves, put higher requirements on this technique.

### 14.6.1 Easy to Learn Instructions

Application instructions must be easy-to-learn. The older dial phones required no time to learn. A simple touch phone, with a few additional buttons, requires at most 10 minutes to master. An ISDN telephone, unfortunately, often requires more than 20 minutes. A telephone application should require at most 10 minutes to understand its main functions. This is achieved through the homogeneous interfaces of different applications provided by a window system. A multimedia application must support similar mechanisms which are known to the user from other applications.

### 14.6.2 Context-sensitive Help Functions

A context-sensitive help function using hypermedia techniques is very helpful, i.e., according to the state of the application, different help-texts are displayed. For example, after selecting the *call re-routing* function, the help function provides a brief explanation of call re-routing.

### 14.6.3 Easy to Remember Instructions

A user-friendly interface must also have the property that the user easily remembers the application instruction rules. Easily remembered instructions might be supported by the intuitive association to what the user already knows. For example, the user knows the phone book (register). Hence, the user interface of a telephone service, implemented in a multimedia system, can show the participant a list on the screen. The user can simultaneously select and call another user through a double-click of the button. With a simple click in a window system, generally, an element is highlighted. The data of the selected callee can be displayed and, if necessary, changed, or additional data can be appended. The designer of such a user interface must put him/herself in the user's situation. Thus, different user-classes need to be considered. In addition to both sporadic and everyday users, there are also users in office areas and homes.

### 14.6.4 Effective Instructions

The user interface should enable effective use of the application. This means:

- Logically connected functions should be presented together and similarly. For example, *call re-routing* and *call forwarding* are two such functions of a telephone service; both functions require the input of a phone number.

- Graphical symbols or short video clips are more effective than textual input and output. They trigger faster recognition. For example, the notions trash and short cuts can be replaced by symbols; people can be identified by their pictures, as well as by their names.

- Different media should be able to be exchanged among different applications. For example, the same address book is used for facsimile, telex, teletex and mailing applications. A simple clipboard function is generally insufficient. Hypertext and hypermedia provide good links for such an approach.

- Actions should be activated quickly. For example, in a telephone service the selection of a callee must be very fast. It is possible with the input of the callee's last name or his/her telephone number. This is an alternative to opening the electronic telephone book (list), scrolling the list and then double-clicking.

- A configuration of a user interface should be usable by both professional and sporadic users.

### 14.6.5 Aesthetics

With respect to aesthetics, the color combination, character sets, resolution and form of the window need to be considered. They determine a user's first and lasting impressions.

It is desirable to develop only one application for different users and languages. This is achieved by separating (either in the window system or application) the text, graphics and actual program.

### 14.6.6 Effective Implementation Support

To achieve effective implementation of a user-friendly human-computer graphical interface, the user's requirements must be considered. This influences the cost of the implementation.

An effective implementation of a user-friendly interface can be influenced by the following:

- If the user's requirements are missing, *Rapid Prototyping* should be used. This means that the user-interface is developed, changed and tested without filling in the contents of the actual programs. Object-oriented programming tools are good environments for this approach.
- If window systems are used, the user interface becomes hardware-independent and the development effort is shorter. Also maintenance-friendliness increases if program generators are available, or uniformly accessible programming environments are used.

### 14.6.7 Entry Elements

User interfaces use different ways to specify entries for the user:

- *Entries in a menu*

  In current menus there are visible and non-visible entry elements Entries which are relevant to the particular task are visible. For example, the xv (Figure 14.4) entry *TextView* is not initially displayed because xv is an X-window image/video grabber. However, if the user clicks on *Load*, the current directory files are displayed in the working window. If a text file is then chosen from the directory, *TextView* becomes visible.

- *Entries on a graphical interface*

  - If the interface includes text, the entries can be marked through color and/or a different font (e.g., NCSA Mosaic's blue color and underlined text). Figure 14.2 shows the NCSA Mosaic user interface, displaying a hypertext document, where the entries are underlined. The user clicks the underlined text and a more detailed description appears in the NCSA Mosaic working window.

– If the interface includes images, the entries can be written over the image. An example is an intelligent training system for tutoring technicians to repair computers (Visual Repair [Goo93]). The system presents images of different computer parts, and by clicking on text written over the parts, the help tool accesses information about the parts and the particular operations that can be applied to them.

– If the interface includes images, the functions can be activated through direct positioning of the cursor on the image object. This is done, for example, with city maps or building images. The user clicks on a certain object (street or room) and a new image, audio and/or text describes the object.

### 14.6.8 Meaningful Location of Functions

Individual functions must be placed together in a meaningful fashion. This occurs through (1) alphabetic ordering or (2) logical grouping.

For example, entries in the telephone book are sorted alphabetically, whereas the *call re-routing* and *call forwarding* functions are logically connected, similarly processed and displayed. In the case of a telephone application, using pull-down menus fo certain functions may be critical. If a graphical interface is available, alphabetic order can be used, but the general rule is to provide a balanced interface which is aesthetically satisfying [Gai86].

### 14.6.9 Presentation

The presentation, i.e., the optical image at the user interface, can have the following variants:

- Full text

- Abbreviated text
- Icons, i.e., graphics
- Micons, i.e., motion video

Each possibility has its advantages and disadvantages, often depending on the individual user. For example, the full text (e.g., *Call Waiting*) can be easily understood but not clearly displayed. An abbreviation (e.g., CW for *Call Waiting*) may be obvious to the frequent user, but not to a sporadic user. Icons must have a uniform semantics inside of the window system (e.g., a trash container is associated with a delete function). In the case of micons, the reduced content of the motion picture must be recognizable.

### 14.6.10 Dialogue Boxes

Different dialogue boxes should have a similar construction. This requirement applies to the design of: (1) the buttons *OK* and *Abort*; (2) joined windows; and, (3) other applications in the same window system [Ber88]. Semantically similar entry functions can be located in one dialogue box instead of several dialogue boxes.

It is important to decide how many dialogue boxes should be opened at the same time, how the entry should be visible and how a new requirement can be expressed through an additional box. For example, the *Abort* button in a window should never be positioned in the same location as the *Save* button of the underlying window.

### 14.6.11 Additional Design Criteria

Some additional useful hints for designing a user-friendly interface should be mentioned:

- The form of the *cursor* can change to visualize the current state of the system. For example, a rotating fish instead of a static pointer shows that a task is in progress.

- If *time intensive tasks* are performed, the progress of the task should be presented. For example, during the formatting of a disk, the amount formatted is displayed through a filling bar; during the remote retrieval of a file, the number of transmitted bytes in relation to the whole size of the file is presented. (In NCSA Mosaic, where large image and sound files are transmitted from the servers to the client, this is an useful display.) This display allows the user to evaluate the state of the task and react to it, i.e., let the task continue or cancel it. Thus, the *Abort* function to cancel the activity should always be present during a time-intensive task.
- A *selected entry* should be immediately highlighted as "work in progress" before performance actually starts. This approach ensures that no further input is given to the entry.

### 14.6.12 Design-specific Criteria

In addition to the above described general criteria for the design of a user interface, the problem specific properties of the actual task need to be considered. These properties are demonstrated in our telephone service example.

The telephone network and telephone-specific end-devices are provided by the telephone companies. They specify the user interface characteristics:

1. The end-device must have the *basic function* of dialing a number. The requirement may be that the dialing is performed using keys and that there is an alphanumeric, single-line display. This requirement provides *compatibility* among different phone devices.

   In a multimedia system, dialing with keys can be programmed, but it is not very meaningful; the main advantages of the different media are unused. To provide compatibility, a key set with corresponding user procedures should be emulated.

2. *Ongoing tasks* should be signaled. For example, if the call re-routing function is activated, this function should be signaled optically on the device. In the case of a telephone (computer) application, its state does not have to be

displayed on the whole screen. A *telephone icon* can be used if no window is opened, but the application is still active.

3. A telephone device must always be *operational*. This requirement influences the corresponding hardware and software.

   If a telephone service is implemented on PCs as a multimedia application, these devices are not always meant to be operational for 24 hours. It also cannot easily become operational when a call arrives. The simplest solution is external storage of the telephone hardware which is operational without the PC being turned on. In the context of communication-capable workstations, a solution that activates the computer through external events (e.g., arriving call) is best. The hard disk can then also serve as the voice storage. When the PC boots, the telephone application must be loaded, i.e., become operational.

4. The *state* of the telephone-device (i.e., telephone application) must be always visible.

   While working with the telephone application, it gets into different *states*. In different states different functions are performed. Some states imply that a function can be selected, some states imply that a function cannot be selected.

   The nonselective functions can be:

   - *Nonexistent*: The function disappears when no activation is possible.
   - *Displayed*: The function is displayed, but marked as deactivated and any interaction is ignored; for example, deactivated menu functions are displayed in gray, the active functions are displayed in black.
   - *Overlapped*: If a function is overlapped with another window which is designed as the *confirmer*, this function cannot be selected. First, after closing the confirmer, other input can be taken.

   It is important to point out that the functions most often used are always visible in the form of a *control panel*. It is necessary to pick carefully which functions will belong in the control panel.

5. When a call request arrives, it must be immediately signaled (e.g., ringing).

For a telephone application on a workstation, the window system provides a preemptive scheduling algorithm. Each process of the window system must be able to interrupt after a certain time span, independent of the task currently being performed. Therefore, arriving calls can be signaled promptly. An intermediate solution can be achieved if the arrival of the call is signaled acoustically by the telephone hardware or at the low system interrupt level. After arrival of the call is signaled, the user can interrupt his/her tasks and activate the telephone application.

Design of a user interface is also influenced by a specific implementation environment. For example, in addition to the primitives of the particular window system, the quality of the graphical terminal with its resolution, size and color-map is important.

## 14.7 Comments

We have discussed in this chapter several issues regarding multimedia user interfaces. The main emphasis has been on video and audio media because they represent *live information.* At the user interface, these media become important because they help users learn by enabling them to choose how to distribute research responsibilities among applications (e.g., on-line encyclopedias, tutors, simulations), to compose and integrate results and to share learned material with colleagues (e.g., video conferencing). Additionally, computer applications can effectively do less reasoning about selection of a multimedia element (e.g., text, graphics, animation or sound) since alternative media can be selected by the user.

Another important issue, that of user-friendly interfaces, was also discussed. This property is crucial, especially with multimedia. Different media provide many possibilities and opportunities to express functionalities at the human-computer interface, but if not implemented correctly, can also lead to confusion and problems.

# Chapter 15

# Synchronization

## 15.1 Introduction

Advanced multimedia systems are characterized by the integrated computer-controlled generation, storage, communication, manipulation and presentation of independent time-dependent and time-independent media [Ste93b, HS91]. The key issue which provides integration is the digital representation of any data and the synchronization of and between various kinds of media and data.

The word synchronization refers to time. *Synchronization* in multimedia systems refers to the temporal relations between media objects in the multimedia system. In a more general and widely used sense some authors use synchronization in multimedia systems as comprising content, spatial and temporal relations between media objects. We differentiate between time-dependent and time-independent media objects. A time-dependent media object is presented as a media stream. Temporal relations between consecutive units of the media stream exist. If the presentation durations of all units of a *time-dependent media object* are equal, it is called *continuous media object.* A video consists of a number of ordered frames; each of these frames has a fixed presentation duration. A *time-independent media object* is any kind of traditional media like text and images. The semantic of the respective content does not depend upon a presentation according to the time domain.

Synchronization between media objects comprises relations between time-dependent media objects and time-independent media objects. A daily example of synchronization between continuous media is the synchronization between the visual and acoustical information in television. In a multimedia system, the similar synchronization must be provided for audio and moving pictures. An example of temporal relations between time-dependent media and time-independent media is a slide show. The presentation of slides is synchronized with the commenting audio stream. To realize a slide show in a multimedia system, the presentation of graphics has to be synchronized with the appropriate units of an audio stream.

Synchronization is addressed and supported by many system components including the operating system, communication system, databases, documents and even often by applications. Hence, synchronization must be considered at several levels in a multimedia system.

The operating system and lower communication layers handle single media streams with the objective to avoid jitter at the presentation of the units of one media stream (e.g., [NS95c, DHH94, PZF94, OT93]). For example, users will be annoyed if an audio presentation is interrupted by pauses or if clicks result in short gaps in the presentation of the audio clip.

On top of this level is the run-time support for the synchronization of multiple media streams is located (e.g., [AH91b, CGCH92, AC91, IBM92b]). The objective at this level is to maintain the temporal relations between various streams. In particular the skew between the streams must be restricted. For example, users will be annoyed if they notice that the movement of the lips of a speaker does not correspond to the presented audio

The next level holds the run-time support for the synchronization between time-dependent and time-independent media together with the handling of user interactions (e.g., [MHE93, Bla92, KG89, Lit93]). The objective is to start and stop the presentation of the time-independent media within a tolerable time interval, if some previously defined points of the presentation of a time-dependent media object are reached. The audience of a slide show is annoyed if a slide is presented before the audio comment introduces a new picture. A short delay after the start of the introducing comment is tolerable or even useful.

The *temporal relations* between the media objects must be specified. The relations may be specified implicitly during capturing of the media objects, if the goal of a presentation is to present the media in the same way as they were originally captured. This is the case of audio/video recording and playback.

The temporal relations may also be specified explicitly in the case of presentations that are composed of independently captured or otherwise created media objects (e.g., [BHLM92, BZ93b, IBM90]). In the slide show example, a presentation designer selects the appropriate slides, creates an audio object and defines the units of the audio presentation stream where the slides have to be presented. Also, the user interactivity may be part of a presentation and the temporal relations between media objects and user interactions must be specified. The tools that are used to specify the temporal relations are located on top of the previous levels.

In recent years, in nearly every multimedia workshop and conference, many synchronization-related contributions have been provided. Most of the contributions address only issues of one or a subset of the levels or regard synchronization only from a specific viewpoint and they are partly overlapping.

The objective of this chapter is to provide an integral view to the area of multimedia synchronization. Therefore, we focus on a consistent definition of synchronization-related terms, synchronization requirements, the synchronization specification, synchronization between media objects and the synchronization related to structuring of multimedia systems. An emphasis is also put on the synchronization in a distributed environment that introduces additional complexity but is very important regarding client/server architectures and future teleservices like access to information bases using an information highway.

Descriptions of low-level technical support for media synchronization, like EDF (Earliest Deadline First) or rate monotonic scheduling in the operating system, isochronous transport services and support for single media streams, are not part of this chapter.

In Section 15.2, the basic terms of synchronization are defined. Subsequently, in Section 15.3, the requirements for synchronization resulting from user perception of multimedia presentations are described. A synchronization reference model is presented in Section 15.4 that allows the structuring of the levels of synchronization and the classification of existing synchronization systems. Section 15.5 provides an overview about synchronization specification methods. Some prominent and representative systems are presented and classified according to the synchronization reference model in Section 15.6. A summary and outlook are given in the last section.

## 15.2 Notion of Synchronization

### 15.2.1 Multimedia Systems

Several definitions for the terms multimedia application and multimedia systems are described in the literature. Three criteria for the classification of a system as a multimedia system can be distinguished: the number of media, the types of supported media and the degree of media integration.

The most simple criterion is the number of media used in an application. Using only this criterion, even a document processing application that supports text and graphics can be regarded as a multimedia system [HKN89]. This is not, however, our definition of multimedia (see Chapter 2, Section 2.3).

The types of supported media are an additional criterion [HS91]. In this case, we distinguish between time-dependent and time-independent media. A time-independent media object is usually presented using one presentation unit. An example is a bitmap graphic. Time-dependent media objects are presented by a sequence of presentation units. An example is a motion picture sequence without audio (i.e., a video sequence) presented frame after frame. Because the integration of time-dependent media objects is a new and essential aspect in information processing, some authors define a multimedia system as a system that supports the processing of more than one medium with at least one time-dependent medium [BB91a].

The degree of media integration is the third criterion [HS91]. In this case, integration means that the different types of media remain independent but can be processed and presented together.

Combining all three criteria, we propose the following *definition of a multimedia system*: a system or application that supports the integrated processing of several media types with at least one time-dependent medium.

Figure 15.1 classifies applications according to the three criteria. The arrows indicate the increasing degree of multimedia capability for each criterion.

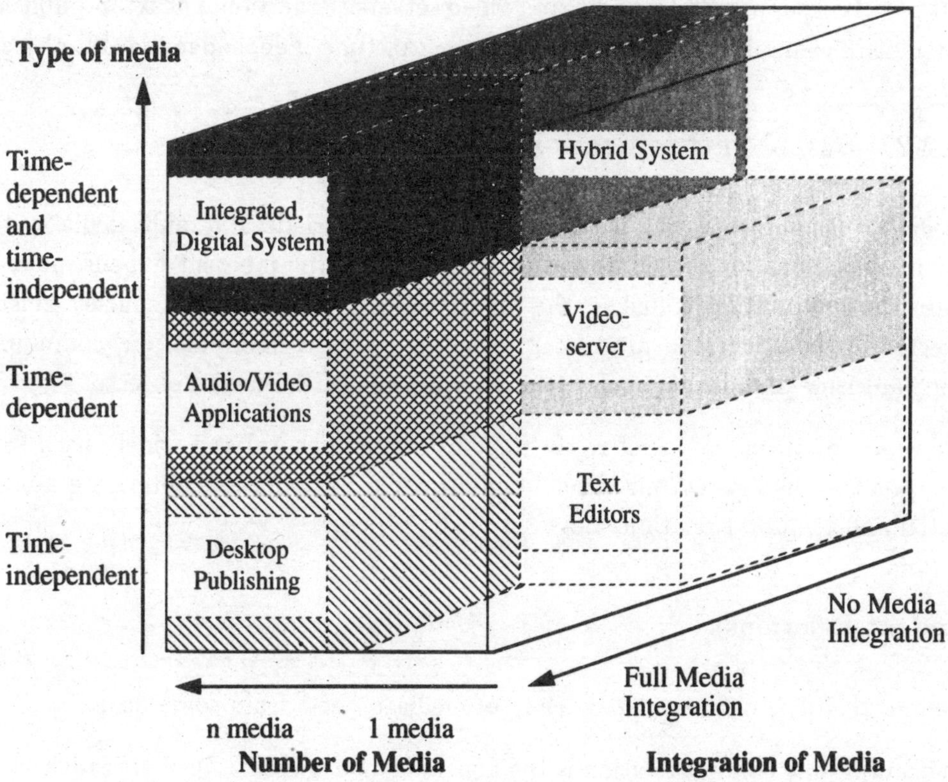


Figure 15.1: *Classification of media use in multimedia systems.*

Integrated digital systems can support all types of media, and due to digital processing, may provide a high degree of media integration. Systems that handle time-dependent analog media objects and time-independent digital media objects are called *hybrid systems* [SSSW89, HSA89]. The disadvantage of hybrid systems is that they are restricted with regard to the integration of time-dependent and time-independent media, because, for example, audio and video are stored on different devices than time-independent media objects and multimedia workstations must comprise both types of devices. The same applies to the interconnection between workstations. Audio/Video-applications that implement functionalities of consumer devices, like video recorders, often do not support the integration of audio and video and time-independent media objects. In addition, they often do not support the separate handling of audio and video media objects. Single time-dependent media objects are often supported by audio and video servers. Traditional desktop-publishing systems are examples of integrated processing of time-independent media objects.

### 15.2.2 Basic Synchronization Issues

Integrated media processing is an important characteristic of a multimedia system. The main reasons for these integration demands are the inherent dependencies between the information coded in the media objects. These dependencies must be reflected in the integrated processing including storage, manipulation, communication, capturing and, in particular, the presentation of the media objects.

The word *synchronization* refers to time. In a more general and widely used sense, some authors use synchronization in multimedia systems as comprising content, spatial and temporal relations between media objects.

#### Content Relations

*Content relations* define a dependency of media objects from some data.

An example of a content relation is the dependency between a filled spreadsheet and a graphic that represents the data listed in the spreadsheet. In this case, the same data are represented in two different ways. Another example is two graphics that are based on the same data but show different interpretations of the data.

For integrated multimedia documents, it is useful to express these relations explicitly to enable an automated update of different views of the same data. In this case, only the data are edited and for the views, the kind of dependencies of the data and the presentation rules are defined. All views of the data are generated automatically and cannot be edited directly. An update of the data triggers an update of the related views. This technique is, for example, used in database systems and may also be used for the different media of a multimedia system.

In general, the implementation of content relations in multimedia systems is based on the use of common data structures or object interfaces that are used to present objects using different media.

### Spatial Relations

The *spatial relations* that are usually known as layout relationships define the space used for the presentation of a media object on an output device at a certain point of time in a multimedia presentation. If the output device is two-dimensional (e.g., monitor or paper), the layout specifies the two-dimensional area to be used.

In desktop-publishing applications, this is usually expressed using *layout frames.* A layout frame is placed and a content is assigned to this frame. The positioning of a layout frame in a document may be fixed to a position in a document, to a position on a page or it may be relative to the positioning of other frames.

The concept of frames can also be used to specify where the presentation units of a time-dependent media object are placed. For example, video frames may be positioned using layout frames. In window-oriented systems, a frame or group of frames may be represented by a window. A window may be resized, moved, iconified, etc. and gives the user additional manipulation freedom to adapt the presentation to the requirements.

Experimental three-dimensional output devices like holographic experiments and three-dimensional projection allow the user to create three-dimensional presentations. In usual window systems, the third dimension is only expressed in terms of overlapping windows. Stereo audio output devices also have layout that defines the positioning of an audio source in a presentation. This is, for example, used in audio and video conferences to give a participant the impression of a seat ordering [LPC90] that is related to the placement of pictures or videos of the other conference participants. This gives the user a more natural communication impression, makes it easier to follow a discussion and therefore, increases the user's acceptance.

**Temporal Relations**

*Temporal relations* define the temporal dependencies between media objects. They are of interest whenever time-dependent media objects exist.

An example of temporal relations is the relation between a video and an audio object that are recorded during a concert. If these objects are presented, the temporal relation during the presentations of the two media objects must correspond to the temporal relation at the recording moment.

These time relations are what we will understand to be synchronization in multimedia systems.

**Comment**

All three types of synchronization relations are important for integrated digital multimedia systems and are meanwhile subject to standardization efforts like MHEG [MHE93] and HyTime [Org92].

Content and spatial relations are well-known from publishing and integrated application systems with databases, spreadsheets, graphical tools and word processing systems. The key aspect in multimedia systems is the temporal relations derived from the integration of time-dependent media objects. Therefore, the rest of this chapter addresses temporal relations only.

### 15.2.3 Intra- and Inter-object Synchronization

We distinguish between time relations within the units of one time-dependent media object itself and time relations between media objects. This separation helps to clarify the mechanisms supporting both types of relations, which are often very different.

- *Intra-object synchronization:* intra-object synchronization refers to the time relation between various presentation units of one time-dependent media object. An example is the time relation between the single frames of a video sequence. For a video with a rate of 25 frames per second, each of the frames must be displayed for 40 ms. Figure 15.2 shows this for a video sequence presenting a bouncing ball.

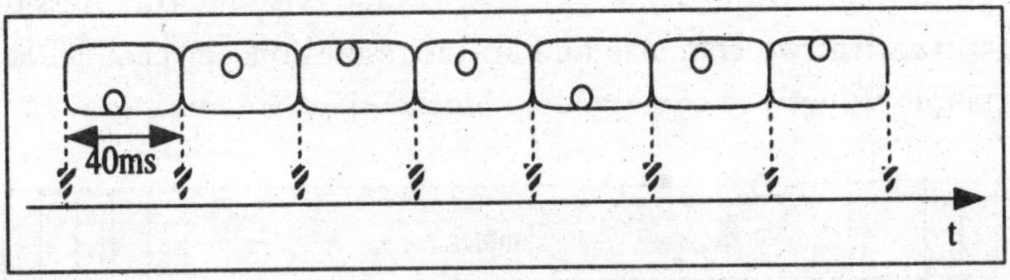


Figure 15.2: *Intra-object synchronization between frames of a video sequence showing a jumping ball.*

- *Inter-object synchronization*: inter-object synchronization refers to the synchronization between media objects. Figure 15.3 shows an example of the time relations of a multimedia synchronization that starts with an audio/video sequence, followed by several pictures and an animation that is commented by an audio sequence.

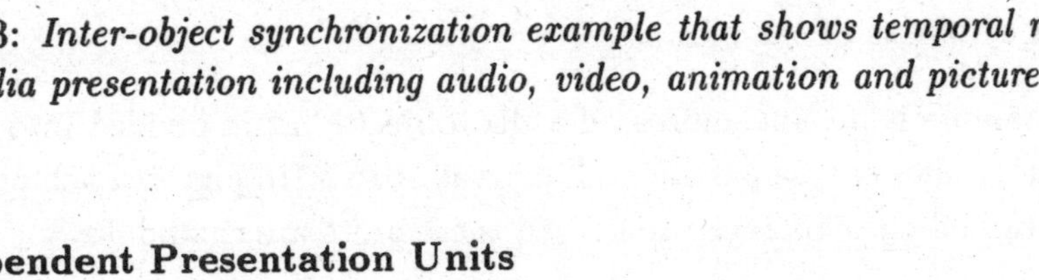


Figure 15.3: *Inter-object synchronization example that shows temporal relations in a multimedia presentation including audio, video, animation and picture objects.*

### Time-dependent Presentation Units

Time-dependent media objects usually consist of a sequence of information units. Such information units are known as *Logical Data Units (LDUs)*.

In many cases, several granularity levels of LDUs in a media object exist. An example is the symphony "The bear" by Joseph Haydn (Figure 15.4). It consists of four movements: vivace assai, allegretto, minuet and finale. Each of these movements is an independent, self-closed part of a composition. It consists of sequences of notes for different instruments. In a digital system, each note is a sequence of sample values. In the case of CD-quality with PCM coding without compression, a sample rate of 44100 Hz with two channels and 16-bit resolution per channel is used. On a CD, these sample values are combined to blocks of 1/75 s duration.

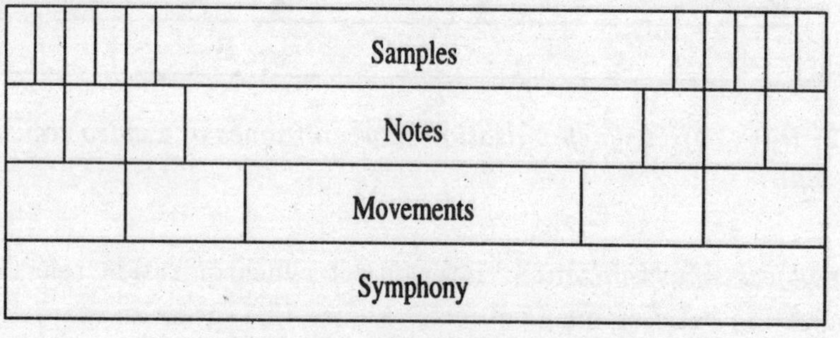


Figure 15.4: *The LDU hierarchy.*

The level of granularity used is application-dependent. It is possible to look at the whole symphony, the movements, the notes, the samples or the combined samples as LDUs. The selection of the LDUs depends on the operations that should be performed on a media object. For simple presentation operations like "play," the whole symphony or the movements are the useful LDUs. For applying instrument-based playing techniques, the notes as smallest description units in the musical area are the useful granularity. For the signal processing task, the operations are based on samples or blocks of samples.

Another example is an uncompressed video object that is divided into scenes and frames. The frames can be partitioned in areas of 16 × 16 pixels. Each pixel consists of luminance and chrominance values. All these units are candidates for LDU units.

In a video sequence coded in the MPEG [ISO93a] format, redundancies within subsequent frames may be used to reduce the amount of digital data used to represent the media object (inter-frame compression). In this case, a sequence of frames that are inter-frame compressed can be regarded as LDU.

The levels of granularity imply a hierarchical decomposition of media objects. Often there are two kinds of hierarchies. The first is a content hierarchy that is implied by the content of the media object. This is the hierarchy of symphony, movement and notes in the symphony example. The second is the coding hierarchy based on the data encoding. For the symphony example, the hierarchy may be a media object representing a movement, that is divided into blocks of samples. The samples are the lowest level of the coding hierarchy.

In addition, LDUs can be classified into closed and open LDUs. *Closed LDUs* have a predictable duration. Examples are LDUs that are parts of stored media objects of continuous media like audio and video, or stored media objects with a fixed duration. The duration of *open LDUs* is not predictable before the execution of the presentation. Open LDUs typically represent input from a live source, for example, a camera or a microphone, or media objects that include a user interaction.

### Classification of Logical Data Units

For digital video, often the frames are selected as LDUs. For example, for a video with 30 pictures per second, each LDU is a closed LDU with a duration of 1/30 s (Figure 15.5).

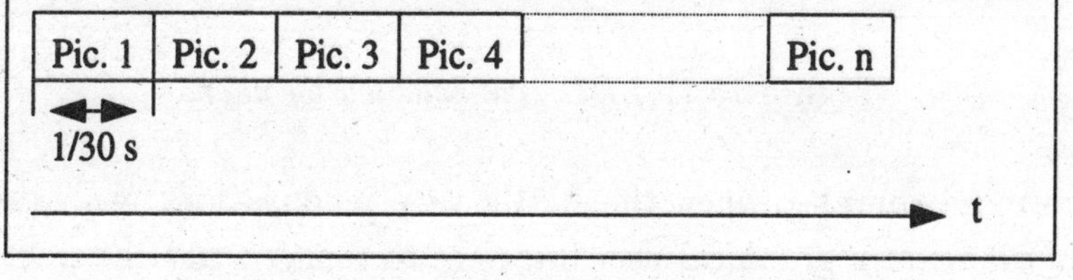


Figure 15.5: *Example of video LDUs.*

In the case of the basic physical unit being too small to handle, often LDUs are selected that block the samples into units of a fixed duration. A typical example is an audio stream where the physical unit duration is very small, therefore, LDUs are formed comprising 512 samples. In the example shown in Figure 15.6, one sample is coded with one Byte, and hence, each block contains 512 Bytes.

Captured media objects usually have a natural basic duration of an LDU. In computer-generated media objects, the duration of LDUs may be selected by the user. An

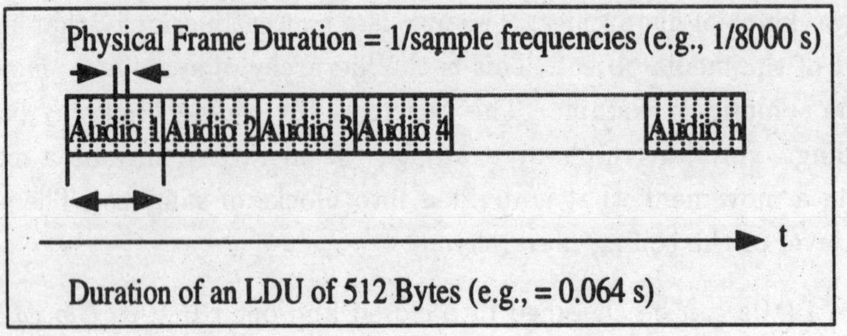


Figure 15.6: *Example of audio LDUs.*

example of these user-defined LDU durations is the frames of an animation sequence. For the presentation of a two-second animation sequence, 30 to 60 pictures may be generated depending on the necessary quality. Thus, the LDU duration depends on the selected picture rate (Figure 15.7).

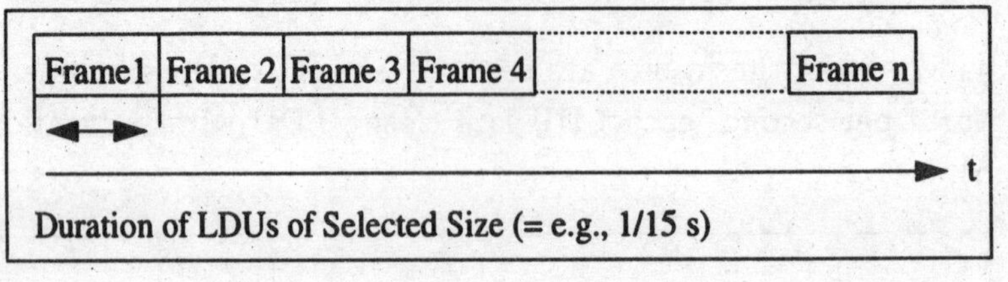


Figure 15.7: *LDU size selected by user.*

Streams are more complex when the LDUs vary in duration. An example is the recording of events at a graphical user interface to replay a user interaction. In this case, an LDU is an event with a duration lasting until the next event. The duration of LDUs depends on the user interaction and varies accordingly (Figure 15.8).

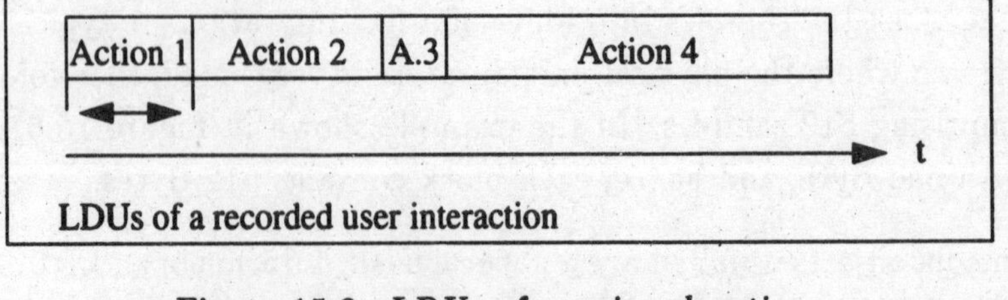


Figure 15.8: *LDUs of varying duration.*

| | LDU Duration Defined During Capturing | LDU Duration Defined by the User |
|---|---|---|
| Fixed LDU Duration | Audio, Video | Animation, Timer |
| Variable, Unknown LDU Duration | Recorded Interaction | User Interaction |

Table 15.1: *Types of LDUs.*

Open LDUs of unpredictable duration are given in the case that the LDU has no inherent duration. An example of an open LDU (i.e., an LDU with no inherent duration) is a user interaction in which the duration of the interaction is not known in advance (Figure 15.9).

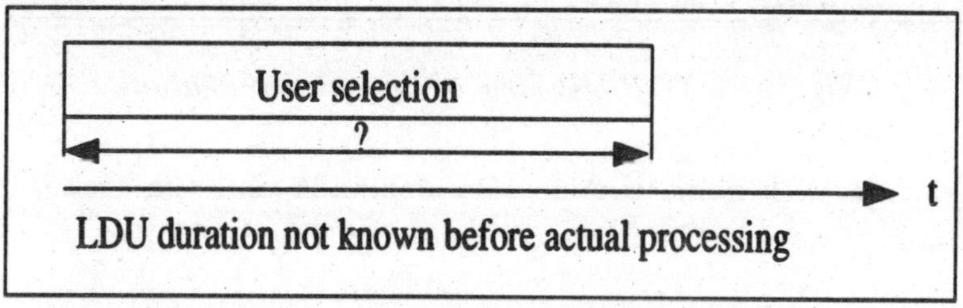


Figure 15.9: *An open LDU representing a user interaction.*

Timers can be regarded as streams of empty LDUs with a fixed duration (Figure 15.10).

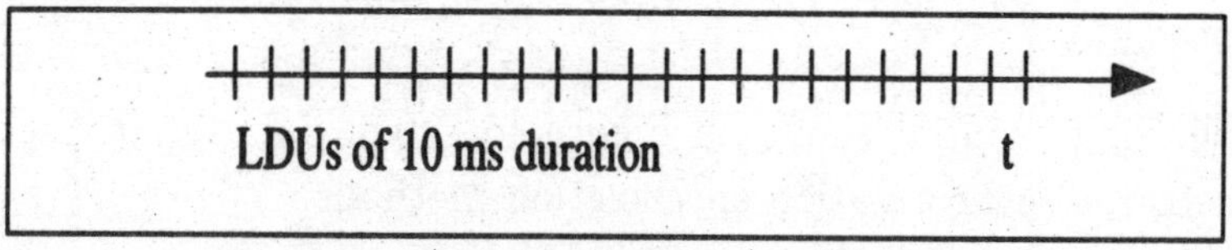


Figure 15.10: *LDUs of a timer.*

Table 15.1 gives an overview of the types of LDUs discussed above.

**Further Examples**

The following three examples show synchronization based on LDUs.

1. Lip synchronization demands tight coupling of audio and video streams. Synchronization can be specified by defining a maximal skew between the two media streams (Figure 15.11).

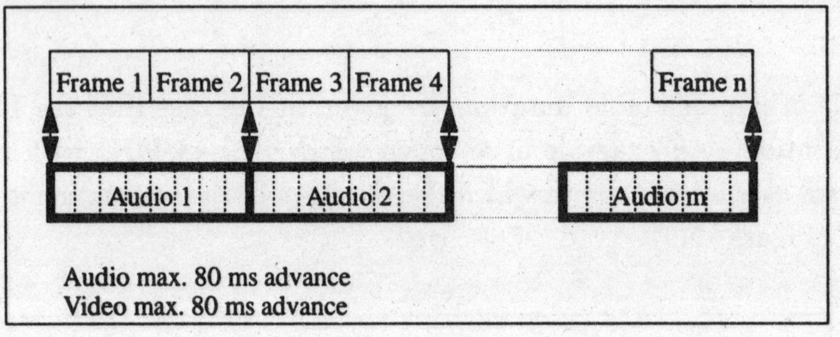


Figure 15.11: *LDU view of lip synchronization.*

2. A slide show with audio commentary demands that the change of slides be temporally related to the audio commentary (Figure 15.12).

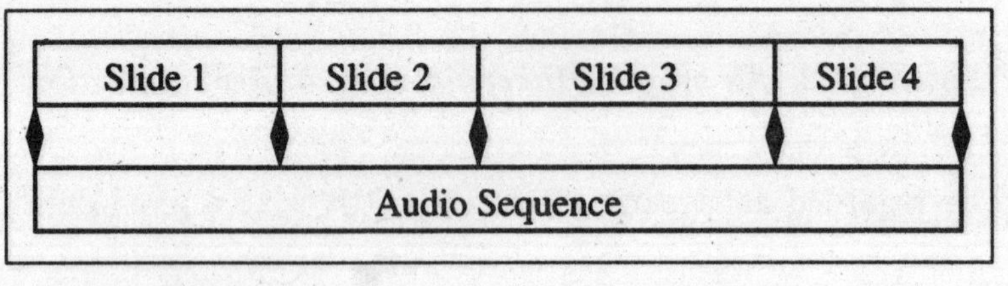


Figure 15.12: *LDU view of a slide show.*

3. The following example shown in Figure 15.13 will be used in Section 15.5 to demonstrate synchronization specification methods.

   A lip synchronized audio/video sequence (Audio1 and Video) is followed by the replay of a recorded user interaction (RI), a slide sequence (P1 - P3) and an animation (Animation), which is partially commented using an audio sequence (Audio2). Starting the animation presentation, a multiple choice question is presented to the user (Interaction). If the user has made a selection, a final picture (P4) is shown.

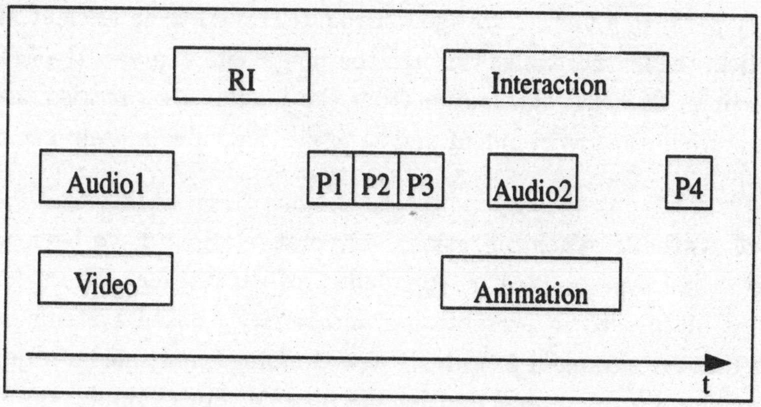


Figure 15.13: *Synchronization example.*

### 15.2.4 Live and Synthetic Synchronization

The live and synthetic synchronization distinction refers to the type of the determination of temporal relations. In the case of live synchronization, the goal of the synchronization is to exactly reproduce at a presentation the temporal relations as they existed during the capturing process. In the case of synthetic synchronization, the temporal relations are artificially specified [LG90b].

The following example shows aspects of *live synchronization*:

Two persons located at different sites of a company discuss a new product. Therefore, they use a video conference application for person-to-person discussion. In addition, they share a blackboard where they can display parts of the product and they can point with their mouse pointers to details of these parts and discuss some issues like: "This part is designed to ..."

This example covers two live synchronization aspects: video conference demands lip synchronization of the audio and video, and the movement of the mouse pointer must be synchronized to the corresponding explanation given in the video conference.

An example of *synthetic synchronization* is a learning environment of a city realized by the Bank Street College of Education, New York [Pre90]:

A learner may perform a virtual voyage (surrogate travel) to an ancient Mayan city. Using a joystick, the learner walks through the jungle and explores the Mayan ruins. At the same time, he hears the sounds from the jungle. He can also take a closer look at the nature in the environment and can "visit" a video museum to get further information.

In the case of synthetic synchronization, temporal relations have been assigned to media objects that were created independently of each other. The synthetic synchronization is often used in presentation and retrieval-based systems with stored data objects that are arranged to provide new combined multimedia objects. A media object may be part of several multimedia objects. For example, the same video clip about Germany may be part of a multimedia object that presents the countries of the European Union, as well as of a multimedia object that presents the countries qualified for the soccer world cup. Media objects of a multimedia object may be stored/located at different servers.

For synthetic synchronization, it is necessary to use a model for the specification and manipulation of temporal synchronization conditions and operations. Common examples [LG90a] of such operations are:

- Presenting media streams in parallel.
- Presenting media streams one after the other (serial).
- Presenting media stream independent of each other.

### Live Synchronization

A typical application of live synchronization is conversational services. In the scope of a source/sink scenario, at the source, volatile data streams (i.e., data being captured from the environment) are created which are presented at the sink (Figure 15.14). The common context of several streams on the source site must be preserved at the sink. The source may be comprised of acoustic and optical sensors, as well as media conversion units. The connection offers a data path between source and sink. The sink presents the units to the user. A source and sink may be located at different sites.

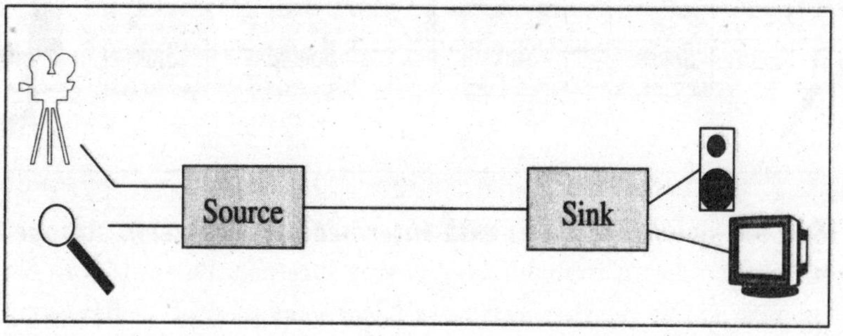


Figure 15.14: *Live synchronization without intermediate long-term storage.*

The goal of synchronization in such a scenario is to reproduce at the sink the signals in the same way as they appeared at the source. A possible manipulation by the sink is to adapt the presentation to the available resources. This may be, for example, a change of resolution or a lower frame rate. To reduce resource usage, it is preferable that such adaptations be already performed at the source, in particular if the source and sink are distributed and connected by a network.

Another type of live synchronization is shown in Figure 15.15 and includes storage which holds the encoded data. The presentation goal is the same as before, but the capturing and presentation are decoupled. In this case, it is possible to manipulate the presentation of the media. The presentation speed may be changed, and random access is possible (which is not possible in the scenario shown in Figure 15.14).

In summary, we must emphasize that the primary demand of live synchronization is to present data according to the temporal relations which existed during the capturing process of the media objects.

### Synthetic Synchronization

The emphasis of synthetic synchronization is to support flexible synchronization relations between media. In synthetic synchronization, two phases can be distin-

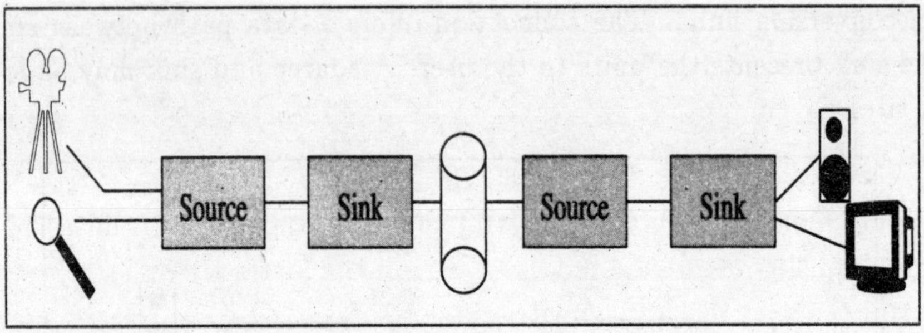


Figure 15.15: *Live synchronization with intermediate long-term storage and delayed presentation.*

guished:

- In the specification phase, temporal relations between the media objects are defined.
- In the presentation phase, a run-time system presents data in a synchronized mode.

The following example shows this for the creation of a multimedia presentation:

Four audio messages are recorded that relate to parts of an engine. An animation sequence shows a slow 360 degree rotation of the engine. With a software tool (e.g., a synchronization editor), time relations between the animation and matching audio sequences are defined. The media objects with the synchronization specification can be used by a presentation tool that executes the synchronized presentation.

In the specification phase of synthetic synchronization, the captured or created media objects are explicitly synchronized. Media objects that are stored in a live synchronization scenario can also be included in a synthetic synchronization playback.

Another variation of synthetic synchronization is the synchronization specification at run-time, such as:

In a railway time-table information system, a user specifies his demands. An automatically-generated audio sequence presents this information to the user. During the presentation, a video sequence is displayed that shows how to go to the departure gateways and how to proceed at the arrival station. The synchronization between the generated audio and video is performed at run-time.

### 15.2.5 Comment

In the case of live synchronization, the synchronization specification is implicitly defined during capturing. In the case of synthetic synchronization, the specification is done explicitly. If media objects are presented as delayed, presentation manipulations like changing the presentation speed and direction and direct access to a part of the object are possible. Adapting the presentation quality to the user demands or the capacity of the underlying system resources is possible in both cases.

User interaction in live synchronization includes only the interaction during capturing. Synthetic synchronization can include user interactions, for example, for navigation.

## 15.3 Presentation Requirements

For delivering multimedia data correctly at the user interface, synchronization is essential. It is not possible to provide an objective measurement for synchronization from the viewpoint of subjective human perception. As human perception varies from person to person, only heuristic criteria can determine whether a stream presentation is correct or not. In this section, results of some extensive experiments are presented that are related to human perception of synchronization between different media.

Presentation requirements comprise, for intra-object synchronization, the accuracy concerning delays in the presentation of LDUs and, for inter-object synchronization, the accuracy in the parallel presentation of media objects.

For intra-object synchronization, we try to avoid any jitter in consecutive LDUs. Whereas processes can wait for each other, using the method of blocking (e.g., in CSP - Calculus of Sequential Programming), a data stream of time-independent

LDUs can also be stopped.

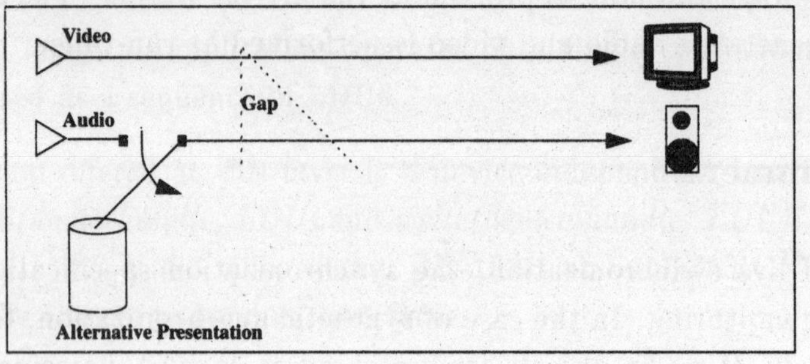


Figure 15.16: *The gap problem, restricted blocking.*

There is a different situation when looking at sequences of audio and moving pictures:

- What does the blocking of a stream of moving pictures mean for the connected output device?
- Should and can the last picture of a stream be shown during the blocking?
- Should, in the case of speech or music, a previous part be repeated during the blocking?
- How long can such a gap, as shown in Figure 15.16, exist?

This situation has become known as the *gap problem* [Ste90]. In the case of moving pictures, existing systems are solving the problem by simply switching the output device to dark or white, or by showing the last moving picture as a still picture. A practical solution must regard the factor time. It is significant, whether the duration of such a gap is a couple of milliseconds, a couple of seconds or even a couple of minutes. Only the actual application (and not the system) is able to select the best solution. Therefore, alternatives must be available that are selected independently of the expected blocking time. The concept of alternative presentations is indicated in Figure 15.16. In this example, it is shown that in the case that the gap between the late video and audio exceeds a predefined threshold, the audio presentation is switched to an alternative presentation. In the case that the gap is shorter, the audio presentation may be stopped until the gap is closed. In general, in the case of blocking, alternative single pictures, sequences of pictures or audio signals can be presented, or simply previously used presentation units can be repeated. This method of process blocking, respectively streams of audio and video, is known as *restricted blocking*.

Restricted blocking uses as a means for resynchronization the repeated presentation of the last sample(s), or an alternative presentation. Another possibility is the *re-sampling* of a stream. The basic idea of re-sampling is to speed up or slow down streams for the purpose of synchronization. We distinguish off-line and on-line re-sampling. *Off-line re-sampling* is used after the capturing of media streams with independent devices. An example is a concert which is captured with two independent audio and video devices. If these devices, like many real-world devices, have insufficient accurate crystal clocks, the theoretic playback duration according to the sample rate of the stored audio and video sequences may differ. Before the execution of the presentation, it is possible to re-sample them to the same theoretic playback duration. *On-line re-sampling* is used during a presentation in the case that, at run-time, a gap between media streams occurs.

Methods for re-sampling are to re-define the playback rate, to duplicate, to interpolate or to skip samples or to re-calculate the whole sequence. The human perception of the re-sampling depends strongly on the media. Video sequences can be re-sampled by adding or deleting single frames in a stream, as is done in NTSC/PAL conversions. If the output device supports different playback rates, the playback rate can be directly adjusted.

Audio streams are more complex. A user will be annoyed by duplicated or deleted blocks of audio. Also, changes in the playback rate can easily be noticed by the user, especially in the case of music playback because the frequency is changing. The same is true for simple interpolation of samples. Algorithms exist that can stretch or widen an audio sequence without this frequency change, but they do not support real-time demands and are only suitable for off-line re-sampling.

For inter-object synchronization, more detailed results of studies in the lip synchronization and pointer synchronization [SE93] areas are described in the following to make clear the importance of user perception aspects for presentation accuracy. A summary of requirements for other synchronization methods follows.

### 15.3.1 Lip Synchronization Requirements

*Lip synchronization* refers to the temporal relationship between an audio and video stream for the particular case of humans speaking. The time difference between related audio and video LDUs is known as the *skew*. Streams which are perfectly "in sync" have no skew, i.e., 0 ms. Experiments at the IBM European Networking Center [SE93] measured skews that were perceived as "out of sync." In their experiments, users often mentioned that something was wrong with the synchronization, but this did not disturb their feeling for the quality of the presentation. Therefore, the experimenters additionally evaluated the tolerance of the users by asking if the data out of sink affected the quality of the presentation.

In discussions with experts that work with audio and video, the experimenters came to realize that generally, subjects responded to or remembered particular parts of the clips, therefore the experimenters observed a wide range of skews (up to 240 ms). A comparison and general usage of these values are somewhat doubtful because the environments from which they resulted were not comparable. In some cases, the experimenters encountered the "head view" displayed in front of some single color background on a high resolution professional monitor, whereas in others a "body view" in a video window at a resolution of 240 × 256 pixels was seen. To get accurate and good skew tolerance levels, the experimenters selected a speaker in a TV news environment in a head and shoulder shot (Figure 15.17). In this orientation, the viewer is not disturbed by background information and the viewer should be attracted by the gesture, eyes, and lip movement of the speaker.

Their study was performed in the news environment in which the experimenters recorded the presentation and then re-played it with artificially introduced skews created with professional editing equipment skewed at intervals of 40 ms, i.e., -120 ms, -80 ms, -40 ms, 0 ms, +40 ms, +80 ms, +120 ms. Steps of 40 ms were chosen for:

1. The difficulty of human perception to distinguish any lip synchronization skew with a higher resolution.

2. The capability of multimedia software and hardware devices to refresh motion video data every 33ms/40ms.

Figure 15.17: *Left: head view; middle: shoulder view; right: body view.*

Figure 15.18 provides an overview of the results. The vertical axis denotes the relative number of test candidates who detected a synchronization error, regardless of being able to determine if the audio was before or after the video. Their initial assumption was that the three curves related to the different views would be very different, but as shown in Figure 15.18, this is not the case.

A careful analysis provides us with information regarding the asymmetry, some periodic ripples and minor differences between the various views.

Left of the central axis, the graph relates to negative skew values where the video is ahead of the audio. On the right, the graph shows where the audio is ahead of the video. Day to day we often experience the situation where the motion of the lips is perceived a little before the audio is heard, due to the greater velocity of light than sound. This is indicated by the right-hand side of the curves being steeper than the left side.

The "body view" curve is broader than the "head view" curve, as at the former a small skew is easier to notice. The "head view" is also more asymmetric than the "body view," due to the fact that the further away we are situated, the less noticeable an error is.

At a fairly high skew the curves show some periodic ripples; this is more obvious in the case where audio is ahead of video. Some people obviously had difficulties in

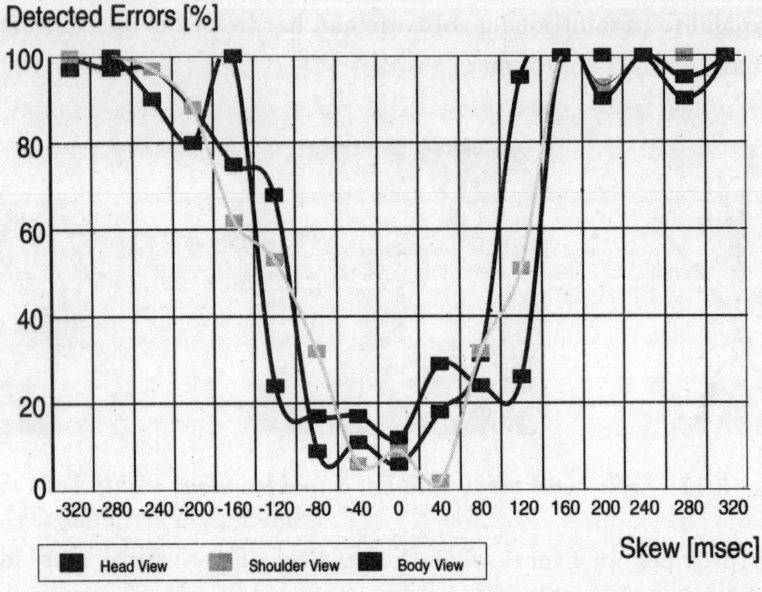


Figure 15.18: *Detection of synchronization errors with respect to the three different views. Left part: negative skew, video ahead of audio; right part: positive skew, video behind audio.*

identifying the synchronization error even with fairly high skew values. A careful analysis of this phenomenon is difficult due to the sample volume (few more than a 100), the media content to be synchronized and the human mind and mood. However, one plausible explanation could be: at the relative minima, the speech signal was closely related to the movement of the lips, which tends to be quasi periodic. Errors were easy to notice at the start and end of pauses, as well as whenever a change in tone was introduced (a point being emphasized). Errors in the middle of sentences were more difficult to notice. Also, we tended to concentrate more at the start of a conversation than once the subject was clear. A subsequent test containing video clips with skews according to these minima (without pauses and not showing the start, end and changes in tone) caused problems in identifying if there was indeed a synchronization error.

Figure 15.19 shows the following areas compiled according to the level of annoyance shown in Figure 15.20:

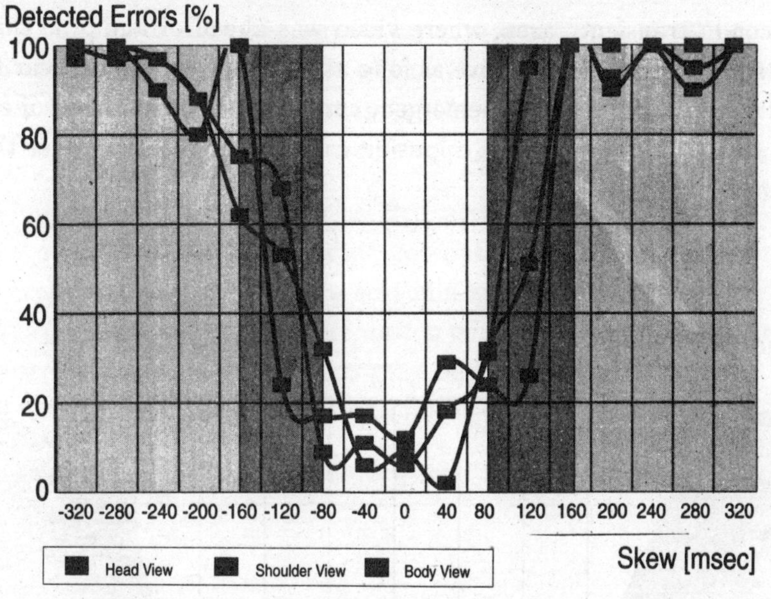


Figure 15.19: *Detection of synchronization errors.*

- The "in sync" region that spans a skew between -80 ms (audio behind video) and +80 ms (audio ahead of video). In this zone, most of the test candidates did not detect the synchronization error. Very few people said that if there was an error it affected their notion of the quality of the video. Additionally, some results indicated that the perfect "in sync" clip was "out of sync." Their conclusion is that lip synchronization can be tolerated within these limits.

- The "out of sync" areas span beyond a skew of -160 ms and +160 ms. Nearly everyone detected these errors and were dissatisfied with the clips. Data delivered with such a skew was in general not acceptable. Additionally, often a distraction occurred; the viewer/listener became more attracted by this "out of sync" effect than by the content itself.

- In the "transient" area where audio was ahead of video, the closer the speaker was, the easier errors were detected and described as disturbing. The same applied to the overall resolution, the better the resolution was, the more obvious the lip synchronization errors became.

- A second "transient" area, where video was ahead of audio, is characterized by a similar behavior as above as long as the skew values are near the in sync area. One interesting effect emerged, namely that video ahead of audio could be tolerated better than the opposing case. As above, the closer the speaker, the more obvious the skew.

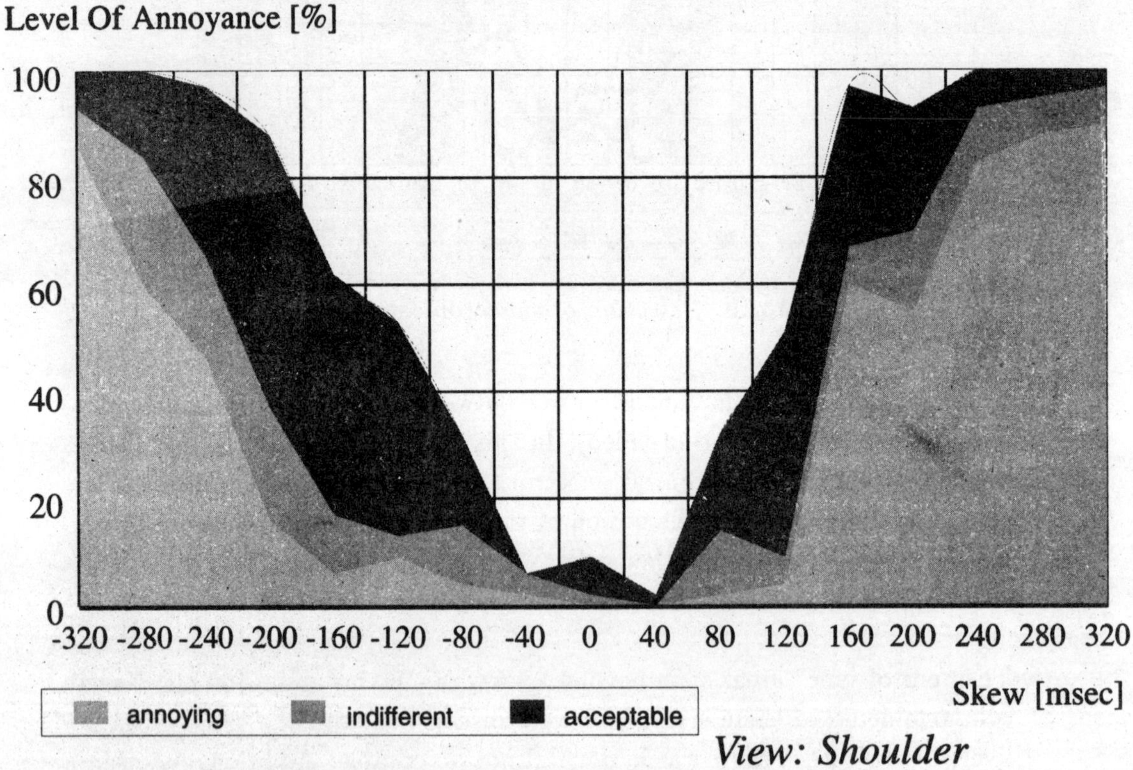


Figure 15.20: ***Level of annoyance of audio/visual skew.***

This asymmetry is very plausible. In a conversation where two people are located 20 m apart, the visual impression will always be about 60 ms ahead of the acoustics due to the fast light propagation compared to the acoustic wave propagation. The experimenters are just more used to this situation than the ones in the test.

### 15.3.2 Pointer Synchronization Requirements

In a Computer-Supported Co-operative Work (CSCW) environment, cameras and microphones are usually attached to the users' workstations. In the next experiment, the experimenters looked at a business report that contained some data with accompanying graphics. All participants had a window with these graphics on their desktop where a shared pointer was used in the discussion. Using this pointer, speakers pointed out individual elements of the graphics which may have been relevant to the discussion taking place. This obviously required synchronization of the audio and remote telepointer.

Figure 15.21: *Pointer synchronization experiment based on a map and technical sketch.*

The experimenters conducted two experiments:

- The first was to explain some technical parts of a sailing boat, while a pointer located the area under discussion (Figure 15.21, right side). The shorter the explanation, the more crucial the synchronization; therefore, the experimenters selected a fast-speaking person who used fairly short words.
- Additionally, the experimenters held a second experiment with the explanation of a traveling route on a map (Figure 15.21, left side). This involved the

continuous movement of the pointer.

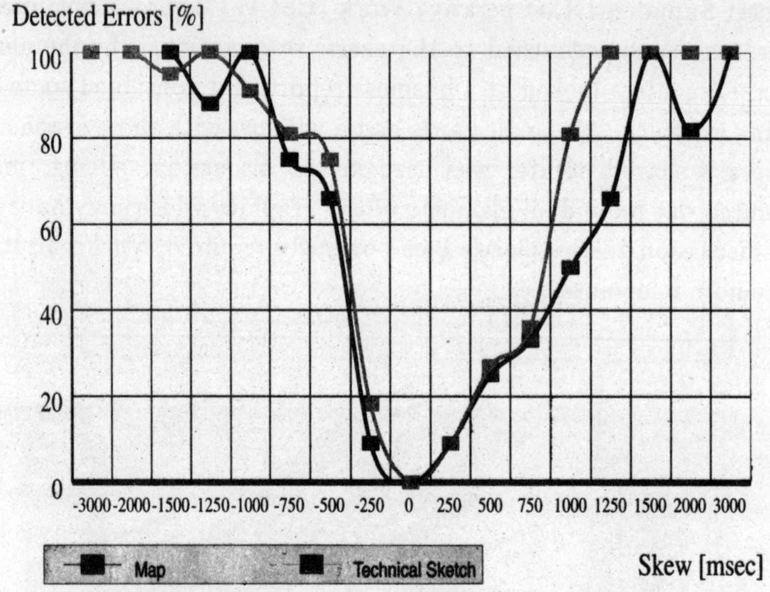


Figure 15.22: *Detection of the pointer synchronization errors.*

From the human perception point of view, pointer synchronization is very different from lip synchronization as it is much more difficult to detect the "out of sync" error at skew values near the error-free case. While a lip synchronization error is a matter of discussion for skews between 40 ms and 160 ms, for a pointer, the values lie between 250 ms and 1500 ms; Figure 15.22 shows some results.

Using the same judgement technique as in their first experiments, the "in sync" area related to audio ahead of pointing is 750 ms and for pointing ahead of audio it is 500 ms (Figure 15.22). This zone allows for a clear definition of the "in sync" behavior, regardless of the content.

The "out of sync" area spans a skew beyond -1000 ms and +1250 ms. At this point, the test candidates began to mention that the skew made the attempted synchronization worthless and became distracted unless the speaker slowed down or moved the pointer more slowly. From the user interface perspective, this is not acceptable. Quite clearly, the practice of pointing to one location on the technical figure while discussing another is virtually impossible.

In the "transient" area, the experimenters found that many test candidates noticed the "out of sync" effect but it was not mentioned as annoying. This is certainly different from "lip sync" where the user was more sensitive to the skew and, without question, found it annoying.

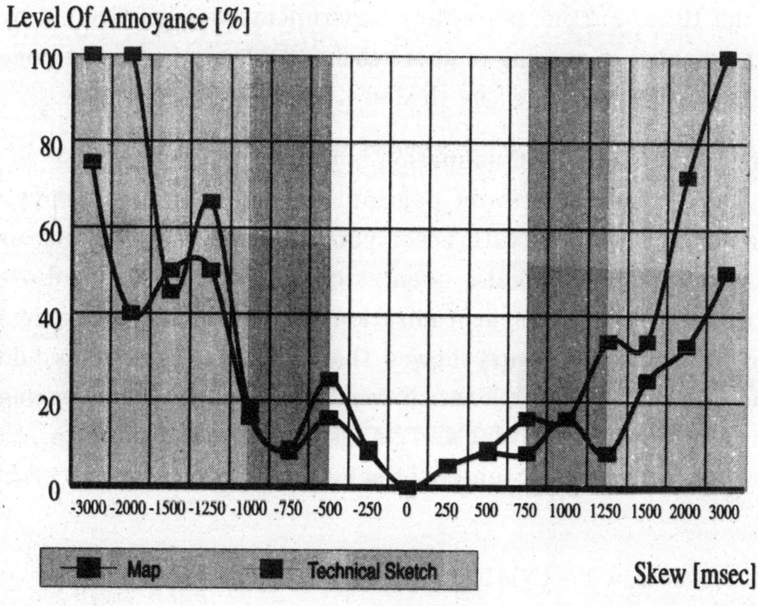


Figure 15.23: *Level of annoyance of the pointer synchronization errors.*

Figure 15.23 shows the number of people who disliked or were indifferent regarding the pointer synchronization error. It is worth mentioning that for several skew values, most of the test candidates detected the fault but did not object to such a skew, hence the broad "in sync" and "transient" areas.

### 15.3.3 Elementary Media Synchronization

Lip synchronization and pointer synchronization were investigated due to inconsistent results from available sources. The following summarizes other synchronization results to give a complete picture of synchronization requirements.

Since the beginning of digital audio, the *jitter* to be tolerated by dedicated hardware has been studied. Dannenberg provided some references and explanations of these studies. In [Ble78], the maximum allowable jitter for 16-bit quality audio in a sample period is 200 ps, which is the error equivalence to the magnitude of the LSB (Least-Significant Bit) of a full-level maximum-frequency 20-KHz signal. In [Sto72], some perception experiments recommended an allowable jitter in an audio sample period between 5 and 10 ns. Further perception experiments were carried out by [Lic51] and [Woo51], the maximum spacing of short clicks to obtain fusion into one continuous tone was given at 2ms (as cited by [RM80]).

The combination of audio and animation is usually not as stringent as lip synchronization. A multimedia course on dancing, for example, could show the dancing steps as animated sequences with accompanying music. By making use of the interactive capabilities, individual sequences can be viewed over and over again. In this particular example, the synchronization between music and animation is particularly important. Experience showed that a skew of +/- 80ms fulfills the user demands despite some possible jitter. Nevertheless, the most challenging issue is the correlation between a noisy event and its visual representation, e.g., the simulated crash of two cars. Here we encounter the same constraints as for lip synchronization, +/- 80 ms.

Two audio tracks can be tightly or loosely coupled. The effect of related audio streams depends heavily on the content:

- A stereo signal usually contains information about the location of the sources of audio and is tightly coupled. The correct processing of this information by the human brain can only be accomplished if the phases of the acoustic signals are delivered correctly. This demands for a skew less than the distance between consecutive samples leading to the order of magnitude of 20 ms. [DS93] reports that the perceptible phase shift between two audio channels is 17 ms. This is based on a headphone listening experiment. Since a varying delay in one channel causes the apparent location of a sound's source to move, Dannenberg proposed to allow an audio sample skew between stereo channels within the boundaries of +/- 11 ms. This is derived from the observation that a one-sample offset at a sample rate of 44kHz can be heard.

- Loosely coupled audio channels are a speaker and, e.g., some background music. In such scenarios we experience an affordable skew of 500 ms. The most stringent loosely coupled configuration has been the playback of a dialogue where the audio data of the participants originate from different sources. The experienced acceptable skew was 120 ms.

The combination of audio with images has its initial application in slide shows. By intuition, a skew of about 1 s arises which can be explained as follows [Dan93]: consider that it takes a second or so to advance a slide projector; however, people sometimes comment on the time it takes to change transparencies on an overhead projector, but rarely worry about automatic slide projectors.

A more elaborate analysis leads to the time constraints equivalent to those of pointer synchronization. The affordable skew decreases as soon as we encounter music played in correlation with notes, e.g., for tutoring purposes. [Dan93] points out that here an accuracy of 5 ms is required. Current practice in music synthesizers allows delays ranging up to 5 ms, but jitter is less than total delay. A 2 ms number refers to the synchronization between the onset times of two nominally simultaneous notes, or the timing accuracy of notes in sequence (see also [Cly85, RM80, Ste87]).

The synchronized presentation of audio with some text is usually known as *audio annotation* in documents or, e.g., part of an acoustic encyclopedia. In some cases, the audio provides further acoustic information to the displayed or highlighted text in terms of "audio annotation." In an existing "music dictionary," an antique instrument is described and simultaneously played. An example of a stronger correlation is the playback of a historical speech, e.g., a speech of J.F. Kennedy with simultaneous translation into German text. This text is displayed in a separate window and must relate closely to the actual acoustic signals. The same applies to the teaching of a language where in a playback mode the spoken word is simultaneously highlighted. Karaoke systems are another good example of necessary audio and text synchronization.

For this type of media synchronization, the affordable skew can be derived from the duration of the pronunciation of short words which last in the order of magnitude of 500 ms. Therefore, the experimentally verified skew of 240 ms is affordable.

The synchronization of video and text or video and image occurs in two distinct fashions:

- In the overlay mode, the text is often an additional description to the displayed moving image sequence. For example, in a video of playing billiards, the image is used to denote the exact direction of the ball after the last stroke. The simultaneous presentation of the video and overlaid image is important for the correct human perception of this synchronized data. The same applies to a text which is displayed in conjunction with the related video images. Instead of having the subtitles always located at the bottom, it is possible to place text close to the respective topic of discussion. This would cause an additional editing effort at the production phase and may not be for the general use of all types of movies but, for tutoring purposes, some short text nearby the topic of discussion is very useful. In such overlay schemes, this text must be synchronized to the video to assure that it is placed at the correct position. The accurate skew value can be derived from the minimal required time. A single word should appear on the screen for a certain time period to be correctly perceived by the viewer: 1 s is certainly such a limit. If the media producer wants to make use of the flash effect, then such a word should be on the screen for at least 500 ms. Therefore, regardless of the content of the video data, we encounter 240 ms to be absolutely sufficient.

- In the second mode, no overlay occurs and skew is less serious. Imagine some architectural drawings of medieval houses being displayed in correlation with a video of these building. While the video is showing today's appearance, the image presents the floor plan in a separate window. The human perception of even simple images requires at least 1 s. We can verify this value with an experiment with slides: the successive projector of non-correlated images requires about 1 s as the interval between the display of a slide and the next one in order to catch some of the essential visual information of the slide. A synchronization with a skew of 500 ms (half of this mentioned 1 s value) between the video and the image or the video and text is sufficient for this type of application.

Consider the billiard ball example from before: a video shows the impact of two billiard balls and the image of the actual "route" of one of the balls is shown by an animated sequence. Instead of a series of static images, the track of the second ball can be followed by an animation which displays the route of the ball across the table. In this example, any "out of sync" effect is immediately visible. For humans to be able to watch the ball with the perception of a moving picture, this ball must be visible in several consecutive adjacent video frames at slightly different positions. An acceptable result can be achieved if every three subsequent frames the ball moves by its diameter. A smaller frame rate may result in the problem of continuity, as often seen in tennis matches on television. As each frame lasts about 40 ms and three subsequent frames are needed, an allowable skew of 120 ms would be acceptable. This is very tight synchronization, which was suitable for the examples the experimenters looked at. Other examples where video and animation are combined include computer-generated figures in films.

Multimedia systems also incorporate the real-time processing of control data. Telesurg is a good example where graphical information is displayed based on readings taken by probes or similar instruments. No overall timing demand can be stated as these issues highly depend on the application itself.

## 15.4 A Reference Model for Multimedia Synchronization

A reference model is needed to understand the various requirements for multimedia synchronization, identify and structure run-time mechanisms that support the execution of the synchronization, identify interfaces between run-time mechanisms and compare system solutions for multimedia synchronization systems.

To this end, we first describe existing classification and structuring methods. Then, a four-layer reference model is presented and used for the classification of multimedia synchronization systems in our case studies. As many multimedia synchronization mechanisms operate in a networked environment, we also discuss special synchronization issues in a distributed environment and their relation to the reference model.

### 15.4.1 Existing Classification Approaches

An overall classification was introduced by Little and Ghafoor [LG90b]. They identified a physical level, system level and human level, but gave no detailed description or classification criteria. Other classification schemes distinguish between intrastream (fine-grain) synchronization and interstream (coarse-grain) synchronization, or between live and synthetic synchronization [LG90b, SM92a].

The model of Gibbs, Breiteneder and Tschichritzis [GBT93] maps a synchronized multimedia object to an uninterpreted byte stream. The multimedia objects consist of derived media objects comprised of rearranged media sequences, e.g., scenes from a complete video. The parts of the media sequences are themselves part of an uninterpreted byte stream.

Ehley, Furth and Ilyas [EFI94] classify intermedia synchronization techniques that are used to control jitter between media streams according to the type and location of the synchronization control. They distinguish between a distributed control based on protocols, distribution based on servers and distribution on nodes without server structure. For local synchronization control, they distinguish control on several layers and the use of local servers.

These classification schemes seem to be orthogonal, and each one of them only captures some specific aspects. They do not fulfill the above stated requirements of the synchronization reference model.

An improved three-layer classification scheme has been proposed by Meyer, Effelsberg and Steinmetz [MES93]. The layers are: the media layer for intrastream synchronization of time-dependent media, the stream layer for interstream synchronization of media streams, the object layer for the presentation, including the presentation of time-independent media objects and the specification layer for authoring complex multistream multimedia applications. At each layer, typical objects and operations are identified. Each layer can be accessed directly by the application or indirectly through higher layers. This approach fulfills the demands of a reference model approach and we will enhance and interpret it appropriately in the following.

### 15.4.2 The Synchronization Reference Model

A four-layer synchronization reference model is shown in Figure 15.24. Each layer implements synchronization mechanisms which are provided by an appropriate interface. These interfaces can be used to specify and/or enforce the temporal relationships. Each interface defines services, i.e., offering the user a means to define his/her requirements. Each interface can be used by an application directly, or by the next higher layer to implement an interface. Higher layers offer higher programming and Quality of Service (QoS) abstractions.

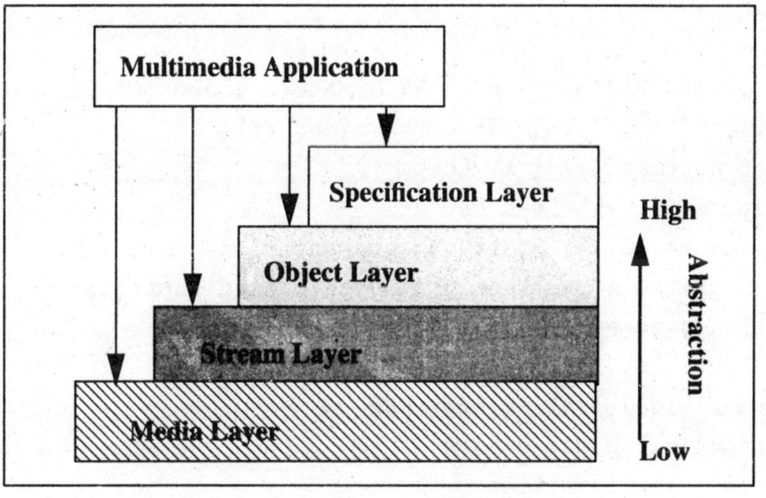


Figure 15.24: *Four-layer reference model.*

For each layer, typical objects and operations on these objects are described in the following. The semantics of the objects and operations are the main criteria for assigning them to one of the layers.

Detailed programming examples derived from a real interface provided by a real product, prototype or standard demonstrate how synchronization can be achieved through this layer. The scenario for the programming example is to display subtitles at predefined times during the playout of a digital movie.

### Media Layer

At the *media layer*, an application operates on a single continuous media stream, which is treated as a sequence of LDUs.

The abstraction offered at this layer is a device-independent interface with operations like *read(devicehandle, LDU)* and *write(device-handle, LDU)*. Systems such as ActionMedia/II$^{TM}$'s audio-video kernel [IBM92a] or SunSPARC$^{TM}$'s audio device [TP91] provide the corresponding interfaces.

To set up a continuous media stream using the abstractions offered by the media layer, an application executes a process for each stream in the manner shown in the following example:

```
window = open(''Videodevice"); \\ Create a video output window
movie = open(''File"); \\ Open the video file
while (not eof(movie)) { \\ Loop
read(movie, &ldu); \\ Read LDU
if (ldu.time == 20) \\ Start the presentation
 print(''Subtitle 1"); \\ of the synchronized subtitles
else if (ldu.time == 26)
 print(''Subtitle 2");
write(window, ldu);} \\ Present LDU
close(window); \\ Close window
close(movie); \\ Close file
```

The process reads and writes LDUs in a loop as long as data are available. Synchronous playout of a subtitle is achieved by polling the timestamps of the LDUs to have a certain value.

Using this layer, the application itself is responsible for the intrastream synchronization by using flow-control mechanisms between a producing and a consuming device [RR93]. If multiple streams run in parallel, the sharing of resources may affect their real-time requirements. Usually, a resource reservation and management scheme allows for guaranteeing intrastream synchronization [VHN92]. The operating system schedules the corresponding process in real-time [MSS92]. In distributed systems, the networking components are taken into account [AHS90, Fer91]. In the special case of lip synchronization, the interstream synchronization can be provided easily, where simultaneous audio and video frames are interleaved within the same LDU (e.g., ActionMedia-II's audio-video support system [IBM92a] and the MPEG data stream [ISO93a]). Finally, the synchronous playout of time-independent media objects and user interactions are tasks to be performed by the application.

Media layer implementations can be classified into simple implementations and implementations that provide access to interleaved media streams.

### Stream Layer

The *stream layer* operates on continuous media streams, as well as on groups of media streams. In a group, all streams are presented in parallel by using mechanisms for interstream synchronization.

The abstraction offered by the stream layer is the notion of streams with timing parameters concerning the QoS for intrastream synchronization in a stream and interstream synchronization between streams of a group.

Continuous media is seen in the stream layer as a data flow with implicit time constraints; individual LDUs are not visible. The streams are executed in a Real-Time Environment (RTE), where all processing is constrained by well-defined time specifications [Her92]. On the other hand, the applications themselves that are using the stream layer services are executed in a Non Real-Time Environment (NRTE), where the processing of events is controlled by the operating system scheduling policies.

Typical operations invoked by an application to manage streams and groups from the NRTE are: *start(stream)*, *stop(stream)*, *create_group(list_of_streams)*, *start(group)* and *stop(group)*. The interaction with time-independent media objects and user interactions is performed by the attachment of events to the continuous media streams (e.g., *setcuepoint(stream/group, at, event)*). Such an event is sent to the application whenever the stream reaches the specified point during playback. At this layer, the application is furthermore in charge of any time-independent media object and user interaction processing. This leads to different application interfaces for continuous media and for time-independent media and user interactions.

The Sync/Stream Subsystem of IBM's MultiMedia Presentation Manager™(MMPM) for OS/2™provides a set of services which can be used to implement data streaming and synchronization. This subsystem, which can be understood as the RTE, is comprised of the Sync/Stream Manager and several stream handlers [IBM92b]. Stream handlers are responsible for controlling the continuous data flow in real-time. The Sync/Stream Manger provides a resource management and controls the registration and activities of all stream handlers.

The following programming example for the use of the stream layer uses the string command interface provided by MMPM.

```
open digitalvideo alias ex \\ Create video descriptor
load ex video.avs \\ Assign file to video descriptor
setcuepoint ex at 20 return 1 \\ Define event 1 for subtitle 1
setcuepoint ex at 26 return 2 \\ Define event 2 for subtitle 2
setcuepoint ex on \\ Activate cuepoint events
play ex \\ Start playing

switch readevent() { \\ Event handling
case 1: display(''Subtitle 1") \\ If event 1 show subtitle 1
case 2: display(''Subtitle 2") \\ If event 2 show subtitle 2
}
```

In MMPM/2™, interstream synchronization for synchronized playback of multiple streams within a group is achieved by a master/slave algorithm, where one stream (the master) controls the behavior of one or more subordinate streams (the slaves). The skip/pause algorithm introduced in [AH91a] gives a detailed discussion of the implementation of such a behavior. The synchronization mechanism in ACME [AH91b], as well as the Orchestration Service [CGCH92], support stream layer abstractions for distributed multimedia systems.

The stream layer abstraction was derived from the abstraction normally provided by the integration of analog media in the computer system. In the Muse and Pygmalion systems of MIT's Project Athena [HSA89] or in the DiME [SM92b] system, continuous media were routed over separated channels through the computer. The connected devices could be controlled by sending commands via the RS-232C interface to start and stop the media streams. In such systems, live synchronization between various continuous media streams is directly performed by the dedicated processing devices.

Stream layer implementations can be classified according to their support for distribution, to the types of guarantees that they provide and to the types of supported streams (analog and/or digital).

An application using the stream layer is responsible for starting, stopping and grouping the streams and for the definition of the required QoS in terms of timing parameters supported by the stream layer. It is also responsible for the synchronization with time-independent media objects.

### Object Layer

The *object layer* operates on all types of media and hides the differences between discrete and continuous media.

The abstraction offered to the application is that of a complete, synchronized presentation. This layer takes a synchronization specification as input and is responsible for the correct schedule of the overall presentation. From our understanding, the abstractions are similar to the "object model" presented in [Ste90].

The task of this layer is to close the gap between the needs for the execution of a synchronized presentation and the stream-oriented services. The functions located at the object layer are to compute and execute complete presentation schedules that include the presentation of the non-continuous media objects and the calls to the stream layer. Further, the object layer is responsible for initiating preparation actions that are necessary for achieving a correctly synchronized presentation. The object layer does not handle the interstream and intrastream synchronization. For these purposes, it uses the services of the stream layer.

An example of interfacing this layer is an MHEG specification [MHE93]. The scope of the MHEG standard is the coded representation of final form multimedia and hypermedia information objects. In the following, we give a rudimentary example of how our scenario might be coded in the MHEG standard (using a simple notation to demonstrate the essentials of our reference model):

```
Composite { \\ Composite object
start-up link \\ How to start the
\\  presentation

viewer start-up
viewer-list \\ Virtual views on
Viewer1: reference to Component1 \\ component objects
Viewer2: reference to Component2
Viewer3: reference to Component3
Component1 \\ Component objects
reference to content ''movie.avs" \\ of the composite
Component2
reference to content ''Subtitle1"
Component3
reference to content ''Subtitle2"
Link1 \\ Temporal relations
''when timestone status of Viewer1
becomes 20 then start Viewer2"
Link2
''when timestone status of Viewer1
becomes 26 then start Viewer3"
}
```

A possible implementation of the object layer is an MHEG run-time system, the *MHEG engine.* The MHEG engine evaluates the status of the objects and performs operations (actions) like prepare, run, stop or destroy on these objects. In the case of time-dependent media objects, the run operation may be mapped to the initiation of a media stream on the stream layer. In the case of a time-independent media object, this call directly demands the object to be presented. Prepare times are necessary, for example, to allow the stream layer to build up a stream connection, or in the case of time-independent media objects, to prefetch the presentation, e.g., to adapt the picture color maps to the maps of the output device. The preparation is started by the prepare action.

Object layer implementations can be classified according to distribution capabilities and the type of presentation schedule computation. It can be distinguished whether the implementation calculates a schedule and, if it calculates one, whether the schedule is computed before the presentation or at run-time of the presentation. Concerning distribution, implementations may be local and may support distribution based on a server structure or full distribution without restriction.

The task of the application using the object layer is to provide a synchronization specification.

### Specification Layer

The *specification layer* is an open layer. It does not offer an explicit interface. This layer contains applications and tools arc located that allow to create synchronization specifications. Such tools are synchronization editors, multimedia document editors and authoring systems. Also located at the specification layer are tools for converting specifications to an object layer format. An example of such a conversion tool is a multimedia document formatter that produces an MHEG specification as proposed by Markey [Mar91a].

For example, the synchronization editor of the MODE system [BHLM92] may be used to specify the synchronization example. It offers a graphical interface to select the video and text objects to use, to preview the video, to select suitable points where the subtitles have to be shown, to specify the temporal relation of this point to the subtitle and to store the synchronization specification.

The specification layer is also responsible for mapping QoS requirements of the user level to the qualities offered at the object layer interface.

Synchronization specification methods can be classified into the following main categories:

- *Interval-based specifications,* which allow the specification of temporal relations between the time intervals of the presentations of media objects.
- *Axes-based specifications,* which relate presentation events to axes that are shared by the objects of the presentation.
- *Control flow-based specifications,* in which at given synchronization points, the flow of the presentations is synchronized.
- *Event-based specifications,* in which events in the presentation of media trigger presentation actions.

### 15.4.3 Synchronization in a Distributed Environment

*Synchronization in a distributed environment* is more complex than in a local environment. This is mainly caused by the distributed storage of synchronization information and the different locations of the media objects involved in the presentation. The communication between the storage and presentation site introduces additional delays and jitter. Often, we also encounter multi-party communication patterns.

#### Transport of the Synchronization Specification

At the sink node, the presentation component needs to have the synchronization specification at the moment an object is to be displayed. We distinguish between three main approaches for the delivery of the synchronization information to the sink:

- *Delivery of the complete synchronization information before the start of the presentation*: This approach is often used in the case of synthetic synchronization. Typically, the application at the sink node accesses the object layer interface with the specification or a reference to the specification as a parameter. The implementation of this approach is simple and it also allows easy handling in the case of several source nodes for the media objects. The disadvantage is the delay caused by the transport of the synchronization specification before the presentation, especially if it is stored on another node. The transport of the synchronization specification is a duty of a component located at the object layer or above.

- *Use of an additional synchronization channel*: This approach, shown in Figure 15.25, is useful in the case of one source node only. It is used and is preferable in the case of live synchronization when all the synchronization information is not known in advance. No additional delays are caused by this method. A disadvantage is that an additional communication channel is needed that may cause errors due to delay or loss of synchronization specification units. It is often forgotten that the information on the synchronization channel must be decoded at the time the respective object is to be displayed, i.e., data communication at this channel must obey certain time behavior. Also, the case of multiple source nodes for synchronized media objects is difficult to handle. The synchronization channel must be handled by the object layer and possibly supported by the stream layer if the synchronization channel is to be defined as a stream.

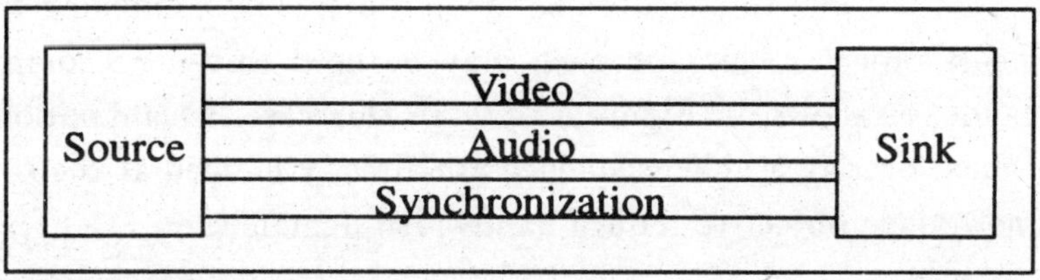


Figure 15.25: *Use of a separate synchronization channel.*

- *Multiplexed data streams*: The advantage of multiplexing data streams on one communication channel (Figure 15.26) is that the related synchronization information is delivered together with the media units. No additional synchronization channel is necessary and no additional delay is caused by this approach. An important problem regarding multiplexed media and synchronization information is the difficulty of selecting an appropriate QoS which matches the requirements of all involved medias, e.g., reliability is dominated by the most stringent media objects. This method is also difficult to use for multiple source nodes. It must be supported by the stream layer. The use of multiplexed data streams may be implied by coding standards like MPEG. MPEG defines a bitstream that combines video, audio and the related synchronization information. Hence, this type of bitstream can be regarded as one medium on the stream layer and for the synchronization with other media, the other approaches can also be chosen.

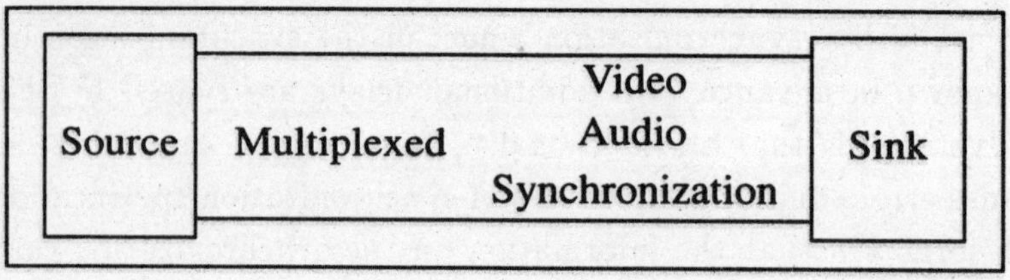


Figure 15.26: *Multiplexed media and synchronization channels.*

### Location of Synchronization Operations

In some cases it is possible to synchronize media objects by combining the objects into a new media object. This approach may be used to reduce communication resource demands, as shown in Figure 15.27. In this case, an animation and two bitmaps that must overlay a video sequence are already merged at the source node to become a new video object to reduce bandwidth demands.

The mixing of objects, including time-independent media objects, must be supported by the object layer. The mixing of media streams, like mixing audio channels, must be supported by the stream layer.

### Clock Synchronization

In distributed systems, the synchronization accuracy between the clocks of the source and sink nodes must be considered. Many synchronization schemes demand knowledge about the timing relations. This knowledge is the basis for global timer-based synchronization schemes, as well as for schemes that demand that operations on distributed nodes are timely and coordinated to ensure, on one hand, in-time deliv-

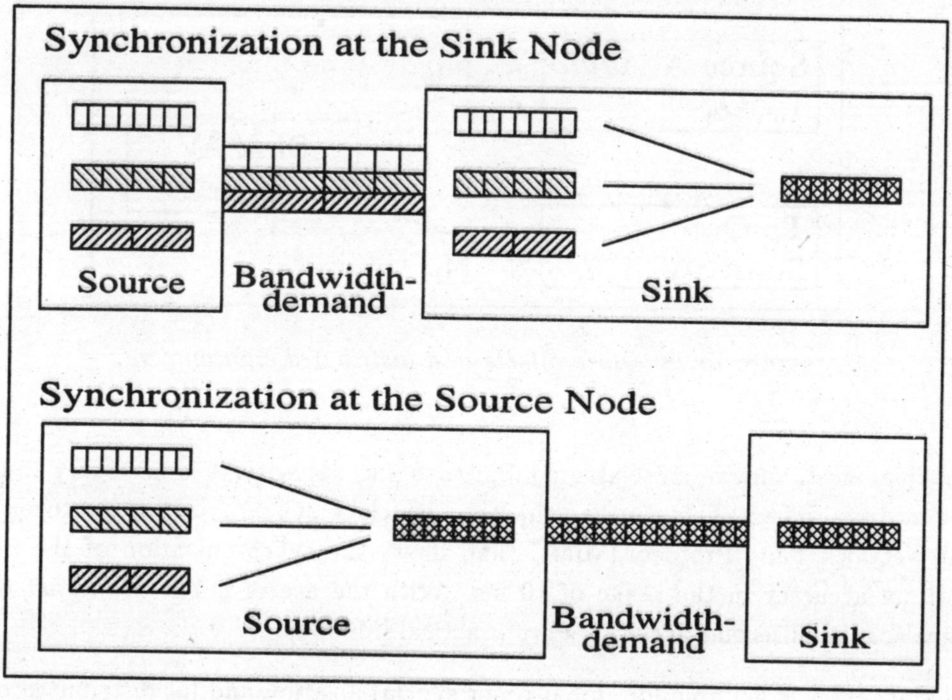


Figure 15.27: *Combining objects to reduce communication resource demands.*

ery and on the other hand, that operations are not performed too early to avoid a buffer overflow.

This problem is especially important for the synchronization in the case of multiple sources (Figure 15.28). If a synchronized audio-video presentation should start at time $T_{av}$ at the sink node, the audio transmission of Source $A$ must start at $T_a = T_{av} - N_{la} - O_a$, with $N_{la}$ as the known net delay and $O_a$ as the offset of the clock of node $A$ with respect to the clock of the sink node. For source node $B$, the start time of the video transmission is $T_v = T_{av} - N_{lv} - O_v$.

The offsets $O_a$ and $O_v$ are not known. The resulting problem of delivery to the sink in time can be solved if the maximal possible values for $O_a$ and $O_v$ are known. It is possible to allocate buffer capacities at the sink and to start the transmission of the audio and video in advance to guarantee that the required media units are available. Because the necessary buffer capacity at the sink node depends on the

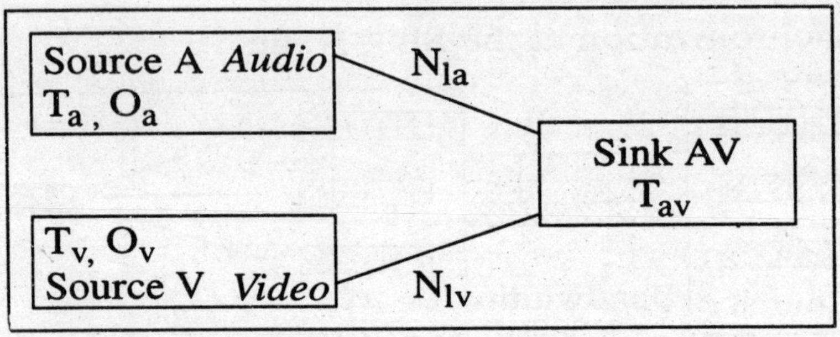


Figure 15.28: *Clock offsets in a distributed environment.*

possible offset, and we must assume limited buffer capacity, it is necessary to limit the maximal offset. This can be achieved with clock synchronization protocols like the Network Time Protocol [Mil91] that allows the synchronization of the clocks with an accuracy in the range of 10 ms. With the use of public broadcast timer signals, submillisecond accuracies are practical [Mil93a].

This accuracy is suitable for global timer synchronization and for distributed operation scheduling.

The in-time delivery of LDUs of a stream is a task of the stream layer that must handle the clock offsets. For in-time delivery of time-independent media objects, the object layer is responsible.

### Multiple Communication Relations

Possible communication patterns are shown in Figure 15.29. Patterns with multiple sinks demand that at run-time, multicast and broadcast mechanisms be used to reduce resource requirements, in particular network resources. Also inefficient multiple executions of the same operation at different sinks should be avoided. The multicasting of streams is the task of the stream layer. Efficient planning of operation execution in the different communication patterns is a responsibility of the object layer.

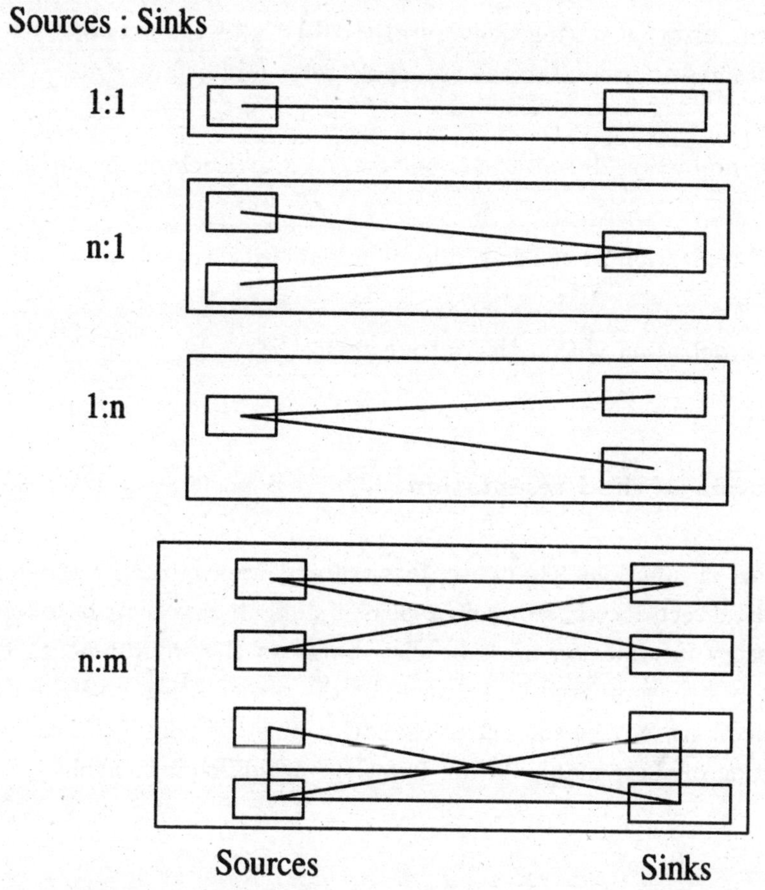


Figure 15.29: *Multiple communication relations.*

### Multi-Step Synchronization

Synchronization in a distributed environment is typically a multi-step process. During all steps of the process, the synchronization must be maintained in a way that enables the sink to perform the final synchronization. The steps of the process are:

- Synchronization during object acquisition, e.g., during digitizing video frames.
- Synchronization of retrieval, e.g., synchronized access to frames of a stored video.

- Synchronization during delivery of the LDUs to the network, e.g., delivering the frames of a video to the transport service interface.

- Synchronization during the transport, e.g., by isochronous protocols.

- Synchronization at the sink, i.e., synchronized delivery to the output devices.

- Synchronization within the output device.

### Manipulation of the Presentation

The support of functions like pause, forward and backward with different presentation speeds, direct access, stop and repeat is difficult in a distributed environment. The necessary information must be distributed in the environment. Objects that have already been prepared in advance for the presentation must be deleted. Network connections may be subject to change or must be rebuilt. Therefore, delays in the execution of these manipulation functions are difficult to avoid.

### Consequences for Synchronization in a Distributed Environment

To achieve synchronization in a distributed environment, many decisions must be made. A first decision is the selection of the type of transport for the synchronization specification. In run-time, decisions must be taken concerning the location of the synchronization operations, handling of the offsets of the clocks and the handling of multicast and broadcast mechanisms. Especially, coherent planning of the steps in the synchronization process, together with the necessary operations on the objects, e.g., decompression, must be done. In addition, presentation manipulation operations demand additional re-planning at run-time.

In general, the execution of synchronized distributed presentations is a complex planning problem. The resulting plan is often known as a schedule.

### 15.4.4 Aggregate Characteristics of the Synchronization Reference Model

The reference model allows for the structuring and classifying of synchronization systems. The identification of the interfaces and layers enables one to combine existing solutions into complete systems. Table 15.2 provides an overview of the interface abstractions and tasks of all layers of our reference model. The classification of mechanisms and methods in the layers is summarized in Table 15.3.

## 15.5 Synchronization Specification

The synchronization specification of a multimedia object describes all *temporal dependencies* of the included objects in the multimedia object. It is produced using tools at the specification layer and is used at the interface to the object layer. Because the synchronization specification determines the whole presentation, it is a central issues in multimedia systems. In the following, requirements for synchronization specifications are described and specification methods are described and evaluated.

A synchronization specification should be comprised of:

- Intra-object synchronization specifications for the media objects of the presentation.
- QoS descriptions for intra-object synchronization.
- Inter-object synchronization specifications for media objects of the presentation.
- QoS descriptions for inter-object synchronization.

The synchronization specification is part of the description of a multimedia object. In addition, for a multimedia object, it may be described in which presentation form, respectively in which alternative presentation forms, a media object should be presented. For example, a text could be presented as text on the screen or as

| Layer | Interface Abstraction | Tasks |
|---|---|---|
| Specification | • The tools performing the tasks of this layer have interfaces; the layer itself has no upper interface | • Editing<br>• Formatting<br>• Mapping user-oriented QoS to the QoS abstraction at the object layer |
| Object | • Synchronization Specification<br>• Objects that hide types of enclosed media<br>• Media-oriented QoS (in terms of acceptable skew and jitter) | • Plan and coordinate presentation scheduling<br>• Initiate presentation of time-dependent media objects by the stream layer<br>• Initiate presentation of time-independent media objects<br>• Initiate presentation preparation actions |
| Stream | • Streams and groups of streams<br>• Guarantees for intrastream synchronization<br>• Guarantees for interstream synchronization of streams in a group | • Resource reservation and scheduling of LDU processing |
| Media | • Device-independent access to LDUs<br>• Guarantees for single LDU processing | • File and device access |

Table 15.2: *Overview of the synchronization reference model layers.*

| Layer | Classification Items |
|---|---|
| Specification | Synchronization specification method:<br>• Interval-based synchronization<br>• Axes-based synchronization<br>• Control flow-based synchronization<br>• Event-based synchronization |
| | Type of tool:<br>• Textual specification tool<br>• Graphical specification tool<br>• Converter |
| Object | Type of distribution:<br>• Local<br>• Distributed, based on servers<br>• Distributed without server usage |
| | Type of schedule computation:<br>• No computation<br>• Compile-time computation<br>• Run-time computation |
| Stream | Type of distribution:<br>• Local<br>• Distributed |
| | Type of guarantees for stream QoS:<br>• No guarantees for QoS, best effort<br>• Guarantees for QoS by resource reservations |
| Media | Type of accessible data:<br>• Single medium data<br>• Interleaved, complex data |

Table 15.3: *Classification of methods and mechanisms at the synchronization reference model layers.*

generated audio sequence. A specification may allow only one of these or a selection of the presentation form at run-time.

In the case of live synchronization, the temporal relations are implicitly defined during capturing. QoS requirements for single media are defined before starting the capture.

In the case of synthetic synchronization, the specification must be created explicitly. Several synthetic synchronization specification methods have been described in the literature. The most important are classified, surveyed and evaluated in the following sections.

### 15.5.1 Quality of Service

The necessary QoS depends on the media and application.

#### Quality of Service for a Media Object

The QoS specification for a media object includes the quality concerning single LDUs of a media object and the accuracy with which the temporal relations between the LDUs of this media object must be fulfilled if the media object is a time-dependent object.

Table 15.4 shows some QoS parameters for a media object. The white boxes contain qualities that are independent of temporal relations. The light shaded boxes contain timing related qualities that are under the limited influence of the presentation system because the quality depends on the quality selected during capture. Usually, only quality degradation via the presentation system is possible. The dark shaded boxes contain timing qualities which are potentially under full control of the presentation environment.

| Media | Image (e.g., bitmap) | Video | Audio |
|---|---|---|---|
| Quality of Service | Color Depth | Color Depth | Lin. or log. sampling |
| | Resolution | Resolution | Sample Size |
| | | Frame Rate | Sample Rate |
| | | Jitter | Jitter |
| | | Error Rate | Error Rate |

Table 15.4: *Some QoS for the presentation of a media object.*

### Quality of Service of Two Related Media Objects

Synchronization requirements can be expressed by a QoS specification. One QoS parameter can define the acceptable skew within the concerned data streams; namely, it defines the affordable synchronization boundaries. The notion of QoS is well established in communication systems, in the context of multimedia, it also applies to local systems. If audio and video parts of a film are stored as different entries in a database, lip synchronization according to the above-mentioned results should be taken into account.

In this context we want to introduce the notion of *presentation- and production-level synchronization*:

- *Production-level synchronization* refers to the QoS to be guaranteed prior to the presentation of the data at the user interface. It typically involves the recording of synchronized data for subsequent playback. The stored data should be captured and recorded with no skew at all, i.e., "in sync." This is particularly applicable if the file is stored in an interleaved format. At the participant's site, the actual incoming audiovisual data is "in sync" according to the defined lip synchronization boundaries. Assuming the data arrive with a skew of +80 ms, and if audio and video LDUs are transmitted as a single multiplexed stream over the same transport connection, then it will be displayed as apparently "in-sync." Should the data be stored on the hard disk and presented simultaneously at a local workstation and to a remote spectator, then for correct delivery, the QoS should be specified as being between -160 ms and 0 ms. At the remote viewer's station without this additional knowledge of the actual skew the outcome might be that by applying these boundaries twice, data are not "in sync." In general, any synchronized data which will be further processed should be synchronized according to a production-level quality, i.e., with no skew at all.

- The presentation requirements discussed in Section 15.3 identify *presentation-level synchronization.* This synchronization defines whatever is reasonable at the user interface. It does not take into account any further processing of the synchronized data; presentation-level synchronization focuses on the human perception of the synchronization. As shown in the above paragraph, by recording the actual skew as part of the control information, the required QoS for synchronization can be easily computed. The required QoS for synchronization is expressed as the allowed skew. The QoS values shown in Table 15.5 relate to presentation-level synchronization. Most of them result from exhaustive experiments and experiences, others are derived from literature as referenced. To their understanding, they serve as a general guideline for any QoS specification. During the lip and pointer synchronization experiments, we learned that many factors influenced these results. We understand this whole set of QoS parameters as a first-order result to serve as a general guideline. However, these values may be relaxed depending on the actual content.

### Quality of Service of Multiple Related Media Objects

So far, media synchronization has been evaluated as the relationship between two kinds of media or separate data streams. This is the canonical foundation of all types of media synchronization. In practice, we often encounter more than two related media streams; a sophisticated multimedia application scenario incorporates the simultaneous handling of various sessions. An example is a video conference where a window displays the actual speaker and the audio emerges from an attached pair of speakers.

| Media | | Mode, Application | Quality of Service |
|---|---|---|---|
| Video | Animation | Correlated | +/- 120 ms |
| | Audio | Lip Synchronization | +/- 80 ms |
| | Image | Overlay | +/- 240 ms |
| | | Non-overlay | +/- 500 ms |
| | Text | Overlay | +/- 240 ms |
| | | Non-overlay | +/- 500 ms |
| Audio | Animation | Event Correlation (e.g., dancing) | +/- 80 ms |
| | Audio | Tightly Coupled (stereo) | +/- 11 µs |
| | | Loosely Coupled (dialogue mode with various participants) | +/- 120 ms |
| | | Loosely Coupled (e.g., background music) | +/- 500 ms |
| | Image | Tightly Coupled (e.g., music with notes) | +/- 5 ms |
| | | Loosely Coupled (e.g. slide show) | +/- 500 ms |
| | Text | Text Annotation | +/- 240 ms |
| | Pointer | Audio Related to the Item to Which the Pointer Points | - 500 ms, + 750 ms[a] |

a. Pointer prior to audio for 500 ms; audio prior to pointer for 750 ms.

Table 15.5: *Quality of Service for synchronization purposes.*

Video and audio data are related by lip synchronization demands. Audio and the telepointer are related by the pointer synchronization demands. The relationship of video data and the telepointer is then yielded by a simple combination. In this example, we will define the following skews:

```
max skew (video ahead_of audio) = 80 ms
max skew (audio ahead_of video) = 80 ms
max skew (audio ahead_of pointer) = 740 ms
max skew (pointer ahead_of audio) = 500 ms
```

leading to the skew

```
skew (video ahead_of pointer) =< 820 ms
skew (pointer ahead_of video) =< 580 ms
```

In general, these requirements can be derived easily by the accumulation of the canonical skew as shown in the above example. The information gathered by the aggregation of media is of interest for the user, as well as for the multimedia system which must provide service according to these values.

In some cases, too many specifications of a synchronization skew exist; for example, a language lesson that includes audio data in English and Spanish, as well as the related video sequences. The course builder enforces lip synchronization between video and audio regardless of the language (+-80 ms). Additionally, the sentences need to be synchronized to switch from one language to the other (we chose a figure of 400 ms for this case). As lip synchronization is more demanding than the synchronization between the languages, this would lead to the following skew specification:

```
1. max skew (video ahead_of audio_english) = 80 ms
2. max skew (audio_english ahead_of video) = 80 ms
3. max skew (video ahead_of audio_spanish) = 80 ms
4. max skew (audio_spanish ahead_of video) = 80 ms
5. max skew (audio_english ahead_of audio_spanish) = 400 ms
6. max skew (audio_spanish ahead_of audio_english) = 400 ms
```

This specification consists of a set of related requirements in all need to be fulfilled, i.e., we must find "the greatest common denominator." For each canonical form, the derived skews are computed as follows:

```
1+2+3+4:
max skew (audio_english ahead_of audio_spanish) = 160 ms
max skew (audio_spanish ahead_of audio_english) = 160 ms

1+2+5+6:
max skew (video ahead_of audio_spanish) = 480 ms
max skew (audio_spanish ahead_of video) = 480 ms

3+4+5+6:
max skew (video ahead_of audio_english) = 480 ms
max skew (audio_english ahead_of video) = 480 ms
```

In the second step, the most stringent set of all requirements are selected:

```
1. max skew (video ahead_of audio_english) = 80 ms
2. max skew (audio_english ahead_of video) = 80 ms
3. max skew (video ahead_of audio_spanish) = 80 ms
4. max skew (audio_spanish ahead_of video) = 80 ms
5. max skew (audio_english ahead_of audio_spanish) = 160 ms
6. max skew (audio_spanish ahead_of audio_english) = 160 ms
```

In the following step, any set of synchronization requirements can be chosen from the above derived calculations:

```
max skew (video ahead_of audio_english) = 80 ms
max skew (audio_english ahead_of video) = 80 ms
max skew (audio_english ahead_of audio_spanish) = 160 ms
max skew (audio_spanish ahead_of audio_english) = 160 ms
```

In summary, the above procedures allow us to solve two related problems:

- If the applications impose a set of related synchronization requirements on a multimedia system, we are now able to find the most stringent demands.
- If a set of individual synchronization requirements between various data streams is provided, we are now able to compute the required relationships between each individual pair of streams.

Both issues arise in non-trivial systems when estimating, computing or negotiating the QoS as it is outlined in the next section.

### 15.5.2 Multimedia Synchronization Specification Methods

For the complex specification of multiple object synchronization, including user interaction, sophisticated specification methods must be used. The following requirements should be fulfilled by such a specification method:

- The method shall support object consistency and maintenance of synchronization specifications. Media objects should be kept as one logical unit in the specification.
- The method should supply an abstraction of the contents of a media object that allows the specification of temporal relations that refer to a part of the media object, but on the other hand regard, the media object as one logical unit.
- All types of synchronization relations should be easily described.
- The integration of time-dependent, as well as time-independent, media objects must be supported.
- The definition of QoS requirements must be supported by the specification method. It should preferably be expressed in the method directly.
- Hierarchical levels of synchronization must be supported to enable the handling of large and complex synchronization scenarios.

In the following sections, specification methods are assessed according to the criteria described above.

### 15.5.3 Interval-based Specifications

In the interval-based synchronization specification, the presentation duration of an object is regarded as interval. Two time intervals may be synchronized in 13 different modes [All83, Ham72]. Some of these types are invertible like before and after. Figure 15.30 shows a reduced set of seven non-invertible types according to [LG90a]. A simple synchronization specification method for two media objects is to use these seven types.

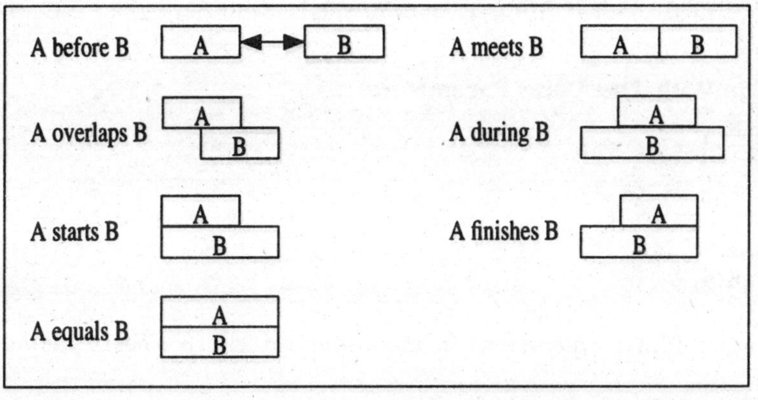


Figure 15.30: *Types of temporal relations between two objects.*

The enhanced interval-based model [WR94] is based on interval relations. The basic interval relations have already been shown in Figure 15.30. In the enhanced approach, 29 interval relations that are defined as disjunctions of the basic interval relations have been identified as relevant for multimedia presentations. To simplify the synchronization specification, ten operators have been defined that can handle these interval relations. These operations are shown in Figure 15.31. The duration of a presentation like A or B, as well as the delay $d_i$, are subsets of +0 because the duration of a presentation, as well as of a delay, may not be known in advance. In addition, the operations *beforeendof, delayed, startin, endin, cross* and *overlaps* $d_i$ must not be 0.

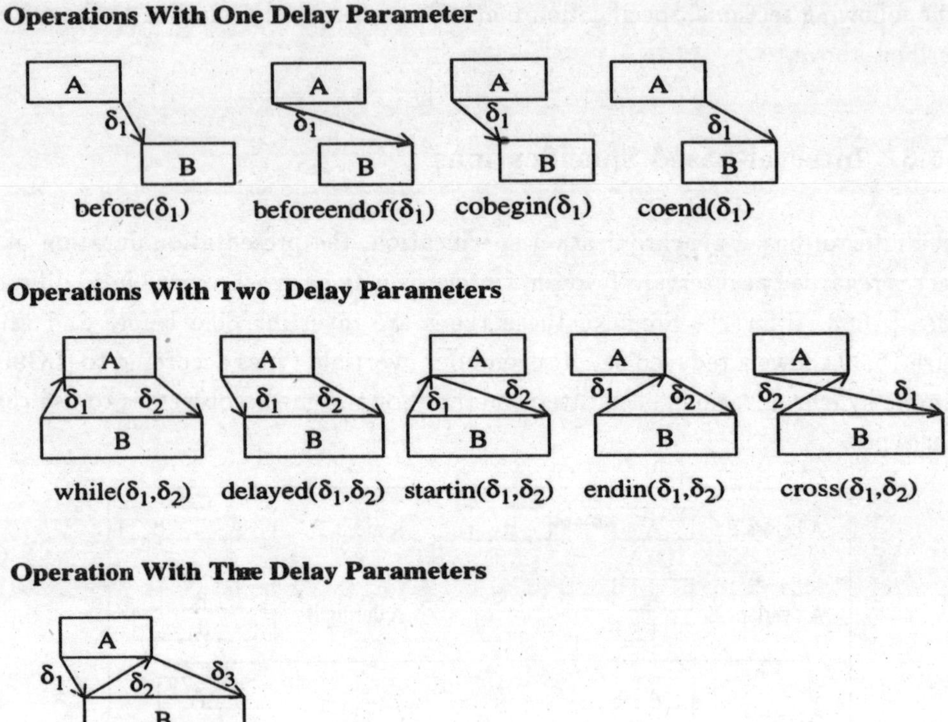


Figure 15.31: *Operations in the enhanced interval-based method.*

A slide show with slides $Slide_i$ $(1 \leq i \leq n)$ and an audio object *Audio* can be specified in this model by:

$$Slide_1\ cobegin(0)\ Audio$$

$$Slide_i\ before(0)\ Slide_{i+1}\ (1 \leq i \leq n-1)$$

Lip synchronization between an audio object *Audio* and a video object *Video* is simply specified by:

$$Audio\ while(0,0)\ Video$$

The application example can be sketched as follows:

```
Audio1 while(0,0) Video
Audio1 before(0) RecordedInteraction
RecordedInteraction before(0) B1
P1 before(0) P2
P2 before(0) P3
P3 before(0) Interaction
P3 before(0) Animation
Animation while(2,5) Audio2
Interaction before(0) P4
```

This model allows the definition of a duration for time-dependent and time-independent media objects. This duration is used in the example to specify the duration of the presentation of the objects picture 1 to picture 3. The open duration of the user interaction can be specified by defining the duration as +0.

The advantage of this model is that it is easy to handle open LDUs, and therefore user interaction. It is possible to specify additional indeterministic temporal relations by defining intervals for durations and delays. Disjunction of operators can be used for specifications of presentation relations like not parallel. Therefore, it is a very flexible model that allows the specification of presentations with many run-time presentation variations.

The model does not include skew specifications. Despite the direct specification of time relations between media objects, it does not allow the specification of temporal relations directly between subunits of objects. Such relations must be defined indirectly by delay specifications, as shown in the while operation for the animation and audio in the application example, or by splitting the objects. The flexibility of specifiable presentations may lead to inconsistencies in run-time. For example, for two video objects A and B a *not* parallel relation has been defined. In run-time, A may be running and B may be coupled by a *before(0)* relation to the end of a user interaction. If this user interaction ends, video B must be started, but on the other hand, it may not be started because of the *not* parallel relation. It must be defined in the model how such inconsistencies must be handled in run-time or such potential inconsistencies must be detected before run-time and the specification must be rejected. Building of hierarchies is easily definable. The assessment of the enhanced

| Advantages | Disadvantages |
|---|---|
| Logical objects can be kept | Complex specification |
| Good abstraction for media content | Additional specifications for skew QoS necessary |
| Easy integration of time-independent objects | Direct specification of time relations between media objects, but not for subunits of the media objects |
| Easy integration of interactive objects | Resolving of indeterminism at run-time may lead to inconsistencies |
| Specification of indeterministic temporal relations supported | |

Table 15.6: *Assessment of the enhanced interval-based synchronization specification.*

interval-based method is summarized in Table 15.6.

### 15.5.4 Axes-based Synchronization

In an axes-based specification, the presentation events like the start and end of a presentation are mapped to axes that are shared by the objects of the presentation.

#### Synchronization Based on a Global Timer

For synchronization based on a *global timer*, all single-medium objects are attached to a time axis that represents an abstraction of real-time. This specification method is used, for example, in the Athena Muse project [HSA89], where synchronization is described by attaching all objects, independently of each other, to a time axis. Removing one object does not affect the synchronization of the other objects.

With modifications, this kind of specification is also used in the model of active media [TGD91]. A world time is maintained, which is accessible to all objects. Each object can map this world time to its local time and moves along its local time axis. When the distortion between world time and local time exceeds a given limit, resynchronization with world time is required. A time axis mechanism is also used in QuickTime [DM92].

Synchronizing objects by means of a time axis allows a very good abstraction from the internal structure of single-medium objects and nested multimedia objects. Defining the beginning of a subtitle presentation relative to a scene in a video stream requires no knowledge of the related video frames. Since synchronization can only be defined based on fixed points of time, problems arise if objects include LDUs of unpredictable duration.

Moreover, synchronization based on one common global timer may not be sufficient for expressing the synchronization relations between different presentation streams. Depending on the coherence of these presentation streams, synchronization based on a common time axis might be either too strong or too weak. A possible solution is to define for each pair of media streams an additional QoS.

The use of the global timer demands that the media streams are able to synchronize themselves to the global timer. This may be difficult for audio streams because of the re-sampling problems. Therefore, the audio stream is often used as the global timer, but this still causes difficulties if several audio streams must be synchronized.

Figure 15.32 shows the specification of the application example. It can be seen that there is no natural possibility to handle the unpredictable duration of a user interaction.

The assessment of the time axis method is summarized in Table 15.7.

### Synchronization Based on Virtual Axes

*Virtual time axes*, as used in the project Athena [HSA89] or the HyTime standard [Org92], are a generalization of the time axis approach. In this specification method, it is possible to specify coordinate systems with user-defined measurement units. A synchronization specification is performed according to these axes. It is also possible

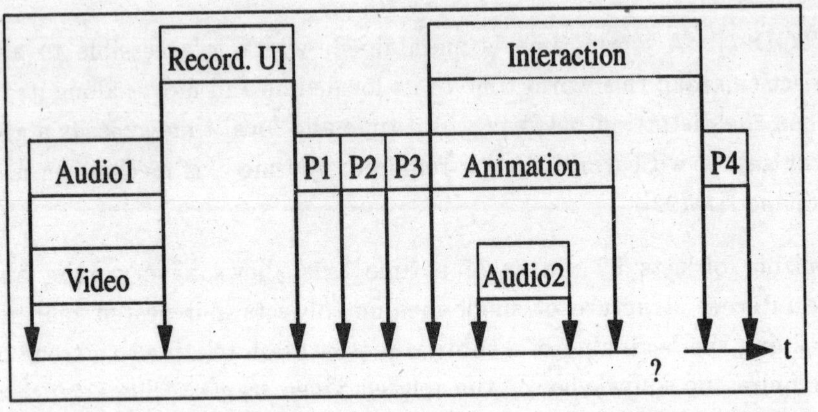


Figure 15.32: *Time axis synchronization specification example.*

to use several virtual axes to create a virtual coordinate space. An example is a music description by notes as shown in Figure 15.33. The tune frequency is defined by the position on the note lines. The sequence and duration is defined on the axis with the measurement unit beat.

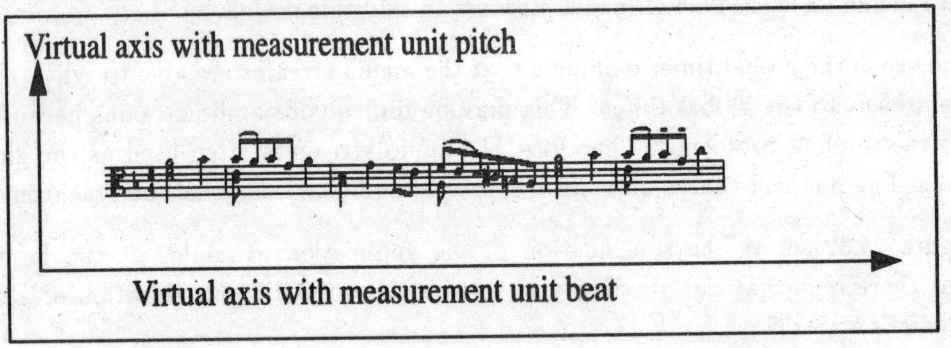


Figure 15.33: *Musical notes as an example of virtual axis.*

The mapping of the virtual axes to real axes is done in run-time. In the example shown in Figure 15.33, the pitch axis is mapped to the audio frequency and the beat axis is mapped to a timer.

The application example of Figure 15.13 can be realized in this approach by two time axes and an interaction axis (Figure 15.34). The latter should have interaction events as measurements units. The assessment of the virtual axes method is summarized

| Advantage | Disadvantages |
|---|---|
| Easy to understand | Objects of unknown duration cannot be integrated, extensions to the model are required |
| Support of hierarchies easy to realize | Skew QoS must be specified indirectly by using the common time axis or additional QoS specifications must be given |
| Easy to maintain because of the mutual independence of objects | |
| Good abstraction for media contents | |
| Integration of time-independent objects is easy | |

Table 15.7: *Assessment of the time axis synchronization specification.*

in Table 15.8.

### 15.5.5 Control Flow-based Specification

In *control flow-based specifications*, the flow of the concurrent presentation threads is synchronized in predefined points of the presentation.

#### Basic Hierarchical Specification

*Hierarchical synchronization* descriptions [Gro89, SS90] are based on two main synchronization operations: *serial synchronization* of actions and *parallel synchronization* of actions (Figure 15.35). In a hierarchical synchronization specification, multimedia objects are regarded as a tree consisting of nodes which denote serial or parallel presentation of the outgoing subtrees.

An action can be either atomic or compound. An atomic action handles the presen-

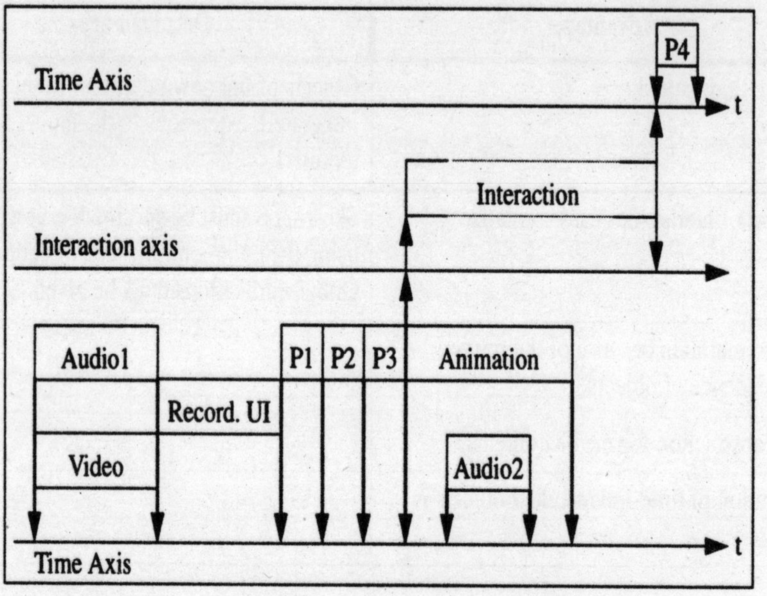


Figure 15.34: *Virtual time axis specification example.*

tation of either a single-media object, user input or delay. Compound actions are a combination of synchronization operators and atomic actions.

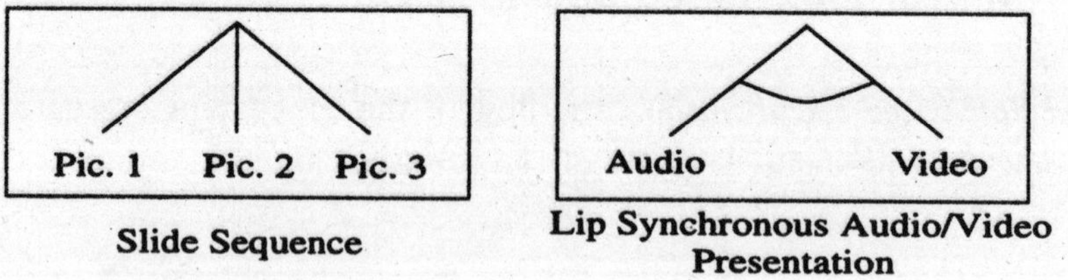


Figure 15.35: *Serial and parallel presentations.*

The introduction of a delay as a possible action [LG90a] allows the modeling of further synchronization behavior like delays in serial presentations and delayed presentations of objects in a parallel synchronization.

Hierarchical structures are easy to handle and widely used. Restrictions from the hierarchical structure arise from the fact that each action can only be synchronized at its beginning or end. This means, for example, that the presentation of subtitles at

| Advantages | Disadvantages |
|---|---|
| Easy to understand | Skew QoS defined only indirectly or through additional specifications |
| Often specification is made according to the problem space possible | Specification may become complex with many axes |
| Good possibility for building hierarchies | Mapping of axes at run-time may be complex and time-consuming |
| Easy to maintain because objects are kept as units and mutually independent objects | |
| Good abstraction for media content | |
| Easy integration of time-independent media objects | |
| Interactive objects can be included using specialized axes | |

Table 15.8: *Assessment of the virtual axis synchronization specification.*

parts of a video stream requires the video stream to be split into several consecutive components. This can be seen in Figure 15.36 for the synchronization specification of the animation and audio block in the example introduced in Section 15.2.3.3. The animation must be split into the parts Animation 1, Animation 2 and Animation 3 to be correctly synchronized with the audio block.

Accordingly, a synchronized multimedia object used as a component in another synchronization can no longer be regarded as an abstract unit if it has to be synchronized between the beginning and end of its presentation. That is to say, hierarchical structures do not support adequate abstraction for the internal structure of multimedia objects. In addition, there are synchronization conditions which cannot be represented using hierarchical structures. For example, the three objects shown in Figure 15.37 are presented in parallel, where any pair of objects is synchronized but always independently of the third object. To specify this synchronization, additional synchronization points must be used.

The assessment of the basic hierarchical method is summarized in Table 15.9.

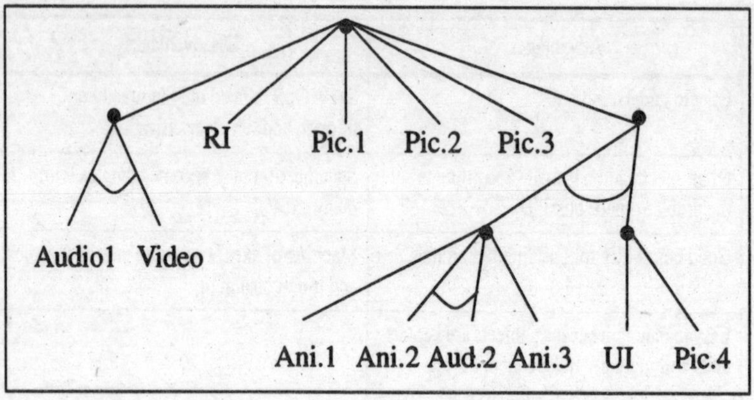


Figure 15.36: *Hierarchical specification example (RI = Recorded Interaction, Pic = Picture, Aud. = Audio, Ani. = Animation, UI = User Interaction).*

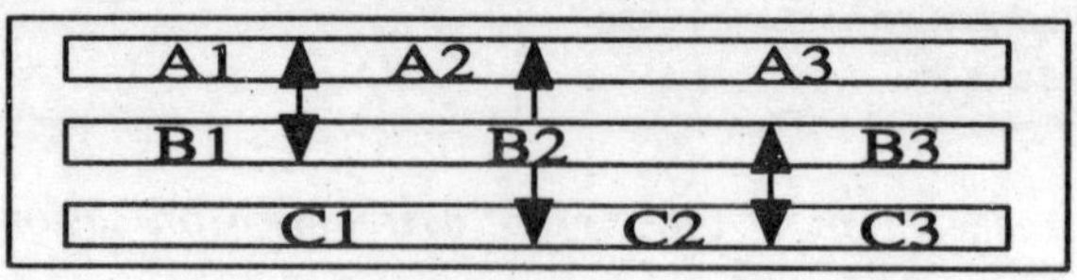


Figure 15.37: *Non-describable synchronization.*

### Reference Points

In the case of synchronization via reference points [Ste90, BHLM92], time-dependent single-medium objects are regarded as sequences of closed LDUs. The start and stop times of the presentation of a media object, in addition to the start times of the subunits of time-dependent media objects, are called *reference points.* Synchronization between objects is defined by connecting reference points of media objects. A set of connected reference points is called a *synchronization point.* The presentation of the subunits that participate in the same synchronization point must be started or stopped when the synchronization point is reached. This approach to synchronization specifies temporal relations between objects without explicit reference to time.

Like synchronization based on a time axis, this description allows synchronization at any time during the presentation of an object; moreover, object presentations of

| Advantages | Disadvantages |
|---|---|
| Easy to understand | Additional description of skew QoS necessary |
| Natural support of hierarchies | For the presentation of time-independent media objects, presentation durations must be added |
| Integration of interactive objects is easy | Splitting of media objects for synchronization purposes is necessary |
| | No adequate abstractions for media object contents |
| | Some synchronization scenarios cannot be described |

Table 15.9: *Assessment of the basic hierarchical synchronization specification.*

unpredictable duration can be integrated easily. This type of specification is also very intuitive to use.

A drawback of reference point synchronization is that it requires mechanisms for detecting inconsistencies. In addition, synchronization based on reference points does not allow for specification of delays in a multimedia presentation. To solve this problem, Steinmetz [Ste90] proposes time specifications which specify explicit real-time-based delays. The inclusion of timers also solves this problem. The specification based on a global timer can be regarded as a subset of the reference point synchronization: a timer according to Figure 15.10 can be used as global timer and all objects refer only to this timer.

In a reference point synchronization specification, the coherence between data streams can be described by specifying a suitable set of synchronization points between the two data streams. A close lip synchronization with a maximal skew of +/- 80 ms can be realized by setting a synchronization point, for example, every second frame of a video (Figure 15.38). If no lip synchronization is required, it may be sufficient to set a synchronization point every 10 frames of the video. Therefore, the specification of the skew QoS is directly integrated into this specification method.

An example of the synchronized integration of time-dependent and time-independent media objects is shown in Figure 15.39. Starting and stopping a slide presentation are initiated by reaching suitable LDUs in the audio presentation.

The application example can be completely specified with the reference point synchronization model shown in Figure 15.40.

Hierarchies in the reference point synchronization method can be created by regarding a set of synchronized objects as one object, with the start of the first object and end of the last object as reference points. Virtual reference points for this presentation can be specified and mapped to the reference points within the hierarchy. The semantic of this mapping can become complex in the case that objects of unknown duration are included in the hierarchy. The assessment of the reference point method is summarized in Figure 15.41.

### Timed Petri Nets

Another type of specification is based on *petri nets* [LG92, LG91b] that are extended with duration specifications at various places, a kind of *timed petri net.*

The rules for a timed petri net are:

- A transition fires, if all input places contain a nonblocking token.
- If a transition fires, a token is removed from each input place and a token is added to each output place.
- A token that is added to a new place is blocked for the duration that is assigned to this place.

A slide show can be specified by assigning corresponding durations to the places (Figure 15.42).

For time-dependent media objects, each place in the petri net represents an LDU. Lip synchronization can be modeled on the basis of connecting appropriate LDUs

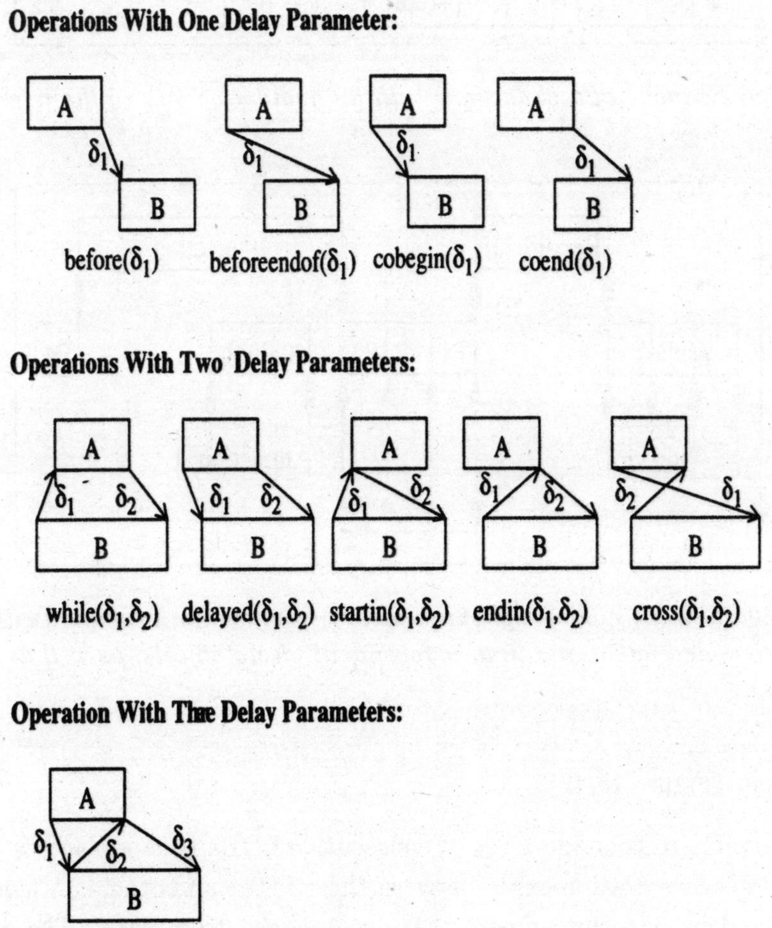


Figure 15.38: *Lip synchronization in the reference point synchronization model.*

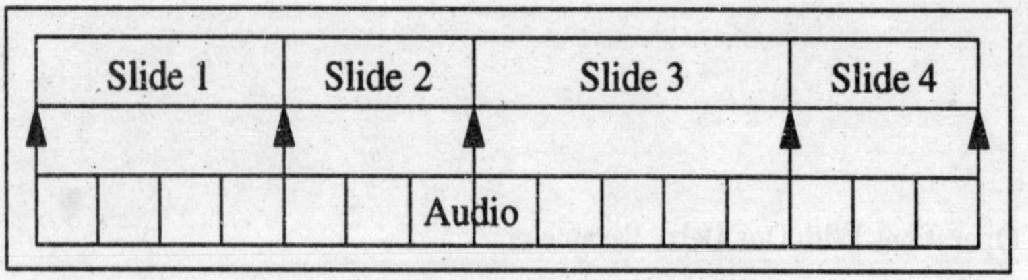


Figure 15.39: *Example of a slide show with an audio sequence in the reference point model.*

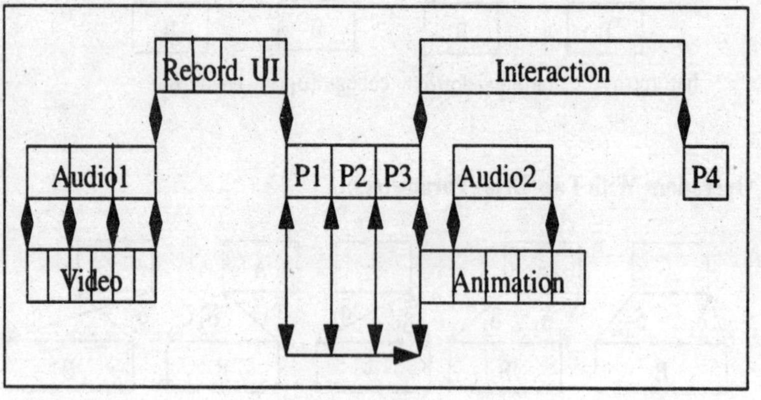


Figure 15.40: *Reference point synchronization specification example (with the integration of time-dependent and time-independent media objects, as well as closed and open LDUs).*

by transitions (Figure 15.43).

It is also possible to combine a set of consecutive LDUs to one place as long as no inter-object synchronization exists between these LDUs and others. A hierarchy can be constructed by creating subnets that are assigned to a place. The duration of the longest path in the subnet is assigned to the place (Figure 15.44).

The application example of Figure 15.13 can be modeled as shown in Figure 15.45. The subnets are not shown because they can be created by the straightforward use of the techniques described above.

Timed petri nets allow all kinds of synchronization specifications. The main drawbacks are the complex specifications and the insufficient abstraction of media object

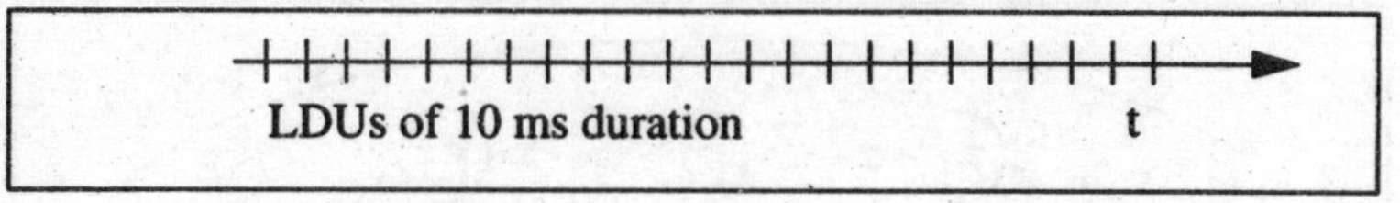


Figure 15.41: *Assessment of the reference point synchronization specification.*

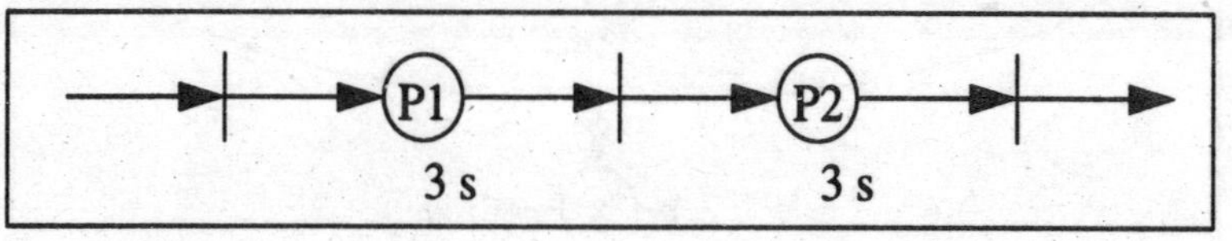


Figure 15.42: *Petri net specification of a slide show.*

content because, much like the hierarchical specification, the media objects must be split into subobjects. The assessment of the timed petri net method is summarized in Table 15.10.

### 15.5.6 Event-based Synchronization

In the case of event-based synchronization, presentation actions are initiated by synchronization events, e.g., as in HyTime and HyperODA [App89]. Typical presentation actions are:

- Start a presentation.
- Stop a presentation.
- Prepare a presentation.

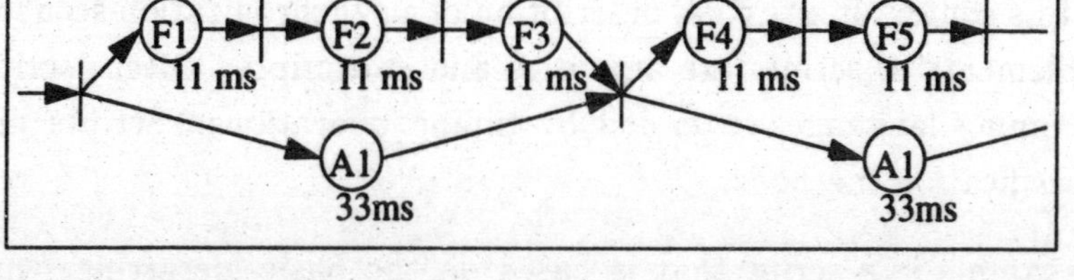


Figure 15.43: *Petri net lip synchronization.*

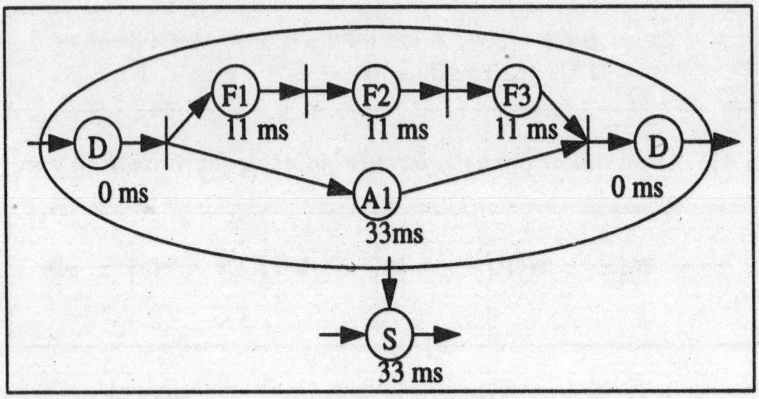


Figure 15.44: *Petri net hierarchy comprised of the synchronization of A1 and F1 to F3.*

The events that initiate presentation actions may be external (e.g., generated by a timer) or internal to the presentation generated by a time-dependent media object that reaches a specific LDU.

Table 15.11 sketches an event-based synchronization for parts of the application example.

This type of specification is easily extended to new synchronization types. The major drawback is that this type of specification is difficult to handle in the case of realistic scenarios. The user is lost in this state transition type of synchronization specification, hence creation and maintenance becomes difficult. The assessment of the event-based method is summarized in Table 15.12.

### 15.5.7 Scripts

A *script* in this context is a textual description of a synchronization scenario [IBM90, TGD91]. Elements of scripts are activities and subscripts. Often, scripts become full programming languages extended by timing operations. Scripts may rely on different specification methods.

A typical example is a script that is based on the basic hierarchical method and supports three main operations: serial presentation, parallel presentation and the

| Advantages | Disadvantages |
|---|---|
| Hierarchies can be created | Difficult to handle |
| Easy integration of time-independent objects | Complex specification |
| Easy integration of interactive objects | Splitting of media objects |
| Integrated skew QoS | Insufficient abstraction of media object content |

Table 15.10: *Assessment of the petri net synchronization specification.*

| Event / Action | Start | Audio1.stop | Timer1. ready | ... |
|---|---|---|---|---|
| Audio1 | start | | | |
| Video | start | | | |
| Pic.1 | | start | stop | |
| Timer1 | | start(3) | | |
| Pic.2 | | | start | |
| ... | | | | |

Table 15.11: *Event-based specification example.*

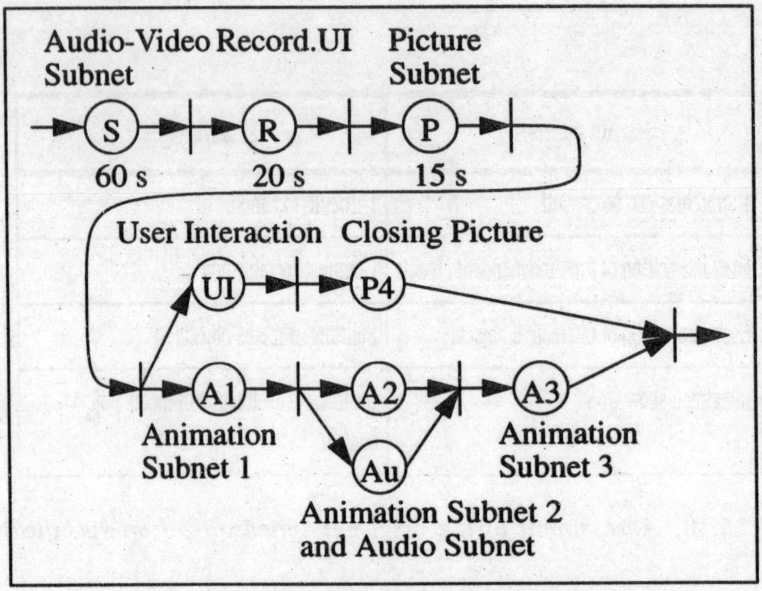


Figure 15.45: *Petri net specification example.*

repeated presentation of a media object.

The following example sketches a script for the application example from Figure 15.13. >> denotes a serial presentation, & denotes a parallel presentation and *n* denotes a presentation repeated *n* times. ([TGD91]):

```
activity DigAudio Audio(``video.au");
activity SMP Video(``video.smp");
activity XRecorder Recorder(``window.rec");
activity Picture Picture1(``picture1.jpeg");
activity Picture Picture2(``picture2.jpeg");
activity Picture Picture3(``picture3.jpeg");
activity Picture Picture4(``picture4.jpeg");
activity StartInteraction Selection;
activity DigAudio AniAudio(``animation.au");
activity RTAnima Animation(``animation.ani");
```

| Advantages | Disadvantages |
|---|---|
| Easy integration of interactive objects | Difficult to handle |
| Easily extensible by new events | Complex specification |
| Flexible because any event can be specified | Hard to maintain |
| | Integration of time-dependent objects by using additional timers |
| | Separate descriptions of skew QoS necessary |
| | Difficult use of hierarchies |

Table 15.12: *Assessment of the event-based synchronization specification.*

```
script Picture_sequence  3Pictures=  Picture1.Duration(5) >>
Picture2.Duration(5) >>
Picture3.Duration(5);

script Lipsynch AV = Audio & Video;
script AniComment AA = Animation & AniAudio.Translate(2);
script Multimedia Application_example {
AV >>
Record. UI >>
3Pictures >>
( (Selection >> Picture4) &
  AA )
```

Scripts are very powerful because they represent full programming environments. A disadvantage is that this method is more procedural than declarative. The declarative approach seems to be more easy for the user to handle. The assessment of the script method is summarized in Table 15.13.

| Advantages | Disadvantages |
|---|---|
| Good support for hierarchies | Difficult to handle |
| Logical objects can be kept | Complex specification |
| Easy integration of time-independent objects | Implicit usage of common timers necessary |
| Easy integration of interactive objects | Special constructs for skew QoS necessary |
| Easily extensible by new synchronization constructs | |
| Flexible because programmable | |

Table 15.13: *Assessment of the script synchronization specification.*

### 15.5.8 Comment

The presented synchronization specification methods have different specification capabilities and are different from the point of user-friendliness, but many of them just present different "views" of the same problem.

The different specification capabilities restrict the mapping between specifications of different methods to the common subset.

The selection of an appropriate specification method depends on the targeted application and on the existing environment. As the temporal behavior of multimedia objects is only one part of a presentation, we must keep in mind the context as it may be an audio/video editor or an MHEG presentation tool. The selected method must fit into the selected environment. There is no "best" or "worst" solution. For simple presentations without user interaction, the method based on a global timer seems to be appropriate. For complex structures with interaction, for example, the reference point model seems to be suitable.

In many cases, users will not directly specify the synchronization using a specific specification method. They will instead use a graphical authoring system that may produce specifications based on different methods. Experience shows that usually one of these specification methods underlies the construction of the user interface and therefore indirectly the advantages and disadvantages of the method reflect themselves at the user interface. In addition, many authoring systems allow the author to step out of the high-level graphical representation and to specify a complex synchronization directly at the lowest synchronization specification level, e.g., the textual level provided by the underlying method, which is not the best way to proceed.

## 15.6 Case Studies

Some interesting approaches to multimedia synchronization are described in this section and classified according to the reference model presented previously. In particular, we analyze synchronization aspects in standards of multimedia information exchange and the respective run-time environments and prototype multimedia systems which comprise several layers of the synchronization reference model.

### 15.6.1 Synchronization in MHEG

The generic space in *MHEG* provides a virtual coordinate system that is used to specify the layout and relation of content objects in space and time according to the virtual axes-based specification method. The generic space has one time axis of infinite length measured in *Generic Time Units (GTUs)*. The MHEG run-time environment must map the GTUs to *Physical Time Units (PTUs)*. If no mapping is specified, the default is one GTU mapped to one millisecond. Three spatial axes (X=latitude, Y=longitude, Z=altitude) are used in the generic space. Each axis is of finite length in an interval of $[-32768, +32767]$. Units are *Generic Space Units (GSUs)*. Also, the MHEG engine must perform mapping from the virtual to the real coordinate space.

The presentation of content objects is based on the exchange of action objects sent to an object. Examples of actions are prepare to set the object in a presentable state, run to start the presentation and stop to end the presentation.

Action objects can be combined to form an action list. Parallel action lists are executed in parallel. Each list is composed of a delay followed by delayed sequential actions that are processed serially by the MHEG engine, as shown in Figure 15.46.

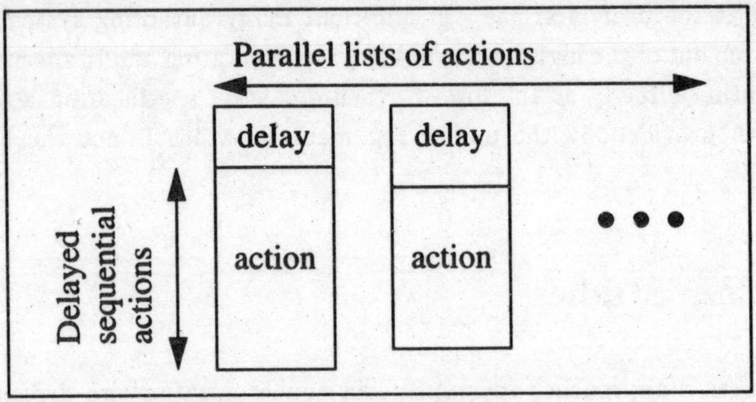


Figure 15.46: *Lists of actions.*

By using links it is possible to synchronize presentations based on events. Link conditions may be associated with an event. If the conditions associated with a link are fulfilled, the link is triggered and actions assigned to this link are performed. This is a type of event-based synchronization.

### MHEG Engine

At the European Networking Center in Heidelberg, an MHEG engine [Gra94] has been developed. The MHEG engine is an implementation of the object layer. The architecture of the MHEG engine is shown in Figure 15.47.

The *Generic Presentation Services* of the engine provide abstractions from the presentation modules used to present the content objects. The *Audio/Video-Subsystem* is a stream layer implementation. This component is responsible for the presentation of the continuous media streams, e.g., audio/video streams. The *User Interface Services* provide the presentation of time-independent media, like text and graphics, and the processing of user interactions, e.g., buttons and forms.

The MHEG engine receives the MHEG objects from the application. The *Object*

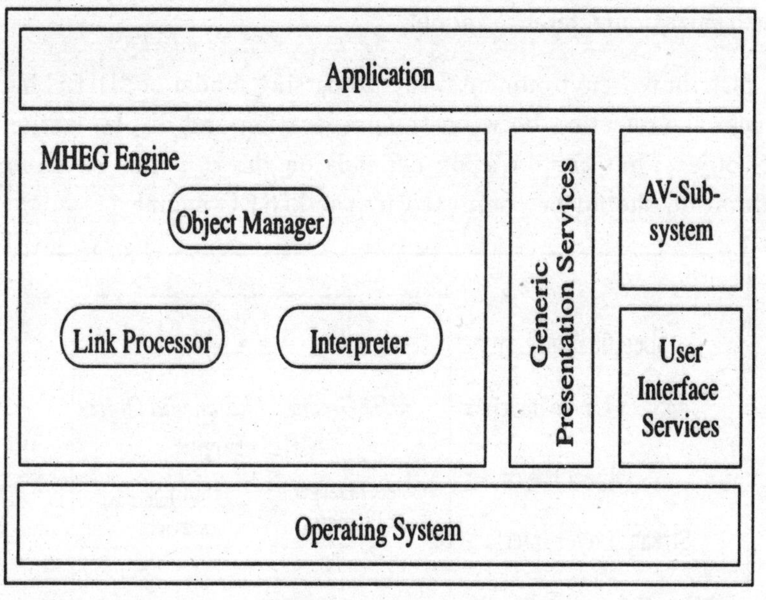


Figure 15.47: *Architecture of an MHEG engine.*

*Manager* manages these objects in the run-time environment. The *Interpreter* processes the action objects and events. It is responsible for initiating the preparation and presentation of the objects. The *Link Processor* monitors the states of objects and triggers links, if the trigger conditions of a link are fulfilled.

The run-time system communicates with the presentation services by events. The *User Interface Services* provide events that indicate user actions. The *Audio/Video-Subsystem* provides events about the status of the presentation streams, like end of the presentation of a stream or reaching a cuepoint in a stream.

### Summary

MHEG is a standardized exchange format that is used as the exchange format at the object layer. The synchronization is based on the virtual axes- and event-based methods. An MHEG engine represents the object layer run-time environment. The object layer implementation of the described engine is based on media servers. The Audio/Video-Subsystem represents the stream layer. Figure 15.48 shows the relation to the synchronization reference model.

Regarding distributed environments, the processing model of MHEG has the following drawback: the duration between the preparation and display action is coded in the MHEG object, but the duration depends on the run-time environment; therefore, this duration should be computed by the MHEG engine.

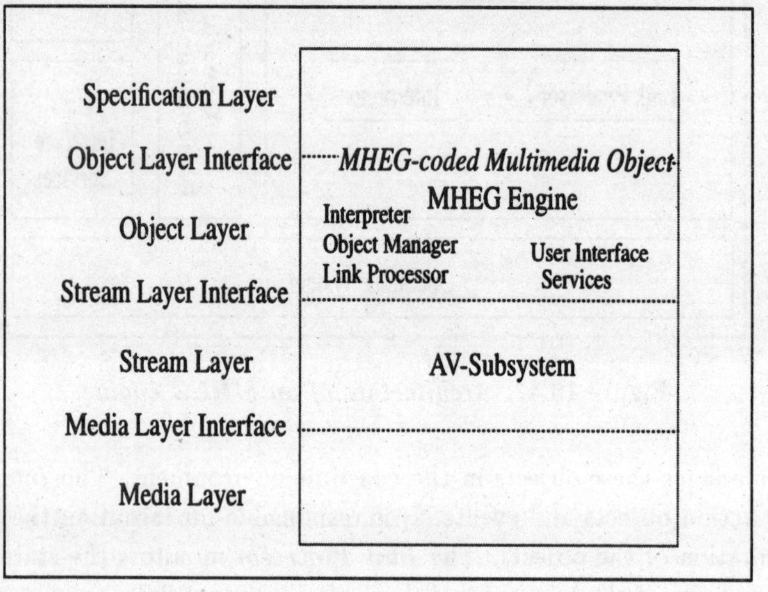


Figure 15.48: *Classification of MHEG and MHEG engine components according to the reference model.*

### 15.6.2 HyTime

HyTime (Hypermedia/Time-based Structuring Language) is an international standard (ISO/IEC 10744) [Org92] for the structured representation of hypermedia information. HyTime is an application of the *Standardized General Markup Language (SGML)* [Smi89] (see also Section 13.3).

SGML is designed for document exchange, whereby the document structure is of great importance, but the layout is a local matter. The logical structure is defined by markup commands that are inserted in the text. The markups divide the text into SGML elements. For each SGML document, a *Data Type Definition (DTD)* exists which declares the element types of a document, the attributes of the elements and how the instances are hierarchically related. A typical use of SGML is the publishing industry where an author is responsible for the content and structure of the document, and the publisher is responsible for the layout. As the content of the document is not restricted by SGML, elements can be of type text, picture or other multimedia data.

HyTime defines how markup and DTDs can be used to describe the structure of hyperlinked time-based multimedia documents. HyTime does not define the format or encoding of elements. It provides the framework for defining the relationship between these elements.

HyTime supports addresses to identify a certain piece of information within an element, linking facilities to establish links between parts of elements and temporal and spatial alignment specifications to describe the relationships between media objects.

HyTime defines architectural forms that represent SGML element declaration templates with associated attributes. The semantic of these architectural forms is defined by HyTime. A HyTime application designer creates a HyTime-conforming DTD using the architectural forms he/she needs for the HyTime document. In the HyTime DTD each element type is associated with an architectural form by a special HyTime attribute.

The HyTime architectural forms are grouped into the following modules:

- The *Base Module* specifies the architectural forms that comprise the document.

- The *Measurement Module* is used to add dimensions, measurement and counting to the documents. Media objects in the document can be placed along with the dimensions.

- The *Location Address Module* provides the means to address locations in a document. The following addressing modes are supported:

  - *Name Space Addressing Schema:* Addressing to a name identifying a piece of information.
  - *Coordinate Location Schema:* Addressing by referring to an interval of a coordinate space if measuring along the coordinate space is possible. An example is to address to a part of an audio sequence.
  - *Semantic Location Schema:* Addressing by using application-specific constructs.

- The *Scheduling Module* places media objects into Finite Coordinate Spaces (FCSs). These spaces are collections of application-defined axes. To add measures to the axes, the measurement module is needed. HyTime does not know the dimension of its media objects. So-called events are used for the presentation of media objects. An event is an encapsulation of a media object and comprises the layout specification related to an FCS. The events can be placed absolutely or relatively to other events within the FCSs.

- The *Hyperlink Module* enables building link connections between media objects. Endpoints can be defined using the location address, measurements and scheduling modules.

- The *Rendition Module* is used to specify how the events of a source FCS, that typically provides a generic presentation description, are transformed to a target FCS that is used for a particular presentation. During the mapping, presentation-related modifications are executed, e.g., changing the color representation, projection of the dimensions from the source to the target FCS or scaling of the presentation.

### HyTime Engine

The task of a HyTime engine is to take the output of an SGML parser, to recognize architectural forms and to perform the HyTime-specific and application-independent processing. Typical tasks of the HyTime engine are hyperlink resolution, object addressing, parsing of measures and schedules, and transformation of schedules and dimensions. The resulting information is then provided to the HyTime application.

The HyTime engine, HyOctane [BRRK94], developed at the University Massachusetts at Lowell, has the following architecture: an SGML parser takes as input the application data type definition that is used for the document and the HyTime document instance. It stores the document object's markups and contents, as well as the applications DTD in the SGML layer of a database. The HyTime engine takes as input the information stored in the SGML layer of the database. It identifies the architectural forms, resolves addresses from the location address module, handles the functions of the scheduling module and performs the mapping specified in the rendition module. It stores the information about elements of the document that are instances of architectural forms in the HyTime layer of the database. The application layer of the database stores the objects and their attributes, as defined by the DTD. An application presenter gets the information it needs for the presentation of the database content, including the links between objects and the presentation coordinates to use for the presentation, from the database.

### Summary

HyTime is applicable to many application areas. It does not standardize content formats, encoding, document types or specific SGML DTDs. It provides a framework for addressing portions of hypermedia document contents and the definition of linking, alignment and synchronization. In the context of the synchronization reference model, a HyTime document, together with its DTD, can be used as input to the object layer. The synchronization is based on the virtual axes synchronization method. The SGML- and HyTime-related preprocessing is done by the HyTime engine in the object layer. The application presenter provides the other object layer and stream layer functionalities. Figure 15.49 shows the relation to the synchronization reference model.

Other classification possibilities are to regard the database as an object layer interface format or to use the database to generate an MHEG specification. In the latter case, the HyTime engine can be regarded as part of a format conversion tool.

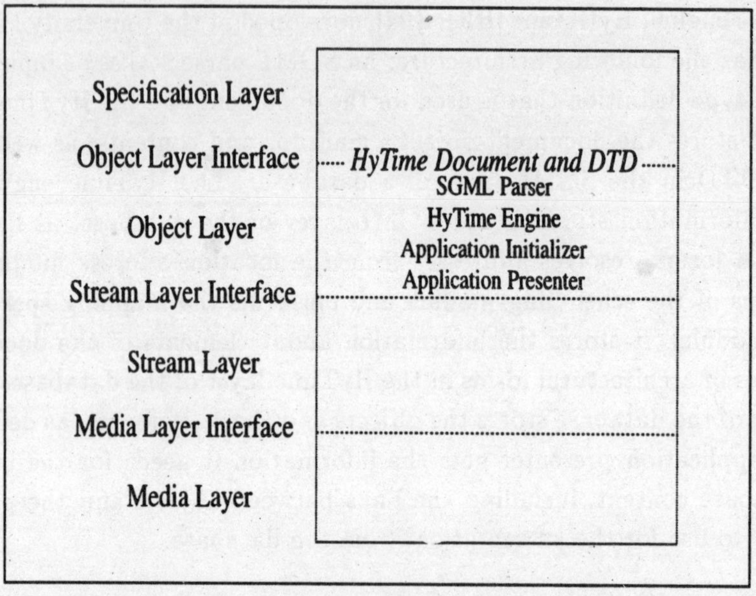


Figure 15.49: *Classification of HyTime and the HyTime engine according to the synchronization reference model.*

### 15.6.3 Firefly System

The objective of the approach of Buchanan and Zellweger [BZ93a, BZ93b] is to automatically generate consistent presentation schedules for interactive multimedia documents that comprise media objects of predictable behavior (like audio and video) and objects of unpredictable behavior (like user interactions). The generation algorithm is comprised of two phases. At the first phase, before execution of the presentation, high-level temporal specifications for a document are used to compute a presentation schedule, as far as possible without knowing the unpredictable durations. In the second phase during the presentation, the scheduling, depending on unpredictable durations, is incorporated.

The specification of the temporal constraints distinguishes media-level specifications that describe the temporal behavior of individual media objects and document-level specifications that describe the temporal behavior of a complete multimedia document, in particular the temporal relations between single media objects. Media items are used for the media-level specification. They provide a reference to a media object and are used to describe the temporal behavior of this media object. A media item consists of:

- *Events,* which represent points in time at the presentation of a media object. They are comparable to a reference point.
- *Durations,* which specify the duration between two subsequent events in a media object. A duration is represented by a triple of values: *minDuration, optDuration* and *maxDuration.* If the three values are equal, the presentation duration is fixed. If they specify an interval, the presentation is adjustable. No values are assigned for an unpredictable duration.
- *Costs,* which can be used as measurement for the degree of degradation in the case of stretching the presentation toward the maximal duration, and respectively shrinking it toward the minimum duration.

A document-level specification consists of:

- *Media items,* which are involved in the presentation.
- *Temporal constraints,* which are used to describe explicit temporal relations between events in one or more media items. Temporal constraints are classified into temporal equalities that describe a fixed temporal relation between two events (e.g., same time, one event 10 s before the other), and temporal inequalities that describe a temporal relation without a specified time (e.g., one event before the other, one event at least 10 s and at last 20 s before the other).
- *Operations,* which can be associated with an event and include non-altering presentation-related operations, like increase volume of an audio presentation, and time-altering operations, like increase-playback-speed.
- *Duration and costs,* which can be described according to the media level. At the document level, this is used to describe a different behavior for several instances of one media item in a document.

- *Unpredictable event control,* which allows activation and deactivation of unpredictable events.

To support the development of temporal specifications, a graphical representation of the specification is supported. The synchronization specification method is a combination of reference point and interval-based synchronization. The scheduler for the presentation that is located at the object layer is divided into two parts: the compile-time scheduler and the run-time scheduler. The compile-time scheduler constructs a main schedule that controls the parts of a document that are predictable, and auxiliary schedules that control the parts of the document that depend on unpredictable events. It is an example of off-line schedule computation at the object layer.

The algorithm contains three parts:

- In the obtaining durations and costs step, the duration and costs for each media item are obtained. To do this, the media and document-level specifications for a media item are unified and time-altering operations are incorporated into the computation of the durations.

- In the finding connected components step, a union-find algorithm is used to find connected parts of a document. Two events are in the same connected component if they are related by a predictable duration or a temporal constraint. The connected components are called predictable, if there are no unpredictable events that trigger events of the component. Otherwise, they are called unpredictable.

- The assigning times to events step computes for each event in a connected component the time for that event with respect to the start time of the component. It uses a simplex algorithm with the durations and temporal constraints as constraints for the algorithm and the minimization of the costs as its objective function.

- In the creating commands step, the previous results are used to create the commands for the execution. A command includes a time when it must be executed, the media item to process, an associated event, the list of unpredictable events to be activated or deactivated and the operations to be executed. All commands of the predictable components are integrated in the main schedule. For each unpredictable component, a separate auxiliary schedule is constructed. To improve performance for a continuous media object with units of fixed durations, only the start of the complete media object and events that refer to other media objects are considered, not every single event within the media item. It is assumed that this stream, like presentation scheduling, is done separately.

The run-time scheduler is an example of on-line schedule computation at the object layer and controls the document clock, the execution schedule and handles the unpredictable events. After the compile-time scheduler has produced the schedules, the run-time scheduler copies the main schedule into the execution schedule and starts the document clock. If the document clock reaches a time with an associated command, it initiates the command. If an activated unpredictable event occurs that triggers an unpredictable component, the run-time scheduler merges the corresponding schedule into the execution schedule taking the actual document time as start time for the first command in the schedule to merge. Because unpredictable components may be triggered several times, the run-time scheduler marks the instances in the execution schedule to be able to distinguish the commands for the different instances of an unpredictable schedule.

### Summary

The Firefly system provides complete synchronization support. At the specification layer, an editor is provided. The temporal relations based on the reference point and interval-based specification methods are used at the object layer interface. The Scheduler provides off-line and on-line computation of presentation schedules at the object layer. The schedule of streams is only initiated at the object layer, the execution is located at the stream layer. Figure 15.50 shows the relation to the synchronization reference model.

The system provides well-organized scheduling planning and integration of unpredictable durations. Currently, the system does not consider media preparation durations, presentation restrictions by insufficient or missing local resources or delays introduced by networks.

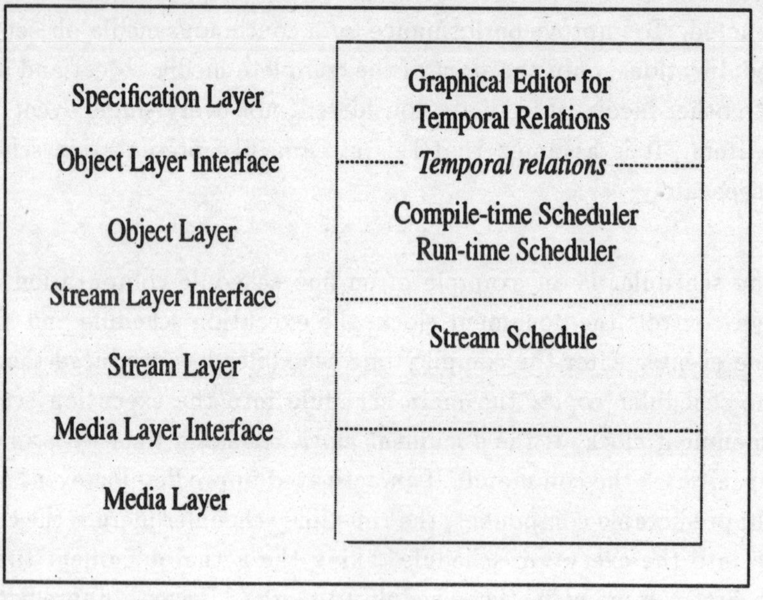


Figure 15.50: *Classification of the Firefly system according to the synchronization reference model.*

### 15.6.4 MODE

The *MODE (Multimedia Objects in a Distributed Environment)* system [Bla93], developed at the University of Karlsruhe, is a comprehensive approach to network transparent synchronization specification and scheduling in heterogeneous distributed systems. The heart of MODE is a distributed multimedia presentation service which shares a customized multimedia object model, synchronization specifications and QoS requirements with a given application. It also shares knowledge about networks and workstations with a given run-time environment. The distributed service uses all this information for synchronization scheduling when the presentation of a compound multimedia object is requested from the application.

Thereby, it adapts the QoS of the presentation to the available resources, taking into account a cost model and the QoS requirements given by the application.

The MODE system contains the following synchronization-related components:

- The *Synchronization Editor* at the specification layer, which is used to create synchronization and layout specifications for multimedia presentations.
- The MODE *Server Manager* at the object layer, which coordinates the execution of the presentation service calls. This includes the coordination of the creation of units of presentation (presentation objects) out of basic units of information (information objects) and the transport of objects in a distributed environment.
- The *Local Synchronizer*, which receives locally the presentation objects and initiates their local presentation according to a synchronization specification.
- The *Optimizer*, part of the MODE Server Manager, which performs the planning of the distributed synchronization and chooses presentation qualities and presentation forms depending on user demands, network and workstation capabilities and presentation performance.

### Synchronization Model

In the MODE system, a synchronization model based on synchronization at reference points is used [BHLM92]. This model is extended to cover handling of time intervals, objects of unpredictable duration and conditions which may be raised by the underlying distributed heterogeneous environment.

A synchronization specification created with the Synchronization Editor and used by the Synchronizer is stored in textual form. The syntax of this specification is defined in the context-free grammar of the Synchronization Description Language. This way, a synchronization specification can be used by MODE components, independent of their implementation language and environment.

MODE distinguishes between dynamic basic objects and static basic objects. A presentation of a dynamic basic object is composed of a sequence of presentation objects. This corresponds to a stream of LDUs. The index of each presentation object is called a reference point. The presentation of a static basic object, that may be a time-independent media object, as well as an interactive object, has only two reference points, the beginning and the end of the presentation. The description of a reference point, together with the corresponding basic object, is called a synchronization element, denoted in the form BasicObject.ReferencePoint. Two or more synchronization elements can be combined into a synchronization point. An entire inter-object synchronization is defined by the list of all synchronization points.

A presentation quality can be specified for each basic object. It is described by a set of attributes comprising an attribute name, preferred value and value domain that describes all possible values for this attribute.

### Local Synchronizer

The Local Synchronizer performs synchronized presentations according to the synchronization model introduced above. This comprises both intra-object and inter-object synchronization. For intra-object synchronization, a presentation thread is created which manages the presentation of a dynamic basic object. Threads with different priorities may be used to implement priorities of basic objects. All presentations of static basic objects are managed by a single thread.

Synchronization is performed by a signaling mechanism. Each presentation thread reaching a synchronization point sends a corresponding signal to all other presentation threads involved in the synchronization point. Having received such a signal, other presentation threads may perform acceleration actions, if necessary. After the dispatch of all signals, the presentation thread waits until it receives signals from all other participating threads of the synchronization point; meanwhile, it may perform a waiting action.

### Planning and Execution of the Distributed Presentation

Before starting any presentation, the Optimizer is invoked. The Optimizer uses a heuristic search algorithm taking the special conditions of a distributed environment like multiple steps of the synchronization in a distributed environment, multiple communication patterns, buffering requirements and merging into account. It uses information about the network, like the available bandwidth, service qualities and available resources at the workstation, as well as information about the processing demands for media objects. This information is provided to the Optimizer by environment and application media descriptions [Bla92].

The planning result determines the achievable quality value for each presentation attribute according to both user demands and network and workstation resources. The result of the planning process is the MODE Flow Graph [Bla91b] that describes the times and nodes at which operations must be executed. The partitioned Flow Graph is delivered to the involved nodes and executed at run-time by the distributed MODE Server Manager.

### Exceptions Caused by the Distributed Environment

The correct temporal execution of the plan depends on the underlying environment, if the workstations and network provide temporal guarantees for the execution of the operations. Therefore, MODE provides several guarantee levels. If the underlying distributed environment cannot give full guarantees, MODE considers the possible error conditions. Three types of actions are used to define a behavior in the case of exception conditions, which may be raised during a distributed synchronized presentation: 1) A waiting action can be carried out if a presentation of a dynamic basic object has reached a synchronization point and waits longer than a specified time at this synchronization point. Possible waiting actions are, for example, continuing presentation of the last presentation object ("freezing" a video, etc.), pausing or cancellation of the synchronization point. 2) When a presentation of a dynamic basic object has reached a synchronization point and waits for other objects to reach this point, acceleration actions represent an alternative to waiting actions. They move the delayed dynamic basic objects to this synchronization point in due time. Possible actions include temporarily increasing the presentation speed or skipping all objects in the presentation up to the synchronization point. 3) When a presentation object does not arrive in time, it is possible to skip the object and to present the next one.

Priorities may be used for basic objects to reflect their sensitivity to delays in their presentation. For example, audio objects will usually be assigned higher priorities than video objects because a user recognizes jitter in an audio stream earlier than jitter in a video stream. Presentations with higher priorities are preferred over objects with lower priorities in both presentation and synchronization.

**Summary**

MODE is a complete synchronization system especially designed to support synchronization in a distributed environment. MODE provides a Synchronization Tool at the specification layer. The output of the tool is used as reference point-based interface format between the specification and the object layer. The Optimizer is part of the object layer and performs an off-line computation of the presentation schedule before the start of the presentation. The MODE Server Manager and the Synchronizer are also part of the object layer. The threads generated by them for the handling of dynamic media objects are part of the stream layer. Figure 15.51 shows the relation to the synchronization reference model.

### 15.6.5 Multimedia Tele-orchestra

At the University of Ottawa, the Multimedia Communication Research Laboratory (MCRLab) of Prof. Nicolas D. Georganas has developed a multimedia synchronization system known as *multimedia tele-orchestra.* This system is comprised of a sophisticated specification schema, the Time Flow Graph (TFG) [LKG94], and an implementation of this synchronization in a distributed environment [KG89]. In contrast to many other specification methods, the TFG takes into account that temporal knowledge may often be relative, i.e., it cannot be described by exact time parameters. The authors call this a fuzzy scenario. In addition, the duration of presentation parts may be imprecise and not known in advance. Hence, neither the exact occurring time points nor the duration are required to specify synchronization.

The notion of intervals serves as a basis for the TFG. In [LKG94] it is shown that all temporal relationships between intervals can be represented with TFGs. This leads to a partial sequential ordering which is used by the actual processing of

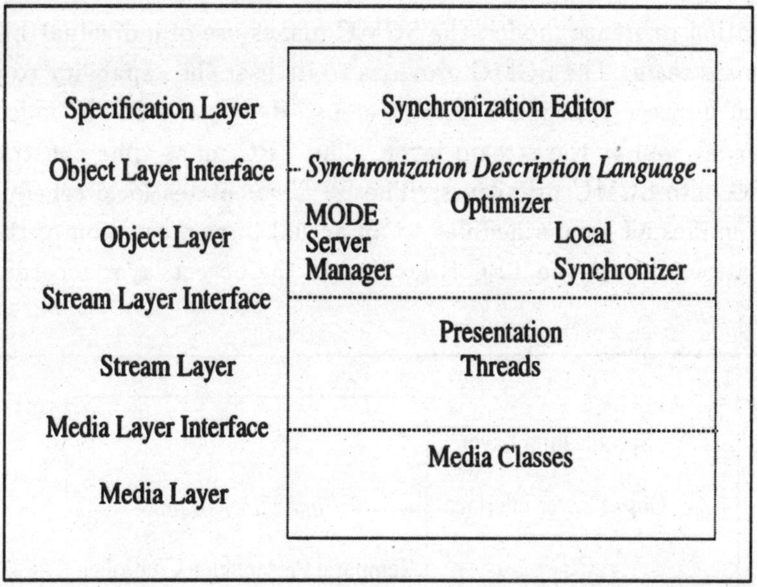


Figure 15.51: *Classification of the MODE system according to the synchronization reference model.*

synchronization at presentation time. With respect to our synchronization reference model, the TFG is an interval-based method located at the specification layer and also covers the interface between this layer and the object layer (see Figure 15.52).

Based on the TFG, a distributed multimedia synchronization schema was developed and became known as the *Synchronization Controller for Multimedia Communication (SCMC)* [KG89]. As a key feature, it takes into account that data may be originated by different sources located at different places. SCMC is targeted to run over ATM networks. However, the same algorithms can be used to operate on top of other multimedia-capable network configurations like Ethernet 10 Base-T, 100 Base-T and IsoEthernet.

In the tele-orchestration approach, a second component, the *Temporal Presentation Controller (TPC)*, is in charge of calculating a schedule with the earliest possible time to present objects at a remote computer. The result of the TPC, i.e., the respective schedule, is subsequently passed to the SCMC, which will actually control data processing to match the synchronization specification. In terms of the synchronization reference model, the SCMC makes use of individual LDUs. It does not rely on a stream. The SCMC provides to its user the capability to provide synchronization between individual data streams. Hence, the SCMC is located at the media layer, as well as the stream layer. The TPC maps time constraints defined by the TFG onto SCMC primitives. The TPC calculates local schedules, whereas the SCMC unifies all local schedules to an actual implementation of the demanded synchronization. Hence, the TPC is located in the object layer according to Figure 15.52.

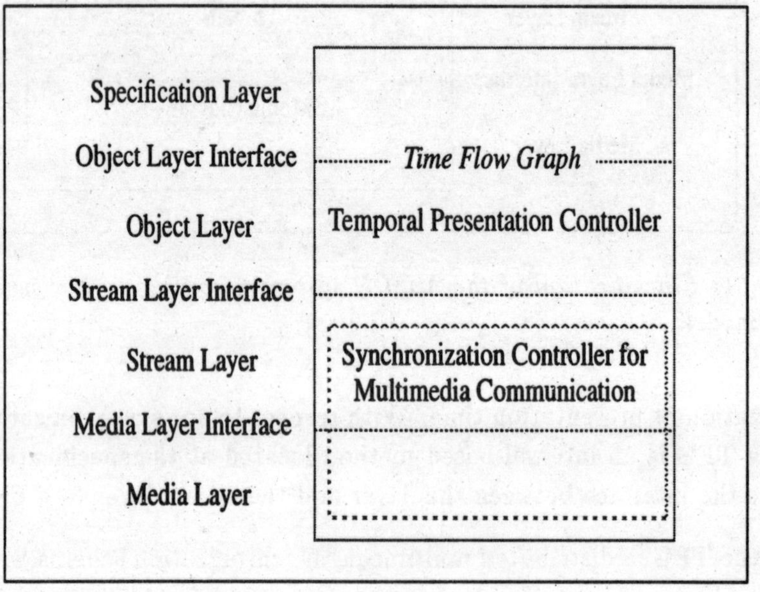


Figure 15.52: *Classification of the Tele-orchestra system according to the synchronization reference model.*

### Summary

Tele-orchestra nicely covers the aspects of all layers of our synchronization reference model. Distribution is known and handled at the specification and stream layers. In [LLKG93], performance analysis results of this synchronization schema are presented.

### 15.6.6 Littles Framework

The main objective of this framework, currently integrated at the University of Boston [Lit93] to a multimedia information system, is to support the retrieval and delivery of multimedia data. This system is comprised of methods for synchronization specification, data representation, temporal access control and run-time intermedia synchronization. Especially, it provides mechanisms to overcome delays caused by storage, communication and computations on media objects. It also provides mechanisms for scalability and graceful degradation of multimedia services.

The specification of the synchronization is based on petri nets [LG90a] and global timer-based specifications that are mapped to the *Temporal-Interval-Base (TIB)* modeling approach. The temporal relations in this model include a start time for a data element, the duration of its presentation and the end time for it. Relative positioning is defined by delays between the start times of presentations.

Based on this specification, static and dynamic presentation scheduling is computed at the object layer. As an example of a simple planning algorithm in an environment with resource restriction, we present the static playout schedule computation algorithm [Lit92, LG92]. It assumes that the data elements are stored in a remote database. The data must be transported to the presentation workstation via a packet-switched network with restricted capacity. In a first step, the synchronization specification is used to compute the point of time for the start of the presentation ($p_i$) for each data unit. This is easily possible using the duration of the presentations ($m_i$). Using the start points of the presentations, it is necessary to compute the point of times to access the data units ($q_i$) from the database because they need a time ($T_i$) to be transported.

Let $D_p$ be the constant propagation delay, $D_t$ the delay proportional to the packet size (medium packet size / channel capacity) and $D_v$ the variable load-dependent delay. Then, $T_i$ is defined as $T_i = D_p + D_t + D_v$.

The following conditions must be fulfilled:

- $p_i \geq q_i + T_i$ (The data units must be available in time.)
- $q_{i-1} \leq q_i - T_{i-1} + D_p$ (Data should be accessed when previous sending of data

is finished.)

The following algorithm is used to compute $q_i$:

```
q[m] = p[m] - T[m] // Start with the last data unit.

for i = 0 to m-2
if q[m-i] < p[m-i-1] - Dp  // Collision
q[m-i-1] = q[m-1] - T[m-i-1] + Dp // Resolve collision
else
q[m-i-1] = p[m-i-1] - T[m-i-1] // No collision
end
end
```

Because static scheduling does not consider dynamic changes in the environment, as well as commands from the user that alter, for example, the presentation speed, dynamic scheduling is introduced. The dynamic scheduling approach is called *Limited A Priori (LAP) scheduling.* It performs the scheduling and reservation of resources only for a short period of time. The multimedia presentation is split into components of similar resource usage. For these components, the schedules are computed and statistical resource reservation is used. Subsequently, the session scheduler executes the presentation of the components. In the case of user-initiated presentation manipulation operations or of load changes, the schedules are recalculated.

To support interstream synchronization, skew control mechanisms are supported. They are based on dropping and duplicating data units, in the case that a queue representing the stream processing reaches low or high threshold values.

The petri net and time-line specifications in the specification layer are mapped to a TIB specification as an object layer interface format that is a type of interval-based synchronization. The off-line and on-line scheduling is located at the object layer. Additional skew control is provided at the stream layer.

**Summary**

The Littles framework represents a well-defined approach combining several layers. Its conception is concentrated on the retrieval of multimedia objects on one server and considers only a reduced set of distribution relevant parameters.

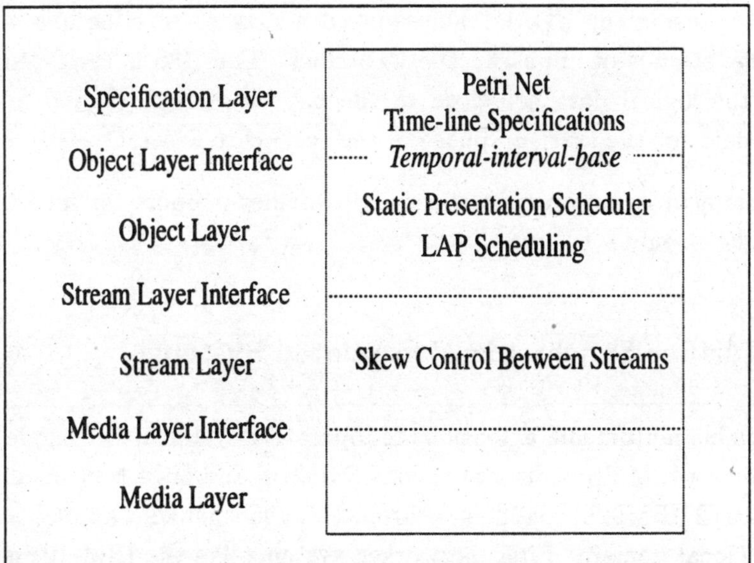


Figure 15.53: *Classification of Littles Framework according to the synchronization reference model.*

### 15.6.7 ACME

*ACME (Abstractions for Continuous MEdia)* [AH91b] is an I/O server for continuous data streams in the stream layer. The server controls a set of physical devices. Users can define logical devices as abstractions from physical devices. A stream path is build up by connecting input and output devices. The connection may be a real network connection. The stream consists of LDUs with an assigned time stamp.

A *Logical Time System (LTS)* synchronizes the I/O of logical devices. An LTS owns a clock that can be bound to the device which is most sensitive against delays, or it may be driven by a specified connection. Each LDU will be processed by a logical device, if the time stamp matches the LTS clock.

A blocking caused by a connection may occur. In this case, the connection's input device is blocked and must buffer more and more units. The output device is starving, because it does not get enough LDUs. The blocking is resolved by skipping LDUs or by pausing the LTS in the case that a max skew value has been reached between time stamps of units and the LTS clock. The LTS is restarted if the time stamps of the logical data are close to the paused LTS clock and an additional amount of data for the start-up phase of the resynchronization was received.

ACME offers a programming interface and provides support for media streams at the stream layer only.

### 15.6.8 Further Synchronization-related Systems

Today, available multimedia extensions for operating systems, like Apple QuickTime [DM92], Microsoft Multimedia Extensions [Mic91a] and IBM Multimedia Presentation Manager/2 [IBM92b] contain synchronization mechanisms applied at the stream layer in the local domain. First, networked systems like the IBM Ultimedia Server cover some synchronization issues in a distributed environment.

The Orchestration Service [CGCH92] provides a stream-oriented interface for synchronized playout of continuous media in a distributed environment. Nicolai [Nic90], Little [LG91a], Escobar [EDP92], Shepherd [SS90], Ramanathan [RR93] and Anderson (as described in Section 6.7) have proposed techniques to control jitter among media streams in the stream layer. An evaluation and classification of these techniques is given in [EFI94].

Stefani, Harzad and Horn [SHH92] have proposed the use, at the object layer, of the synchronous language ESTEREL for the programming of multimedia synchronization. The language and its run-time environment provide support for fast event processing.

At the University of Geneva [TGD91], an object-oriented system with a global timer-based synchronization specification has been developed. At run-time, a global timer is available to all objects. Each object maps this time to its own local time that it uses for its intra-object synchronization. If the skew of the local time and the world time of the global timer exceeds a maximal value, a resynchronization with the world time is performed.

Bultermans framework [Bul93] handles the problems of sharing network resources, synchronizing data coming from multiple sources and representation of data on heterogeneous hosts in a distributed environment. The components of the framework can manage the resources of the distributed environment for all active applications. The necessary information is provided by a specification of the applications resource and synchronization demands.

The Tactus system [DNN+93] includes a server for the synchronization of media at the sink node and an interface toolkit extented to support computation and controlling of streams and to deliver them to the presentation server. The scheduling is computed in advance to avoid delays at run-time. An introduced cut operation allows for low-latency reaction to user interactions by selecting between pre-computed schedules.

The use of traditional event-based user interface servers can be the reason for synchronization failures caused by the delay between calling the server to do a presentation and the actual presentation performance of the server. The time relations of demanded presentations get lost quite often. A proposal to handle this problem is to extend the window server to delay the execution of a presentation until a client-defined event occurs. This allows the reintroduction of the time relations between presentations in the server.

HyperODA [App89] is a standardization activity that defines a multimedia document exchange format. It is an extension of the *Open Document Architecture (ODA)* [BB91b]. The extension of ODA to a multimedia and hypermedia document architecture requires new content architectures, e.g., for audio and video, and the definition of a model for the layout in time and integration with the layout in space. Intra-object synchronization is included in the content architectures, for example, in the audio content architecture. Inter-object synchronization is realized by event-based synchronization in prototypes. HyperODA is still in development.

### 15.6.9 Comment

A large number of synchronization supporting systems have been developed. Commercially available synchronization support is mainly restricted to the support of streams in local systems. Many research efforts are directed towards support of distributed environments, the development of presentation scheduling strategies and the integration of user interaction. The analysis of existing systems has confirmed that the synchronization reference model matches the structuring needs of multimedia synchronization systems.

## 15.7 Summary and Outlook

### 15.7.1 Summary

In integrated multimedia systems, several aspects regarding synchronization must be considered. Unfortunately, the same term is used by many authors to denote different issues. In this chapter, synchronization-related terms have been defined and the layers of synchronization processing in multimedia systems have been classified in a synchronization reference model.

Intra-object synchronization has been defined as the synchronization of the LDUs of one media object. Inter-object synchronization is the synchronization between the media objects.

For live synchronization, the synchronization specification directly results from the temporal relations during the capturing of the objects. In synthetic synchronization, the temporal relations between media objects are explicitly created.

Several methods for the synthetic synchronization specification have been discussed which have been developed over the last years. The enhanced interval-based method specifies relations between presentation intervals. The axis methods specify synchronization using a mapping of media objects to one or more common axes. The basic hierarchical method uses operations like parallel and serial to define relations between media objects. The reference point approach allows for specification by defining relations between the LDUs of media objects. Petri nets can be used to specify the flow of a presentation by using places with durations and attaching the start of presentation operations to the firing of transitions. The event-based method couples presentation operations to events. Scripts are a programming-oriented approach which make use of synchronization operations. All of these methods have been shown to provide different specification capabilities as outlined in the previous sections. Conversions or mappings of specifications between the different methods are possible, but often they are restricted to a common subset of the specification capabilities. In most cases, the user uses a graphical editor to specify the synchronization. The underlying specification methods usually reflect themselves in the user interface abstraction and the editors allow for direct access to these specification methods.

The required QoS of the temporal relationships to be presented to the viewer/listener is derived from the user's perception. Experiments have shown that a skew of more than +/- 80 ms between an audio and a video stream is annoying, if lip synchronization is necessary. Further QoS requirements and a method for combining QoS requirements for multiple concurrent media have been presented.

A synchronization reference model has been defined that classifies synchronization facilities and interfaces in layers and allows the identification and classification of media synchronization issues and approaches. The specification layer is comprised of tools for the creation and conversion of synchronization specifications. The object layer takes at its service interface synchronization specifications as input. It plans and organizes the presentation, and initiates the presentation of time-independent media objects and of user interactions. For the presentation of continuous media, it uses the stream layer services. The stream layer supports at its interface abstractions of streams. It handles the intra-object synchronization and the synchronization between continuous media streams. The media layer hides at its interface access to the multimedia devices.

A distributed execution environment causes many additional challenges because of the distribution of the synchronization specification and the respective media objects, the required communications and delays in the distributed environment and the demanded use of multi-party communication. Synchronization in the distributed environment is a multi-step synchronization process and planning problem.

The most well-known systems have been classified according to this synchronization reference model. This case study results in a comparison of the capabilities of the various approaches. On the other hand, it has proved the usefulness of the synchronization reference model.

### 15.7.2 Future Topics

The expansive development of multimedia applications demands that presentations be executed on heterogeneous platforms. For that purpose, standards like MHEG and ScriptX are used that support exchangeable synchronization specifications. The success of multimedia exchange standards depends on the availability of run-time environments for the exchange formats. Which standard will be the most important in the future is still open. The availability of a standard format will also lead to the availability of supporting authoring systems.

The upcoming availability of multimedia teleservices demands an open distributed environment. For that purpose, an open stream mechanism and open object layer services are required. Initial work in the area of open streams in a heterogeneous environment has been done by the Interactive Multimedia Association, an industry-driven approach to open multimedia services. Additional efforts are required for the development of open object layer services.

### 15.7.3 Conclusion

In summary, we classified and compared the major approaches. Here, we focused on the demands, the various specification methods and basic run-time support concepts of the regarded approaches. Many more ideas, prototypes and products have implemented some kind of synchronization. However, it is still a matter of research to find out which are the most appropriate approaches for performing synchronization, especially in distributed environments.

# Chapter 16

# Abstractions for Programming

Most of the current commercially available multimedia applications are implemented in procedure-oriented programming languages (structural languages) such as C. In the past, multimedia-specific functions (e.g., changing the volume while playing an audio passage) were called, and respectively controlled, through hardware-specific libraries or device drivers.

Unfortunately, the application code of most commercial multimedia application programs are still highly dependent on hardware. The exchange of a multimedia device still often requires a re-implementation of important parts of the application program. This also happens when devices produced by different companies with similar or identical functionalities are exchanged. Consider, for example, video cards. Cards with the same functionalities are produced by companies like Apple, IBM, Parallax and RasterOps. However, the functions for accessing the cards are completely different. With the advent of common operating system extensions, this problem is attacked.

Some applications are implemented with the help of *tools.* These tools either directly generate the code or manage routines which can be used by the application in order to integrate the device units into the application. When these devices are exchanged, these applications often require either generation of new code or the tool must be changed and new interaction methods with the device units are needed.

A comparison can be made to the technique of programming with floating point numbers. Different computers, which support floating point numbers, differ in their architectures, instructions and interfaces. Sometimes, RISC architectures or parallel processors are used. Despite the variety of architectures, only a few standard formats, such as the IEEE format, are used for the presentation of numbers. The programmers mostly use the so-called *built-in functions* of higher programming languages to make use of floating point processing capabilities.

In contrast to multimedia environments, well-defined abstractions in higher programming languages can be found in the form of *data types* (e.g., float type in C). This approach hides the actual hardware configuration from the application without any major loss of performance.

In research, object-oriented approaches to the programming of multimedia systems and especially applications, have been used [Bla91a, GBD$^+$91, RBCD91, FT88, LG90a, SHRS90, SM92a]. Also, interfaces to communication systems are often implemented via object-oriented approaches.

*Multimedia objects* allow a fast integration in their environment despite their different capabilities, properties and functions. Development of a separate language or extensions of a compiler are not necessary. Multimedia can become an integral part of the programming environment if the proper class hierarchy is used. Unfortunately, the various currently used class hierarchies are very different. There is no generally accepted optimal class hierarchy.

This chapter describes different programming possibilities for accessing, and respectively representing multimedia data. Further, this chapter gives an overview of abstraction levels such as *libraries*, *system software*, *higher procedural programming languages* and *object-oriented approaches* going into more detail in some of the approaches.

## 16.1 Abstraction Levels

*Abstraction levels* in programming define different approaches with a varying degree of detail for representing, accessing and manipulating data. We describe in this chapter the abstraction levels with respect to multimedia data and their relations among each other (shown in Figure 16.1). A multimedia application may access

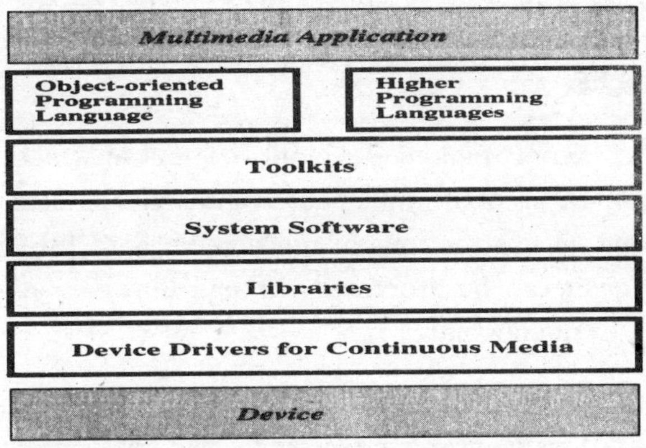


Figure 16.1: *Abstraction levels of the programming of multimedia systems.*

each level.

A *device* for processing continuous media can exist as a separate component in a computer. In this case, a device is not part of the operating system, but is directly accessible to every component and application. A *library*, the simplest abstraction level, includes the necessary functions for controlling the corresponding hardware with specific device access operations.

As with any device, multimedia devices can be bound through a device driver, respectively the operating system. Hence, the processing of the continuous data becomes part of the *system software.* This requires several properties described in Chapter 9 from the multimedia operating system, for example, appropriate schedulers, such as rate monotonic scheduler or earliest-deadline-first scheduler. Multimedia device drivers embedded in operating systems simplify considerably the implementation of device access and scheduling. For example, an operating system could resolve the register allocation for individual devices so that no collision occurs. In the case where allocation of registers for some devices (e.g., ATM host interface) is controlled through the Operating System (OS) and for other devices through applications (e.g., video card), the application programmer must be careful when assigning the registers.

Dedicated programming languages, such as programming for *Digital Signal Processing* (DSP), allow for the implementation of real-time programs. The corresponding program mostly runs in a *Real-Time Environment* (RTE) separate from the actual application. It is not very common today that an application software is programmed in the RTE.

*Higher procedural programming languages* build the next abstraction level. They are the languages most often used to implement commercial multimedia applications. Further, they can contain abstractions of multimedia data [SF92]. The code generated from the compiler can be processed through libraries, as well as through a system interface for continuous data.

More flexibility for the programmer is provided via the abstraction level – *an object-oriented environment.* This environment provides the application with a class hierarchy for the manipulation of multimedia. Also in this case, the generated or interpreted code can be processed and controlled through libraries, as well as through a system interface for continuous media (see Figure 16.1).

## 16.2 Libraries

The processing of continuous media is based on a set of functions which are embedded into libraries. This is the usual solution for programming multimedia data. These libraries are provided together with the corresponding hardware.

The device driver and/or library, which controls all available functions, also supports each device. (In the early DiME project at IBM Heidelberg, for example, a large number of different audio and video components were supported by corresponding hardware cards which were either connected directly to the workstation or were implemented as extension cards [SSSW89].) Here, the libraries differ very much in their degree of abstraction. Some libraries can be considered as extensions of the graphical user interface, whereas other libraries consist of control instructions passed as control blocks to the corresponding driver. Consider, for example, some functions supporting the IBM's early *Audio Visual Connection (AVC)*:

```
acb.channel = AAPI_CHNA
```

```
acb.mode = AAPI_PLAY
...
aud_init(&acb)  /* acb is the audio control block */
...
audrc = fab_open(AudioFullFileName,AAFB_OPEN,AAFB_EXNO, 0,&fab,0,0,0,0);
fork(START IN PARALLEL)
aud_strt(&acb)
displayPosition(RelativeStarttime, Duration)
...
acb.masvol = (unsigned char) Volume
audrc = aud_crtl(&cb)
...
```

Libraries are very useful at the operating system level, but there is no agreement (and may never be) over which functions are best for different drivers, i.e., which functions should be supported. As long as neither sufficient support of operating systems for continuous data nor further integration into the programming environment exist, there will always be a variety of interfaces and hence, a set of different libraries.

## 16.3 System Software

Instead of implementing access to multimedia devices through individual libraries, the device access can become part of the operating system. An example of access to multimedia devices and support for continuous media processing implemented in operating system is the experimental *Nemo* system from the University of Cambridge [Hyd94] (shown in Figure 16.2). The Nemo system consists of the Nemo Trusted Supervisor Call, running in supervisor mode, and three domains running in user mode: *system*, *device driver* and *application*.

The *Nemo Trusted Supervisor Call (NTSC)* code implements those functions which are required by user mode processes. It provides support for three types of processes. *System processes* implement the majority of the services provided by the operating system. *Device driver processes* are similar to system processes, but are

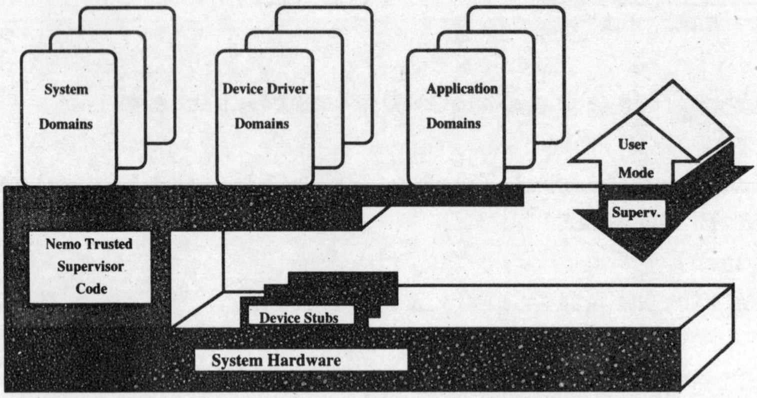


Figure 16.2: *Structure of the Nemo system.*

distinguished by the fact that they are attached to device interrupt stubs which execute in supervisor mode. Application processes contain user programs. Processes interact with each other via the system abstraction – InterProcess Communication (IPC) – which is implemented using low-level system abstractions *events* and, if required, *shared memory.* These system abstractions support the continuous media communication among processes [Hyd94].

The NTSC calls are separated into two classes, one containing calls which may only be executed by a suitable privileged system process such as kernel, the other containing calls which may be executed by any process. Further, NTSC is responsible for providing an interface between a multimedia hardware device and its associated driver process. This device driver implementation ensures that if a device has only a low-level hardware interface to the system software, code can be implemented within a device driver stub to implement a higher level interface. This allows the system builder to trade off hardware complexity and cost against the processor cycles required to implement a high-level device interface.

### 16.3.1 Data as Time Capsules

Some special abstractions, such as the *time capsule* [Her90], are seen in multimedia systems as being related to files systems. These file extensions serve as storage, modification and access for continuous media. Each *Logical Data Unit (LDU)* carries in its time capsule, in addition to its data type and actual value, its valid life span.

This concept is more useful for video than for audio. For example, if a video has 25 frames per second, each frame has a valid life span of 40 ms. The read access during a normal presentation occurs at this rate. The presentation rate changes for fast forward, slow forward or fast rewind processes. This can be achieved as follows:

1. The presentation life span of a data unit (e.g., a video frame) can change. For example, in a slow forward process, each frame is valid for a longer period of time.

2. The valid life span is not considered. Instead, the choice of the LDUs, which are specified through the time capsule, is influenced. In the fast forward process, some data units are skipped, but the valid life span for each frame is not changed. In the slow forward process, the presentation of individual frames occurs twice or several times. Note that this simple implementation is possible with uncompressed data. In the case of compressed motion pictures (e.g., MPEG), the information change of the consecutive frames needs to be considered and therefore an arbitrary individual frame cannot be skipped. However, access to I-frames can only be implemented.

The *time capsule* work can be extended by the refinement of LDUs (e.g., pixel, image frame, video sequence, etc.). The modification of the data rate should not follow for each sample value, but for a sequence of sample values. At the video output device, each frame must have the same valid life span because the modification of the physical rate is not possible. A similar concept, connection of data with rate, is presented in [GBD+91].

### 16.3.2 Data as Streams

A well-known, used and implemented abstraction at the system level is the *stream.* A stream denotes the continuous flow of audio and video data. Prior to this flow, the stream is established between source(s) and sink(s). This is equivalent to the setup of a connection in a networked environment. Subsequently, operations on a *stream* can be performed such as play, fast forward, rewind and stop.

In Microsoft Windows, a *Media Control Interface (MCI)* provides the interface for processing multimedia data [Mic91b, Mic91c]. It allows the access to continuous media streams and their corresponding devices.

For further considerations of streams and any kind of operating system requirements and basic system support of abstractions for programming continuous media application (e.g., page locking, preemptive scheduling, system call timeouts, etc.), Chapter 9 provides sufficient guidance.

## 16.4 Toolkits

A simpler approach (from the user perspective) in a programming environment than the system software interface for control of the audio and video data processing can be taken by using *toolkits* [AGH90, AC91]. These toolkits are used to:

- Abstract from the actual physical layer (it is also done in a limited way by the libraries).
- Allow a uniform interface for communication with all different devices of continuous media (with eventual input of quality of service parameters).
- Introduce the client-server paradigm (here, the communication can be hidden from the application in an elegant way).

Toolkits can also hide process-structures. It would be of great value for the development of multimedia application software to have the same toolkit on different system platforms, but according to current experiences, this remains to be a wish, and it would cause a decrease in performance.

Toolkits should represent interfaces at the system software level. In this case, it is possible to embed them into the programming languages or object-oriented environment. Hence, we describe the available abstraction in the subsequent section on programming languages and object-oriented approaches.

## 16.5 Higher Programming Languages

In the following, procedural higher programming languages will be called *High-Level Languages (HLL)*. In such an HLL, the processing of continuous media data is influenced by a group of similar constructed functions. These calls are mostly hardware- and driver-independent. Hence, their integration in HLLs leads to a wishful abstraction, supports a better programming style and increases the productivity. Programs must be capable of supporting and effectively manipulating multimedia data. Therefore, the programs in an HLL either directly access multimedia data structures, or communicate directly with the active processes in a real-time environment. The processing devices are controlled through corresponding device drivers. Compiler, linker and/or loader provide the required communication between the application program and the processing of continuous data. There does not yet exist a programming language which includes special constructs for the manipulation of multimedia data, besides possibly programming languages in the digital signal processing domain, which exist mostly at the assembler level to achieve the best time behavior of a program.

Media can be considered differently inside a programming language. In the following subsections, different developed variants are discussed. First results have been published in [SF92] and [Ste93b].

### 16.5.1 Media as Types

The following example shows the programming expression in an OCCAM-2 similar notation [Lim88, Ste88]. OCCAM-2 was derived from *Communication Sequential Processes (CSP)* [Hoa85]. This language is used for the programming of transputers [Whi90]. This notation was chosen in the following examples because of its simplicity and embedded expressions of parallel behavior. This does not mean that programming must be enforced this way or that this is a better way of processing multimedia data.

```
a,b REAL;
ldu.left1, ldu.left2, ldu.left_mixed AUDIO_LDU;
```

```
...
WHILE
  COBEGIN
     PROCESS_1
        input(micro1,ldu.left1)
     PROCESS_2
        input(micro2,ldu.left2)
  ldu.left\_mixed := a * ldu.left1 + b * ldu.left2;
  ...
END_WHILE
...
```

One of the alternatives to programming in an HLL with libraries is the concept of *media as types*. Here, the data types for video and audio are defined. In the case of text, character is the type (the smallest addressable element). A program can address such characters through functions and sometimes directly through operators. They can be copied, compared with other characters, deleted, created, read from a file or stored. Further, they can be displayed, be part of other data structures, etc. There is no plausible reason, known to the authors, why the same functionality cannot be applied to continuous media. The smallest unit can be the LDU. As described in Section 2.6, these data units can be of very different granularity (and therefore of different size and duration). In the above described example, two LDUs from microphones are read and mixed. The following example describes the merging of a text and motion picture. It is interpreted as the overlay of the text onto the motion picture:

```
subtitle TEXT_STRING;
mixed.video, ldu.video VIDEO_LDU;
...
WHILE
  COBEGIN
      PROCESS_1
            input(av_filehandle,ldu.video)
            IF new_video_scene
```

```
            input(subtitle_filehandle,subtitle)
        mixed.video := ldu.video + subtitle
    PROCESS_2
        output(video_window,mixed.video)
    ...
END_WHILE
...
```

An application for the merging example is a provision of subtitles in a video clip. For example, a distribution service can transmit a movie parallel with audio and subtitles in many languages. The user decides the combination. It is already done with stereo tone where two languages are partially provided. The mixture of two visual media, except the case of having a picture inside another picture, is not provided in this form. The mixture of text and video can already be implemented in a simple way through using, e.g., the teletext-decoder integrated in television devices. Note, that in the above described subtitle example, an implicit type conversion must occur. Variables of different types (VIDEO_LDU, TEXT_STRING) are added (ldu.video + subtitle) and at last again assigned to a variable (mixed.video) of one of these types (VIDEO_LDU). During the merge, respectively the adding process, their relative position and duration can be specified. Besides a standard value (e.g., center the subtitle in the lower part of the picture) specified a priori, this relative position can be defined freely by the programmer at the initialization phase. The duration is determined in the program through an explicit fade-in operation. It can also be defined relative to the scene duration at the initialization. Note that several possibilities for the duration specification are described in Chapter 15.

In this area, we gathered the following experiences:

- The real-time processing of LDUs with a very fine granularity is complicated in an HLL, respectively there are only conditionally predictable. An example of an LDU at very fine granularity is an individual audio sample. The following solutions are possible:
  - The HLL actually consists of two programming environments, which are mixed together in an application program. The real-time environment

contains digital signal processing algorithms, which are generated, modified, improved, etc. [RS78]. The non-real-time environment contains the whole conventional programming. The application programmer does not notice that he deals with those two environments. Both environments are concealed for the programmer. Hence, the code of both environments can be mixed.

- As an alternative, the algorithms of the corresponding environments can be contained in different functions or procedures. It is possible to call all real-time functions through a *Real_ Function*, and all remaining functions through a *Function*. Both kinds of functions can be used together. How far a *Call by Reference* of continuous data is possible, depends on the processing model of the continuous data, which is not easy to implement. If a dedicated memory space is handled by a special-purpose signal processor, then this approach becomes even more difficult to be implemented. Using a main processor in real-time mode, it can be implemented.

- A communication concept between the two programming environments can be introduced in an HLL. An application would exist of two separate modules where each module is defined for one programming environment. These modules, which consist of at least one process, would exchange the necessary information through the multimedia communication concept.

- An LDU with a gross granularity exists when, for example, a video or audio sequence is accessed only as a whole unit. In this case, the individual media elements cannot be accessed (e.g., beginning of the second scene).

- With respect to the *granularity of the LDU,* it is important to find the proper size of an LDU as the data type:

  For example, in the case of audio, the audio blocks (75 per second), known from CD technology, should be the accessible units. In the case of video, the minimal granularity should be the video frames (i.e., not image segments, lines, columns, pixels, etc.). Also, short video clips up to duration of two seconds can be defined as an LDU. This makes sense, for example, for compressed video, where besides an intraframe compression image, also images with difference values, interframe coded, are transmitted. A typical sequence contains two intraframe coded images per second, the rest (28 images) are interframe coded. Hence, an LDU would have the duration of 0.5 seconds.

From a pragmatic point of view, a manipulation of pixels for a discrete cosine-transformation or a fast Fourier transformation should not be part of an HLL. This should further consist as part of the digital signal processing with the corresponding software and hardware. But the HLL should have access to the DSP algorithms as a whole.

- The meaning of the operators + *(addition)*, - *(removal)*, etc. is not only media-dependent, but also application-specific. The addition of two video images can mean an overlapping of two images (with transparent colors) or only a mixture of luminance values. Here, a consent for the general interpretation is necessary.

### 16.5.2 Media as Files

Another possibility of programming continuous media data is the consideration of continuous media streams as *files* instead of data types.

```
file_h1 = open(MICROPHONE_1,...)
file_h2 = open(MICROPHONE_2,...)
file_h3 = open(SPEAKER,...)
...
read(file_h1)
read(file_h2)
mix(file_3, file_h1,file_h2)
activate(file_h1, file_h2, file_h3)
...
deactivate(file_h1, file_h2, file_h3)
...
rc1 = close(file_h1)
rc2 = close(file_h2)
rc3 = close(file\_h3)
```

The example describes the merging of two audio streams. The physical file is associated during the open process of a file with a corresponding file name. The program receives a *file descriptor* through which the file is accessed. In this case, a device unit, which creates or processes continuous data streams, can be associated with a file name.

*Read* and *write functions* are based on continuous data stream behavior. Therefore, a new value is assigned continuously to a specific variable which is connected, for example, with one read function. On the other hand, the read and write functions of discrete data occur in separate steps. For each assignment of a new value from a file to the corresponding variable, the read function is called again.

In a *seek function*, the pointer in a file can be positioned to particular places which correspond to the beginning of an LDU. Continuous data are also often played from a source of non-persistent data. A microphone and camera are examples of such sources. For these files, a seek function cannot be performed. This can be compared with the reception of discrete data from a keyboard. This kind of file processing is widespread in the UNIX$^{TM}$environment. Here, the most device units are handled at their interfaces to the applications as files (either as a *stream device* or as a *block device*). The programming of devices must be extended corresponding to Leungs *active devices* [LLM+88]. All file-similar functions can be used, additionally it is also possible to activate and deactivate a device. An *activate function* means that the actual data transmission starts and a *deactivate function* means that the transmission stops.

Using this kind of programming of continuous data, the number and functionality of the operations with continuous data (in comparison to programming with media data types) is limited. This approach can be seen as the programming of data streams.

### 16.5.3 Media as Processes

The processing of continuous data contains a time-dependency beçause the life span of a process equals to the life span of a connection(s) between source(s) and destination(s). A connection can exist locally, as well as remotely. Under this consideration, it is possible to map continuous media to processes and to integrate them in an HLL.

```
    PROCESS cont_process_a;
    ...
    On_message_do
        set_volume ...
        set_loudness ...
        ...
    ...
  [main]
pid = create(cont_process_a)
send(pid, set_volume, 3)
send(pid, set_loudness)
...
```

In the above example, the process *cont_process_a* implements a set of *actions (functions)* which apply to a continuous data stream, Two of them are the modification of the volume *set_volume* and the process of setting a volume, dependent from a band filter, *set_loudness.*

During the creation of the process, the identification and reservation of the used physical device(s) occur. The different actions of the continuous process are controlled through an IPC mechanism. For example, the transmission of continuous data is controlled by sending signals and messages. The continuous media process determines itself how the accessed actions are performed.

Thus, the processing can be done either once or continuously, meaning that during the entire transmission of continuous data:

- The loudness is determined once by a device driver call. The driver loads a certain storage content which is used by the running process controlling an audio board.
- If the main processor passes the audio data further from a file to the communication system, then the loudness can be changed here. Thus, the compression

and coding must be considered. In this example, it is assumed that an uncompressed PCM-coded audio signal with 64 Kbits/s is present. The continuous process transmits these data and changes, as well as the loudness, according to the desired value.

The present variants for the integration of a multimedia programming in an HLL require the properties of the programming language described in the section below.

### 16.5.4 Programming Language Requirements

The processing of continuous data is:

- Controlled by the HLL through pure asynchronous instructions (typically, through the use of a library).
- An integral part of a program through the identification of the media, respectively data streams with data types, variables, files or processes.

Therefore, the HLL should support a *parallel processing* as was presented in all examples of HLL programming of continuous media. Thus, it is of secondary importance if the number of processes is known at compile time or if it is defined dynamically at run-time.

#### Interprocess Communication Mechanism

Different processes must be able to communicate through an Inter-Process Communication mechanism (IPC). This IPC mechanism must be able to transmit audio and video in a timely fashion because these media have a limited life span. Therefore, the IPC must be able to:

- Understand a priori and/or implicitly specified time requirements. These requirements can be specified using QoS parameters or they can be extracted from the data type (if a medium is implemented as a data type).

- Transmit the continuous data according to the requirements.

- Initiate the processing of the received continuous process on time.

The generated heap from the compiler is limited in its size, the location and properties are determined by the compiler. The processing of time-critical data requires a careful assignment and manipulation of the storage space. The IPC and communication between different programs must happen effectively. The performance analysis in the multimedia and high-speed communication systems show that the most time-consuming operation is the *copying of data* operation. System-wide uniform *buffer management* at the system software layer extracts this problem. A virtual copying means that the access rights onto the buffer spaces are passed to other components. For example, this approach was implemented in the multimedia communication system HeiTS [HHS91]. The HLL compiler for continuous media must use this buffer management. The same is true for the IPC implemented in this language.

Audio and video *processes* require the availability of *real-time* processing. This can be implemented, as described in Section 16.4.1, by combining two programming environments. The HLL should support a clear data type specification.

**Language**

The authors see no demand for the development of a new dedicated language. A partial language replacement is also quite difficult because cooperation between the real-time environment and the remaining programs requires semantic changes in the programming languages. The IPC must be designed and implemented in real-time, the current IPC can be omitted.

A language extension is the solution proposed here. For the purpose of simplicity, in the first step, a simple language should be developed which satisfies most of the above described requirements. An example of such a language is OCCAM-2. Some real-time systems are implemented in this parallel programming language today. An alternative is a parallel C-variant for the transputer. In the long run, ADA still provides a good concept as a language basis.

## 16.6 Object-oriented Approaches

The object-oriented approach was first introduced as a method for the reduction of complexity in the software development and it is used mainly with this goal today. Further, the reuse of software components is a main advantage of this paradigm. The basic ideas of object-oriented programming are: *data encapsulation* and *inheritance,* in connection with *class* and *object* definitions. The programs are implemented, instead of using functions and data structures, by using classes, objects, and methods.

### Abstract Type Definition

The definition of data types through abstract interfaces is called ***abstract type definitions.*** The abstract type definition is understood as an interface specification without a knowledge and implementation of internal algorithms. This data abstraction hides the used algorithm.

In a distributed multimedia system, abstract data types are assumed for virtual and real device units such as cameras and monitors. For example, an interface, which contains a function *zoom*, can also contain a parameter which specifies the actual position in an area from 10 ... 500. However, this specification does not describe the actual implementation.

### Class

The implementation of abstract data types is done through *classes.* A class specification includes an interface provided to the outside world.

For example, in a class *professional_camera*, the operations *zoom* and *set_back_light* are defined and implemented. If the objects, which represent a closed class, use only relative position entries, the implementation of the *zoom* operation needs to transform the absolute values into the necessary relative parameters.

### Object

An *object* is the instance of the class. Therefore, all objects, derived from the same class include the same operations as an interface to the outside world. An object is created at run-time of the system. It includes a set of operations, which are called *methods.* Additionally, each object has an *internal state,* which exists during the life span of the object, but it can only be accessed using the methods associated with this object. It can be compared with a global variable assigned to a process, but not with local variables of functions and procedures (as is implemented in most programming languages). Objects communicate among each other through the exchange of messages. Thus, a *message* calls the corresponding method of the target object.

In a distributed multimedia environment, virtual units are considered to be objects. Thus, corresponding methods represent operations on the devices. The method *play* of a VCR object (*Video Cassette Recorder*) is mapped to the *play_operation* of the corresponding VCR device driver. Multimedia data units (the LDU's images, audio and video clips) can also be considered objects.

### Inheritance

One of the most important properties of object-oriented systems is *inheritance.* Classes contain, besides the root and leaves of the hierarchy, superclasses and subclasses (fathers and sons).

For example, let the class *professional_camera* be a subclass of the class *camera.* Methods such as *autofocus_on* and *focus* are defined in the class *camera.* The *professional_camera* class also has the method *zoom.* An object, which is derived from the *professional_camera*, can use the method *zoom,* as well as the operations *focus* and *autofocus_on.*

The main problem has been and remains to be the design of a clear and uniform class hierarchy for a multimedia system.

Until now, only simple inheritance was considered. For example, for the application interface of a conference application, it is not possible to explicitly combine all necessary devices for each conference. Such an application would be dependent on a certain set of device types which are bound together in the required configuration. Device binding often includes different basic devices. A conference object inherits properties of different objects in an object-oriented environment, therefore a multi-inheritance is often useful.

Another type of inheritance is used by the consideration of interfaces. The same interface is provided for different classes, but the implementations can be very different. So, the operator *+ (addition)* could contain, according to the used data type, slightly different semantics and implementation. The addition of audio LDUs means the mixing of audio signals. Additionally, when applied to two video data streams, it can mean, for example, simultaneous presentation of both information streams in different halves of a window.

### Polymorphism

*Polymorphism* is related to the property of inheritance indicating when the same name of a method is defined in several classes (and objects) with different implementations and functionalities. For example, the function *play* is used with audio and video data. It uses different device units for each medium. The data can come either from a file of a local file environment or from an audio-video sequence of an external device. Inside of the object-oriented approach, for example, *play* is defined in different classes. According to which object must perform the operation, the corresponding method is chosen.

This concept is especially useful with respect to system use because the complexity of different types and device units is reduced and there is a common set of method names for classes and objects of different media. On the other hand, polymorphism can also very easily cause programming errors that are difficult to find. Hence, this abstraction strongly complicates the implementation. This can occur easily through unwanted, multiple identical method names. In an object-oriented environment, according to Wegener's definition [Weg87, Nie89], multimedia programming is achieved through the implementation and extension of class hierarchies.

The following sections describe different class hierarchies that support multimedia systems and applications. The examples and actual implementations were developed in the language C++, but the results are independent of a specific language [SF92]. In the authors' opinion, there will be many different class hierarchies in the future and they will be connected through complex relations to provide required interactions. However, the resulting complexity will not be easy to handle.

### 16.6.1 Application-specific Metaphors as Classes

An application-specific class hierarchy introduces abstractions specifically designed for a particular application. Thus, it is not necessary to consider other class hierarchies. This approach leads to a number of different class hierarchies. Furthermore, using this approach, one very easily abandons the actual advantage of object-oriented programming, i.e., the reuse of existing code.

Unfortunately, this is currently the most used solution, which has led to different kinds of class hierarchies. Although, for similar applications, similar class hierarchies can be implemented. Therefore, a catalog of similar applications is necessary to use the existing knowledge for the development of a new application.

### 16.6.2 Application-generic Metaphors as Classes

Another approach is to combine similar functionalities of all applications. These properties or functions, which occur repeatedly, can be defined and implemented as classes for all applications. An application is defined only through a binding of this class. For example, basic functions or functional units can create classes. The methods of these classes inherit the general methods through integration of application-specific subclasses. In theory this approach sounds easy to follow. In practice, we have not yet a very useful set of basic/generic application classes looks like, because known implementations of application-generic classes only work well for a very restricted set of applications.

### 16.6.3 Devices as Classes

In this section we consider objects which reflect a physical view of the multimedia system. The devices are assigned to objects which represent their behavior and interface.

Methods with similar semantics, which interact with different devices, should be defined in a device-independent manner. The considered methods use internally, for example, methods like *start*, *stop* and *seek*. Some units can manipulate several media together. A computer-controlled VCR or a Laser Disc Player (LDP) are storage units which, by themselves, integrate (bind) video and audio. In a multimedia system, abstract device definitions can be provided, e.g., camera and monitor. We did not say anything until now about the actual implementation. The results show that defining a general and valid interface for several similar audio and video units, as well as input and output units, is quite a difficult design process. This is also demonstrated by the following abbreviated C++ program [SF92]:

```
class media_device
      {char *name;
       public:
               void on(), off();
      }; /* end media_device */

class media_in_device :
public media_device
      {private:
               DATA data;
       public:
               refDATA get_data();
      }; /* end media_in_device */

class media_out_device :
      {public:
               void put_data(refDATA dat);
      }; /* end media_out_device */
```

```
class answering_machine:
public media_device
       {private:
           list my_list; //  class for ADT list
           media_in_device recorder;
           media_out_device message_for_caller, message_from_caller;
           RefDATA information; //  text a caller hears
           void display_position();
        public:
           void answer()
                {message_for_caller.on();
                 message_for_caller.put_data(information);
                 message_for_caller.off();
                 recorder.on();
                }
           void play()
                {message_from_caller.on();
                 message_from_caller.put_data(my_list.head());
                 display_position();
                 message_from_caller.off();
                 my_list.dequeue()
                }
       } /* end answering machine */
main(){ };
```

The concept of *devices as class hierarchies* provides a simple parallel performance of the methods. Note, synchronization is not supported in this hierarchy and must be provided through other components; multiple inheritance is often needed.

### 16.6.4 Processing Units as Classes

This abstraction comprises source objects, destination objects and combined source-destination objects which perform intermediate processing of continuous data. With this approach, a kind of "lego" system is created which allows for the creation of a data flow path through a connection of objects. The outputs of objects are connected with inputs of other objects, either directly or through channel objects.

As an example of this concept, the *processing unit* as a class is presented. (It was originally implemented as part of the DiME project of the IBM European Network Center in Heidelberg, Germany [SHRS90].). It was used at the beginning of the application implementation of a remote camera control system in Heidelberg. It should be understood that it is as an example only.

Similar considerations are discussed in [AC91] with the node types of COMET, in [GBD+91] with sources, destinations and filters, and in [SS91] with modules of a variable number of input and output channels.

### Multimedia Object

A multimedia application processes and controls (respectively generates) the interactions and information of different continuous and discrete media. From the object-oriented viewpoint, an application is considered to be a *multimedia object.* Such an object uses or consists of many other objects which contribute to the solution of the task. These objects are connected to, for example, representation of different media and device units. Such a *Compound Multimedia Object (CMO)* consists of other CMOs and *Basic Multimedia Objects (BMOs).* The *Basic Multimedia Class (BMC)* typically represents an individual medium of an input type (e.g., data from a camera, stored audio sequences from a file) or output type (e.g., data output to a video window or speaker). A *Compound Multimedia Class (CMC)* can control, and respectively represent several media and devices. BMOs are instances of BMCs; CMOs are instances of CMCs.

Data can be either *transient* or *persistent.* For example, if an image is read from a hard disk, the following properties are connected with each other: *life span, input type* and *medium* image. Generally, the media are *text, image, audio* and *video.* Further, it is possible to consider other media such as *tables* or *drawings* which need to be included in the range of BMCs.

For clarification of the properties of this approach, an encyclopedia example is discussed below. Instead of presenting the example in an object-oriented language, the example specification is chosen in an easy-to-understand notation for didactical reasons:

```
Lexicon: compound_object;
     DATA: Explain external;
           Animation external;
     ACCESS_POINTS: VIDEO_SOURCE Animation.VIDEO_SOURCE;
                    AUDIO_SOURCE Animation.AUDIO_SOURCE;
                    TEXT_SOURCE Explain.TEXT_SOURCE;
     METHODS:
           start: display(Explain);
           play: play(Animation);
           pause: pause(Animation);
           stop: stop(Animation);
           ...
Animation: compound_object;
     DATA: Speech external;
           Scene external;
     ACCESS_POINTS: VIDEO_SOURCE Scene.VIDEO_SOURCE;
                    AUDIO_SOURCE Speech.AUDIO_SOURCE;
     METHODS:
           play: play(Speech), play(Scene) in_parallel;
           pause: pause(Speech), pause(Scene) in_parallel;
           stop: stop(Speech), stop(Scene) in_parallel;
           ...   ...
     EVENTS:
           audio_end: wait(video_end); stop(Scene);
           video_end: wait(audio_end); stop(Speech);
 Scene: basic_object;
     DATA: VIDEO_filename at node_1;
     ACCESS_POINTS: VIDEO_SOURCE;
     METHODS:
```

```
            play;
            pause;
            top;
            ....
        EVENTS:
            at_end: display(LAST_PICTURE), inform_PARENT(video_end);
            ....  ...
    Speech: basic_object;
        DATA: AUDIO_filename at node_2;
        ACCESS_POINTS: AUDIO_SOURCE;
        METHODS:
            play:
            pause:
            stop:
        EVENTS:
            at_end: inform_PARENT(audio_end);
    Explain: basic object;
        DATA: TEXT_filename at node_1;
        ACCESS_POINTS: TEXT_SOURCE;
        METHODS:
            display;
            ....
        EVENTS:
            ....
```

In the above example, the actual classes of the lexicon are presented. Instead of *Explain: basic_object*, actually *Explain: basic_class* should be given; instead of *Animation: compound_object*, *Animation: compound_class* should be considered. The reason why objects instead of classes were considered is just simplicity. This way, the example shows its run-time behavior better. BMOs are used as processing elements with the sources, destinations and combined sources-destinations of media streams. Corresponding to the *class hierarchy of BMOs*, different properties can be chosen at the highest level of the classification.

In Figure 16.3, a division of source, destination and combined source-destination is

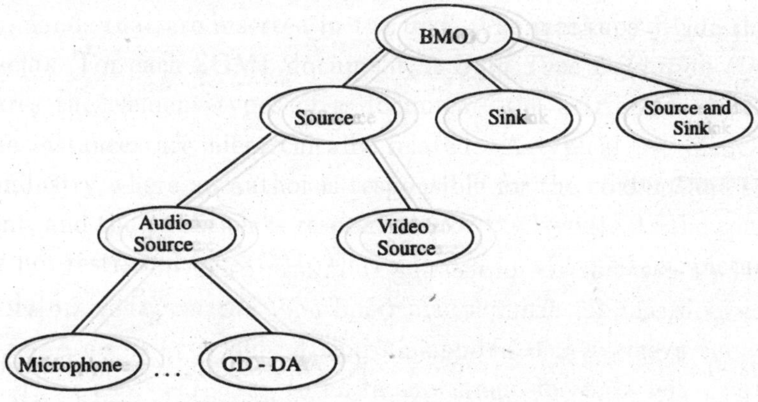


Figure 16.3: *Example of a multimedia class hierarchy.*

shown as the primary qualification attribute. The medium is defined as a secondary attribute. It is important to point out that in other examples, several BMOs from the same BMC can coexist simultaneously.

### Data Specification DATA

The *data specification* DATA specifies the BMO's binding to a file, a device unit and their place. A *device unit* mostly consists of hardware and software, although a device unit may only consist of a software module. There can be objects at different places which point to remote BMOs. In the data specification, the lexicon example shows the binding of the object *Scene* to the *VIDEO_filename* at the place *node_1*.

### Methods

Each BMO contains a set of *methods* that is dependent on its class. Some methods, which repeat themselves, are *play* and *stop.* The internal state of all multimedia objects which process continuous media is constantly renewed with current values because the actual data (for example, a picture of a video scene) are valid only during a certain time interval. Therefore, some methods also support time-dependent functions such as *slow motion*, *presence* of a scene during two seconds or *volume increase* during five seconds.

#### Event Processing

BMOs include event-driven processing to inform other objects about certain states of their own objects, for example, *start* and *end.* Further, they are used to transmit asynchronous events which happen during the life span of an object. Therefore, events are special kinds of operations of an object. They can be compared to *exceptions* in real-time programming languages such as CHILL. A BMO, connected to a continuous data stream, contains in our model its own defined time-scale and events. A priori-defined events are *start* and *end.* Additionally, there can be defined user-specific events. The relation between events and their event processing is specified for each BMO.

#### Access Points

Continuous data of a data stream can be processed from several objects consecutively. The corresponding BMOs must be connected with each other. Therefore, each BMO contains one or several *ports* which are called *access points.* Access points for BMOs are objects which consist not only of local addresses, but also of protocols with entries concerning the required data coding and compression. They include all source- and destination-specific information which is necessary for their connection. BMOs can have access points such as *VIDEO_SOURCE*, and *VIDEO_SINK.* The application can pass the multimedia data to storage, communication, presentation and processing units through access points.

Transparent to the manipulation of multimedia objects, is the control of adequate transmission over the network(s). The network component takes the necessary information, including the QoS parameters for connection setup and for data transmission from the object-control-information. The required resource management is interfaced by this processing.

### Channel Object

A binding between one or several sources and one or several destinations can be implemented. A *channel object* is created with dedicated and communication-supportive methods to bind sources and destinations. After creations of such a channel, sources and destinations can be bound to each other through a *bind* call to the particular channel. This approach allows the implementation of not only multicast, but also $n$-to-$m$ connections ($n, m > 0$). The access rights of the particular object are assigned during the *bind* call. Destinations and sources can be bound to the same channel independently through this mechanism.

Depending on the channel object implementation, one or several sources can be connected to it. Usage with an individual source is the same as in the case of a normal TV transmission channel: a channel is created, the data of the source object are recorded and each authorized user can connect to this channel and can receive the continuous data.

In a general case with several sources, the channel serves as a mixer of data and it must also guarantee synchronization. Using channel objects, it is possible to dynamically change the bindings among different multimedia objects. They always contain the methods *connect* and *disconnect*. To fully integrate BMOs into the system, this multimedia connection management must be implemented as a multimedia communication system.

### CMO, BMC and CMC

Given that different media are not only supported separately, but also simultaneously, some device-dependent media combinations must be integrated into the object-oriented model.

An application should additionally find predefined *Compound Multimedia Classes (CMCs)* and their corresponding CMOs, as well as create them itself. In this section, this extension of the model is discussed.

An application implements a new CMC by using content-containing BMCs and

CMCs. This new class contains other classes inside its data specification, access points, methods and/or event processing. With respect to methods, this property is called inheritance.

The *activation* of a CMC creates a CMO. A binding inside of the data specification can be set inside the class, as well as for a specific object. Additionally, information, such as life span, access rights and distribution aspects can be assigned to an object.

The *methods of CMOs* can be set up application-specifically. They are developed using methods of content-containing BMCs and CMCs and private algorithms. In our example, the method *play* of the CMO *Animation* uses the methods *play* of the objects *Speech* and *Scene.*

Similar to the method specification, the *event processing of CMOs* is defined. Typically, either methods of the *content-containing* object (see *stop(Scene)* of the CMO *Animation*) are called or an event is sent to other objects (see *inform_PARENT (video_end)* of the CMO *Scene*). Events inform the called objects about the state of the calling object.

The use of methods and events allows the application to create a script which expresses the interactions of different objects precisely and relatively simply. Thus, the presentation of multimedia data can be determined.

### Distribution of BMOs and CMOs

Another aspect is the *distribution of BMOs and CMOs.* A CMO can consist of objects which are distributed over different computer nodes.

The channel object with the methods *create_connection* and *delete_connection* supports the possibility to manage connections of several media together. Internally, the transmission can be implemented either through integration and interleaving of different media over one connection or through several individual connections. Thus, the access rights of data can be examined. For example, consider the class of a CMO, called *lexicon*, as shown in Figure 16.4. BMOs and CMOs (the same as BMCs and CMCs) contain the four areas *DATA, ACCESS_POINTS, METHODS* and *EVENTS.* This example shows BMOs, as well as CMOs. The data of the BMO

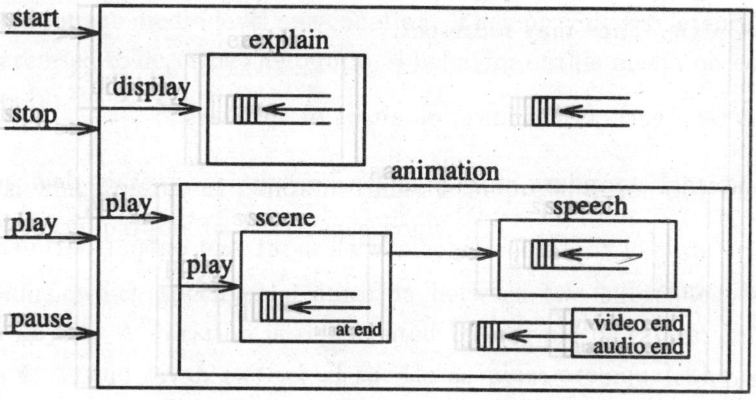


Figure 16.4: *Example of a CMC.*

specification are abbreviated with *_filename*. At the moment when the CMO *lexicon* is activated, or started, a text of the text object *Explain* is displayed. The user can call the method *play* in the application which activates the corresponding method in the CMO *Lexicon*. *Play* starts the presentation of a combined audio-video sequence of the object *Animation*. The application also allows the user to access methods like *pause* or *stop*. Thus, the corresponding method in the lexicon is called. The CMO *Animation* is a composition of audio and video objects.

If one assumes that the audio and video information output do not posses the same length, then certain actions must be performed when one of the media finishes earlier than the other(s). The method *play* of the object *Animation* starts the video scene and the audio passage concurrently. If the audio passage finishes before the video scene, the event *audio_end* is sent from the object *Speech* to the object *Animation*. If the video scene finishes before the audio passage, the last image of the video sequence is displayed and the signal *video_end* is sent to the object *Animation*.

All events of the object *Animation* cause a data flow to be stopped, some media-dependent methods to be performed, and the waiting of an event of another object. At the end, the combined audio-video information as a whole unit is stopped. This kind of synchronization is known as *conditional blocking* [Ste90].

In the preceding paragraphs, *sources* were specified as BMOs and CMOs. In the same way, destinations and combined source-destination objects can also be specified as BMOs and CMOs. They may represent:

- *Output devices* such as windows, monitors or speakers.
- *Files* of internal secondary storage devices or external storage devices.
- *Processing units* of continuous media with input and output ports (hardware and/or software).

The above described model served as the basis for the development of a remote camera control [WSS94]. This application (remote camera control), implemented in C++, includes communication support which allows the control of different kinds of cameras from a remote place. In another recent approach at the EPFL (Lavosanne), a language, called *Sync C++* has been implemented as a concurrent version of C++ [CDP94]. There, Petitpierre defined active objects which were used for real-time programming of multimedia data. These objects had their own life span (as threads of execution) and hence, worked independently from the others. Sync C++ was shown to be very efficient in writing multimedia applications with a large amount of user interface handling.

### 16.6.5 Media as Classes

The *Media Class Hierarchy* defines a hierarchical relation for different media. The following example shows such a class hierarchy. Thus, the individual methods of the class hierarchy will not be described. The class *Pixel* in the class hierarchy uses, for example, multiple inheritance.

```
Medium
    Acoustic_Medium
      Music
        Opus
          Note
            Audio_Block
              Sample_Value
```

```
      Speech
        ...
      ...
    Optical_Medium
      Video
        Video_Scene
          Image
            Image_Segment
              Pixel
            Line
              Pixel
            Column
              Pixel
     Animation
       ...
     Text
       ...
     ...
   ...
   other_continuous_medium
   discrete_medium
```

Another example shows the following class hierarchy (note, so far we have not found a *best* class hierarchy because different class hierarchies are better suited for different applications):

```
Medium
  continuous_medium
    Audio
      Audio_Passage
        Music
        Speech
        Noise
  Video
```

```
      Video_Scene
    Animation
      Animation_Scene
    Pointer_Information
    Further_Realtime_Data
  discrete_medium
    Image
      Image_Segment
        Pixel
      Line
        Pixel
      Column
        Pixel
    Text
    Formula
    Table
      Line
        Attribute
        Formula
        Value
    ...
```

A specific property of all multimedia objects is the continuous change of their internal states during their life spans [SHRS90, GBD+91]. Data transfer of continuous media is performed as long as the corresponding connection is activated. A *connection* can be either a connection for local data transfer between source(s) and destination(s) (e.g., from a disc to a video window), or a connection for remote data transfer. Data can also be transmitted when a method does not exist for the object (besides the methods *new* and/or *init*), respectively a message was not sent. The activation happens implicitly in this case. Thus, the internally managed storage areas of continuous media always take new values. This is also valid for the control information, for example, time stamps.

Besides the class hierarchy, the main attributes (expressed or retrieved through methods) need to be considered for different classes. Typical methods used by all continuous media are, for example, *play* and *stop*. We have implemented these methods for different classes and different devices. The lesson learned is that it is relatively easy to enforce the same or similar semantics for different implementations.

Some programming environments already provide languages based on the object-oriented approach with processing units or media as classes. For example:

- *Gibbs' Multimedia Programming Environment* has a strong media relation [GBD+91]. It is implemented through a *scripting language* extension at the user interface. This language belongs to the category *processing units* as classes. Here, constructs for input of parallel, sequential, repetitious processing are included ($a >> b$, a & b, $n \times b$).
- The *Rendezvous*™ *Environment* includes graphical classes [HBP+93]. The primitive graphical classes include the full range of drawing primitives available to the X Window System™, such as lines, rectangles, polygons, arcs, ovals, text and color and monochrome images. In this environment, the application programmer uses the *Rendezvous Language*, which is an object-oriented language extended with features that simplify the construction of multi-user interfaces using the Rendezvous Architecture. The structure of the major Rendezvous Language components, including the interface to the X Window System via CLX (Common Lisp X), is shown in Figure 16.5.

Considering media as classes is a general approach. As a part of each application there can also be further multimedia-specific class hierarchies.

### 16.6.6 Communication-specific Metaphors as Classes

Communication-oriented approaches often consider objects in a *distributed environment* through an explicit specification of classes and objects tied to a communication system. Blakowski specifies, for example, information, presentation and transport classes [Bla91a]. The information, contained in the information objects, can build a presentation object which is later used for presentation of information. Information objects can be converted to transport objects for transmission purposes (see [Bla91a] for the complete state-transition graph). Possible extension to this model would be

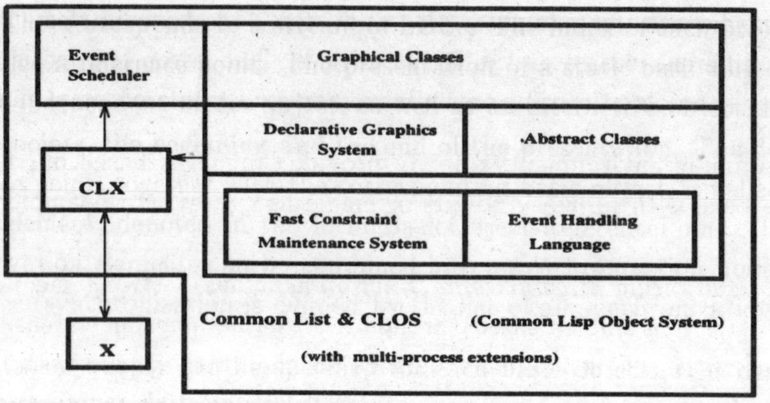


Figure 16.5: *Structure of Rendezvous Language components [HBP+93].*

a *storage class.* Information is often processed differently. It depends on whether the information should be presented, transmitted or stored. With storage objects, it is necessary to consider the different storage formats. Relevant formats are the coding and compression formats, format of interleaved data streams and formats such as CD-ROM ISO 9660.

## 16.7 Comments

The current research in programming of multimedia applications leads to the following conclusions:

- There are too few proper data abstractions for structural programming of multimedia data.
- The abstraction level for *higher procedural programming languages,* which is used for the programming of continuous media has been considered only to a very small extent.
- There is a great number of object-oriented and toolkit approaches based on very different class hierarchies. Consolidation is needed.

Hence, the following comparisons can be made:

- *Libraries* represent the simplest integration of multimedia devices and functions in a system. The functions of such a library can be called from the system software level, as well as by a programming language. Different devices (often with the same functionality) provide different interfaces. Hence, portability of multimedia programs tends to be difficult.

  Using this library approach, multimedia products can be brought to market in a short time with *new and already improved functions.* However, after some time, the complexity of the application development increases because of different hardware which slows down the further spread of this approach. Therefore, other abstraction levels are necessary.

- *System software interfaces* integrate multimedia functions into the operating system. Currently, approaches are tied to specific operating systems and to one kind of multimedia data processing.

  Instead of providing devices in the form of libraries for processing of continuous media, it is necessary to integrate device drivers into the operating system. The main problem is current operating systems: most of them do not provide real-time processing. Today, it is still necessary to find tricky ways to provide multimedia processing.

- *Higher procedural programming languages* can rely on library functions when continuous media programming is integrated. However, these libraries are product-specific and very different. Therefore, a corresponding programming language needs to communicate with several libraries. This requires a high development effort.

  As an alternative, it is possible to access abstractions such as *constraints* and *event handlers* in the operating system. However, because this alternative is available only in special cases (e.g., the Rendezvous Environment and Nemo system ), this approach will take time to catch on. Thus, it is not clear how these abstractions will differ in various operating systems. The development of current commercial multimedia applications is done mostly using higher procedural programming languages. Here, the functions of existing libraries can be called directly. Integrated programming of applications with continuous media inside higher programming languages leads to simpler and clearer programming.

- *Object-oriented approaches* are the most widespread abstractions for research in programming of multimedia applications today. Existing system software is most often used for integration with physical devices. Therefore, as a first step, all functions of this system software is tied to its class hierarchy. The same happens with communication systems. Thus, the developed class hierarchies are very different, and one cannot currently identify the *best* class hierarchy. The combination of the media-related class hierarchy with the "lego" approach of processing units may satisfy several applications.

There is no *best* approach to the abstraction of multimedia data (according to current experiences and results). Different abstraction levels will coexist; however, to mutually use the respective results, these layers must build on one another (as shown in Figure 16.1).

# Chapter 17

# Multimedia Applications

## 17.1 Introduction

The availability of multimedia hardware and software components has driven the enhancement of existing applications towards being more user-friendly (known as re-engineering) It has also initiated the continuous development of new multimedia applications. Applications are crucial for the whole domain of multimedia computing and communications because they are the only reason why anybody would invest in this area. However, so far no serious attempt has been made to classify these applications. Because of the burgeoning number of multimedia applications, with this chapter we aim to provide a structured view on the field of multimedia applications.

Data regarding projects, products and other issues discussed in this chapter were collected from a variety of sources: several computer magazines, sets of product catalogues, project descriptions in the context of the U.S. Federal *High Performance Computing and Communications (HPCC)* program, the European *ESPRIT* program, RACE, ACTS, DELTA and other programs, worldwide-supported initiatives such as the *World Wide Web Initiative*, market surveys and extensive customer feedback.

### 17.1.1 Programs

Several programs for the development of multimedia applications have been established during the last few years, some well-known from the U.S. and Europe are outlined below.

- *USA*

  The High Performance Computing and Communication *(HPCC)* program accelerates the development of scalable, high-performance computers, advanced high-speed computer communications networks and advanced software – all critical components of a new *National Information Infrastructure (NII)* initiative [HPC94]. The HPCC program evolved in the early 1980's out of recognition by American scientists, engineers and leaders in government and industry. One of the most significant program components in the HPCC program is the *Information Infrastructure Technology and Applications (IITA)* program. The IITA's research and development efforts are directed towards *National Challenge* problems such as *civil infrastructure, digital libraries, education and lifelong learning, energy management, the environment, health care, manufacturing processes and products, national security* and *public access to government information.* IITA technologies will support advanced applications such as:

  - *Tele-medicine*

    An individual's medical records (including X-ray and CAT scan images) will be sent to a consulting physician located miles away.

  - *Remote Education and Training*

    The access and study of books, films, music, photographs and works of art in the Library of Congress and in the nation's great libraries, galleries and museums will be available on a regular basis to teachers and students anywhere in the country.

  - *Tele-operation*

    The flexible incorporation of improved design and manufacturing, which may be performed in a distributed manner, will produce safer and more energy-efficient cars, airplanes and homes.

– *Information Access*

Universal access to government data and information products by industry and the public will be supported.

HPCC program management consists of several working groups coordinating activities in specific areas. The application group, led by NASA (the National Aeronautics and Space Administration), coordinates activities related to national challenge applications, software tools needed for application development and software development at high performance computing centers. The education group, led by the National Institute of Health and Department of Health and Human Services, coordinates HPCC education and training activities. The communication group, led by NSF (National Science Foundation), coordinates network integration activities. The research group, led by ARPA (the Advanced Research Projects Agency, Department of Defense), focuses on basic research, technology trends and alternative approaches to address the technological limits of information technology.

- *Europe*

ESPRIT (European Strategic Program for Research in Information Technology) is a well-known scientific program of the European Community. The primary goal is to support development of technology and science similar to the HPCC program. The smaller RACE (Research in Advanced Communication in Europe) program is similar to ESPRIT, but focuses on communication issues. In the second phase, the RACE II program focused on the residential and small business user market to use multimedia communication applications (tele-applications) [RAC93]. *ACTS* (Advanced Communication Technology)is the follow-up to the RACE program. Emphasis is on the customer's access connection, which is the most cost-sensitive issue of the whole network and the one most closely related to the service demand. The RACE projects, for example, cover applications such as:

– *Tele-interaction*

Tele-services will be used in information systems (e.g., information kiosks) and entertainment (e.g., telegames) as part of the information age.

– *Tele-shopping*

Shopping through remote electronic catalogues will support faster and more convenient sale and advertisement of products.

– *Thematic channels with interactive TV and electronic newspaper*

The development of current TV technology towards interactive TV and the use of thematic channels will make it possible to create new programs for education and entertainment. Thematic channels might provide access to electronic newspapers and other information.

– *Tele-working*

Further development of interactive tele-services will provide an environment for the reliable setup of home offices, as well as industrial collaboration and remote education. Already today, services such as videotelephony and video-conferencing are part of collaborations among remotely located laboratories and colleagues.

For these applications, new tools and system components are being implemented for incorporation into commercial products.

Among the national programs, the German Telekom project *BERKOM* (BERliner KOMmunikationssystem) is one of the most prominent, having run over five years and incorporating the multimedia work of the most active researchers in the field.

### 17.1.2 Structure

There are many views on how multimedia applications should be classified. For example, a market-oriented view and pragmatic view may divide the current multimedia applications into ***kiosk applications***, ***educational applications*** and applications in the area of ***cooperative work***. Another view would be a communication-oriented view, dividing multimedia applications into ***interactive*** or ***distribution-oriented applications***. A third possibility is some view derived from the hypertext/hypermedia area.

Our classification evolves mainly from the need to describe and present a coherent view on this important area, discussed at numerous commercial and scientific events;

it looks at *multimedia processing* from the computer user perspective. Hence, we distinguish among tools and applications which support the user in *media preparation, media composition, media integration and media communication.* Furthermore, the user is exposed through multimedia applications to *media consumption* and *media entertainment.* This has become known, colloquially, as the "media food chain."

## 17.2 Media Preparation

Media preparation is performed by multimedia I/O hardware and its supporting software. Therefore, hardware and software are the basic components for introducing media into the digital world of a computer. Appropriate hardware is the prerequisite for working with multimedia applications. The software creates the environment to work actively with the multimedia applications. It allows the computer user to use and interactively work with the multimedia hardware. We discussed system software issues in Chapters 8, 9, 11 and 12 and application software issues in Chapters 13, 14 and 16. We shall also present some application-specific software issues in this chapter when we discuss different kinds of user interaction with media. For the purpose of better understanding, we concentrate in this section on some specialized multimedia devices.

### 17.2.1 Means

New hardware technology is needed for multimedia applications and their interactive experience. Chapters 3, 4 and 5 discuss the basic principles of media and their hardware support in more detail. Here we want to expand briefly on other devices also available for media preparation.

#### Audio Support

Some *audio* support with *multiple-channel digital sound tracks* is already available. For example, a six-channel digital sound track (front-left, center, front-right, surround-left, surround-right and subwoofer) has been developed. In the area of virtual reality entertainment, sound interaction occurs via a *helmet*. The same degree of attention was paid to the design and development of digital stereo sound.

### Video Support

*Video boards* and *digitizers* aim toward a high-resolution picture presentation. The ultimate goal is high resolution and a film rate of 60 frames per second (HDTV) or faster, "a la Showscan," which provides an extremely clear picture. An important capability of the video hardware is to provide a constant frame rate with a minimum of jitter. This property is more important than a faster rate or even increased color or pixel resolution because a large amount of jitter between frames causes the perception of jerky motion video, which is more disturbing than a slower frame rate with minimal jitter. For example, the video compression technique MPEG creates frame-differencing. Because the differences in content between frames are not really controllable, a constant delivery rate of frames to the viewer is not always maintained, thereby causing a perception of jerky MPEG-compressed motion video.

*Graphical displays* provide high resolution for graphical, image and motion video applications. An important component of the raster system display (see Figure 4.2 for the architecture of a raster display) is the *video controller*, which constantly refreshes the display. For applications where *mixing of video* is required, the video controller provides this function. Two images, one defined in the frame buffer and the other defined by a video signal coming from a television camera, recorder or other source, can be merged to form a composite image. Examples of this kind of merging are regularly seen on television news, sports and weather shows.

Currently, several basic kinds of displays are used in virtual reality applications [Tri87, FDFH92, Cla94]:

- *Head-Mounted Displays (HMD)*

  An HMD includes one or two displays. Special lenses allow the user to focus on the display as if they were further away.

- *Surround Displays*

Surround displays surround the user, meaning the user is situated in a room with walls serving as displays. To provide stereoscopy and sensitivity to head motions, a stereoscopic display system and head position tracker are used.

- *Digital Holography*

  Holography is a method for displaying 3D images without using special headgear or tracking the viewer's location. Traditional holograms are produced by exposing photographic film simultaneously to laser light scattered from the object to be recorded, and to a reference beam from the same laser. The interference patterns recorded on the film encode the object's appearance from a range of viewpoints. The hologram is viewed by illuminating it with laser light from the opposite direction.

### Scanner Devices

*Image scanners* and *photo CD devices* support input and output of images and photographs. Although *data tablets* can be used to manually digitize existing line drawings, this is a slow process, unsuitable for more than a few simple drawings. Image scanners provide an efficient solution. A television camera, in conjunction with a digital frame grabber, is an inexpensive way to obtain moderate resolution ($1000 \times 1000$ pixels, with multiple intensity levels) raster images of black-and-white or color photographs. Slow-scan Charge-Coupled-Device (CCD) television cameras can produce an image of $2000 \times 2000$ pixels in about 30 seconds [FDFH92].

For high-quality publication work, a *photo scanner* is used. The photograph is mounted on a rotating drum. A light beam is directed at the photo, and the amount of light reflected is measured by a photocell. For a negative, transmitted light is measured by a photocell inside the drum. As the drum rotates, the light source slowly moves from one end to the other, thus doing a raster scan of the entire photograph. The highest resolution scanners use laser light sources, and have resolutions greater than 2000 pixels per inch.

Another type of scanner uses a long thin strip of CCDs, called a *CCD array*. A drawing is digitized by passing it under the CCD array. A single pass, taking one or two minutes, is sufficient to digitize a large drawing. Resolution of the CCD array is 200 to 1000 pixels per inch, which is less than the photo scanner technique.

### Recognition Devices

*Recognizers* are built to recognize different media. An example is the *object-oriented character recognition engine AQUIRE* [KW93b]. AQUIRE is used in a pen-based computer environment. From a programmer's point of view replacing a keyboard with a pen requires a pen-based user interface that provides a complete control mechanism for a pen as a central input device. To support the same user interface methods, where the user is accustomed to a keyboard as the input device, a highly sophisticated character recognition engine must be embedded in the pen-based applications. This recognizer can be used to transform drawings (e.g., cup drawing) into their semantics (e.g., cup meaning).

Other recognizers may perform, for instance, *image recognition* to convert images into text, or *speech recognition* to convert audio into text.

### Tracking Devices

*Trackers* report information about position, orientation, acceleration, pressure or joint angles of tracked objects [MAB92]. There are several technologies which have been deployed:

- *Electromagnetic trackers* produced by, for example, Polhemus and Ascension, determine the receiver's position and orientation using coils, pulsed with an electrical signal, in the transmitter and receiver for producing and sensing a magnetic field.

- *Ultrasonic trackers* use ultrasonic pulses in the transmitter and receiver to determine the orientation of the receiver.

- *Optical tracking systems* use video cameras to track objects. Camera-based approaches may track hands and bodies without requiring that users wear special apparatus [Ino93].

Other tracking systems are used, such as coarser-grained, position-only tracking, finger-joint-angles tracking with various sensory gloves or eye tracking technologies. Eye tracking is employed to focus a camera onto the object envisaged by the photograph itself.

#### Motion-based Devices

*Motion-bases* are typically hydraulic systems that manipulate the viewer along several axes of motion (up to six degrees-of-freedom of lateral or rotational). The movement of the platform, vehicle or chair is programmed to mimic the real-world motion that would correspond to the visual image. A motion-base is best at simulating acceleration. For instance, quick movement of a motion-base simulates bumps and impacts. The challenge is to implement a synchronized motion-base with its visual reality.

### 17.2.2 Remarks on the Current Status

An important issue in multimedia performance is the proper selection of media based on the media hardware availability. This means that depending on what the multimedia application should achieve, the computing system with its devices and particular media quality is selected. It is crucial to point out that this approach is still very dependent on hardware, and causes problems with portability of multimedia applications.

Another important problem is that the currently available multimedia computer hardware is still not fast enough to meet the goals of applications, such as *virtual reality entertainment* and *motion-based simulators.*

## 17.3 Media Composition

Media composition involves *editing* single media, i.e., changing its objects, such as characters, audio sentences, video frames and attributes such as the font of a character, recording speed of an audio sentence or color of an image.

### 17.3.1 Text and Graphics Editors

#### Text Editors

Text editors provide writing and modifying facilities to compose text in a document. There are either separate text editors (e.g., GNU emacs text editor in combination with the LaTeX document preparation tool on workstations, WordPerfect on PCs) or text is embedded in graphical tools such as drawing programs – *xfig, MacDraw, CorelDRAW (Corel Corp.), etc.*. When editing text, one must deal with the issues of font selection, text style and text effects:

- *Fonts*

  The exact description of each character of text is determined by its font. Font files contain these descriptions, either in bitmap or vector form. Vector fonts are mathematical descriptions of the characters, which can be rendered in a wide range of sizes. Bitmap fonts are stored as bitmaps in predefined sizes.

- *Text Styles*

  Text can be presented in different styles, such as italicized, emboldened, underlined, etc. There are many possible text styles. Therefore, a writer of a document should make a careful choice for its uniform use.

- *Text Effects*

  More advanced text processing systems provide text effects such as shadowing, extrusion, textured fills, text-on-curve, etc. Such possibilities are offered in *CorelDRAW*.

Text editors are also beginning to be enhanced through other media, such as graphic objects. This is the same trend we see in the expansion of graphical tools with text manipulation capabilities. An example of an advanced word processor with graphical capabilities is *Microsoft Word.* This tool provides, in addition to text capabilities, a new toolbar and ribbon that can be customized for the creation of tables, envelopes, bullets and more. Furthermore, a built-in drawing program allows one to work with graphics without leaving the *Word* application.

### Graphics Editors

*Graphics editors* use facilities at the user interface for editing structural representations of graphical objects (structure-level editing) and for modifying higher-level operations on graphical objects (object-level editing). These two levels of editing are possible because the graphical system stores object primitives and their structural representations, which can be manipulated. A simple example of a graphical editor is *xfig* – an X Windows drawing program running on UNIX machines. This drawing application, also called a *layout editor or graphical illustrator* [FDFH92], supports editing of structural representations (the box to the right in Figure 17.1), as well as editing through the use of graphical icons (the two columns of graphical icons to the left in Figure 17.1). Graphical objects can be drawn, moved, copied, etc. via the user interface. Similar interactive programs that allow users to assemble complex 3D

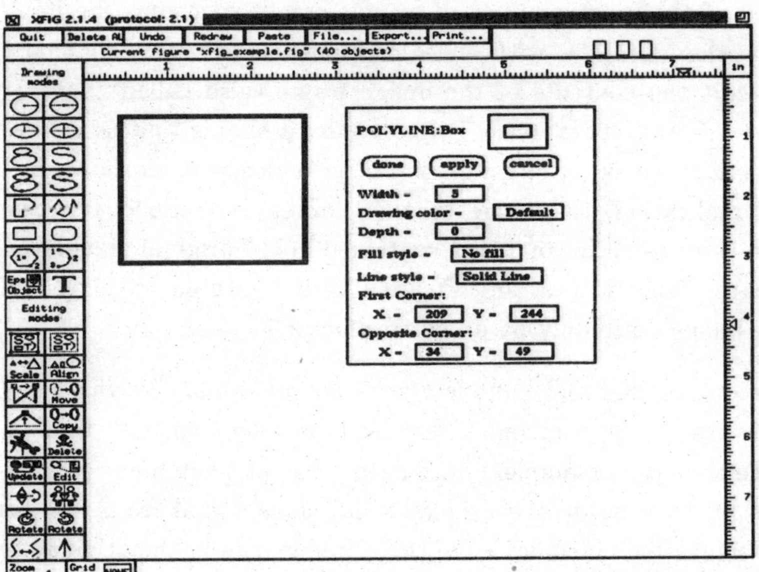


Figure 17.1: *Drawing application (xfig) with graphical and structural editing capabilities.*

objects from simpler objects are called *geometric editors* or *construction programs.* Object-level editing, screen refreshing and scaling in graphical editors require storage and re-specification of primitives by the application or by the graphics package. If the application stores the primitives, it can perform the re-specification; thus, these object-level operations are more complex. For example, in a graphics application with motion or update dynamics, the editor can modify an object database, which involves modifications of viewing, modeling transformations and changes in or replacement of objects.

### 17.3.2 Image Editors

Image editors are suitable for applications when neither the application nor the underlying software package keeps a record of the primitives (as is typical in most painting programs).

*Scaling* (one of the functionalities of an image editor) cannot be implemented by re-specifying the primitives with scaled endpoint coordinates. All that can be done is to scale/edit the contents of the image frame (also called canvas) using *read-pixel* and *write-pixel* operations. For example, a simple and fast way to scale up a bitmap/pixmap (make it larger) is via *pixel replication,* as shown in Figure 17.2. With pixel replication, the image becomes larger, but also coarser, since no new information is provided beyond that contained in the original pixel-level representation (compare Figure 17.2(a) and Figure 17.2(b)). Moreover, pixel replication can increase an image's size only by an integer factor.

Hence, a second scaling technique is used – *sampling and filtering* [FDFH92]. *Sampling* is the process of selecting a finite set of values (pixels) from a continuous signal. Once the pixels (samples) have been selected, they must be displayed, using *reconstruction,* to recreate the original continuous signal from the samples. The continuous signal itself includes noise (high frequencies in the original signal), hence to get a clear image, a *filtering* process (removal of the high frequencies) must be used either before sampling (pre-filtering) or after reconstruction of the image (post-filtering) to remove the noise.

One technique of pre-filtering is *aliasing.* Here, the high frequency components are converted into lower frequency components. The visual artifact of this is that the observed image is *staircasing*, i.e., some edges are not smooth. This visual artifact

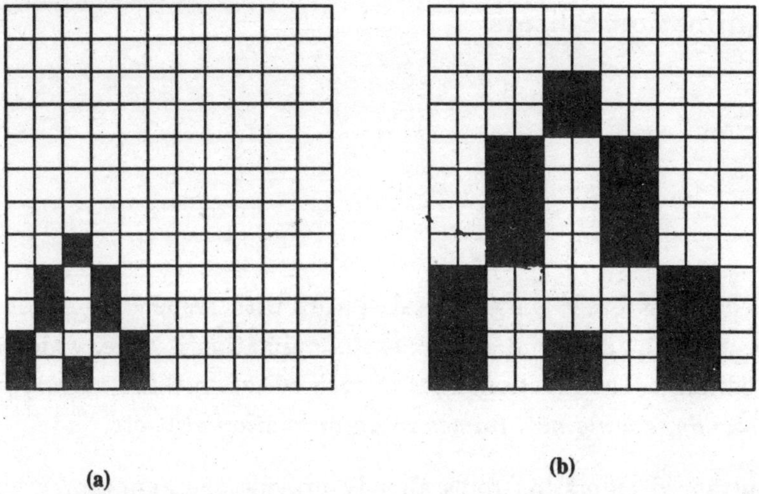

Figure 17.2: *Effect of pixel replication (a) original image at screen resolution. (b) zoomed (double size) image at the same screen resolution.*

must be removed. One possibility for removing *staircasing* is to increase the screen resolution. Another possibility to remove *staircasing* is to use different methods of *anti-aliasing* (see [FDFH92]).

Image editors provide other functionalities such as *increase of resolution, change of intensity, modification of RGB (Red, Green, Blue) colors, colormap editing*, etc. These functionalities can be found in an image editor such as *xv*, developed for UNIX workstations by John Bradley of the University of Pennsylvania in 1993.

An example of a graphics/image editor is *Adobe's Photoshop*™. This tool allows one to draw, edit and paste objects on several layers. Experimenting with different combinations of graphics, text and special effects without altering the original background image is possible. Furthermore, new filters let the user create 3D lighting effects, and remove dust and scratches from scanned images.

Another example of a photograph editor is Aldus *PhotoStyler*™. This tool edits photographic images created by different types of scanners and includes several editing options, such as editing of resolution, scaling of the photographic images, and providing access to various image processing techniques to apply them to the image after it has been scanned for producing a proper photographic image.

### 17.3.3 Animation Editors

Animation editing is based on graphical editors with respect to 2D or 3D spatial graphic objects. The additional component in animation is time, which can also be edited (4D editing). The functionalities of such editors include *cutting frames from an animation clip, adding new frames to an animation clip*, etc.

The most advanced animation tools already provide the animator with the capability to draw only the key frame. The intermediate frames are then drawn by the computer animation program. This process is called *tweening*. Further, some animation tools include *morphing* (polymorphic tweening), which is a transformation from one shape to another. This transformation can be seen in the cartoon *The Lion King* from Disney studios (1994). With this technique, many special effects can be created.

A general problem in temporal editing of animations is *temporal aliasing* (*staircasing* in time). The temporal aliasing problem in animation can be partially solved by increasing temporal resolution (i.e., increase the frame rate). In another approach, *temporal anti-aliasing* takes multiple samples of a signal and computes their weighted average. In this case, however, the multiple samples must smooth the time continuity and not the space continuity (as was the case in image editors), so the intensity at a point in the image for several sequential times is computed and these are weighted to get a value at a particular frame. Many other approaches have been developed to address temporal aliasing: supersampling, box filtering in the time domain, etc. [FDFH92].

Note that animation tools may include several integrated media editors. For example, Gold Disc, Inc. offers *Animation Works Interactive (AWI)* [Lut94] where *Movie Editor* is used for the assembly of complete animations, *Cel Editor* for building cels (this is an old name for an animation object drawn on a sheet of celluloid) and actors, and *Background Editor* (painting tool) for building the background.

### 17.3.4 Sound Editors

Sound tools support a number of operations that let the user access, modify and play sound data. The operations fall into four categories:

- *Locating and Storing Sounds*

  Location and storage of sounds can be done in four ways: (1) *record* a sound using an A/D audio device (analog-to-digital converter), (2) *read* sound data from a sound file, (3) *retrieve* a sound from a pasteboard, and (4) *create* sound data algorithmically.

- *Recording and Playback*

  The record operation continuously records sound from a microphone input until it is stopped or paused. Recorded sound is *m-law encoded*, which corresponds to CCITT G.711 and is the standard for voice data used by telephone companies in the U.S., Canada and Japan. *A-law and $\mu$-law encoding* is also part of G.711, and it is the standard encoding for telephony elsewhere in the world. The data are sampled at a rate of 8000 samples per second with 12-bit precision, but if the digitized sound is being compressed, then 8-bit precision per sample is achieved.

  The playback operation plays a sound using a D/A audio device (digital-to-analog converter) speaker output.

- *Editing*

  The editing operation allows one to copy/paste, cut, delete, insert or replace sampled sound data. One problem ought to be pointed out here: audio data are normally contiguous in memory. However, when a sound object is edited, its data can become *fragmented* or discontiguous. Fragmented sounds are played less efficiently. Hence, it is important to have an operation which *compacts* the samples into a contiguous object. Note that compacting a large sound object that has been considerably fragmented can take quite some time.

Digital music tools may include, for example, MIDI editors for music data stored as a *midi-file* – a music representation format that supports the conventions of the standard MIDI audio. MIDI audio is a series of commands for controlling a music synthesizer to produce, for example, orchestral music.

Generally, music editors include functionalities such as modification of loudness, amplitude, tone control, retrieval of a note from a part, removal of a note from a part, addition and removal of groups of notes, etc.

With music editors, special effects such as hall echos can be created. Furthermore, if *Digital Signal Processors (DSP)* are available, music can be synthesized on the DSP and new music can be created with a particular music tool (e.g., MusicKit [Tec89]).

### 17.3.5 Video Editors

Video editors are based on image editors for editing individual frames, but as in the case of animation editing, temporal considerations are important. Therefore, time resolution (time aliasing) is solved if frames are deleted, added or replaced. Editing functionalities of video editors may combine several cuts into one sequence, adjust audio separately from video and add video transition effects. An example of such a motion video editor is *VidEdit,* which works with Microsoft *Video for Windows* [Lut94].

Some advanced motion video editors (e.g., *D/Vision Pro* from TouchVisionSystems, a PC-based professional video editor running under DOS), can open several windows with different source videos. The editor can roll through each video source at variable speeds and select *edit-cut points.* This kind of editing causes fragmentation of the video. In the case of a conventional videotape, the edited sequence of video frames must be recorded to a new tape to view the new video clip. This kind of editing is called *linear* editing. An advanced video editor (e.g., D/Vision Pro) provides an *Edit Decision List (EDL)* from which the final video can be reconstructed, i.e., the edited video does not have to be recorded to a new tape because it can be played continuously using the EDL. This is called *non-linear* editing. Such tools may have further editing capabilities, e.g., adding dynamic transitions such as wipes, dissolves or fades between cuts.

Advanced motion video editors include several editors for editing video, sound and music in an integrated fashion. Examples of such tools come with Macintosh's

*QuickTime.*

## 17.4 Media Integration

Media integration specifies relationships between various media elements to represent and manipulate a multimedia object (e.g., document). Integration is still very much dependent on technology, i.e., platform-specific and format-specific, although there are attempts to provide tools which will integrate media on any platform with any format. An example of media integration in a multimedia application can be found in an authoring tool (Section 17.4.3). In this application, some levels of integration are platform-independent, but others, such as authoring languages, are not.

### 17.4.1 Multimedia Editors

*Multimedia editors* support the ability to manipulate multimedia documents that include structured text, multi-font text, bitmap images, graphics, video, digitized voice and other modifiable objects. Most editors use the *What You See Is What You Get* (WYSISYG) editing approach. An example of an early multimedia editor is the BBN's *Diamond Multimedia Editor* [CFLT87].

Several design issues need to be considered when implementing editors for multimedia documents:

- *Document Structure*

  The editor's functionality depends on the structure of the multimedia documents. To enable the exchange of documents and to be prepared for CSCW (Computer-Supported Cooperative Work), the document structure should be compatible with international standards, such as SGML (HTML) or ODA.

- *Media Editor Integration*

  Each medium has its own structure, therefore a multimedia editor actually consists of a collection of powerful and complex editors for individual media provided in an integrated fashion. There are several different issues regarding integration:

1. *Display Surface*

   Different media should be viewed in an integrated fashion, although for editing purposes either an integrated surface or separate window can be used.

2. *Processes*

   A design choice must be made with respect to the implementation of individual editors. They can be implemented as separate processes and the multimedia editor serves then as a parent process for management, or all the editors are implemented within a single monolithic process.

3. *User Interface*

   Media editors should be consistent with respect to the appearance of menus, dialogues, and terminology for commands and prompts.

4. *Data Levels*

   It should be possible to transfer data from one media type to another.

- *Multiple Buffers and Multiple Panes*

  It may be necessary to simultaneously manage multiple documents during one editing session. This can be done by providing *multiple buffers within the editor.* However, with a windowed environment (where multiple instances of an editor can run), several documents can be processed too.

  The capability of viewing multiple parts of the same document can also be provided. *Multiple panes* allow a single window to be split into multiple views. Panes are useful as lightweight devices for allocating screen space without suffering the overhead of going through the window manager. Their existence is often short-lived.

- *Large Documents*

  The multimedia editor must be able to handle large documents, perhaps stored in a distributed fashion. It might even happen that we need to work on *partial* documents because the editor does not have access to the whole document, only to parts of it.

- *External Representation*

  The individual media should be stored in their standardized formats.

The editor framework provides facilities for managing multiple buffers and panes and dispatching events to the individual media editors. It provides functions which operate on entire objects and documents, as well as a set of services which are used by the media editors. Each media editor makes available an array of generic functions, often addressed as the editor framework, as well as defined whatever media-specific editing operations are appropriate.

### 17.4.2 Hypermedia/Hypertext Editors

Hypermedia/hypertext documents consist of multimedia and non-linear links among the information. The documents are stored in multimedia databases in a structured representation (e.g., HTML database for HTML documents). Hence, the editing process means *accessing* document structures through links (associations) and *editing* objects according to their characteristics (text editors, graphics editors and others are executed).

Hypermedia/hypertext documents might be created and modified through hypermedia/hypertext tools such as:

- Apple's *Hypercard* runs on a Macintosh. It follows the card model (the page size of the document is the same as the size of a card), but has scrolling fields too (for more explanation, see Chapter 13). The documents incorporate text and graphics. Other media are accessible through extensions. The system provides a powerful scripting language.

- *DynaText* is a hypertext system based on SGML and a large number of graphics standards. It comes from Electronic Book Technology. DynaText is now available for SUN workstations.

- *NoteCard* (Xerox PARC) uses the card metaphor, meaning that it structures information in card-size chunks at a hypertext node.

- *Hyperbole* is a flexible, extensible *Personal Information Manager* (PIM) tool, which runs on top of the GNU Emacs text editor, available on any UNIX system. It is written in the programming language Lisp. It is the first step towards a distributed multimedia architecture which will create a *Personalized Information Environment (PIR)*. Hyperbole brings techniques of associative information management offered by hypertext systems to the domain of PIMs. Hyperbole allows the user to use any comfortable tool to generate information. At any point, the information can be easily integrated and further adapted for use within Hyperbole. Rather than the structured approach taken by most PIMs, Hyperbole offers an open framework under which many styles of information and task management can be performed [Wei91a].

- *Guide* is a hypertext editor running on Macintoshs and PCs using Windows. The tool uses an SGML-compatible language called HML. Documents may contain text and graphics.

The editors of hypermedia documents should not only include the editing facilities of the individual media, but also networking capabilities for accessing distributed hypermedia documents. Hence, a *tele-service* that follows logical links should be included. There already exist such hypermedia systems, for example, on the *World Wide Web (WWW)* and *HyperBase*.

### 17.4.3 Authoring Tools

Consider an application which coordinates a *multimedia presentation*. This application needs to provide a dynamic behavior and support several users' actions to integrate media to a required multimedia presentation. To implement an application with such dynamic support requirements, several processes must be programmed. This kind of application can be either written in a programming language, or implemented using an *authoring system*.

Hence, an authoring system is a set of software tools for creating multimedia applications embedded in an authoring environment. A person who creates applications for multimedia integration, for example, presentation, is called an *author*. The processes together are called *authoring* [Lut94]. There are also other components which belong to the authoring environment, such as multimedia *hardware*, *firmware* (software that is permanently built into the hardware) and an *assembly tool* (an authoring tool that arranges multimedia objects into a presentation or an application, dealing with their relationships in space and time).

When a multimedia application is produced via an authoring system, the author goes through several stages. Note that often at the various steps, a user's feedback is needed which might imply some additional work at any previous step:

- *Concept*

  This step identifies the *application audience*, the *application type* (presentation, interaction, etc.), the *application purpose* (inform, entertain, teach, etc.) and the general subject matter. At this stage, the authoring system cannot help.

- *Design*

  The style and content of the application must be specified. The object should include and generate enough detail so that the following stages of content collection and assembly can be carried out by the authoring system without further interruptions. However, the authoring system should still be tolerant of some kind of revisions. At this stage, the design parameters are entered into the authoring system. The authoring system can take over the task of documenting the design and keeping the information for the next steps of outlining, storyboarding, flow charting, slide sorting, and scripting.

  The other task in the design stage is to decide which data files will be needed in the application, such as audio, video and image files. A list of the material should be generated. The authoring system is only rarely involved in this task (a few authoring systems include entries for dummy file names).

- *Content Collection*

  The content material is collected and entered into the authoring system. In general, this includes taking pictures, making a video clip and producing an audio sequence. When the existing content is available either from internal or external sources, no creation tools are needed. It may be necessary to use a conversion tool to convert external source formats into formats with which the authoring system works. If the author creates the content himself/herself, creation tools are needed, such as word processing, paint and drawing software, image capture hardware and software, audio capture hardware and software and video animation hardware/software. Some authoring systems have some of these features, but with limited capabilities compared to the stand-alone tools.

- *Assembly*

  The entire application is put together in the assembly stage. Presentation packages, for example, do their assembly while the author is entering the content for the various screens. Once the screens are defined and placed in order, the presentation is ready to run. The limitation of this approach is that the author has little or no chance to interact with the authoring system. When the application includes a lot of interaction and very complex or dynamic screens, most authoring tools require details of the work, sometimes even programming. Most high-end authoring software packages, especially those which have a full authoring language, can be operated in a modular mode. In this case, a programmer can create customized modules that fit the specific needs of the particular application.

- *Testing*

  The created application must be tested. More sophisticated authoring systems provide advanced features such as single-stepping or tracing the program flow.

As is clear from the above steps, authoring tools are still platform-dependent, although they are closer to the goal of independence than editors or hypermedia tools. It is worthwhile to mention Kaleida Labs, a joint venture between Apple Computer and IBM for multimedia technologies. One of their major projects is *ScriptX*, a universal language that will allow multiple digital platforms to play the same digital file without modification. Because different platforms have different features and capabilities, the *ScriptX* run-time environment includes *dynamic adaptation* that allows an application to query the environment of the current platform and decide in real-time how it can best present itself. *ScriptX* is fully object-oriented with the capability for the user to combine objects at run-time, similar to MHEG, described in Chapter 13. Authoring tools might use this language to become more platform-independent.

Several authoring products are currently available which help to develop applications, such as:

- Information delivery applications can be developed using the authoring tools *Mediascript OS/2 Pro* (Network Technology Corp.), *IconAuthor* (Unisys), *ToolBook* (Asymetrix / ADI), *Authorware Professional*, IBM's *InfoDesigner 2* and others.

- Professional presentations can be developed using presentation authoring tools such as *PowerPoint* (Microsoft, Inc.), *FreeLance Graphics* and *Harward Graphics*. All the tools provide many features for enhancing the presentation by adding professional styles, images, graphics, audio, video, animation or charts.

- QuickTime movies and interactive projects can be created by movie authoring tools such as *MovieWorks* (from Interactive Solutions, Inc.). MovieWorks has several advanced capabilities: first, MovieWorks allows the user to create and edit objects in text, sound and paint; second, the user determines the project's look and feel; third, the user uses the *Composer* component to integrate the objects into a scene, and to add animations and special effects (scaling and transitions); and fourth, scenes can be linked together, either sequentially or interactively, to create a project.

## 17.5 Media Communication

Media communication denotes applications which exchange different media over a network via *tele-services* (e.g., video conferencing, cooperative work, mailing, etc.) to multimedia application end users.

The advantage of tele-services in multimedia applications is that the end users can be located in different places, and (1) still interact closely in a quite natural way or (2) operate on remote data and resources in the same way as with local data and resources. The disadvantage (currently) is that the delivery time of the tele-services is longer than the processing time of local multimedia applications. For example, the retrieval of a video clip takes longer when the information must be retrieved from a remote video server than if it is located on the video disc of a local computer. Therefore, the tradeoff between location and time needs to be kept in mind.

In the following section (17.5.1), we briefly describe *tele-service* mechanisms. In Sections 17.5.2 through 17.5.6 we present some implementation architectures for tele-services, and in Section 17.5.7 discuss some tele-applications.

### 17.5.1 Tele-Services

Tele-services are services provided by communication systems which are based on and make use of audio and video data. With current networks and the further development of high-speed networks, technology will enable distributed multimedia applications which need tele-services.

In this section we concentrate only on basic communication paradigms, such as tele-interaction and retrieval of information, without going into the details of communication systems. The details and basic principles of communication systems with respect to multimedia are described in Chapters 10 and 11.

#### Interactive Services

Interactive services include an exchange of control data between remote sites to influence the presentation of continuous media data. Communication between the sender and receiver can be performed either *synchronously*, which means that data arrive with a well-defined end-to-end delay, or *asynchronously*, which means that data arrive at any time. For example, a video conferencing application uses synchronous communication when remote conference participants are viewing a speaker. Mailing systems use asynchronous communication.

With respect to their task, interactive services are roughly divided into *conversational services* (e.g., used in video conferencing), *messaging services* (e.g., used in mailing systems), *retrieval services* (e.g., used in document retrieval systems), *tele-action services* (e.g., used in banking systems) and *tele-operation services* (e.g., used in tele-robotics systems). We will briefly describe the communication behavior of each service below:

- *Conversational Service*

  A conversational service supports *conversation* between remotely located end users. The service uses a two-way communication connection between the sender and receiver. The bi-directional delivery of multimedia is done in synchronous mode. Another feature of a conversational service is the time of the data delivery. The data must be delivered quickly (i.e., end-to-end delay must be minimal) in both directions so that conversation among the users can flow smoothly and in real-time without disturbing the human perception of a dialogue.

- *Messaging Service*

  A messaging service provides an exchange of messages between a sender and receiver where the end users are human users. The exchange of messages in both directions is done asynchronously, such that the time of delivery can be pre-determined. Since the end users can send messages whenever they like, fast delivery time is not required (i.e., end-to-end delay does not have to be minimal). The content of a message, a mail, can include all kinds of media data.

- *Retrieval Service*

  A retrieval service provides an exchange of messages between a sender and receiver, where the sender, also called the *client*, is a human user and the receiver, also called the *server*, is a computer with database provision. The client requests information from the server, where the information is stored; the server retrieves the information and sends it back.

  There is two-way communication, but the communication has the following characteristics. From the client to the server, the communication is asynchronous because the request from the client does not comply to timing constraints. The communication from the servers to the client may require a synchronous or asynchronous mode of operation depending on the information retrieved. If the retrieved information includes continuous media, the delivery must be synchronous. For example, if a user requests a movie from a remote video server, the video and audio delivery must occur according to stringent timing constraints. If the retrieved information includes a text file,

| General Categories | Applications |
|---|---|
| Transaction Processing | credit cards, lottery, automatic teller machines, medical insurance claims |
| Alarm and Surveillance | burglary, fire, smoke, medical, disabled persons, environmental surveillance |
| Business Automation | information access, data processing |
| Utility Resource Management | automatic meter reading, time-of-day rate information |
| Control and Command | appliances, thermostats, lights, vending machines, industrial equipment monitoring, hospital equipment |
| Interactive Video Support | home shopping |

Table 17.1: *Tele-action services [Sco94].*

then the delivery can be asynchronous. There is a strict requirement on the reliability of the transmitted data, while the requirement on the delivery time is relaxed. Although, to provide an acceptable user service, the delivery time (response time) from the server to the client should be minimal.

- *Tele-action Service*

  Tele-action means to act at a distance [Sco94]. Such actions include reading or writing some information to a remote location, or possibly both. Instead of sending a person to write or read information on a device, it is done remotely via a communication network. This form of data collection is useful when coupled with a computer system that can use the data to initiate an action (e.g., generate a bill). The tele-action services can be further classified with respect to their relation to the industry as shown in Table 17.1.

  - *Transaction Processing*

Transaction processing services perform business transactions. They remotely check databases for available funds (possibly transferring the funds) and print receipts. Some applications which use these services are listed in Table 17.1.

– *Alarm and Surveillance*

Alarm and surveillance is a service that monitors factors affecting individual or public safety.

– *Business Automation*

Business automation services provide information access to medical or legal databases, real state listings, etc. Furthermore, they can be used for management of databases for individual distributors and suppliers.

– *Utility Resource Management*

Utility resource management services provide better management and a distribution of resources, such as gas, water and electricity. These services help, for example, a utility company track and control consumption, as well as monitor safety factors.

– *Control and Command*

Control and command services, often called *tele-metry* services (telemetry means to measure at a distance), are used to remotely read data and monitor the status of remote control equipment.

– *Interactive Video Support*

A growing number of industries are trying to develop services that offer smart control of a television set. In particular, there is interest in services that provide interactive control of video services.

• *Tele-operation Service*

Tele-operation services have bi-directional communication. They allow the user to perform a task at a distance, typically by manipulating a master controller that causes a slave effector to move remotely mimicking the master controller's movement.

### Distribution Services

Distribution services are services for the distribution of information to different remote sites. They are one-way communication from the broadcasting source to the remote destinations. For example, TV broadcasting or radio broadcasting use distribution services. There are two kinds of subservices: ***distribution services without individual user presentation control*** and ***distribution services with individual user presentation control.***

The development of these services continues to move towards interactive services [Ran94]. The reason is that with the new technology of *video on demand* over cable TV networks, several types of control have been and will be given to the viewer:

- *Pay-per-view*

  Cable subscribers can order movies and programs using today's *set-top decoder box.* However, these set-top boxes do not give the viewers any freedom other than the choice off whether to view the program or not. The viewer has no control over the movie shown.

- *Near Video-On-Demand*

  This service is achieved by having many channels broadcast the same program, but with a definite temporal variation or delay between the channels. With this approach, the viewer can simulate forward and reverse functions by changing channels appropriately. One suggestion for the time delay is to start the same video clip every ten minutes. This gives the user some control over the time at which (s)he can view the movie. In the case of a live program, a *deferred airing* has been suggested to give the user the possibility: (1) to decide if (s)he wants to watch the program, and (2) to see the live program later in case the user missed the first specified broadcasting time. *Deferred airing* is a concept in which live programs are broadcast after a specific time delay.

- *True Video-On-Demand*

  This service provides the functions of a VCR and hence gives the user complete freedom to temporally alter the viewing. Further steps are *Interactive TV* and

*Cyber Vision,* where the user is involved in the content and can at least make choices of how the movie will proceed.

The first two types of services do not require many changes in current cable TV networks. The third service will require a switching system to be installed to support bi-directional signaling.

### 17.5.2 Implementation of Conversational Services

Conversational services are implemented as tools like multimedia conferencing, video-telephony or computer-supported cooperative work. These tools are then used, for example, in a group of applications called *tele-working.*

#### Video Conferencing

*Tele-conferencing systems* allow the user to achieve most of the efficiency and productivity of traditional meetings with one main difference: the user can stay at his/her desk as can the remote conference participants. A multimedia conferencing system enables people to work together across geographically distant locations without the need to meet at one site. They communicate among each other in multi-party or face-to-face mode using motion video, audio and textual information in each direction. The audio and video quality heavily depends on the platform. Therefore, a big factor in the success of a tele-conferencing system is to achieve high media quality over any platform and interconnectivity among various platforms and vendors. A possible setup of a video conferencing system is shown in Figure 17.3.

Video conferencing is used either in an office environment, where the video is displayed on a PC or workstation screen, or in a conference room, where the video is displayed on a *video wall* (large TV screen). For the office environment, desktop video conferencing systems have been developed. The name suggests that the PCs or workstations in offices are placed at users' desks so that they can easily communicate any time. For a conference room environment, large TV screens in conference rooms are used for meetings of groups located at different geographical places. We will discuss some of the conference room solutions in Section 17.5.7.

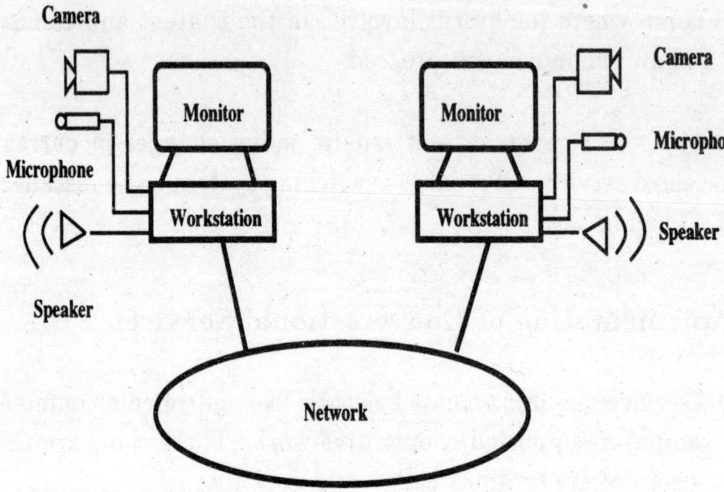


Figure 17.3: *Video conferencing system.*

Desktop video conferencing systems often include a dedicated shared white-board application (i.e., drawing and writing software support for multiple users) [MR94]. *Application sharing* denotes techniques which replicate the user interface of the particular software (e.g., the user's favorite text processor) so that the software can be used simultaneously by all participants of a conference. The concurrency in the activities underlies the mechanisms of "floor passing" (also called "chalk passing") to determine which one of the users may actually interact with the software at a given time (see Chapter 11).

Some examples of conferencing tools are *vat* for audio conferencing and *nv* for video conferencing running on SUN workstations, and BERKOM's *MMC (Multimedia Conferencing)* on a network of UNIX-based machines such as IBM's RISC System/6000, SUN, HP and further workstations [KW93a].

### Video-phone with Conversational Service

A video-phone is basically a sophisticated telephone with a screen for the presentation of the caller(s). A video-phone with conversational services supports *video-telephony* applications. Video-telephony is used for telephone meetings between two or more persons in which image transfer may be voice-controlled, such that the speaker is seen by the others. A possible architecture is shown in Figure 17.4.

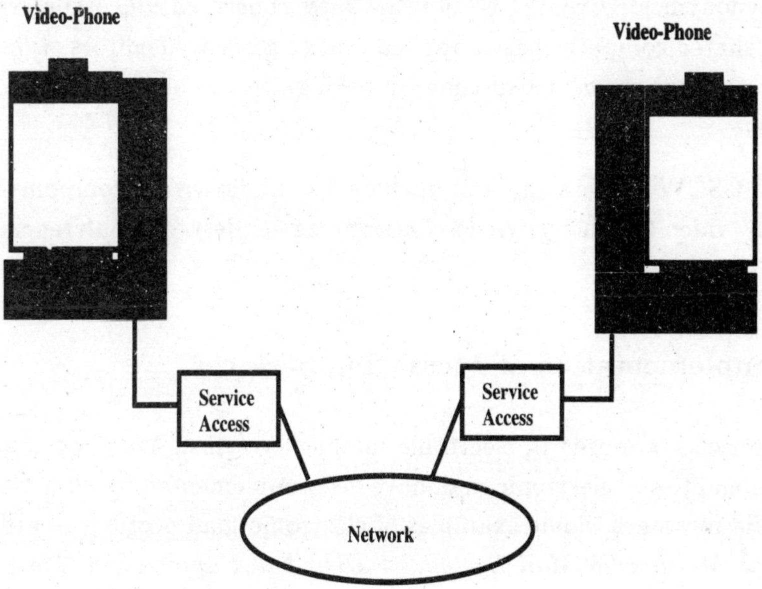


Figure 17.4: *Video-telephony system.*

### Computer Supported Cooperative Work (CSCW)

The current infrastructure of networked workstations and PCs makes it easier for people to cooperate. The cooperative work done in this environment is called *Computer Supported Cooperative Work* (CSCW). CSCW systems allow several people at different locations to work on the same data, most often a document.

CSCW systems are divided into *asynchronous CSCW* and *synchronous CSCW* systems. *Asynchronous cooperative work* specifies processing activities which do not happen at the same time. A typical example is a health insurance claim for coverage of surgery expenses processed separately by persons responsible for different functions in the insurance company. *Synchronous cooperative work* happens at the same time. The fast development of multimedia has established video conferencing as an integral part of CSCW systems.

Systems that support group collaboration are called *groupware*. The essence of groupware is the creation of a shared workspace among collaborators and it is often used as a synonym for CSCW. Groupware may consist of video conferencing, together with shared computer-based applications (e.g., shared editors, white-boards). If groupware is supported in real-time, it belongs to the area of *synchronous telecollaboration.*

Commercial CSCW applications still include few audio-visual components and are built as only video-telephony, video-conferencing or desktop-conferencing applications.

### 17.5.3 Implementation of Messaging Services

Messaging services are used in electronic mailing systems. A number of extensions to the functionalities of electronic mail have been implemented to allow the exchange of multimedia messages. Some examples of electronic mail prototypes are DARPA's experimental *Multimedia Mail System, a Distributed Inter-office Mail System* or *Diamond Mail* from BBN.

We will present two approaches implementing multimedia mail systems: *MIME (Multipurpose Internet Mail Extension)* (Internet Standard) and *the Multimedia Mail Tele-service* based on CCITT recommendation X.400 (88) [Sch94b].

#### MIME

MIME is an extension of Internet Mail defined by the Internet Engineering Task Force (IETF) working group [BF93]. It offers a simple standardized way to represent and encode a wide variety of media types. MIME messages can include seven types of media – text, images (image/gif, image/jpeg), audio, video (video/mpeg), message for encapsulated messages, multiparts for including multiple types of data in a single message and application data (application/PostScript).

Various strategies for MIME implementation are possible. A flexible approach is to use *metamail.* It is a simple program which is called when the mailing program gets non-textual information. Metamail does not understand any MIME data type, but instead knows how to read a set of configuration files, called *mailcap files*. The mailcap program, handling the mailcap file, recognizes the data type and calls the particular program for viewing the message. For example, if the message includes an image, mailcap may call the image viewing program *xv*.

### Multimedia Mail Tele-service

Multimedia Mail Tele-service, developed within the BERKOM project [RK92], is based on the X.400/88 CCITT recommendation. This service supports message types such as ASCII text, PostScript, teletext and other *body part* types of the X.400 standard. The BERKOM profile defines externally-defined body parts for audio, video and image as new information types.

The mailing system is implemented as follows: the X.400 *Message Transfer System* (MTS) delivers messages submitted from either a *Multimedia Mail User Agent* (MM-Mail UA) or a *Global Store Server (GSS)* to one or more recipient UAs or MSs and returns notification to the originator, if requested. The transfer system is based on the *store-and-forward* principle. The user agent includes composers, editors, viewers or converters for multimedia messages. The storage server stores multimedia components and makes any data, especially high-volume data, accessible worldwide. It can be considered as a public or private service for the temporary deposition of bulk data in a global network. Major components of this multimedia mail system are shown in Figure 17.5. Unlike text messages, the size of multimedia messages may range from a few Kbytes to many Mbytes. Messages of many Mbytes might be too large for MTS, as well as for the storage capacities at the recipient's site. A possible solution is to include *references* to large message components within the message rather than include the contents. These references are like pointers to a remote store that can be accessed by originators and recipients using specialized protocols for data transfer.

## 17.5.4 Implementation of Retrieval Services

Multimedia retrieval systems allow users to access large multimedia storage and databases, located at servers, and to view this information. The servers are shared

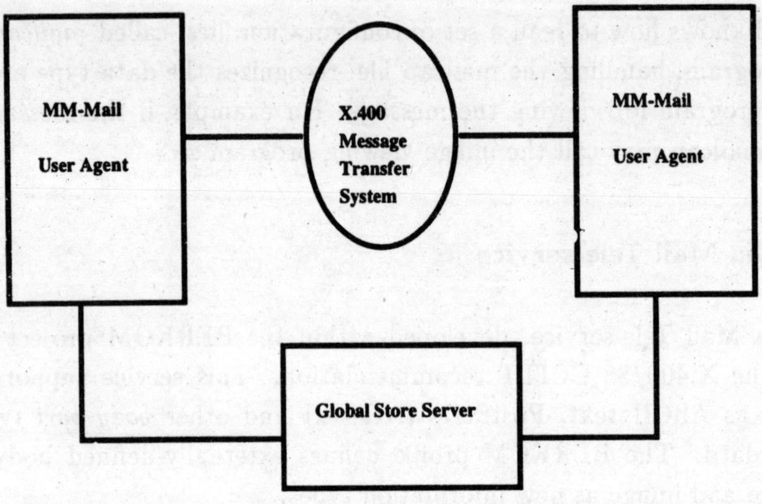


Figure 17.5: *Multimedia mail system.*

among the clients. We will describe a multimedia retrieval system with the focus on video retrieval. Multimedia retrieval services are used in applications such as the World Wide Web and Internet Gopher, which we briefly describe.

### Video Server

The main types of information stored in video servers are movies and other video information. It is more economical to store videos on central servers because of the considerable amount of valuable disk space they consume. To retrieve video data from the central server over today's computer networks, a software, which carefully manages resources in networks, end-systems and routers, is necessary. Client workstations and PCs, which are used to retrieve and display data, are connected to the video server using, for example, local area networks.

The communication protocol to retrieve video from a video server is as follows: the user issues a request, which may include the name of the video; the server sends the required video over the network and the video is then presented in a client window. A similar protocol applies to audio and other media. All multimedia data should be retrieved from a server in real-time. A possible video retrieval system setup is shown in Figure 17.6.

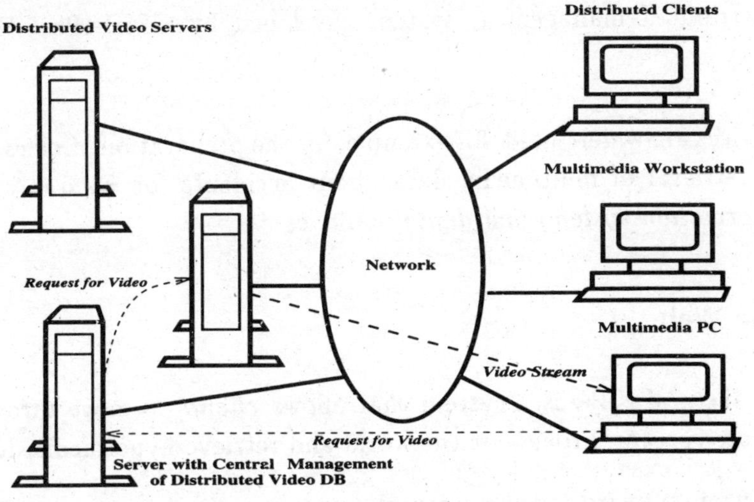


Figure 17.6: *Multimedia retrieval system.*

Examples of video server prototypes are:

- The *Ultimedia Server/6000*, which allows users to store, record, share and retrieve multimedia data using IBM Heidelberg's HeiTS communication technology.
- The $V^3$ *video server* [RM93], which allows a user to interactively store, retrieve, manipulate and present analog and short digital video clips. The picture and sound data of a video clip are stored in a database in digital form or on a laser as analog streams. The conventional properties of database systems, such as queries, multiple-user access and recovery, are supported. Digital and analog data are transported via digital and analog networks, respectively. Video clips can be accessed by methods that initialize, present and control them. For example, the presentation of a clip can be started by the operation *play* and interrupted by the operation *stop*. Due to the storage of analog video clips on laser discs and their WORM (Write Once Read Many) characteristics, picture and sound data cannot be edited. The video data of a digital clip, modeled as a sequence of frames, can be manipulated by inserting, cutting

and moving parts. The server system is developed on top of the VODAK database management system. VODAK is a prototype of an object-oriented and distributed management system developed by GMD-IPSI, Darmstadt, Germany.

Retrieval services are widely used, for example, for the preparation of *news broadcast*, storage and retrieval of multimedia data about accidents for *insurance purposes*, *employee information systems* and *digital libraries*.

### World Wide Web

*World Wide Web (WWW)* is a system that allows *clients* to move through many different remote *servers* throughout the world and retrieve hypermedia documents.

It has a body of software (clients, servers, gateways, library, tools) and a set of protocols and conventions such as: a *WWW Server* is a program, like *ftp server*, that responds to an incoming caller request and provides a service to the caller. An example of a WWW server is the CERN (the European Laboratory for Particle Physics) server or the NCSA (the National Center for Supercomputing Applications) server. *Gateways* are servers that provide data extracted from other systems. For example, the *VMS Help* gateway allows any VMS help file to be made available to WWW clients. The *Common WWW Code Library* is the basis for most WWW browsers because it contains network access and format handling. *WWW and HTML (HyperText Markup Language)* tools are parts of the available WWW software whose purpose is to manage WWW servers, generate hypertext, view retrieved information, etc. For example, the user can view a hypermedia document (a HTML document) with the *NCSA Mosaic*©tool for X Windows running on SUN workstations.

### Internet Gopher

The Internet Gopher is a client/server-based worldwide information delivery service from the University of Minnesota. The user can search and retrieve various information, using the *Internet Gopher protocol*, such as newspapers, newsletters, weather forecasts, phone-books, libraries, information about universities, etc. This information can include media types, such as text, sound and/or image. Furthermore, gopher objects can be files (e.g., UNIX uuencoded files, BinHexed Macintosh files), images (in GIF format), MIME information (multimedia mailing format) or HTML documents (hypertext format).

### 17.5.5 Implementation of Tele-action Services

We will briefly outline two possible architectures for the implementation of tele-action services. One architecture demonstrates the implementation of utility resource management and the other architecture demonstrates the implementation of an alarm and surveillance system.

#### Message Switch and Store for Utility Resource Management

A possible (and quite common) setup for the implementation of utility resource management is shown in Figure 17.7. The system is based on a *Message Switch and*

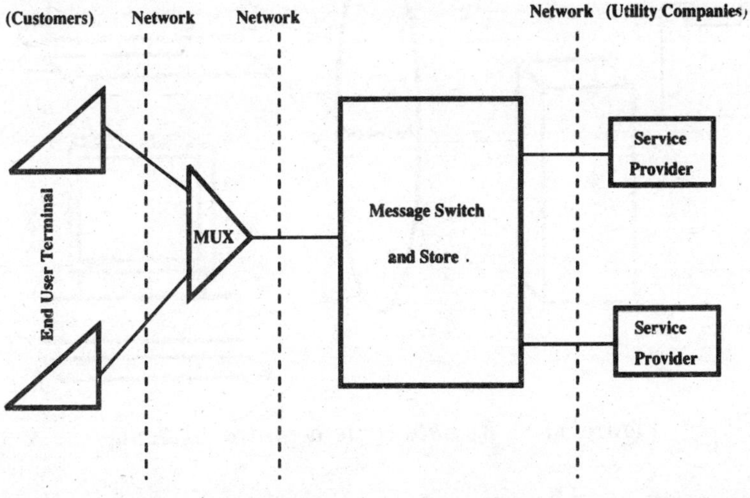


Figure 17.7: *Message switch and store for utility resource management.*

*Store* device that provides much of the functionality of the message delivery service.

It is a key component because it collects messages from the multiplexer and sends them to the service provider, which is the utility company. The multiplexers are typically located in the local exchanges and are remotely controlled by the *message switch and store* device. Permanent monitoring and polling of the end user terminals (e.g., tariff meter, pulse meter) is performed by the multiplexer.

### Remote Camera Control for an Alarm and Surveillance Service

One possible implementation of an *alarm and surveillance* service is a *remote camera control system* and it is used in areas such as: *production monitoring*, *computer-integrated manufacturing* or *monitoring of security areas.* The architecture of such a system is shown in Figure 17.8. The camera is located at a remote site in need of

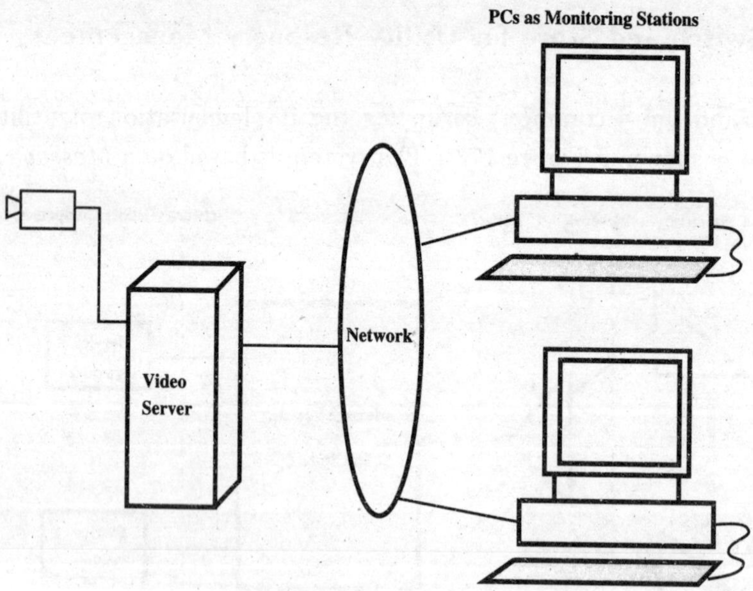


Figure 17.8: *Remote camera control system.*

monitoring. It is connected to a video server which digitizes the motion video and sends it over a communication network to a user (observer). The user views the motion video on his/her PC or workstation [WSS94].

### 17.5.6 Implementation of Tele-operation Services

Tele-operation used, for example, in a tele-robotics application presents challenges quite distinct from tele-conferencing. It allows a remote operator to exert force or to impart motion to a slave manipulator. The operator experiences the force and resulting motion of the slave manipulator, known as *kinesthetic feedback*. An operator is also provided with visual feedback and possible audio feedback as well. An example of such a system is shown in Figure 17.9 [NS93].

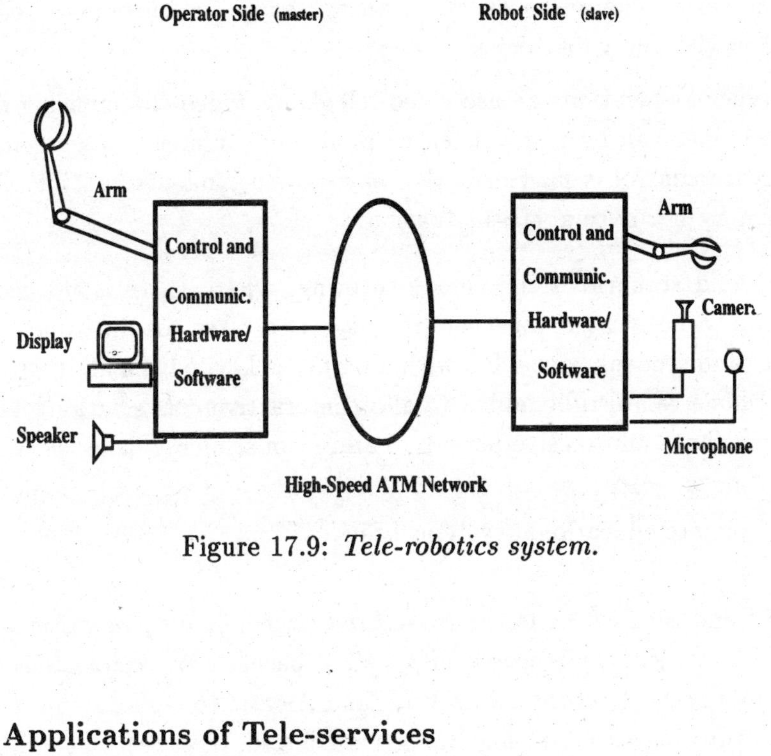


Figure 17.9: *Tele-robotics system.*

### 17.5.7 Applications of Tele-services

The services discussed above are used in our society in many ways. One group of applications that use these services are *tele-working* applications. People can stay at their work or home and connect with other people for different purposes. Tele-working includes tele-activities such as *remote education*, *offices in the home*, *tele-collaboration* and *tele-medicine*.

### Remote Education

There are two remote education scenarios:

- The first scenario is a group of people sitting together in one location with the necessary equipment needed for their remote education. The remotely located teacher gives a lecture to the group. The visual equipment in the classroom (i.e., room where the group is gathered) is most often a *video wall.* A video wall is a large TV screen connected to a computer for video reception and transmission. The audio can be transmitted either through a telephone or together with the video signal.

  This type of education can use video-telephony, video-conferencing or just live (cheap) video can be transmitted without any conference management. If no conference control is provided, the teacher and students control the communication as in a normal class situation.

- The second scenario is individual tutoring, where there is no need for the students to be located together (in space and often also in time). Both the teacher and student have a PC with a monitor, keyboard and other devices. A video-phone can also be added to allow interactive conversation. The teacher may distribute and receive papers to and from students using electronic mail.

Examples of remote educational systems are:

- *BETEL* and *BETEUS* – In the *Broadband Exchange for Trans-European Links (BETEL)* project, high-speed links (ATM-based, cross connected) were provided by France Telecom, Swiss PTT and Alcatel to demonstrate multimedia remote tutoring services (and further advanced services). The EPFL (Lausanne) and Eurocom (Sophia-Antipolis) jointly provide a tele-teaching application [BDG+94]. As a successor of BETEL, the *Broadband Exchange for Trans-European USage (BETEUS)* project supports the interconnection of six locations in Europe through the ATM pilot network. In the summer of 1995, this network will be used for tele-teaching among four sites [BDG+94]. Further research at EPFL, under the guidance of J.P. Hubaux, will be devoted to an open architecture for advanced multimedia services over ATM with emphasis on network management issues.

- *CO-LEARN* – a multimedia system for distributed teaching and learning with participants at different sites (PCs running MS Windows or UNIX workstations) connected by an ISDN network [Hau93]. This system offers four scenarios: tele-teaching, real-time tele-assistance, real-time multimedia conferencing and an asynchronous forum for exchange of multimedia and learning material.

- *Tele-mentoring System* – a system for interactive distance learning using the Asynchronous Transfer Mode (ATM) network of the AURORA Gigabit Testbed [SDF+94]. The experimental trial for distance learning used tele-conferencing hardware (Video-Window from Bellcore), which converts NTSC television and audio signals to and from ATM cells. This hardware connected Bellcore's and University of Pennsylvania's video walls with other apparatus to create a realistic two-way interaction.

### Tele-office

Currently, employees can work at home and still access various information sources and communicate with their colleagues, management and others via telecommunication networks. A home office might consist of a telephone, PC, printer (the minimal configuration), video-phone, fax (the advanced configuration) and telecommunication services such as conversational services, retrieval services and/or messaging services.

### Tele-collaboration

Tele-collaboration has become an important part of our working environment. To make this service successful, a *media space* [BBI93] – a collaborative work environment – is created. A *media space* may consist of a network supporting the transmission of audio, video and other data, fixed connections (local or remote) to employees' offices, a crossbar switch that links cameras, monitors and microphones in each office and computers that allow switched access to persons in each office. The possible architecture of a media space is shown in Figure 17.10.

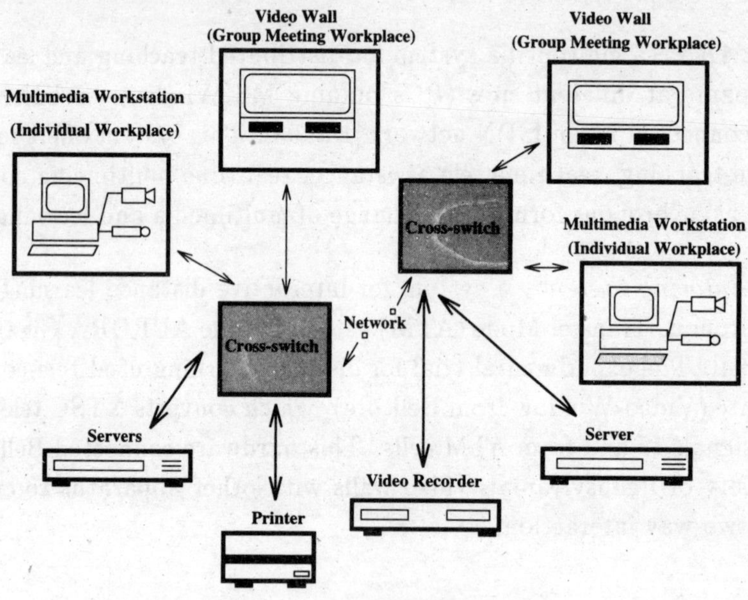


Figure 17.10: *Media space as the example for tele-collaboration.*

In addition to the hardware, a media space may support conversational service capabilities for one-on-one conversations (e.g., video-telephony, e-mail), many-to-one conversations (e.g,, bulletin board newsgroups, e-mail, tele-conferencing), many-to-many conversations for group meetings (e.g., video-conferencing, groupware), shared applications (e.g., white-board) and recording and retrieving video records.

There are several research projects that have implemented a media space into their working environment and have included trials to evaluate the effectiveness of the media space:

- *Media Space at Xerox PARC*

  This media space uses cameras, monitors, microphones and computing to connect employees' offices. Media space in this project is geographically split between Palo Alto, California and Portland, Oregon. It is important to note that during the trial, the media space was constantly in use, functioning like an extension of physical space. It was not something that was turned off or on during the day, but was continually available. The office cameras were most often open and in one of three states: *open and on* (the user is visible); *open but focused on some nonuser location* (friendly but not personally visible); and *closed* (lens cap was on and/or the camera was off). Microphones were often off, but could be switched on quickly as needed. The media space was mostly used for project and lab meetings.

- *VideoWindow at Bellcore*

  The VideoWindow system provides a large screen display with live audio between two public areas on different floors of a research lab building. During the trial, the system was on 24 hours a day for three months to support informal interactions among researchers and staff. People typically came to the area for some specific task (e.g., to pick up mail) and could engage in conversation with others who happened to coincidentally appear either in the same space or in the space provided by the VideoWindow.

- *Cruiser at Bellcore*

  Media space in the Cruiser system [FKRR93] connects research offices for informal interactions. It uses a desktop video-telephony system. Cruiser is based on the model of walking down a hallway and popping one's head into a doorway. During a cruise, either the observed or the observer have the option of changing the cruise activity to a two-way conversation activity.

There are also other research projects, such as CAVETAT/Telepresense from the University of Toronto, RAVE from Rank Xerox EuroPARC, Kasmer from Xerox PARC, and TeleCollaboration from US West Advanced Technologies.

### Tele-medicine

*Tele-medicine services* address elderly, sick or disabled people who cannot leave their homes. Over the telecommunication network, these people can consult their doctor (tele-diagnosis) and get medical information and other administrative health information. Tele-diagnosis uses a conversational service implemented, for example, through video-telephony. Access to medical and health care information can be achieved through retrieval services.

*Tele-surgery* allows one to consult a specialist on demand for crucial and difficult operations performed at local hospitals. The easiest way to implement this application is to provide remote camera control with conferencing capabilities.

## 17.6 Media Consumption

Media consumption is the act of *viewing, listening or feeling multimedia information.* Viewing and listening are the most common ways users consume media. Feeling multimedia information can be experienced in motion-based entertainment parks, for example, through virtual reality. This is still a very new area in computer science and there are few results. Therefore, we will discuss it only briefly in Section 17.7 and Chapter 18.

The major emphasis of this section is on viewing multimedia information (presentation). Presentation of multimedia information is often done through authoring tools, as well as by other tools. One major requirement of media consumption, which needs to be considered by each public multimedia application, is the *simplicity of presentation.* Especially, when user interfaces with new media are introduced, it is important to convince users to consume them because people like to do things the same or in ways similar to how they used to do them in the past. Therefore, (1) familiar human user interfaces must be created, (2) the users need to be educated, and (3) the users need to be carefully navigated through the new application.

We will analyze some design issues with respect to viewing multimedia documents and then discuss some applications where proper media consumption is important (e.g., books, electronic newspapers, kiosks).

### 17.6.1 Viewing Multimedia Documents

Multimedia documents can be viewed ("consumed") in two modes: by *browsing* and by *detailed media consumption.*

*Browsing* means that the user goes quickly through the document to get an overview of what the document includes. For example, the user may just read the titles of articles in a newspaper, table of contents of a book or a brief abstract of a scientific article. To browse through text, graphics or image information, the viewing tool provides a *menu* (e.g., table of contents), *sliding bars* on the side of the window where the document is displayed in a *highlighted phrase* (colored or underlined), *graphical icons* (e.g., arrow icon, audio icon), *search functions* or *small images.* Highlighted phrases, graphical icons and small images are hyperlinks to other information. For browsing through video information, the tool provides functions such as *move forward, move backward, search for a certain scene* or *play a short video clip.* For audio information, the tool provides analogous functions such as *move forward, move backward, play a short audio clip* or *search for a certain song/musical passage.*

*Detailed media consumption* means a detailed reading, viewing or listening of the multimedia entity. This mode requires functions such as *display a document, quit, play video/audio, stop video/audio.*

Many viewing tools provide additional functions which help the user view multimedia information:

- *Navigation* includes prespecified steps to view a document. The *navigate* menu may, for example, specify how to get to the beginning of a document, bibliography or other specific part of the document.

- *Annotation* allows the user to add personal annotations to any document during the viewing process. Annotations in the *Mosaic* tool are inlined as hypertext links at the end of the document. The annotation can be *personal, public* or *workgroup*-oriented.

Section 17.5.4 already discussed the implementation of retrieval services. We now extend the discussion with respect to consumption issues by the two following examples.

#### Music Consumption

Music consumption is widespread among PC users. Current music tools offer various functionalities for working with MIDI and WAVE audio data.

Music tools provide opportunities to: (1) learn the basic theory necessary to understand music (MIBAC's Music Lessons), (2) create a powerful recording studio (OpCode Systems' Musicshop), (3) manipulate sounds and CD audio tracks (OpCode Systems' Audioshop), (4) compose, play, record, edit and print out music on a PC (Passport Designs' MusicTime), (5) mix and edit MIDI instruments (Master Tracks Pro 5), and (6) learn to play musical instruments (e.g., The Pianist, The Jazz Guitarist).

#### NCSA Mosaic

NCSA Mosaic is an Internet-based *global hypermedia* information browser and World Wide Web client developed at the National Center for Supercomputing Applications (NCSA) at the University of Illinois, Urbana-Champaign.

A single-click with the left mouse button on a hyperlink (i.e., a highlighted phrase or icon) causes Mosaic to retrieve the document associated with that link and display it in the *Document View* window. A single-click with the middle mouse button also causes Mosaic to follow the link and open a new Document View window on top of the existing one. From that point, either Document View window can be used for further navigating and viewing of hypermedia documents.

### 17.6.2 Books, Proceedings and Newspapers

Books, proceedings and newspapers can be interactive multimedia documents which may be electronically distributed to the home. The user may either print the data or navigate through the information on some computer. Instead of simply broadcasting the same newspaper to all readers, the user accesses the electronic versions of newspapers, magazines, book, etc. The access can be customized according to individual profiles. This approach saves paper, has a potential for personal selection and provides fast delivery. It means that news can be written into the server as soon as it arrives in the news studio and the reader gets the most recent information. Despite the advantages, experiments have shown that customization is not always wanted and readers often tend to prefer paper over electronic versions.

### 17.6.3 Kiosks

Recent technological advances have made possible the high-quality delivery of video and audio integrated into the desktop computing environment. This capability, combined with the increasingly common use of digital information acquisition and storage, provides an opportunity to create public information services known as *multimedia kiosk systems.*

Kiosk systems are often located in public areas, accessible to visitors or customers. The kiosk are controlled by a computer that allows the user to interactively control the information or service (s)he wants to obtain. Since kiosk customers might be unskilled users, the user interface must be simple and easy to handle.

A further requirement for a kiosk system is that response time must be short. At present, this can be achieved only if the kiosk system is local or connected to its server by a local area network. The kiosk applications use the retrieval services (query mode) or some tele-action services for communication with the servers.

The equipment constituting a multimedia kiosk system might take a variety of forms. The hardware requirements include a processor, storage device, display, speakers and a touch screen. An advanced configuration could also include a video disk player, high-speed network connection, high-resolution screen, keyboard, printer and camera, plus any other hardware needed for the specific application, such as a device to accept money and dispense change.

Applications of information-providing services within the realm of multimedia kiosk systems include *airport or train station kiosks* with maps of terminals, arrival/departure times and gate numbers; *museum showcase kiosks* with preview information of forthcoming exhibits and schedules of forthcoming attractions; *bank assistant kiosks* with information on banking products and worksheets for planning savings accounts; *cinema information kiosks* with information on times and places of movies, selected clips from movies and movie trivia; *retail store kiosks* with information on product highlights, special pricing, and store layout; and *real-estate catalog kiosks* with information on real estate categorized by price, location, information about schools, libraries, stores in the neighborhood, pictures and videos of objects.

Some examples of kiosk systems as information manipulators are: a *ticket counter* that provides reservation and purchase of plane/concert/etc. tickets, and interactive seating according to a floor plan; a *bank teller* that supports sale of life-insurance, transfer of funds, and tracking of investments; an *education* system that supports an on-line student interaction with lessons and immediate feedback/review (learning tools); a *cooperative work* system that supports team development of document draft, dynamic work assignment and status reports.

### 17.6.4 Tele-shopping

Multimedia tele-shopping enables users to shop from their homes. For example, a household installs a PC and a tele-service (retrieval service) to set up a connection to a database or multimedia catalogue. The service allows the user to search for different products from the catalogue. The products may be presented either with video and sound or as a text accompanying still images. Analogous to kiosk systems, the user interface and manipulation of information during the viewing process must be easy to work with because of the broad range of users. A product may also be ordered and paid for electronically (i.e., tele-action service).

Examples of tele-shopping applications are: home ordering/shopping of goods, ticket reservation (theater, cinema, concerts, shows, travels, etc.) and advertising with multimedia.

## 17.7 Media Entertainment

Virtual Reality entertainment (VR), Location-Based Entertainment (LBE), motion-based simulators, large-screen film and games (based on interactive audiovisual support) are applications that use multimedia for entertainment and bring a different and more involved entertainment experience than what is available with a standard TV or movie theater.

### 17.7.1 Virtual Reality

The term *Virtual Reality* (VR) promises far more than our technology can currently deliver. It has been variously used to describe user interfaces ranging from synthesized physical environments presented on Head-Mounted Displays (HMDs), to ordinary graphics displayed on conventional CRTs, to text-based multi-user games.

Computer-based VR systems are three-dimensional, interactive as opposed to passive, and use one or more devices in an attempt to provide the user with a sense of presence, be it visual, auditory or tactile[HPC94, Ear93]. Among these devices are head-tracked displays and stereo displays (both visual and audio), hand trackers and haptic displays (devices which provide force feedback).

The first VR systems appeared before computers were used for VR. Morton Heilig developed a machine called the Sensorama [Hei62], which involved all of the senses except taste in a virtual motorcycle ride through Manhattan. Early flight simulators also created virtual environments without the aid of computers. They used movies or created live video by shooting model boards with TV cameras [Sch83].

Currently, the hardware platform of virtual environments consists of color stereo HMDs, haptic displays, spatial sound, data gloves and 3D graphics [Bro88, WF90]. The software architectures for virtual environments have been developed to support a single hardware platform or a small number of tightly coupled platforms. As a result, systems were originally modeled after traditional interactive programs. Current systems still ignore issues that would arise if such applications were used on a larger scale, as will be required for the real world. The first virtual environment applications were simple event-loop-based programs. There are several problems with this approach because the following requirements need to be satisfied:

1. VR displays should respond to changes in tracked objects, especially the user's head, at least ten times per second for the virtual environment to be convincing

[FD94]. A solution to this requirement is to distribute the VR system over multiple processes, decoupling the simulation steps from the redisplay loop.

2. VR systems should not have tightly coupled distributed processes because this approach does not scale towards new hardware and system software solutions. A solution is to use structured applications (modular approach), i.e., applications structured as a large set of asynchronous, event-driven processes. Each process is independent of the others and communication is performed via a well-defined message protocol. Hence, as the VR technology advances, individual modules (processes) can be independently modified.

3. VR systems should scale up gracefully. Solutions for this requirement can be achieved using adaptive algorithms, dynamic environments and adaptive protocols (e.g., the DIS protocol used in SIMNET [FD94]).

4. VR systems should have immersive, fully synthesized, photo-realistic graphical displays. The solution for this requirement is still far away because current technology still does not provide such displays. Partial solutions to this requirement might be in a graphical display with (a) rendering of fully scenes, (b) rendering of selected objects, or (c) rendering images from the viewpoint of a given user.

There are many VR systems based on various types of implementation approaches. One implementation approach is demonstrated in *MR Toolkit* [SGLS93], where a VR system decouples the simulation steps from the redisplay loop. Since the simulation determines what is displayed and the user's head position determines from which angle it is displayed, MR Toolkit distributes the VR system over multiple processes. Another implementation approach took toolkits such as *dVS* (Division) [Gri91], *VR-DECK* [CJKL93] or *DIVE* [CH93]. They implemented VR systems as a large set of asynchronous, event-driven processes. This approach allowed the system to be more easily reconfigurable at run-time and more fault-tolerant. A third approach is taken in the *WAVES* system [Kaz93], where a large-scale distribution of virtual environments over communication media of varying bandwidth is supported.

### 17.7.2 Interactive Video

Interactive video research addresses various problems in the area of *interactive TV* and *Video-On-Demand.* Interactive TV research concentrates on cable and public television, whereas Video-On-Demand concentrates computer-oriented television. Since both areas merge, in the future we will see the results of both areas in one *interactive video* service. We described the individual steps in Section 17.5.1 on distributed services.

#### Interactive TV

*Interactive TV* specifies that the TV viewer can become a more active participant than is the case today. There are several types of interactivity. The simplest is when the viewers can "produce" the programs they are watching. For instance, the user might select one out of several camera angles from a televised sporting event, or ask for supplementary information about the teams or players. Another example could be an educational program where one out of several educational levels could be selected and/or extra tutorials could be requested.

Interactive TV is an application that may require different types of technological solutions because the interactive programs would be too specialized to be transmitted on ordinary channels. This means that one has to subscribe either to special cable TV channels, or to a telecommunication service. Both cases require a decoder for receiving the TV signal and equipment for communicating with the TV/producer studio.

#### Video-On-Demand

Video-On-Demand (VOD) services represent a class of applications where video information is accessed from one or more video servers.

More generally, VOD systems include many more components that are necessary for the provision of a complete service, such as video server(s), administration and maintenance systems, networking services, backbone networks for linking geographically distributed video servers and set-top units for receiving, demodulating, decoding and converting video for television playback. Elements of a VOD system are shown in Figure 17.11 [CCP+94].

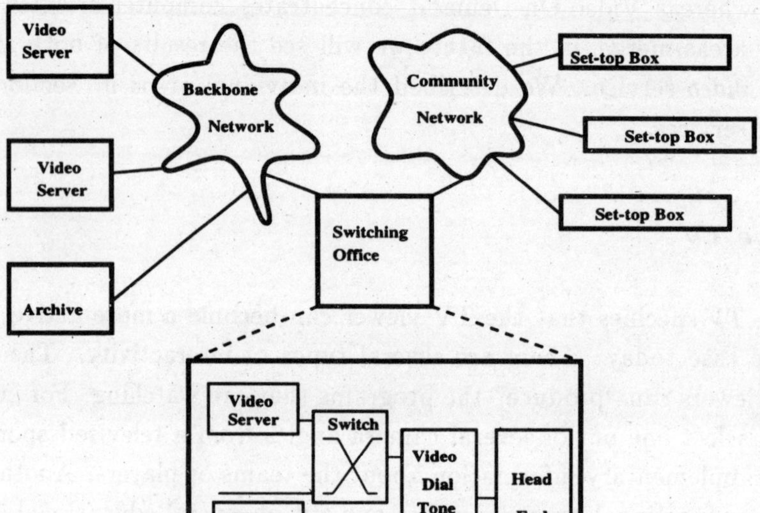


Figure 17.11: *Video-On-Demand system.*

VOD services need *retrieval* tele-services. Furthermore, the video service is an asymmetrically switched service in which the customer chooses among a wide selection of video material and receives, on-demand, a real-time response. The service is asymmetric in the sense that the downstream (to the customer) channel is much higher bandwidth than the upstream channel.

The best-known application of VOD is the *video library* which uses *Interactive VOD.* Interactive VOD allows a user to gain access to a movie (i.e., digitized video sequence stored on a storage medium such as hard disk) via point-to-point connection. This connection allows the user individual and instantaneous control of the storage medium in terms of *start, fast-forward, pause* and *rewind* actions.

There are two basic types of interactive VOD service [DVV94]:

- *Interactive VOD with instantaneous access*, whereby the user can instantly retrieve and individually control program information from a library instantly, with instant control response. The service is provided as follows: the customer selects a movie out of a large set of movies; the transmission starts within a few seconds; the user can stop and continue the transmission instantaneously; the functions *fast forward* and *rewind* are performed instantaneously, and; the user gets uninterrupted response. To provide this service, a video load buffer must be created at the start of the program so that responses to different functions can be performed immediately.

- *Interactive VOD with delayed access*, whereby users retrieve and individually control program information from a library, but there is a waiting time depending on the available bandwidth resources in the network, and/or popularity index of the requested program. In this case, the user needs to wait a few minutes before the movie starts, while (s)he still has full pause control capability. For this case, the video load buffer is only created when the function pause is performed and not at the start of the program. Therefore, this service consumes less video buffer resources and does not require fast load.

### 17.7.3 Interactive Audio

Similar to interactive video services, *CD-on-Demand* is likely to be established. The audio server will store music libraries, and the listeners will be able to retrieve their requested song from such a library. An example of such a system is the *LyricTime* research prototype from Bellcore [LHB92]. *LyricTime* is a personalized music system that allows the listeners to select songs (using a filter function) from a music server. The songs are played at a listener's workstation using its built-in audio capability. At the same time, a still image from the album cover is presented on the display. The listener is free to stop and start playing at any time, step forward and backward through the list of selected songs, change the volume, tell the filter function what mood (s)he is in and provide evaluative feedback on the current song.

Another interactive audio application might be the availability of *thematic audio channels* , for example, to car drivers. Over these channels, specific information (news) on road conditioning can be requested from the driver, although future development in this area is headed towards *Intelligent Vehicle Highway Systems*, where an instrumented car enters an instrumented line and the driver becomes a passenger. Already, route guidance systems based on digital maps, such as the U.S. system marketed by Oldsmobile [Col94], can pilot drivers through optimal routes with timely voice instructions.

### 17.7.4 Games

The modern computer game is an audiovisual engine capable of keeping an internal model of some dynamic system. Unlike a real application, a game often deliberately hides certain pieces of information about its internal state, working against the user to create a greater challenge. Games are based on *interactivity* between the user and the computer [Joi94].

Games can be divided according to storage location, environment sophistication and number of players. With respect to the storage location, electronic games can be stored on a *local* computer or a *remote* computer (tele-games). With respect to the environment, games can be placed in an *interactive environment with audio-visual components* and/or *an interactive environment with advanced technology components,* such as movies and VR groupware, etc.

With respect to the number of players, there are *one-on-one games* and *terminal-sharing games* with two players, where each player has a different input device and they play at the same time. We also experience games which make use of communication networks and allow players to interact remotely (tele-games).

#### Games in an Interactive Environment

One interactive game technique is referred to as *branching.* Using this technique in a game, the player experiences short, linear story segments. At the end of each segment, there are a small number of choices, each leading to a new linear segment, etc. The games use CD-ROM technology to store massive amounts of artwork, music, sound effects and animation on a single disc.

Most interactive games do not use the branching technique at all. They are based on *clever algorithms.* An example of an algorithm-based game with a rich interactivity is the highly acclaimed game *Sim City.* This product simulates the growth and development of an urban metropolis, with the player in the role of a city mayor. At each point in the game, the player can perform various operations on the landscape, such as zoning land, demolishing buildings and layering down roads, water mains and electric power lines. Since the game map is large, and since the player can perform these operations almost everywhere on the map, the number of possible moves at any given moment in time is clearly immense. Here, algorithms from the game theory, and other application domains, such as the networks' routing algorithms, genetic algorithms, neural nets and cellular automata are used.

### Tele-games

The main use of tele-games is for video games and VR games. A video game menu might be connected via a network to a centralized video game machine, from which a game is chosen. A scenario is then sent from the central machine to a PC monitor in the home, and the home participant seemingly has control over one or more objects within the scenario. As the game starts, only the new coordinates of the game object and moving targets are sent from the machine to the PC at home, while the actions performed by the home participant are sent to the central machine. Instead of playing with a centralized machine, one could also play games against another home participant, or several participants, over the network.

VR games might be similar to the video game described above, but will give the user the illusion of actually being in the game by using a helmet with an HMD and headphones, so that (s)he will be surrounded by a synthetically generated environment. The user might also be wearing a data glove with motion sensors, or using haptic displays, which enhance the user's sense of natural participation even further.

Networked graphical games (like DOOM) are proliferating rapidly, using a range of technologies. Much of the current development is in 3D *Distributed Interactive Simulation (DIS).* The basis for today's DIS is SIMNET, a large-scale tactile training environment developed by DARPA (Defense Advanced Research Projects Agency) in the early 1980's. In this environment, vehicle simulators, each incorporating real-time simulation and high resolution image generation systems, interact over local and wide area networks. However, there are still considerable obstacles to achieving the goals of DIS. In the meantime, shared 3D database gaming will continue to evolve on-line (e.g., Gemie's Air Warrior) and begin to appear on LAN, in themed arcades, family entertainment centers and festival retail locations [Dod94].

An example of a WAN (Wide Area Network) game environment is the MUD (Multi-User Dungeon) game environment. Other game environments are created over commercial networks, such as ImagiNation and MPGNet, which allow users to have a fully graphical, multi-player experience in their home for an hourly fee.

## 17.8 Trends

We observe several trends in multimedia applications:

- Applications are going from reengineering of existing applications to establishing new application domains. The new applications may require reengineering of user-interfaces, new integration techniques, etc. The problem is that the multimedia application designers and developers do not always know what will be the future applications.

- Multimedia applications are moving from a single PC user environment to either a multi-user environment or to a personalized user environment using PowerBooks and other personalized tools.

- Multimedia applications are designed less and less for local environments only and more and more for distributed environments.

- The solutions of current applications are often platform-specific and system-dependent. The trend is going toward open solutions, so that applications are portable across various platforms.

- Media consumption is going from a passive mode of user-computer interaction to an active mode of interaction, although not every user is comfortable with this change.

- Media communication services are going from unidirectional to bidirectional information flow. Interactive-TV is the best example.

- Technical improvements and changes in multimedia applications improve productivity through better collaboration opportunities, visualization of different manufacturing processes, etc.

Last but not least, we enthusiasts in multimedia research and development must always keep in mind that even the best and most advanced system features are only visible to the user by exciting and productive applications. Going back to the roots when Alexander Graham Bell invented the telephone, the major application – also advertised at that time – was listening to a concert (and not to act as the synchronous communication vehicle as it is today). Therefore, we surveyed and categorized this plethora of applications without giving our personal impression of the "best" multimedia application domain.

# Chapter 18

# Future Directions

## 18.1 Where Are We Today?

*Multimedia* represents the features and capabilities of a large number of computer components and systems. We have looked at multimedia systems from a scientific point of view focusing on the processing of audio, video and in part, images and graphics. However, since audio, video, graphics, image processing and real-time processing are not new areas, a question needs to be answered:

*Is the simple composition of existing concepts, techniques, components and systems a global multimedia solution?*

In the following section we provide a few examples of today's state-of-the-art technologies and in so doing, provide an answer to the above question.

### 18.1.1 User Interface

Until recently, *audio* has been well-known at the user interface level in connection with special speech analysis and synthesis systems. For example, speech analysis applications typically emphasize menu-control, i.e., for hands-free operation.

If audio is going to be part of a multimedia system, audio input and output methods should be dedicated for all applications. Further, the audio I/O (input/output) operations should be connected with known window system paradigms because this connection increases user acceptance. This requirement implies *spatial placement* of the audio output that corresponds to a video window. For example, if a video window is moved to the left, the corresponding sound should also be moved to the left stereo channel. Audio in multimedia systems is as much a part of the user interface as the window systems are of today's workstations.

Hence, current workstations and operating systems need to be modified, and in the next step, new workstation architectures and new operating systems are needed to provide adequate hardware and system support for this simple example of stereo channels and spatial placement of audio.

### 18.1.2 Operating Systems

Because of their *real-time requirements,* audio and video streams cannot be properly processed with traditional non-real-time operating systems. Moreover, current real-time operating systems satisfy different requirements than multimedia need, i.e., they provide reliability and their end-systems are most often dedicated systems in which the processing paths are known a priori. Multimedia workstations as end-systems do not require such a high degree of reliability, but they need operating systems which should be able to be configured and programmed by the user. Real-time routines shall be plugged in, the way we incorporate device drivers today.

Hence, the current operating systems need to be modified, and in the next step, new operating systems are needed to satisfy multimedia requirements.

### 18.1.3 Multimedia Documents

Available text processing systems do not embed the attribute *time* as a part of their internal processing.

In multimedia documents, however, the parameter of *time* is an additional component to content and spatial relations. Hence, a multimedia document is more than a mixture of movies and data in a traditional document.

Here, new solutions need to be found which answer questions such as: *How must multimedia documents be structured to be easily read and how can the authoring process be supported in this way?*

### 18.1.4 Synchronization

Currently, synchronization among individual data streams is most often implicitly included, for example, in the application or in the compression scheme (e.g., MPEG-2). It is almost always achieved through interleaving or fixed coupling (time or frequency multiplexing) of data units from different media during the transmission or storage process. Television, video recorders and stereo radios exhibit this kind of behavior to achieve synchronization. Additionally, for the most part, only time-dependent data streams are inter-related and synchronized. For example, TV subtitling is an integral part of video (if the subtitle is not displayed through a videotext service).

In a multimedia system, different kinds of streams need to be synchronized because services such as TV, video recorder, stereo radio, etc. will be integrated as the end-devices. Hence, the current mechanisms for synchronization are not sufficient.

New synchronization mechanisms to synchronize all the different media will need to be developed so that, for example, a presentation of a certain image could be coupled with the call of a procedure, implemented by an application developer.

### 18.1.5 Programming

Further questions need to be answered regarding the *programming* of audio and video processing. Current programming is based on traditional languages such as C, C++, ADA and others. Also, the programming of real-time algorithms for signal processors has been known for a long time.

Programming of multimedia requires structures and control mechanisms so that a programmer can specify continuous types similar to the character type in a text string, and control audio and video flow from the existing environment in a similar way as a character is controlled in a text string.

Hence, new programming languages need to be developed which should include all possibilities known from C, C++ or ADA, but also include new properties such as the handling of continuous media.

## 18.2 What Are the Next Steps?

All the above examples make clear the necessity of including temporal considerations into existing concepts, techniques, components, and systems. Hence:

*The simple composition of existing systems and methods is* **not** *a global multimedia solution.*

In the following paragraphs, let us – without certainly discussing all next steps – outline some developments we foresee and believe are crucial:

All currently known multimedia systems (either products or research projects) consider only partial aspects of the time-critical processing of audio and video. Only those critical components that allow for the correct processing of particular multimedia applications and system configurations are implemented. For example, it is always assumed that the system bus capacity is sufficient or that higher priority interrupts will not cause problems during the processing of continuous data. However, interrupts can considerably disrupt the processing of audio and video data because the process management does not include these interrupts in the same way as the other real-time processing. Therefore, resource guarantees are only provided for the most critical resources.

The goal is to integrate all hardware and software components into time-critical processing. This book is intended to be used as a starting point for accomplishing such a challenging goal.

Trends in several areas such as communication systems, operating systems, user interfaces, compression, etc., already indicate the directions, solutions and approaches.

Strong forces, which drive the development of multimedia systems, are multimedia applications. One of the main driving forces is the media entertainment industry. Therefore, based on the example of the Virtual Reality (VR) environment, we show which new challenges are imposed on multimedia systems.

A *Virtual Environment (VE)* can be viewed as a multi-modal, interactive and spatially-oriented user interface, where a *multi-modal user interface* is simply defined as a human/machine interface that actively or purposely fully utilizes interactions and display techniques in multi-sensory modalities (e.g., visual and auditory display, tracking and haptic interface devices). We discuss some of the future directions in the hardware and software components to provide such VEs.

### 18.2.1 Devices

Major improvements of *hardware* support are expected, because important hardware issues, such as computer performance, mobility and speed, are centers of research and development. This implies that in the future, multimedia devices could be used as mobile end-points. However, the current mobility of multimedia applications is still limited by display, computer architecture, network and tracking technologies. Hence, work needs to be done in these four areas:

- *Displays*

  The trend in displays for VR systems is the HMD (Head-Mounted Display). The most obvious requirement for HMDs is to have a *resolution and field of view* that approaches the fidelity of the human visual system. A display that allows a wide field of view at a low resolution and simultaneous display of a high-resolution inset that follows the user's gaze would be effective. Furthermore, the *depth of field* is also important. Current HMDs all have pixels focused at the same depth. Stereoscopic displays provide depth information using visual cues (stereoscopic images), but present the whole of the images at a single focal length.

  Clearly, HMDs must be made smaller, lighter and non-tethered; and *see-through displays* (see-through HMDs or see-through hand-held displays), used in augmented reality systems, must eventually be constructed so that they allow individual pixels to be transparent or opaque.

- *Processors*

  Workstation processors need to handle real-time manipulation of video streams, real-time creation of textures from raw images, etc. Processing performance is still slow on available multimedia computers. For example, current high-end graphics hardware, such as the Silicon Graphics Reality Engine [Ake93], allow textures to be mapped to 3D surfaces without significant overhead in the graphics pipeline, but creating texture from raw images is slow on these machines.

- *Networks*

  Virtual environments place demands on networks that are similar to those of other multimedia applications. The necessity of low latency will be partially solved by the availability of high-speed networks.

- *Trackers*

  The problems with current tracking systems are ones of *range*, *latency* and *accuracy*. For all systems, low *latency* is important, especially if the user's head is being tracked. The *range* and *accuracy* parameters depend on the particular VR application. For example, desktop VEs do not require a significant range because the user must be able to see the stationary display. On the other hand, *augmented reality systems*, where the user's view of the real world is overlaid with computer-generated graphics, require extremely high accuracy and low latency. These requirements need to be ensured so that the virtual images register properly with the real world.

Further developments can be seen in the provision of devices that *physically interact* with the environment. For example, in the case of a remote manipulation application, if a user grabs an object with a data glove in a simulated environment, a *robot hand* at the remote site may perform the same action on a real object.

Other trends in devices include the implementation of *locomotion interfaces*. Locomotion interfaces can provide the experience of moving around in space while actually being confined in a small space. Examples of locomotion devices are, in addition to *visual displays*, *haptic devices for feet and hands* and *auditory displays.* We briefly describe the haptic and auditory displays. Visual displays were described in Chapter 4.

- *Haptic Displays*

  A ground surface interface (*haptic interface for the feet*) is a device that permits the user to experience the active sensations of walking, running, climbing, etc., in a constrained space. Such a device allows the user to move his or her feet in a natural fashion and provide feedback to the user matching the space-time characteristics of the simulated surface (e.g., an inclined plane). It also senses the behavior (e.g., positions, forces) of the user to control the actions of the device and to provide appropriate information to the other display systems in the VE. Examples of such interfaces are *treadmill displays* and *haptic interfaces for individual feet.*

  A surface pad (*haptic interface for the hand*) is a device that permits the user to read information stored in the computer by experiencing, for example, vibrations from the pad. The computer information is transformed into tactile feedback presented on the output haptic display.

- *Auditory Displays*

  Auditory displays play sound(s) to the user. There are two VE techniques that use this technology. The first technique is where the auditory display presents sounds which exhibit the same spatial and temporal patterns as when listening to sounds in a natural environment. An example is the illusion of self-rotation simulated by a sound field rotating around the head of a stationary subject [Lac77].

  The second technique is cognitive cuing where, for example, visually induced self-motion is augmented by the sound of a virtual wind or engine aircraft [PKG91].

  The trend here is to create a synthesized acoustic field relevant to the illusion of moving through the real acoustic field. Aside from simulating changes in the direction of sound sources (Section 18.1.1), changes in the apparent distance of the sources and changes in the apparent location of the individual within the reflecting environments are important.

### 18.2.2 Visualization

*Real-time 3D visualization* is required by certain multimedia applications. Video will play an ever-increasing role in the visualization process at the multimedia interfaces. The integration of video cameras with display devices will allow for tracking people in front of the display.

Using two cameras, stereo vision can be achieved. If the cameras are positioned appropriately for the remote viewer's interocular distance, a reasonable stereo pair of images can be displayed. Alternatively, it may be possible to dynamically construct a 3D model of the visual part of the user's head and transmit this information [OKKT93].

### 18.2.3 Mobility

Increased multimedia consumption will require the creation of *ubiquitous computing* environments. *Ubiquitous computing* is a term coined by Mark Weiser [Wei91b] to describe a future in which we are surrounded in our everyday life by a multitude of computers so numerous, yet so unremarkable, that we barely know they are there. Hence, a ubiquitous computing environment will consist of a large number of computers integrated into seamless immediate surroundings, connected by high-speed wireless networks.

To provide such an environment, mobile computing and multimedia will have to be integrated. An example of such an application is the playback of stored video on both mobile devices and conventional workstations. A system supporting such an application must provide performance-guaranteed delivery of video data to mobile clients [MSK+93].

The issue which needs to be resolved to create this environment is: how existing connections must be rerouted to maintain current conversations and how various routing databases must be updated to allow new connections to be established when a Mobile Host (MH) moves into the network. There are several algorithms for performing rerouting in connection-oriented networks, for example, *incremental re-establishment* [MSK+93], or *multicast-based re-establishment* [KMS+93], which might be applied to connectionless networks.

### 18.2.4 Interactivity

VEs require *high frame rates* and *fast response time* because of their inherently interactive nature. The frame rates need to be faster than 10 frames/s and response times must be kept below 0.1 seconds; otherwise, performance severely degrades the illusion of presense.

One major source of delays is the *data access*, which will need to be bounded. For example, in applications which use video servers (Video-On-Demand), the delays in data management come from the seek time to search for data on the disk and from the available bandwidth to move data during the reading process. The trend is to use *Redundant Arrays of Inexpensive Disks (RAIDs)* for efficient storage and retrieval of large amount of data [Lee92]. RAIDs use parallel transfer from an array of drives to support high data transfer rates and high request rates. Their throughput can reach bandwidths of 100 Mbytes/s, although for some VE applications, the necessary data bandwidth is in the range of 300 to 500 Mbytes/s. This implies that, for some applications, the only viable storage medium for data is physical memory, which given the storage requirements, is currently too expensive to be practical (current memories can achieve a capacity of 16 gigabytes).

### 18.2.5 Operating Systems

Operating Systems (OSs) should support lightweight shared memory processes, thus minimizing the time required for context switching and inter-process communication. The OS should be capable of assuming that high-priority processes can be serviced at very short and regular intervals. Further, developers should be given the capability to determine scheduling through tunable parameters.

### 18.2.6 Further Issues in Virtual Environments

The main requirements which will need to be satisfied in a virtual environment are *interacting, navigating and communicating* in the visual domain, as well as in the acoustic and haptic domains. Further, *modeling* (geometric, physical and behavioral) and inclusion of hypermedia need to be considered. These requirements set challenges on multimedia interfaces, hypermedia documents and other overlapping areas. Therefore, we briefly discuss the trends in multimedia interfaces and the inclusion of hypermedia into the virtual environment.

### 18.2.7 Multimedia User Interface

There are several research and development directions which will dominate in multimedia interfaces implementations:

- *Behavioral Modeling*

  Computers will be used more and more to facilitate communication among people. Education and training become more effective and engaging with multimedia interfaces that incorporate video and audio. Hence, behavioral modeling in social settings, which influences the design of multimedia user interfaces, will continue not only in CSCW environments, but also in education and training [Bla94].

- *Intelligent Multimedia Interfaces*

  Multimedia planning based on Artificial Intelligence (AI) techniques holds increasing importance for research. An intelligent interface should provide automation of routine tasks, enhance services, style and clarity. Intelligent interfaces will be essential when we face the prospect of retrieving information from thousands of on-line databases.

- *Using Existing User Interface Paradigms*

  Information we work with is often most effectively displayed using 2D techniques, even in a virtual environment. The most common 2D interfaces use so-called *WIMP (Windows, Icons, Menus, Pointers)* techniques. In the future, ubiquitous computing and virtual environments will provide management of 3D environments; hence, it is important to examine how 2D WIMP techniques can be applied to 3D environments [FDFH92, Lut94, May93a].

- *Personalized Multimedia Services*

  Personalized multimedia services promise a new era in which clients no longer have to search, locate and schedule media presentations. Rather, intelligent *Personal Service Agents (PSA)*, acting on behalf of clients, provide presentations at the client's preferred viewing times [RR94]. Personalized multimedia services are expected to access other services such as storage providers (multimedia servers), network providers and content providers (e.g., publishing houses, news distributors).

### 18.2.8 Hypermedia

Hypermedia should be embedded in VE because its techniques would allow for linking physical and virtual objects [Mey89]. For example, if a hypermedia node is embedded into the structure of a virtual world, the node can be accessed and audio played or compressed video displayed. This implies that hypermedia capabilities should be available throughout the operating system rather than in separate hypermedia applications.

Another direction in this area is *hyper-navigation.* Hyper-navigation involves the use of nodes as *travel agents* in the virtual terrain. They would allow travel at either accelerated speed in VE or at slow speed using hypermedia links with their node connections.

### 18.2.9 Multimedia Applications

New VE applications are emerging that present new challenges to multimedia processing.

Tele-robotics and remote manipulation have become more and more important in fields such as hazardous environments, natural disaster management, hospitals, police and fire stations, distributed nursing and education. The basic principles of the tele-robotics and remote manipulation are described in Chapter 17.

Other multimedia applications, where VEs play a part, come from the entertainment area where the development goes toward *location-based entertainment* and *distributed games.*

### Location-Based Entertainment

*Location-Based Entertainment* (LBE) means an intelligent environment for the user's entertainment. LBE's attractions will be the most publicly visible applications of digital graphics, visualization and other disciplines. In the entertainment industry, convincing sensory illusion and natural interactivity can translate into fascination for players and profit for owners. LBEs could be used to help promote cooperative learning by exploiting "the strong web of connections joining commercial play and cultural cohesion" (Nasaw [Har94]).

Generally, LBE will need technology which provides: (1) several degrees of freedom for haptic displays, (2) film frame sizes and HDTV quality for visual displays, (3) VR, (5) cybermotion (computer-driven animated mechanism), (6) mechatronics (electro-mechanical apparatuses), (7) human interface, (8) performance support, (9) automatic translation, (10) CSCW, and (11) groupware.

Further, to create LBE for cooperative behavior, new structural components will be helpful:

- Players might assume new characteristics or other identities. There could be a sort of *personality construction kit* for building customized identities that players can elaborate between play sessions, as in Internet-hosted MUD (Multi-User Dungeons and Dragons) games.

- Each player could have a different custom *view* of the same LBE. For example, one player might be piloting a futuristic spaceship, while another might be riding a wild animal.

- Players could build and modify games themselves. With sufficiently flexible simulation engines and a common specification language, LBEs could include tools to build and modify the flow of play.

### Games

Trends in game development include new algorithms and a change in emphasis from local games to distributed games.

*Algorithms* for games are still poor at simulating realistic behavior. Even the most sophisticated adventures rely heavily on prescripted dialogs for character interaction.

*Distributed Interactive Simulations* (DISs) represent various simulation systems spread over networks which interactively run different scenarios of a specific problem. Before such a large scale of various simulation systems and home platforms sharing a 3D database can occur, DIS protocols must be adopted and severe problems of heterogeneous platform interoperability must be solved, among other things.

## 18.3 What Are the Multimedia Research Issues?

Many research issues regarding multimedia technologies need to be solved to make any significant progress. Some of them are:

- Random access of optical storage devices still takes too long. Magnetic storage devices are too expensive for the storage of multimedia data. Hence, the research issue is to decrease access time of CD devices, as well as to lower the cost of magnetic storage devices.

- The compression of audio and video sequences, using mode-based techniques, is expected to compress audio and video data at VCR quality to less than 128 kbits/s. Scalability remains a crucial issue.

- The query (and search) for audio and video entries in a database should be content-oriented.

- Communication protocols and networks should support all the different media providing the demanded guarantees. Further, communication and coding methods must allow for interoperability among different systems.

- Operating systems should consider all components which take part in the processing of multimedia data. This should also include distributed system paradigms, such as distributed shared memory and remote procedure call.

- Currently, there is no agreement over the optimal programming interface within a programming environment.

- New metaphors should be explored with respect to user interface audio and video.

- Most multimedia applications have been implemented as improvements on existing technologies. New applications should be researched. An example is an *individual newspaper*, the content and media of which is customized to the individual reader profile.

Many of the above issues require a solid and comprehensive knowledge of multimedia processing. Hence, this book can be used as a working material for learning about current multimedia technologies and for attacking new multimedia research tasks.

# Appendix A

# Abbreviations

| | |
|---|---|
| AAL | ATM Adaptation Layer |
| AC | Access Control |
| ACME | Abstractions for Continuous MEdia (name of a project) |
| ACTV-I | Advanced Compatible Television, Fist System |
| A/D | Analog/Digital (Analog-to-Digital Conversion) |
| ADC | Analog-to-Digital Converter |
| ADPCM | Adaptive Difference Plus Code Modulation |
| AI | Artificial Intelligence |
| AIMI | An Intelligent Multimedia Interface |
| ANSI | American National Standards Institute |
| API | Application Programming Interface |
| ARP | Address Resolution Protocol |
| ARQ | Automatic Repeat ReQuest |
| ART | Available Resource Table |
| ARTS | Advanced Real-time Technology Operating System |
| ATM | Asynchronous Transfer Mode |
| AT&T | American Telephone and Telegraph |
| AS | Autonomous Systems |
| AU | Access Unit |
| AVC | Audio Visual Connection |
| AVK | Audio Visual Kernel |
| AVSS | Audio/Video Support System |
| AWI | Animation Works Interactive |

| | |
|---|---|
| BCH | Bose-Chadhuri-Hocquenghem |
| BERKOM | BERliner KOMmunikationssystem |
| B-ISDN | Broadband Integrated Service Data Network |
| BGP | Border Gateway Protocol |
| BMC | Basic Multimedia Class |
| BMO | Basic Multimedia Object |
| BWB | BandWidth Balancing |
| | |
| CAT | Computerized Axial Tomography |
| CAV | Constant Angular Velocity |
| CBDS | Connectionless Broadband Data Service |
| CBR | Constant Bit Rate |
| CCD | Charge Coupled Device |
| CCIR | Consultative Committee International Radio |
| CD | Compact Disc |
| CD | Committee Draft (of an ISO standard) |
| CD-DA | Compact Disc Digital Audio |
| CD-I | Compact Disc Interactive |
| CD-MO | Compact Disc Magneto Optical |
| CD-ROM | Compact Disc Read Only Memory |
| CD-ROM/XA | Compact Disc Read Only Memory EXtended Architecture |
| CD-RTOS | Compact Disc Real-Time Operating System |
| CD-WO | Compact Disc Write Once |
| CDTV | Commodore Dynamic Total Vision |
| CERN | European Laboratory for Particle Physics |
| CGA | Color Graphics Adapter |
| CGEG | Computer Graphics Expert Group |
| CIF | Common Intermediate Format |
| CIRSC | Cross Interleaved Reed Solomon Code |
| CLUT | Color Look-Up Table |
| CLV | Constant Linear Velocity |
| CMC | Compound Multimedia Class |
| CMFS | Continuous Media File System |
| CMIS | Common Management Information Service |
| CMIP | Common Management Information Protocol |
| CMO | Compound Multimedia Object |
| CMTP | Continuous Media Transport Protocol |

| | |
|---|---|
| COMET | Columbia Operations and Maintenance Explanation Testbed |
| CON | CONcentrator |
| cps | cycles per second |
| CPU | Central Processing Unit |
| CRT | Cathode Ray Tube |
| CS | Convergence Sublayer |
| CSMA/CD | Carrier Sense Multiple Access with Collision Detection |
| CSCW | Computer-Supported Cooperative Work |
| CSP | Communication Sequential Process |
| DA | Destination Address |
| DAB | Digital Audio Broadcasting |
| D/A | Digital/Analog |
| DAC | Digital-to-Analog Converter |
| DAP | Document Application Profile |
| DARPA | Defense Advanced Research Projects Agency |
| DAT | Digital Audio Tape |
| DBS | Direct Broadcast Satellite |
| DCA | Document Content Architecture |
| DBMS | DataBase Management System |
| DCT | Discrete Cosine Transformation |
| DFT | Discrete Fourier Transformation |
| DIN | German National Intitute for Standardization |
| DIS | Distributed Interactive Simulation |
| DIS | Draft International Standard (at ISO) |
| DM | Delta Modulation |
| DQDB | Distributed Queue Dual Bus |
| DPCM | Difference Pulse Code Modulation |
| DPG | Dedicated Packet Group |
| DSP | Dedicated Signal Processor |
| DSP | Digital Signal Processing |
| DSSSL | Document Style Semantics and Specification Language |
| DTD | Data Type Definition |
| DVB | Digital Video Broadcasting |
| DVI | Digital Video Interactive |
| DVMRP | Distance Vector Multicast Routing Protocol |
| D2-MAC | Duobinary Multiplexed Analog Components |

| | |
|---|---|
| EDD | Earliest Due Date |
| EDF | Earliest Deadline First |
| EDL | Edit Decision List |
| EDTV | Enhanced Definition TeleVision System |
| EGA | Enhanced Graphics Adapter |
| EGP | Exterior Gateway Protocol |
| ELV | Edit Level Video |
| ENC | European Networking Center |
| | |
| FAT | File Allocation Table |
| FBAS | Farb-Bild-Austast-und Synchronsignal (German abbrev. for Composite Video Signal) |
| FCFS | First Come First Served |
| FCS | Finite Coordinate Space |
| FDCT | Forward Discrete Cosine Transformation |
| FDDI | Fiber Distributed Data Interface |
| FEC | Forward Error Correction |
| FFT | Fast Fourier Transformation |
| FIFO | First In First Out |
| fps | frames per second |
| FRESS | File Retrieval and Editing SyStem |
| | |
| GBW | Guaranteed Bandwidth |
| GC | Group Communication |
| GE | General Electric |
| GHz | GigaHertz |
| GIF | Graphical Interchange Format |
| GKS | Graphical Kernel System |
| GSS | Global Store Server |
| GSS | Group Sweeping Scheduling |
| GSU | Generic Space Unit |
| GTU | Generic Time Unit |
| | |
| HAM | Hypertext Abstract Machine |
| HD-MAC | High Definition Multiplexed Analog Components |
| HDTV | High Definition TeleVision |
| HeiTS | Heidelberg Transport System |
| HeiRAT | Heidelberg Resource Administration Technique |

| | |
|---|---|
| Hz | Hertz |
| HID | Hop IDentifier |
| HLL | Higher Level Language |
| LPC | Linear Predictive Coding |
| HMD | Head Mounted Displays |
| HP | Hewlett-Packard Company |
| HPCC | High-Performance Computing and Communication |
| HRC | Hybrid Ring Control |
| HSLAN | High-Speed Local Area Network |
| HTML | HyperText Markup Language |
| | |
| IDCT | Inverse Discrete Cosine Transformation |
| IDRP | Inter-Domain Routing Protocol |
| IDTV | Improved Definition Television |
| IEEE | Institute of Electrical and Electronics Engineers |
| IETF | Internet Engineering Task Force |
| IGP | Interior Gateway Protocol |
| IITA | Information Infrastructure Technology and Applications |
| IMAL | Integrated Media Architecture Laboratory |
| I/O | Input/Output |
| IP | Internet Protocol |
| IP | Index Point |
| IPC | InterProcess Communication |
| IS | International Standard |
| ISDN | Integrated Service Data Network |
| ISI | Information Science Institute |
| ISO | International Standard Organization |
| | |
| JBIG | Joint Bi-level Expert Group |
| JPEG | Joint Photographic Expert Group |
| | |
| kHz | kiloHertz |
| | |
| LAN | Local Area Network |
| LAP | Limited A Priori |
| LBAP | Linear Bounded Arrival Processes |
| LBE | Location-Based Entertainment |

| | |
|---|---|
| LCD | Liquid Crystal Display |
| LDU | Logical Data Unit |
| LED | Light Emitting Diode |
| LLF | Least Laxity First |
| LP | Long Play |
| LSP | Link State Packet |
| LTS | Logical Time Systems |
| | |
| MAC | Medium Access Control |
| MAN | Metropolitan Area Network |
| MBone | Multicast Backbone |
| MCI | Media Control Interface |
| MCS | Multimedia Communication System |
| MCU | Minimum Coded Unit |
| MDBMS | Multimedia DataBase Management System |
| Memex | Memory Extender |
| MH | Mobile Host |
| MHEG | Multimedia and Hypermedia Information Coding Expert Group |
| MIB | Management Information Base |
| Micon | Moving Icon |
| MID | Message Identification |
| MIDI | Musical Instrument Digital Interface |
| MIME | Multi-purpose Internet Mail Extensions |
| MIN | Multi-stage Interconnection Network |
| MIPS | Music Information Processing Standard |
| MM | MultiMedia |
| MMC | MultiMedia Conferencing |
| MMPM/2 | MultiMedia Presentation Manager/2 |
| MO:DCA | Mixed Object Document Content Architecture |
| MPEG | Motion Picture Expert Group |
| MS | Message Store |
| MTS | Message Transfer System |
| MUD | Multi-User Dungeon |
| | |
| NAK | Non-AcKnowledgment |
| NASA | National Aeronautics and Space Administration |
| NCSA | National Center for Supercomputing Applications |

| | |
|---|---|
| N-ISDN | Narrowband Integrated Service Data Network |
| NFSNET | National Science Foundation NETwork |
| NIH | National Institute of Health |
| NII | National Information Infrastructure |
| NLS | ON Line System |
| NRTE | Non Real-Time Environment |
| NRZI | Non Return to Zero Inverted |
| NTP | Network Time Protocol |
| NTSC | Nemo Trusted Supervisor Call |
| NTSC | National Television Systems Committee |
| OCR | Optical Character Recognition |
| ODA | Open Document Architecture |
| ODIF | Open Document Interchange Format |
| ODL | Open Document Language |
| OS | Operating System |
| OSI | Open System Interconnection |
| OSPF | Open Shortest Path First |
| OWL | Office Workstations Limited |
| QCIF | Quarter Common Intermediate Format |
| PAL | Phase Alternating Line |
| PARC | Palo Alto Research Center |
| PC | Personal Computer |
| PCM | Pulse Coded Modulation |
| PDD | Physical Device Driver |
| PDU | Protocol Data Unit |
| PES | Packetized Elementary Stream |
| PH | Physical Layer |
| PHIGS | Programmer's Hierarchical Interactive Graphics System |
| PHY | PHYsical Layer Protocol |
| PIM | Personal Information Manager |
| PIR | Personalized Information Environment |
| PLV | Presentation Level Video (formerly Production Level Video |
| PMD | Physical Layer Medium-Dependent |
| PRT | Priority Token Ring |

| | |
|---|---|
| PSA | Personal Service Agent |
| PTI | Payload Type Information |
| PTU | Physical Time Unit |
| | |
| QoS | Quality of Service |
| QA | Queued Arbitrated |
| | |
| RAID | Redundant Arrays of Inexpensive Disks |
| RCAP | Real-time Channel Administration Protocol |
| RDA | Remote Data Access |
| R-DQDB | Reactive Distributed Queue Dual Bus |
| RFC | Request For Change (at IETF) |
| RGB | Red Green Blue (composite video signal) |
| RI | Recorder User Interaction |
| RIFF | Resource Interchange File Format |
| RMTP | Real-time Message Transport Protocol |
| RTE | Real-Time Environment |
| RTIP | Real-Time Internet Protocol |
| RTP | Real-Time Transport Protocol |
| RTCP | RTP Control Protocol |
| RTV | Real-Time Video |
| | |
| SA | Sender Address |
| SAR | Segmentation And Reassembly |
| SCEFO | SCEne FOrmat |
| SCMP | ST Control Message Protocol |
| SCMC | Synchronization Controller for Multimedia Communication |
| SCO | Santa Cruz Operation |
| SDU | Service Data Unit |
| SECAM | SEquential Coleur Avec Memoire |
| SGML | Standard Generalized Markup Language |
| SMT | Station ManagemenT |
| SDH | Synchronous Digital Hierarchy |
| SIGCHI | Special Interest Group for Computer Human Interaction |
| SJF | Shortest Job First |
| SMDL | Standard Music Description Language |
| SMDS | Switched Multi-megabit Data Service |

| | |
|---|---|
| SMPTE | Society of Motion Picture and Television Engineers |
| SNMP | Simple Network Management Protocol |
| SONET | Synchronous Optical NETwork |
| SPDL | Standard Page Description Language |
| SPI | Stream Programming Interface |
| SRGP | Simple Raster Graphics Package |
| SRI | Stanford Research Institute |
| SSTF | Shortest Seek Time First |
| ST-II | Stream Protocol, Version 2 |
| STM | Synchronous Transfer Mode |
| SVGA | Super VGA |
| | |
| TC | Transmission Convergence |
| TCP | Transmission Control Protocol |
| TDM | Time Division Multiplexing |
| TDS | Time Driven Scheduler |
| TEXTPLAN | TEXTual Explanation Planner |
| THz | TeraHertz |
| TIFF | Tagged Image File Format |
| TIB | Temporal Interval Base |
| TPC | Temporal Presentation Controller |
| TRT | Token Rotation Time |
| TTRT | Target Token Rotation Time |
| TV | TeleVision |
| | |
| UA | User Agent |
| UC | University of California |
| UDP | User Datagram Protocol |
| UNI | User Network Interface |
| | |
| VE | Virtual Environment |
| VBR | Variable Bit Rate |
| VC | Virtual Circuit |
| VCI | Virtual Connection Identifier or Virtual Channel Identifier |
| VDP | Video Display Processor |
| VE | Virtual Environment |
| VGA | Video Graphics Array |

| | |
|---|---|
| VLP | Video Long Play |
| VOD | Video On Demand |
| VPI | Virtual Path Identifier |
| VR | Virtual Reality |
| VRAM | Video RAM |
| | |
| WAN | Wide Area Network |
| WAS | Workahead Augmenting Set |
| WBC | Wide Band Channels |
| WIMP | Windows, Icons, Menus, Pointers |
| WO | Write Once |
| WORM | Write Once Read Many |
| WME | Window Multimedia Extension |
| WWW | World-Wide Web |
| WYSIWYG | What You See Is What You Get |
| | |
| XGA | EXtended Graphics Array |
| XTP | Xpress Transport Protocol |
| | |
| YARTOS | Yet Another Real-Time Operating System |

# Bibliography


[AA93] G. J. Armitage and K. M. Adams. Using the Common LAN to Introduce ATM Connectivity. In *Proceedings of 18th Conference on Local Computer Networks*, pages 34–43, Minneapolis, Minnesota, September 1993.

[Abb84] C. Abbott. Efficient Editing of Digital Sound on Disc. *Journal of Audio Engineering*, 32(6):394–402, 1984.

[AC91] D. Anderson and P. Chan. Toolkit Support for Multiuser Audio/Video Applications. In R.G. Herrtwich, editor, *Proceedings from 2nd International Workshop on Network and Operating System Support for Digital Audio and Video*, pages 230–241, Heidelberg, Germany, November 1991. Springer Verlag.

[AC93] J. W. Atwood and G. C. K. Chung. Error Control in the Xpress Transfer Protocol. In *Proceedings of 18th Conference on Local Computer Networks*, pages 423 - 431, Minneapolis, Minnesota, September 1993.

[ACD+93] R. Aravind, G. L. Cash, D. L. Duttweiler, H. Hang, B. G. Haskell, and A. Puri. Image and Video Coding Standards. *AT&T Technical Journal*, 72(1):67–89, January/February 1993.

[Ace93] A. Acero. *Acoustical and Environmental Robustness in Automatic Speech Recognition*. Kluwer Academic Publishers, Boston, 1993.

[ACG93] B. S. Atal, V. Cuperman, and A. Gersho, editors. *Speech and Audio Coding for Wireless and Network Applications*. Kluwer Academic Publisher, Dodrecht, 1993.

[ACM88] ACM. Special Issue on Hypertext. *Communications of the ACM*, 31(7), July 1988.

[ACM89] ACM. Special Section on Interactive Technology. *Communications of the ACM*, 32(7), July 1989.

[ACM91] ACM. Special Section on Digital Multimedia Systems. *Communications of the ACM*, 34(4), April 1991.

[ACT93] K. Amer, K. Christensen, and T. Toher. Experiments with Client/Server Multimedia on Token Ring. In *Proceedings of 18th Conference on Local Computer Networks*, pages 2–7, Minneapolis, Minnesota, September 1993.

[AFG+93] E. Andre, W. Finkler, W. Graf, T. Rist, A. Schauder, and W. Wahlster. WIP: The Automatic Synthesis of Multimodal Presentations. In Mark T. Maybury, editor, *Intelligent Multimedia Interface*, pages 75–93. AAAI Press / The MIT Press, 1993.

[AFN90] Y. Ashikaga, K. Fukuoka, and M. Naitoh. CD-ROM Premastering System Using CD-Write Once. *Fujitsu Scientific Technical Journal*, 26(3):214–223, October 1990.

[AGH90] D.P. Anderson, R. Govindan, and G. Homsy. Abstractions for Continuous Media in a Network Window System. Technical Report UCB/CSD 90/596, Computer Science Division, UC Berkeley, Berkeley, CA, September 1990.

[AH91a] D. P. Anderson and G. Homsy. Synchronization Policies and Mechanisms in a Continuous Media I/O Server. Technical Report 91-003, International Computer Science Institute, Berkeley, CA, 1991.

[AH91b] D.P. Anderson and G. Homsy. A Continuous Media I/O Server and its Synchronization Mechanism. *IEEE Computer*, 24(10):51–57, October 1991.

[AHS90] D. P. Anderson, R. G. Herrtwich, and C. Schaefer. A Resource Reservation Protocol for Guaranteed Performance Communication in the Internet. Technical Report 90/006, International Computer Science Institute, Berkeley, CA, February 1990.

[Ake93] K. Akeley. RealityEngine Graphics. *Computer Graphics*, 27:109 –116, 1993. SIGGRAPH '93 Proceedings.

[All83] J. F. Allen. Maintaining Knowledge about Temporal Intervals. *Communications of the ACM*, 26(11):832–843, November 1983.

[All85] J. B. Allen. Cochlear Modelling. *IEEE ASSP Magazine*, pages 3–29, 1985.

[And93] D. P. Anderson. Meta-scheduling for distributed continuous media. *ACM Transaction on Computer Systems*, 11(3), August 1993.

[Ann94a] Announcement. 3D Digitizing Systems. *Computer Graphics World*, page 59, April 1994.

[Ann94b] Announcement. Kodak Expands Photo CD System. *Computer Graphics World*, page 59, April 1994.

[Ann94c] Announcement. Video Accelerator Boards. *Computer Graphics World*, page 53, May 1994.

[ANR74] N. Ahmed, T. Natarajan, and K. R. Rao. Discrete Cosine Transform. *IEEE Transactions on Computers*, 23:90–93, January 1974.

[AOG91] D. P. Anderson, Y. Osawa, and R. Govindan. Real-Time Disk Storage and Retrieval of Digital Audio/Video Data. Technical Report UCB/CSD 91/646, Computer Science Division, University of California, Berkeley, CA, September 1991.

[App89] W. Appelt. HyperODA. ISO/IEC/JTC1/SC18/WG3, 1989.

[App90] W. Appelt. *Dokumentenaustausch in Offenen Systemen*. Springer Verlag, Berlin, Heidelberg, New York, 1990.

[As90] H. van As. Performance Evaluation of the Bandwidth Balancing in the DQDB MAC Protocol. In *Proceedings of 8th Annual EFOC/LAN Conference*, pages 231–239, Munich, Germany, June 1990.

[ATW+90] D. P. Anderson, S. Tzou, R. Wahbe, R. Govindan, and M. Andrews. Support for Continuous Media in the DASH System. In *Proceedings of the 10th ICDCS*, Paris, France, May 1990.

[Bae69] R. M. Baecker. Picture Driven Animation. In *SJCC*, pages 273–288, Montvale, NJ, 1969. AFIPS Press.

[Bas90] G. A. J. Bastiaens. Compact Disc Interactive. *Computer Education*, February 1990.

[BB91a] U. Bormann and C. Bormann. Offene Bearbeitung multimedialer Dokumente. *Informatik-Spektrum*, 14:249–260, October 1991.

[BB91b] U. Bormann and C. Bormann. Standards for Open Document Processing: Current State and Future Developments. *Computer Networks and ISDN Systems*, 21:149–163, May 1991.

[BBI93] S. A. Bly, S. A. Bly, and S. Irwin. Media Space: Bringing People Together in a Video, Audio, and Computing Environment. *Communications of the ACM*, 36(1):28–45, January 1993.

[BCG+90] P. B. Berra, C. Y. R. Chen, A. Ghafoor, C. C. Lin, T. D. C. Little, and D. Shin. Architecture for Distributed Multimedia Database Systems. *Computer Communications*, 13(4):217–231, May 1990.

[BCS93] B. Braden, D. Clark, and S. Shenker. Integrated Services in the Internet Architecture: an Overview. Internet Draft, October 1993.

[BD92] M. M. Blattner and R. B. Dannenberg. *Multimedia Interface.* ACM Press, 1992.

[BDG+94] E. Biersack, P. Dubois, M. Goud, J.P. Hubaux, and Y.-P. Pusztaszeri. Teletutoring over Betel Network. In *15th Speedup Workshop*, Lugano, March 1994.

[Ber88] R. E. Berry. Common User Access – a consistent and usable human-computer interface for SAA environments. *IBM System Journal*, 27(3):281–300, 1988.

[BF91] K. B. Benson and D. G. Fink. *HDTV - Advanced Television for the 1990s.* Intertext Publications, McGraw-Hill Publishing Company, Inc., 1991.

[BF93] N. Borenstein and N. Freed. Mime (Multipurpose Internet Mail Extensions) Part One: Mechanism for Specifying and Describing the Format of Internet Message Bodies. *Internet draft RFC-1521*, September 1993.

[BG87] D. Bersekas and R. Gallager. *Data Networks.* Prentice Hall, 1987.

[BH93] M. F. Barnsley and L. P. Hurd. *Fractal Image Compression.* AK Peters, Ltd., Wellesley, Massachusetts, 1993.

[BHLM92] G. Blakowski, J. Hubel, U. Langrehr, and M. Muhlhauser. Top Support for the Synchronization and Presentation of Distributed Multimedia. *Computer Communication*, 15:611–618, December 1992.

[BHS91] G. Blair, D. Hutchison, and D. Shepard. Multimedia Systems. In *Tutorial Proceedings of 3rd IFIP Conference on High-Speed Networking*, Berlin, Germany, March 18–22, 1991.

[Bie93] E. W. Biersack. Performance Evaluation of Forward Error Correction in an ATM Environment. *IEEE JSAC*, 11(4):631–640, May 1993.

[Bin93] R. Binder. Summary of the Gigabit TCP workshop. e-mailing list, April 1993.

[BK93] S. Barilovits and J. Kadambi. FDDI-2 Packet Services and Latency Adjustment Buffers. In *Proceedings of 18th Conference on Local Computer Networks*, pages 176–185, Minneapolis, Minnesota, September 1993.

[Bla91a] G. Blakowski. Concept of a Language for the Description of Transport and (Re-)presentation properties of Multimedia Objects. *(in German) Informatik Fachberichte*, (293):465–474, 1991. Springer Verlag.

[Bla91b] G. Blakowski. The MODE-FLOW-GRAPH: A Processing Model for Objects of Distributed Multimedia Applications. In *Proceedings of International Symposium on Communication*, pages 646–649, December 1991.

[Bla92] G. Blakowski. High Level Services for Distributed Multimedia Applications based on Application Media and Environment Descriptions. *Australian Computer Science Communications*, 14:93–109, January 1992.

[Bla93] G. Blakowski. *Development and Runtime Support for Distributed Multimedia Applications.* Verlag Shaker, German edition, 1993.

[Bla94] M. M. Blattner. In Our Image: Interface Design in the 1990s. *IEEE Multimedia*, Spring, 1994.

[Ble78] B. Blesser. Digitization of Audio: A Comprehensive Examination of Theory, Implementation, and Current Practice. *Journal of the Audio Engineering Society*, 26:739–771, October 1978.

[BM91] A. Banerjea and B. Mah. The Real-Time Channel Administration Protocol. In *Proceedings of 2nd International Workshop on Network and Operating System for Digital Audio and Video*, Heidelberg, Germany, November 1991.

[BM93] J. D. Burger and R. J. Marshall. The Application of Natural Language Models to Intelligent Multimedia. In M. T. Maybury, editor, *Intelligent Multimedia Interface*, pages 75–93. AAAI Press / The MIT Press, 1993.

[BN93] Ch. Baber and J. M. Noyes, editors. *Interactive Speech Technology: Human Factors Issues in the Application of Speech Input/Output to Computers.* Taylor & Francis, Bristol, PA, 1993.

[Boo87] M. Boom. *Music Through MIDI.* Microsoft Press, 1987.

[Bor79] A. Borning. Thinglab - A Constraint-Oriented Simulation Laboratory. Technical Report SSI-79-3, Xerox Palo Alto Research Center, Palo Alto, CA, July 1979.

[Bor92] N. S. Borenstein. Computational Mail as Network Infrastructure for Computer-Supported Cooperative Work. In *Proceedings of ACM Conference on Computer-Supported Cooperative Work, CSCW'92*, pages 67 –73, Toronto, Canada, October 1992.

[BPSWL93] C. C. Bisdikian, B. Patel, F. Schaffa, and M. Willebeek-LeMair. On the Effectiveness of Priorities in Token Ring for Multimedia Traffic. In *Proceedings of 18th Conference on Local Computer Networks*, pages 25–31, Minneapolis, Minnesota, September 1993.

[Bra87] S. Brand. *The Media Lab, Inventing the Future at MIT*. Viking Penguin, 1987.

[Bri86] G. Bristow, editor. *Electronic Speech Recognition: Techniques, Technology, and Applications*. New York: McGraw-Hill Publishing Company, Inc., 1986.

[Bro88] F. Brooks, Jr. Grasping Reality Through Illusion – Interactive Graphics Serving Science. In *Proceedings of CHI'88*, pages 1–10, Washington DC, 1988.

[BRRK94] J. Budford, L. Rutledge, J. Rutledge, and C. Kestin. HyOctane: A HyTime Engine for a MMIS. *Multimedia Systems*, 1(4):173–185, 1994.

[BS92] W. Borner and G. Schnellhardt. *Multimedia: Grundlagen, Standards, Beispielanwendungen*. TE-WI Verlag GmbH, 1992.

[Bul93] D.C.A. Bulterman. Specification and Support of Adaptable Networked Multimedia. *Multimedia Systems*, 1(2):68–76, 1993.

[Bur93] J. Burger. *Desktop Multimedia Bible*. Addison-Wesley Publishing Company, Inc., 1993.

[BW76] N. Burtnyk and M. Wein. Interactive Skeleton Techniques for Enhancing Motion Dynamics in Key Frame Animation. *CACM*, 19(10):564–569, October 1976.

[BW86] B. Bleser and J. Ward. Human Factors Affecting the Problem of Machine Recognition of Hand-Printed Text. In *Computer Graphics '86 Conference Proceedings*, volume 3, pages 498 –514, Fairfax, VA, 1986.

[BZ93a] C. Buchanan and P. T. Zellweger. Automatic Temporal Layout Mechanisms. In *Proceedings of the 1st ACM International Conference on Multimedia*, Anaheim, CA, August 1993.

[BZ93b] M. C. Buchanan and P. T. Zellweger. Automatically Generating Consistent Schedules for Multimedia Applications. *Multimedia Systems*, 1(2):55–67, 1993.

[CB88] J. Conklin and M. L. Begeman. gIBIS: A Hypertext Tool for Exploratory Policy Discussion. *ACM Transaction on Office Information Systems*, 6(4):303–331, October 1988.

[CCH93a] A. Campbell, G. Coulson, and D. Hutchison. A Multimedia Enhanced Transport Service in a Quality of Service Architecture. In *Workshop on Network and Operating System Support for Digital Audio and Video '93*, Lancaster, England, November 1993.

[CCH+93b] J. Crowcroft, S. Chuang, S. Hailes, M. Handley, N. Ismail, D. Lewis, and I. Wakeman. Multimedia Application Requirements for Multicast Communications Services. In *Proceedings of INET 93*, San Francisco, CA, August 1993.

[CCP+94] Y. Chang, D. Coggins, D. Pitt, D. Skellern, M. Thapar, and Ch. Venkatraman. An Open-Systems Approach to Video on Demand. *IEEE Communications*, 32(5):68–80, May 1994.

[CDP94] G. Caal, A. Divin, and C. Petitpierre. Active Objects: a Paradigm for Communications and Event Driven Systems. In *Proceedings of the GLOBECOM Conference*, San Francisco, CA, November 1994.

[CFLT87] T. Crowley, H. Forsdick, M. Landau, and Virginia Travers. The Diamond Multimedia Editor. Report from BBN Laboratories, Inc., 1987.

[CG87] B. Campbell and M. Goodman. HAM: A General Purpose Hypertext Abstract Machine. In *Hypertext '87*, November 1987.

[CGCH92] G. Coulson, F. Garcia, A. Campbell, and D. Hutchison. Orchestration Services for Distributed Multimedia Synchronization. In *Proceedings of the 4th IFIP International Conference on High Performance Networking (HPN)*, Liege, Belgium, December 1992.

[CGR90] G. Champine, D. Geer, and W. Ruh. Project Athena as a Distributed Computer System. *IEEE Computer*, 23(9):40–51, September 1990.

[CH93] C.F. Carlsson and O. Hagsand. DIVE - A Multi-User Virutal Reality System. In *Proceedings of IEEE Virtual Reality Annual Internaional Symposium*, pages 394 –400, 1993. IEEE Neural Networks Council.

[Cha93] Y. Chang. RFC 1453 - XTP instead of RTCP: Discussion. rem-conf mailing list posting, April 16, 1993.

[Che86] P. P-S. Chen. The compact disk ROM: how it works. *IEEE Spectrum*, 23(4):44–49, April 1986.

[Che92] G. Chesson, et al. XTP Protocol Specification Revision 3.6. Protocol Engine, Inc., available from XTP Forum, 1900 State Street, Santa Barbara, CA 93101, January 1992.

[CJKL93] C. F. Codella, R. Jalili, L. Koved, and J. B. Lewis. A Toolkit for Developing Multi-User, Distributed Virtual Environments. In *Proceedings of IEEE Virtual Reality Annual International Symposium*, pages 401 –407, 1993.

[CJRS89] D. D. Clark, V. Jacobson, J. Romkey, and H. Salwen. An Analysis of TCP Processing Overhead. *IEEE Communications Magazine*, pages 23–29, June 1989.

[CKY93] M. S. Chen, D. D. Kandlur, and P. S. Yu. Optimization of the Group Sweeping Scheduling (GSS) with Heterogeneous Multimedia Streams. In *Proceedings of the First ACM International Conference on Multimedia*, pages 235–241, Anaheim, CA, 1993.

[CL88] J. Y. Chung and J. W. S. Liu. Algorithms for Scheduling Periodic Jobs to Minimize Average Error. In *IEEE Real-Time Systems Symposium*, pages 142–151, Huntsville, Alabama, 1988.

[CL89] J. Y. Chung and J. W. S. Liu. Performance of Algorithms for Scheduling Periodic Jobs to Avoid Timing Faults. In *Proceedings of 22nd Hawaii International Conference on System Sciences*, pages 683–692, Hawaii, 1989.

[Cla94] S. Clarke-Wilson. The Design of Virtual Environments – Value Added Entertainment. *Computer Graphics*, 28(2), May 1994.

[Cly85] M. Clynes. Secrets of Life in Music: Musicality Realized by Computer. In *Proceedings of the 1984 International Computer Music Conference*, San Francisco, CA, 1985. International Computer Music Association.

[Col94] C. Collier. Smart Cars, Smart Highways. *IEEE Spectrum*, pages 27–33, April 1994.

[CSA+89] D. Corey, J. Schmidt, M. Abel, S. Bulick, and Steve Coffin. Multimedia Communications: The US West Advanced Technologies Prototype Telecollaboration System. In *5th IEEE International Workshop on Telematics*, Denver, Colorado, September 1989.

[CSR88] S. C. Cheng, J. A. Stankovic, and K. Ramamritham. Scheduling Algorithms for Hard Real-Time Systems – A Brief Survey. In J.A. Stankovic and K. Ramamritham, editors, *Hard Real-Time Systems*, pages 150–178, Washington, DC, 1988. IEEE Computer Society Press.

[CSZ92] D.D. Clark, S. Shenker, and L. Zhang. Supporting Real-Time Applications in an Integrated Services Packet Network: Architecture and Mechanism. In *SIGCOMM'92*, pages 14–22, Baltimore, MD, August 1992.

[CW90] D. W. Craig and C. M. Woodside. The Rejection Rate for Tasks with Random Arrivals, Deadlines and Preemptive Scheduling. *IEEE Transactions on Software Engineering*, 16(10):1198–1208, October 1990.

[Dan93] R. Dannenberg. Sound Effects and Video Synchronization, Music Playback and Visualization of the Corresponding Strokes. Personal Communication, 1993.

[DBB+93] A. Danthine, O. Bonaventure, Y. Baguette, G. Leduc, and L. Leonard. QoS Enhancements and the New Transport Services. In *Local Networks Interconnection*, pages 1–22, Raleigh, NC, October 1993. eds.: R.O. Onvural, A.A. Nilsson, Plenum Press, NY (1993).

[Dee89] S. Deering. Host Extensions for IP Multicasting. RFC 1112, August 1989.

[Dep89] Marketing Department. Brochure. Showscan Film Corporation, 1989.

[Der74] M. L. Dertouzos. *Control Robotics: The Procedural Control of Physical Processing*, volume 74 of *Information Processing*. North Holland Publishing Company, 1974.

[DG82] B.I. Slikvood D. Goedhart, R. J. van de Plassche. Digital to Analog Conversion in Playing a Compact Disc. *Philips Technical Review*, 40(6), August 1982.

[DG90] P. Duhamel and C. Guillemot. Polynomial Transform Computation of the 2-D DCT. In *Proceedings of IEEE ICASSP-90*, pages 1515–1518, Albuquerque, New Mexico, 1990.

[DHH+93] L. Delgrossi, Ch. Halstrick, D. Hehmann, R. G. Herrtwich, O. Krone, J. Sandvoss, and C. Vogt. Media scaling for audiovisual communication with the heidelberg transport system. Technical Report 43.9305, IB¡ ENC Heidelberg, Heidelberg, Germany, 1993.

[DHH94] L. Delgrossi, R. G. Herrtwich, and F. O. Hoffmann. An Implementation of ST-II for the Heidelberg Transport System. *Internetworking Research and Experience*, 5, 1994.

[DHVW93] L. Delgrossi, R. G. Herrtwich, C. Vogt, and L. C. Wolf. Reservation Protocols for Internetworks: A Comparison of ST-II and RSVP. Technical Report 43.9315, IBM European Networking Center, Heidelberg Germany, 1993.

[DLW93] B. J. Dempsey, J. Liebeherr, and A. C. Weaver. A New Error Control Scheme for Packetized Voice over High-Speed Local Area Networks. In *Proceedings of 18th Conference on Local Computer Networks*, Minneapolis, Minnesota, September 1993.

[DM92] D. L. Drucker and M. D. Murie. *QuickTime Handbook*. Hayden, Carmel, CA, 1992.

[DNN+93] R. D. Dannenberg, T. Neuemdorffer, J. M. Newcomer, D. Rubine, and D. A. Anderson. Tactus: Toolkit-Level Support for Synchronized Interactive Multimedia. *Multimedia Systems*, pages 77–86, 1993.

[Dod94] C. Jr. Dodsworth. Digital Illusion: Networked Interactive Entertainment. *Computer Graphics*, 28(2):91, May 1994.

[DS93] R. Dannenberg and R. Stern. Experiments Concerning the Allowable Skew of Two Audio Channels Operating in the Stereo Mode. Personal Communication, 1993.

[DVV94] D. Deloddere, W. Verbiest, and H. Verhille. Interactive Video on Demand. *IEEE Communications*, 32(5):82–88, May 1994.

[DZ90] C. Dobrian and D. Zicarelli. *MAX Development Package Manual.* Opcode Systems, Inc., Mentlo Park, CA, 1990.

[Ear93] R. A. Earnshaw et al., eds. *Virtual Reality Systems.* Academic Press, London, 1993.

[ECM88] ECMA. *Data Interchange on Read-Only 120mm Optical Data Disks (CD-ROM).* European Computer Manufacturers Association Standard ECMA-130, 1988.

[EDP92] J. Escobar, D. Deutsch, and C. Patridge. Flow Synchronization Protocol. In *Proceedings of IEEE Globecom*, pages 1381–1387, 1992. vol. 3.

[EFI94] L. Ehley, B. Furth, and M. Ilyas. Evaluation of Multimedia Synchronization Techniques. In *Proceedings of the International Conference on Multimedia Computing and Systems*, pages 110–119, Boston, MA, May 1994. IEEE Computer Society Press.

[EH92] A. D. N. Edwards and S. Holland. *Multimedia Interface Design in Education.* NATO ASI Series, Springer Verlag, 1992.

[Fal85] F. Fallside. *Computer Speech Processing.* Englewood Cliffs, NJ: Prentice-Hall International, 1985.

[FD94] E. Foxlin and N. Durlach. An Inertial Head-Oriented Tracker with Automatic Drift Compensation for Us with HMDs. In *VRST'94: The ACM Symposium on Virtual Reality Systems and Technology*, 1994.

[FDFH92] J. D. Foley, A. van Dam, S. K. Feiner, and J. F. Hughes. *Computer Graphics – Principles and Practice.* Addison-Wesley Publishing Company, Inc., 2 edition, 1992.

[FE88] E. A. Fox and M. E. Williams (Editor). *Optical disks and CD-ROM: Publishing and Access.* Elsevier Science Publishers, 1988.

[Fei85] S. Feiner. APEX: An Experiment in the Automated Creation of Pictorial Explanations. *IEEE Computer Graphics and Application*, 5(11):29–37, 1985.

[Fei90] E. Feig. A Fast Scaled DCT Algorithm. In K. S. Pennington and R. J. Moorhead II, editors, *Image Processing Algorithms and Techniques*, volume 1244, pages 2–13, Santa Clara, CA, February 11–16, 1990. Proc. SPIE.

[Fel90] L. Feliclan. Simulative and Analytical Studies on Performances in Large Multimedia Databases. *Information Systems*, 15(4):417–427, April 1990.

[Fer91] D. Ferrari. Design and Application of a Delay Jitter Control Scheme for Packet-switching Internetworks. In *Proceedings of 2nd International Workshop on Network and Operating System Support for Digital Audio and Video*, Heidelberg, Germany, November 1991. Also published in Vol. 614 of Lecture Notes in Computer Science, pages 72–83, Springer Verlag.

[Fin91] G. G. Finn. An Integration of Network Communication with Workstation Architecture. *ACM Computer Communication Review*, 21(5):18–29, October 1991.

[FKRR93] R. S. Fish, R. E. Kraut, R. W. Root, and R. E. Rice. Video as a Technology for Informal Communication. *Communications of the ACM*, 36(1):48–61, January 1993.

[Fla72] J. L. Flanagan. *Speech Analysis, Synthesis and Perception.* Springer Verlag, 1972.

[FM93] S. K. Feiner and K. R. McKeown. Automating the generation of coordinated multimedia explanations. In M. T. Maybury, editor, *Intelligent Multimedia Interface*, pages 75–93. AAAI Press / The MIT Press, 1993.

[For79] J. Forgie. ST - A Proposed Internet Strem Protocol. IEN 119, MIT Lincoln Laboratory, September 1979.

[Fre82] S. French. Sequencing and Scheduling: An Introduction to the Mathematics of the Job Shop. Ellis Horwood Limited, Chichester, 1982.

[Fre92] R. Frederick. nv, Network Video Tool. UNIX manual pages, 1992.

[Fri87] M. E. Frisse. Searching for Information in a Hypertext Medical Therapeutics Manual. Technical report, Medical Information Group, Stanford University, Palo Alto, CA, 1987.

[Fri92] J. R. Frick. Compact Disc Technology. Internal Publication, 1992. Disc Manufacturing, Inc.

[FS92] S. Furui and M. M. Sondhi, editors. *Advances in Speech Signal Processing.* Marcel Dekker Inc., New York, Hong Kong, 1992.

[FSB82] S. Feiner, D. Salesin, and T. Banchoff. DIAL: A Diagrammatic Animation Language. *CG&A*, 2(7):43–54, September 1982.

[FT88] E. Fiume and D. Tsichritzis. Multimedia Objects. In D. Tsichritzis, editor, *Active Object Environment*, pages 121–128. June 1988.

[FV90] D. Ferrari and D. C. Verma. A Scheme for Real-Time Channel Establishment in Wide-Area Networks. *IEEE JSAC*, 8(3):368–379, April 1990.

[FWC84] J. D. Foley, V. L. Wallace, and P. Chan. The Human Factors of Computer Interaction Techniques. *IEEE Computer Graphics and Applications*, 11(11):13–48, November 1984.

[Gai85] J. Gait. An Aspect of Aesthetics in Human-Computer Interaction: Pretty Windows. *IEEE Transactions on Software Engineering*, 11(8):714–717, August 1985.

[Gai86] J. Gait. Pretty Pane Tiling of Pretty Windows. *IEEE Software*, 3(5):9–14, September 1986.

[GBD+91] S. Gibbs, Ch. Breiteneder, L. Dami, V. de May, and D. Tscichritzis. A Programming Environment for Multimedia Applications. In *2nd International Workshop on Network and Operating System Support for Digital Audio and Video*, Heidelberg, Germany, November 1991.

[GBT93] S. Gibbs, C. Breiteneder, and D. Tsichritzis. Data Modeling of Time-based Media. In *Visual Objects*, pages 1–21, Geneve: Univerite de Geneve, Centre Universitaire d'Informatique, June 1993.

[GC89] P. Ghislandi and A. Campana. In Touch with XA. Some Considerations on Earlier Experiences of CD-ROM XA Production. In *Proceedings of 13th International Online Information Meeting*, pages 211–226, 1989.

[GC92] J. Gemmel and S. Christodoulakis. Principles of Delay Sensitive Multi media Data Storage and Retrieval. *ACM Transactions on Information Systems*, 10(1), January 1992.

[GCB88] A. Ghafoor, C. Y. R. Chen, and P. B. Berra. A Distributed Multimedia Database System. In *Proceedings of Workshop on the Future Trends of Distributed Computing Systems in the 1990s*, pages 461–469, Hong Kong, September 1988.

[Ger85] German national standardization body, Berlin–Köln. *Terminology in Computing*, DIN 4300 edition, 1985.

[Gia92] M. Giardina. *Interactive Multimedia Learning Environments, Human Factors and Technical Considerations on Design Issues.* Springer Verlag, 1992.

[GO91] D. W. Gifford and J. W. O'Toole. Intelligent File Systems for Object Respositories. In *Operating Systems of the 90s and Beyond, International Workshop Proceedings*, pages 20–24, Dagstuhl Castle, Germany, July 1991. Springer-Verlag, Heidelberg.

[Gol91a] Ch. F. Goldfarb. HyTime: A Standard for Structured Hypermedia Exchange. *IEEE Computer*, 24(8):81–84, August 1991.

[Gol91b] Ch. F. Goldfarb. *The SGML Handbook.* Claredadon Press, Oxford, 1991.

[Goo93] B. A. Goodman. Multimedia Explanation for Intelligent Training Systems. In Mark T. Maybury, editor, *Intelligent Multimedia Interfaces*, pages 148–173. AAAI Press/The MIT Press, 1993.

[Gra81] J. Gray. The Transaction Concept: Virtues and Limitations. In *Proceedings of the 7th International Conference on VLDB*, pages 370–382, Cannes, France, 1981.

[Gra84] R. M. Gray. Vector Quantization. *IEEE ASSP Magazine*, 1(2):4–29, April 1984.

[Gra94] G. Grassel. Object-oriented Design and Implementation of a MHEG Runtime Environment for the Interactive Presentation of Multimedia Documents in a Distributed Environment. Master's thesis, University of Mannheim, March 1994. Master thesis in German.

[Gri91] G. Grimsdale. DVS – Distributed Virtual Environment System. In *Proceedings of Computer Graphics '91*, 1991.

[Gro89] AFNOR Expert Group. *Multimedia Synchronization: Definitions and Model, Input Contribution on Time Variant Aspects and Synchronization in ODA-Extensions.* ISO IE JTC 1/SC 18/WG3, February 1989.

[Gup94] A. Gupta. Design scheme 2 - A Multicast Realtime Protocol Scheme. Talk at the XUNET'94 Meeting, February 1994.

[GV92] C. Gonzales and E. Viscito. Flexible Digital Video Coding. Personal Communication, 1992.

[Ham72] C. Hamblin. Instants and Intervals. In *Proceedings of the 1st Conference of the International Society for the Study of Time*, pages 324–331, 1972.

[Har89] L. Hardman. Evaluating the Usability of the Glasgow Online Hypertext. *Hypermedia*, 1(1):34–63, 1989.

[Har94] M. Harris. Entertainment Driven Collaboration. *Computer Graphics*, 28(2), May 1994.

[Hau93] M. Hauck. Progammierschnittstelle für den Datenbankzugriff durch Klienten im CO-EARN System. Technical University at Darmstadt, 1993.

[HBP+93] R. D. Hill, T. Brinck, J. F. Patterson, S. L. Rohall, and W. T. Wilner. The Rendezvous Language and Architecture. *Communications of the ACM*, 36(1):62–67, January 1993.

[HD90] R. G. Herrtwich and L. Delgrossi. ODA-Based Data Modeling in Multimedia Systems. Technical Report 90–043, International Computer Science Institute, Berkeley, CA, 1990.

[Hei62] M. L. Heilig. Sensorama Simulator. United States Patent Number 3,050,870, August 1962.

[Her90] R. G. Herrtwich. Time Capsules: An Abstraction for Access to Continuous-Media Data. In *IEEE Real-Time Systems Symposium*, pages 11–20, Orlando, Florida, December 1990.

[Her92] R. G. Herrtwich. An Architecture for Multimedia Data Stream Handling and its Implication for Multimedia Transport Service Interface. In *3rd IEEE Workshop on Future Trends of Distributed Computing Systems*, Taipei, Taiwan, April 1992.

[HH91] R. Händel and M. Huber. *Integrated Broadband Networks*. Addison-Wesley Publishing Company, Inc., 1991.

[HHS91] D. Hehmann, R. G. Herrtwich, and R. Steinmetz. Creating HeiTS: Objectives of the Heidelberg High-Speed Transport System. Technical Report 439102, IBM ENC Heidelberg, Heidelberg, Germany, 1991.

[HKL+91] K. Harney, M. Keith, G. Lavelle, L. D. Ryan, and D. J. Stark. The i750 Video Processor: A Total Multimedia Solution. *Communications of the ACM*, 34(4):64–78, April 1991.

[HKN89] R. Hunter, P. Kaijser, and F. Nielsen. ODA: A Document Architecture for Open Systems. *Computer Communication*, 12:69–79, April 1989.

[HL88] K. S. Hong and J. Y. T. Leung. On–Line Scheduling of Real-Time of Tasks. In *IEEE Real-Time Systems Symposium*, pages 244–258, Huntsville, Alabama, 1988.

[HL90] C. Hemrick and L. Lang. Introduction to Switched Multi-Megabit Data Services (SMDS), an Early Broadband Service. In *ISS 90*, Stockholm, Sweden, June 1990.

[HLG93] J. M. Hyman, A.A. Lazar, and G.Pacifici. A Separation Principle between Scheduling and Admission Control for Broadband Switching. *IEEE JSAC*, 11(4):605–616, May 1993.

[HM91] M. Hayter and D. McAuley. The Desk Area Network. *ACM Operating Systems Review*, 25(4):14–21, October 1991.

[HM93] W. S. Hiles and D. T. Marlow. Experimentation on the Concentrator Tree with Loopback. In *Proceedings of 18th Conference on Local Computer Networks*, pages 147–156, Minneapolis, Minnesota, September 1993.

[Hoa85] C. A. R. Hoare. *Communication Sequential Processes.* Prentice-Hall International, 1985.

[Hof91] M. Hoffman. *Benutzerunterstützung in Hypertextsystemen durch privated Kontexte.* PhD thesis, Naturwissenschaftliche Fakultät der Technischen Universität Carolo-Wilhelmina, Braunschweig, Germany, 1991.

[Hol88] F. Holtz. *CD-ROM: Breakthrough in Information Storage.* TAB Books, Inc., 1988. ISBN 0–8306–1426–5.

[Hou88] H. S. Hou. A Fast Recursive Algorithm for Computing the Discrete Cosine Transform. *IEEE Trans. Acoust. Speech and Signal Processing*, ASSP–35(10):1455–1461, 1988.

[HPC94] HPCC. High Performance Computing & Communications: Towards a National Information Infrastructure. A Report by the Committee on Physical, Mathematical and Engineering Sciences, 1994.

[HR93] M. Hamdaoui and P. Ramanathan. Improved Non-Real-Time Communication in FDDI Networks with Real-Time Traffic. In *Proceedings of 18th Conference on Local Computer Networks*, pages 157–166, Minneapolis, Minnesota, September 1993.

[HS82] J. P. J. Heemskerk and K. A. Schouhamer Immink. Compact Disc: System Aspects and Modulation. *Philips Technical Review*, 40(6), August 1982.

[HS89] D. Haban and K. G. Shin. Application of Real-time Monitoring to Scheduling Tasks with Random Execution Times. In *IEEE-Real-Time Systems Symposium*, pages 172–180, Santa Monica, 1989.

[HS91] R. G. Herrtwich and R. Steinmetz. Towards Integrated Multimedia Systems: Why and How. *Informatik-Fachberichte*, (293):327–342, 1991. Springer Verlag.

[HS92] R. M. Haralick and L. G. Shapiro. *Computer and Robot Vision*, volume 1. Addison-Wesley Publishing Company, Inc., 1992.

[HS93] M. E. Hodges and R. M. Sasnett. *Multimedia Computing, Case Studies from MIT Project Athena.* Addison-Wesley Publishing Company, 1993.

[HSA89] M. E. Hodges, R. M. Sasnett, and M. S. Ackerman. Athena Muse: A Construction Set for Multimedia Applications. *IEEE Software*, pages 37–43, January 1989.

[HTM92] T. Hoshi, Y. Takahashi, and K. Mori. An Integrated Multimedia Desktop Communication and Collaboration Platform for Broadband ISDN: The Broadband ISDN Group Tele-Working System. In *Proceedings of Multimedia'92*, pages 28 –37, April 1992.

[HTV82] H. Hoeve, J. Timmermas, and L. B. Vries. Error Correction and Concealment in the Compact Disc System. *Philips Technical Review*, 40(6), August 1982.

[Huf52] D. A. Huffman. A Method for the Construction of Minimum Redundancy Codes. In *Proceedings of IRE 40*, pages 1098–1101, September 1952.

[HVWW94] R. G. Herrtwich, C. Vogt, H. Wittig, and L. Wolf. Resource Management for Distributed Multimedia Systems. Technical Report 43.9403, IBM European Networking Center, IBM Heidelberg, Heidelberg, Germany, 1994.

[HW94] M. J. Handley and I. Wakeman. CCCP: Conference Control Channel Protocol: A Scalable Base of Building Conference Control Applications. Technical report, Department of Computer Science, University College London, London, England, March 1994. in preparation.

[Hyd94] E. A. Hyden. *Operating System Support for QoS.* PhD thesis, Wolfson College, University of Cambridge, February 1994.

[Hyp88] Hypertext. Special issue on hypertext. *Communications of the ACM*, 31(7), July 1988.

[HYS88] G. Hudson, H. Yasuda, and I. Sebestyen. The International Standardization of a Still Picture Compression Technique. In *Proceedings of IEEE Global Telecommunications Conference*, pages 1016–1021, November 1988.

[IBM90] Corporation IBM. *Audio Visual Connection User's Guide and Authoring Language Reference.* IBM Corporation, Version 1.05, IBM Form S15f-7134-02 edition, August 1990.

[IBM91] Corporation IBM. *AIX Version 3.1: RISC System/6000 as a Real-Time System.* IBM International Technical Support Center, Austin, March 1991.

[IBM92a] Corporation IBM. *ActionMedia/II - Technical Reference.* IBM Corporation, version 1.0 edition, 1992.

[IBM92b] Corporation IBM. *IBM Multimedia Presentation Manager Programming Reference and Propgramming Guide 1.0.* IBM Corporation, IBM Form: S41G-2919 and S41G-2920 edition, March 1992.

[IBM92c] IBM Corporation. *The IBM OS/2 Programming Guide, Volume I, Control Program Interface*, March 1992.

[IBM92d] IBM Corporation. *Multimedia Presentation Manager/2, Programming Guide*, 1992.

[IBM92e] IBM Corporation. *The OS/2 Multimedia Advantage*, 1992.

[IET94] IETF. Minutes of the multipart multimedia session control working group (mmusic). Proceedings of 29th Internet Engineering Task Force, March 1994.

[Inc85] Symbolics Inc. *S-Dynamics.* Symbolics, Inc., Cambridge, MA, 1985.

[Ino93] H. Inoue. Vision Based Behaviour: Observation and Control of Robot Behavior by Real-Time Tracking Vision. In *6th International Symposium Robotics Research*, Hidden Valley, PA, 1993.

[INR93] INRIA. *H. 261 Software Codec for Videoconferencing over the Internet.* INRIA, Sophia-Antipolis, France, January 1993. Research Report No. 1834.

[Int89] B. V. Phillips International. *Compact Disc-Interactive - A Designer Overview.* Kluwen,Technische Boeken B.V., Deventer, Netherlands, 1989.

[ISO93a] ISO. Information Technology – Coding of Moving Pictures and Associated Audio for Digital Storage Media up to about 1.5 Mbit/s, 1993. ISO IEC JTC1/SC29.

[ISO93b] ISO. Information technology – coding of moving pictures and associated audio for digital storage media, test model 4. Draft, MPEG 93/255b, February 1993. ISO IEC JTC 1.

[ITUC90] The International Telegraph International Telecommunication Union and Telephone Consultative Committee. Line Transmission on non-Telephone Signals: Video Codec for Audiovisual Services at p x 64 kbit/s. CCITT Recommendation H.261, 1990.

[Jan85] P. A. Janson. *Operating Systems, Structures and Mechanisms.* Academic Press Inc., Orlando, Florida, 1985.

[JB88] V. Jacobson and R. Braden. TCP Extension for Long-Delay Path. RFC 1072, October 1988.

[JB89] D. Jaffe and L. Boynton. An overview of the sound and music kit. *Computer Music Journal*, 13(2):48–55, 1989.

[JBZ90] V. Jacobson, R. Braden, and L. Zhang. TCP Extension for High-Speed Path. RFC 1185, October 1990.

[Jef90] K. Jeffay. Scheduling Sporadic Tasks with Shared Resources in Hard-Real-Time Systems. Technical Report TR90-039, University of North Carolina at Chapel Hill, Department of Computer Science, Chapel Hill, North Carolina, November 1990.

[JM92] V. Jacobson and S. McCanne. vat, Video Audio Tool. UNIX manual page, 1992.

[JM93a] V. Jacobson and S. McCanne. sd, Session Directory tool. UNIX manual page, 1993.

[JM93b] V. Jacobson and S. McCanne. wb, Whiteboard. UNIX manual page, 1993.

[JMF93] V. Jacobson, S. McCanne, and S. Floyd. A Conferencing Architecture for Light-Weight Sessions. MICE Seminar Series, University College London, UK, 1993.

[JN84] N. S. Jayant and Peter Noll. *Digital Coding of Waveforms*. Prentice-Hall, 1984.

[Joi94] D. "Talin" Joiner. Interactive Entertainment. *Computer Graphics*, 28(2), May 1994.

[JSA92a] JSAC. Special Section on Signal Processing and Coding for Recording Channels. *IEEE Journal On Communications*, 10(1), January 1992.

[JSA92b] JSAC. Special section on speech and image coding. *IEEE Journal On Communications*, 10(5), June 1992.

[JSP91] K. Jeffay, D.L. Stone, and D.E. Poirier. YARTOS: Kernel Support for Efficient, Predictable Real-Time Systems. In *Proceedings of IFAC, Workshop on Real-Time Programming*, Atlanta, Georgia, May 1991. Pergamon Press.

[Kaz93] R. Kazman. Making Wawes: On the Design of Architectures for Low-End Distributed Virtual Environments. In *Proceedings of IEEE Virtual Reality Annual International Symposium*, pages 443 –449, 1993. IEEE Neural Networks Council.

[Kes92] S. Keshav. Report on Workshop on QoS Issues in High-Speed Networks. *Computer Communication Review*, 22(5):74–85, October 1992.

[KG89] A. Karmouch and N. D. Georganas. Multimedia Document Architecture and Database Design for Medical Applications. In *2nd IEEE COMSOC International Multimedia Communications Workshop*, Montebello, Quebec, Canada, April 1989.

[KGTM90] P.H. Kao, W. A. Gates, B. A. Thompson, and D. K. McCluskey. Support for the ISO 9669/HSG CD-ROM File System Standard in the HP-UX Operating System. *Hewlett-Packard Journal*, pages 54–59, December 1990.

[KJ93] M. Keshtgary and A. P. Jayasumana. Bandwidth Allocation in FDDI-II for Isochronous, Synchronous and Asynchronous Traffic. In *Proceedings of 18th Conference on Local Computer Networks*, pages 196–204, Minneapolis, Minnesota, September 1993.

[KL91] C. M. Krishna and Y. H. Lee. Real-Time Systems. *IEEE Computer*, pages 10–11, May 1991.

[Kle92] B. Klee. CD-ROM/WO also Kompatibles Publishing Medium. In *Proceedings of DGB-Online Tagung*, Frankfurt, Germany, April 1992.

[KMR93] H. Kanakia, P. P. Mishra, and A. Reibman. An Adaptive Congestion Control Scheme for Real-Time Packet Video Transport. In *Proceedings of SIGCOMM '93*, Baltimore, MD, August 1993.

[KMS+93] K. Keeton, B. Mah, S. Seshan, R. Katz, and D. Ferrari. Providing Connection-Oriented Network Services to Mobile Hosts. In *Proceedings of USENIX Symposium on Mobile and Location-Independent Computing*, 1993.

[Koe94] J. F. Koegel Buford, editor. *Multimedia Systems.* ACM Press/Addison-Wesley Publishing Company, Inc., 1994. contributing editor.

[KR82] A. C. Kak and A. Rosenfeld. *Digital Picture Processing*, volume 1. Academic Press, 2 edition, 1982.

[Kra88] S. Krakowiak. *Principles of Operating Systems.* MIT Press, Cambridge, MA, 1988.

[KS95] S. Keshav and H. Saran. Semantics and Implementation of a Native-Mode ATM Protocol Stack. Internal technical memo, AT&T Bell Laboratories, Murray Hill, NJ, January 1995.

[KSN+87] S. Komatsu, T. Sampel, T. Nishihara, T. Furuuya, and Y. Yamada. The Multimedia CD-ROM System for Educational Use. *IEEE Transactions on Consumer Electronics*, 33(4):531–539, November 1987.

[KW93a] T. Kaeppner and L. Wolf. Architecture of HeiPhone: A Testbed for Audio/Video Teleconferencing. Technical Report 43.9316, IBM ENC, Heidelberg, Germany, 1993.

[KW93b] B. Klauer and K. Waldschmidt. An Object-Oriented Character Recognition Engine. In *Proceedings of European Informatik Congress, Euro-ARCH'93.* Springer Verlag, October 1993.

[KWY94] A. Karmouch, R. Wang, and T. Ycap. Design and Analysis of a Storage Retrieval Model for Audio and Video Data. Technical report, Multimedia Information Systems, Department of Electrical Engineering, University of Ottawa, Ottawa, Canada, 1994.

[Lab93] Bellcore Information Networking Research Laboratory. The Touring Machine System. *Communications of the ACM*, 36(1):68–77, January 1993.

[Lac77] J. R. Lackner. Induction of Illusory Self-Rotation and Nystagmus by a Rotating Sound Field. *Aviation Space and Environmental Medicine*, 48:129–131, 1977.

[Lan84] G. Langdon. An Introduction to Arithmetic Coding. *IBM Journal of Research and Development*, (28):135–149, March 1984.

[LBH+90] W. H. Leung, T. J. Baumgartner, Y. H. Hwang, M. J. Morgan, and S. C. Tu. A Software Architecture for Workstation Supporting Multimedia Conferencing in Packet Switching Networks. *IEEE JSAC*, 8(3):380–390, April 1990.

[LD87] L. F. Ludwig and D. F. Dunn. Laboratory for Emulation and Study of Integrated and Coordinated Media Communication. In *Frontier in Computer Technology, Proceedings of the ACM SIGCOMM '87*, August 1987.

[Le 91] D. Le Gall. MPEG: A Video Compression Standard for Multimedia Applications. *Communications of the ACM*, 34(4):46–58, April 1991.

[LE91] B. Lamparter and W. Effelsberg. X-MOVIE: Transmission and Presentation of Digital Movies under X. In *Proceedings of 2nd International Workshop on Network and Operating System Support for Digital Audio and Video*, pages 18–19, Heidelberg, Germany, November 1991.

[Lee84] B. G. Lee. A New Algorithm to Compute the Discrete Cosine Transform. *IEEE Transactions on Acoustic Speech and Signal Processing*, ASSP-32(6):1243–1245, December 1984.

[Lee92] E. Lee, et al. RAID-II: A Scalable Storage Architecture for High-Bandwidth Network File Service. Technical Report UCB/CSD 92/672, UC Berkeley, Berkeley, CA, 1992.

[LEM92] B. Lamparter, W. Effelsberg, and N. Michl. MTP: A Movie Transmission Protocol for Multimedia Applications. In *Proceedings of the 4th IEEE ComSoc International Workshop on Multimedia Communications*, pages 260–270, Monterey ,CA, April 1992.

[Lev89] R. Levin, et al. Operating Systems Review. *ACM Press, Operating Systems Review*, 23(3), July 1989.

[LF91] E. N. Linzer and E. Feig. New DCT and Scaled DCT Algorithms for Fused Multiply/Add Architectures. In *Proceedings of IEEE ICASSP*, pages 2201–2204, Toronto, Canada, May 1991.

[LG90a] T. D. C. Little and A. Ghafoor. Synchronization and Storage Models for Multimedia Objects. *IEEE JSAC*, 8(3):413–427, April 1990.

[LG90b] T.D.C. Little and A. Ghafoor. Network Considerations for Distributed Multimedia Objects Composition and Communication. *IEEE Network Magazine*, 4:32–39, November 1990.

[LG91a] T. D. C. Little and A. Ghafoor. Multimedia Synchronization Protocols for Broadband Integrated Services. *IEEE JSAC*, 8:1368–1382, December 1991.

[LG91b] T. D. C. Little and A. Ghafoor. Spatio-temporal Composition of Distributed Multimedia Objects for Value Added Networks. *IEEE Computer*, 24:42–50, October 1991.

[LG92] T. D. C. Little and A. Ghafoor. Scheduling of Bandwidth-constrained Multimedia Traffic. *Computer Communication*, 15:381–387, July 1992.

[LHB92] S. Loeb, R. Hill, and T. Brinck. Lessons from LyricTime: A Prototype Multimedia System. In *Proceedings of Multimedia'92*, pages 106–110, April 1992.

[Lic51] J. Licklider. Basic Correlates of the Auditory Stimulus. In S. S. Stevens, editor, *Handbook of Experimental Psychology.* Wiley, 1951.

[Lim88] Inmos Limited. *OCCAM Programming Manual.* Prentice-Hall International, 1988.

[Lio91] Ming Liou. An overview of the px64 kbit/s video coding standard. *Communications of the ACM*, 34(4):59–63, April 1991.

[Lip91] A. Lippman. Feature sets for interactive images. *Communications of the ACM*, 34(4):92–101, April 1991.

[Lit92] T. D. C. Little. Protocols for Bandwidth-constrained Multimedia-traffic. In *Proceedings of the 4th IEEE ComSoc International Workshop on Multimedia Communications*, pages 150 –159, April 1992.

[Lit93] T. D. C. Little. A Framework for Synchronous Delivery of Time-Dependent Multimedia Data. *Multimedia Systems*, 1(2):87–94, 1993.

[Liu93] P. Liu. The official status of mpeg-2 and mpeg-4. Personal Communication, 1993.

[LKG94] L. Li, A. Karmouch, and N. Georganas. Multimedia Teleorchestra with Independent Sources: Part 1 - Temporal Modeling of Collaborative Multimedia Scenarios. *Multimedia Systems*, 1(4):143 – 153, 1994.

[LL73] C. L. Liu and J. W. Layland. Scheduling Algorithms for Multiprogramming in a Hard Real-Time Environment. *Journal of the ACM*, 20(1):46–61, January 1973.

[LL89] W. F. Leung and G. W. R. Luderer. The Network Operating System Concept for Future Services. *AT&T Technical Journal*, 68(2):23–35, April 1989.

[LLKG93] L. Li, L. Lamont, A. Karmouch, and N. Georganas. A Distributed Synchronization Control Scheme in a Group-oriented Conferencing Systems. In *Proceedings of the 2nd International Conference on Broadband Islands*, Athens, Greece, June 1993.

[LLM+88] W. H. Leung, G. W. Luderer, M. J. Morgan, P. R. Roberts, and S. C. Tu. A Set of Operating System Mechanisms to Support Multimedia Applications. In *Proceedings of International Seminar on Digital Communication*, pages 71–76, Zürich, Switzerland, March 1988.

[LLN87] J. W. S. Liu, K.-J. Lin, and S. Naturajan. Scheduling Real-Time, Periodic Jobs Using Imprecise Results. In *IEEE Real-Time Systems Symposium*, pages 252–260, San Jose, CA, 1987.

[LLSY91] J. W. S. Liu, K.-J. Lin, W.-K. Shin, and A. C. Yu. Algorithms for Scheduling Imprecise Computations. *IEEE Computer*, pages 58–68, May 1991.

[LM80] J. Y. T Leung and M. L. Merrill. A Note on Preemptive Scheduling of Periodic Real-Time Tasks. *Information Processing Letters*, 11(3):115–118, November 1980.

[LM89] V. Y. Lum and K. Meyer–Wegener. A Multimedia Database Management System Supporting Contents Search in Media Data. Naval Postgraduate School, March 1989.

[LM90] V. Y. Lum and K. Meyer–Wegener. An Architecture for a Multimedia Database Management System Supporting Content Search. In *Proceedings of Conference on Computing and Information*, Niagara Falls, Ontario, Canada, May 1990.

[LMY88] A. Leger, J. Mitchell, and Y. Yamazaki. Still picture compression algorithm evaluated for international standardization. In *Proceedings of IEEE Global Telecommunications Conference*, pages 1028–1032, November 1988.

[Loc90] P. C. Lockemann. Multimedia Databases: Paradigm, Architecture, Survey and Issues. University of Karlsruhe, Fakultät für Informatik, 1990.

[LOW91] A. Leger, T. Omachi, and G. K. Wallace. JPEG Still Picture Compression Algorithm. *Optical Engineering*, 30(7):947–954, July 1991.

[Loy85] C. Loy. Musicians Make a Standard: The MIDI Phenomenon. *Computer Music Journal*, 9(4), 1985.

[LPC90] L. Ludwig, N. Pincever, and M. Cohen. Extending the Notion of a Window System to Audio. *IEEE Computer*, 23(8):66–72, August 1990.

[LR86] S. Lambert and S. Roplequet. *CD-ROM: The New Papyrus*. Redmond WA: Microsoft Press, 1986.

[LR93] D. C. Lynch and M. T. Rose, editors. *Internet System*. Addison-Wesley Publishing Company, Inc., 1993.

[LS86] J. P. Lehoczky and L. Sha. Performance of Real-Time Bus Scheduling Algorithms. *ACM Performance Evaluation Review*, 14(1):44–53, May 1986.

[LS93] P. Lougher and D. Shepherd. The Design of a Storage Service for Continuous Media. *The Computer Journal*, 36(1):32–42, 1993.

[LSST91] J. P. Lehoczky, L. Sha, J. K. Strosnider, and H. Tokuda. Fixed Priority Scheduling Theory for Hard Real-Time Systems. In *Foundations of Real-Time Computing, Scheduling and Resource Management*, pages 1–30. Kluwer Academic Publishers, Norwell, 1991.

[Lu93] G. Lu. Advances in digital image compression techniques. *Computer Communications*, 16(4):202–214, April 1993.

[Luk94] M. E. Lukacs. The Personal Presence System – Hardware Architecture. In *Proceedings of 2nd ACM Conference on Multimedia*, October 1994.

[Lut91] A. C. Luther. *Digital Video in the PC Environment.* Intertext Publications McGraw-Hill Publishing Company, Inc., New York, 1991.

[Lut94] A. C. Luther. *Authoring Interactive Multimedia.* Academic Press, 1994.

[LW82] J. Y. T. Leung and J. Whitehead. On the Complexity of Fixed-Priority Scheduling of Periodic Real-Time Tasks. *Performance Evaluation (Netherland)*, 2(4):237–350, 1982.

[MAB92] K. Meyer, H.L. Applewhite, and F.A. Biocca. A Survey of Position Trackers. *Presence: Tele-operators and Virtual Environments*, 1:173–200, 1992.

[Mac86] J. D. Mackinlay. Automating the Design of Graphical Presentations of Relational Information. *ACM Transactions on Graphics*, 5(2):110–141, 1986.

[Mah93] B. A. Mah. A Mechanism for the Administration of Real-Time Channels. masters thesis, The Tenet Group, University of California at Berkeley and International Computer Science Institute, Berkeley, CA, May 1993.

[Mam93] R. J. Mammone, editor. *Artificial Neural Networks for Speech and Vision.* Chapman & Hall, London, New York, 1993.

[Mar91a] B.D. Markey. Emerging Hypermedia Standards – Hypermedia Market Place Prepares for HyTime and MHEG. In *Proceedings of the USENIX Conference about Multimedia - For Now and The Future*, pages 59–74, June 1991.

[Mar91b] J. Marks. *Automating the Design of Network Diagrams.* PhD thesis, Harvard University, 1991.

[Mar91c] J. Marks. A Formal Specification Scheme for Network Diagrams that Facilitates Automated Design. *Journal of Visual Languages and Computing*, 2(4):395–414, 1991.

[May93a] M. T. Maybury. Introduction to Intelligent Multimedia Interfaçes. In M. T. Maybury, editor, *Intelligent Multimedia Interfaces*, pages 1–8. AAAI Press / The MIT Press, 1993.

[May93b] M. T. Maybury. Planning Multimedia Explanations Using Communicative Acts. In M. T. Maybury, editor, *Intelligent Multimedia Interfaces*, pages 75–93. AAAI Press / The MIT Press, 1993.

[MB94] M. Macedonia and D. Brutzman. MBONE, the Multicast Backbone. *IEEE Computer*, 27(4):30–36, April 1994.

[MDR90] C. McKnight, A. Dillon, and J. Richardson. Problem in Hyperland? A Human Factors Perspective. Technical report, HUSAT Research Center, Loughborough University of Techn. Leics., 1990.

[ME94] T. Meyer-Boudnik and W. Effelsberg. MHEG: An Interchange Format for Interactive Multimedia Presentations. Informatik Berichte, Computer Science Department, University Mannheim, Mannheim, Germany, February 1994.

[Mei83] B. Meier. BRIM. Technical report, Computer Graphics Group, Computer Science Department, Brown University, Providence, RI, 1983.

[Mel94] L. Melatti. Fast ethernet: 100 mbit/s made easy. *Data Communications*, pages 111–113, November 1994.

[MES93] T. Meyer, W. Effelsberg, and R. Steinmetz. A Taxonomy on Multimedia Synchronization. In *Proceedings of the 4th International Workshop on Future Trends in Distributed Computing Systems*, Lisabon, Portugal, September 1993.

[Mey89] N. Meyrowitz. *The Missing Link: Why We're All Doing Hypertext Wrong.* MIT Press, 1989. The Society of Text: Hypertext, Hypermedia, and the Social Construction of Information.

[Mey91] K. Meyer-Wegener. *Multimedia Datenbanken.* B. G. Teubner, Stuttgart, Germany, 1991.

[MGC82] J. P. Sinjou M. G. Carasso, J. B. H. Peek. The Compact Disc Audio System. *Philips Technical Review*, 40(6), August 1982.

[MHE93] MHEG. *Information Technology – Coded Representation of Multimedia and Hypermedia Information (MHEG), Part 1: Base notation (ASN.1).* Committee draft ISO/IEC CD 13522-1, iso/iec jtc1/sc29/wg12 edition, June 1993.

[Mic91a] Corporation Microsoft. *Microsoft Windows Multimedia Authoring and Tools Guide.* Microsoft Press, 1991.

[Mic91b] Corporation Microsoft. *Microsoft Windows Multimedia Programmer's Reference.* Microsoft Press, 1991.

[Mic91c] Corporation Microsoft. *Multimedia: Programmer's Workbook.* Microsoft Press, 1991.

[Mil91] D.L. Mills. Internet Time Synchronization. *IEEE Transactions on Communications*, 38(10):1482–1493, October 1991.

[Mil93a] David M. Mills. Precision Synchronization of Computer Network Clocks. *ACM Computer Communication Review*, 24(2):28–43, April 1993.

[Mil93b] I. Milouchewa. RFC 1453 - XTP some comments: Discussion. rem-conf mailing list, April 21, 1993.

[MK93] S. Mirchandi and R. Khana. *FDDI Technology and Applications.* John Wiley & Sons, Inc., 1993.

[Mok84] A. K. Mok. The Design of Real-Time Programing Systems Based on Process Models. In *IEEE Real-Time Systems Symposium*, Austin, Texas, 1984.

[Moo90] D. J. Moore. Multimedia Presentation Development using the Audio Visual Connection. *IBM Systems Journal*, 29(4):494–508, 1990.

[Moo94] G. Moon. New video and multimedia products. Internet – Electronic Mail, February 1994. from rem-conf&.es.net news group.

[Mos82] J. E. B. Moss. Nested Transactions and Reliable Distributed Computing. In *Proceedings of the 2nd Conference on Reliability of Distributed System Software and Database Systems*, pages 33–39, 1982.

[Moy93] J. Moy. Multicast routing extensions for ospf. In *Proceedings of INET 93*, San Francisco, CA, August 1993.

[MP91] J. L. Mitchell and W. B. Pennebaker. Evolving JPEG Color Data Compression Standard. In M. Nier and M. E. Courtot, editors, *Standards for Electronic Imaging Systems*, volume CR37, pages 68–97. SPIE, 1991.

[MR93a] P. Martini and M. Rumekasten. MAN/WAN Integration – the ATM-to-DQDB Case. In *Proceedings of 18th Conference on Local Computer Networks*, pages 102–109, Minneapolis, Minnesota, September 1993.

[MR93b] B. C. McKellar and J. Roos. Buffer management in communication systems. Technical Report 43.9312, IBM European Networking Center, IBM Heidelberg, Germany, 1993.

[MR94] M. Mulhäuser and T. Rüdebusch. Context Embedding and Reuse in Cooperative-Software Development. In Jose L. Encarnacao, James D. Foley, and Ralf Guido Herrtwich, editors, *Perspectives of Multimedia Systems*, July 1994. Position Papers of the Dagstuhl Multimedia Seminar.

[MSK+93] B. A. Mah, S. Seshan, K. Keeton, R. H. Katz, and D. Ferrari. Providing Network Video Service to Mobile Clients. In *Proceedings of the Fourth Workshop on Workstation Operating Systems*, Napa, CA, October 1993.

[MSS92] A. Mauthe, W. Schultz, and R. Steinmetz. Inside the Heidelberg Multimedia Operating System Support: Real-Time Processing of Continuous Media in OS/2. Technical Report 43.9214, IBM European Networking Center, IBM Heidelberg, Germany, 1992.

[MT90] C. W. Mercer and H. Tokuda. The ARTS Real-Time Object Model. In *IEEE Real-Time System Symposium*, pages 2–10, Lake Buena Vista, Florida, 1990.

[MTA+89] W. E. Mackay, W. Treese, D. Applebaum, B. Gardner, B. Michon, E. Schlusselberg, and D. Davis. Pygmalion: An Experiment in Multimedia Communication. In *Proceedings of SIGGRAPH '89*, Boston, MA, July 1989.

[Mue89] M. Muehlhäuser. Requirements and Concepts for Networked Multimedia Courseware Engineering. In *International Conference on Computer Aided Learning 89*, Dallas, Texas, 1989.

[Mul91] S. J. Mullender. Systems of the Ninties - Distributed Multimedia Systems. In *Systems of the 90s and Beyond, International Workshop*, pages 273–278, Dagstuhl Castle, Germany, July 1991. Springer Verlag, Heidelberg.

[Mur84] G. M. Murch. Physiological principles for the effective use of color. *IEEE Computer Graphics and Applications*, 11(11):49–54, November 1984.

[Mus90] H. G. Musmann. The ISO audio coding standard. In *IEEE Globecom 90*, pages 511–517, San Diego, CA, December 1990.

[Mye84] B. A. Myers. The User Interface for Saphire. *IEEE Computer Graphics and Applications*, 11(12):13–32, December 1984.

[MZ93] N. Malcolm and W. Zhao. Guaranteeing Synchronous Messages with Arbitrary Deadline Constraints in an FDDI Network. In *Proceedings of 18th Conference on Local Computer Networks*, pages 186–195, Minneapolis, Minnesota, September 1993.

[Nah93] K. Nahrstedt. Network Service Customization: An End-Point Perspective. Technical Report MS-CIS-93-100, CIS, University of Pennsylvania, Philadelphia, PA, December 1993.

[NBH88] R. M. Newman, Z. L. Budrikis, and J. L. Hullet. The DQDB MAN. *IEEE Communication Magazine*, 26(4):20–28, April 1988.

[Nev82] R. Nevatia. *Machine Perception.* Prentice-Hall, Inc., Englewood Cliffs, NJ, 1982.

[Ngu93] G. D. Nguyen. Reliability Analysis for FDDI Dual Homing Networks. In *Proceedings of 18th Conference on Local Computer Networks*, pages 140–146, Minneapolis, Minnesota, September 1993.

[NH88] A. N. Netravali and B. G. Haskell. *Digital Pictures: Representation and Compression.* Plenum Press, New York, 1988.

[NHNW93] J. Nieh, J. G. Hanko, J. D. Northcutt, and G. A. Wall. SVR4 UNIX Scheduler Unacceptable for Multimedia Applications. In *Proceedings of 4th International Workshop on Network and Operating System Support for Digital Audio and Video*, pages 35–47, Lancaster, UK, 1993.

[Nic90] C. Nicolau. An Architecture for Real-Time Multimedia Communication Systems. *IEEE JSAC*, 8:391–400, April 1990.

[Nie89] O. M. Nierstra. A Survey of Object Oriented Concepts. *SIGMOD Record*, 18(1), March 1989.

[Nie90a] J. Nielsen. The Art of Navigating through Hypertext. *Communications of the ACM*, 33(3):298–310, 1990.

[Nie90b] J. Nielsen. *Hypertext and Hypermedia.* Academic Press, 1990.

[Nor91] D. A. Norman. Cognitive artifacts. In J. M. Carroll, editor, *Designing Interaction*, pages 17–38. Cambridge University Press, 1991.

[NP78] N. J. Narasinha and A. M. Peterson. On the computation of the discrete cosine transform. *IEEE Trans. Communications*, COM-26(6):966–968, October 1978.

[NS92] K. Nahrstedt and J. M. Smith. Integrated Multimedia Architecture for High-Speed Networks. In *Proceedings of Multimedia '92*, Monterey, CA, April 1992.

[NS93] K. Nahrstedt and J. Smith. An Application-Driven Approach to Networked Multimedia Systems. In *Proceedings of 18th Conference on Local Computer Network*, Minneapolis, Minnesota, September 1993.

[NS95a] K. Nahrstedt and J. M. Smith. The QoS Broker. *IEEE Multimedia*, 2(1):53–67, Spring 1995.

[NS95b] K. Nahrstedt and J.M. Smith. Design, Implementation and Experiences of the OMEGA End-point Architecture. Technical Report MS-CIS-95-22, CIS, University of Pennsylvania, Philadelphia, PA, May 1995.

[NS95c] K. Nahrstedt and R. Steinmetz. Resource Management in Networked Multimedia Systems. *IEEE Computer*, pages 52–64, May 1995.

[NTDS89] J. G. Neal, C. Y. Thielman, Z. Dobes, and S. M. Shapiro. Natural Language with Integrated Deictic and Graphic Gestures. In *Proceedings of 1989 DARPA Workshop on Speech and Natural Language*, pages 410–423, Harwich Port, 1989. Morgan Kaufman.

[NV92] R. Nagarajan and C. Vogt. Guaranteed-Performance Transport of Multimedia Traffic over the Token Ring. Technical Report 43.9201, IBM European Networking Center, IBM Heidelberg, Germany, 1992.

[OC89] S. Oberlin and J. Cox, editors. *Microsoft CD-ROM Yearbook 1989–1990.* Microsoft Press, 1989.

[OF93] S. O'Shea and J. Finucane. Reactive DQDB. In *Proceedings of 18th Conference on Local Computer Networks*, Minneapolis, Minnesota, September 1993.

[OG93] R. Ochsle and M. Graf. The Internet Protocol Family over atm. Technical Report 43.9301, IBM ENC, Heidelberg, Germany, 1993.

[OKKT93] J. Ohya, Y. Kitamura, F. Kishino, and N. Terashima. Real-time Reproduction of 3D Human Images in Virtual Space Teleconferencing. In *Proceedings of IEEE Virutal Reality Annual International Symposium*, pages 408–414, 1993. IEEE Neural Networks Council.

[OMS+92] T. Ohmori, K. Maeno, S. Sakata, H. Fukuoka, and K. Watabe. Distributed Cooperative Control for Application Sharing Based on Multiparty and Multimedia Desktop Conferencing System: MERMAID. In *Proceedings of Multimedia '92*, pages 112– 131, April 1992.

[Org86] International Standard Organization. *Information Processing – Standard Generalized Markup Language.* ISO, Genf, 1986.

[Org89] International Standard Organization. *Information Processing – Office Document Architecture and Interchange Format.* ISO, Genf, 1989.

[Org92] International Standard Organization. *Hypermedia/Time-based Document Structuring Language (HyTime).* ISO/IEC, is10744 edition, 1992.

[Org93] International Standards Organization. Information technology – digital compression and coding of continuous-tone still images. International Standard ISO/IEC IS 10918, 1993. ISO IEC JTC 1.

[O'S90] D. O'Shaughnessy. *Speech Communication.* Addison-Wesley Publishing Company, Inc., Reading Massachusetts, 1990.

[OT93] S. Oikawa and H. Tokuda. User-Level Real-Time Threads: An Approach towards High Performance Multimedia Threads. In *Proceedings of the 4th International Workshop on Network and Operating System Support for Digital Audio and Video*, pages 61 –71, November 1993.

[PA91] A. Puri and R. Aravind. Motion compensated video coding with adaptive perceptual quantization. *IEEE Trans. on Circuits and Systems for Video Technology*, 1:351, December 1991.

[Par87] Parallax Graphics. *The Parallax 1280 Series Videographics Processor*, 1987.

[Par94] C. Partridge. *Gigabit Networking.* Addison-Wesley Publishing Company, Inc., 1994.

[Per93] R. Perlman. *Interconnections: Bridges and Routers.* Addision-Wesley, New York, 1993.

[PF92] D. Paulisson and H. Frater. *Multimedia Mania.* Data Becker GmbH, Dusseldorf, Germany, 1992.

[Phi73] Phillips. Laser vision. *Phillips Technical Review*, 33:187–193, 1973.

[Phi82] Phillips and Sony Corporation. *System Description Compact Disc Digital Audio*, 1982. Red Book.

[Phi85] Phillips and Sony Corporation. *System Description Compact Disc Read Only Memory*, 1985. Yellow Book.

[Phi88] Phillips and Sony Corporation. *CD-I Full Functional Specification*, 1988. Green Book.

[Phi89] Phillips and Sony Corporation. *System Description CD-ROM/XA*, 1989.

[Phi91] Phillips and Sony Corporation. *System Description Recordable Compact Disc Systems*, 1991. Orange Book.

[PKG91] F. H. Previc, R. V. Kenyon, and K. K. Gillingham. The Effect of Dynamic Visual Roll on Postural and Manual Control and Self-control Perception. In *2nd Annual Scientific Meeting of the Aerospace Medical Society*, Cincinnati, OH, 1991.

[PM93] W. B. Pennebaker and J. L. Mitchell. *JPEG Still Image Data Compression*. Van Nostrand Reinhold, New York, 1993.

[PMJA88] W. B. Pennbaker, J. L. Mitchell, G. Langdon Jr., and R. B. Arps. An Overview of the Basic Principles of the Q-Coder Binary Arithmetic Coder. *IBM Journal of Research Development*, 32(6):717–726, November 1988.

[Pre90] L. Press. Computer or Teleputer? *Communications of the ACM*, 33(9):29–36, September 1990.

[Pry89] M. de Prycker. Impact of Data Communication on ATM. In *ICC 89*, Boston, MA, June 1989.

[Pry93] M. de Prycker. *Asynchronous Transfer Mode – Solution for Broadband ISDN*. Ellis Horwood Limited and Market Cross House, 2 edition, 1993.

[PS83] J. Peterson and A. Silberschatz. *Operating System Concepts*. Addison-Wesley Publishing Company, Inc., 1983.

[PZF92] C. Parris, H. Zhang, and D. Ferrari. A Mechanism for Dynamic Rerouting of Real-Time Services on Packet Networks. Technical report, UC Berkeley, Berkeley, CA, 1992.

[PZF94] C. Parris, H. Zhang, and D. Ferrari. Dynamic Management of Guaranteed Performance Multimedia Connections. *Multimedia Systems*, 1(6), 1994.

[RAC93] RACE. TITAN - Tool for Introduction Scenario & Techno-economic Evaluation of Access Network. Report of RACE II - Project Summaries, 1993.

[Ran93] P. V. Rangan. Video Conferencing, File Storage, and Management in Multmedia Computer Systems. *Computer Networks and ISDN Systems*, March 1993.

[Ran94] P. V. Rangan. C2 Interactive Multimedia Services on Cable TV Networks. In Jose L. Encarnacao, James D. Foley, and Ralf Guido Herrtwich, editors, *Perspectives of Multimedia Systems*, July 1994. Position Papers of the Dagstuhl Multimedia Seminar.

[RB90] I. Rubin and J. E. Baker. Media Access Control for High-Speed Local Area and Metropolitan Area Communication Networks. *Proc. of the IEEE*, 78(1), January 1990.

[RBCD91] L. Ruston, G. Blair, G. Coulson, and N. Davies. A Tale of Two Architectures. In *2nd International Workshop on Network and Operating System Support for Digital Audio and Video*, Heidelberg, Germany, November 1991.

[Rei82] C.W. Reinholds. Computer animation with scripts and actors. In *SIGGRAPH 82*, pages 289–296, 1982.

[RG90] Herrtwich R. G. ODA-Based Data Modelling in Multimedia Systems. Technical Report TR–90–043, International Computer Science Institute (ISCI), Berkeley, CA, August 1990.

[RH93] S. Roth and W. Hefley. Intelligent Multimedia Presentation Systems: Research and Principles. In M. T. Maybury, editor, *Intelligent Multimedia Interface*, pages 13–59. AAAI Press / The MIT Press, 1993.

[RHA+85] C. Rose, B. Hacker, R. Anders, K. Wittney, M. Metzler, S. Chernicoff, C. Espinosa, A. Averill, B. Davis, and B. Howard. *Inside Macintosh,*, volume 1. Addison-Wesley Publishing Company, Inc., Reading, MA, 1985. I-35–I-213.

[Ril89] Michael D. Riley. *Speech Time-Frequency Representation.* Boston: Kluwer Academic Publishers, 1989.

[Rip89] G. D. Ripley. DVI – A Digital Multimedia Technology. *Communications of the ACM*, 32(7):811–822, July 1989.

[RJ85] J. W. Reedy and J. R. Jones. Methods of Collision Detection in Fiber Optic CSMA/CD Networks. *IEEE Journal on Selected Areas in Communication*, 3:890–896, November 1985.

[RJ91] M. Rabbani and P. Jones. Digital image compression techniques. In *Tutorial Texts in Optical Engineering*, volume TT7. SPIE Press, 1991.

[RK82] A. Rosenfeld and A. C. Kak. *Digital Picture Processing*, volume 1. Academic Press, 2 edition, 1982.

[RK92] H. Ricke and J. Kanzow, editors. *BERKOM – Broadband Communication within the Optical Fibre Network in Telecom Research.* R. v. Decker's Verlag, G. Schenk, Heidelberg, Germany, 1992.

[RKV92] P. V. Rangan, T. Kaeppner, and H. W. Vin. Techniques for Efficient Storage of Digital Video and Audio. In *Proceedings of 1992 Workshop on Multimedia Information Systems,*, Tempe, Arizona, February 1992.

[RM80] D. Rubinea and P. McAvinney. Programmable Finger-tracking Instrument Controllers. *Computer Music Journal*, 14(1):26–41, Spring 1980.

[RM91] S. F. Roth and J. Mattis. Automating the Presentation of Information. In *Proceedings of the IEEE Conference on AI Applications*, pages 90–97, Miami Beach, FL, 1991.

[RM93] T. C. Rakow and P. Muth. The $v^3$ Video Server – Managing Analog and Digital Video Clips. In *Proceedings of ACM SIGMOD'93 Conference*, pages 556 –557, Washington, DC, May 1993.

[RMM91] S. F. Roth, J. Mattis, and X. Mesnard. Graphics and Natural Language Generation as Components of Automatic Explanation. Technical report, Sullivan and Tyler, 1991.

[Row93] R. Rowe. *Interactive Music Systems.* MIT Press, Cambridge, MA, 1993.

[Roy94] K. Roy, editor. In Person Desktop Conferencing Software: An Overview. *Pipeline*, 5(3):16–18, May/June 1994.

[RR93] S. Ramanathan and V. Rangan. Feedback Technique for Intra-media Continuity and Intra-media Synchronization in Distributed Multimedia Systems. *Computer Journal*, 36(1):19–31, 1993.

[RR94] S. Ramanathan and P. V. Rangan. Architectures for Personalized Multimedia. *IEEE Multimedia*, Spring, 1994.

[RS78] L.R. Rabiner and L.W. Schafer. *Digital Processing of Speech Signals.* Prentice-Hall International, 1978.

[RSSS90] J. Rückert, H. Schmutz, B. Schoner, and R. Steinmetz. A Distributed Multimedia Environment for Advanced CSCW Applications. In *IEEE Multimedia 90*, Bordeaux, France, November 15-17, 1990.

[RSV94] W. Reinhard, J. Schweitzer, and G. Volksen. CSCW Tools: Concepts and Architectures. *CACM*, 27(5):28–36, May 1994.

[RV91] P. V. Rangan and H. M. Vin. Designing File Systems for Digital Video and Audio. *Operating Systems Review*, 25(5):81–94, October 1991.

[RVG+93] K.K. Ramakrishnan, L. Vaitzblit, C. Gray, U. Vahalia, D. Ting, P. Tzelnic, S. Glaser, and W. Duso. Operating System Support for Video-On-Demand File Services. In *Workshop on Network and Operating System Support for Digital Audio and Video '93*, Lancaster, England, November 3-5, 1993.

[RW93] A. L. N. Reddy and J. Wyllie. Disk Scheduling in a Multimedia I/O System. In *Proceedings of the first ACM International Conference on Multimedia*, pages 225–233, Anheim, CA, 1993.

[Sal91] J. H. Salzer. File Sytems Indexing and Backup. In *Operating Systems of the 90s and Beyond, International Workshop*, pages 13–19, Dagstuhl Castle, Germany, July 1991. Springer-Verlag, Heidelberg.

[SC92] E. M. Schooler and S. L. Casner. An Architecture for Multimedia Connection Management. In *Proceedings of Multimedia'92*, pages 271–274, April 1992.

[SCFJ94] H. Schulzrinne, S. Casner, R. Frederick, and V. Jacobson. RTP: A Transport Protocol for Real-Time Applications. Internet Draft of IETF - Working Draft, July 18 1994.

[Sch83] B.J. Schachter. *Computer Image Generation.* John Wiley, New York, 1983.

[Sch87] B. Schneiderman. User Interface Design for the Hyperties Electronic Encyclopedia. In *Hypertext '87*, November 1987.

[Sch92] M. E. H. Schouten, editor. *The Auditory Processing of Speech: from sounds to words.* Mounton de Gouyter, Berlin, New York, 1992.

[Sch93] E. M. Schooler. The Impact of Scale on a Multimedia Connection Architecture. *ACM Journal Multimedia Systems*, 1(1):2–9, 1993.

[Sch94a] H. Schulzrinne. Conferencing and collaborative computing. In Jose L. Encarnacao, James D. Foley, and Ralf Guido Herrtwich, editors, *Perspectives of Multimedia Systems*, July 1994. Position Papers of the Dagstuhl Multimedia Seminar.

[Sch94b] G. Schürmann. Multimedia documents and mailing. In Jose L. Encarnacao, James D. Foley, and Ralf Guido Herrtwich, editors, *Perspectives of Multimedia Systems*, July 1994. Position Papers of the Dagstuhl Multimedia Seminar.

[Sco94] H. A. Scott. Tele-action Services: An Overview. *IEEE Communication*, 32(6):50–53, June 1994.

[SDF+94] J. M. Smith, S. B. Davidson, D. J. Farber, I. Lee, and I. Winston. Tele-Mentoring Annual Report II. Annual Report NSF CDA-92-14924, University of Pennsylvania, Philadelphia, PA, July 1994.

[SDW92] W.T. Strayer, B. Dempsey, and A. Weaver. *XTP: The Xpress Transfer Protocol.* Addison-Wesley Publishing Company, Inc., July 1992.

[SE93] R. Steinmetz and C. Engler. Human Perception of Media Synchronization. Technical Report 43.9310, IBM European Networking Center Heidelberg, Heidelberg, Germany, 1993.

[SF91] D. Seligmann and S. Feiner. Automated Generation of Intent-Based 3D Illustrations. In *Proceedings of the ACM SIGGRAPH '91*, pages 123-132, Las Vegas, NV, July 28-August 2, 1991. Also in Computer Graphics 25(4).

[SF92] R. Steinmetz and Ch. Fritzsche. Abstractions for Continuous Media Programming. *Computer Communication*, 15(4), July 1992.

[SG88] R. Steinmetz and G. Gremler. Designkriterien einer graphisch orientierten Telephon-Benutzerschnittstelle. In *ITG-Fachtagung "Nutzung und Technik von Kommunikationendgeräten*, Bad Nauheim, September 13-16, 1988.

[SG90] L. Sha and J. B. Goodenough. Real-time Scheduling Theory and ADA. *IEEE Transactions on Computers*, 23(4):53–64, April 1990.

[SGC94] W.T. Strayer, S. Gray, and R.E. Cline,Jr. An Object-Oriented Implementation of the Xpress Transfer Protocol. In R. Steinmentz (Ed.), editor, *Multimedia: Advanced Teleservices and High-Speed Communication Architectures, 2nd International Workshop, IWACA'94*, pages 387–400, Heidelberg, Germany, September 1994. Lecture Notes in Computer Science, No. 868.

[SGLS93] C. Shaw, M. Green, J. Liang, and Y. Sun. Decoupled Simulation in Virtual Reality with the MR Toolkit. *ACM Transactions on Information Systems*, 11(3):287–317, 1993.

[SGN88] R. W. Scheifler, J. Gettys, and R. Newman. *X Window System.* Digital Press, 1988.

[SH86] N. Suehiro and M. Hatori. Fast Algorithms for the DFT and other Sinusoidal Transforms. *IEEE Transactions on Acoustics, Speech and Signal Processing*, ASSP-34(3):642–644, June 1986.

[SHH92] J.B. Stefani, L. Hazard, and F. Horn. Computational Model for Distributed Multimedia Applications Based on a Synchronous Programming Language. *Computer Communication*, 15:114–128, March 1992.

[SHRS90] R. Steinmetz, R. Heite, J. Rückert, and B. Schöner. Compound Multimedia Objects – Integration into Network and Operating Systems. In *International Workshop on Network and Operating System Support for Digital Audio and Video*, Berkeley, CA, November 1990.

[SJ87] K. C. Sevcik and M. J. Johnson. Cycle Time Properties of the FDDI Token Ring Protocol. *IEEE Transactions on Software Engineering*, SE-13(3), 1987.

[Ska94] K. Skarakis. *IRIX REACT*. Silicon Graphics, Inc., Mountain View, CA, March 1994.

[SKG91] L. Sha, M. H. Klein, and J. B. Goodenough. Rate monotonic analysis for real-time systems. In *Foundations of Real-Time Computing, Scheduling and Resource Management*, pages 129–156. Kluwer Academic Publisher, Norwell, 1991.

[SM92a] R. Steinmetz and T. Meyer. Modelling Distributed Multimedia Applications. In *IEEE International Workshop on Advanced Communications and Applications for High-Speed Networks*, München, Germany, March 1992.

[SM92b] R. Steinmetz and T. Meyer. Multimedia Synchronization Techniques: Experiences based on Different System Structures. In *Proceedings of 4th IEEE ComSoc International Workshop on Multimedia Communications*, pages 305 –314, Monterey, CA, April 1992.

[Smi89] J. M. Smith. Standard Generalized Markup Language and Related Standards. *Computer Communication*, 12:80–83, April 1989.

[SP90] J. Sterbenz and G. Parulkar. Axon: Application-oriented Lightweight Transport Protocol Design. In *ICCC'90*, New Delhi, India, November 1990.

[SPI94] SPIE. Symposium on Electronic Imaging. In *Conference on Digital Video Compression on Personal Computers: Algorithms and Technologies*, volume 2187, February 1994. SPIE/IS&T.

[Spr90] B. Sprunt, et al. Implementing Sporadic Servers in ADA. Technical report, Carnegie-Mellon University, Pittsburgh, PA, May 1990.

[SR89] L. Sha and R. Rajkumar. Real-time systems. A Tutorial of the Rate-Monotonic Scheduling Framework with Bus-Related Issues P896.3, Draft 4.0, Futurebus+, 1989.

[SRB+92] K. Srinivas, R. Reddy, A. Babadi, S. Kamana, V. Kumar, and Z. Dai. MONET: A Multi-media System for Conferencing and Application Sharing in Distributed Systems. CERC Technical Report Series CERC-TR-RN-91-009, Concurrent Engineering Research Center, West Virginia University, Morgantown, WV, February 1992.

[SRN+83] R. V. Schmidt, E. G. Rawson, R. E. Norton, S. B. Jackson, and M. D. Bailey. Fibernet II - A Fiber Optic Ethernet. *IEEE Journal on Selected Areas in Communication*, 1:702–710, November 1983.

[SS90] M. Salmony and D. Shepherd. Extending OSI to Support Synchronization Required by Multimedia Applications. *Computer Communication*, 13:399–406, September 1990.

[SS91] D. Steinberg and J. Sirota. Components: A Multimedia Programming Model. In *2nd International Workshop on Network and Operating System Support for Digital Audio and Video*, Heidelberg, Germany, November 1991.

[SS94] P. Sander and R. Steinmetz. A New Remote Camera Control User Interaction Technique. Patent, 1994.

[SSL89] B. Sprunt, L. Sha, and J. Lehoczky. Aperiodic Task Scheduling for Hard Real-Time Systems. *The Journal of Real-Time Systems*, 1:27–60, 1989.

[SSS+93] D.C. Schmidt, B. Stiller, T. Suda, A.N. Tantawy, and M. Zitterbart. Language Support for Flexible, Application-Tailored Protocol Configuration. In *Proceedings of 18th Conference on Local Computer Networks*, Minneapolis, Minnesota, September 1993.

[SSSW89] R. Steinmetz, H. Schmutz, B. Schoner, and M. Wasmund. Generic Support for Distributed Multimedia Applications. Technical Report 43.8910, IBM European Networking Center, Heidelberg, Germany, November 1989.

[Sta92] W. Stalling. *ISDN and Broadband ISDN.* Macmillan Publishing Company, 2 edition, 1992.

[Ste83] G. Stern. Bbop – A System for 3D Keyframe Figure Animation. In *SIGGRAPH 83*, pages 240 –243, New York, July 1983. Introduction to Computer Animation, Course Notes 7.

[Ste87] M. Stewart. The Feel Factor: Music with Soul. *Electronic Musician*, 3(10):55–66, 1987.

[Ste88] R. Steinmetz. *OCCAM 2: Die Programmiersprache für parallele Verarbeitung.* Hüthig Verlag, Heidelberg, Germany, 1988.

[Ste90] R. Steinmetz. Synchronization Properties in Multimedia Systems. *IEEE JSAC*, 8:401–412, April 1990.

[Ste92] B. Steinbrink. *Multimedia: Einstieg in eine neue Technologie.* Markt-und-Technik Verlag, 1992.

[Ste93a] R. Steinmetz. Enabling Multimedia Communications over the Token Ring: A New Distributed Resource Management Protocol. Technical Report GE 892-0096, IBM ENC, Heidelberg, Germany, 1993.

[Ste93b] R. Steinmetz. *Multimedia Technology: Introduction and Fundamentals (in German).* Springer Verlag, 1993.

[Ste94a] R. Steinmetz. Data Compression in Multimedia Computing: Standards and Systems. *ACM Multimedia Systems Journal*, 1(5), March 1994.

[Ste94b] R. Steinmetz. Multimedia Operating Systems: Resource reservation, Scheduling, File Systems, and Architecture. Technical Report 43.9402, IBM ENC, Heidelberg, Germany, March 1994.

[Sto72] T. Stockham. A/D and D/A Converters: Their Effect on Digital Audio Fidelity. In L. Rabiner and C. Rader, editors, *Digital Signal Processing*, pages 55–66. IEEE Press, New York, 1972.

[Sto88] J. A. Storer. *Data Compression Methods and Theory.* Computer Science Press, 1988.

[Str88] P. Strauss. BAGS: The Brown Animation Generation System. Ph.D. Thesis CS-88-22, Computer Science Department, Brown University, Providence, RI, May 1988.

[Stu94] H. J. Stuttgen. Network evolution and multimedia communication. Technical Report 43.9404, IBM European Networking Center Heidelberg, Heidelberg, Germany, 1994.

[Sun90] Sun. *VideoPix.* Sun Corporation, Inc., 1990.

[Sut63] I. E. Sutherland. Sketchpad: A Man-Machine Graphical Communication System. In *SJCC, Spartan Books*, Baltimore, MD, 1963.

[SvdM91] F. Sijstermans and J. van der Meer. CD-I Full-Motion Video Encoding on a Parallel Computer. *Communications of the ACM*, 34(4):81–91, April 1991.

[SW94a] E. Schooler and A. Weinrib. Multiparty Multimedia Session Control WG. Minutes from the 29th IETG, Seattle, WA, posted on rem-conf, March 1994.

[SW94b] S. Shenker and A. Weinrib. Managing Shared Ephemeral Teleconferencing State: Policy and Mechanism. ftp site from thumper.bellcore.com:pub/abel/agree.ps, March 1994.

[Swi87] D. C. Swinehart. Telephone Management in the Etherphone System. In *IEEE Globecom '87*, pages 30.3.1–30.3.5, 1987.

[SZ87] K. E. Smith and S. B. Zdonik. A Case Study of the Differences between Relational amd Object-Oriented Database Systems. In *Conference on Object-Oriented Programming Systems, Languages and Applications*, October 1987.

[TAC+94] D. L. Tennenhouse, J. Adams, D. Carver, H. Houh, M. Ismert, Ch. Lindblad, B. Stasior, D. Weatherall, D. Bacher, and T. Chang. A Software-Oriented Approach to the Design of Media Processing Environments. In *Proceedings of International Conference on Multimedia Computing and Systems*, Boston, MA, May 1994.

[Tan87] A. S. Tanenbaum. *Operating System, Design and Implementation.* Prentice-Hall, Inc., Englewood Cliffs, NJ, 1987.

[Tan88] A. S. Tanenbaum. *Computer Networks.* Prentice-Hall, Englewood Cliffs, NJ, 2 edition, 1988.

[TBR92] D. P. Tranchier, P. E. Boyer, and Y. M. Rowand. Fast Bandwidth Allocation in ATM Networks. In *ISS 92*, Yokohama, Japan, October 1992.

[Tec89] Technical Manual, NeXT, Inc. *NeXT 0.9 Technical Documentation: Concepts*, 1989.

[TG90] M. Teener and R. Gvozdanovis. FDDI II operation and architectures. In *Proceedings of 14th Conference on Local Computer Networks*, pages 49–61, July 1990.

[TGD91] D. Tsichritzis, S. Gibbs, and L. Dami. Active Media. In *Object Composition (D. Tsichritzis, ed.)*, pages 115 –132, Universite de Geneve, Centre Universitaire d'Informatique, Geneve, June 1991.

[Tin89] M. Tinker. DVI Parallel Image Compression. *Communications of the ACM*, 32(7):844–851, July 1989.

[TK91] A. M. Van Tilborg and G. M. Koob, editors. *Foundations of Real-Time Computing, Scheduling and Resource Management.* Kluwer Academic Publisher, Norwell, 1991.

[Top90] C. Topolocic. Experimental Internet Stream Protocol, Version 2 (ST II). Internet Network Working Group, RFC 1190, October 1990.

[TP90] E. Tirtaatmadha and R. Palmer. The Application of Virtual Path to the Interconnection of IEEE 802.6 Metropolitan Area Network. In *ISS 90*, Stockholm, Sweden, June 1990.

[TP91] R. Terek and J. Pasquale. Experiences with Audio Conferencing Using the X Window System, UNIX and TCP/IP. In *Proceedings of USENIX 91*, pages 405–418, Nashville, TN, June 1991.

[Tri87] G. Tricoles. Computer generated holograms: An historical review. *Applied Optics*, 26(20):4351–4360, 1987.

[TS93] C. B. S. Traw and J. M. Smith. Hardware/Software Organization of a High-Performance ATM Host Interface. *IEEE JSAC, Special Issue on High-Speed Computer/Network Interfaces*, 11(2):240–253, February 1993.

[TTCM92] H. Tokuda, Y. Tobe, S. T. C. Chou, and J. M. F. Moura. Continuous Media Communication with Dynamic QOS Control Using ARTS with an FDDI Network. In *ACM SIGCOMM 92*, pages 88–98, Baltimore, MD, 1992.

[TYL93] Z. Tsai, K. Yu, and F. Lai. Design and Analysis of a Hierarchical and Modular Local ATM Switch. In *Proceedings of 18th Conference on Local Computer Networks*, pages 44 –51, Minneapolis, Minnesota, September 1993.

[UNI93] UNIFORUM. UNIX Leaders Announce Common Open Software Environment. Press Release, San Francisco, CA, March 17 1993.

[V. 93] V. Rosenborg, et al. *A Guide to Multimedia.* New Riders Publishing, Carmel, Indiana, 1993.

[Vet85] M. Vetterli. Fast 2-D Discrete Cosine Transform. In *Proceedings of IEEE ICASSP-85*, pages 1538 - 1541, Tampa, Florida, March 1985.

[VG91] E. Viscito and C. Gonzales. A Video Compression Algorithm with Adaptive Bit Allocation and Quantization. In *Proceedings of SPIE Visual*

*Communications and Image Processing*, volume 1605 205, Boston, MA, November 1991.

[VHC89] F. W. P. Vreeswijk, M. R. Haghiri, and C. M. Carey-Smith. HDMAC Coding for Compatible Broadcasting of High Definition Television Signals. In *CCIR*, Geneva, Switzerland, January 1989.

[VHN92] C. Vogt, R. G. Herrtwich, and R. Nagarajan. HeiRAT: The Heidelberg Resource Administration Technique, Design Philosophy and Goals. In *Proceedings of Conference on Communication in Distributed Systems*, München,Germany, 1992. Also published in Informatik aktuel, Springer.

[vLZ89] B. A. G. van Luyt and L. E. Zegers. The Compact Disc Interactive System. *Phillips Technical review*, 44(11/12):326–333, November 1989.

[VN84] M. Vetterli and H.J. Nussbaumer. Simple FFT and DCT Algorithms with Reduced Number of Operations. *Signal Processing*, August 1984.

[VR93] H.M. Vin and P. V. Rangan. Techniques for Efficient Storage of Digital Video and Audio. *Computer Communications*, 16:168–176, March 1993.

[VZ91] D. Verma and H. Zhang. Design documents for RTIP/RMTP. unpublished report, University of California at Berkeley and International Computer Science Institute, Berkeley, CA, May 1991.

[Wai88] A. Waibel. *Prosody and Speech Recognition.* London: Pitman, San Mateo, CA: Morgan Kaufmann Publishers, 1988.

[Wal91] G. K. Wallace. The JPEG Still Picture Compression Standard. *Communications of the ACM*, 34(4):30–44, April 1991.

[WB85] J. Ward and B. Blesser. Interactive Recognition of Handprinted Characters for Computer Input. *CG&A*, 5(9):24–37, September 1985.

[WBV92] L. Wolf, W. Burke, and C. Vogt. Cpu scheduling in multimedia systems. Technical Report 439404, IBM European Networking Center, IBM Heidelberg, Germany, 1992.

[WC87] C. M. Woodside and D. W. Craig. Local Non-Preemptive Scheduling Policies for Hard Real-Time Distributed Systems. In *IEEE-Real-Time Systems Symposium*, pages 12–17, San Jose, 1987.

[Weg87] P. Wegner. Dimensions of Object-Based Language Design. In *Proceedings of OOPSLA'87*, October 1987.

[Wei91a] B. Weiner. Hyperbole Draft Report. Wolrd Wide Web, May 1991.

[Wei91b] M. Weiser. The Computer of the 21st Century. *Scientific American*, 265(3):94–104, 1991.

[WF90] E. Wenzel and S. Forster. Real-time Digital Synthetis of Virtual Acoustic Environments. In *Proceedings of 1990 Symposium on Interactive 3D Graphics*, pages 139–140, Snowbird, UT, 1990.

[WH94] L. Wolf and R. G. Herrtwich. The System Architecture of the Heidelberg Transport System. *ACM Operating Systems Review*, 28(2), April 1994.

[Whi90] C. Whitby-Strevens. Transputers – Past, Present, and Future. *IEEE Micro*, 10(6):16–19 & 78–82, December 1990.

[Wil89] C. J. Williams. Creating Multimedia CD-ROM. In *Proceedings of 7th Conference on Interactive Instructions Delivery*, pages 88–92, March 1989.

[Win91] Microsoft Windows. *Multimedia: Programmer's Workbook.* Microsoft Press, 1991.

[Wod92] R. Wodaski. *Multimedia Madness!* Sams Publishing, 1992.

[Woo51] H. Woodrow. Time Perception. In Stevens S. S, editor, *Handbook of Experimental Psychology.* Wiley, 1951.

[WPD88] D. Waitzman, C. Patridge, and S. Deering. Distance Vector Multicasting Routing Protocol. FRC 1175, November 1988.

[WR94] T. Wahl and K. Rothermel. Representing Time in Multimedia Systems. In *Proceedings of International Conference on Multimedia Computing and*

*Systems*, pages 538–543, Boston,MA, May 1994. IEEE Computer Society Press.

[WSM+91] K. Watabe, S. Sakata, K. Maeno, H. Fukuoka, and T. Ohmori. Distributed Desktop Conferencing System with Multi-user Multimedia Interface. *IEEE JSAC*, 9(4):531–539, May 1991.

[WSS94] M. Wieland, R. Steinmetz, and P. Sander. Remote Camera Control in a Distributed Multimedia System. In *GI Conference*, Hamburg, Germany, September 1994.

[WVP88] G. Wallace, R. Vivian, and H. Poulsen. Subjective Testing Results for Still Picture Compression Algorithms for International Standardization. In *IEEE Global Telecommunications Conference*, pages 1022–1027, November 1988.

[YH93] M. C. Yuang and Y. R. Haung. Assessment and Aternative Design of FDDI II MAC Protocol. In *Proceedings of 18th Conference on Local Computer networks*, pages 205 –212, Minneapolis, Minnesota, September 1993.

[YV92] J. Yee and P. V. Vatarya. Disk Scheduling policies for Real-Time Multimedia Applications. Technical report, University of California, Berkeley, CA, August 1992.

[ZDE+93] L. Zhang, S. Deering, D. Estrin, S. Shenker, and D. Zappala. RSVP: A new Resource ReSerVation Protocol. *IEEE Computer*, September 1993.

[Zic87] D. Zicarelli. M and Jam Factory. *Computer Music Journal*, 11(4):13–29, 1987.

[ZK91] H. Zhang and S. Keshav. Comparison of Rate-Based Service Disciplines. In *SIGCOMM'91*, pages 113–122, Zürich, Switzerland, September 1991. ACM Press, Computer Communication Review 21(4).

[ZLB+87] T. Zimmerman, J. Lanier, C. Blanchard, S. Bryson, and Y. Harvill. A Hand Gesture Interface Device. In *Proceedings of CHI + GI*, pages 189–192, New York, NY, 1987. ACM.

# Index